ENCYCLOPÆDIA

Britannica®

ENCYCLOPÆDIA BRITANNICA (INDIA) PVT. LTD., NEW DELHI
AND
IMPULSE MARKETING, NEW DELHI

INTRODUCTION

**Was the 'Trojan horse' really a horse? What's inside a camel's hump?
Where did jazz come from? Are aliens waiting for us in outer space?
When...? How...? Why...? Why not...?**

In the 17 exciting sections of the new *Britannica Learning Library,* you will find answers to these and many more of your questions. Through articles, pictures, teaser questions, and fun facts, you'll learn about our world and its people, animals, places, events, cultures, arts, technological advances, and so on. To help you on your journey, we've provided the following signposts.

■ **Subject Tabs**—The coloured box on the top of each page will quickly tell you the article subject.

■ **Search Lights**—Try these mini-quizzes before and after you read the article and see how much – and how quickly – you can learn. You can even make this a game with a reading partner. (Answers are upside down at the bottom of the page.)

■ **Did You Know?**—Check out these fun facts about the article subject. With these surprising 'factoids', you can entertain your friends, impress your teachers, and amaze your parents.

■ **Picture Captions**—Read the captions that go with the photos. They provide useful information about the article subject.

■ **Vocabulary**—New or difficult words are in **bold type**. You'll find them explained in the Glossary at the end of the book.

Have a great trip!

TABLE OF CONTENTS

Journey through the solar system and beyond

Exploring Space

Exploring Space

TABLE OF CONTENTS

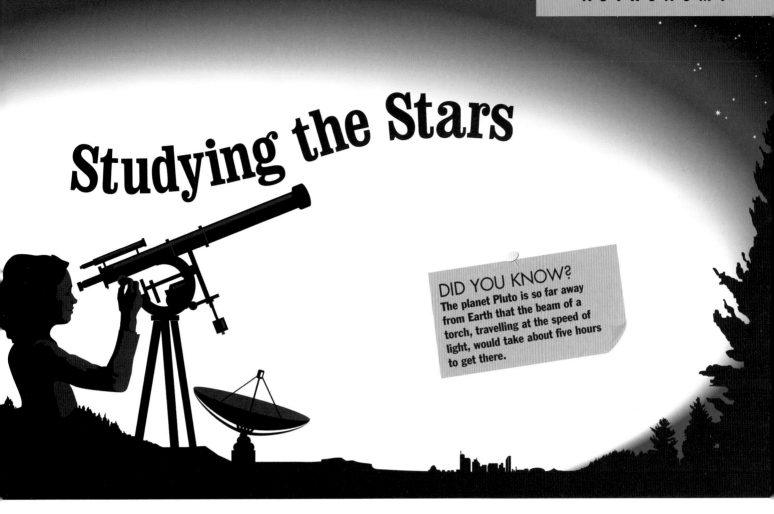

Studying the Stars

DID YOU KNOW?
The planet Pluto is so far away from Earth that the beam of a torch, travelling at the speed of light, would take about five hours to get there.

Look at the sky. What do you see?

If it's day you'll see the Sun. If it's night you'll see the Moon. And if the sky is clear you'll see stars. In big cities you may see only a few hundred stars. But out in the country or on the ocean you'll see many thousands. You may even see planets and, if you're lucky, a **comet**.

There are people who look at the sky for hours and hours, night after night. They study the stars, the planets, and other objects in the sky. These people are called 'astronomers'. The word 'astronomy' comes from the Greek for 'star' and 'arrangement'.

Astronomers study the universe in many different ways. Some watch faraway objects. Others work in **laboratories** where they look at samples of **meteorites**, rocks from the Moon, and space **debris** from other planets. Some try to make models of the different objects people have studied.

Not all astronomers get paid for the work they do. Some do it for a hobby. Such people are called 'amateur astronomers'.

How do astronomers study objects that are millions, even billions, of kilometres away? They use powerful telescopes that make things look large enough to be seen in detail. Some telescopes are small enough to be held in the hand. Others are as big as a bus!

SEARCH LIGHT

Which of these things do astronomers study?
- stars
- planets
- moons
- astronauts
- comets

Answer: They study all of these except for astronauts.

Infinite Space

The universe is a vast **expanse** of space that contains all matter and energy, from the smallest particle to the biggest galaxy. It contains all the planets, the Sun, stars, asteroids, our Milky Way galaxy, and all the other galaxies too.

No one knows how big the universe is. Astronomers believe that it is still growing outwards in every direction.

How did it all begin? No one is really sure of that either.

Most scientists believe that at first everything was one incredibly solid, heavy ball of matter. This ball exploded billions of years ago - and the universe was born. The moment of this explosion is called the 'big bang'. It is from this moment that time began.

After the explosion, the early universe was small and extremely hot. As it cooled, it expanded and pieces spread out. Small pieces formed the basic **elements** hydrogen and helium. Other pieces began to join together, and objects began to form. Over billions of years, the objects became galaxies, stars, and planets.

How the universe was formed is still only a theory (an idea). But different parts of it have proved to be true over the years. Astronomers continue to **investigate** the theory. One way they do this is by using a 'spectroscope'. A spectroscope measures the colour of light coming from an object. Changes in the colour indicate whether an object is moving away from or towards the Earth.

Because of spectroscope readings, scientists believe that the universe is still growing outwards in every direction.

SEARCH LIGHT

If the universe is still growing, is it moving towards or away from the Earth?

Answer: Everything in the universe is moving away from everything else. You can see how this works by drawing black dots on a balloon, then blowing it up and watching the dots spread apart.

The Invisible Magnet

SEARCH LIGHT

Why do you think a ballpoint pen won't work when you try to write with its point facing upwards?

Raise your arm. Keep it in that position for as long as you can. What happens?

After some time, your arm begins to hurt. Something seems to be pulling it down. Soon you will have to lower your arm.

A force called 'gravity' causes you to lower your arm. Gravity acts a bit like a magnet, tugging at your arm as if it were a piece of metal.

We can't see gravity or touch it. We can only feel it. The Earth has gravity that pulls down on everything on or near it. It is this force that keeps us all on the Earth.

The Moon and the Sun also have gravity. All bodies in the universe have gravity. In fact, gravity helps hold all of them together. Sir Isaac Newton first introduced the idea of gravity, and Albert Einstein added to Newton's ideas.

Gravity works in a two-way system. This means that all bodies exert a pull on each other. For example, Earth's gravity forces the Moon to circle around it all the time. In return, the Moon's gravity attracts the waters of Earth's oceans to cause tides.

The force of gravity becomes weaker and weaker as you move away from its source. That is partly why astronauts can float around in outer space. They are too far away for the Earth to have much pull on them.

What do you think would happen if there were no gravity on Earth?

DID YOU KNOW?
A 1961 Disney film, The Absent-Minded Professor, introduced a particularly far-fetched antigravity idea - flubber, a super-bouncy 'flying-rubber'.

Answer: Gravity causes the ink in a ballpoint pen to flow to the wrong end of the pen when its point is facing away from the ground. The upside-down pen's point soon runs out of ink.

Star Clusters

When we look at the sky at night, we can sometimes see thousands of stars shining brightly. They look as if they have been scattered around the sky. But actually, most stars are clustered together in huge groups. These groups are called 'galaxies'.

Our Sun is part of a galaxy. It is the Milky Way Galaxy. On a very clear night, if you look carefully at the sky, you might see part of this whitish band of stars stretching from one side to the other.

The universe is so huge that the Milky Way Galaxy is only one of many galaxies. Astronomers think that there are billions of galaxies in the universe. Each of these galaxies may contain trillions of stars, many much bigger than our Sun! The Milky Way itself contains several billion stars.

Some galaxies have no regular shape. Others, like the Milky Way, are shaped a bit like a giant merry-go-round. Each one has a centre around which stars move in circles.

It is hard to see the other galaxies in the sky with the naked eye. Even though they are incredibly large, they are also incredibly far away. Scientists must use powerful telescopes to study other galaxies. For this reason it takes a long time to learn even a little bit about another galaxy. And there's still a great deal we haven't learned about our own galaxy.

SEARCH LIGHT

Find and correct the mistake in the following sentence:
There are many, many universes in the galaxy.

DID YOU KNOW?
Unlike galaxies, constellations are groups of stars. People used to imagine connecting the stars to make pictures in the night sky. Most constellations are named after animals and mythological figures. They still help astronomers and navigators locate certain stars.

Our galaxy, the Milky Way, is shaped a bit like a giant merry-go-round. Its billions of stars move in circles around the centre.
© Myron Jay Dorf/Corbis

Answer: There are many, many galaxies in the universe.

Distant Fire

DID YOU KNOW?

After our own Sun, the nearest star to Earth is Alpha Proxima Centauri. It is 4.3 light-years away, or almost 1.3 billion kilometres from Earth.

All stars are basically enormous balls of fire. They are made up of gases that give off both heat and light as they burn. Their power comes from nuclear energy, the same source that both powers atomic bombs and produces electricity in many parts of the world.

The life of a star spans billions of years. A star is born from clouds of dust and the **element** hydrogen. This cloud mass forms a spinning ball and becomes extremely hot. It becomes so hot that the hydrogen gas begins to glow. The glowing gas ball is called a 'protostar' ('proto' means 'beginning' or 'first').

A protostar slowly becomes bigger until eventually it stops growing. It is then a star, and it can continue to glow for millions of years. But eventually it starts to cool off. It turns red and grows larger once more. It becomes a 'red giant'. Then the star begins to die. How long a star lives depends on how big it is. The bigger the star, the longer it lives.

In large stars, the heat inside the star produces iron. This iron acts like a sponge and soaks up the star's energy. The energy eventually causes a big explosion called a 'supernova'. In some cases, what is left may become a black hole. Black holes are like giant vacuum cleaners in space that suck up everything around them, including light.

Our Sun is still a young star, although it is already billions of years old. It will be many more billions of years before it begins to die. So there's still time to finish your homework!

SEARCH LIGHT

True or false? Black holes were once stars.

When you look up at the night sky, it's hard to believe that all those twinkling stars are actually enormous balls of fire.
© Matthias Kulka/Corbis

Answer: TRUE. Black holes are former stars that have collapsed inwards and now swallow up all material and light around them.

Wanderers
in the Sky

SEARCH LIGHT

Group the nine planets according to whether they're made of *Gas, Ice*, or *Rock/Metal*.
Jupiter - Saturn - Mars - Venus - Uranus - Pluto - Earth - Mercury - Neptune

Billions of years ago, there was an enormous swirling cloud of gas and dust. This cloud packed together and became extremely hot. Eventually, the centre of the cloud formed our Sun. The rest of the cloud clumped together until it formed planets.

The nine planets in our solar system revolve (or circle) around our Sun. Beginning with the one closest to the Sun, they are: Mercury, Venus, Earth, Mars, Jupiter, Saturn, Uranus, Neptune, and Pluto.

The planets have been divided into two basic groups. There are Earth-like planets and Jupiter-like planets.

Earth-like planets are close to the Sun and are made up of rock and metal. These planets are Mercury, Venus, Earth, and Mars. The other planets are larger and farther away from the Sun. These planets are Jupiter, Saturn, Uranus, and Neptune. These four planets haven't got a solid surface. They are made up of gases and liquids.

But that's only eight planets. Pluto, the farthest from the Sun, is neither Earth-like nor Jupiter-like. It is a frozen planet, the only one.

Each planet **rotates** on its **axis**. An axis is like an imaginary pole going through a planet's centre from one end to the other. The planet spins as if a giant hand had given this pole a great twist.

Most planets rotate from west to east. Only Venus, Uranus, and Pluto rotate from east to west. On these three planets the Sun seems to rise in the west and set in the east.

DID YOU KNOW?
Scientists have found three planets orbiting the star Upsilon Andromedae, a star much like our Sun. Some think this means there could be life on one of the planets.

Answer: *Gas:* Jupiter, Saturn, Uranus, Neptune
Ice: Pluto
Rock/Metal: Mars, Venus, Earth, Mercury

Minor Planets

On January 1st in 1801, a man named Giuseppe Piazzi found a new object in the sky. It was circling the Sun out beyond the planet Mars, and Piazzi thought it might be a comet. Some people thought that it was a new planet. Over the next few years many more objects were seen. All of these were much smaller than a planet. Astronomers now call these objects 'asteroids' or 'minor planets'.

There are thousands of asteroids in our solar system. They tend to vary in shape, ranging from large **spheres** to smaller slabs and potato-shaped objects. Some asteroids are big. Most are the size of a boulder. The asteroid that Piazzi found, called Ceres, is the biggest discovered so far. Its **diameter** is about 930 kilometres. Smaller asteroids form when two big asteroids smash into each other and break up. Astronomers think that there are millions of tiny asteroids in the solar system.

Like planets, all asteroids in our solar system circle the Sun. The path that a planet or an asteroid follows when it circles the Sun is called an 'orbit'. Most asteroids are found farther from the Sun than Earth, between the orbits of Mars and Jupiter. Some, though, come quite close to the Sun.

Many people believe that millions of years ago an asteroid hit Earth and led to the dinosaurs' dying out. Some filmmakers in Hollywood have even made popular science-fiction films using the idea of an asteroid hitting Earth.

SEARCH LIGHT

Fill in the gap:
An asteroid might have been involved in the disappearance of the dinosaurs when it crashed into _____.

DID YOU KNOW?
Here's a surprise: not all asteroids are in outer space! Starfish are also called asteroids. The name that these two very different things share means 'starlike'.

Answer: An asteroid might have been involved in the disappearance of the dinosaurs when it crashed into Earth.

Rocketing Masses
with Fuzzy Tails

The word 'comet' comes from a Greek word that means 'hairy one'. A comet sometimes looks like a star with a hairy tail. But a comet is not a star. Like the Moon, a comet has no light of its own. A comet shines from the sunlight bouncing off it. Like the Earth, a comet goes around the Sun, so it may appear again and again.

But if a comet isn't a star, what is it?

Some scientists think that a large part of a comet is ice. The rest is bits of iron and dust and perhaps a few big chunks of rock. When sunshine melts the ice in a comet, great clouds of gas go streaming behind it. These clouds make the bright fuzzy-looking tail.

Long ago when there were no streetlights and the air was very clean, everyone could see comets. Unlike the stars that shone every night, comets seemed to appear quite suddenly. People thought that they would bring bad luck such as floods, hungry times, or sickness.

The English astronomer Edmond Halley, who lived over 200 years ago, discovered about 24 different comets. One that keeps coming back was named for him because he worked out when it would return. Halley first saw it in 1759, and it reappeared in 1835, 1910, and 1986. The next time it comes near the Earth will be in the year 2060.

How old will you be then?

SEARCH LIGHT

If Halley's Comet came around in 1759, 1835, 1910, and 1986, about how many years does it take to appear?

Derke/O'Hara/Stone

DID YOU KNOW?
American author Mark Twain, who wrote *Tom Sawyer*, was born in 1835 on a day when Halley's Comet could be seen in the sky. Just as he predicted, he died when Halley's Comet was again seen in the sky, in 1910.

Answer: Halley's Comet generally comes around every 76 years, though sometimes it takes just 75.

Family of the Sun

Pluto · Uranus · Jupiter · Mercury · Earth · Sun · Mars · Neptune · Saturn · Venus

DID YOU KNOW?
The Sun's temperature on the surface is about 5,537 to 6,093°C. That's 100 times hotter than a really hot day on Earth!

Imagine a huge black space. The Sun moves through this vast space, taking many smaller bodies with it. These bodies include planets, asteroids, comets, meteors, and tiny **molecules** of gases. The Sun and its companions are known as a 'solar system'. Many solar systems and stars clustered together make up a galaxy.

Astronomers do not know how far out our solar system extends. We think that Pluto is the last planet to **orbit** the Sun, but there could still be more. At its farthest point from the Sun, Pluto is about 7.2 billion kilometres away.

The Sun provides energy for the rest of the solar system. It also provides the heat and light necessary for life on our planet. And its **gravity** keeps the planets, comets, and other bodies in orbit.

After the Sun, the planets are the largest and most **massive** members of the solar system. There are nine known planets: Mercury, Venus, Earth, Mars, Jupiter, Saturn, Uranus, Neptune, and Pluto.

Asteroids, known as 'minor planets', are smaller bodies. Most asteroids lie between Mars and Jupiter. Ceres is the largest asteroid.

A comet appears in the sky as a fuzzy spot of light with a tail streaming after it. It is made up of dust and frozen gases. As this giant dirty snowball moves closer to the Sun, the ice melts, making what looks like a tail. Halley's Comet is probably the most famous of all the comets.

SEARCH LIGHT

Which of these would you *not* find in the solar system?
- galaxy
- star
- planet
- comet
- asteroid

Answer: Galaxies are made up of stars and solar systems, not the other way around.

17

The Planet Nearest to the Sun

Mercury is the first of the nine planets in our solar system and the closest to the Sun. Because it seems to move so quickly across the night sky, it was named after the wing-footed Roman god. Mercury is visible to the naked eye from Earth, just before dawn and just after sunset.

Mercury is only slightly bigger than Earth's Moon. Its entire surface is airless, though many different gases surround the planet. Mercury is also a place of extreme temperatures. Its hottest temperature is 400°C and its coldest is −175°C.

In 1974 and 1975 the spacecraft Mariner 10 flew as close to Mercury as possible, sending back pictures and other information. Scientists found the planet's surface covered with a layer of broken rock called 'regolith'. Mercury also has large ice patches at its north pole.

Some regions of Mercury are filled with heavy **craters**, probably created when the planet ran into other bodies as it was forming. Other regions show gently rolling plains. These may have been smoothed by the flow of volcanic lava. The planet also features long

Mariner 10 space probe, which sent valuable pictures of and other data about Mercury.
© Corbis

steep cliffs called 'scarps' in some areas.

Mercury takes 88 Earth days to go around the Sun once, which gives it a very short year. But it takes 1,416 hours to complete one **rotation** about its **axis**, so it has a very long day.

Mercury has a sunrise only once in every two of its years. This is because, after one of its very long days, the Sun is in a different place in Mercury's sky. It takes three of Mercury's days (about 176 of our days) for the Sun to rise once again in the morning sky.

NASA/Roger Ressmeyer/Corbis

DID YOU KNOW?
It's not surprising that Mercury was named after the speedy messenger of the gods. The planet travels at an incredible 48 kilometres per second.

Answer: Being so close to the intense heat and bright light of the Sun makes Mercury hard to study. It's difficult to look at it and hard to send a probe there that won't melt.

A Morning and Evening Star

Venus is the second planet from the Sun. It is named after the Roman goddess of love and beauty, perhaps because it shines so brightly. It shines brightly sometimes in the western sky as the 'evening star' and at other times in the pre-dawn eastern sky as the 'morning star'.

Magellan space probe being launched by the space shuttle *Atlantis* in 1989.
© NASA/Roger Ressmeyer/Corbis

Although Venus is the closest planet to Earth, it is difficult to study because it is completely covered by thick layers of clouds. Venus' dense cloud layers do not allow much sunlight to reach the planet's surface. They do, however, help keep the surface very hot, as do the planet's active volcanoes. The temperature on the Venusian surface reaches about 464°C. The highest clouds, by contrast, have a daily range of 25 to −149°C.

Of all the planets, Venus is closest to Earth in size. In fact, Earth and Venus were once regarded as sister planets. Some scientists have suggested that Venus could support some form of life, perhaps in its clouds. However, people could not breathe the air there.

Several spacecraft have visited and sent back information about Venus, beginning with Mariner 2 in 1962. The immensely powerful Hubble Space Telescope has also provided considerable **data** about the planet.

Scientists have learned that the surface of Venus is marked with hundreds of large meteor **craters**. These craters suggest that since it formed, the surface of Venus has changed in a different way from Earth's surface. Earth has only a few large craters that are easy to recognize.

Venus is different from Earth in another way too. It hasn't got a moon.

SEARCH LIGHT

How are Venus and Earth alike? What makes them different?

NASA/JPL/Caltech

DID YOU KNOW?
Some scientists think that an unusual positioning of the planets Venus and Jupiter may have been the bright Star of Bethlehem reported at the time of Jesus Christ's birth.

Answer: Earth and Venus are roughly the same size, and both planets have active volcanoes. Venus might also be able to support some form of life, though probably in its clouds. But Earth is different because it's got water, a moon, and breathable air.

A Trip to the Moon

Would you like to go to the Moon? One day you may be able to.

Astronauts have already visited the Moon. They took their own food, water, and air. You would have to take these things with you too, because the Moon doesn't have them.

Compared with the planets, the Moon is very close to the Earth. It is only 400,000 kilometres away. Spaceships travel fast enough to cover this distance in a matter of hours.

One day there may be little towns on the Moon. The first ones will probably be covered over and filled with air. When you're inside a Moon town, you'll be able to breathe normally without a spacesuit or air tank. But you will need to wear a spacesuit and an air tank outside.

When you walk outside the Moon town, you will feel a lot lighter. You will be able to take giant steps of more than three metres. You'll be able to throw a ball almost out of sight. This is because the Moon has fairly weak gravity, the force that prevents things from flying off into space.

Astronaut Edwin E. ('Buzz') Aldrin on 20 July 1969, one of the first two people to walk on the Moon.
NASA/JPL/Caltech

SEARCH LIGHT

Find out what you would weigh on the Moon. Take your weight and divide by 7.

Gravity is also what gives your body weight. You will not weigh as much on the Moon as you do on Earth. If you weigh 20 kilos on Earth, you'll weigh only around 3 kilos on the Moon!

From the Moon you'll see many more stars than you can see from Earth. They'll also seem much brighter because you won't be looking through layers of air and pollution. And you'll be able to enjoy this view for two whole weeks at a time. That's the length of the Moon's night!

NASA/JPL/Caltech

DID YOU KNOW?

Since there's no wind or water on the Moon, the astronauts' footprints could still be there in 10 million years.

Answer: If your Earth weight is 28 kilos, for example, your Moon weight would be only about 4 kilos.

The Red Planet

SEARCH LIGHT

Which surface feature on Mars holds a record?

Mars is the fourth planet from the Sun. It is named after the ancient Roman god of war. Since the planet is red in colour, it is also called the 'red planet'.

The first spacecraft to fly close to Mars was Mariner 4, in 1965. In the 1970s two Viking spacecraft landed there, and in July 1997 Mars Pathfinder touched down. These efforts sent back soil sample reports, pictures, and other **data** from Mars - but no proof of life.

Because of similarities between Mars and Earth, however, scientists think there could be some form of life on Mars.

Martian surface of rocks and fine-grained material, photographed in 1976 by the Viking 1 spacecraft.
NASA

Mars is half the size of Earth. Its thin air is made up mainly of carbon dioxide and other gases, so we wouldn't be able to breathe it. And the Martian surface is much colder than Earth's would be at that distance from the Sun. Two small moons, Phobos and Deimos, **orbit** Mars.

Like Earth, Mars has ice caps at both poles. But its ice caps are composed mostly of solid carbon dioxide, or dry ice. Liquid water has not been seen on the surface of Mars. However, billions of years ago there may have been large lakes or even oceans on Mars.

Also like Earth, Mars has different seasons. Mars takes 687 Earth days to go around the Sun once. This means that its year is almost twice as long as ours. But since it spins on its **axis** once every 24 hours and 37 minutes, its day is just about the same length.

Despite being small, Mars has the largest volcano in our solar system, Olympus Mons. It stands about three times higher than Earth's highest point, Mount Everest, and covers an area just a bit smaller than the entire country of Poland.

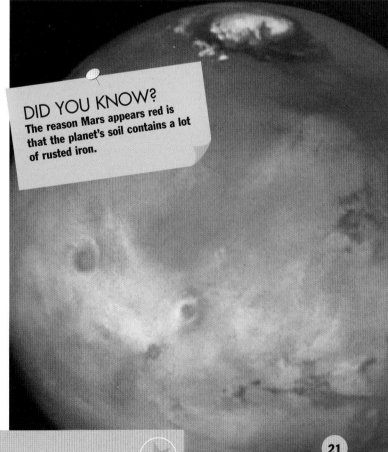

DID YOU KNOW?
The reason Mars appears red is that the planet's soil contains a lot of rusted iron.

In this image taken by the Hubble Space Telescope in 1997, you can see the north polar ice cap (white area) at the top and some huge volcanoes (the darker red spots) in the left half of the photo.
Phil James (Univ. Toledo), Todd Clancy (Space Science Inst., Boulder, CO), Steve Lee (Univ. Colorado), and NASA

King of the Planets

Jupiter is the biggest planet in our solar system. It is so big that all the other eight planets could fit inside it at the same time and there would still be some space left. The planet is named after the king of the Roman gods.

Jupiter is a giant ball of gases, mostly the **elements** hydrogen and helium. Helium is the gas that makes balloons float in air, and hydrogen is one part of water. The centre of the planet is probably made of a hot liquid, like a thick soup.

Jupiter isn't a very welcoming place. It is extremely hot. It is thousands of times hotter than the hottest place on Earth.

Also, storms rage on Jupiter's surface almost all the time. Scientists have seen one storm there that is almost twice as

Jupiter's Great Red Spot (colours improved) as seen by Voyager I spacecraft, 1979.
Jet Propulsion Laboratory/NASA

wide as the Earth! It is called the Great Red Spot. It has been raging on Jupiter's surface for at least a few hundred years.

Jupiter definitely has over 50 moons, and probably more. Some of them are much bigger than Earth's Moon. One is even bigger than the planet Mercury! Others are tiny, only a few miles across.

Astronomers have found something very exciting on one of Jupiter's moons, called Europa. They believe that it has a huge ocean of water below its surface that may have simple life forms in it.

DID YOU KNOW?
Jupiter has more than 50 known moons and Earth has only 1. But that seems fair because Jupiter is 1,500 times bigger than Earth!

SEARCH LIGHT

Find and correct the mistake in this sentence:
A storm known as the Big Red Dog has been raging on Jupiter's surface for hundreds of years.

NASA

Answer: A storm known as the Great Red Spot has been raging on Jupiter's surface for hundreds of years.

The Ringed Planet

Saturn is the sixth planet from the Sun. It is named after the god of **agriculture** in Roman mythology. Saturn is easily visible through a small telescope, and its famous spectacular rings are quite clear. The astronomer Galileo was the first to see the rings through his telescope.

Saturn is a gas planet, like Jupiter, Neptune, and Uranus. Very little of it is solid. Most of Saturn consists of the **elements** hydrogen and helium. It is covered with bands of coloured clouds and surrounded by a number of thin rings made up of water ice and ice-covered **particles**. Photographs taken by the Voyager 1 and 2 spacecraft show that these rings range in size from a speck of dust to the size of a house. Voyager 2 took the photograph you see here.

Because Saturn is made of different substances, different parts of the planet **rotate** at different rates. The upper atmosphere swirls around the planet at rates of between 10 hours and 10 minutes (Earth time) and about 10 hours and 40 minutes. The inner core, which is probably made of hot rocks, rotates in about 10 hours and 39 minutes.

Saturn takes 29 years and 5 months in Earth time to go around the Sun just once. The Earth goes around the Sun once every 365 days. Saturn's year is so much longer because the planet is so much farther away from the Sun than Earth is.

Astronomers have found that at least 30 moons **orbit** Saturn. The largest of these is Titan, which is almost as large as the planet Mercury or Mars. In our photograph, you can see two of the moons as tiny white spots to the lower left of (Dione) and below (Rhea) the planet. Other satellites include Mimas, Enceladus, and Tethys.

SEARCH LIGHT

Saturn's many rings are made of
a) ice.
b) dust.
c) gas.
d) rock.

DID YOU KNOW?
Saturn is more than ten times the size of Earth. But the planet is so light that it could float on an ocean of water.

Jet Propulsion Laboratory/NASA

Answer: a) ice.

King George's Star

Uranus is the seventh planet from the Sun. It's named after the god of the heavens in ancient Greek mythology.

When William Herschel discovered this planet in March 1781, he named it Georgium Sidus (George's Star) in honour of King George III of England. Others called it Herschel. In about 1850, scientists began to use the name Uranus.

The spacecraft Voyager 2 visited Uranus about 200 years after Herschel discovered it. Findings confirmed that Uranus is a large gas planet. Small amounts of methane gas in its upper atmosphere give the planet a blue-green colour.

It takes Uranus 84 of Earth's years to go once around the Sun, so its year is 84 times as long as ours. But the planet takes only about 17 hours to spin on its **axis** once, so its day is shorter.

Voyager 2, the spacecraft that reported Uranus' makeup.
© Corbis

Unlike other planets, Uranus lies on its side at an odd angle. It points first one pole towards the Sun, then its equator, and then the other pole. So it is not yet clear which is the planet's 'north' pole.

As with other gas planets, such as Jupiter, Saturn, and Neptune, Uranus has a system of rings. In some places, the rings are so thin that they seem to disappear.

The planet has 20 known moons that are made mostly of ice and have many **craters**. The five major ones are Miranda, Ariel, Umbriel, Titania, and Oberon. Their names are those of characters from works by William Shakespeare and Alexander Pope.

DID YOU KNOW?
Between Uranus and Saturn lies Chiron, an object first considered to be an asteroid, then reclassified as a comet. Its name reflects its confused identity: Chiron was a centaur - a half man, half horse in Greek mythology.

SEARCH LIGHT

Find and correct the mistake in the following sentence: When William Herschel discovered Uranus in 1781, he named it Georgium Sidus after his dog.

Jet Propulsion Laboratory/NASA

Answer: When William Herschel discovered Uranus in 1781, he named it Georgium Sidus after his king.

The Eighth Planet

Neptune is the eighth planet from the Sun. It is named after the Roman god of the sea.

The planet Neptune was discovered in 1846, but little was known about it until the spacecraft Voyager 2 visited it in August 1989.

Artist's impression of the Voyager 2 spacecraft leaving Neptune after it visited that planet (seen in the background).
© Corbis

Neptune has a shorter day than Earth. So why is Neptune's year so much longer than ours? (Hint: Neptune is the eighth planet from the Sun, and Earth is only the third.)

Neptune is made up mostly of gases. Its bluish colour comes from its thick atmosphere of hydrogen, helium, and methane. Like other gas planets, such as Jupiter and Saturn, Neptune has rapid winds and big storms. The winds on Neptune are the fastest known in our solar system, reaching speeds of about 2,400 kilometres per hour.

The planet rotates quickly - once every 16.1 hours. This means that its day is about two-thirds as long as ours. But it has a much longer year. There are about 60,225 days in one Neptune year. That's how many days it takes the planet to **orbit** the Sun. It has been in the same year since its discovery in 1846. Each season on Neptune lasts for 41 years.

Like Saturn, Neptune has rings - but they aren't as noticeable. Neptune also has 11 known moons. Triton is the largest moon. Triton is slowly drawing closer to Neptune. It is thought that it will one day crash into the planet.

DID YOU KNOW?

It's more than just a little chilly on Neptune. The average temperature is −225°C. By comparison, Antarctica - the coldest place on Earth - has recorded a mere −90°C at its coldest.

NASA

Answer: Neptune is so much farther than Earth from the Sun that it takes the eighth planet about 165 times as long to orbit the Sun.

The Lonely Planet

In Roman mythology, Pluto was the god of the underworld. Pluto is the name given to another dark mystery: the smallest planet in our solar system. Pluto is smaller than the Earth's Moon and is the farthest planet from the Sun - most of the time.

Every 248 years, Pluto's odd **orbit** takes it closer to the Sun than the planet Neptune goes. For 20 years Neptune becomes the farthest planet, as happened from 1979 to 1999.

Pluto is so far away and small that it wasn't discovered until 1930. It is the only planet that hasn't been visited by a spacecraft. Only recently have very strong instruments like the Hubble Space Telescope given us some details about this mysterious faraway planet.

Tiny Pluto is only about 2,390 kilometres across from pole to pole. It's not entirely clear what the planet is made of, but scientists think it may be 50 to 75 per cent rock and the rest frozen water and gases. Pluto is so far from the Sun's warmth that all of it is permanently frozen. Because of its small size and icy

One of the very first photos of Pluto's surface, taken with the Hubble Space Telescope.
Alan Stern (Southwestern Research Institute), Marc Bule (Lowell Observatory), NASA, and the European Space Agency

makeup and because it travels in a part of the solar system where some comets are thought to come from, scientists wonder if Pluto is really more like a giant comet than a planet.

Pluto spins in the opposite direction from most of the other planets. If you were on the planet, you would see the Sun rise in the west and set in the east. A day on Pluto is equal to six days and 25 minutes on Earth. Pluto's year takes more than 90,155 of our days.

Pluto's moon, Charon, wasn't discovered until 1978. As you can see from the large photo, Charon is about half the size of Pluto - quite large for a moon. In fact, some scientists consider Pluto and Charon to be a double planet.

DID YOU KNOW?
Walt Disney's dog character Pluto was named after the ninth planet. Pluto the dog first appeared in 1930, the same year that the planet Pluto was discovered.

SEARCH LIGHT

Fill in the gaps: Pluto is so _____ that it wasn't discovered until _____.

NASA/European Space Agency

Answer: Pluto is so far away that it wasn't discovered until 1930.

Ancient
Mathematician-Astronomer

SEARCH LIGHT

More than 1,500 years ago the Indian scientist Aryabhata came up with some rules and ideas in mathematics that we still use today, as well as some important facts about astronomy.

Aryabhata wrote *Aryabhatiya*, his major work, when he was only 23 years old. Part of the book discusses two kinds of mathematics: geometry (a kind of maths for measuring shapes and objects) and algebra (which solves some number problems).

Fill in the gap: Aryabhata worked out how long the _____ is without using a clock.

The rest of the *Aryabhatiya* talks about the planets, the stars, and space. Aryabhata was the first astronomer to state that the Earth is round and **rotates** on its **axis**. He explained that the Sun and the night sky only seem to move across the sky from east to west each day because the Earth rotates the other direction, from west to east.

Aryabhata worked out that one Earth rotation lasts 23 hours, 56 minutes, and 4 1/10 seconds. That is, he worked out how long one day is. Today's exact measurement is only a tiny fraction different! Of course, to simplify things we count our day as having 24 hours.

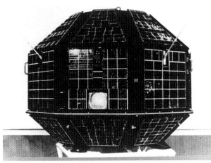

Aryabhata, India's first unmanned satellite.
Indian Space Research Organization

Aryabhata also explained events called '**eclipses**', which happen when the Sun or the Moon goes dark. Hindu mythology says eclipses occur when Rahu, a planet, gobbles up the Sun or Moon. But Aryabhata realized that eclipses happen because of shadows cast by the Earth or the Moon on one another.

The Indian government honoured this great scientist in 1975 by naming the country's first satellite after him.

DID YOU KNOW?

Like many ancient scientific works, Aryabhata's great book, *Aryabhatiya*, was written in verses as a kind of poetry.

These are the ruins of Nalanda, the ancient Buddhist learning centre where Aryabhata studied and worked. Khagola, the observatory at Nalanda, gave its name to the term in India for astronomy: *khagola-shastra*.
© Lindsay Hebberd/Corbis

Student of the Sky

Hundreds of years ago many people thought that the Earth stayed still and the Sun went around it. Then came a man named Nicolaus Copernicus, who said that it was the Sun that stayed still and the Earth that moved. And he was mostly right.

Copernicus was born on 19 February 1473 in Poland. His father died a few years after Copernicus was born, and a wealthy uncle brought the young boy up. He sent him to the University of Kraków to study mathematics. There Copernicus also studied the stars and planets.

Copernicus didn't believe that the Earth was the centre of the universe and that all the other planets and stars circled around it. He studied the sky for years and finally decided that the Sun sat at the centre of the universe. The Earth and the other planets spun around the Sun.

Some of what Copernicus said wasn't correct. We know today that all the planets and the stars, including the Sun, move constantly. We also know that the Sun is the centre not of the universe but rather of the solar system. Yet Copernicus was right in some ways. It is true that the Earth circles the Sun.

An image of the solar system as Copernicus imagined it.
© Stefano Bianchetti/Corbis

Copernicus presented his ideas in a book called *On the Revolutions of the Celestial Spheres*. The book wasn't published for 13 years because the Roman Catholic church opposed it. It is said that Copernicus received the first copy as he was dying - on 24 May 1543.

DID YOU KNOW?
Andreas Osiander, who was in charge of getting Copernicus' last book printed, made some changes and added a note to the front saying that the book wasn't meant to be true— all without the author's permission!

SEARCH LIGHT

Find and correct the error in the following sentence: Copernicus studied the skies and finally decided that the Sun circles the Earth.

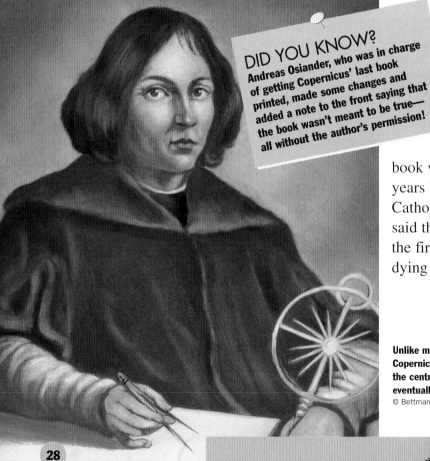

Unlike most people in his day, Nicolaus Copernicus didn't believe that the Earth was the centre of the universe. And his studies eventually showed that he was right.
© Bettmann/Corbis

Answer: Copernicus studied the skies and finally decided that the Earth circles the Sun.

Stargazer

Johannes Kepler was born on 27 December 1571 in Germany. He was to grow up to be an important astronomer who made many discoveries about the stars. Astronomers study the movements of planets, stars, comets, and meteors. However, for most of his life Kepler studied and taught mathematics.

When he was 23 years old, Kepler became an official calendar maker. Calendar making was a difficult job because certain church holy days had to happen just as a particular star was in a particular spot in the sky. It took a lot of complicated maths to make a good calendar.

In 1597 Kepler published his first important work, *The Cosmographic Mystery*. Kepler's book explained the distance of the planets from the Sun. Kepler also said that all the planets revolve around the Sun and that the Sun remains in one position - an idea that built on those of the earlier astronomer Nicolaus Copernicus.

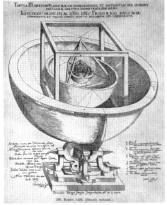

Diagram of Kepler's first model of the universe.
© Bettmann/Corbis

In 1600 Kepler moved to Prague, where he soon became Emperor Rudolf II's **imperial** mathematician, the most important mathematics post in Europe. Kepler discovered that Mars's orbit is an ellipse (an oval-like shape) rather than a circle. He also explained important laws for the motion of all of the planets around the Sun.

Kepler's scientific work focused on astronomy. But he also studied other sciences and mathematics so he could learn everything possible about the stars.

DID YOU KNOW?
Kepler's grave was lost during a war, but the words he composed for his gravestone still survive:
I used to measure the heavens,
now I shall measure the shadows of the earth.
Although my soul was from heaven,
the shadow of my body lies here.

Johannes Kepler became the official mathematician to Emperor Rudolf II. This picture shows him explaining some of his discoveries to the emperor.
© Bettmann/Corbis

Answer: c) maths.

An Apple, an Idea

When you throw a ball into the air, do you wonder why it always comes back down? Why doesn't it keep going up?

One man did more than wonder. He was Sir Isaac Newton.

There is a story that says Newton was sitting under an apple tree when an apple struck him on the head. He wondered why the apple fell down instead of up. Was there a force that no one could see, pulling the apple to the ground?

Actually, it was Newton's observation of the motions of the planets that contributed most importantly to his great discovery: the *Law of Universal Gravitation*. This 'natural law' helps explain why the Earth, the Moon, and the planets don't bump into each other. It explains why things feel light or heavy and what makes them fall to the ground.

Newton's reflecting telescope, made in 1668.
© James A. Sugar/Corbis

What Newton decided was that everything has gravity. And every object's gravity has a pull on everything else around it. Heavy things pull harder than light ones.

Newton worked out many other things too. Did you know that white light is actually made of seven colours? These are the colours that make up a rainbow. Newton discovered this. He let the light pass through a **prism**, and the seven colours all came through separately. He then let the colours pass through another prism and they combined back into white light.

Newton's investigations also led him to invent the first reflecting telescope, which uses mirrors to gather light to improve a telescope's capability. His design is still used by amateur telescope makers.

Isaac Newton was one of the greatest scientists who ever lived. He died in 1727 and was buried in Westminster Abbey in London, England. He was the first scientist to be honoured in this way.

SEARCH LIGHT

Find and correct the mistake in the following sentence: Newton's *Theory of Reflecting Telescopes* helped explain why the planets don't bump into each other.

DID YOU KNOW?
The story of Newton and the apple isn't true, but it is a good way to remember something important about someone famous.

Sir Isaac Newton's theory of gravity contributed to his lasting reputation as one of the greatest scientists of all time.
© Bettmann/Corbis

Answer: Newton's *Theory of Gravitation* (or *Gravity*) helped explain why the planets don't bump into each other.

A Brilliant Wonderer

Young Albert Einstein didn't always do well in school in Germany. His teachers thought he took too long to answer questions. And often they got upset because Albert thought of questions they couldn't answer.

Find and correct the error in the following sentence: Albert Einstein invented gravity.

The more Albert learned, the more things he thought about. The more he thought, the more questions he had. By age 12 he had decided that he would solve the riddle of the 'huge world' - the universe.

Einstein thought there must be some rules to explain why everything in the universe, big and little, acts as it does. How can gravity attract distant objects through empty space? What makes tiny atoms stick together to form all the different things there are?

The Einstein Memorial, a sculpture in honour of the great scientist, in Washington, D.C., U.S.
© Roman Soumar/Corbis

He thought and thought until he believed he had some of the answers for things that scientists had long tried to work out - such as what makes gravity work and how fast light can travel. Einstein even proved such unexpected things as the fact that light bends under the force of gravity.

You may have heard of Einstein's famous formula $E = mc^2$. This stands for a complex idea called 'relativity'. But in the simplest terms it shows that a small **particle** of matter is equal to an enormous quantity of energy.

Einstein introduced entirely new ways of thinking about time, space, matter, energy, and gravity. His ideas guided such scientific advances as space exploration and the control of atomic energy. One of the concepts he explained, the **photoelectric effect**, led to something most people enjoy daily: television.

DID YOU KNOW?
One story about Einstein has it that he once used a check for $1,500 as a bookmark - and lost it.

Albert Einstein, shown here in his study, introduced entirely new ways of thinking about time, space, matter, energy, and gravity.
© Bettmann/Corbis

Answer: Albert Einstein explained gravity.

Discovering
How Stars Grow

Astronomer Subrahmanyan Chandrasekhar was born in Lahore, India (now in Pakistan). He studied at home, then attended universities in India and England. He traveled to the United States to work and became a U.S. citizen in 1953.

Chandrasekhar's work on stars helped explain how the strange space **phenomena** called 'black holes' are born.

By the early 1930s scientists had decided that over billions of years a star changes its **chemical** makeup and its energy drains away. The star then starts to shrink, pulled into a tight ball by its own **gravity**. It ends up about the size of the Earth and becomes a 'white dwarf' star.

Chandrasekhar, however, showed that this process happens only to stars about one and a half times the size of our Sun or smaller. Larger stars actually continue to fall in on themselves. Finally their gases explode in a **supernova**, shining a billion times brighter than the Sun. These larger stars become neutron stars after their explosions. A neutron star is only about 19 kilometres across, but it has as much matter in it as the Sun.

Lalitha Chandrasekhar at the unveiling of the Chandra X-Ray Observatory, named to honour her husband.
© Reuters NewMedia Inc./Corbis

Even bigger stars than those will collapse into black holes. Black holes have so much gravity in such a small amount of space that nothing can escape from them, not even light!

Chandrasekhar's discoveries were so important that they were named the 'Chandrasekhar limit' after him. And in 1983 he was awarded the Nobel Prize for Physics for his contributions to scientific knowledge.

DID YOU KNOW?
Some scientists think it might be possible to travel through black holes to other parts of the universe, assuming you could somehow survive the crushing gravity.

SEARCH LIGHT

True or false? Chandrasekhar is known for his work on the Sun.

At the University of Chicago campus where he taught, Subrahmanyan Chandrasekhar sits at the base of a statue named 'Nuclear Energy', created by sculptor Henry Moore.
© Bettmann/Corbis

Answer: FALSE. Chandrasekhar is known for his work on stars bigger than the Sun - stars that become black holes when they die.

First American Woman in Space

Sally Kristen Ride was the first American woman to fly into outer space. Only two other women had ever flown into space before - both from the former Soviet Union.

Ride did not grow up wanting to be an astronaut. She actually started out as an athlete and was a talented tennis player. But she decided to go to university instead, studying first English and then science.

Ride was one of about a thousand women who applied to be an astronaut and serve as a scientist on the new space shuttle flights. Whilst still at university, Ride was chosen by NASA (the National Aeronautics and Space Administration) to be one of six new female astronauts.

In 1979 she completed her NASA training, earning her pilot's licence at the same time. Four years later, on 18 June 1983, she became the first American woman to go into space. Ride was chosen as the flight engineer aboard the space shuttle *Challenger*. Her work as a scientist meant that she could **monitor** and run the shuttle's complicated equipment.

Ride says that 'the flight was the most fun I'll ever have in my life'.

She flew into space a second time on 13 October 1984. This time, her childhood friend Kathryn Sullivan made history by becoming the first American woman to walk in space.

Sally Ride has shared her exciting experiences and knowledge in books for children, including *To Space and Back* in 1986 (written with Susan Okie) and *Voyager: An Adventure to the Edge of the Solar System* in 1992 (written with Tam O'Shaughnessy).

> **DID YOU KNOW?**
> Other 'female firsts' in space include Valentina Tereshkova of Russia (formerly the Soviet Union), the very first woman in space (1963), and Mae Jemison, the first African American woman astronaut, aboard the space shuttle *Endeavor* (1992).

SEARCH LIGHT

True or false? Sally Ride is famous for being the first woman in space.

Before Sally Ride became the first American woman in space, she was part of the team on the ground, communicating with the astronauts in space. It must have been exciting to experience those calls from both sides.
© Bettmann/Corbis

Answer: FALSE. She is famous for being the first *American woman in space.*

Exploring the New Frontier

SEARCH LIGHT

Why is a space station called a satellite?

Once, the Moon was the only important thing in **orbit** around planet Earth. Today, many objects circling the Earth have been launched into space by people. All these orbiters, including the Moon, are called '**satellites**'. Those launched by people are called '**artificial** satellites'.

Communications satellites send telephone, television, and other electronic signals to and from different places on Earth. Weather satellites take pictures of the clouds and wind systems. Various scientific satellites gather information about outer space. There are even 'spy' satellites which take pictures for the military. And there are space stations.

In the late 20th century, the United States, Russia, the European Space Agency, Japan, and Canada joined forces to build the International Space Station (the ISS). It is meant to have people on it all the time. In 1998, the first two ISS **modules** were launched and joined together in space. In November 2000, the first three-person crew, an American and two Russians, occupied the station, which was still being added to.

Large space stations are planned for the future. These will have many people working in them all the time. They could be like airports are today, where a person changes planes to go to a specific destination. But from a spaceport, people would change spacecraft to travel to the Moon, another planet, or another space station.

In November 2000 the first three-person crew - an American and two Russians - occupied the still-growing International Space Station.
© NASA

DID YOU KNOW?

In order to leave the Earth's gravity and visit a space station, you have to travel at a speed of 11 kilometres per second.

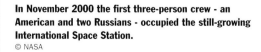

Answer: Since space stations orbit a planet, they are considered to be satellites.

Going Up in Space

Space is what we call the area that's 160 kilometres or more above Earth's surface. Below that boundary is Earth's **atmosphere** - the layer of gases including the air we breathe. In space there is no air to breathe. And it is very, very cold.

Russia and the United States were the first countries to send people into space. Russia's space travellers are called 'cosmonauts', which means 'space sailors'. Those from America are called 'astronauts', meaning 'star sailors'.

In 1961 cosmonaut Yuri Gagarin became the first man to travel into space. In 1969 astronaut Neil Armstrong became the first man to walk on the Moon. Sally Ride, in 1983, was the first American woman astronaut.

Today people travel into space inside **space shuttles** that ride piggyback on a rocket into space. After blastoff, the Earth outside the shuttle moves farther and farther away until it looks like a big blue-and-white sea outside the astronauts' window.

In space anything not tied down will float - including the astronauts themselves! Earth's gravity has become too weak to hold things down. In fact, it's hard to tell what 'down' means in space.

The shuttle's many special machines help astronauts live in space. The main computer helps fly the shuttle and control conditions within it. A long metal arm lets the astronauts handle things outside their ship. And many other machines are carried along for experiments. Today most space shuttle trips are to space stations, where astronauts and cosmonauts can live while they work in space.

DID YOU KNOW?
Because different planets have different gravities, an astronaut's weight would change from planet to planet. For example, an astronaut weighing 75 kilos on Earth would weigh only 28 kilos on Mars but 177 kilos on Jupiter.

SEARCH LIGHT

Space is the area
a) more than 160 kilometres out from Earth.
b) more than 16 kilometres out from Earth.
c) more than 16,000 kilometres out from Earth.

Imagine you are lying on your back inside a space shuttle. Two long rockets will help your heavy spaceship get off the ground. With five seconds to go, the fuel in your spaceship starts burning. 'Five...four...three...two...one'.
NASA

Answer: a) more than 160 kilometres out from Earth.

In addition to an atmosphere, which three things are needed for life?
a) water, heat, and air
b) dirt, heat, and light
c) water, heat, and light

Life Beyond the Earth

Could there be life elsewhere in the universe? There are some people who think that it's possible. They have given the idea a name, extraterrestrial life. 'Extra' means 'beyond' and 'terrestrial' means 'of the Earth', so altogether the name means 'life beyond the Earth'.

Most scientists believe that for another planet to have life on it, it must have an **atmosphere** (air), light, heat, and water like the Earth does.

We get our light and heat from the Sun. The universe is filled with millions of stars like our Sun. Scientists are trying to find out if these stars have planets - perhaps Earth-like planets. If there is such a planet, then it could have life on it.

It's not easy to find extraterrestrial life. The universe is an immense place to search. Some scientists believe that if there is intelligent life elsewhere, it may send radio signals to us. So far, the only signals that scientists have found are the natural ones that come from stars and planets themselves.

Whether it is possible or not, the idea of beings on other planets has excited people for years. Some believe that aliens from other worlds have even visited Earth. They call these aliens 'extraterrestrials' or 'ETs'. Some even claim to have seen ETs and their spaceships, which are called 'unidentified flying objects' or simply 'UFOs'.

What do you think? Are there creatures living on other planets? And how do you think they would live?

DID YOU KNOW?
World War II American pilots gave the name 'foo fighters' to mysterious UFOs - floating lights they saw over Germany. Today an American rock band has borrowed the name.

Discover and understand our world's natural wonders

Planet Earth

Planet Earth

TABLE OF CONTENTS

Learning About the Earth

Geography is the science of the Earth's surface. It helps us learn about what makes the different shapes and colours of the Earth - the ground, rocks, and water, what does and does not grow.

If you look at the Earth as a geographer does, then you might see it as a colourful map. Much more than half of it is blue with oceans, lakes, rivers, and streams. In some places it is tan-coloured with the sands of dry deserts. In other places it is green with forests. There are purple-grey mountains and white snow-capped peaks. And there are the soft yellow of grain fields and the light green of leafy crops.

Part of learning about the Earth is learning where people can and can't live. The different colours of your Earth map can help you discover this.

You won't find many people in the tan, white, or larger blue parts - deserts, the snowfields, and oceans. Not many people live in the deserts, because deserts are hot and dry. Very few plants can grow there. In the high mountains and at the North and South poles, it is very cold. Most plants don't like the cold, and most people don't either.

You will find people in and near the green and yellow parts and the smaller blue parts - the farmlands, forests, rivers, and lakes. To those regions you can add brown dots and clusters of dots, for towns and cities.

There's a lot to learn about the Earth, just as there's a lot to learn about a friend. Geography helps you become the Earth's friend.

SEARCH LIGHT

Areas where not many people live are also the areas where few plants grow. Why do you think that is? (Hint: What do you do with lettuce, beans, and apples?)

DID YOU KNOW?
The 'big blue marble' is one nickname for the planet Earth. This is because, from space, our world looks like a big round marble - all blue with swirling white streaks of clouds.

The coast of Nova Scotia, in Canada, shows some of Earth's many shapes and colours. Geography looks closely at what makes these different shapes and colours.
© Raymond Gehman/Corbis

Answer: If few plants grow in an area, then few animals will live there. This is because animals need either plants or other animals to eat. And without plants or animals, there's nothing for people to eat.

The Largest Pieces of Land

SEARCH LIGHT

Name the seven continents.

The continents are the largest bodies of land on the Earth. Look at a globe. Whatever is blue is water. Most of the rest is land: the continents.

There are seven continents. From biggest to smallest, they are Asia, Africa, North America, South America, Antarctica, Europe, and Australia.

Some continents, such as Australia and Antarctica, are completely surrounded by water. And some continents are joined together, as Asia and Europe are.

Continents are physical bodies, defined by their shape, size, and location. They have mountains, rivers, deserts, forests, and other physical features. But people have divided them into **political** groupings, called 'countries' or 'nations'.

Large continents, such as Asia, may include both very large countries, such as China, and very small countries, such as Nepal. Australia, the smallest continent, is also a country - one of the world's largest.

North America contains three countries - Canada, the United States, and Mexico - and a few small countries, in a region known as Central America. Europe, on the other hand, is the world's second-smallest continent but has about 50 countries.

Africa, the second-largest continent, is believed to be where the very first humans appeared. The continent of Antarctica is all by itself down at the South Pole. It is rocky and is covered by thick ice that never melts. Only a few plants and animals can be found along its seacoasts.

Earth scientists believe that the continents began forming billions of years ago. Lighter parts of Earth's **molten** core separated from heavier parts and rose to the top. As they cooled off and became solid, the land that eventually became the continents formed.

Most scientists agree that the individual continents were at first joined together and then drifted apart. One theory suggests that there were once two 'supercontinents': Gondwanaland in the south and Laurasia in the north.

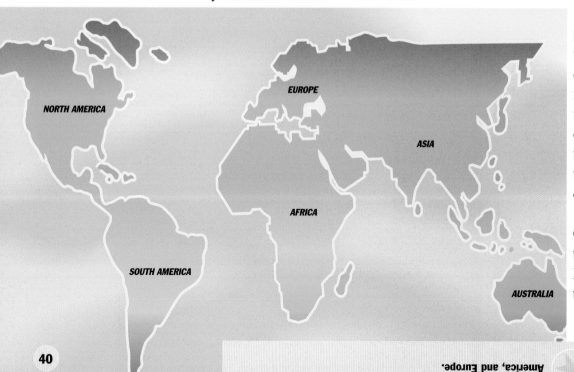

NORTH AMERICA

EUROPE

ASIA

AFRICA

SOUTH AMERICA

AUSTRALIA

A Continent of Extremes

Antarctica is the coldest, windiest, and highest **continent** in the world. It lies at the bottom of the world, surrounding the South Pole. The name Antarctica means 'opposite to the Arctic', referring to the Arctic Circle on the other side of the world.

The coldest temperature recorded in Antarctica is also the world's lowest, at −89.2°C. A sheet of ice covers the entire continent. At its thickest point, the ice is almost 5 kilometres deep - and that's on *top* of the ground. The continent contains most of the world's ice and much of the world's freshwater. Toward the edges of the continent, the ice becomes glaciers, creeping rivers of ice.

Strange and wonderful Antarctica has only one day in the entire year. The Sun generally rises on 21 September and sets on 22 March. This one long day is the summer. From 22 March until 21 September, the South Pole is dark and Antarctica has its night, or winter.

People do not live permanently in Antarctica. Only scientists and some adventurous tourists visit. There are, however, 45 species of birds in Antarctica, including the emperor penguin and the Adélie penguin, that live near the seacoast. Also, four species of seals breed only in Antarctica.

Whales live in the water around the **frigid** continent. The killer whale, the sperm whale, the rare bottle-nosed whale, the pygmy whale, and seven species of baleen whales can all be found off the coast.

Oddly, there are active volcanoes in Antarctica. That means you can find not just the world's coldest temperatures here but, deep down, some of the hottest too.

These emperor penguins are some of Antarctica's very few inhabitants. So in a way, they might indeed be considered the 'rulers' of this harsh and beautiful frozen desert continent.
© Galen Rowell/Corbis

DID YOU KNOW?
Antarctica is a desert - a 'frigid desert'. It's extremely cold, unlike the more common hot sandy deserts. But like them, it gets so little moisture during the year that very little life can survive.

SEARCH LIGHT

Match the numbers with the correct labels. You may have to do some working out and clever thinking!

45	coldest temperature
−89.2	bird species
182.5	thickness of ice
5	length of one day

Answer: −89.2 (°C) — *coldest temperature*
45 — *bird species*
5 (kilometres) — *thickness of ice*
182.5 (days) — *length of one day*

Building Earth's Giant Landscapes

What makes mountains? Several different processes contribute to mountain building. And most mountains are formed by a combination of these - usually over millions of years.

Deep inside, the Earth is so incredibly hot that everything is melted, or molten. This molten material, or lava, escapes to the Earth's surface when volcanoes erupt. The lava cools and becomes hard and solid. This happens again and again, collecting until there is a volcanic mountain.

Mount Fuji in Japan and Mount St. Helens in Washington state, U.S., are volcanic mountains. There are also many undersea volcanic mountains - much taller than anything on land!

In some cases, strong earthquakes caused the surface rock for miles and miles to break. Part of the surface was then lower and part of it was higher.

SEARCH LIGHT

Mountains are made when
a) volcanoes erupt.
b) earthquakes happen.
c) the Earth pushes together.
d) all of the above.

More earthquakes moved the lower parts down and the upper parts up. Eventually, the high parts became tall enough to make mountains.

Still other mountains were pushed up from the bottom of an ocean when two enormous portions of the Earth crashed together - *very slowly*, over millions and millions of years. Some of the largest mountain chains formed this way. The Andes of South America is an example.

Another mountain-building process is called 'folding'. If you push a rug up against a wall, it folds and rumples. That's basically the way the Appalachian Mountains in eastern North America were formed.

At first, most mountains were steep and sharp. But even hard rocks can be worn away. Slowly, with the wind and the rain rubbing at them, steep sharp mountains grew smoother, shorter, and rounder.

DID YOU KNOW?
To be considered a mountain, the land must rise at least 610 metres above its surroundings. Mount Everest, the world's highest mountain, rises 8,850 metres above sea level.

© David Muench/Corbis

When Water Is Stronger than Stone

Caves are natural openings in the Earth large enough for a person to get in. Most have been made when rainwater or streams have worn away rock - usually a softer rock such as limestone. The wearing-away process is called 'erosion'.

Slowly, over millions of years, the water works away at the soft rock, making a small tunnel-like opening. As more and more rock wears away, the opening grows wider and deeper. Soon even more water can flow in. In time, many of these openings become huge caves, or caverns.

Mammoth Cave-Flint Ridge in Kentucky, U.S., is a linked system of caverns. It is 555 kilometres long, one of the longest in the world. In France the Jean Bernard, though much shorter (17.9 kilometres long), is one of the world's deepest caves, reaching down more than 1,535 metres.

Some caves have beautiful craggy formations called 'stalactites', like those pictured here, that hang from the cave's roof. These are made by water seeping into the cave. Each drop leaves a very tiny bit of dissolved rock on the ceiling of the cave. After thousands and thousands of years, an icicle-shaped stalactite forms.

When water drips to the cave's floor, it deposits small **particles** of solids. These slowly build up into a stalagmite, which looks like an upside-down icicle.

There are other kinds of caves that are made in different ways. When lava flows out of a volcano, it sometimes leaves gaps, making volcanic caves. When ice melts inside a glacier, glacier caves result. And ocean waves pounding on the shore year after year can wear away a cave in the face of a cliff.

SEARCH LIGHT

Which of the following is *not* a way that caves are formed?
ocean waves
lava
lightning
water erosion
ice melts

DID YOU KNOW?
Here's a good rhyming way to remember which formation is a stalactite and which is a stalagmite.
Stalactites hold 'tight' to the ceiling.
Stalagmites 'might' reach the roof.

© David Muench/Corbis

Answer: Caves aren't formed by lightning.

Lands of Little Water

Deserts are places that get very little rain each year - so little rain that most trees and plants cannot grow there. Some deserts will go for years without rain. They are difficult places to live in, and the few plants, animals, and people who live there have to be tough to survive. Every continent except Europe has a desert. Even Antarctica has one, a **frigid** desert.

Most deserts, however, are arid or dry deserts with mile after mile of sand, baked earth, and barren rock. In the daytime, these places look like lost worlds - hot, dry, and silent. Usually, the only plants growing there are low thorny ones. These plants store most of the water they are able to collect. It may be a long time before their next drink.

At night it can be quite cold in the desert. That's when creatures that have been hiding from the Sun's burning rays come out of their homes. Many of the creatures are lizards and insects such as scorpions. There are also different kinds of rats as well as other, larger animals.

Golden desert snapdragons, or yellow Mojave flowers, in Death Valley, California, U.S.
© Darrell Gulin/Corbis

You can hear the animals squeaking and growling near water holes and springs. That's where the coyotes, badgers, bobcats, foxes, and birds gather - all hunting for food and water. When the rare spring does bubble up in the desert, plants and trees begin to grow. An island of green like this is called an 'oasis'.

Many people choose to live in the desert. In the late afternoon the sky turns crimson and gold, and the mountains make purple shadows. And at night the stars seem close enough to touch.

DID YOU KNOW?
Desert sands are known to 'sing'. For some reason that scientists do not yet fully understand, sand sometimes makes a booming, barking, or humming noise when walked upon or moved by some other natural force.

SEARCH LIGHT

Fill in the gap: Every continent except _____ has a desert.

This desert in California, U.S., called Death Valley, is both beautiful and dangerous. It's also the lowest point below sea level in the Western Hemisphere.
Joseph Sohm—Chromosohm/Photo Researchers

Answer: Every continent except Europe has a desert.

Water in the Desert

Probably the most precious thing in the world is fresh water. If a person was lost in a desert without any special equipment or supplies, he or she would soon die from lack of water.

It is therefore not surprising that very few people live in the desert. But some people do. Where do they stay? Obviously, they stay where there is water.

A place in the desert with a natural supply of fresh water is called an 'oasis'. An oasis has enough water to support a variety of plants.

Most oases (the plural of 'oasis') have underground water sources such as springs or wells. Al-Hasa is the largest oasis in the Middle Eastern country of Saudi Arabia. It has hectares and hectares of palm groves and other crops.

But not all oases have a constant supply of water. Some areas have dry channels called 'wadis', where springs sometimes flow. And desert areas at higher elevations sometimes receive extra rain to support plant life.

In the Sahara, people can live year-round in the oases because the water supply is permanent. The oases allow crops to be watered, and desert temperatures make crops grow quickly. The date palm is the main source of food. However, in its shade grow citrus fruits, figs, peaches, apricots, vegetables, and cereals such as wheat, barley, and millet.

The Siwa Oasis in western Egypt has about 200 springs. It is a very fertile oasis, and thousands of date palms and olive trees grow there. In fact, the people living in this oasis export dates and olive oil to other places in the world.

SEARCH LIGHT

How is an oasis like an island?

DID YOU KNOW?
Few people realize just how extreme desert weather can be. The hottest desert temperature recorded is 58°C, in Libya. And in Chile there is a desert that apparently hasn't had any rain for the last 400 years.

In the Sahara desert an oasis like this depends heavily on date palms. They provide both food and enough shade to grow other plants that are too sensitive to grow directly in the desert sun.
Robert Everts–Stone/Getty Images

Answer: An oasis is like an island of water surrounded by a sea of sand. It's like a reverse island.

45

Fingers of Land

A peninsula is a body of land surrounded by water on three sides. The word 'peninsula' comes from the Latin *paene insula*, which means 'almost an island'. There are peninsulas on every **continent**, but each one is different. Most peninsulas of any significance extend into the sea or very large lakes.

In the United States, Florida is a peninsula. The state of Alaska qualifies as one and has several smaller peninsulas of its own.

One of the last great wilderness areas in the United States is on the Olympic Peninsula in Washington state. It is surrounded by the Pacific Ocean, the Strait of Juan de Fuca, and Puget Sound. It has a rainforest, rivers, **alpine** peaks, glaciers, and such creatures as salmon and elk.

In Mexico there are two main peninsulas, the Yucatán Peninsula in the east and Baja California in the west. The Yucatán Peninsula draws tourists to the ruins of great Mayan cities such as Uxmal and Chichén Itzá.

Another famous peninsula is the Sinai Peninsula in Egypt. It is triangular in shape. The peninsula links Africa and Asia. In Jewish history the Sinai Peninsula is known as the site where God appeared before Moses and gave him the Ten Commandments.

Europe too has several peninsulas. In northern Europe the Scandinavian Peninsula contains the countries of Norway and Sweden. Denmark forms another. And the Iberian Peninsula in southern Europe is made up of Spain and Portugal. Italy and part of Greece are peninsulas as well.

The world's largest peninsula is Arabia, at over 2.6 million square kilometres. Other important peninsulas in Asia include Korea and Southeast Asia.

> **DID YOU KNOW?**
> Peninsulas in warm climates, such as Iberia (Spain and Portugal), Italy, and Florida, tend to be popular tourist destinations owing to their miles of beaches.

SEARCH LIGHT

Which of the following are peninsulas? (Feel free to consult your classroom map or globe.)

Korea	Britain
Portugal	Arabia
Italy	Florida
Hawaii	Denmark

This peninsula in the U.S. state of Michigan is small by some standards. But it's an excellent example of what a peninsula looks like.
© James L. Amos/Corbis

Answer: The only two that are *not* peninsulas are Hawaii and Britain. They are islands.

Endangered Ecosystems

Imagine a forest with a carpet of wet leaves littering the ground. If you look up, you see only a **canopy** of broad green leaves. There are wildflowers on the trees. You can hear water drops, insects, birds, and, perhaps, the distant screech of a monkey. The place you are picturing is a rainforest.

View of the Venezuelan rainforest canopy from the air.
© Fotografia, Inc./Corbis

A rainforest is a kind of **ecosystem** - a community of all the living things in a region, their physical environment, and all their interrelationships.

Rainforests are dense, wet, and green because they get large amounts of rain. The Amazon Rainforest in South America is the world's largest rainforest. Other large rainforests lie in Central Africa and Southeast Asia. Northeastern Australia's 'dry rainforest' has a long dry season followed by a season of heavy rainfall.

In a rainforest nothing is wasted. Everything is **recycled**. When leaves fall, flowers wilt, or animals die on the forest floor, they decay. This releases nutrients into the soil that become food for the roots of trees and plants. Water **evaporates** in the forest and forms clouds above the trees. Later this water falls again as rain.

SEARCH LIGHT

What's one important way that rainforests help people? (Hint: Think of aspirin.)

Rainforests are rich in plants and animals. Many have not even been discovered yet. Some rainforest plants have given us important medicines. These include aspirin, which is a pain reliever, and curare, used to help people relax during medical operations.

Unfortunately, the rainforests are being destroyed rapidly. The trees are felled for **timber** and to clear land for farming. Animals living in these forests are facing extinction. And once lost, these animals and forests cannot be replaced.

© Gary Braasch/Corbis

DID YOU KNOW?
Rainforests are being cut down or burned at an alarming rate. Scientists estimate that every day a rainforest the size of New York City is lost.

Answer: Rainforest plants have helped unlock the secrets of many of the drugs we use to keep ourselves healthy today. Aspirin is one of these.

Grassy Wetlands

A marsh is a wetland - an area of land containing much soil moisture that does not drain well. Swamps are also wetlands. The main difference is that while trees grow in a swamp, grasses grow in a marsh. Marsh grasses have shallow roots that spread and bind mud together. This slows the flow of water, which drops rich soil deposits and encourages the growth of the marsh.

There are two main types of marshes - freshwater marshes and salt marshes. Freshwater marshes are found at the mouths of rivers. These marshes are famous as bird **sanctuaries**. They provide an important **habitat** for many birds, mammals, and insects. If we didn't have the marshes, then we would lose many of these animals. There simply isn't anywhere else where they can survive.

SEARCH LIGHT

What's one way that swamps and marshes are alike? What's one way that they're different?

The Amazon in South America, the Congo in Africa, the Nile in Egypt, the Tigris and Euphrates in Iraq, and the Mekong in Vietnam all have large freshwater marshes.

Did you know that the rice you eat grows in freshwater marshes? Rice is the most important of all marsh plants. It provides a major portion of the world's food.

Salt marshes are formed by seawater flooding and draining flat land as tides go in and out. The grasses of a salt marsh will not grow if the ground is permanently flooded. Salt marshes are found along the east coast of the United States, in the Arctic, in the U.K., in northern Europe, in Australia, and in New Zealand.

The Ruby Marshes in the state of Nevada, U.S., provide a great example of what these grassy wetlands look like.
© David Muench/Corbis

DID YOU KNOW?
The largest marsh in the world is the Florida Everglades. This marsh-swamp combination is somewhat more than 3,200 square kilometres and is home to many extraordinary animals, including the very rare Florida panther.

Answer: Both swamps and marshes are wetlands and support a lot of wildlife. But while trees grow in swamps, grasses grow in marshes.

The Power
of Flowing Water

DID YOU KNOW?
People first looking at Mars through modern telescopes thought that it was covered with rivers or canals. Satellite photographs now suggest that parts of Mars once had flowing water. Water could have meant there was life on Mars.

It seems fairly obvious what rivers are for. They give us water to drink and fish to eat. They do these things for many animals too. But it might surprise you to learn that rivers have some even bigger jobs.

For one thing, rivers deliver water to lakes and oceans. Another major task is changing the face of the land, and this second job makes a huge difference. No other force changes as much of the world's surface as running water does. In fact, the world's rivers could completely **erode** the face of the Earth, though it might take them 25 million years to do it.

We can see rivers' **handiwork** all around us. Valleys are carved out when rivers slowly cut through rock and carry off soil. Canyons and gorges are young valleys.

Another impressive bit of river handiwork is the waterfall. Waterfalls happen when a river wears away soft rock and then drops down onto hard rock that it can't erode. Some falls are **harnessed** to produce electricity.

The world's tallest waterfall is Angel Falls in Venezuela. It drops an incredible 979 metres. Khone Falls on the Mekong River in Southeast Asia sends 9.5 million litres of water over the edge every second - the most of any falls and nearly double the flow of North America's Niagara Falls.

The world's longest river is the Nile in North Africa. The Amazon in South America is a little shorter but carries more water than any other river.

SEARCH LIGHT

Fill in the gap: You could describe one of a river's main jobs as being a sculptor of _____.

Answer: You could describe one of a river's main jobs as being a sculptor of land.

Engulfed by Water

Take a small bowl and place a sponge in it. Now slowly pour water into the bowl. The sponge soaks up the water. But once the sponge is full, the bowl begins to fill up with water. If you pour more water, the bowl will overflow.

This is what happens in a flood. The ground is like a giant sponge that soaks up rainwater until it is full. Some of the water dries and goes back into the air. The rest, called 'runoff', can't be soaked up and can cause floods.

There are different types of flood. Spring floods occur when heavy winter snows melt rapidly. Floods caused by heavy rains can occur at any time of the year. Rivers overflow their banks, and the ground can't soak up the extra water.

The rain and wind accompanying hurricanes (or typhoons, in the Pacific Ocean) can also cause floods. Huge ocean waves **overwhelm** coastal towns, and the heavy rains cause rivers and streams to flood nearby areas. Hurricane-created floods struck Central America in 1998, killing more than 20,000 people and leaving one and a half million homeless.

A flash flood, however, comes without warning. When a **cloudburst** occurs in a hilly region or in a dry riverbed, the runoff is fast. The ground doesn't have time to soak up the rainwater. Destructive flash floods happen when a great deal of water overflows all at once.

Volcanic eruptions and earthquakes at sea may cause huge waves called 'tsunamis', which may swamp coasts. The volcanic eruption of Krakatoa in 1883 formed waves that flooded whole districts in Indonesia.

DID YOU KNOW?
A disastrous flood in 1919 in Boston, Massachussetts, U.S., had nothing to do with water. A molasses tank exploded, and over 7.5 million sticky litres poured out in a 4.5-metre-high wave. Twenty-one people died, and for years Boston smelled of molasses.

In 1999 these people and others suffered losses in the floods that followed Hurricane Irene in Florida, U.S.
© AFP/Corbis

Rivers of Ice

In high mountains there are places that are packed full of ice. These ice packs are called 'glaciers' and look like giant frozen rivers. And like rivers, glaciers flow - but usually so slowly you can't see them move.

It takes a long time to make a glacier. First, snow falls on the mountains. It collects year after year, until there is a thick layer called a 'snowfield'.

In summer the surface of the snowfield melts and sinks into the snow below it. There it freezes and forms a layer of ice. This too happens year after year, until most of the snowfield has been changed into ice. The snowfield is now a glacier.

The snow and ice in a glacier can become very thick and heavy. The glacier then begins to actually move under its own weight and creeps down the mountain valley. It has now become a valley glacier.

SEARCH LIGHT

A valley glacier is
a) a glacier that has grown up in a valley.
b) a thick layer of snow.
c) a glacier that has started to move down a mountain.

The valley glacier moves slowly but with enormous force. As it moves, it scrapes the sides of the mountain and tears off pieces of it. Sometimes it tears off chunks as big as a house. As the glacier moves down the mountain into warmer regions, the ice begins to melt. The icy water fills rivers and streams.

Many thousands of years ago, much of the Earth's surface was covered with moving glaciers. This period is sometimes called the Ice Age. As the world warmed, most of the ice melted away and formed many of the rivers, lakes, and seas around us today - including the Great Lakes in North America, which have an area greater than the entire United Kingdom.

DID YOU KNOW?
In 1998 Christian Taillefer of France set a cycling speed record. He rode down the face of a glacier on a bicycle and reached a speed of 212 kilometres an hour.

In Alaska's Glacier Bay National Park, the 16 glaciers that descend from the mountains present an amazing sight.
© Neil Rabinowitz/Corbis

Answer: c) a glacier that has started to move down a mountain.

The Rainforest River

On a map of South America a thick line cuts across the country of Brazil all the way from the Andes Mountains in Peru to the Atlantic Ocean. That line traces the mighty Amazon River. The other lines that lead into it are major rivers too. Altogether they make up one of the world's greatest river systems, carrying more total water than any other.

Why is the river called 'Amazon'? Many years ago, in 1541, a Spanish soldier named Orellana sailed down the river. He had to fight many women soldiers who lived by the river. It made him think of the Amazons, who were the mighty women soldiers of Greek mythology. So he called the river 'Amazon'.

Along the banks of the river are miles of trees, all tangled together with bushes and vines. This region is known as a 'rainforest'. You can hear the sound of water dripping from leaves because it rains here almost every day. This is the largest tropical rainforest in the world.

In the rainforest there are very tall trees, some as tall as 60 metres. They spread out like giant umbrellas and catch most of the sunlight. There are rubber trees, silk cotton trees, Brazil nut trees, and many others. Many animals, some quite rare, make their homes among the tree branches. These include **exotic** parrots and **mischievous** monkeys - as well as giant hairy spiders!

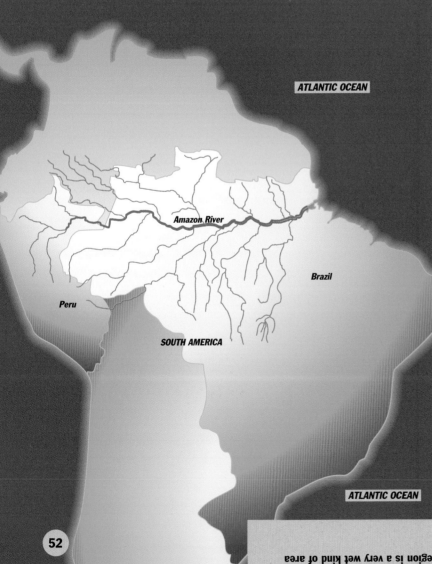

ATLANTIC OCEAN

Amazon River

Brazil

Peru

SOUTH AMERICA

ATLANTIC OCEAN

SEARCH LIGHT

True or false? It rains almost every day in the Amazon.

DID YOU KNOW?

You may hear 'Amazon' used for a totally different thing: Amazon.com or Amazon.co.uk. Perhaps this Internet store wants to be the greatest of its kind, just as the Amazon River is.

Answer: TRUE. The Amazon region is a very wet kind of area known as a 'rainforest'.

Egypt's Gift

There's one country that depends almost entirely on the river that flows through it. That country is Egypt, and the river is the Nile.

Life would be **drastically** different in Egypt if there was no Nile. The river is the source of all the water used for farming in Egypt. That is why people call Egypt the 'gift of the Nile'.

People farm on the banks of the river. Two of the most important things they grow are rice and cotton. Egyptian cotton is one of the finest cottons in the world.

It rains very little in Egypt. Where it does, it's not much more than 17 centimetres a year. There are very dry deserts on both sides of the Nile. The plants you will find there are mostly thorny bushes and desert grass.

Long ago even Egypt's seasons depended on the river. There were just three seasons. *Akhet* was when the river was flooded. During *peret* the land could be seen after the flood. And *shomu* took place when the river's waters were low.

The Nile is **teeming** with different kinds of fish. The most common is the Nile perch. And the river is also an important waterway. Canals, or man-made streams, act as a highway **network** for small boats and ships during the flood season.

After its long journey across North Africa, the Nile empties into the Mediterranean Sea.

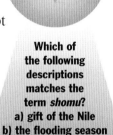

SEARCH LIGHT

Which of the following descriptions matches the term *shomu*?
a) gift of the Nile
b) the flooding season
c) the low-water season
d) the season after the flood

'The Smoke That Thunders'

It is difficult to stand in front of this spectacular African waterfall without feeling small. Victoria Falls is about twice as high as Niagara Falls in North America and about one and a half times as wide. It inspires awe and respect in all who see it.

Victoria Falls lies on the border between Zambia and Zimbabwe in southern Africa along the course of the Zambezi River.

The falls span the entire **breadth** of the Zambezi River at one of its broadest points. There is a constant roaring sound as the river falls. A dense blanket of mist covers the entire area. The Kalolo-Lozi people who live in the area call this mist Mosi-oa-Tunya, 'the Smoke That Thunders'.

The first European to set eyes on this wonder of nature was the British explorer David Livingstone. He named it after Queen Victoria.

The waters of Victoria Falls drop down a deep **gorge**. All the water of the Zambezi River flows in through this gorge. At the end of the gorge is the Boiling Pot, a deep pool into which the waters churn and foam during floods. The river waters then emerge into an enormous zigzag channel that forms the beginning of the Batoka Gorge.

The Victoria Falls Bridge is used for all traffic between Zambia and Zimbabwe. When it opened in 1905, it was the highest bridge in the world.

In 1989 Victoria Falls and its parklands were named a World Heritage site.

© Patrick Ward/Corbis

SEARCH LIGHT

The average height of Niagara Falls is about 50 metres. So what height would you estimate for Victoria Falls? (Hint: Look in the first paragraph.)

DID YOU KNOW?
Victoria Falls is huge, but another waterfall takes the record for being the tallest. Angel Falls in Venezuela dwarfs Victoria at an amazing 979 metres tall.

Answer: Victoria Falls is about twice as high as Niagara Falls. So you can estimate Victoria Falls at 100 metres.

Thunder of Waters

Horseshoe Falls, the Canadian section of Niagara Falls.
© Dave G. Houser/Corbis

Niagara Falls, one of the most spectacular natural wonders in North America, is more than 25,000 years old. The falls are on the Niagara River, which flows between the United States and Canada, from Lake Erie to Lake Ontario.

It is awesome just to be near the waterfall and watch the force of so many litres of water plunging down the steep cliff. More than 2.3 million litres per second pour over the falls. As the water thunders down, it fills the air with a silvery mist in which you can see many shining rainbows. A ceaseless roar fills the air as all this water strikes the bottom. The Iroquois Indians called this waterfall Niagara, meaning 'thunder of waters'.

The falls are divided into two parts by Goat Island. The larger portion is the Canadian section, known as the Horseshoe Falls. It measures 790 metres along its curve and drops 49.4 metres. The American Falls are smaller and rockier. Their width is 305 metres across, and they drop about 51 metres.

Between the American Falls and Goat Island are the small Luna Island and the small Luna Falls, also called Bridal Veil Falls. There are caves behind the curtain of water of both these falls. One of these is the Cave of the Winds.

The best views of the falls are from Queen Victoria Park on the Canadian side, Prospect Point on the U.S. side, and Rainbow Bridge, which crosses between the two.

DID YOU KNOW?
The great Niagara Falls once stopped running. On the evening of 29 March 1848, ice blocked the Niagara River, and the falls stopped for about 30 hours.

SEARCH LIGHT

Find and correct the error in the following sentence: Niagara Falls is more than 2,500 years old.

© Hubert Stadler/Corbis

Answer: Niagara Falls is more than 25,000 years old.

Nature's Masterpiece

A canyon is a deep steep-walled valley cut through rock by a river. The word 'canyon' comes from the Spanish word *cañón*, which means 'tube'. Such valleys are found where river currents are strong and swift. A smaller valley cut out in the same way is called a 'gorge'.

The Grand Canyon, in northern Arizona state in the United States, is the most beautiful and awesome canyon in the world. It is cut about a kilometre and a half deep into the earth and is known for its fantastic shapes and colours. Swiftly flowing water, sand, gravel, and mud gave the rocks their interesting shapes. Each of its rock layers has a different shade of colour, including **buff**, grey, green, pink, brown, and violet.

Rafting through the Grand Canyon on the Colorado River.
© Kevin Fleming/Corbis

The canyon is 446 kilometres long and has been carved through the Arizona landscape by the Colorado River. It stretches in a zigzag course from the northern end of Arizona to the Grand Wash Cliffs near Nevada.

Many ancient pueblos - Native American cliffside dwellings - and other ruins in the canyon show that prehistoric peoples lived there. The Grand Canyon was first discovered by Europeans in 1540. It was established as a national park in 1919.

Visitors to the park can take a mule-pack trip down to the bottom of the canyon. People can even go river rafting, taking a thrilling trip over the rapids.

DID YOU KNOW?
In geological terms the Grand Canyon is fairly young, at about 6 million years old. But the rocks it cuts through date back as far as 2 billion to 2.5 billion years ago.

SEARCH LIGHT

Fill in the gap: The word 'canyon' comes from the Spanish word for '_____'.

If you visit the canyon, you'll probably see some of the many animals that live there. Squirrels, coyotes, foxes, deer, badgers, bobcats, rabbits, chipmunks, and kangaroo rats all make their homes near the canyon.

In 1979 the Grand Canyon was named a World Heritage site.

The Colorado River, seen here in the Marble Canyon portion of the Grand Canyon, cut the whole canyon - over millions of years.
Gary Ladd

Answer: The word 'canyon' comes from the Spanish word for 'tube'.

The World of Water

Did you know that nearly three-fourths of the Earth's surface is under water? And almost all of that water is in one of the four major oceans. From biggest to smallest the oceans are: the Pacific, the Atlantic, the Indian, and the Arctic. Seas, such as the Mediterranean and the Caribbean, are divisions of the oceans.

© Kennan Ward/Corbis

The oceans are in constant motion. The **gravity** of the Moon and the Sun pulls on the oceans, causing tides - the regular rising and falling of the ocean along beaches and coastlines. The Earth's **rotation** makes the oceans circulate clockwise in the Northern **Hemisphere** and **anticlockwise** in the Southern Hemisphere. And winds cause waves to ripple across the ocean surface, as well as helping currents to flow underneath.

Currents are like rivers within the ocean. Some are warm-water currents, which can affect temperatures on land, and some are cold-water currents, which generally flow deeper. Major ocean currents, such as the Gulf Stream off the North American coast, also make for faster ocean travel.

We know less about the oceans than we do about the Moon. The ocean depths hide dramatic deep trenches and enormous mountain ranges. The Mid-Oceanic Ridge is a 65,000-kilometre range that circles the globe.

Oceans affect our lives in important ways. They provide fish to eat. They add moisture to the air to form clouds. And the clouds then make the rain that helps plants grow. Some scientists are even working on affordable ways to turn salt water into fresh water for drinking, cooking, washing, and watering crops. If they succeed, it will be one of the most important inventions of our time.

SEARCH LIGHT

How do the oceans help plants grow?

DID YOU KNOW?

The Mariana Trench near the island of Guam has the deepest spot measured so far, at nearly 11 kilometres. The world's highest mountain, Mount Everest, could sink in that spot and still have a mile of water above it.

© Doug Wilson/Corbis

Answer: Ocean water helps plants grow by adding moisture to the air, which turns into clouds. When the clouds gather enough moisture, it rains, which helps plants grow.

Dry Spots in a Watery World

Small island in the South Pacific Ocean.
© Craig Tuttle/Corbis

Islands are areas of land surrounded on all sides by water. Islands come in all shapes and sizes. The very smallest are too small to hold even a house. The largest islands contain whole countries.

If you live in the United Kingdom, Iceland, Australia, or Japan, you live on an island. But these islands are so large that you might walk all day and never see water.

How do islands develop in the first place?

Some islands begin as fiery volcanoes in the ocean. Hot lava pours out of the volcano, making the island bigger and bigger. Slowly, as the lava cools, it becomes solid land, and when it rises above the water, it becomes an island. These are the volcanic islands.

Other islands are actually parts of the world's **continents**. Some of the land towards the edge of the continent may have been worn away over many, many years by wind or rain, or perhaps some of it sank. Then water from the ocean came in to fill the low places and made a new island.

A row of islands may once have been the tops of mountains in a mountain range. The Aleutian Islands off the coast of North America were probably once a part of a mountain range that connected Alaska with Asia.

Perhaps most surprising are the islands that are built up from the bottom of the ocean from the skeletons of tiny, tiny sea animals called 'coral'. As some corals die, others live on top of them. After thousands of years, a coral island rises to the ocean surface. And these islands go on living!

DID YOU KNOW?
If you try to count the number of islands in the world by looking at a globe, you'll probably come up with 300 or so. But that's only the major islands. Altogether the total is closer to 130,000.

SEARCH LIGHT

Find and correct the error in the following sentence: Coral islands are made of tiny ocean rocks that have piled on top of each other for thousands of years.

This photo from the air shows one of the islands of the Maldives, a country made up of about 1,300 islands in the Indian Ocean.
© Lawson Wood/Corbis

Answer: Coral islands are made of tiny ocean creatures [or creatures' skeletons] that have piled on top of each other for thousands of years.

The Islands at the End of the World

One of the many varieties of finches on the Galapagos Islands.
© Galen Rowell/Corbis

A tortoise as big as a bathtub! Giant lizards that look like dragons! These are only a few of the special things that make the Galapagos Islands different from any other place on Earth. The islands lie in the Pacific Ocean, far away from any other land. People have called them 'the world's end'. Like some other natural wonders, the Galapagos have been named a World Heritage site.

DID YOU KNOW?
The Galapagos finches all developed from the same ancestor. But to share such a small area, different groups developed beaks suited to different feeding habits. This fact helped Darwin understand how species change.

The Galapagos Islands were formed from volcanoes that erupted in the sea. The bare and rocky islands look as if no creature could ever live there. But thousands of animals do, including many found nowhere else in the world. One animal that lives there is the giant tortoise, or land turtle. In fact, the islands got their name from these tortoises. The word *galápagos* means 'tortoises' in Spanish.

The Galapagos Islands were especially important to the famous British scientist Charles Darwin. When Darwin visited the islands, he discovered that there were creatures living there that did not live anywhere else in the world. He saw metre-long lizards - land iguanas that looked like small dragons. And he saw amazing **marine** iguanas - lizards that had actually learned to swim. He also found a great many birds called 'finches' that were all much the same except for differences in their beaks. These differences meant that they all ate different things, which allowed them all to share the same **habitat**.

Darwin decided that all plants and animals evolve, or change little by little, as the world around them changes. One plant or animal group will usually be more successful than another. Darwin called this process 'natural selection'. And he called the overall change through time the 'theory of evolution'.

Do you think people are evolving? What do you think we might look like in a million years?

SEARCH LIGHT

Darwin's famous theory is called
a) natural selection.
b) good versus evil.
c) the big bang.

The giant Galapagos tortoise can live as long as 150 years - longer than almost any other animal. Sadly, few are left today.
© Craig Lovell/Corbis

Answer: a) natural selection.

Island of Reefs
Within Reefs

The Great **Barrier** Reef is one of the great natural wonders of the world. It is actually a system of many individual reefs and islets (small islands). Altogether there are 2,100 individual reefs in the Great Barrier Reef. This huge ridge of coral reefs is separated from land by a **channel** of water 48 kilometres wide.

Exploring the Great Barrier Reef at low tide.
© Staffan Widstrand/Corbis

The Great Barrier Reef was formed over millions of years from mounds of coral. A coral is a soft animal that supports its body inside a hard hollow shell. When the coral died, its shell remained and other corals grew on top of it. Over those millions of years, the corals remained hardened and became cemented together. Slowly they were covered with underwater plants, **debris** from the ocean, and other corals.

The Great Barrier Reef lies in the Pacific Ocean off the coast of Queensland in north-eastern Australia. From north to south its length is equal to the entire Pacific Coast of the United States - extending more than 2,000 kilometres! The water is so clear and pollution-free at the Great Barrier Reef that people can glimpse the wonderful **marine** life deep underwater.

Besides the 400 types of coral, there are such animals as anemones, snails, lobsters, prawns, jellyfish, giant clams, and dugongs. And there are more than 1,500 **species** of saltwater fish. Many of the small fish have brilliant colours and unusual shapes.

The Great Barrier Reef was named a World Heritage site in 1981.

DID YOU KNOW?
Though it isn't truly a single structure, the 350,000-square-kilometre Great Barrier Reef is often referred to as the largest structure ever built by living things. And people had no hand in it!

SEARCH LIGHT

True or false?
The Great Barrier Reef is made of rock.

From north to south, the length of Australia's Great Barrier Reef is equal to that of the entire Pacific Coast of the United States!
© Australian Picture Library/Corbis

Answer: FALSE. It's made of coral skeletons and live coral.

The Biggest Ice Cubes

DID YOU KNOW?
On 14-15 April 1912, just before midnight, the ocean liner *Titanic* struck an iceberg and sank on its very first voyage. Only 705 people survived, and 1,522 of the passengers and crew died.

You can see from the size of the boat how big some icebergs actually are. But the much larger part of an iceberg is under the water!
Pal Hermansen—Stone/Getty Images

Icebergs are simply broken-off pieces of glaciers or polar ice sheets that float out into the ocean. Very big pieces. Even little icebergs called 'growlers' are as big as buses. Big ones are longer than freight trains and as high as skyscrapers.

One especially surprising thing about an iceberg is that the part you see above the water is only a small bit of the whole iceberg. Most of the iceberg is underwater. You can see the way an iceberg floats by doing an easy experiment at home.

Fill a clear glass half full of very cold water. Drop an ice cube into the glass. Notice how most of the ice cube stays below the water.

The ice cube floats just the way an iceberg floats. And as the cube melts, it turns over, just as an iceberg does. Icebergs melt when they float away from freezing waters into warmer waters. Icebergs always start in the parts of the world where it stays cold all the time, near the North or the South Pole.

Icebergs can be very dangerous when they float, big and silent, into the path of a ship. In the past many ships were wrecked because they hit an iceberg. Fortunately, this hardly ever happens anymore. This is because most modern ships have radar that finds the icebergs before they become a problem.

In addition, special airplanes from the International Ice Patrol watch for icebergs in likely areas, and satellites scan the oceans every day. Maps and warnings are regularly sent by radio to all the ships in nearby waters.

SEARCH LIGHT

Icebergs are broken-off pieces of
a) islands.
b) glaciers.
c) ice cubes.

Answer: b) glaciers.

The Ocean's Rise and Fall

Perhaps you have been to the beach and put your towel very close to the water. Then, when it was time to leave, the water seemed to have shrunk and was now far away from your towel.

What actually happens is even more surprising. At high tide the water creeps up the beach. At low tide the water slips down. So the water really doesn't shrink; it simply goes away! But how, and where?

Most seashores have about two high tides and two low tides per day. It takes a little more than 6 hours for the rising waters to reach high tide. It takes another 6 hours for the falling waters to reach low tide. This 12-hour rise and fall is called the 'tidal cycle'.

Tides are caused mainly by the gravity of the Moon and the Sun pulling on the Earth. This causes ocean waters to pile up in a big bump of water directly

At low tide the water slips low down on the beach. At high tide it will creep back up.
© Tim Thompson/Corbis

beneath the Sun and the Moon. As the Earth **rotates**, the tidal bumps try to follow the two heavenly bodies.

The Sun and the Moon are in line with the Earth during a full moon or a new moon. Their gravity added together causes higher-than-normal high tides called 'spring tides'. When the Moon and the Sun are farthest out of line, their gravity forces offset each other. This causes lower-than-normal high tides, called 'neap tides'.

The tides in the Bay of Fundy in Canada rise higher than 16 metres. Beach towels and umbrellas at the Bay of Fundy don't stand a chance!

At high tide the water creeps high up on the beach.

© Tim Thompson/Corbis

SEARCH LIGHT

It takes 6 hours for the tide to rise or fall. When the tide has both risen and fallen, that makes one tidal cycle. How long does it take for two tidal cycles?

DID YOU KNOW?

Some narrow rivers that empty into the sea develop large waves when extremely high tides rush into them. These waves, called 'tidal bores', force the river's flow to change direction as they pass.

Answer: Each tidal cycle has got one rising tide and one falling tide. It takes 6 hours for the tide to rise or fall, so it takes 12 hours for it to do both. That is, 12 hours for one tidal cycle. Two tidal cycles then take 24 hours.

EUROPE

The Youngest Ocean

DID YOU KNOW?
Legend says that the Atlantic Ocean hides the remains of Atlantis, an island that supposedly sank beneath the sea. People have believed stories of Atlantis for many hundreds of years and have spent almost as much time searching for it.

SOUTH AMERICA

AFRICA

The Atlantic Ocean is the world's second largest ocean, after the Pacific. It covers nearly 20 per cent of the Earth. If you tasted water from all the oceans, you'd find the Atlantic to be the saltiest. And even though it is very old, it is actually the youngest ocean.

The Atlantic Ocean lies between Europe and Africa on one side of the globe and North and South America on the other. It reaches from the Arctic Ocean in the north to Antarctica in the south.

Like all oceans, the Atlantic has large movements of water **circulating** in it called 'currents'. Atlantic water currents move **clockwise** in the northern half of the world, but **anticlockwise** in the southern half. The Gulf Stream, a powerful and warm current in the North Atlantic, moves along the east coast of North America. There and elsewhere, the Gulf Stream has important effects on the weather.

Millions of tons of fish are caught each year in the waters of the Atlantic Ocean. In fact, more than half of all the fish caught in the world come from the Atlantic. The Atlantic is also used for activities such as sailing, wind surfing, and whale watching.

But despite the usefulness and magnificence of the Atlantic Ocean, the level of pollution has increased. People have allowed fertilizers, **pesticides,** and waste from toilets and sinks and factories to get into the ocean waters. As people and businesses try harder to stop pollution, the Atlantic will again become a healthier home for its animal and plant life.

SEARCH LIGHT

True or false?
The Atlantic is the saltiest ocean.

Answer: TRUE.

Ocean Between Many Continents

Millions of years ago there was one huge mass of land in the Southern **Hemisphere**. It was the continent of Gondwanaland. But over many, many years Gondwanaland slowly broke up into the continents of South America, Africa, Antarctica, and Australia, as well as most of India.

The water that filled the growing space between these continents is now the Indian Ocean. The Indian Ocean is a huge body of salt water. It is the third largest ocean in the world - about five and a half times the size of the United States!

People from India, Egypt, and ancient Phoenicia (now mostly in Lebanon) were the first to explore this ocean. Later, Arabian merchants set up trade routes to the east coast of Africa. And Indian traders and priests carried their civilization into the East Indies. The dependable winds from the rainy season known as the 'monsoon' made these voyages possible.

Today the Indian Ocean has major sea routes. They connect the Middle East, Africa, and East Asia with Europe and the Americas. Ships carry tanks of **crude oil** from the oil-rich Persian Gulf and Indonesia. The oil is important to modern society, but spills from these oil tankers can endanger ocean life.

The Indian Ocean is alive with plants, as well as animals such as sponges, crabs, brittle stars, flying fish, dolphins, tuna, sharks, sea turtles, and sea snakes. Albatross, frigate birds, and several kinds of penguins also make their home there.

Arabian Peninsula

India

AFRICA

PACIFIC OCEAN

AUSTRALIA

ANTARCTICA

SEARCH LIGHT

Fill in the gap with the correct number: The Indian Ocean is _____ times as big as the United States.

Answer: The Indian Ocean is 5½ times as big as the United States.

EUROPE

Bosporus

Italy

Turkey
(ASIA)

Dardanelles

The Sea in the
Middle of Land

AFRICA

DID YOU KNOW?
Various Mediterranean regions have special marriage customs. One area's custom is to cut the groom's tie into many pieces, which are then sold to the wedding guests for honeymoon money.

Egypt

The Mediterranean Sea gets its name from two Latin words: *medius*, meaning 'middle', and *terra*, meaning 'land'. The Mediterranean Sea is almost entirely surrounded by land. It's right between Africa, Europe, and Asia.

The Mediterranean is a bit larger than the African country of Algeria. But more important than its size is its location. Its central position made the Mediterranean an important waterway for a number of classical cultures, such as those of Italy, Greece, Egypt, and Turkey.

Many **channels** connect the Mediterranean with other bodies of water. The Strait of Gibraltar connects the Mediterranean with the Atlantic Ocean. The Dardanelles and the Bosporus connect it with the Black Sea, between Europe and Asia. And the Suez Canal is a man-made channel connecting the Mediterranean Sea with the Red Sea, which lies between the Arabian **Peninsula** and North Africa.

Three major rivers also lead into the Mediterranean Sea: the Rhône in France, the Po in Italy, and the Nile in Egypt. But the water from most of the rivers **evaporates** quickly. Instead, the Mediterranean Sea gets most of its water from the Atlantic Ocean. So Mediterranean water is very salty.

There are many popular tourist **resorts** along the Mediterranean. These include some of the Mediterranean's many islands, such as Corsica, Sardinia, Sicily, Malta, Crete, and Cyprus. Tourists often like to take a **cruise** across the Mediterranean. They get to visit many different countries all at once, try lots of different food, and see the **remains** of various ancient civilizations.

SEARCH LIGHT

Which ocean provides the most water to the Mediterranean?

Answer: The Atlantic Ocean supplies most of the Mediterranean's water.

65

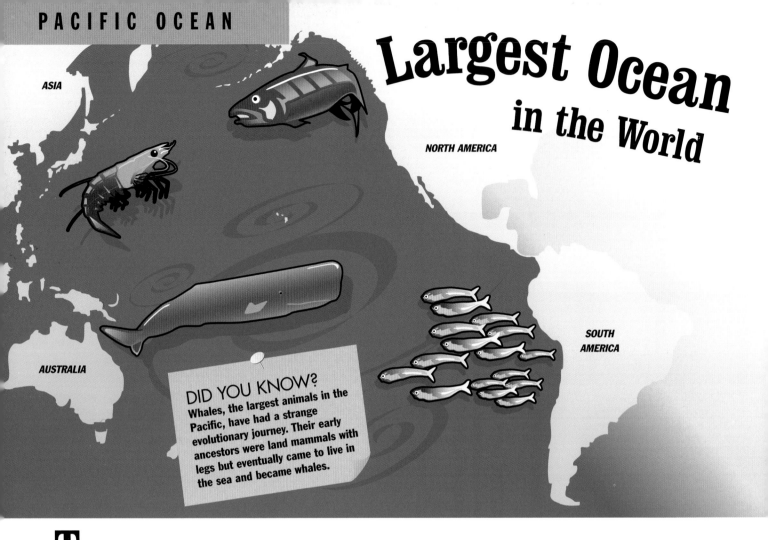

Largest Ocean in the World

ASIA

NORTH AMERICA

AUSTRALIA

SOUTH AMERICA

DID YOU KNOW?
Whales, the largest animals in the Pacific, have had a strange evolutionary journey. Their early ancestors were land mammals with legs but eventually came to live in the sea and became whales.

The Pacific Ocean is the largest ocean in the world. It covers nearly one-third of the Earth. The Pacific is also deeper than any other ocean. The Pacific Ocean lies between the **continents** of Asia and Australia on the west and North and South America on the east.

The Pacific's deepest parts are the ocean trenches. These trenches are long, narrow, steep, and very deep holes at the bottom of the ocean. Of the 20 major trenches in the world, 17 are in the Pacific Ocean. The deepest trench is the Mariana Trench. It is deeper than Mount Everest (the highest mountain on land) is tall.

There are also many islands in the Pacific Ocean. Some islands were once part of the continents. Some that were part of Asia and Australia include Taiwan, the Philippines, Indonesia, Japan, and New Zealand.

Other Pacific islands have risen up from the floor of the ocean. Many of them are born from volcanoes. These islands are built over thousands of years by the lava that comes out of the volcanoes. The Hawaiian Islands and the Galapagos, for example, started as volcanoes.

The Pacific Ocean is very rich in **minerals.**
It also has large supplies of oil and natural gas. And there is rich **marine** life in the Pacific. Fish such as salmon in northwestern America, bonito and prawns in Japan and Russia, and anchovy in Peru are all major food sources for people worldwide.

SEARCH LIGHT

Fill in the gaps:
The Pacific is the
_____
and the
_____
of all the oceans.

Answer: The Pacific is the largest and the deepest of all the oceans.

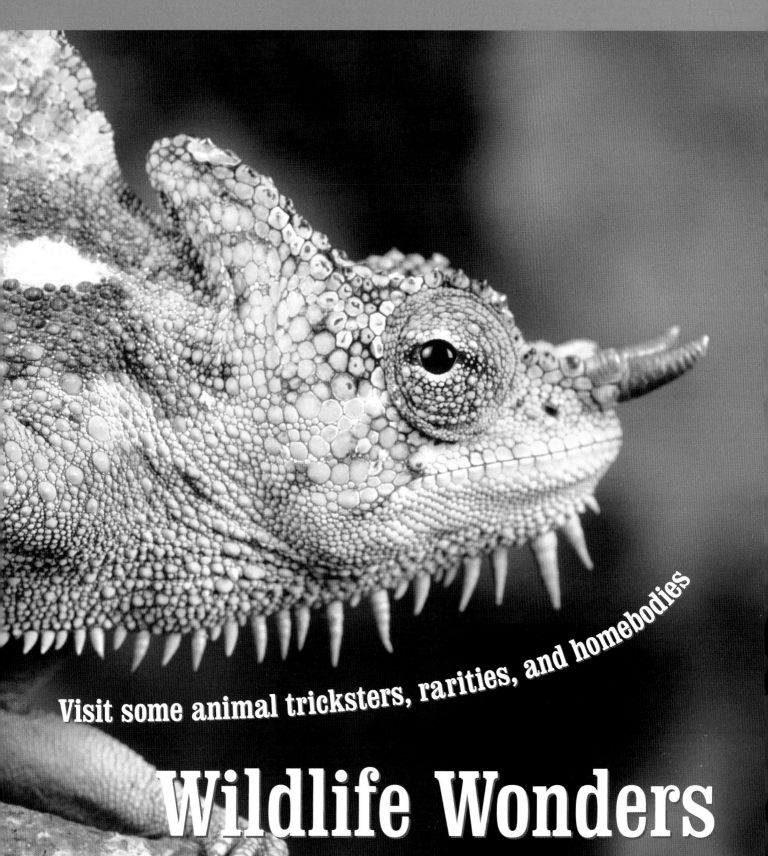

Visit some animal tricksters, rarities, and homebodies

Wildlife Wonders

Wildlife Wonders

TABLE OF CONTENTS

© Paul A. Souders/Corbis

The Armoured Animals

Can you imagine an animal covered in armour from head to toe, like a **medieval** knight? Meet the armadillo. The word 'armadillo' means 'little armoured one' in Spanish.

Armadillo of the Andes Mountains in South America.
© Galen Rowell/Corbis

Armadillos are round creatures with short legs. They are about the size of a small dog. They have strong curved claws, and yes, their bodies are covered with armour. This armour is made of hard plates or scales connected by bands that stretch. If they didn't stretch, the armadillo would have great difficulty moving around.

The armour helps protect the armadillo from its enemies. But its main job is to protect the armadillo from being cut and scratched by thorns and cactuses that grow where it lives.

Central and South America are home to many kinds of armadillo. There you'll find the pichi armadillo, Burmeister's armadillo, and the pink fairy armadillo. You'll also find the giant armadillo, which is nearly 1.5 metres long. One **species**, the nine-banded armadillo, is found in Texas and several other U.S. states.

Armadillos can't see very well and are almost toothless. They hunt mostly at night and eat insects and worms, soft roots and fruits, and occasionally dead animals.

When enemies appear, the armadillo usually runs away into the tough undergrowth, where its **predators** can't follow. Sometimes the armadillo will jump straight into the air to scare its enemies.

As a last resort it will roll itself up into a hard ball.

You may not believe it, but armadillos are very good swimmers. They stay afloat by swallowing a lot of air. In fact, under all that armour, armadillos are full of surprises!

SEARCH LIGHT

Fill in the gaps: The word 'armadillo' is Spanish for '_____ _____'.

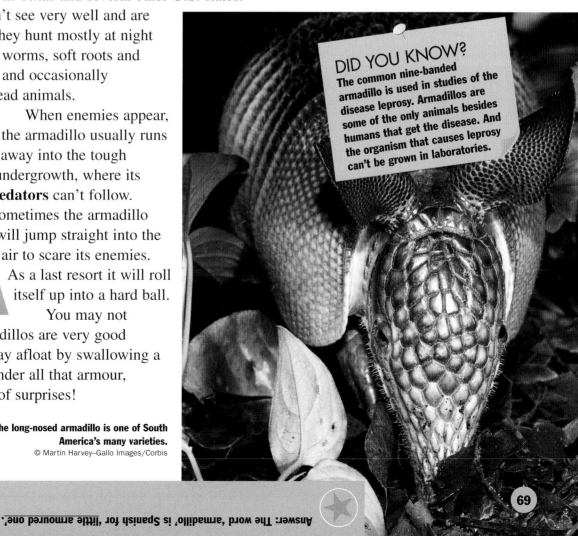

DID YOU KNOW?
The common nine-banded armadillo is used in studies of the disease leprosy. Armadillos are some of the only animals besides humans that get the disease. And the organism that causes leprosy can't be grown in laboratories.

The long-nosed armadillo is one of South America's many varieties.
© Martin Harvey–Gallo Images/Corbis

Answer: The word 'armadillo' is Spanish for 'little armoured one'.

The Colour-Wizard Lizards

Many people believe that the lizard known as the 'chameleon' can make its colour change to match its surroundings. It's true that the colour of a chameleon's skin can change, but not as a result of the chameleon's decision. The colour change may help the chameleon avoid its enemies. The colour change is a form of **camouflage**, a disguise that lets something blend in with its surroundings.

Chameleon of South Africa.
© Erice Reisinger–Gallo Images/Corbis

Chameleon skin contains colour-causing substances called 'pigments' that change under certain conditions. For instance, on a day when there is no bright sunlight, chameleons appear grey or green. Bright sunlight causes the skin to darken. On cool nights the colour fades to a creamy colour. The skin also changes colour when chameleons are excited, angry, or afraid.

There are many types of chameleon. About half are found only on the African island nation of Madagascar. The others are found mostly south of Africa's Sahara desert, with another few in western Asia and southern Europe. The 'false chameleon', or anole, is often sold in pet stores. This lizard of the Americas changes colour, but not as dramatically as a true chameleon.

Chameleons live in trees, where they usually eat insects. They catch their prey with the help of their long and slender tongue. They shoot the tongue out, grab the prey on the sticky end, and then draw the tongue back into their mouth. Very large chameleons may even use their sticky tongues to catch birds.

Another unusual thing about chameleons is that each eye can move independently of the other, so they can see in different directions at once. This makes it very hard to sneak up on a chameleon.

The Parson's chameleon, from Madagascar, is one of the largest of its family.
© Royalty-Free/Corbis

SEARCH LIGHT

What's wrong with the following statement: Chameleons can make their skin colour change in order to match their surroundings.

DID YOU KNOW?

Some say that the chameleon's eyes helped inspire the invention of the military turret, a revolving tower. You can see turrets today on the tops of tanks.

Answer: Chameleons' skin colour does change. But they don't decide to change it, and it doesn't always change in order to match their surroundings.

Reptile Royalty

The king cobra is the world's largest poisonous snake. It may grow to twice the length of a Ping-Pong table. Its **venom** is so powerful that elephants have died within three hours of a bite on the toe or trunk.

King cobras are olive-yellow to brownish black, sometimes with lighter bands across the back. Like other cobras, the king cobra is known for its unique 'threat display'. When it is angered or disturbed, it raises its head and **flares** its narrow, unmarked hood. This shows its yellow or red throat, which often is striped.

The king cobra can raise its head to a third of its entire length and may even move forward while upright. It is very curious by nature and often sits upright to see farther. It may be the most intelligent of all snakes.

The king cobra hunts in forests, fields, and villages. It usually eats other snakes and normally does not bite people. In **captivity** it is aggressive to strangers but recognizes its keeper and knows when it's mealtime. However, it can become dangerous during the mating season or when cornered or startled.

The female cobra builds a nest for laying eggs. Using a loop of her body as an arm, she pulls leaves, soil, and ground litter into a mound. In this nest she lays 20 to 40 eggs. She coils above or near the eggs for about two months and fiercely defends them.

The king cobra is found in parts of Asia from southern China to the Philippines, Indonesia, and India.

DID YOU KNOW?
The king cobra has an unusual hiss that is much lower than other snakes' - more like a growl than a hiss.

SEARCH LIGHT

People are afraid of cobras and as a result often kill the snakes. Why do you think people are scared of cobras? (Hint: What would you worry about if you came face to face with a cobra?)

The king cobra (like other cobras) performs the famous 'threat display' by pulling the ribs of the neck sideways and forward. This flattens the neck into a hood.
© E. Hanumantha Rao/NHPA

Answer: Because cobras are poisonous and have occasionally killed people with their bite, many consider the snake a danger to humans. Cobras also have a flaring 'hood' that makes them look threatening. Actually, far more snakes are injured and killed by people each year than the other way around.

Spotted American Cats

When we think of cats, we usually think of small domestic cats or big cats like lions and tigers. But there are many kinds of cat of all sizes still living in the wild. One such cat is the ocelot. The ocelot is about twice the size of a domestic cat.

The ocelot is found in the Western Hemisphere, from Texas in the south-western United States down to Argentina in South America. It lives in several different habitats, including tropical forests, grasslands, and brush.

Ocelot of Costa Rica, in Central America.
© Kevin Schafer/Corbis

SEARCH LIGHT

Look at the small photo. Why do you think it's hard to know just how many ocelots there are in some areas? (Hint: What do the spots on the ocelot's fur do for it?)

The ocelot's fur is short, smooth, and yellowish grey. There are small black spots on its head, two black stripes on each cheek, and four or five black stripes along its neck. This coat is good **camouflage** for the ocelot. It makes the animal hard to see in the leafy shade, for example. But its patterned fur is also attractive to humans. People hunt the ocelot for its fur, and so the number of ocelots in the wild has shrunk. In the United States, it's illegal to hunt ocelots or to sell their fur.

In the wild, ocelots generally like to live alone. They sleep during the day, usually in a tree or in other heavy plant cover. At night they hunt for rodents, birds, reptiles, and fish. However, they will also kill pets and other small **domestic** animals left outdoors.

Ocelot kittens start hunting with their mother when they are about three months old. When they are a year old, they leave the mother and start living on their own.

Some people try to keep ocelots as pets, since they are easily tamed when they're kittens. But when they grow up, the adult ocelots can sometimes be bad-tempered.

DID YOU KNOW?
Unlike its cousin the domestic cat, the ocelot doesn't mind a swim now and then. It's quite good at it!

© Tom Brakefield/Corbis

Answer: Ocelots sleep during the day in trees and other areas with dense leaf cover. An ocelot's spotted coat helps it blend into a leafy background and makes it difficult to see, day or night.

Playing Dead to Stay Alive

An opossum 'playing possum'.
© Joe McDonald/Corbis

An opossum is a grey creature about the size of a domestic cat. It has a long, pointy white face and beady little eyes. The opossum sleeps in the daytime and comes out at night.

Opossums are marsupials, which are mammals that carry their young in pouches on their bellies. Like kittens and puppies, baby opossums are born blind. So the first thing they do is snuggle inside their mother's built-in belly pouch. About 13 baby opossums can fit and feed inside the pouch at one time. They stay in there and go everywhere with the mother.

While they're in the pouch, the tiny opossums grow until they are the size of little mice. Then, after five weeks, they crawl out and ride piggyback on the mother's back. They hold on to her thick silvery-black fur with special grabbing thumbs.

Loaded with babies on her back, the mother opossum scampers through the woods and scurries up trees. She scrambles through bushes looking for fruits and berries. She climbs trees to find insects, birds' eggs, and little creatures to eat. When one of the babies gets tired, it just tumbles back into the pouch for a rest.

Opossums - or 'possums', as they're sometimes called - have another strange behaviour. Most **predatory** animals like to eat live food and will lose interest in animals that are already dead. So the opossum sometimes escapes its enemies by pretending to be dead. It will freeze like a statue and then topple over to the ground. When the predator loses interest and leaves, the opossum calmly gets up and walks away. This clever trick has become known as 'playing possum'.

SEARCH LIGHT

How many babies can a mother opossum carry in her pouch at one time?

© W. Perry Conway/Corbis

DID YOU KNOW?
People often picture opossums hanging from tree branches by their tails. Although they wrap them around branches to help keep their balance, opossums don't actually hang by their tails.

Answer: A female opossum can carry about 13 babies in her pouch at one time.

73

Touch Me Nots

The porcupine's name comes from words meaning 'pig' and 'spines'. This small rodent's body is covered with dark fur and the sharp quills, or spines, that give it its name. Some porcupine quills are attached in bunches, and others are attached singly. But all quills are used to protect against enemies.

Porcupines can't actually shoot their quills through the air. When it's threatened, a porcupine puffs out its quills. The quills easily come loose if touched and stick in an enemy's skin. They can cause painful wounds and may kill if they make their way into vital organs or cause infection.

There are 25 **species** of porcupine, divided into Old World and New World porcupines.

Baby New World porcupine.
© D. Robert & Lorri Franz/Corbis

Old World porcupines include the **crested** porcupines of Africa, Asia, and Europe. Long-tailed porcupines are also found in Asia. Brush-tailed porcupines are found in Asia and Africa.

The best-known New World species is the forest-dwelling North American porcupine. Other species found in the tropical forests from Mexico to South America use their long tails to grab onto branches. Porcupines shelter in tree branches and roots, hollow logs, burrows, and caves. Old World species like to stay on the ground more than New World porcupines do.

Old World porcupines like this one have quills embedded in clusters. New World porcupines have quills interspersed with hair, underfur, and bristles.
© Vittoriano Rastelli/Corbis

SEARCH LIGHT

Why do you think an axe handle would have salt in it that a porcupine would want?

Porcupines are most active at night. They eat almost any tree part they can reach, including the bark. North American porcupines prefer a tender layer beneath the bark. In trying to get at it, they may chew away the bark in a ring, which kills the tree. Porcupines sometimes gnaw antlers and wooden tools such as axe handles and canoe paddles for the salt and oil they contain.

DID YOU KNOW?
Baby porcupines have very soft quills when they're born, kind of like cooked spaghetti. The quills stiffen quickly after the baby is born.

Answer: People sweat through their hands when they work. An axe handle would soak up the sweat as well as the salt in the sweat.

The Swinging Singers

Gibbons are in the family of apes, but they are 'lesser apes'. That's because they are smaller and less intelligent than great apes, such as the chimpanzee and the gorilla.

White-handed gibbon, also called Malayan lar.
© Tom McHugh/Photo Researchers

Gibbons are found in the tropical rainforests of Southeast Asia. There, the gibbon uses its long arms to swing from branch to branch in the jungle's thick **canopy**. Its long, thin hands and feet help make the gibbon a very good **aerial acrobat**. The gibbon's thumb starts at the wrist and not the palm of its hand. This means the thumb acts like a hook on branches. The gibbon's feet also have a long split between the big toe and the other toes. This split provides a firm foothold on branches.

Because they are so well suited to tree climbing, gibbons spend most of their time travelling along branches. And they don't have to leave the trees for dinner. Gibbons eat fruit, leaves, vegetables, and insects, all of which are found in the canopy.

Gibbons live in small family groups of a male, a female, and their young. The male and female 'sing' in the morning and evening, and the males sometimes give solo performances. Gibbons are **territorial**, and singing lets everyone know that they are at home. The moment the family home is threatened, gibbons hoot and leap and swing with great excitement.

Gibbons are a great attraction at zoos because they are such fun to watch. Unfortunately, they are in danger of disappearing altogether in the natural world.

The grey gibbon lives on the island of Borneo in Southeast Asia.
© Uwe Walz/Corbis

SEARCH LIGHT

Why is it a useful thing for gibbons to sing?

Answer: When gibbons sing, they are letting other gibbons know where they are.

Fierce but Shy Apes

Although gorillas look **ferocious**, they are actually very quiet and shy. They live in family groups in the thickest parts of jungles, where they are not likely to be disturbed. At night, the father gorillas sleep on the ground while the mother and baby gorillas sleep in big nests of sticks and leaves. Sometimes they sleep in the lower branches of trees, where they are safe from **prowling** animals.

If you were to visit a gorilla's home, the male head of the group would try to protect his family. His first step would be to beat his chest, grunt, hoot, and roar to scare you away. Rather than fight you, the gorilla would hope that you left on your own.

Mountain gorilla family in Rwanda.
© Yann Arthus-Bertrand/Corbis

A gorilla's feet, hands, and wrinkled face are bare and black. Its arms are so long they almost touch the ground, even when it is standing up. A gorilla's fur may be short or long, depending on where it lives. The short-haired gorilla lives in the hot, damp jungles of western Africa. The long-haired gorilla lives in the cooler high mountains of central Africa. There are not many gorillas of either kind left in the wild.

Gorillas and chimpanzees are the closest living animal 'relatives' to humans. Along with the bonobos and the orangutans, these animals make up the 'great apes'. Like the other great apes, gorillas are very clever and can solve problems. They have good memories, and some can even learn sign language. You never know, one day you may sit down and have a chat with our cousin the gorilla!

SEARCH LIGHT

Why do you think people would make the mistake of thinking that gorillas are naturally fierce? (Hint: Look at the face of the gorilla in the large photo.)

DID YOU KNOW?
A gorilla called Koko has learned some basic American Sign Language. Not everyone agrees that she is actually communicating, but most agree that she has a large sign-language vocabulary.

A male mountain gorilla like this one may weigh as much as 180 kilos. Females are smaller at up to about 90 kilos.
© Kennan Ward/Corbis

Answer: When we see someone with a heavy brow, we usually suppose that person is frowning and angry. People who aren't used to seeing gorillas often think that the gorillas' expressions mean they have the same feelings as people.

Meet the King and Queen of Beasts

Unlike all the other big cats, lions live in groups, called 'prides'. Prides of lions can be found on grasslands, in desert areas, and on rocky hills. But except for African animal parks, there are few places left in the world where lions still roam free. Today the only wild lions outside Africa are a few hundred protected animals in the Gir Forest National Park in north-western India.

The male lion in the smaller photo has a big shaggy mane. Why do you think male lions have manes? (Hint: Male lions guard and protect the pride's territory.)

Each pride is made up of lionesses (female lions) of different ages but all related to each other, plus their cubs, and one or two adult male lions. A pride may have as few as 4 or as many as 37 members, but about 15 is the usual number.

Male lion.
© Randy Wells/Corbis

During the day lions lie in the shade or climb trees and rest on the branches. But they become very active at night. Like other cats, they can see well in dim light and like to hunt in the dark. Lions hunt grazing animals, such as zebras, antelopes, buffaloes, and gazelles.

Most lions will not attack a human or a large animal such as a giraffe or a hippopotamus. But lions that live near villages may carry away donkeys, goats, or even small cows. Imagine how strong a lion's teeth and neck have to be to lift a cow over a fence!

Female lions such as these do most of the hunting. The males usually roar to 'scare up' the prey while the females lie in wait.
© Tom Brakefield/Corbis

DID YOU KNOW?
A lion's tongue is so rough that it could lick the skin off your body.

A male lion is usually identified by its big fur collar, called a 'mane', and by the dark **tuft** of hair on its tail. Females are the same sandy colour as males, but they are a little smaller. Lion cubs have dark spots when they are born.

You may think that lions only roar, but they also growl, grunt, and cough. Sometimes they even purr like giant pussycats.

Answer: A male lion has to look fierce and strong to scare off other animals. The mane makes him look bigger and scarier.

Noble Hunters, Strong Families

DID YOU KNOW?

Wolves have often proved helpful wherever they live. They help control the numbers of rodents and deer. And by leaving dead prey remains behind, wolves provide meals for many other animals.

Wolves are very intelligent animals. They are also quite social - living and hunting in family packs. They have a strict ranking system, with a **dominant** female and male - the alpha pair - leading the pack. Only the alpha pair mate and have puppies, though the whole pack helps raise the young. Four to seven pups are born at a time.

Packs have 7 to 30 members, depending on how much **prey** is available. Each pack patrols a home territory of 100 to more than 1,000 square kilometres. They define their territory with scent markings and with growls, barks, and their legendary howl.

Even though they're not terribly fast, wolves are excellent hunters. They tackle much larger animals and can even bring down huge moose and bison. Usually they hunt caribou and elk, but they might even eat mice if that's all they can find.

Adult grey wolves and cub.
© Tom Brakefield/Corbis

The grey wolf is also known as the 'timber wolf'. In spite of its name, the grey wolf may be brown, reddish, black, or whitish on its back.
© Tom Brakefield/Corbis

© Wes Thompson/Corbis

SEARCH LIGHT

Fill in the gap: The alpha male and female are the pack _____.

Wolves hunt by using their keen senses and group cooperation. They work by tiring out their prey, sometimes chasing them all night. At the end they encircle their prey, waiting for the chance to attack unexpectedly. As soon as the animal is brought down, the pack will feed. The highest-ranking members eat first and get all the tastiest bits.

Wolves belong to the canine family. Their relatives include jackals, coyotes, dingoes, New Guinea singing dogs, wild dogs of Africa, and the **domestic** dogs people keep as pets.

Scientists believe that wolves may be the original canine from which the others descended. However, only three **species** of wolves remain today. There are grey wolves in Europe, Asia, Canada, Alaska, and Yellowstone Park (U.S.). A few hundred Ethiopian wolves live in a small part of Africa. Red wolves now survive mostly in **captivity**, but they used to roam the south-eastern United States.

The Bears That Aren't Really Bears

This roly-poly little animal has shiny black eyes that look like wet liquorice. Its funny black nose is pressed against its face between bushy grey ears. If you found this animal in your bedroom, you might think it was a toy teddy.

Fill in the gap: Koalas are marsupials. This means the mothers feed and carry their babies in a _____ on their bellies.

But this is a real animal (though it isn't a real bear), and it's called the koala. It is found only in Australia. The koala drinks dew and eats nothing but leaves of the eucalyptus tree, as shown in the large photo. It is famously slow-moving and gentle, and it sleeps up to 16 hours a day. Even when they're being **aggressive**, koalas rarely use their energy to fight. Instead they'll make loud croaking sounds known as 'bellowing'.

Mother koala carrying baby on her back.
© David and Eric Hosking/Corbis

Koalas are related to kangaroos. Both are marsupials. Marsupial mothers carry and feed their young in a pouch on their bellies. It's like a built-in baby sling.

When they're born, koala babies are blind, hairless, and smaller than your little finger. Usually only one baby is born at a time, but sometimes there are twins. After about six months in the pouch, the koala baby is ready to explore the world - but not on its own feet. At first, it climbs up on its mother's back. It rides on her back for the next six months, until it's almost as big as she is.

Mothers and babies communicate with gentle squeaks, clicks, and hums. A grunt indicates irritation or impatience. After a year the young koala leaves its mother to make its own home. Koalas are very **territorial**, and the young are not encouraged to stay once they can take care of themselves.

DID YOU KNOW?

Koalas are often slow-moving and quiet. Some people believe that their eucalyptus diet has a calming effect on them. The truth is, however, that their digestion rate is slowed down because the leaves take a lot of energy to digest.

© Wes Thompson/Corbis

Snakes' Feared Rivals

Curled up in its soft burrow, the shaggy-haired mongoose looks gentle and harmless. But when it's hungry, a mongoose is a very dangerous creature. Some people call the mongoose 'furred lightning' because it can move faster than a snake can strike. This makes the mongoose the most famous snake killer in the world.

There are over 40 species of mongoose living in Asia, Africa, and Europe. India is home to both the mongoose and the cobra, a highly poisonous snake. When a mongoose meets a cobra, the mongoose uses its speed and sharp teeth to grab the snake behind the head. Then it hits the cobra against the ground until the snake is dead.

Because of their snake-fighting ways, mongooses are very welcome in places where there are many poisonous snakes. Sometimes people in these places keep mongooses as pets. But mongooses aren't allowed in most countries of the world, not even to be kept in zoos. It is dangerous to bring even a few mongooses into a country where they do not naturally live.

Yellow mongoose, also called meerkat.
© Martin Harvey–Gallo Images/Corbis

Some countries have made the mistake of **importing** mongooses to help kill snakes and rats. The problem is that once the mongooses have killed and eaten most of the snakes and rats, they still need food. So the mongooses hunt the other small animals that they can catch, and they can catch almost anything. No bird, rabbit, or squirrel is safe from the 'terror of the fields'. Few small animals are quick enough to escape a hungry mongoose.

This yellow mongoose in Botswana has just won its battle with a snake.
© Gallo Images/Corbis

SEARCH LIGHT

Can you tell from the large picture how a mongoose keeps from getting bitten by snakes? (Hint: The snake's tail is still on the ground.)

DID YOU KNOW?
The children's story 'Rikki-Tikki-Tavi' by Rudyard Kipling is about a mongoose that saves a human family from a cobra.

Answer: The mongoose grabs the snake just behind the head so that the snake can't reach it with its fangs.

Cuddly Exotic
Bears

Lesser panda.
© Keren Su/Corbis

In the wild, giant pandas get most of their food from bamboo plants. What will happen if people in China keep cutting down the bamboo forests?

When you think of pandas, you probably picture a big cuddly black-and-white bear. But there are actually two kinds of panda: the giant panda and the lesser panda. The giant panda is the familiar black-and-white animal, which is found mostly in the forests of China and Tibet. The lesser panda looks rather like a raccoon.

The giant panda grows to about 1.5 metres long and 100 kilos. Its favourite food is bamboo, and it eats almost nothing else. It needs to consume large quantities of bamboo to get the nourishment that its body needs, so it spends about 10 to 12 hours a day eating. **Captive** pandas, like those found in zoos, have a broader diet. In addition to bamboo, they may eat cereals, milk, and garden vegetables.

The lesser panda is smaller and has rich reddish brown fur on its back and black fur on its belly. It has a bushy ringed tail that makes it look a little like a raccoon. The lesser panda is sometimes called a 'cat bear' or 'red bear cat'. It's found in China, as well as in the South Asian countries of Myanmar, Nepal, and India. Like its giant cousin, the lesser panda also eats bamboo. But it also eats grasses, fruits, other plant material, and, sometimes, small animals.

Giant pandas are endangered animals. Their natural habitat keeps shrinking each year. But many countries are trying to help China preserve its bamboo forests so that pandas have a place to live. People are also working to increase the number of pandas by breeding them in zoos.

There are probably only about 1,000 giant pandas left in the wild. Another 100 or so live in zoos.
© Keren Su/Corbis

DID YOU KNOW?
Many people call the panda a 'panda bear', but for a long time scientists weren't sure if it really *was* a bear. Today, in spite of some non-bear traits, the panda is usually classified in the bear family.

Answer: If people continue to cut down the bamboo forests, then giant pandas will starve and die out. They simply couldn't adjust to a life without bamboo.

81

Intelligent Creatures
...Like Us!

Apes are the most humanlike of all animals. Like people, apes do their work during the day and sleep at night. They also live in families and communities like we do. And like humans, apes sometimes fight each other. Great apes, like humans, can learn to use tools.

Family of chimpanzees.
© Paul A. Souders/Corbis

In the wild, some of the apes known as 'chimpanzees' use twigs and leaves as tools. They cleverly poke a twig inside the nests of ants and termites. Then they pull up the twig and eat the insects that cling to it. They make leaf cups to scoop up water. They also use leaves and twigs to clean themselves.

There are two types of ape: great apes and lesser apes. The great apes include orang-utans, gorillas, chimpanzees, and bonobos. The lesser apes include gibbons and siamangs. Apes live mostly in the tropical forests of Africa and Asia. The orang-utan, whose name means 'person of the forest', is found today only on the islands of Borneo and Sumatra.

Gibbons and orang-utans live in trees. Chimpanzees and bonobos live in trees and on the ground. Gorillas spend most of their time on the ground but sometimes sleep in trees. Most apes like to eat shoots, fruits, leaves, seeds, and grass. But while most apes will eat insects, little birds, birds' eggs, rodents, and other young animals, gorillas don't eat meat at all.

Chimpanzees and gorillas are intelligent animals. Scientists have even taught some of them to solve problems and use sign language.

Can you guess what the most noticeable physical difference between an ape and a monkey is? Apes don't have tails! And they don't have claws either. They have flat nails like we do.

DID YOU KNOW?

One type of special behaviour that humans and great apes share is the ability to recognize themselves in mirrors. The only other animals known to do this are the bottle-nosed dolphins.

SEARCH LIGHT

Why do you think that the ability to learn to make and use tools may indicate intelligence? (Hint: What do tools help you do?)

Orang-utans, such as these from Sumatra, are among the group called the 'great apes'. Great apes are considerably more intelligent than the 'lesser apes' (gibbons).
© Tom Brakefield/Corbis

Answer: Tools help animals - including people - control and change their environment. Many animals have adapted to their surroundings in amazing ways. But very few besides apes and humans are able to make their surroundings adapt to them.

Fliers by Night

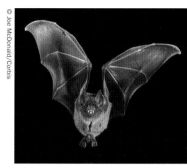

(Top) Leaf-nosed bat; (bottom) fruit bat.

Bats are mammals, and like all mammals they have fur, give birth to live young, and produce milk for their young. But bats are also the only **mammals** that really fly.

Bats live all over the world, but they prefer warm climates. They like to live in huge groups, or colonies, sometimes with 1,000 bats or more in a colony. Bats sleep in caves, hollows in trees, and empty buildings.

There are many kinds of bats, in many sizes. The flying fox bat, when it stretches its wings, is wider than you are tall. But the tiny Philippine bamboo bat's wings are barely 15 centimetres from tip to tip.

Most bats eat insects. The Mexican bats of Texas can eat millions and millions of insects every year! Other bats eat fruit, honey, and **pollen**. But whatever they eat, all bats look for their food at night.

You may have heard the term 'blind as a bat'. Bats actually see very clearly, but they don't rely on their eyes. When a bat flies, it makes sounds that we can't hear. These sounds bounce off objects in the bat's path, creating echoes which the bat's large ears can hear. The echoes tell the bat what lies ahead and help it locate food and enemies.

Some people fear bats, but in fact they are very helpful. Not only do they eat insects that pester us, but bats also help **pollinate** many flowers and plants. Without bats, many plants, especially some kinds of cactus, wouldn't be alive.

> **DID YOU KNOW?**
> There's a bridge in Austin, Texas, U.S., that provides a roosting place for Mexican bats. More than a million at a time make this bridge their home.

SEARCH LIGHT

True or false? Bats are solitary animals.

Answer: FALSE. Bats live in huge groups, or colonies.

The Silk Spinners

Spiders belong to a large group of animals called 'arthropods'. This group also includes crabs, centipedes, and insects. Arthropods have their skeletons on the outside of their bodies.

Though they're part of the same larger group, spiders are not insects. Insects have six legs, while spiders have eight. This makes them part of a smaller group, the arachnids. Arachnids - including **scorpions** and ticks - have eight walking legs. Many spiders and other arachnids use **venom** to kill their prey.

Jumping spider ready to pounce.
© Robert Pickett/Corbis

Spiders also spin silk. In fact, the word 'spider' comes from an old English word that means 'to spin'. Spiders have silk-making organs called 'spinnerets' near the back of their bodies. They spin silk from a liquid made by special **glands**. It becomes solid thread after the spider pushes it out of its body.

Spiders spin different types of silk for different uses. Some silk is stronger than steel wire. Spiders use silk for webs to trap food, for lining their nests, and to hold the eggs they lay. When a spider has to escape from an enemy, it may quickly spin a getaway thread and drop out of sight on it.

Not all spiders catch food in a web. Some, such as the jumping spider, pounce like a cat to capture insects. Others spin silk funnels, where they hide during the day before going hunting at night. The brightly coloured crab spider hides between flower petals and grabs insects looking for nectar. Pirate spiders creep inside the webs spun by other spiders and then eat them up.

> **DID YOU KNOW?**
> Spiders live everywhere, even underwater. Water spiders are called 'diving bells' because they build bell-shaped webs underwater. The bell webs trap air bubbles for the spider to breathe.

SEARCH LIGHT

How does the pirate spider catch its food?

Many spiders spin webs to trap food - most often insects such as this unfortunate butterfly.
© Tecmap Corporation—Eric Curry/Corbis

Answer: A pirate spider eats other spiders out of their own webs.

New Zealand's
Feathered Favourites

The kiwi is a strange little bird found only in the forests of the island nation of New Zealand. During the day it sleeps in its burrow, and at night it looks for food, as the one in the large photo is doing. Kiwis eat worms, insects, **larvae**, spiders, and berries.

Kiwis have a strong sense of smell and a touch-sensitive bill. They are the only birds whose nostrils are at the very end of the bill. The kiwi's bill is long and narrow, and there are sensitive whiskers at the base of it. Having noses at the very end of their bills is a big help when they are hunting!

Kiwis also have a good sense of hearing, but they have poor vision in daylight. To escape enemies they rely on their strong legs. Kiwis are fast runners and fierce fighters. They have four toes on each foot, each with a large claw. The claws are very useful when kiwis are facing enemies.

The kiwi is an unusual bird. It is greyish brown and about as big as a chicken. It has wings that are not fully formed, so it does not fly. The wings are hidden in its feathers, which are shaggy and hair-like.

The bird is much loved by the people of New Zealand, even though they don't see it very often. New Zealanders themselves are sometimes called Kiwis. A fruit, a breakfast cereal, and an airline are named after the kiwi too. Pictures of the bird can be seen on New Zealand's postage stamps and coins.

'Kiwi crossing' road sign in New Zealand.
© Paul A. Souders/Corbis

DID YOU KNOW?

Compared with the size of the bird, the kiwi's egg isn't just large, it's enormous. The egg is about 20 percent of the mother's weight. It fills almost her entire body right before it's laid.

SEARCH LIGHT

Fill in the gap: The kiwi is an unusual bird. Its _____ are not fully formed, so it does not fly.

© Geoff Moon—Frank Lake Picture Agency/Corbis

Answer: The kiwi is an unusual bird. Its wings are not fully formed, so it does not fly.

The Biggest Birds in the World

Male ostrich protecting eggs in a nest.
© Kevin Schafer/Corbis

The ostrich is the largest living bird in the world. Ostriches are about 2.5 metres tall and may weigh as much as 155 kilos. They have very short wings, which means ostriches are too heavy to fly. Ostriches' wings can't get them into the air, but flapping their wings while they run helps the birds go faster on the ground. Ostriches can run up to 65 kilometres an hour. This makes them not just the biggest but also the fastest bird on the ground!

Ostriches don't use their speed to catch food. Instead, they run to keep away from their enemies. But the first thing ostriches do when they see an enemy is hide. To avoid being seen, ostriches generally lie flat on the ground with their necks outstretched. This makes them look like just another bush. People sometimes say that ostriches bury their heads in the sand when they sense danger. But this isn't true. You just can't see their heads when ostriches are lying down.

Ostriches don't always hide or run away from trouble. If their young are in danger, ostriches will fight. They use their beaks, and they kick with their very powerful legs. An ostrich could easily kill a person with a few kicks of its feet.

Wild ostriches live in groups in Africa. Sometimes there are as many as 50 birds in a single group. Ostriches eat mostly plants, fruits, and berries, but once in a while they'll also eat small animals and insects.

A tame ostrich that's been treated well may do a very special thing: it can be trained to carry people on its back. In fact, in some parts of the world people have ostrich races.

© Wolfgang Kaehler/Corbis

DID YOU KNOW?
In the days when fashionable women wore very big hats, they were often decorated with ostrich feathers.

SEARCH LIGHT

Which of the following can be said about ostriches?
- Ostriches eat a lot of meat.
- Ostriches are the biggest bird.
- Ostriches are great runners.

Answer: Ostriches are the biggest bird and are great runners too.

Egg-Laying
Mammals

If someone asked you to describe a mammal, you might say a mammal is a warm-blooded animal with hair or fur. You'd add that mammals give birth to live babies instead of laying eggs and that they feed their young with milk.

Well, the platypus feeds its babies milk. And the platypus is warm-blooded and has brown fur. But the platypus breaks a big mammal rule - it lays eggs. Platypuses and Australian spiny anteaters are the only members of an egg-laying mammal group called 'monotremes'.

Platypuses are found in the lakes and streams of Tasmania and of eastern and southern Australia. They spend their lives feeding along the bottoms of rivers, streams, and lakes and resting in burrows dug into banks.

SEARCH LIGHT

Which of the following statements about the platypus are true?
- It has fur.
- It is warm-blooded.
- It gives birth to live babies.

DID YOU KNOW?

The official name of the spiny anteater, the only other monotreme besides the platypus, is 'echidna'.

The platypus, so awkward and peculiar on the ground, is perfectly adapted for underwater hunting.
© Joe McDonald/Corbis

A platypus has a big appetite. The amount of food it eats every day is almost equal to its own weight. A platypus meal may consist of insects, worms, shellfish, fish, frogs, **molluscs**, tadpoles, or earthworms.

The platypus often looks for food underwater. But in the water, the platypus's eyes and ears are closed. Since it can't see or hear underwater, the platypus depends entirely on its snout to find its food. But what a snout! A platypus snout looks like a duck's bill, which is why the platypus is sometimes called the 'duckbill'.

The platypus also has webbed feet like a duck and a tail like a beaver. When you look at it, the platypus doesn't seem to be a single animal but rather several different animals put together.

Answer: It has fur and is warm-blooded, but it doesn't give birth to live babies.

87

Shy Cousins of the
Horse and Rhino

The tapir is a strange-looking animal. It has a stumpy tail and a soft flexible snout like a short elephant trunk. Some tapirs are brown or grey. Others have a black head and legs, with a dirty-white back and belly. Its feet have hooves, just like a horse.

In fact, tapirs are related to horses, and to rhinos too. You wouldn't know it to look at them, since tapirs don't look much like either animal. But when it's feeding, the tapir uses its nose to move things aside and graze on plants, like a horse does.

South American tapir of Ecuador.
© Michael & Patricia Fogden/Corbis

This Malayan tapir is related to the horse, but it looks more like a pig. To add to the confusion, its baby is called a 'calf', like a cow's baby.
© Kevin Schafer/Corbis

SEARCH LIGHT

What are three reasons that tapirs are becoming endangered?

DID YOU KNOW?
A mother tapir carries her baby for about 13 months before it is born. That might seem like a lot to us humans, who take only nine months. But it's nothing to the elephant, which carries its baby for 24 months.

The shy, **solitary** tapir is found in Myanmar, Malaysia, Thailand, and Sumatra. It also lives in the forests of Central and South America. The tapirs of Central America are the largest, about as big as a donkey.

Tapirs usually live deep in the forest near swamps and rivers. They're good swimmers and often escape from enemies into the water. In South America the tapir's main enemy is the jaguar. In Asia it has to beware of tigers.

But the tapir's greatest enemy, no matter where it lives, is people. Tapirs are endangered, which means their numbers in the wild are decreasing. This is because people cut down forests for wood and clear land to grow crops, destroying the home of the tapir and of many other animals as well. And besides the threat from tigers and jaguars, tapirs also face human hunters who kill them for food and sport.

With luck, people will soon pay more attention to preserving this unusual animal in the wild.

Answer: They are hunted by jaguars and tigers.
They are hunted by people.
People cut down their forest homes.

Packed and Ready to Go

Did you know that a camel's hump is like a lunch box? After a good feed, a camel changes the extra food and water into fat and keeps it safe in its hump. A camel can then go for days without food or water, living on that fat. That is why people use them for crossing deserts. Camels don't have to stop all the time for a drink or a bite to eat.

When camels do get hungry, they're definitely not hard to feed. Camels eat all kinds of grass and plants, even those that are dry and thorny. In fact, a hungry camel will gobble up tents, straw baskets, and even leather belts and will drink 95 litres of water in just a few minutes!

The dromedary, or Arabian camel, has one hump. You'll find the dromedary in North Africa, the Middle East, and India. The Bactrian camel, which lives mostly in Central Asian countries, has two humps. Both camels can carry people and heavy loads. They are excellent for making long journeys. But camels can be quite bad-tempered. They bellow, bite, or kick hard if you tease them. They even spit when they're unhappy!

Camels are useful in other ways, too. Their hair is used to make tents, blankets, rugs, ropes, and clothes. Camel skin is used to make footwear and bags. Cheese and other foods are made from camel milk.

Here's an **oddity**: camels have a double set of eyelashes. These help to keep the camels' eyes safe from sand during desert sandstorms. The camel just closes its nose while long hair protects its eyes...and its ears, too.

© Hans Georg Roth/Corbis

Bactrian camel.
© Corbis

Dromedary, or Arabian camel.
© Jose Fuste Raga/Corbis

DID YOU KNOW?
If a mother camel has to go on a journey when her baby is very young, the baby is put inside a carrier on a 'nurse' camel beside the mother. If the mother can't see the baby, she'll run away, perhaps thinking her baby is lost and she needs to find it!

Answer: TRUE.

The Largest Animals on Land

Can you tell the difference between an African elephant and an Indian elephant?

First look at the ears: African elephants have much larger ears than Indian elephants. African elephants are altogether larger and stronger and have thicker skin than their Indian cousins. In fact, African elephants are the largest animals on land. They can grow to more than 3.4 metres tall and weigh more than 5,400 kilos!

Indian elephants, found in South and Southeast Asia, are smaller, gentler, and easier to train. Most elephants in zoos and circuses are Indian. Elephants and people have long worked together. Usually, one man trains one elephant. In India, the trainer is called a *mahout*. In Myanmar (Burma), he's called an *oozie*. Both African and Indian elephants have been used in wartime.

Both kinds of elephants eat fruits, nuts, grass, and vegetables, but trees are their favourite food. To get to the best tree leaves, elephants break off branches with their trunks or sometimes just knock the whole tree down. Elephants also breathe, smell, and trumpet through their trunks. When they're hot, elephants have a bath to cool off. They swim underwater and stick their trunks up in the air so they can breathe. Elephants also have showers, using their trunks to suck up water and spray it on themselves.

Male elephants have huge tusks for digging, carrying things, and sometimes fighting. But their tusks also cause elephants problems. Hunters have killed so many elephants for the ivory in their tusks that there are not many elephants left.

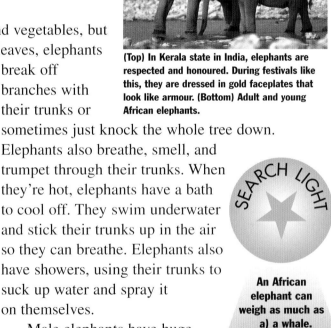

(Top) In Kerala state in India, elephants are respected and honoured. During festivals like this, they are dressed in gold faceplates that look like armour. (Bottom) Adult and young African elephants.

DID YOU KNOW?
The famous general Hannibal, of ancient Carthage in North Africa, led a battle company that included 37 elephants into the Alps on his way to fight the Roman army.

Indian elephants in Sri Lanka.
© Lindsay Hebberd/Corbis

SEARCH LIGHT

An African elephant can weigh as much as
a) a whale.
b) a bus.
c) a big snail.

Answer: b) a bus.

Bounty of the Andes

(Top) Herding llamas in the highlands of Peru; (bottom) Quechua Indian girl with llama.

SEARCH LIGHT

Which of the following do people get from llamas?
- meat
- milk
- wool
- fuel
- transportation

The llama is closely related to the alpaca, the guanaco, and the vicuña. This group of animals is called 'lamoids'. They are part of the camel family, but lamoids do not have humps like camels.

Llamas are the largest lamoids. They are about 1.2 metres tall and can weigh 113 kilos, and they have long legs and a long neck. Their coat is usually white, but some llamas are black, brown, or white with black markings.

Today most llamas are **domestic** animals. Most of them are kept by South American Indians in the mountains of Bolivia, Peru, Ecuador, Chile, and Argentina. The llama has many uses. It is a source of food and milk. It also provides wool and hair that can be used to make knitted clothing, woven fabrics, rugs, and rope. Llama **dung** can be dried and used as fuel.

The llama is also an important transport animal. It's strong, and it can go a long time without water. Also, the llama eats many kinds of plants. These traits make the llama perfectly

suited for travelling over the plateaus and mountains of the Andes, where there is very little water or vegetation. A llama can carry a 45-kilo load and travel up to 32 kilometres a day!

The llama is usually gentle, but it will hiss, spit, or even kick if it is ill-treated. And a llama can be stubborn. It will refuse to work if it feels too much is being asked of it.

This llama, one of Peru's great treasures, stands in front of a man-made Peruvian treasure, the ruins of Machu Picchu.

DID YOU KNOW?

Llamas like to live in groups and will even live with sheep if there are no other llamas around. Shepherds often use llamas as 'watchdogs' because llamas will fight off any animal that threatens their herd.

Answer: Llamas provide people with all of these things.

Shaggy Beasts of Tibet

A yak is a heavy, strong ox with shaggy black hair and humped shoulders. Yaks and other oxen are part of the animal family that includes cattle, buffalo, antelopes, and goats. They live on the high Himalayan mountain **plateaus** of Tibet (part of China), Nepal, and Bhutan. Yaks graze on grass and need a lot of water. They often eat snow in winter.

Some yaks live in the wild. But their numbers have decreased so much that soon none may be left. Bulls (male yaks) in the wild can grow as tall as 1.8 metres and may weigh twice as much as a horse. Cows (female yaks) are usually smaller and weigh less. Wild yaks live in large herds of cows, young bulls, and calves. Older bulls stay together in smaller groups.

Nepalese boy leads yak.
© Nik Wheeler/Corbis

Like the camel and the donkey in other cultures, the Himalayan yak is an extremely important beast of burden.
© Keren Su/Corbis

People have also **domesticated** yaks, and these animals are plentiful. Domestic yaks are often patched black and white, and they are smaller than wild yaks. They also have longer hair than wild yaks.

In the lives of Himalayan mountain people, the domestic yak is extremely useful. People eat its meat and drink its milk. They make leather from its hide and twist its long hair into ropes and cords. Even the tail is not wasted - it is used as a flyswatter!

Because trees don't grow on the higher areas of the windy plateaus, there's very little wood available. So the yak's dried **dung** is an important fuel source to make fires for warmth and cooking. The yak is also useful for transport. Tibetans and Nepalese travel in the plateaus and mountains on the yak's back. They also use this valuable animal to carry or pull heavy loads.

SEARCH LIGHT

Which of the following are ways that people use the yak?
- to provide flyswatters and rope
- to supply fuel
- for milk and meat
- to carry things and people

Answer: All of these things are ways people have found to make use of the yak.

The Bouncers

Gazelles are a graceful fast-moving antelope - part of a group that includes cattle and sheep. Gazelles live on the open plains and **semi-desert** regions of Africa. They're usually found in herds of 5 to 20 animals. Sometimes hundreds of gazelles move together, forming one large herd.

Gazelles are herbivores. That means they eat mainly herbs, bushes, and rough desert grasses. Some gazelles need more water than many plains animals. These gazelles often eat early in the morning or at night, when leaves contain more water than they do in the heat of the day.

Gazelles do one very unusual thing. As

SEARCH LIGHT

What are the two reasons for the decline in the number of wild gazelles?

Thomson's gazelle in Tanzania.
© Tom Brakefield/Corbis

they travel in the herd, some of them bounce on all four legs. They keep their legs stiff, and as they hop, all four legs leave and touch the ground at the same time. It's not clear why they sometimes move this way. Perhaps they're just playing and having a good time. But there may be a more important reason for doing this. As they bounce in the air, the gazelles can see enemies moving toward the herd. The rest of the herd can then be warned of danger, and all can run to a safe place. And gazelles are swift runners.

Gazelle meat is a good source of food for local people. The gazelle is also food for **predators** on the plains. But the population of some kinds of gazelle is shrinking because they are often overhunted for their meat. Their **habitat** is also disappearing. Desert areas are becoming drier with fewer trees, so these areas are becoming less suitable for gazelles.

Tanzania's Serengeti Plain is rich in wildlife. These male Grant's gazelles live in Serengeti National Park.
© Kevin Schafer/Corbis

Answer: The number of gazelles in the wild has declined because they are being hunted too much for their meat and because their natural habitat is disappearing.

93

Australia's Amazing Leapers

The kangaroo and its relatives are called marsupials. The mother animals among most marsupials have a pouch, or pocket, attached to their bellies. The pouch is part of their furry skin. It's where the babies stay while they are nursing. Most marsupials are found in Australia and on nearby islands.

When a kangaroo is born, it's about as long as your little finger. While it's growing, it stays safe and well fed in its mother's pouch. A baby kangaroo is called a 'joey'.

As you can see from the large photo, when the joey is big enough, it can poke its head out of the pouch. It can then eat leaves that are close enough to reach without climbing out. As it grows bigger, it can slip out of the pouch to nibble grass. Then it climbs back into the pouch at night or whenever it is tired of hopping. If there is danger while the joey is out of

Kangaroos visiting a golf tournament.
© AFP/Corbis

the pouch, the mother kangaroo picks up her baby, stuffs it into the pouch, and hops away.

Except for the small rat kangaroo and tree kangaroo, kangaroos have extremely strong back legs. The strong legs help it make the giant leaps it is known for. Its long tail helps it keep its balance while the legs are in the air. Kangaroos are herbivores, which means they eat only plants.

Kangaroos are usually gentle and timid. But if they are cornered, they'll stamp their hind feet and growl. They can grab an enemy with their front paws and kick it with their powerful back feet.

DID YOU KNOW?
Joeys aren't born inside their mother's pouch. They have to climb there first. Quite a feat, considering they're born blind, furless, and very, very tiny.

SEARCH LIGHT

Find and correct the mistake in the following sentence: Kangaroos use their tails to fight.

© Michael S. Yamashita/Corbis

Answer: Kangaroos use their back feet to fight.

Monkeys' Primitive Cousins

Lemurs have lived on Earth for a very long time, but they are found in only two places: Madagascar and the Comoro Islands, off the eastern coast of Africa. Millions of years ago, the island of Madagascar broke away from the continent of Africa. On the continent the monkeys were smarter than the lemurs, and the lemurs all died out. But no monkeys ever reached Madagascar, so the lemurs did well there without any competition.

Mother and baby ring-tailed lemurs.
© Kevin Schafer/Corbis

The best-known **species** of lemur, the ring-tailed lemur, has a long striped tail, with rings of black and white. Like most lemurs, it lives in trees but looks for food on the ground. When walking on the ground, the ring-tailed lemur waves its tail back and forth, high in the air over its back. But lemurs don't hang from trees by their tails, as some monkeys do. Instead lemurs' tails help them keep their balance and sail through the air from tree to tree, like the ring-tailed lemur in the large photo.

Lemurs are mild, shy animals, but they can be very curious when there is food around. They have a better sense of smell than monkeys have, and they use it to find fruits, leaves, insects, and small birds to eat. Most of this activity takes place at night, because lemurs like to sleep during the day.

Lemurs usually have only one baby at a time. The baby clings to its mother's underside and travels with her through the treetops. After a while, the baby lemur rides on its mother's back.

SEARCH LIGHT

Which of the following statements about lemurs are true?
- Lemurs live throughout Africa.
- Lemurs live side by side with monkeys.
- Lemurs hang from their tails like monkeys do.

DID YOU KNOW?
The word 'lemur' comes from the Latin word meaning 'ghost'. Perhaps this is because they move about silently at night and have large, mysterious eyes.

© Wolfgang Kaehler/Corbis

Answer: None of these statements are true.

Surefooted
Mountain Climbers

People raise goats for their milk, hair, and meat. Such goats are **domesticated**. But several types of goat live in the wild - such as the ibex, the markhor, the tahr, and the goral. Domesticated goats may have descended from these wild varieties.

The ibex is a sturdy wild goat living in the mountains of Europe, Asia, and north-eastern Africa. Though ibex live in herds, old males usually live alone. The European ibex has brownish grey fur. The male has a beard and large horns shaped like half circles. Other ibex include the walia and the Siberian ibex.

Mountain goats in the Rocky Mountains of Olympic National Park, Washington, U.S.
© W. Wayne Lockwood, M.D./Corbis

The markhor is a large goat once found throughout the mountains of southern and central Asia. Now only small numbers are found, and in only a few places. The markhor is about as tall as a donkey. Unlike the ibex, its horns are long and wound like a **corkscrew**. Its coat is reddish brown in summer and long, grey, and silky in winter.

Ibex have dwindled in number in recent years. These male ibex stand in front of a glacier in their native Austria.
© K.M. Westermann/Corbis

SEARCH LIGHT

Which of the following wild goats have backward-curving horns?
a) ibex
b) goral
c) markhor
d) tahr

The surefooted tahr lives in herds and is usually found on steep wooded mountainsides. It can be as tall as the markhor, though it often is much smaller. Three species of tahr are found from India to Arabia. The smallest is the Arabian tahr, with its short brownish grey coat. Tahr horns are short, flat, and backward curving.

The goral is found from the Himalayas to eastern Siberia. Its horns also curve backward. And like the ibex and tahr, it has a coarse coat that is brownish grey in colour. It is smaller than these other two goats, however.

Answer: b) goral and d) tahr

Get to know the animals that live closest to us

Familiar Animals

Familiar Animals
TABLE OF CONTENTS

Britannica
LEARNING
LIBRARY

The Tiger in Your House

If a cat lives with you, you have a member of a proud, sometimes fierce family as a pet. A tiger is a cat. So are lions, leopards, and cheetahs. Jaguars, lynx, panthers, and pumas are cats too.

All cats have five toes on their front paws and four on their back paws. They have long sharp claws. They use their claws for climbing trees, catching food, and protecting themselves against other animals. All cats except the cheetah can move their claws in and out.

All cats purr, making a low, continuous, rattling hum. The purr is a relaxing, self-comforting sound that can signal a friendly mood. Many cats also meow, though 'big cats' (such as lions and tigers) roar. Most cats don't like to go in water, but they can all swim if they have to. Cats can hear even faraway things. And they can see at night when it's very dark. They are also among the fastest animals on Earth. In fact, the cheetah can run faster than any other animal, but only for a short distance.

Though **domestic** cats are usually fed by their owners, cats naturally get their food by hunting. They'll eat anything from mice to zebras, depending on how big a cat they are. Some will eat fish, clams, and snails. When house cats play with string and small toys, they're displaying their ancient family hunting **instinct**.

Cats have existed on the Earth for a very long time. The people of Egypt were the first to keep cats as pets. They gave them milk in gold saucers and made statues of cats. When cats died, they were often buried in special graveyards or even made into mummies!

Pet cat being cuddled.
© Jose Luis Pelaez, Inc./Corbis

SEARCH LIGHT

Name one thing that house cats have in common with lions? How are they different?

The domestic cat (house cat) is one of the most popular house pets. In ancient Thailand, cats lived in kings' castles.
© Craig Lovell/Corbis

DID YOU KNOW?
If you've ever been licked by a cat, then you know that cats have rough tongues. They all do. This is because their tongues are covered with little sharp-edged pockets. The pockets help them lick up water and groom their fur.

Answer: Both lions and house cats eat meat. They also both purr, have five toes on their front feet, and are very quick. But cats can live in your house. Lions are too big and too wild to be pets.

Most Valuable Creatures on Earth

In Iran they were sacrificed to the gods. In India they are treated as **sacred**. In the ancient world they were used as money. Almost everywhere they have been used as a source of milk, butter, cheese, and meat. Cattle have, for thousands of years, been humanity's most valuable animals.

The word 'cattle' once meant all kinds of domestic animals. It comes from the Latin word *capitale*, which means 'wealth' or 'property'. The word 'cattle' is used now only for certain **bovines**, the animal group that includes oxen, bison, and buffalo.

A bull is a male bovine and a cow is a female - though the term 'cow' is often used for both. A calf is the young of either sex. Cattle that are between 1 and 2 years old are called 'yearlings'. The natural lifespan of cattle is about 20 years, but most of them are sent to slaughter long before they reach this age.

Today's domestic cattle in Africa, Asia, and Indonesia are very much like the cattle that lived in those areas 2,000 years ago. In Europe and America, however, cattle farmers have produced new breeds.

Nowadays cattle are classified as dairy, beef, or **dual**-purpose types, which means they are used for both dairy and beef production.

© Hans Georg Roth/Corbis

© Royalty-Free/Corbis

(Top) Cows at a livestock market.
(Bottom) Longhorn resting under a tree.

SEARCH LIGHT

Fill in the gaps:
A _____ is a male bovine and a _____ is a female.

One of the most popular breeds of cattle is the Brown Swiss breed. It is classified as a dairy cow in the United States and as a dual-purpose type in other countries. It may be one of the oldest breeds of cattle. A grown Brown Swiss cow weighs about 680 kilos. Other popular breeds include the Guernsey, the Jersey, and the Holstein.

DID YOU KNOW?
Cattle are ruminants - animals that bring their food back up after it has been swallowed, to be rechewed and reswallowed. This process is known as 'chewing the cud'.

Cattle have served many purposes to human beings over the years. Holstein cows such as these can be a source of dairy products.
© Gunter Marx Photography/Corbis

Answer: A bull is a male bovine and a cow is a female.

The Loyal Companions

For thousands of years, dogs have held a special place in people's hearts. They are known as 'man's best friend'. This is because they are so brave, loving, and loyal. Dogs are used to living in groups called 'packs' and obeying the pack leader. Now humans are their pack leaders. Dogs depend on people for food - mostly meat - and perform services in return.

Since prehistoric times, dogs have worked for people. They have tracked game animals and retrieved them on land and water, guarded houses, and pulled sledges. They have delivered messages, herded sheep, and even rescued people trapped in snow. They sniff out illegal drugs and explosives, help police make arrests, and guide visually impaired people. Fast-running dogs are also used in races.

Dogs have many abilities and characteristics that make them useful. Sharp teeth are one of these. Most dogs can smell fainter odours and hear higher notes than any person. And although dogs don't see many colours, they are very good at noticing movement.

Security guard with police dog examining bags at a convention in Mexico.
© AFP/Corbis

SEARCH LIGHT

About how much difference is there between the tallest dog mentioned in the article and the shortest one mentioned?

Dogs come in many shapes, sizes, and **temperaments**. A big Irish wolfhound stands about 80 centimetres high at the withers, or top of the shoulders. The chihuahua, however, stands about 13 centimetres tall. Herding dogs such as collies tend to be intelligent. Terriers, which were bred to catch rodents, were originally quite fierce. But many different breeds of dogs now make playful family pets.

Dogs have been **domesticated** for much of human history. When Pompeii - the ancient Italian city that was buried by a volcano in AD 79 - was excavated, a dog was found lying across a child. Apparently it was trying to protect the child.

Dogs, some of the most popular animals in the world, come in many shapes and sizes. They were among the first animals to be domesticated, or tamed, by humans.
© Tim Davis/Corbis

DID YOU KNOW?
The ancient Egyptian god known as Anubis had a man's body and the head of a jackal - a member of the same family as dogs and wolves.

Answer: On average, the difference between the Irish wolfhound and the chihuahua is 69 centimetres.

Beasts of Burden

Donkeys were among the first animals to be tamed by humans. The first donkeys probably came from Asia. People ride donkeys and use them to carry heavy loads, or **burdens**. Because they are surefooted, donkeys are useful on rough or hilly ground.

SEARCH LIGHT

What's one way that donkeys are like horses? What's one way that they're different?

Donkey carries load through the streets of Colombia, South America.
© Jeremy Horner/Corbis

Donkeys play an important part in the lives of people in the mountains of Ethiopia and other parts of north-eastern Africa. They are also important to the people in the high plains of Tibet and in parts of South America.

Donkeys can be found in a range of sizes. From the ground to the shoulder, the American donkey can be 168 centimetres tall, while the Sicilian donkey is only about 81 centimetres tall. The donkey's long ears are its most noticeable feature. Donkeys are usually white, grey, or black in colour, or shades in between. Most of them have a dark stripe from their mane to their tail. The mane of a donkey is short and tends to stick out.

Donkeys can survive on almost any kind of plant for food, but usually they eat hay or grass. They are gentle and patient and become fond of their masters if they are treated well. This is why some people prefer donkeys to horses or mules.

DID YOU KNOW?
Donkeys can be famously stubborn. If they don't want to move, then no amount of pushing or pulling will budge them.

The donkey is related to the horse. Sometimes people **crossbreed** a donkey with a horse. When the father is a donkey and the mother is a horse, the baby is called a 'mule'. Another name for a donkey is a burro, which is the Spanish word for the animal.

This donkey shows how important these animals can be to their owners. Donkeys are gentle and patient and become fond of their masters if they are treated kindly.
© Galen Rowell/Corbis

Answer: Donkeys and horses look very much alike, with similar faces, legs, bodies, tails, and manes. Horses, however, are generally much taller than donkeys. And donkeys are generally considered better pack animals and are more patient than horses.

Strong and Graceful Animal Friends

The horse has been a friend to human beings for thousands of years. Long ago, horses were used to carry soldiers onto the battlefield. They have also pulled carriages, carts, and heavy farm machinery. Today people ride horses and use them for hunting, playing **polo**, and racing. Horses even perform in circuses.

The reason horses have been used in so many ways is because they are large and strong. A typical horse weighs more than 450 kilos! It can stand more than 1.5 metres tall at the shoulder. From its nose to its tail, it's about 2.7 metres long.

The legs of a horse are strong even though they look very slender. When a horse is moving, its back legs give it the power to move forward and its front legs give it support.

A horse's foot is really just one large toe, and the hoof is like a thick toenail. The part of the hoof that can be seen when the horse's feet are on the ground is called the 'wall'. A horseshoe is fitted to the underside of the wall to protect it from cracking.

A herd of galloping horses in New Zealand.
© Kit Houghton/Corbis

SEARCH LIGHT

Fill in the gap: The outside part of a horse's hoof is called the '_____'.

A horse's eyes are larger than those of any other land animal. But horses have a problem with sight. A horse sees things first with one eye and then with the other. So even small **stationary** objects appear to move. This frightens the horse. To keep a horse calm, the owner sometimes fits pads called 'blinders', or 'blinkers', on the outer sides of the eyes. This prevents the horse from seeing things that might frighten it.

Many people still enjoy horseback riding. This woman is riding seated in what's called a 'stock saddle'. American ranchers and cowboys developed this comfortable seat. The more formal 'English saddle' is used with many show horses.
© Royalty-Free/Corbis

DID YOU KNOW0?
Ruins of some of the world's earliest civilizations have included pictures and sculptures of horses. This proves that people have been working with horses for thousands of years.

Answer: The outside part of a horse's hoof is called the 'wall'.

Smarties
with Dirty Faces

Did you know that in tests of intelligence, pigs have proved to be among the smartest of all domestic animals - even more intelligent than dogs?

The world's largest population of **domestic** pigs is in China. The second largest population of domestic pigs is in the United States, and the third largest is found in Brazil.

Besides domestic pigs, there are several species of wild pigs found in Europe, Asia, and Africa. The **pygmy** hog is the smallest of the wild pigs. It is found in Nepal and northern India. It is now in danger of becoming extinct. The warty pig and the bearded pig live in parts of Southeast Asia, Malaysia, and the Philippines.

Wild pigs eat a wide variety of foods, including leaves, roots, fruit, and reptiles. Food for domestic pigs includes maize and other grains, and some kinds of rubbish too. A pig's snout ends in a flat rounded disk. Pigs use their snouts to search for food. Both male and female wild pigs have **tusks** on their snouts, which they use for defence.

(Top) Pigs enjoying a mud bath; (bottom) getting friendly with a piglet.

SEARCH LIGHT

Find and correct the mistake in the following sentence: Pigs have proved to be among the least smart of all domestic animals.

DID YOU KNOW?
People think pigs are dirty animals because they so often see pigs wallowing in mud. But pigs cover themselves with mud to stay cool. Given a choice, pigs prefer air-conditioning to mud baths.

A female pig is old enough to have piglets when she is about a year old. Before she gives birth to her first **litter**, the female pig is known as a 'gilt'. After the first litter, she is known as a 'sow'. Sows can have as many as 20 piglets in a litter, but a litter of 10 or 11 is the average. A male pig is called a 'boar'. A young **weaned** pig of either sex is called a 'shoat'.

Female pigs can have as many as 20 piglets in a litter. China holds the record for having the largest population of domestic pigs. The United States is second.
© Royalty-Free/Corbis

© Eye Ubiquitous/Corbis

© Julie Habel/Corbis

Answer: Pigs have proved to be among the smartest of all domestic animals.

Follow the Leader

Like Mary's little lamb, sheep like to follow a leader, usually an old ram (male sheep). They live together in groups called 'flocks'. If the shepherd or farmer who takes care of the sheep can get the leader going in the right direction, the rest will follow. Sometimes well-trained and specially reared dogs called 'sheepdogs' help herd the sheep and keep them from getting lost.

(Top) Dall's sheep, a variety found in Alaska; (bottom) a boy holds a fleecy lamb (young sheep).

Domestic sheep are very useful animals. Their thick, soft fleece, or wool, is used for making clothes and blankets. Some sheep are raised for their meat. In many countries people drink sheep's milk, which is also used for making cheese.

A sheep's wool is cut off with **shears**, much as your hair is trimmed with scissors. Sheep are sheared only once a year, at a time when they won't be too cold without their wool. Sheep do something else that people do: they take baths. They are herded into tanks of water with chemicals in it. This mixture of chemicals and water is called a 'sheep-dip', and it is used to protect the sheep from **parasites**. Sheep also have to have shots from a **veterinarian**.

Did you know that sheep are easily scared? Even a sheet of paper blowing in the wind will frighten them. Thunderstorms also frighten them.

There are wild sheep in many parts of the world. They look a lot like goats, but there are some ways to tell the two apart. Sheep don't have beards, for example, but many goats do. Also, sheep's horns curl around the sides of their heads, but goats' horns arch toward the backs of their heads.

SEARCH LIGHT

Which of the following is *not* a feature that sheep and goats share?
a) giving milk
b) growing a beard
c) producing wool

DID YOU KNOW?
Some breeds of horned sheep may grow more than one pair of horns. For example, Jacob sheep, a British breed that is also raised in the United States, may grow as many as three pairs of horns.

Sheep are raised all over the world. This shepherd in Chile leads his sheep down a mountain road.
© Galen Rowell/Corbis

Answer: b) growing a beard

Birds of a Feather

SEARCH LIGHT

What do birds have that no other animal has?

Like many animals, birds are **warm-blooded**. They have many other features in common with other animals, too. But they have one feature that makes them **unique** among all living animals: birds have feathers.

The entire covering of feathers is called the bird's 'plumage'. Feathers are an important part of why most birds can fly. And feathers help protect all birds from rain, cold, and heat.

The next time it rains, watch for birds outside the window. You may see them standing with wings and tail drooping to the ground. The water simply slides off without soaking through. On a cold winter day you may notice that birds fluff out their feathers. Fluffed-out feathers hold a layer of warm air next to the skin. In hot weather a bird flattens its feathers. This keeps the skin cool by stopping hot air from reaching it.

Birds have different kinds of feathers. In many birds a thick coat of feathers called 'down' lies closest to the skin. Down feathers are soft and warm. Water birds have extra-thick coats of down. That's one reason why ducks can paddle about in icy winter waters without getting cold.

A bird's main body feathers are called '**contour** feathers'. Most contour feathers have many small hooks. The tiny hooks lock together like a zip, which makes the feathers smooth in a single direction. Some contour feathers are colourful and are for show only. Other contour feathers are special 'flight feathers'. These are found on the edges and tips of the wing and in the tail. They can be adjusted as a bird flies to help the bird steer and change speed.

DID YOU KNOW?
A few birds have a curious trick of stroking their feathers with live ants. It's not clear why they do this. One explanation is that an acid produced by the ants seems to kill or drive away insects.

Riders of the Wind

If an eagle spread its wings in your room, it would take up as much space as your bed. Eagles have been called the 'king of birds' because of their **majestic** appearance and power of flight. They fly easily, using air currents to ride the wind.

Golden eagle.
© Royalty-Free/Corbis

Eagles are birds of prey, which means that they hunt other animals for food. One reason they are such good hunters is that they have excellent eyesight. Even when an eagle is so high in the air that it can hardly be seen, it can still see small objects on the ground. When it spots a meal, it swoops down and grabs the animal with its strong claws. Then it uses its hooked beak to tear the animal apart.

Eagles build huge nests of sticks on rocky cliffs or in the treetops. Their nests are big enough to hold people! Eagles use the same nest year after year, returning to it with the same mate.

When there are eggs to hatch, both the mother and the father eagles take turns sitting on them. Both parents care for the little eagles afterward, taking them mice, fish, rabbits, ducks, snakes, and squirrels to eat. But eagles don't always catch their own food. Sometimes they steal food from another bird by chasing the bird until it gets tired and drops whatever it is carrying.

Not all eagles look alike. A golden eagle has a cap of gold feathers on its head. A bald eagle is not really bald, but it looks that way because its head feathers are white and its body feathers are brown.

SEARCH LIGHT

Find and correct the error in the following sentence: Only female eagles take care of the babies.

DID YOU KNOW?
When eagles choose a mate, they do a dramatic high-flying act called cartwheeling. Gripping each other with their claws, they plunge together toward the ground. At the last moment they pull apart and fly upward again.

Near Kenai, Alaska, a bald eagle perches on a branch.
© Theo Allofs/Corbis

Laugh, Kookaburra!

The birds known as kingfishers are found all over the world, but most kinds live in **tropical** areas. Many kingfishers are brightly coloured, especially the ones found in Southeast Asia. All are famous for their swift dives.

Kingfishers are often boldly patterned. Many of them have **crests** on their large heads. Their bodies are squat, and their bills are long and heavy. A kingfisher's long bill helps it to catch fish as it swoops into the water.

(Top) Sacred kingfisher; (bottom) Malachite kingfisher.

The most commonly spotted kingfisher in North America is the belted kingfisher. It ranges from Canada to the Gulf Coast. You can recognize the belted kingfisher by its shaggy black crest. It also has bluish grey feathers on the upper part of its body and white on the under part. Both the male and the female seem to be wearing a belt! The male kingfisher has a belt of grey breast feathers. The female has a chestnut coloured belt.

The belted kingfisher makes its nest in a hole that it digs in the ground close to streams and lakes. The nest is full of fish bones. The belted kingfisher eats only fish, which it catches. Once the fish has been caught, the kingfisher whacks it against a branch a few times and then eats it whole!

Some kingfishers live in forests rather than near water. Among the forest kingfishers is the well known kookaburra of Australia. It eats reptiles, including poisonous snakes. The kookaburra is sometimes called the '**bushman's** clock', because it is heard early in the morning and just after sunset. It has a loud laughing or **braying** voice.

SEARCH LIGHT

Find and correct the error in the following sentence: The most commonly seen kingfisher in North America is the kookaburra.

The diet of the kookaburra includes lizards, insects, and even poisonous snakes.
© Martin Harvey—Gallo Images/Corbis

DID YOU KNOW?
A pair of belted kingfishers will take turns digging a tunnel into a riverbank to create their nest. They dig with their bills and use their feet to kick the loose dirt from the tunnel's mouth.

108

Answer: The most commonly seen kingfisher in North America is the belted kingfisher.

The Nighttime Hunters

Maybe it's because they fly mostly at night that owls seem so mysterious. Some **superstitions** connect them with scary things such as witches. But owls aren't that mysterious, and they aren't scary. They are simply **nocturnal** birds. And they are very helpful to people.

Saw-whet owls.
Ron Austing—Frank Lane Picture Agency/Corbis

Owls are hunters. Some owls eat insects or fish, but most eat rodents, such as mice and rats. Without owls, there would be too many rodents, and rodents are serious **pests.**

Owls can see better at night than most animals. They have excellent hearing and can detect the smallest scratchings of a mouse. When it comes to locating **prey**, their hearing helps them more than their eyesight. Because of their soft feathers, owls fly silently and almost always surprise their prey. Owls catch their prey in their long strong claws and swallow it without chewing.

The only way an owl can look around is to turn its head. It can turn its head almost all the way around, turning it so fast that you can hardly see it move. Sometimes it looks as though the owl is turning its head all the way around in a full circle!

Some people say owls are wise. That is because they were once associated with Athena, the Greek goddess of wisdom.

Owls sleep during the day, hidden among tree branches. If you were to see an owl, you'd probably mistake it for a piece of bark. It would sit still, not moving a feather. It wouldn't even move its eyes. It couldn't, because an owl's eyes can't move! This is why owls seem to stare at you - if you're lucky enough to see one!

SEARCH LIGHT

Why do some people think that owls can turn their heads all the way around in a circle?

DID YOU KNOW?
Owls swallow their food whole, and then afterward they cough up hard balls of the parts they can't eat, such as bones and fur. If you find these hairy lumps scattered under a tree, it's a pretty good bet there's an owl nearby.

Common barn owls live all over the world, except in Antarctica and Micronesia.
© Eric and David Hosking/Corbis

Answer: Owls can turn their heads to the left or the right almost all the way around. It's because the head snaps back so quickly, truly in the blink of an eye, that people think owls can turn their heads all the way around.

Bright Colours
and Brilliant Whites

Citron-crested cockatoo.
© Eric and David Hosking/Corbis

Parrots and cockatoos have long fascinated humans. These lively birds not only are beautiful but they entertain us with their chatter and behaviour as well. Many parrots are brightly coloured, with green feathers and patches of red, orange, or blue. Most cockatoos are white, and all have a patch of long feathers called a 'crest' on their head that stands up straight when the bird is excited.

Parrots and cockatoos belong to the same family as cockatiels, macaws, parakeets, and many other colourful birds. The tiniest parrot is the pygmy parrot, which is only 7 centimetres long. The largest member of the family is a type of macaw that can be as much as 101 centimetres long. All the birds in this family have strong hooked bills that can crack open nuts. Their thick fleshy tongues help them eat. Some birds have brush-tipped tongues that are useful in sucking **nectar** from flowers and juice from fruits.

DID YOU KNOW?
Like many rainforest animals, wild parrots are endangered. This is partly because their homes are destroyed when the forest is cut down or burned. But they are also threatened by people who hunt them in order to sell them as pets.

Parrots and cockatoos have unusual feet. Two toes point forward and two point backward. This lets them climb trees swiftly and grasp their food firmly as they eat it. The birds can also use their strong bills to help them climb.

Parrots and cockatoos are found in most **tropical** regions of the world, especially in rainforests. These birds can live for 30 to 50 years. Some have been known to live for 80 years!

Some parrots talk, sing, laugh, and whistle. They have a sharp sense of hearing and can **echo** human sounds and speech. Cockatoos can talk too. They are very **impish** and like to play tricks - like figuring out how to escape from their cages!

Macaws gather at Manu National Park in Peru to eat clay. The clay adds minerals to the birds' diet.
© Michael & Patricia Fogden/Corbis

Proud Birds

A peacock's feathers are brilliant shades of bronze, blue, green, and gold. It even has a little crown of feathers, called a 'crest', on the top of its head. The centre of attraction, though, is the peacock's long tail. At the tip of each tail feather is a big shiny spot ringed with blue and bronze that looks like an eye.

When the male peacock wants to attract a female peacock (called a 'peahen'), it dances! And again the action is all in the tail. The peacock lifts its tail and spreads it out like a fan. Every feather is shown off this way. At the end of this show, the peacock makes its tail feathers **vibrate**. This makes the quills in the long tail feathers rattle and rustle. The peahen is charmed!

Peahens do not have long tails or crests. They are green and brown in colour and almost as big as the males.

Peacocks live in the wild in Southeast Asia and belong to the pheasant family. Two important kinds of peacock are the green, or Javanese, peacock and the blue, or Indian, peacock. The green peacock is found from Myanmar to Java. The blue is found in India and Sri Lanka. These beautiful birds can also be seen in zoos around the world.

A long time ago, people kept peacocks at home. The ancient Greeks called the peacock 'Hera's bird'. In their religion, Hera was the wife of Zeus, the god of sky and weather. She was thought of as the queen of heaven. According to an old story, the eyelike markings on peacock feathers were the 100 eyes of the giant Argus.

SEARCH LIGHT

The male peacock in the picture is spreading his tail feathers to try to
a) scare the peahen.
b) attract the peahen.
c) hide the peahen.

DID YOU KNOW?
Peacocks may be beautiful birds, but they definitely don't have beautiful voices. Peacocks make a harsh screeching when they 'sing', if you can call it that.

The male peacock displays his feathers to get the attention of the female.
© Terry W. Eggers/Corbis

Answer: b) attract the peahen.

The World's Largest Population

The Earth is home to more insects than any other kind of animal. Insects are unique among all creatures because their bodies are divided into three parts - the head, the thorax, and the abdomen. The head contains the mouth, the eyes, and the **antennas**. Some insects use their antennas for smelling. The thorax is similar to a person's chest. If an insect has wings, they are attached to the thorax. And some insects have ears on the thorax. The abdomen contains a large part of the **digestive system**.

Instead of having bones, insects have an outer covering to support the body. The muscles are attached to this covering. The outer layer of the covering is waxy and **waterproof**.

All insects have six legs. Their legs, like their wings, are attached to the thorax. Each leg has five different bending places. It's like having five knees.

Each kind of insect has features that help it get along in the world. The pond skater has little cups on its feet so that it can walk on water. Dragonflies can hover and turn in the air like little helicopters. They even look like helicopters!

Some insects make sounds like music. Perhaps the most beautiful music is made by the snowy tree cricket. This insect uses one of its front wings as a fiddle and the other as a bow. Locusts have two tiny shell-like drums close to their wings. When the wings flap, these drums sound like fingers tapping on a metal lid. Grasshoppers make sounds by rubbing their wings or their back legs together. In some places people keep crickets or grasshoppers in cages to listen to their songs.

SEARCH LIGHT

What are the three parts of an insect's body?

DID YOU KNOW?
It may seem hard to believe, but in the countryside almost all the noises you hear at night are made by insects and frogs - even the ones that sound like birds or people.

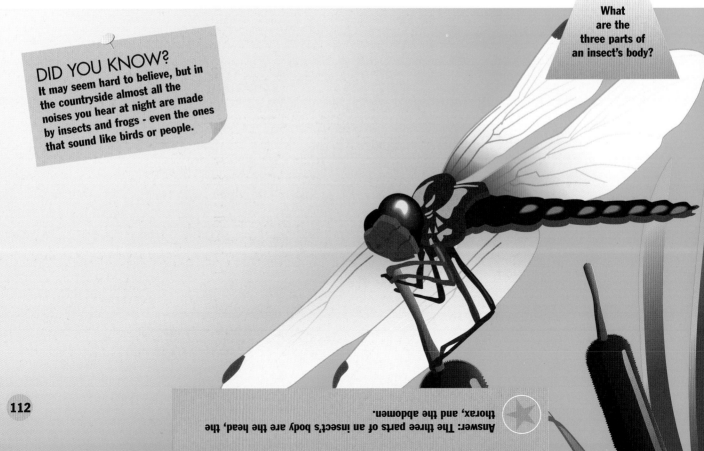

Answer: The three parts of an insect's body are the head, the thorax, and the abdomen.

Insect
Castle Builders

Most ants live in nests that they build in protected places. Many live underground, sometimes under a rock. Some ants live in trees or inside wild plants. Others build their nests on the ground, using tiny sticks, sand, mud, gravel, and even leaves.

Large ant hill in the Northern Territory of Australia.
© Penny Tweedie/Corbis

SEARCH LIGHT

Why do you think ants touch feelers whenever they meet? (Hint: What important function do the feelers, or antennas, serve?)

An ant hill is a mound of sand or dirt where thousands of ants live and work. Inside the hill are special rooms where food is kept and other rooms for baby ants. Tunnels connect the rooms. Worker ants build the nest, make tunnels, and repair any damage to the ant hill.

Soldier ants guard the ant hill day and night and protect it from enemies. An ant has long feelers, called antennas, that stick out from its head. It can give messages to other ants by tapping them with its antennas. Ants smell with their antennas too. They use scents to tell whether another ant is a friend or an enemy. If an ant from another nest wanders into the ant hill, the soldiers will attack it. Deadly wars are often fought between two nests of ants.

The whole nest is ruled by the queen ant, the mother of all the ants. The queen lays her eggs in a special room in the ant hill, while the other ants feed, clean, and protect her.

The 'ant castle' doesn't have a barn or a stable. But in one room certain kinds of ants keep aphids, which are tiny green insects. Aphids are called 'ant cows' because the ants 'milk' them to get a sweet juice the aphids produce. Other ants are like farmers too. They grow fungus inside their nests, and the fungus is all they eat!

Two leafcutting ants are hard at work clipping out pieces of a leaf in a rainforest in Costa Rica. The fragments are transported to an underground nest that can include over 1,000 chambers and house millions of individual ants. The ants physically and chemically create 'gardens' of fungus that grow on the chewed leaves. The fungus then provides them with food.
© Steve Kaufman/Corbis

DID YOU KNOW?
One type of ant travels as an army. Millions of army ants move in lines that look like rivers of ants! These ant armies weigh so much that they can knock over trees and even bring down large animals, which they then eat.

Answer: Ants touch when they meet because that's how they communicate with one another. They also use their feelers to tell if an ant is an enemy or a friend.

113

Inside the Hive

Inside a honeybee hive you'll see bees. But you'll also see hundreds of little six-sided rooms, or 'cells'. The bees build these cells with a wax - beeswax - that they make inside their bodies.

The bees store many things in the wax cells, including honey, **nectar**, and a food called 'bee bread'. Bee bread is made of flower **pollen** mixed with honey. The cells are also used to hold the tiny eggs that will hatch into baby bees.

Most of the bees' work is done in spring and summer. That's when the honey is made and stored and when the queen bee lays most of her eggs. The queen bee is the biggest bee in the hive.

There are two other kinds of bee in the hive: drones and workers. Drones are larger than the workers and have no stingers. They don't do any work, but one drone mates with the queen and is the father of all the hive's workers.

A bee pollinates a flower.
© George D. Lepp/Corbis

SEARCH LIGHT

True or false? Drones have stingers.

Each of the worker bees has a special job. Some build the cells in the hive, and others keep the hive clean. Some workers are soldiers that guard the hive and chase away any bees, wasps, and other insects that might try to steal the hive's honey.

Other worker bees fly out to visit flowers and blossoms. They take pollen and nectar back to the hive to make bee bread and honey. Some bees even stay by the door of the hive and flap their wings quickly to blow cool air through the hive.

DID YOU KNOW?
Bees can tell if an intruder has entered the hive because the intruder smells different. But one kind of moth has found a way to sneak into hives. It fakes the smell of the hive just long enough to get in and steal some honey.

Bees go about their work on a man-made honeycomb.
© Lynda Richardson/Corbis

Answer: FALSE. Only worker bees and queens have stingers.

Fly by Day, Fly by Night

Butterflies and moths are found throughout the world, from deserts to hot jungles to high up in snowy mountains. You can see them on every continent except Antarctica.

Butterflies and moths are insects, and like all insects they have three pairs of legs. Their bodies are divided into three sections: head, **thorax**, and **abdomen**. On either side of the head is a large special eye. These eyes are able to detect the smallest movement. But they cannot see faraway things very clearly.

The thorax, the middle section of the body, has two pairs of wings. The wings in front are usually larger. Dust-like scales cover the wings, body, and legs. If you happen to touch a butterfly or moth, these scales will come off in your hand.

If you want to know whether you are looking at a butterfly or a moth, you should look at its **antennae.** Butterflies and moths use their antennae to hear and smell. Butterfly antennae end in little round knobs. Moth antennae may look like tiny feathers or threads.

The most striking thing about butterflies is their colouring. Most are bright and beautiful. But most moths are dull coloured, with thicker bodies and smaller wings. Butterflies hold their wings straight up over their backs when they rest. Moths rest with their wings spread out. Butterflies are active during the day. But moths usually fly around at night.

Many butterflies and moths seem to like sweet things. **Nectar** from flowers is an important part of their diet. Some will eat mosses and ferns. Others like cones, fruits, and seeds, but some do not eat at all and live for only a short time!

Brown moth.
© Karen Tweedy-Holmes/Corbis

SEARCH LIGHT

When do most butterflies fly, during the day or at night?

DID YOU KNOW?

The viceroy butterfly protects itself by looking like the monarch butterfly, which has an unpleasant taste. So animals often avoid eating the viceroy because it looks so much like the bad-tasting monarch.

A cracker butterfly rests on the leaf of a plant.
© George D. Lepp/Corbis

Indestructible
Insects

Cockroaches have been around for many millions of years. This means that cockroaches lived through times when many other animals disappeared forever. They are very tough insects indeed. One type, the Oriental cockroach, can live for a month without food!

Cockroaches are found nearly everywhere. Some kinds live outside, but others live indoors alongside humans. These kinds are pests. They like warm dark areas in homes, offices, ships, trains, and even airplanes. Their broad flat bodies can squeeze through the narrowest of cracks. Although cockroaches may look like beetles, they are related to crickets. Like them, cockroaches use their long **antennae** on their heads for feeling through dark places.

Cockroaches usually hide during the day and come out at night to feed. They eat all sorts of plant and animal products, including paper, clothing, books, and other insects. Some cockroaches even eat other cockroaches.

SEARCH LIGHT

True or false? Most cockroaches hide at night and come out during the day.

DID YOU KNOW?
Many scientists believe that the cockroach is one of the few animals that could survive a nuclear bomb blast.

Their feeding causes a lot of damage. And they have a nasty smell too. They can also cause allergies and are thought to spread diseases to humans. No wonder cockroaches are considered among the worst household pests.

Humans get rid of cockroaches with common poisons and traps. But cockroaches have many other enemies besides humans. Spiders, frogs, toads, lizards, and birds all feed on them.

There are more than 3,500 types of cockroach. Some are small, while others reach lengths of seven centimetres. Many are colourful. Most have two pairs of wings. Some, such as the American cockroach, can fly long distances. Others, such as the Oriental cockroach, can't fly at all. But all cockroaches have long powerful legs and can run very fast.

Cockroaches usually run and hide when a light is turned on in a dark room.

© Gallo Images/Corbis

Answer: FALSE. Cockroaches usually hide during the day and come out at night to feed.

The Wing Singers

A cricket never opens its mouth to chirp. Instead, it raises its stiff leathery front wings and rubs one over the other to make its high creaking sound. It's a loud noise for such a tiny insect. Some crickets are as small as your thumbnail.

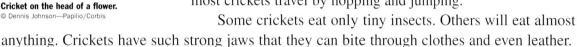

Cricket on the head of a flower.
© Dennis Johnson—Papilio/Corbis

Only male crickets have music-making wings. The chirping lets female crickets know where to find them, and it also keeps other male crickets away. The smooth wings of female crickets make no sound. Some kinds of male and female crickets use their back wings for flying. But most crickets travel by hopping and jumping.

Some crickets eat only tiny insects. Others will eat almost anything. Crickets have such strong jaws that they can bite through clothes and even leather.

Like other insects, a cricket has six legs. On its feet there are tiny claws that help it dig or run along on a tree limb or ceiling. You'll never guess where a cricket's ears are. They're down near the joints of its front legs!

There are many different kinds of cricket. Crickets are black, green-brown, whitish, and straw coloured. There are the field crickets and brown house crickets. Both chirp during the day and night. But the white and green tree crickets and the bush crickets chirp only at night.

A special kind of cricket in North America is called a 'thermometer cricket'. Try counting how many times it chirps in 15 seconds and add 40 to it. Now you know the temperature in Fahrenheit degrees! The crickets chirp faster as the weather gets warmer.

SEARCH LIGHT

True or false? Some crickets can fly.

There are a number of myths about crickets. Some people believe that harming a cricket will lead to bad luck.
© Cordaiy Photo Library Ltd./Corbis

Answer: TRUE.

Garden-Variety Hoppers

Grasshoppers are insects that are found all over the world. They live in all kinds of places but are most common in grasslands and tropical forests. One type spends most of its life on floating plants. But grasshoppers also live in people's gardens. Their brown or green colouring helps them blend in with the plants and soil around them.

Bladder grasshopper.
© Anthony Bannister—Gallo Images/Corbis

The reason grasshoppers are fond of gardens is that they are **vegetarians**. And people grow many things that grasshoppers like to eat. In some parts of the world, grasshoppers called locusts travel in huge swarms that can destroy a whole season's worth of crops.

The grasshopper itself has to be careful as well. Some if its relatives, such as the mantises, will make a meal out of a grasshopper. Many birds, frogs, and snakes also eat any grasshopper they find. In certain parts of the world, even people eat grasshoppers. Whether they are dried, fried, jellied, roasted, dipped in honey, or ground into **meal**, they can be a good source of **nutrients**.

> **DID YOU KNOW?**
> In the story called 'The Ant and the Grasshopper', the grasshopper spends all of its time eating while the ant stores up food for winter. Come winter, the grasshopper is very hungry. Of course, in real life grasshoppers don't act this way at all.

But grasshoppers have their ways of avoiding danger too. They can smell and hear an enemy, and, of course, they can hop. A grasshopper can hop so well because of its long hind legs. And though grasshoppers usually hop or crawl to get around, most kinds can also fly.

Usually, male grasshoppers are the ones that chirp or sing. They rub their wings together, or they rub their hind legs against their front wings. The song is the male's way of calling the female grasshopper.

SEARCH LIGHT

Farmers really don't like some kinds of grasshoppers. What are these grasshoppers called?

Grasshoppers are green, olive, or brown and may have yellow or red markings.
© Karl Switak—Gallo Images/Corbis

Answer: Farmers don't like locusts because they destroy crops.

An Itchy Situation

'**M**-m-m-m-m-m-s-s-z-z-sz-sz-n-n-z-z-zing-ing-ing!'

The humming sound you hear when a mosquito is near your ear comes from the fast beat of the mosquito's wings. Actually, that's the hum of the female mosquito. It is only the female mosquito that bites and leaves those itchy lumps on your arms or legs. The male mosquito seems to be satisfied with a meal of nectar and other plant juices.

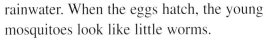

Mosquitoes are insects that are usually found wherever the weather is damp or where there are rivers, lakes, or swamps. That's because mosquitoes must lay their eggs in water. Otherwise, the eggs could not hatch. Mosquitoes sometimes lay their eggs in ponds, and other times they lay them in ditches. They will even lay them in tins partly filled with

Magnified image of young, newly hatched mosquitoes.
© Science Pictures Limited/Corbis

rainwater. When the eggs hatch, the young mosquitoes look like little worms.

Sometimes mosquitoes fly so high up in the air that they even get in through the open windows of tall apartment buildings in big cities. In the far north, near the North Pole, there are so many mosquitoes in summer that when they fly they look like black clouds.

Getting rid of mosquitoes is difficult. One way is to drain all the water out of ditches, swamps, and ponds where they lay their eggs. To destroy full-grown mosquitoes, different kinds of insecticides are used. An insecticide is a powder or liquid for killing harmful insects. Unfortunately, it can be dangerous for animals and people too.

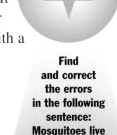

SEARCH LIGHT

Find and correct the errors in the following sentence: Mosquitoes live in dry places such as deserts, because they must lay their eggs in sand.

DID YOU KNOW?
Diseases such as malaria, which kills thousands of people each year, are spread to humans by mosquito bites. This is the main reason that people are so eager to kill mosquitoes.

A female mosquito sucks blood from a human arm.

© Richard T. Nowitz/Corbis

Answer: Mosquitoes live in damp places or near rivers, swamps, and lakes, because they must lay their eggs in water.

Majestic American Beasts

The bison, or American buffalo, is the largest land animal in North America. A bull bison stands 2 metres tall at the shoulder and weighs almost a tonne. Bison once roamed the **vast** plains in herds of many thousands of animals. The shaggy bison were looking for fresh fields of tasty grass.

In order to live on the cold Great Plains, the American Indians needed rich food, warm clothing, and strong shelter. The herds of bison gave them all of these things. Bison meat was their daily food. They made warm clothes and blankets from the thick skins. They also used the skins to make **moccasins** and tents. They used the horns to make containers and the bones to make tools.

The Plains Indians killed just enough bison for their needs. The European settlers were different. With their guns they could kill bison in larger numbers than the Indians had with their arrows and spears. Some of the settlers used the bison they killed. But other people killed for sport or just to keep animals from being used by the Indians.

Bison grazing in Wyoming's Yellowstone National Park.
© Darrell Gulin/Corbis

So there came a time when very few bison were left. Animal lovers tried to make people see how important it was to let the bison live. The governments of Canada and the United States finally put all the bison they could find into national parks and other safe places.

There probably will never be millions of bison again, but there are thousands today. There is also a European bison called the 'wisent'. The wisent is even larger than the American bison - and it is even more scarce.

DID YOU KNOW?
The bison was once so plentiful that it was used on an American coin - the 'buffalo nickel'. On the other side was the head of a Plains Indian.

SEARCH LIGHT

The U.S. Army once killed bison to make the Plains Indians surrender. Why would killing bison achieve this? (Hint: What did the Plains Indians get from bison in addition to food?)

Much like the stampeding herd pictured here, the American bison once roamed the North American plains in great numbers.
© Layne Kennedy/Corbis

Answer: The Plains Indians followed the great bison herds as they moved throughout the year. They got their food, tents, clothing, and tools from the animals. When the army killed the bison, they were killing everything the Plains Indians used for survival.

Howling at the Moon

Alone coyote howling at the Moon is probably familiar to anyone who's watched cowboy movies. It's true that the coyote is famous for its night concerts. Sometimes it utters short yaps and at other times it makes long howls. This is how coyotes communicate, but to people coyotes sound sad.

Coyotes are part of which family?
a) cat
b) dog
c) Jones

The coyote is mostly found in North America. It is sometimes called the 'little wolf' or 'brush wolf'. This is because it is related to the wolf. Both are members of the dog family. But the coyote is smaller than the wolf.

The coyote's fur is long and rough. It is greyish brown in colour, although there is sometimes a patch of white at the throat and belly. The **muzzle** is narrow and has a darker colour. A coyote's legs may be reddish and its tail bushy and black-tipped.

Coyote roaming the forest.
© Royalty-Free/Corbis

The coyote is most active after dark. It hunts for its food alone or in a group called a 'pack'. It generally feeds on **rodents** and **hares**. A coyote can follow and chase animals for long distances. Sometimes coyotes like to eat vegetables, fruit, and insects.

To find a mate, a coyote may travel for miles. The coyote pair, the male and the female, sometimes stay together for life. Both parents look after the pups. The young live with their parents for as long as three years. They help to look after and protect their brothers and sisters that are born after them.

Sometimes coyotes have been hunted and killed to protect farm animals. But they can still be found in many areas where people live.

DID YOU KNOW?
Most people think of the American Wild West when they think of coyotes. But coyotes have been showing up all over the United States. Some have even been seen in New York City.

Coyotes are well known for the various sounds they make. At times it appears that they're howling at the Moon.
© Jeff Vanuga/Corbis

Answer: b) dog

Cousins of the Dinosaurs

When scientists first found remains of dinosaurs, they thought they had found giant lizards. They later realized that dinosaurs and lizards are different types of animals, but they are related. Both are types of reptiles.

There are many kinds of lizard. They may be green, grey, red, brown, blue, yellow, black, or almost any colour! Some are longer than a man, and some are so tiny you could hold them between your fingers. The smallest lizards in the world belong to the skink and gecko families. The largest is the Komodo dragon of Southeast Asia.

Most lizards have a long tail, dry scaly skin, strong short legs, and long toes. They also have sharp claws. Some have spiny scales under their toes, which help them cling to rocks or branches.

Draco lizards are also called the 'flying lizards'. They can't fly the way a bird does, but they have a tough skin that can spread out. They can jump from a tree and sail a long way through the air.

A little lizard called the 'American chameleon' is pretty and friendly. These tiny creatures are helpful to humans because they eat harmful insects. They seem to be able to change colour when they want to. They can't really do that, but their skins do change from brown to green when there are changes in light and temperature.

The Gila monster is one of the few lizards that are dangerous. It is black and pink or orange, which makes it easy to see. And that's a good thing because the Gila has a poisonous bite.

SEARCH LIGHT

True or false? The flying lizard doesn't really fly.

DID YOU KNOW?
If another animal tries to eat the glass lizard by grabbing its tail, the tail comes off. The other animal may then think it has caught the whole lizard.

(Top) Komodo dragon; (bottom) gecko.

The five-lined skink is very small. It usually grows to be only about 13 to 20 centimetres long.

© Buddy Mays/Corbis

Answer: TRUE. It jumps and glides through the air.

Cute Clowns
and Big Bullies

Visitors to a zoo are always attracted by the **antics** of monkeys. Many animals have tails. But none use them in as many ways as monkeys do. And no monkey uses its tail as cleverly as the spider monkey.

The furry spider monkey is the champion **acrobat** of the monkey world. Its long arms help it to swing through trees. Its tail is thin, long, and very strong. It can reach almost all the way around a thick tree trunk. The tail holds onto the tree like a hand, although it doesn't have fingers.

Monkeys can be as small as kittens. The spider monkey is small, but the tiny playful marmoset is smaller - sometimes no larger than a mouse. Howler monkeys are quite big, about as big as a medium-sized dog. And their howl is so loud that they can be heard for miles. These monkeys **roam** through the trees in groups looking for food. Baboons are among the largest of all monkeys. They have dog-like snouts and large sharp teeth. They like to fight each other to see which is the strongest. The winner becomes the leader of the group.

Most monkeys feed mainly on fruits, flowers, and seeds. Some include insects and eggs in their diet. Baboons sometimes eat small mammals. Baboons live in the dry grasslands of Africa. And some macaques live in the Himalayas. But most monkeys live in warm places with lots of trees, such as tropical rainforests.

Monkeys often share their habitat with their close relatives the apes. And though apes are brainier, monkeys have a bonus too: they have tails and apes don't.

© Kennan Ward/Corbis

© Kevin Schafer/Corbis

(Top) Family of baboons in Tanzania, Africa; (bottom) Central American spider monkey sitting on a tree branch.

SEARCH LIGHT

Most monkeys live in
a) the Himalayas.
b) hot deserts.
c) tropical rainforests.

DID YOU KNOW?
A tail that can wrap around things and hold onto them is called 'prehensile'. Having prehensile tails not only has made monkeys into great climbers but has also allowed them to pick up things when their hands are busy - such as an extra banana for later!

Patas monkeys like this one live in bands in the grass and scrub regions of Central America.
© Kennan Ward/Corbis

Answer: c) tropical rainforests.

Long Ears
and Strong Legs

If you see an animal outside that hops and has long ears, it could be a rabbit or a hare. Rabbits have tails that are white on the bottom. That's why some American rabbits are called 'cottontails'. Hares have longer ears and longer legs than rabbits.

European rabbits are the ancestors of all **domestic** rabbits worldwide. Rabbits live together in underground **burrows** called 'warrens'. Inside the warren a mother rabbit carefully shreds leaves and collects grass to line a nest for her babies. Then she pulls bits of fur from her thick coat to make a warm and snug bed. Baby rabbits haven't any fur at first, so the mother must keep them warm.

The nest is usually deep enough in the warren to keep the babies safe. But when a rabbit sees a **predator** looking for the nest, the rabbit will thump its back legs to warn other rabbits.

SEARCH LIGHT

**Fill in the gap:
Rabbits have a tail that is _____ on the bottom.**

Cute and cuddly pet rabbit.
© Kelly-Mooney Photography/Corbis

Rabbit mothers aren't gentle when their babies are in danger from dogs, foxes, snakes, owls, or hawks. They bite and kick hard with their feet!

Hares don't build warrens. Their homes are shallow holes that they dig in the grass, under trees, or in brush heaps. Some hares in cold climates have a white coat during the winter and a brown one in the summer.

Both rabbits and hares love to eat green plants such as clover as well as the bark, buds, and berries of trees and shrubs. They search for food from sundown to dawn and then hide during the day. And if you've heard the story about a rabbit jumping into a thorny bush to stay safe - it's true. Rabbits make twisting paths through thorny underbrush, where their enemies can't follow.

DID YOU KNOW?
Rabbits that live in hot areas usually have bigger ears than those that live in cold areas. Larger ears help animals stay cool, while smaller ears help animals keep from getting too cold.

The American black-tailed jackrabbit is actually a hare. It's easily recognized by its long ears tipped with black colouring.
© Darrell Gulin/Corbis

Answer: Rabbits have a tail that is white on the bottom.

Masked Bandits

The raccoon is a smart and curious animal, easily recognized by the black mask across its eyes and the black bands ringing its bushy tail. These bands give the raccoon its nickname, 'ringtail'.

A raccoon at a pond.
© D. Robert & Lorri Franz/Corbis

To many people in North and South America raccoons are animals that dig through rubbish during the night at campsites and in town rubbish bins. They're **nocturnal** animals, sleeping in the daytime, and they eat many different kinds of foods. Raccoons often search in shallow water for food such as frogs and crayfish, and this once caused people to believe that raccoons washed their food.

Raccoons' bodies usually measure 50 to 66 centimetres long, and their tails are about 30 centimetres long. They weigh about 10 kilos, though a large male may weigh more than twice that amount. A raccoon's **forefeet** look like slender human hands, and the creature can handle objects quickly and easily.

Raccoons range from northern Alberta, in Canada, through most of the United States and into South America. They like wooded areas near water, but many also live in cities. They swim and climb, and they often live together high in hollow trees, in openings in rocks, in tree stumps, or in other animals' burrows. In cities they are often found living in the attics of houses.

In spring a female raccoon usually has three or four babies. When they are 10 or 11 weeks old, the mother starts taking them on short outings. The young stay with their mother for about a year.

Raccoons are considered pests in some areas, and in the eastern United States they are the primary carrier of the disease **rabies**.

DID YOU KNOW?
The name 'raccoon' comes from a Native American Indian word for the animal. Other names taken from Native American Indian languages include caribou, opossum, skunk, and woodchuck.

Raccoons that are used to being around people may seem so friendly and cute that you want to pick them up. Don't! They're still wild animals with sharp teeth, and they may carry diseases.
© Joe McDonald/Corbis

SEARCH LIGHT

Why do you suppose raccoons are sometimes called 'bandits'?

Answer: They are called bandits because they look like they are wearing masks and because they steal food from rubbish bins.

Legless Wonders

(Top) Ghost corn snake; (bottom) woma python.

Aside from worms, almost every animal you see on land has legs. But snakes are different. They don't have legs, or arms either. Most snakes move around by pushing against the ground, scraping it with their tough scales.

Snakes look slippery and slimy, but they're not. Their skin actually feels like cool soft leather. As a snake gets bigger, its skin gets tighter and tighter until the snake wiggles right out of it, wearing a new skin. A snake sheds its skin this way a few times a year.

The smallest snakes are no larger than worms. All snakes are hunters, though. Small snakes eat insects. Larger snakes eat rats or squirrels or rabbits. The huge pythons and anacondas can swallow a deer.

Some snakes use poison called 'venom' to catch animals. They deliver their poison with a bite. Others are constrictors, which means that they wrap themselves around their prey and suffocate it. Still other snakes eat bird eggs. Snakes swallow their food whole, without chewing. The jaws may be hinged so that the snake can eat something larger than its own head. A snake that has just eaten may not need another meal for days and days.

Snakes are eaten by big birds such as eagles, hawks, and owls. The Indian mongoose (a mammal) kills cobras. Wild hogs stamp on snakes to kill them. And, of course, many people kill snakes on sight.

Most snakes avoid people and won't hurt you if you don't bother them. Still, it's a good idea to leave wild snakes alone.

SEARCH LIGHT

True or false? Snakes chew their food.

DID YOU KNOW?
During cold winters, thousands of snakes may sleep together in a hole under ground to keep each other warm. This is called a 'snake pit'.

The sea snake has a flat tail that it can use like an oar to move itself through the water.
© Brandon D. Cole/Corbis

Answer: FALSE. Snakes swallow their food whole.

Learn about the many different kinds of plants we eat

Food Plants

Food Plants

Fruit Tree Royalty

The apple tree is a hardy plant that is grown in more parts of the world than any other fruit tree. That's why the apple has often been called the 'king of fruits'.

Even though it is five-sixths water, the apple has vitamins, minerals, and **carbohydrates**. Before the science of nutrition told us how to eat healthily, people already knew that 'an apple a day keeps the doctor away'.

Apples are grown for eating, cooking, and making juice. 'Eating' apples are crisp and juicy, with a tangy smell. They may be red, green, greenish yellow, pink, or orange. 'Cooking' apples are firm. 'Juice' apples are used to make apple juice and cider. Apples are also preserved as jams, jellies, apple butter, and chutneys. And applesauce - made by stewing and, often, sweetening apples - is popular in many places.

If you plant the seeds of a good-tasting apple, you will probably be disappointed by the fruit that the new tree produces. Branches, as well as seeds, have to be used to produce the best apples. The process is called 'grafting'. Apple trees need well-drained soil to grow. They also need a period of cool winter weather to rest before the fruit-growing season.

There are many signs that humans discovered the apple a long time ago. There are pictures of apples carved on stone by **Stone Age** people. Apples are mentioned in the Bible. Although some kinds of apple grow wild in North America, the apples Americans eat come from varieties that were brought from Europe. John Chapman, an early American planter better known as Johnny Appleseed, helped to spread these varieties far and wide. Apple pie, in fact, is a symbol of America.

Colourful apple varieties.
© Royalty-Free/Corbis

SEARCH LIGHT

Why is the apple called the 'king of fruits'?

DID YOU KNOW?
The French term for 'potato' is *pomme de terre*, which means 'apple of the earth'. This may be because apples and potatoes have a similar texture (feel), size, and shape.

Apples must be handled carefully to avoid bruising. Here a worker gently picks apples ready for harvesting.
© Royalty-Free/Corbis

Answer: The apple is called the 'king of fruits' because apple trees are grown in more places than any other fruit tree.

Fruit of Gold

A banana plant may grow to a height of 6 metres or more, but it is considered to be an **herb** rather than a tree. Instead of a trunk, it has a **stalk** made up of leaves rolled tightly around each other. From the stalk grows a big bunch of 50 to 200 individual bananas. Only one bunch grows on each plant. The bunch is made up of several clusters. Each cluster has 10 to 20 bananas. After harvesting, the plant is cut down. A new one then grows from an underground stem.

Farm worker on a banana plantation in Oman, in the Middle East.
© Christine Osborne/Corbis

Bananas grow only where it is warm and wet all the time, which is why people in cold countries may never see a banana plant. They love to eat the bananas, though. That's why banana farms called **plantations** are a big business in South Asia, Africa, Central and South America, and the islands of the Caribbean Sea. But Asia is where bananas originally came from.

Most everyone knows what happens to a banana that has sat around too long. It gets brown and mushy. So bananas have to be picked while they're still hard and bright green. They may have a long trip ahead of them - usually thousands of kilometres from the plantation to the grocery store. Refrigerated ships keep the bananas from ripening too soon, and then special heat and moisture treatments help them to ripen on schedule.

Bananas are used in making delicious cream pies, cakes, breads, and fruit salads. Many people's favourite banana dessert is the banana split ice-cream treat. But not all bananas are eaten as fruit. Some varieties never get sweet. These bananas, called 'plantains', are cooked and served as a vegetable.

SEARCH LIGHT

Plantains are
a) bananas that aren't sweet.
b) yellow bananas.
c) mushy brown bananas.

DID YOU KNOW?

The largest banana split ever made was reported to be a little over seven kilometres long.

Bunches of bananas hang on a plant before being harvested and exported from the Caribbean island of Grenada in the West Indies.
© Dave G. Houser/Corbis

Answer: a) bananas that aren't sweet.

The 'Head' of a Vegetable Family

Cabbage has been grown for food since ancient times. Nearly 3,000 years ago, the Greek poet Homer mentioned it in his story-poem the *Iliad*.

Wild cabbage is native to the shores of the Mediterranean Sea. It also grows wild on the sea cliffs of Great Britain. The ancient Romans probably planted it there. Cabbages have thick moist leaves with a waxy coating. The leaves are often grey-green or blue-green in colour. Cabbage plants like cool weather and deep rich soil.

Two heads of cauliflower.
© Ed Young/Corbis

Over hundreds of years, many vegetables have been developed from the wild cabbage. Some are used for garden decoration or for feeding animals. But people eat many kinds. The cabbage group includes the common cabbage, cauliflower, broccoli, Brussels sprouts, and several other vegetables. They are rich in vitamins and minerals and low in **calories**.

The common, or head, cabbage has a tight bunch of leaves (the head) around a centre stem. People eat the leaves raw or cook them. Cabbage soup is a popular dish in much of eastern Europe. Finely chopped raw cabbage is the main ingredient in a salad called 'coleslaw'. If sliced-up cabbage is salted and put away for a long time, it goes through a chemical change. The result is sauerkraut, a popular dish in Germany. In Korea cabbage is a major ingredient in the traditional dish called *kimchi.*

Cauliflower has a head of tight thick white flowers. People eat the flowers either raw or cooked. Broccoli has bright green loosely clustered flowers. People eat these flowers along with the tender stalks. Brussels sprout plants have many little cabbage-like heads instead of one large head at the top.

SEARCH LIGHT

Which of the following is not mentioned as a member of the cabbage family?
a) broccoli
b) cauliflower
c) carrot
d) Brussels sprouts

DID YOU KNOW?
In France a popular term for a loved one is *petit choux,* which means 'little cabbage'.

There are more than a hundred varieties of cabbage. Common (or head) cabbage is pictured here.
© Eric Crichton/Corbis

Answer: c) The carrot is not part of the cabbage family.

Poor Man's Food

In Mediterranean countries the fig is used so widely, both fresh and dried, that it is called the 'poor man's food'. The soft juicy fruit of the fig tree cannot remain fresh for long in the hot **climate** where it grows. So it has to be dried in the sun before it is sent to the market. Fresh or dried, the fig is packed with food value.

Figs were first found growing around the Mediterranean Sea. It's no surprise then that figs still grow in the countries bordering the Mediterranean—including Turkey, Greece, Italy, and Spain. Spanish missionaries introduced the fig tree to Mexico and California. The entire fig crop in the United States comes from California.

There are four main types of figs: Caprifig, Smyrna, White San Pedro, and Common. When a fig is introduced into another country, a new name is often given to it. The Smyrna fig became known as the Calimyrna fig in California.

Fig plants are either bushes or small trees. Fig trees are easily grown from **cuttings** off an adult tree. The fruit occurs either singly or in pairs. The trees produce two or three crops a year.

The best-tasting dried figs are those that have been allowed to dry partly on the tree. The figs are then laid out on trays to finish drying in the sun. Turning and moving them about while they dry improves their quality. Most dried figs are eaten in their natural form, though many are ground into a paste to be used in bakery products.

SEARCH LIGHT

Why would the fact that so many people eat figs earn it the nickname 'poor man's food'? (Hint: Food costs money.)

Fig trees grow only in hot dry climates. Shown here is the fruit of the fig tree as it ripens.
© Richard T. Nowitz/Corbis

DID YOU KNOW?
There are more than 900 members of the fig group. One of them, the Bo tree, or pipal, is sacred in India. It is believed to be the tree under which the Buddha sat when he attained enlightenment.

Answer: Poor people can't afford many kinds of food but can always eat the figs found growing wild.

Fruit of the Vine

Grapes grow wild in wooded and warmer regions of the Northern **Hemisphere**. And people have raised grapes in these regions for thousands of years. Grapes have been taken to South Africa, South America, and Australia and grown with great success. There are about 60 different grape plants, as well as thousands of varieties.

Table grapes.
© Craig Lovell/Corbis

The grape plant is a woody vine. A vine is a kind of plant that can't stand up by itself. It has stems called tendrils that cling to things and support the plant. An untrimmed vine may reach a length of 15 metres. Grapes are berries that grow in bunches on the vine. Grapes come in many colours - pale green, yellow, red, purple, or black. Some grapes have a white powdery coating.

The growing of grapes is called 'viticulture'. People don't usually grow grapes by planting seeds. Instead, they take cuttings off a vine that is already growing. These cuttings spend a year or so in **nurseries**, waiting to grow roots. When they have roots, they're ready to grow outside.

Another method of grape growing is called layering. In layering, the branch of a full-grown vine is bent into a curve and made to grow along the ground. New shoots and roots soon grow from this part of the branch. These are cut off from the parent vine and replanted as new vines.

Grapes are high in sugar. Different types are used for different purposes. Some are eaten fresh. Others are dried out to make raisins. But most are squeezed for their juice. Some grape juice is put through a process called 'fermentation' that changes some sugar into alcohol. The product that results is called 'wine'.

The growing
of grapes
is called
a) 'vineculture'.
b) 'viticulture'.
c) 'grapiculture'.

DID YOU KNOW?
One hectare of grapes produces almost 40,000 glasses of wine.

This worker is collecting bunches of grapes at harvest time. Green and red table grapes are an excellent source of vitamin A.
© Ted Streshinsky/Corbis

Answer: b) 'viticulture'.

The Largest Tree-Borne Fruit

The largest fruit that grows on trees is the jackfruit. And when we say it grows on trees, we mean it - the fruit grows on the main trunk of the tree and not on the branches. That's because it is so heavy that the branches can't support it - they would break right off!

So how big is this fruit? Well, a single jackfruit can weigh over 36 kilos! It sometimes reaches 90 centimetres long and almost 60 centimetres around. The jackfruit tree is also very large. It looks something like a large oak tree and grows to a height of 15 to 20 metres.

Jackfruit grows in the warm regions of Asia. It's grown widely in tropical countries where it is warm and rains a lot, such as the Philippines. There are many varieties of jackfruit. Some of the popular ones include Black Gold, Galaxy, and Honey Gold.

A young Indonesian boy carrying jackfruits.
© Bennett Dean—Eye Ubiquitous/Corbis

Like its cousin the mulberry, jackfruit is a compound fruit. This means that it has many, many seeds and that each seed surrounded by its **pulp** is a separate fruit. The big jackfruit you see is like a huge container holding all the little fruits together.

Young jackfruits are green. They turn brownish yellow when ripe. Raw jackfruit is cooked like a vegetable, though the sweet pulp surrounding the seeds can be eaten fresh. The seeds can be boiled or roasted and eaten like chestnuts.

Jackfruit has other uses too. The wood is a valuable hardwood like teak. It is used for making many things, especially furniture. Dried jackfruit leaves are used as fuel for cooking fires, while the green leaves provide **fodder** for goats.

SEARCH LIGHT

Most fruit grows on branches. Where does jackfruit grow?

DID YOU KNOW?
Ripe jackfruits have a strong odour before they're cut open. Some people compare the smell to that of rotting onions! But once you cut into the ripe fruit, it smells more like pineapples or bananas.

Jackfruit is a distant cousin of the fig. It can grow to tremendous size.
© Liu Liqun/Corbis

Answer: Jackfruit grows on tree trunks. It's too heavy for branches.

Sweet, but Oh So Sour!

The lemon is a **citrus** fruit, a family of fruits that includes limes, grapefruit, and oranges. Lemons grow on small trees and spreading bushes. The trees can grow quite tall if they are not trimmed. Their leaves are reddish when young, but they gradually turn green. Some lemon trees have sharp thorns next to the leaves.

Lemon flowers are large and may grow singly or in small clusters. The new buds of the lemon flower have a reddish tint. As they blossom, the inside of the flower turns white. Lemon flowers have a lovely sweet scent. This is one of the reasons that people like to have lemon trees in their gardens.

Lemon trees bloom throughout the year. The fruit is usually picked while it is still green. It can be damaged easily, so pickers wear gloves and have to be careful when handling the fruit. The fruit is stored for three or more months until its colour has changed to an even yellow.

The lemon fruit is oval and covered with a **rind** that is yellow when ripe. Inside, the flesh (or pulp) is divided into eight to ten segments that contain small pointed seeds. The pulp and its juice are rich in vitamin C. Lemon flavour is used in many foods, and many people put it in their tea. But the juice is very sour.

Some other important products provided by the lemon are lemon oil and pectin. In some places, the oil is used in perfumes and soaps. Pectin is what makes jelly so thick and sticky. It is also used in some medicines.

SEARCH LIGHT

What colour are lemons when they are picked from the tree?

DID YOU KNOW?
The substance that makes lemons so sour is called citric acid. In addition to being so sour, it is a very harsh substance - in fact, it's said that there's enough citric acid in a lemon to dissolve a pearl!

Beautiful and fragrant, lemon trees usually bloom throughout the year.
© Ray Juno/Corbis

Answer: Lemons are usually picked while they are still green. They turn yellow after they have aged for a while.

The Regal Tropical Fruit

Sweet, tasty, and wonderfully sticky - that's a mango! So many people like this fruit that it is sometimes called 'the queen (or king) of **tropical** fruits'. And not only does it taste good - it's good for you because it's full of vitamins.

But mangoes didn't always taste so good. Thousands of years ago they were small fruits that tasted like pine needles! At that time they grew only in some parts of Asia, such as India and Myanmar. Today they're grown in most tropical countries. There are even mango farms in the southern United States.

Mangoes come in many shapes, sizes, and colours. They can be oval or round or long and slender. They can be red, yellow, or green. The smallest mangoes are no bigger than plums. The biggest are up to 25 centimetres long and can weigh as much as 2.3 kilos.

No matter what size they are, though, all mangoes have a lot of very juicy yellow or orange fruit underneath a thin skin. In the middle of the fruit is a single flat seed.

Mangoes grow on tall trees. Take five elephants and put them on top of each other, and that's how high mango trees can grow. The trees are evergreen, which means they keep their leaves all year.

You can eat mangoes raw. Just wash them, peel them, cut them, and eat them. Or you can eat mangoes mixed in milk, like a mango smoothie. Mangoes are also used to make sauces and chutneys. In India, during festivals, you'll find mango leaves strung together hanging outside the front doors of many houses. This is because mangoes are believed to bring luck.

SEARCH LIGHT

True or false? Mangoes used to taste awful.

Fresh mangoes.
© W. Wayne Lockwood, M.D./Corbis

DID YOU KNOW?
Fruit bats help spread mangoes by carrying the fruit to another perch, where they eat the flesh and drop the seed. The seed plants itself in the ground, and soon a small mango tree pops up there.

The mango is one of the most important and widely grown fruits of the tropical world. Mangoes are a rich source of vitamins A, C, and D.
© Douglas Peebles/Corbis

Answer: TRUE. Long ago they had a chemical flavour. Unripe mangoes still have that taste.

The Drinkable Fruit

The orange is one of several kinds of small trees and shrubs that belong to the **'citrus'** group. Other common citrus fruits are lemons, limes, grapefruit, and tangerines. The first oranges and other citrus fruits probably grew in the tropical regions of Asia, especially in the islands of Southeast Asia. The practice of growing oranges spread to India, to the east coast of Africa, and then to the Mediterranean regions. Today oranges are also grown in the warm regions of the Americas and Australia.

The orange is a nearly round fruit with a leathery, oily peel and juicy flesh (or pulp) inside. It grows on attractive trees 4.5 to 9 metres tall. Orange trees have sweet-smelling waxy blossoms and leaves that stay green throughout the year. Their branches often have small thorns as well. A single orange tree will bear fruit for 50 to 80 years or longer. Sometimes the age of an orange tree is counted in centuries!

The most popular variety of orange is the China orange. It's also called the sweet orange or common orange. This orange tastes best when it is fully ripe, and it should not be picked before that. Another popular variety, the Seville orange, is not as commonly grown. The Seville is used in making **marmalade**. Other varieties of oranges include the Jaffa from Israel, the blood orange with its red pulp, and the navel, which is usually seedless.

Oranges are also grown to produce juice, either fresh or frozen. Nearly half the oranges produced in the United States are made into frozen **concentrated** juice. Orange juice is rich in vitamin C and also provides some vitamin A.

SEARCH LIGHT

Can you name three citrus fruits?

The seedless navel orange, shown here, became a major fruit in California after it was introduced from Brazil in 1873.
© Ed Young/Corbis

Answer: Oranges, tangerines, lemons, limes, kumquats, and grapefruit are all citrus fruits.

Luscious Fruit Treat

Strawberries are eaten fresh, often with cream. They are also used as a filling for pastries, tarts, and cakes. Strawberry shortcake is made of fresh strawberries, a cake or biscuit base, and whipped cream. Needless to say, strawberries are a very popular fruit.

Strawberry plants can be found throughout most of the United States and Canada, Europe, the United Kingdom, and parts of Africa. They are also grown in New Zealand, Australia, and Japan.

The strawberry is a low **herb** plant that branches off in all directions. At the top of the plant is the 'crown' from which the leaves sprout. The leaves have three sections, each of them hairy with **saw-toothed** edges. The flowers are mostly white and sometimes reddish. They appear in small groups on slender **stalks** arising from the leaves. As the plant gets older, the roots become woody. Then the crown sends out 'runner plants', trailing vines that spread over the ground, making the plant bigger.

Runner plants are planted in autumn for a crop expected the following year. Strawberry plants are usually used to produce fruit for one to four years. In regions with very cold winters, the plants are put out in spring and protected during winter by covering the rows with straw.

Strawberries need to be stored in a cool and dry place after they've been picked. But they still don't remain fresh for very long. Some are frozen or preserved to make them last longer.

DID YOU KNOW?
Strawberries are sweet, but they're good for you too. They're rich in vitamin C, iron, and other minerals.

SEARCH LIGHT

Find and correct the error in the following sentence: Runner plants make the strawberry plant hard to catch.

The heart-shaped red fruits of the strawberry plant are popular all over the world.
© Ed Young/Corbis

Answer: Runner plants make the strawberry plant bigger.

Vegetables or Fruit?

Cooks call the tomato a vegetable, but gardeners say it's a fruit. It's actually both! In the garden the tomato is considered a fruit because it grows from a flower and has seeds in it. But in the kitchen it's considered a vegetable because it isn't sweet like apples or grapes.

Tomatoes were first grown thousands of years ago by South American Indians who lived in the Andes Mountains. In Mexico, Indians **cultivated** tomatoes long before Spanish explorers arrived in the 1500s. The name 'tomato' comes from *tomatl*, a word in the language of the Aztec people of Mexico.

A few tomato varieties.
© Michelle Garrett/Corbis

SEARCH LIGHT

The first Europeans to use the tomato as a food were the
a) Spanish and French.
b) Italians and Aztec.
c) Spanish and Italians.
d) Swiss and Indians.

The Spanish who returned to Europe after their explorations brought the tomato back with them. The tomato was first used as a food in Spain and Italy. From Europe, tomatoes were taken to North America. Today they grow all around the world, wherever winters are not too cold and summers not too hot.

Tomatoes not only taste good - they're also good for you! They're packed with vitamins A and C. Tomatoes can be served cooked by themselves or used as a part of many different meals. They're used to make soups and salads. Tomato juice is popular because of its tangy flavour. Tomatoes also form the base for ketchup, chilli sauce, and spaghetti sauce. And, of course, they're a must for your pizza!

A father and his son taste a tomato they have just picked. Tomatoes come in many different shapes and sizes.
© Ariel Skelley/Corbis

DID YOU KNOW?
For a long time the tomato was believed to be a relative of the poisonous belladonna plant. In fact, the roots and leaves of the tomato plant are poisonous. But the fruit is safe to eat and, in fact, is very good for you!

Tasty Tubers

Yam plants are climbing vines. Long slender stems bear clusters of small green flowers that look quite pretty. The plants need hot wet weather and take rather long to grow. Different varieties of them are grown as food in the tropics. In some parts of West Africa and New Guinea, yams are also used in ceremonies related to farming.

Yams, like potatoes, have thick tubers. A tuber is the thick part of the plant's stem that grows underground and stores food for the plant. And just as with the potato, the tuber is the part of a yam that people eat.

There are hundreds of varieties of yam. They differ greatly in look and taste. The colour of the tuber's flesh may be white, yellow, pink, or purple. Some taste sweet, some bitter, and some quite bland.

Baskets of yams at a market in the Cook Islands.
© Robert Holmes/Corbis

SEARCH LIGHT

Fill in the gap: The part of a yam that is eaten grows _____.

True yams are different from the sweet potato. However, some varieties of sweet potato are often called yams in the United States. Both sweet potatoes and yams are **starchy** foods with a fair amount of sugar in them. Some yams also contain poisons that may make a person sick if the tuber is not properly cooked. The poisons are destroyed by cooking.

Most people eat yams as they would potatoes. Yams are served fried, roasted, baked, and boiled. Cooked yams are often mashed into a sticky paste or dough that can then be further baked or boiled.

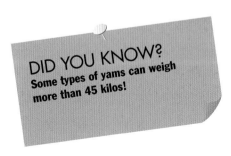

DID YOU KNOW?
Some types of yams can weigh more than 45 kilos!

Women collect yams in Papua New Guinea.
© Caroline Penn/Corbis

Answer: The part of a yam that is eaten grows underground.

A Versatile Cereal

Barley was one of the first plants ever grown as a crop. Like other food plants in the group called 'cereals', barley is a grass that is grown for its **starchy** seeds. Barley has a nutty taste and a lot of food value. People have known for a long time that barley is good to eat. It was probably first grown in **prehistoric** Ethiopia and in Southeast Asia. Egyptian farmers grew barley as far back as 5000 BC. Ancient people of Europe, Asia, and North Africa raised it too.

Barley is an especially widespread crop because it can be grown in so many different climates. It grows and ripens quickly, which makes it just right for areas that have short growing seasons - regions far to the north (such as Canada) or high up in the mountains (such as Tibet). But barley can survive just as well in the dry heat of North Africa.

Ancient people used barley to make bread. Although barley doesn't bake as well as wheat does, the flour is good for making flat breads such as pita. And barley is ideal for making some hot cereals. Polished **kernels** called 'pearl barley' serve to thicken and flavour soups. Barley can also be put through a process that turns it into a flavouring called 'malt'. Barley malt is used in making some vinegars and drinks, especially beer.

Despite all these uses, only about half the barley grown in the world is eaten by people. The rest goes to feed animals.

Barley, one of the world's major cereal plants.
© Doug Wilson/Corbis

DID YOU KNOW?
Ancient Roman gladiators trained on a diet of barley. These professional fighters gained energy and strength from barley's excellent food value.

SEARCH LIGHT

Fill in the gap: Barley was one of the _____ plants grown as a crop.

About half of the world's barley crop is used as animal feed.
© Frank Lane Picture Agency/Corbis

Answer: Barley was one of the first plants grown as a crop.

Grain of the Americas

Maize is a grain, just as wheat and rice are. Maize is known as 'corn' in the United States, Canada, and Australia. It was first found in the Americas. Mayan farmers of Mexico and Central America **cultivated** maize. Early European explorers of the Americas were the first to take maize to Europe. Since that time, maize has been grown all over the world.

Maize grows in areas that have rich soil and cold nights but no frost during the growing season. It also needs plenty of sunshine to ripen. These conditions are found in a large area of the midwestern United States known as the Corn Belt. Similar conditions are also found in parts of Asia, much of Central and South America, the Mediterranean, and southern Africa. The largest producers of maize, after the United States, are China and Brazil.

A boy holding ears of corn in a farm field in South Africa.
© Barbara Bannister–Gallo Images/Corbis

Maize is used to feed cattle and **poultry**. And, of course, it serves as food for humans. The maize that people eat is also called 'sweet corn'. The grains of maize that people eat are the seeds of the plant. The seeds are called 'kernels' and are found along the length of the spike. The spike with the kernels is commonly known as the 'ear' of corn. Leaves called 'husks' wrap around and cover the spike. The seeds, if they are planted, will grow into new maize plants.

Large quantities of maize are used in Latin American cooking. *Masa harina* is a kind of flour made from maize. It makes a dough that's used to make tortillas - a kind of round thin flat bread. They are the wraps for tacos, burritos, and enchiladas.

DID YOU KNOW?
None of the maize plant has to be wasted. For example, the stalks are made into paper and materials for building. And the cobs - the spikes stripped of kernels - are used for fuel and to make charcoal.

SEARCH LIGHT

Find and correct the error in the following sentence: Maize was first found in Europe.

Vast fields of maize like this one in the U.S. state of Nebraska are a common sight in the U.S. Corn Belt.
© Philip Gould/Corbis

Answer: Maize was first found in the Americas.

Food from Water-Grown Grasses

Do you chew grass? Actually, you probably do! The grains that most people eat daily are actually grasses - or at least grass seeds. These include wheat, maize, rye, and rice. More than half the people in the world eat rice almost every day. The grain is so important that millions of people in Asia would starve if they didn't have it. China and India are amongst the largest producers of rice. Rice is also the basic feature of most meals in the islands of the western Pacific and much of Latin America.

Rice plants are carried for planting.
© Michael S. Yamashita/Corbis

Most rice is grown in water. The land under the water has to be smooth and level, like a table top. The water on top must be the correct depth. If it's too deep, the rice will drown. If it's not deep enough, the rice won't grow.

In the countries of Asia, the muddy ground is ploughed by water buffalo pulling wooden ploughs. Then the tiny rice plants are planted in rows. If it doesn't rain enough, water is brought in from lakes and rivers to flood the fields. The rice plant grows under the water, with its green shoots sticking out. A water-filled field planted with rice is called a 'rice paddy'.

When the rice is ripe, the water is drained off the fields. After the ground has dried, the rice **stalks** are cut and tied into bundles. When the stalks have dried, the brown **hulls** are removed from the rice seeds. Many farmers grow rice for their families to eat. Rice to be sold in shops goes to a factory. There it is packed into boxes and then shipped to the shops.

SEARCH LIGHT

When you eat rice, you're eating the seeds of a kind of
a) grass.
b) tea.
c) fruit.

DID YOU KNOW?
Rice was first grown as a crop about 5,000 years ago in India. It later spread from there. It reached southern Europe in the 1400s.

In order to grow rice in hilly areas, giant steps called 'terraces' are dug into the hillsides. Each giant step has a little wall of mud at its edge to hold in the water that covers the rice as it is growing.
© Dave G. Houser/Corbis

Answer: a) grass.

The Bread of Life

Wheat is one of the oldest and most important of the **cereal** crops. Many people eat wheat products at every meal. It is an important ingredient of many breads, pastries, and pastas. Wheat has lots of **nutrients** and is a major source of energy for humans.

Wheat can be eaten simply by soaking and cooking the seeds, or grain. But for many foods the grain has to be turned to flour first. This requires grinding the wheat.

The wheat plant is a kind of grass with long slender leaves. In most kinds of wheat the stems are hollow. The top part of the plant is made up of a number of flowers. Two to six flowers form groups called 'spikelets'. Two to three of the flowers in each spikelet produce grains. It's the grains that are used as food.

Wheat ready for harvesting.
© Bohemian Nomad Picturemakers/Corbis

More of the world's farmland is used for growing wheat than for any other food crop. The world's largest producer of wheat is China. Other leading producers are India, the United States, Russia, France, Ukraine, and Turkey.

Many thousands of varieties of wheat are known. The most important ones are used to make bread and pasta. Club wheat, a soft variety, is used for cakes, biscuits, pastries, and household flour.

Wheat was first grown on farms about 9,000 years ago in the Euphrates River valley of the Middle East. In ancient Egypt, wheat was so important that the people buried some with the pharaohs (kings). In this way, they believed, the pharaohs would never go hungry in the afterlife.

DID YOU KNOW?
Although most wheat is eaten, some of it is used to make paste. (Be careful not to confuse the two!)

SEARCH LIGHT

About how many years ago was wheat first grown on farms?
a) 9,000
b) 900
c) 9,000,000

Large wheat fields cover parts of Kansas, North Dakota, Montana, Oklahoma, and Washington in the United States.
© Joseph Sohm; ChromoSohm Inc./Corbis

Answer: a) 9,000

The Chocolate Tree

DID YOU KNOW?
For hundreds of years, chocolate was enjoyed mainly as a beverage. By the 1500s the Aztec of Mexico were making a bitter cocoa-bean drink. They also used cocoa beans as money.

A chocolate tree may sound like something made up in a book or film, but chocolate really does come from trees. A tree called the 'cacao' is the source of all cocoa powder and chocolate.

Cacao trees grow only in warm areas that get a lot of rain. The trees grow long fruit called 'pods' that range in colour from bright yellow to deep purple. Inside the pods are rows of seeds called 'cocoa beans'. Each is about the size and shape of a big fingernail. It is from these cocoa beans that we get one of the world's favourite foods, chocolate.

But a lot of things have to be done to the beans before they turn into chocolate. After the cocoa beans are taken out of the pods, they are left in a damp place for a few days. The beans turn a rich brown colour and begin to smell like chocolate. Then they are dried and cleaned.

Next the beans are shipped to chocolate factories all over the world. There they are roasted and ground into a paste. This paste contains a fatty yellow liquid called 'cocoa butter'. To make chocolate, you have to add extra cocoa butter to the paste. To make dry cocoa powder, you have to remove all the cocoa butter.

The chocolate is still not ready to eat, though. Cocoa beans are not naturally sweet. In fact, the paste is very bitter. So a lot of sugar must be mixed in. Milk may be added too. The chocolate is then poured into moulds to harden into chocolate bars. Now it is finally ready to eat!

SEARCH LIGHT

True or false? Chocolate is naturally very sweet.

Answer: FALSE. Chocolate is naturally quite bitter. It is the sugar added to it that makes it sweet.

Don't Touch!

Cactus plants nearly always grow in dry areas where it hardly ever rains. In all there are about 1,650 different kinds of cactus plants (cacti). All of them except one live in North and South America, especially in Mexico. Cacti can be very tall or really tiny. Some have strange shapes or features. In the Arizona desert of the United States, you can see miles of giant treelike saguaro cacti. Another type, the old-man cactus, got its name from its woolly white 'hair'. Some prickly pear cacti have a fruit that can be eaten. You can even make sugary sweets from a cactus.

Most plants give off water through their leaves. But water is rare and **precious** in the deserts where cacti live. Cacti save water by having no leaves or only small ones that drop off early. A cactus also stores up water inside its thick stem. Almost every cactus has sharp spines that look like thorns or needles. These help protect it from people and animals that want to eat the moist parts inside. In the old days in the American West, the watery juice inside a barrel cactus often saved people's lives.

Some types of cacti are used for making medicines. Dried-up cacti are sometimes used as firewood, and cacti planted around houses can provide a thorny fence. Many people like to keep cacti as houseplants for their unusual appearance. Some cacti also produce big colourful flowers. Maybe you could grow a cactus garden!

There are more than how many different kinds of cacti in the world?
a) 650
b) 16,500
c) 1,650

DID YOU KNOW?
The saguaro cactus blossom is the state flower of Arizona, U.S., where it is illegal to kill the saguaro cactus.

Answer: c) 1,650

The World's Favourite Cup

SEARCH LIGHT

Which part of the coffee plant is used to make the coffee drink?

Coffee is one of the most popular drinks in the world. Many people think it has a great taste and a wonderful smell. Coffee also contains caffeine, which is a stimulant - that is, a substance that increases the body's activity.

Coffee grows as a bush with sweet-smelling flowers and fleshy fruit called 'coffee cherries'. Within the fruit are two seeds, or 'beans'. The beans are dried, roasted, and ground. The ground coffee is then **brewed** in water to make a drink. Coffee plants need warm weather and plenty of rain, so they grow only in **tropical** regions. There are at least 60 types of coffee plants. But only two kinds, called Arabica and Robusta, are in great demand.

Arabica coffee has more flavour and **fragrance**. It is grown in Central and South America, the Caribbean, and Indonesia. Coffee from Colombia is especially well known. Robusta coffee is grown mainly in Africa. The Robusta plant does not pick up disease easily. It is also useful in making instant coffee. Instant coffee is coffee powder that dissolves completely in water.

Coffee beans ready for purchase.
© Mark Ferri/Corbis

Coffee probably first came from Ethiopia, in north-eastern Africa. From there it was taken to the Middle East. At first it was used as a food, as a medicine, and in wines. People did not begin to drink coffee as we know it for hundreds of years. Coffee was taken to Europe and then to the Americas, starting in about the 1500s.

Today coffee is one of the world's most popular drinks. Rest periods taken during working hours are often called 'coffee breaks'. Many, many people begin each day by drinking a cup of coffee.

DID YOU KNOW?
Many countries have special coffee drinks. Turkish coffee is a strong, thick sweetened drink. Italy's espresso is made by forcing steam through ground coffee beans. France's *café au lait* and Latin America's *café con leche* both mean 'coffee with milk'.

More than 10 billion coffee trees are grown on plantations all over the world. Each tree yields about 450 grams of coffee every year. Trees begin to bear fruit when 3 to 5 years old and continue to do so for another 10 to 15 years. Here, a woman in Thailand handpicks coffee cherries, which contain coffee beans.
© Michael S. Yamashita/Corbis

Answer: The coffee seeds, or beans, are used to make coffee.

Spectacular Leaves, Sensational Syrup

SEARCH LIGHT

Why are the seeds of a maple tree attached to wings?

In parts of the United States and Canada autumn is spectacular as the leaves on the trees turn bright yellow, red, and orange. One tree in particular displays fantastic autumn colours - the maple. Some maple trees even display unusual colours such as burgundy, bronze, and purple.

There are about 200 kinds of maple tree. They can be found throughout most of North America, Europe, and north-eastern Asia. The leaves of most maples grow thickly in a **dome** shape. In summer the thick **foliage** of the maple provides lots of shade. This makes it a popular tree for parks and streets. Many people also plant maple trees in their gardens.

The fruit of maple trees is a hard pebble-sized structure with a pair of thin wings. Each wing has a seed at its tip. The wings help the seeds 'fly' away on the wind, far enough from the tree to grow in the sunlight.

Many maples produce sweet **sap**. In North America the sap of the sugar maple is made into maple syrup. Sugar maples grow slowly. They do not produce sap until they are about 40 years old!

North American Indians long ago learned the secret of tapping maple trees for their sugar. The process is fairly simple. Several holes are drilled into the bark of the tree. **Spouts** are driven into these holes, and the sap flows through the spouts into pails hanging on the spouts. The sap is boiled until it has thickened. Then the maple syrup is ready to pour onto your pancakes!

DID YOU KNOW?
Even though maple sap flows through the trees all spring, summer, and autumn, it is collected for syrup only in the early spring. That's when the trees produce the sweetest sap.

Answer: The wings help the seeds 'fly' on the wind so they can travel to a sunnier place, where they can grow.

The Original Fast Food

Before people learned to hunt or fish, they lived mostly on fruits, nuts, and berries. Nuts were especially important because they are very nourishing and rich in oil and protein. Nuts also keep well and are easy to store. A nut is actually a kind of fruit. It is dry and hard, and it is usually covered with a tough woody shell.

A couple of nuts that you may know about are chestnuts and pistachios. There are several kinds of chestnut tree, including the American, European, Chinese, and Japanese varieties. Chestnuts are an important food for people and animals. The American and European chestnuts provide valuable wood. And some chestnut trees are grown simply for their beauty.

Pistachio trees are from Central Asia, where they have been grown for about 3,000 years. Today they are also grown in North America. Their nuts are greenish and very tasty.

Other kinds of nuts include hazelnuts, beechnuts, and acorns. But some foods that are popularly called 'nuts' aren't true nuts. Peanuts, for example, are actually a type of bean! And coconuts are really a kind of stone fruit called a 'drupe'. The Brazil nut is also called the candlenut because it can be lit and used as a candle. But it's technically a seed.

Walnuts are another 'nut' that's not really a nut. But they too are good food. They have been grown since ancient times. They were highly valued in Persia and Mesopotamia. Today they are grown in many countries. Black walnut trees are also planted as decorations, and their fruit **husks** are used for making dyes. The trees grow slowly and may live for more than 250 years!

SEARCH LIGHT

True or false? Peanuts are tasty and nutritious nuts.

DID YOU KNOW?
The kola nut, grown widely in the tropics, has been used to flavour fizzy drinks. But many of these drinks now contain chemicals that taste like the kola nut instead.

Some foods that are called 'nuts' are actually other kinds of foods. These include walnuts and coconuts.

EB Inc.

Answer: FALSE. The peanut is not really a nut – it's a kind of bean.

149

Plant of Peace and Plenty

Since ancient times people have grown olive trees for their fruit and oil. Today olive trees are found in all the countries bordering the Mediterranean Sea. The trees are also grown in parts of the United States, Australia, and South Africa. But the leading producers of olives and olive oil are Spain, Italy, and Greece. They sell a lot of the fruit and oil to other countries.

The common olive tree has broad leaves and many branches. Its leaves are dark green above and silvery underneath. Olive branches have been a **universal** symbol of peace since the days of ancient Greece.

Olive trees bloom in late spring. The tiny white flowers hang in clusters and develop into fruit that is either picked by hand or shaken from the tree. An olive tree does not always bear fruit every year. The trees may produce a heavy crop one year and no crop the next year.

Olive branches ripe with fruit.
© Vittoriano Rastelli/Corbis

Often the olives are picked when they are still unripe and green coloured. Some crops are allowed to ripen and darken on the trees before they're picked. But fresh olives are very bitter. Before they can be eaten, they must be treated with chemicals and stored, sometimes for several months. By the time they're ready to eat, their colour may be green, black, dark red, or even purplish.

Olives are grown for the production of olive oil as well. The oil is taken from the fruit. It is one of the most widely used oils for cooking and eating, especially by people in the Mediterranean region. In using this oil, they are carrying on a tradition that is as old as civilization.

Groves of olive trees cover the hills near the city of Jaén in southern Spain.
© Michael Busselle/Corbis

SEARCH LIGHT

True or false? People eat olives right off the tree.

DID YOU KNOW?

The olive tree is an evergreen and keeps its leaves all year-round. It can grow to be 15 metres tall and may live more than 500 years!

Answer: FALSE. Olives are bitter right off the tree and have to be processed before they can be eaten.

The Prince of Plants

The palm is one of the most useful plants around, which is why people sometimes call it the 'prince of the plant kingdom'. There are many types of palm. They grow as trees, shrubs, and vines in the tropics and other warm regions.

The trunk of the palm is branchless, with a **tuft** of large leaves on the top. The trunks can be very tall, or they can be so short that the plant is almost trunkless. Often the palm trunk is smooth. But the trunks of some are spiny like a cactus while others are covered with stiff **fibres** that can be made into strong cords. Palm leaves are **pleated** and may be shaped like fans or feathers. Some varieties of palm leaves are very long with prickly tips.

Palm trees grow from sand on a beach in Jamaica.
© Eye Ubiquitous/Corbis

SEARCH LIGHT

Fill in the gap:
The _____ is one of the most valuable palms in the world.

Palms produce dry or fleshy fruits that vary in size, shape, and structure. For example, the date and the betel nut are soft fleshy fruits. The fruit of the coconut is hard on the outside and has moist 'meat' and liquid inside. The coco-de-mer is the largest fruit in the world. This palm fruit can be larger than a human head, with a pair of seeds that look like two coconuts joined together.

The coconut is one of the most valuable palms in the world. It provides vegetable oil for cooking. The fibre of the coconut husk is called 'coir' and can be woven into ropes and mats. The coconut shell is hard and is used to make cups and bottles. The liquid in the centre is called 'coconut milk'. You can drink it and cook with it, much as you would with animal milk.

DID YOU KNOW?
Some island people say there are as many uses for coconuts as there are days in a year.

The leaves of palms are usually clustered at the top of the tree's trunk in a large fan- or feather-shaped crown. The palm trees shown here are growing on a beach in St. Croix.
© Bill Ross/Corbis

Answer: The coconut is one of the most valuable palms in the world.

When Is a Nut Not a Nut?

They look and taste like nuts. They have shells like nuts, and they have skins like nuts. But they're not nuts. They're *peanuts*.

Actual nuts grow mostly on trees or bushes. But peanuts grow underground. That's why peanuts are also called 'groundnuts'. Although they look and taste like nuts, peanuts are really part of a plant group called 'legumes'. Legumes also include peas and beans. The peanut pod is a spongy shell covered with tiny dimples. Inside the shell you will usually find two peanuts. These are the seeds for new peanut plants.

Peanuts grow easily in warm sandy places. They require at least five months of warm weather, with rainfall during the growing season. The peanut plant is a low bush. Some kinds grow long low branches called 'runners'. When the peanuts are ripe, peanut farmers usually dig up the plants and stack them against sticks to dry out. Farmers feed the tops of the dry plants to their animals.

Peanuts may be roasted in their shells before they're eaten. Or they may be shelled and prepared as salted peanuts. Roasted peanuts are used in sweets and baked goods, for peanut butter, and in many other foods. Peanuts are often grown just for their oil.

An important person in the history of the peanut is Dr. George Washington Carver. This American researcher suggested that farmers plant peanuts to help make their worn-out soil healthy again. And then he came up with new uses for peanuts so that the farmers could sell them. By the time he'd finished, Dr. Carver had found more than 300 things that could be made out of peanuts.

A woman harvests peanuts on the island of Mauritius.
© Wolfgang Kaehler/Corbis

DID YOU KNOW?
Dr. George Washington Carver's products from peanuts included peanut milk, cheese, and coffee, as well as plastics, shampoo, and shoe polish.

SEARCH LIGHT

Find and correct the errors in the following sentence: Peanuts are legumes that grow on trees in cold sandy places.

Peanuts are grown in warm temperate or subtropical areas throughout the world. Here workers pick weeds in a peanut field in Samoa.
© Catherine Karnow/Corbis

Answer: Peanuts are legumes that grow underground in warm sandy places.

Hot and Spicy

Garden peppers have been used in cooking since ancient times. Hot peppers contain a substance called 'capsaicin' that gives them a sharp burning taste. Many people enjoy this strong taste and use it to flavour foods. People like to eat peppers fresh, dried, smoked, tinned, powdered, and pickled.

Pepper plants are herbs. The fruit of the plants differs in size, shape, and taste. The colour ranges from green through yellow to deep red and purple. You'll find peppers in the tropics of Asia. They also grow all over Central and South America. In 1493 pepper seeds were carried from South America to Spain. After that, the plants quickly spread all over Europe.

There are two kinds of pepper: mild and hot. Mild peppers are usually large and can be red, green, or yellow in colour. Bell peppers are bell-shaped, wrinkled, and puffy. Pimiento is a mild pepper with a special flavour and is usually used for stuffing other foods, such as olives. Paprika is another mild pepper. It's usually powdered and used as a spice. It is especially popular in Spain and Hungary.

The hot peppers include cherry, red cluster, tabasco, long chilli, and cayenne peppers. These are often served as relishes and pickles or ground into a fine powdered spice. Tabasco peppers are ground and mixed with vinegar to make a spicy hot sauce. Both fresh and dried Mexican chilli peppers are used to flavour stewed meat dishes.

There are two general types of peppers: the mild and the hot varieties.
© Paul Almasy/Corbis

SEARCH LIGHT

Fill in the gap: _____ is what makes hot peppers hot.

DID YOU KNOW?
The spice called 'pepper' doesn't come from pepper plants. It comes from the berries of an unrelated vine. Pepper plants belong to the nightshade family, along with potatoes, tomatoes, and eggplants.

Bell peppers like the ones shown are often used in salads, as cases for fillings, and in other cooked dishes.
© Michelle Garrett/Corbis

Wild Plants of the Ocean

You are in the waves at the seaside when suddenly something that feels cold and clammy slaps you on the back! Is it a friendly fish? No, it's probably just seaweed. These plants grow wild in the sea, just as weeds grow wild on land.

Seaweed grows all over the world. Some kinds float along the top of the water. Others are attached to the sea bottom or to rocks. Seaweed comes in many colours, such as red, brown, purple, and green. It may look like a red carpet or like tree branches with leaves and berries. The 'berries' are actually little gas-filled balloons that help keep the leaves afloat. Some kinds of seaweed, called 'kelp', can grow longer than 30 metres and have tough and leathery branches. Other kinds look like lettuce and are actually called 'sea lettuce'.

Seaweed on a New Zealand beach.
© Richard Hamilton Smith/Corbis

SEARCH LIGHT

There are many different kinds of seaweed. Can you name three of them?

People have found many uses for seaweed. The plants have been used for stuffing furniture and making paper. Giant kelps have been used as ropes. Laver, dulse, gulfweed, sea lettuce, and other kinds of seaweed are eaten, either by themselves or as part of other foods. Brown seaweed is used for making **fertilizers** for plants.

Even animals take advantage of seaweed. Tangled clumps of seaweed provide homes and hiding places for fish and other sea creatures. In the Atlantic Ocean, a huge floating mass of gulfweed between the United States and Africa is a resting place for seabirds. This gulfweed is called *Sargassum*, and this part of the Atlantic is the famous Sargasso Sea.

DID YOU KNOW?
If you like sushi or maki rolls, then you've probably eaten seaweed. Many of these Japanese delicacies are wrapped in seaweed.

Giant kelp grows off the coast of California.
© Ralph A. Clevenger/Corbis

Answer: Kelp, sea lettuce, laver, dulse, and gulfweed are all names for different kinds of seaweed.

A Sweet and Syrupy Plant

The sugarcane plant is a giant grass that grows year-round in warm and wet regions of the world. The island of New Guinea is probably the original home of sugarcane. Gradually, the plant was introduced to Southeast Asia, India, Polynesia, and other areas. Today Asia is the largest producer of sugarcane, followed by South and North America.

Workers harvesting sugarcane.
© Otto Lang/Corbis

The sugarcane plant is grown for its sweet **sap**. Much of the world's sugar and molasses comes from sugarcane sap. And in many parts of the world, people enjoy sucking on a piece of sugarcane for a sweet treat.

Sugarcane grows in clumps of stalks that reach a height of 3 to 6 metres. The colour of the stalk varies from almost white to yellow to deep green, purple, red, or violet.

The sugarcane crop needs at least 150 centimetres of water per year and nine months for the stalks to ripen. Once the stalks are ripe, they are stripped of their leaves and trimmed. The stalks are then washed and cut into short lengths. Most of this work is still done by hand.

Sugar is removed from the cane by two methods. In the first method, the finely cut stalks are put in hot water. This separates the sugar from the stalks. In the second method, the juice is squeezed from the stalks by pressing them between heavy rollers.

The juice taken from the cane is heated until it is boiling. Next, the water in the juice is allowed to **evaporate**. The resulting syrup is boiled again until sugar crystals have formed. The syrup left behind is called 'molasses'.

SEARCH LIGHT

Fill in the gaps: We get _____ and _____ from sugarcane sap.

DID YOU KNOW?

Raw sugar is brown, not white.

Sugarcane is sold at market in a village in India.
© Earl & Nazima Kowall/Corbis

Answer: We get sugar and molasses from sugarcane sap.

The Cup That Cheers

It soothes you when you are upset. And if you're tired, it can lift your spirits. It's tea - the drink that cheers!

Tea was first drunk in China thousands of years ago. At first it was used as a **medicinal** drink, but eventually it became popular to drink anytime. It was later introduced to Japan. European trading ships took it from Asia to England and Holland.

Worker separating tea leaves by hand in Indonesia.
© Owen Franken/Corbis

There are two main varieties of tea - the small-leaved China plant and the large-leaved Assam plant. Mixing the leaves of these produces many other types of tea.

Tea can be named according to where it's grown. For example, there's China tea, Ceylon tea, Japanese tea, Indonesian tea, and African tea. But most tea is known as green, black, or oolong tea. Green tea, made from the China plant, is produced in Japan, China, Malaysia, and Indonesia. Black tea, made from the Assam plant, comes mostly from India. Oolong teas are produced mostly in southern China and Taiwan.

The different kinds of tea are made in different ways. To make black tea, the freshly picked leaves are dried, rolled, and strained. They are then fermented. Fermenting is a way of making the flavour more intense. Finally, the leaves are dried with hot air. This is how the tea becomes black. Unlike black tea, green tea is not fermented. The leaves are just rolled and dried, so they remain green. Oolong is made like black tea. It is sometimes scented with flowers such as jasmine.

Tea is made ready for drinking by soaking its leaves in boiled water. This is called 'steeping'.

> **DID YOU KNOW?**
> Iced tea was made popular by an Englishman at the St. Louis World's Fair of 1904 in the United States. His job was to get people to drink tea. The weather was hot, so he filled tall glasses with ice and poured hot tea over it. Everyone loved it!

SEARCH LIGHT

What's the difference between green tea and black tea?

Tea is made from the young leaves and leaf buds of tea plants. The farmworkers shown here are harvesting tea leaves in Malaysia.
© Neil Rabinowitz/Corbis

Answer: Aside from their different colours, black tea is fermented and green tea is not.

Encounter fascinating animals that live in and around water

Creatures of the Waters

Creatures of the Waters

TABLE OF CONTENTS

Forever Gliding

The albatross is an amazing seabird. It spends most of its life soaring above the water. The only time albatrosses ever go ashore is when they lay eggs and raise their chicks. Groups (called 'colonies') of the birds build nests on the isolated Antarctic islands. A single large white egg is laid in a bowl-shaped nest built from plants and soil. Sometimes the nest is just a patch of bare ground.

Scientists measuring an albatross' wingspread.
© Wolfgang Kaehler/Corbis

A young albatross grows slowly. It takes at least four months for it to develop all the feathers it will need to fly. Once it's able to fly, the albatross will spend the next five to ten years out at sea. The albatross can glide for days at a time, without flapping its long narrow wings. To stay in the air like this, it needs windy weather. In calm weather the albatross has trouble keeping its heavy body in the air, so it rests on the water and floats like a cork. It feeds on small **squid** and fish. But it will also follow fishing boats and eat scraps that are thrown overboard.

Some kinds of albatrosses are brown, but most of them are white with some brown or black markings on their bodies or wings. Albatrosses are the largest of all flying birds. In fact, the wandering albatross has the largest wingspread amongst living birds. The wings of a wandering albatross can measure 3.4 metres from tip to tip.

Albatrosses live very long lives and are one of the few species of bird that die of old age.

SEARCH LIGHT

Which of the following can be said about an albatross?
a) It spends most of its time on land.
b) It eats other birds.
c) It goes to land only to lay eggs.

DID YOU KNOW?

In the past, sailors believed albatrosses had special powers. They believed that killing the bird would bring bad luck.

Albatrosses use their long wings to soar and glide on air currents. They can stay in the air for hours without flapping their wings. The black-browed albatross, shown here in flight, has a dark marking around the eye that makes it look as though it is frowning.

© Peter Johnson/Corbis

159

Dabblers, Divers, and Perchers

Ducks are champion swimmers and are at home almost anywhere near water. Some feed and nest in streams and ponds. Others live near deep wide lakes. Some make their homes on rocky cliffs by the ocean.

There are three kinds of duck:

'**Dabbling** ducks' put their heads under water to eat plants that grow there. This way of feeding is called 'dabbling'. They build their nests in hollows near the water. There they also eat plants and insects found near the shore. Dabbling ducks can fly very fast.

'Diving ducks' dive deep down into the water to find things to eat. They mostly eat fish. They are very strong swimmers.

'Perching ducks' make nests in trees and hold on to the branches with their long-clawed toes. This is called perching. Some may perch on the tall stalks that grow over marshy ponds.

All ducks are graceful fliers and swimmers. But on the ground they waddle from side to side, moving slowly in a funny, jerky way. You usually don't see a duck waddling too far away from water.

In winter many ducks fly south, where the water is warmer and there's more to eat. But icy cold water doesn't bother them. A thick inner layer of soft fluffy feathers called 'down' keeps them warm. And their bigger outer feathers help too. They're **waterproof**. Feathers are a duck's raincoat. Every year ducks lose their old feathers, and new feathers grow in. This is called 'moulting'. Until the new feathers grow, ducks can't fly. So they hide in the grass or on the water to keep safe from enemies.

(Top) A dabbling gadwall duck; (bottom) young girl holding a fluffy duckling.

DID YOU KNOW?
Ducks make their feathers waterproof by rubbing oil on them. They get the oil from special glands on their chests and rub it on their feathers with their bills.

A male wood duck is easily identifiable by his purple and green head, his reddish-brown breast flecked with white, and his bronze sides.
© Gary W. Carter/Corbis

SEARCH LIGHT

Unscramble these words that have to do with a duck.
wsmimre
nblbiadg
dlwaed

© Roger Wilmshurst—Frank Lane Picture Agency/Corbis

© Royalty-Free/Corbis

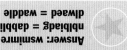

Answer: wsmimre = swimmer
nblbiadg = dabbling
dlwaed = waddle

Fine-Feathered Travellers

Geese are found virtually everywhere. There's the wild Canada goose, and halfway around the world is the snow goose of Siberia. There is the **pied** goose, which lives 'down under' in Australia. The rarely seen Hawaiian goose lives out in the middle of the Pacific Ocean. The little brant goose nests in very cold Arctic areas. The wild goose called the greylag is found in Europe.

SEARCH LIGHT

How do people use down feathers?

(Top) Mother goose nuzzling her gosling (young goose); (bottom) snow geese flying in a V formation.

Geese spend a lot of time in the water. Like ducks, they have a coat of oil on their feathers that keeps them from getting too wet. And the soft feathers beneath, called 'down', keep them warm even in the iciest of waters. Down is so good at keeping things warm that people often use it in ski jackets and in duvets. It's also good in pillows because it's so soft.

Geese are fairly large birds, often standing a metre tall despite their short legs. Geese may look somewhat silly when they waddle on land. But their **sturdy** legs actually help them walk more steadily than ducks or swans do.

Geese have webbed feet that make them strong swimmers. They are also powerful fliers. They can make especially long flights during their annual **migrations** to their winter feeding grounds. You may see groups of geese travelling south in the autumn in lines that make a V shape. This formation helps keep them from getting tired as they fly because each goose gets a lift from the air flowing off the goose ahead.

DID YOU KNOW?
Some people keep geese as guards. Geese make loud honking cries when danger appears. After chasing the enemy away, they cackle triumphantly.

A Canada goose flies close to the water.
© Getty Images

Answer: People use down to stuff pillows, duvets, and ski jackets because the feathers are soft and very warm.

The Ocean's Clean-up Crew

A fishing boat chugs back into the harbour with its day's catch. The gulls follow close behind. They know that the fishermen will be throwing treats overboard as they empty the bait bag and clean the deck. The gulls dip into the waves to scoop up bits of food. They fill the air with their excited cries. This often happens when they are fighting over something good to eat.

SEARCH LIGHT

How are gulls helpful to humans?

Along the shore, gulls are helpful to the people who clean beaches and harbours. They swoop down to pick up messy things. Gulls eat almost anything, from dead fish to crisps and scraps of hot dogs. And they clear away lots of insects too.

Gulls eat all day long. They have to just to stay alive. Gulls are big birds that fly great distances. While flying, they use up a lot of energy. Gulls can fly many kilometres without stopping. They can fly from one end of a country to the other. But all the time they're up there, they're looking down to see if they can find something to eat.

Seagull stands on a rock.
© Guy Motil/Corbis

Gulls are good swimmers too. Their feet are webbed. The little stretches of skin between their toes make their feet act as paddles.

Gulls are also floaters. They stay on top of the water like a piece of wood does. On long trips over the ocean, they drop down onto the water and float while taking a nap.

DID YOU KNOW?
The type of gull called Bonaparte's gull was named after Charles-Lucien Bonaparte, a nephew of the famous French emperor Napoleon Bonaparte. The younger Bonaparte spent much of his life studying the world's birds.

Gulls are among the most common water birds of ocean and coastal zones worldwide. Some gulls travel enormous distances between their summer and winter homes.

© Chris Jones/Corbis

Answer: Gulls clean up a lot of food waste from beaches, harbours, picnic areas, tips, and car parks that would otherwise be left behind as rubbish.

Well-Dressed Swimmers

When a penguin swims, its light-coloured belly and dark-coloured back help hide it from enemies. From underneath, its light belly looks like the sky. This makes it hard for its enemy the leopard seal to see it. From above, its dark back looks like the dark water, which helps hide it from big hunting birds.

Penguins cannot fly, but they swim extremely well. The shape of their bodies, sort of like a submarine, lets them swim very fast. They use their short flat wings like flippers and practically fly through the water. In fact, they often leap out of the water and look as if they are trying to flap through the air.

There are 17 types of penguins. They live in Antarctica and along the cool portions of the coasts of Africa, New Zealand, Australia, and South America. Penguins have a thick layer of fat that helps to protect them from the cold. And although they don't look like they do, they actually have feathers all over their bodies. These short feathers also help to keep them warm.

Members of the emperor penguin species, the largest of the penguins.
© Tim Davis/Corbis

Penguins' short legs give them an odd walk. They do, however, run quickly. Sometimes they'll build up speed and then slide on their bellies to travel quickly over ice and snow.

Penguins live in nesting **colonies**. These colonies can be enormous. Penguins return to the same place, the same nest, and the same partner every year - sometimes travelling long distances. Penguins use the Sun to help them find their direction. Most penguins build a nest on the ground with pebbles, mud, and vegetation. The females lay one or two eggs, and then both parents take turns looking after them.

DID YOU KNOW?

Penguins are the only birds that can swim but not fly.

SEARCH LIGHT

Do penguins have feathers?

Penguins are excellent divers and swimmers. Here, gentoo penguins enjoy a romp through the water.
© George D. Lepp/Corbis

Answer: Like all birds, penguins have feathers. But theirs are so short and close to their bodies that the feathers look more like skin.

Birds of Beauty,
Grace, and Speed

Ducks, geese, and swans are the three main kinds of waterfowl. Swans are the largest of the three, and they are also the fastest flyers and swimmers. They have a stately and dignified appearance when swimming on a pond.

Like the other waterfowl, swans have oily feathers that stay dry in the water. Their webbed feet make them strong swimmers. Swans are heavy-bodied birds that feed by dabbling - dipping the long neck into shallow water for plants. They don't dive for food. They have powerful wings for flying long distances.

The whistling swan and the trumpeter swan are found in North America, while the mute swan lives in Europe and Asia. These birds are white. South America is the home of the black-necked swan, while the beautiful black swan lives in Australia. It is the state emblem of Western Australia.

Mother swan and cygnets.
© AFP/Corbis

SEARCH LIGHT

What's one way that ducks and swans are alike? How are they different?

Swans make a variety of sounds. Even the mute swan often hisses or makes soft snoring sounds. It may even grunt sharply.

The male swan is called a 'cob'. The female is called a 'pen'. They look alike. A pair of swans usually stays together for life. The female swan lays about six pale eggs on a heap of plant material, while the male keeps close guard. The young swans are called 'cygnets'. They can run and swim just a few hours after they hatch. But father and mother swan look after them carefully for several months. Sometimes the cygnets will ride on their mother's back when they get tired from swimming or need protection from enemies.

DID YOU KNOW?
E.B. White's *The Trumpet of the Swan* is a story about a voiceless swan that learns to play a trumpet.

A family of mute swans, with cygnets riding on their mother's back, swim along the water.
© Philip Perry—Frank Lane Picture Agency/Corbis

Answer: Both ducks and swans are water birds with oily feathers and webbed feet for swimming. But swans are considerably bigger than ducks. They fly and swim faster than ducks too.

The Land-and-Water Dwellers

Millions of years ago, a group of fish began to breathe both in and out of the water. Eventually these fish made their way onto land and began to develop legs. These animals became amphibians, the ancestors of frogs, toads, and salamanders.

The word 'amphibian' comes from the Greek words *amphi*, which means 'both', and *bios*, which means 'life'. As their name suggests, amphibians live both in freshwater and on land.

Amphibians are cold-blooded animals. This means that an amphibian's body temperature generally matches the temperature around it. To warm up, amphibians often **bask** in the sun, and to cool off, they move into the shade. Amphibians must also stay near water. If their skin dries out, they will die.

There are three main groups of amphibian. The largest group includes the true frogs, tree frogs, and toads. True frogs have long hind legs and can swim and leap very well. Tree frogs have suction pads on their fingers and toes and can hold on to smooth surfaces. Toads have shorter legs than frogs, and their skin has a warty appearance.

The second group of amphibians is the salamanders, which have tails. The giant salamander of Japan and China is the largest of all amphibians. It can grow to a length of more than 1.5 metres.

The third group is the caecilians. These odd amphibians are rarely seen. They have long slender bodies with no arms or legs. They are also blind. A long flexible structure called a 'tentacle' sticks out next to each of their useless eyes. They use these tentacles to feel and sniff their way around.

SEARCH LIGHT

What's so special about amphibians? (Hint: Remember those Greek words.)

DID YOU KNOW?
Salamanders were once believed to live in fire. The word 'salamander' comes from ancient words that mean 'fire lizard'.

Answer: Amphibians are one of the few groups of animals that can live comfortably both in the water and on the land.

Amazing Changing
Amphibians

Frogs are amphibians. This means they can live both in water and on land. And they have a life cycle that takes place in both environments.

A mother frog lays her eggs in the water. In a few days tiny tadpoles, or polliwogs, wriggle out of the eggs. The tadpoles don't look like frogs at all. They have long tails for swimming and slits called **gills** for breathing.

As a tadpole grows into a frog, it changes in many ways. Its tail gets shorter and shorter until it disappears. At the same time, the frog grows front and hind legs. The hind feet have long toes with webs between them to help in swimming and leaping. Plus, the gills disappear and **lungs** develop. Once these changes are complete, the creature is ready to live on land as well as in the water. It's now a frog. For some kinds of frogs, this process of change takes just two months. For others, it may take as long as three years.

A frog has smooth moist skin. Its eyes are so big that they seem about to pop out of its head. These eyes help it find food. Its hind legs are more than twice as long as its front ones. The frog travels in great leaps on these long strong legs.

Frogs are closely related to toads. What's the difference between a frog and a toad? Well, a toad's skin is dry and bumpy. Its legs are short, so it can only hop, not leap. And toads spend more of their time on land than frogs do.

SEARCH LIGHT

Unscramble the following words that relate to frogs.
daploet
sligl
traew

Red-eyed leaf frog tadpoles.
© Michael & Patricia Fogden/Corbis

DID YOU KNOW?
The Goliath frog of West Africa is nearly 30 centimetres long!

The tree frog has long legs and sticky sucker-like disks on its feet for climbing.
© Darren Maybury—Eye Ubiquitous/Corbis

**Answer: daploet = tadpole
sligl = gills
traew = water**

Modern Dinosaurs

If you're looking for reptiles that have been around since the days of the dinosaurs, try alligators and crocodiles. These large lizard-like animals are related to the giant reptiles of the past.

Alligators and crocodiles are closely related. They look a lot alike, but alligators have a broad flat

Alligators in the Okefenokee Swamp, Georgia, U.S.
© David Muench/Corbis

head with a rounded **snout**. Most crocodiles have a narrow, pointed snout. When a crocodile closes its mouth, the fourth tooth on each side of its lower jaw sticks out. Crocodiles are larger than alligators. They range from 2 to more than 6 metres long, while most alligators are about 1.8 to 2.4 metres long.

Alligators and most crocodiles live along the edges of large bodies of freshwater such as lakes, swamps, and rivers. They spend a lot of time in the water, but they can also be found on land near the water. Large adults can stay under water for over an hour without breathing.

Both animals have long snouts, powerful tails, and thick skin with bony plates underneath. Their eyes, ears, and nostrils are located on top of their long heads. Alligators and crocodiles often float with only their eyes and noses showing.

Crocodiles can be found in **tropical** swamps and rivers in Asia, Australia, Africa, and South America. Alligators are less widespread. The American alligator lives in the south-eastern United States. In South America there are various alligators called caimans. The Chinese alligator lives in the Yangtze River and is smaller than the American alligator.

Adult alligators and crocodiles eat mostly fish, small mammals, and birds. Sometimes they may kill deer or cattle. Crocodiles are more likely than alligators to attack humans, though alligators will attack if cornered.

DID YOU KNOW?

There are saltwater crocodiles living in northern Australia and Southeast Asia. Australians call their crocodiles 'salties'.

Today, many alligators and crocodiles are in danger of becoming extinct. One reason is that many are killed each year for sport or for their skins, which are used to make purses, shoes, and belts. These crocodiles are lying in the grass near Moramanga, Madagascar.
© Wolfgang Kaehler/Corbis

SEARCH LIGHT

True or false? Alligator is another name for a crocodile.

Answer: FALSE. Though they are related, alligators and crocodiles are two different animals.

A Tight Squeeze

The giant anaconda is one of the longest and heaviest snakes in the world. But this South American animal is not poisonous. The anaconda kills its prey by squeezing it so hard that it cannot breathe.

The anaconda spends most of its time in water. When an animal goes to a river to drink, the anaconda grabs it. If the prey is large, the snake wraps itself around the animal and can choke it. The anaconda then drags the body into the water to keep it away from jaguars and biting ants that would be attracted to the **carcass**. When an anaconda eats a large animal, it gets so stuffed that it lies still for weeks to digest its meal!

Giant anaconda.
© Z. Leszczynski/Animals Animals

There are two types of anaconda. The yellow anaconda is the smaller of the two. It is tan or greenish yellow with large black markings across its back and black blotches along its sides. Yellow anacondas are found in the southern Amazon River area. The giant anaconda is twice as big as the yellow anaconda. It's olive green with black spots. The giant anaconda lives in the South American tropics east of the Andes Mountains and on the Caribbean island of Trinidad. Giant anacondas can measure over 10 metres long.

Despite its size, a giant anaconda is not really violent. Scientists can simply pick up an anaconda and carry it off. But it may take several of them to lift the snake, especially if it just ate!

SEARCH LIGHT

Find and correct the error in the following sentence: Anacondas kill their prey with a poisonous bite.

DID YOU KNOW?
Like most snakes, anacondas swallow their food whole. They can open their mouths wide enough to fit around an entire goat.

A yellow anaconda lies on a log at the edge of the water. Although the anaconda spends much of its time in water, it may also crawl on land and even climb into trees to catch birds.
© Joe McDonald/Corbis

Answer: Anacondas kill their prey by squeezing it.

Taking Their Time

Turtles are known as slow-moving animals. They were around during the age of dinosaurs more than 100 million years ago. Dinosaurs are gone now, but turtles are still here. Slow but steady wins the race!

Like the dinosaurs, turtles are reptiles. There are nearly 250 kinds of turtles in the world today. All turtles breathe air at least part of the time, even sea turtles, which spend almost their whole life in the ocean. In addition to the ocean, turtles can live in ponds, lakes, or rivers. Other turtles live in forests or even hot desert sands, far away from water. Some people refer to land turtles as 'tortoises'.

Turtles come in all sizes. Some are no more than 10 centimetres long. At the other end of the scale, the Atlantic leatherback turtle may weigh as much as 680 kilos.

Even sea turtles go ashore to lay their eggs. The newly hatched baby turtles are completely on their own. They scramble from their nest under the sand and walk on their tiny new flippers to the water.

Three painted turtles perched on a rock.
© William Manning/Corbis

SEARCH LIGHT

Fill in the gap: Land turtles are sometimes called _____.

Land and sea turtles can take care of themselves because they carry their houses with them wherever they go. Their houses are their shells. Some turtles can close their shells completely. The snapping turtle can't, but it has a powerful bite for protection.

No matter where they live, turtles don't need to hunt for food or water all the time. Some have a special place inside their bodies where they can store water. And they can store food in the form of fat. Turtles can live for days or even weeks without having anything to eat or drink.

DID YOU KNOW?
Turtles can live longer than people can. Turtles are known to have lived 150 years in the wild, and there are reports of turtles that were even older than that.

A boy kneels to investigate a small turtle. Turtles are found in lakes, ponds, salt marshes, rivers, forests, and even deserts.
© Ariel Skelley/Corbis

Answer: Land turtles are sometimes called tortoises.

Citizens of the Waters

A fish is a cold-blooded animal that has a backbone, lives in water, and breathes by means of **gills**. It normally has two pairs of fins in place of arms and legs, as well as several other fins. Most fish are covered with **scales**.

Fish are fascinating in their variety. The sea horse looks something like a tiny horse standing on its tail. Flounders are as flat as a dinner plate. The rabbitfish, a small relative of the shark, has a head and teeth resembling those of a rabbit. Anglerfish carry their own 'fishing rod' to catch other fish. An extended part of the back fin has wormlike pieces of flesh at the tip, which are the 'bait'. Anglers of the deep sea have bait that lights up to attract victims.

Size differs as much as shape. Some Philippine gobies reach an adult size of less than one and a quarter centimetres. The whale shark, the largest of all fishes, reaches 50 metres in length and weighs about 18 tonnes.

Fish swim mainly by sideways movements of the body and tail. The fins are used for balancing, steering, and braking. To move quickly from a resting position, some fish shoot a stream of water out of the gills, which causes them to lunge forward. The fastest swimmers, such as the tuna, can travel 48 kilometres per hour.

Most fish continue to grow as long as they live. Fish that live to an old age can become very large. Carp are among this group. They may live 100 years!

SEARCH LIGHT

Fill in the gap. Fish breathe through _____.

DID YOU KNOW?
Fish called mudskippers can crawl across mud flats and wet fields in search of food. Lungfish can burrow into mud when their pools dry up. They lie there, for months if necessary, until rain refills the pools.

Answer: Fish breathe through gills.

The Fishy Survivor

The common carp is a fish that lives along the muddy bottoms of ponds, lakes, and rivers. It swallows plants, insects, and anything else it finds to eat. It was first found in Asia but was later taken into Europe and North America. Some people like to eat carp.

SEARCH LIGHT

True or false? Carp live in the ocean.

Sometimes carp can live 100 years and grow to weigh 35 kilos or more. But not all carp grow that old or that heavy. The fish that are caught usually are under 10 years old and do not weigh more than 4.5 kilos.

The carp has a blunt nose and a small thick-lipped mouth. From its upper lip dangle two pairs of feelers that are called 'barbels'.

There are three kinds of common carp. The scale carp has large scales all over its wide heavy body. Its back is olive green, its sides are gold-coloured, and its belly is bright yellow. The mirror carp has only three or four rows of huge scales along its sides. The leather carp is almost without scales, but it has a very thick skin.

Goldfish swimming in a bowl.
© Doug Wilson/Corbis

In some ways the carp is a **nuisance**. In hunting for food, the carp muddies the water. This affects the life of many plants and animals. A carp sometimes pushes more valuable fish away from their food and also eats their eggs. The carp has a habit of pulling out plants from their roots. This keeps ducks away. It is very difficult to get rid of carp. The fish can thrive even in dirty water and can also survive in very warm and very cold water.

DID YOU KNOW?
The common goldfish, often a child's first pet, is a member of the carp family.

Colourful carp swim in a pond outside a restaurant in Japan. In Asia and Europe carp are often raised in ponds because it is possible to grow many fish in a small amount of water.
© Wolfgang Kaehler/Corbis

Answer: FALSE. They live in freshwater rivers, lakes, and ponds.

A Frightening
Little Fish

The piranha is found in the rivers and lakes of South America. It is a meat-eating fish with long, triangular, razor-sharp teeth. When hungry, the piranha can be both bold and **savage**. But for such a frightening fish, it is not very big. Most are about the size of an adult's hand.

Red-bellied piranha.
© Kevin Schafer/Corbis

Some piranhas are silver in colour, with orange undersides. Others are almost totally black. All have blunt heads, saw-edged bellies, and strong jaws.

In the Amazon River, there are 20 different kinds of piranhas. The most famous is the red-bellied piranha. It has the strongest jaws and the sharpest teeth. When water levels are low, this piranha hunts in schools of more than 100 fish. Many schools join in the feast if a large animal has been attacked. But normally red-bellied piranhas prefer **prey** only slightly larger than themselves.

Usually a group of red-bellied piranhas swim around together in search of prey. The moment the prey is found, the fish signal each other. Piranhas have excellent hearing, so it's possible that they signal each other with sounds. Each fish in the group has a chance to take a bite and then swim away, making way for the others.

Most piranhas never kill large animals, and they almost never kill humans. The smell of blood attracts piranhas, but most of them feed on what is left by others rather than making fresh kills. For this reason their reputation for being ferocious is not deserved.

DID YOU KNOW?
The name 'piranha' comes from the Portuguese words for 'fish' and 'tooth'.

SEARCH LIGHT

Why do you suppose that when water levels get low, piranhas hunt in larger schools than they would otherwise? (Hint: How much of your body can you fit underwater in the tub once you start letting the water out?)

Groups of piranhas hide out and chase and attack fish that swim by.
© John Madere/Corbis

Answer: When river water levels are low, there's less room for fish to spread out, so piranhas have to hunt together in large groups.

Leaping Up the Waterfall

These fish aren't going down a waterfall. They're going up! Not much can stop these big strong salmon - not even a waterfall. The salmon are swimming up the river to return to the quiet waters where they hatched. They're returning in order to spawn - that is, to lay their own eggs. They started their journey far out in the sea.

Somehow the salmon manage to find the river they are looking for. Night and day they swim on. They eat nothing at all after getting into their river. Finally, they reach the waters where they came from.

We don't know how salmon can find their way on this long trip up the river. But we know what they do when they reach the end.

Male sockeye salmon.
© Natalie Fobes/Corbis

SEARCH LIGHT

True or false? Salmon travel upstream against the river current to lay their eggs.

At the top of the stream, the mother salmon digs a long hole with her tail and **snout**. She fills the hole with thousands of tiny eggs. She covers the eggs with sand to keep them safe.

The eggs hatch. When the baby salmon are about as long as your finger, they are big enough to start the swim to the ocean. They float backward down the long river - tails first and heads last! They seem to steer better that way.

Many of the babies never reach the ocean because there are too many enemies. Birds, bears, and bigger fish along the way love to eat them. The salmon that do reach the ocean will one day start the long hard trip up the river.

DID YOU KNOW?

Each generation of salmon returns to the same river, to the same spot, to lay their eggs every year. So a salmon's parents, grandparents, and great grandparents all chose the same river.

These Pacific salmon are trying to leap up a waterfall of the Brooks River in Katmai National Park, Alaska, U.S., to spawn upstream.
© Galen Rowell/Corbis

Answer: TRUE.

Predators
of the Sea

When the first dinosaurs walked on Earth, sharks were already swimming in the sea. The dinosaurs are long gone, but sharks are still a force to be reckoned with.

Great white sharks, in particular, are feared as man-eaters. It's hard to fight them, because they are so strong and fast in the water. Their tough skin is protected by tiny toothlike scales. In their big mouths are rows and rows of sharp teeth that rip like the edge of a saw. Sharks continue to grow teeth all their lives. A great white shark can make a quick meal out of almost anything!

The hammerhead shark can also be dangerous. Don't be fooled by its awkward-looking rectangle of a head. In general, most shark attacks take place in shallow water, where sharks sometimes go to hunt for fish. A hungry shark can easily mistake a human arm or leg for a tasty fish.

SEARCH LIGHT

Find and correct the error in the following sentence: Hammerhead sharks got their name because they bash their prey over the head.

(Top) Scalloped hammerhead shark; (bottom) swimming shark.

Most kinds of sharks are not dangerous to people. This includes the largest shark of all, the whale shark. Whale sharks can be 15 metres long, but they feed on small fish and on tiny life forms called plankton. Other sharks eat fish of all sizes. The shark appears out of nowhere, often from below, to take its prey by surprise.

Did you know that a shark has to keep swimming all the time? Its body is made in such a way that if it doesn't swim, it will sink to the bottom of the sea. Good thing sharks know how to sleep while they swim!

DID YOU KNOW?
Unlike most other fish, sharks don't have hard bones. Instead, their skeletons are made of cartilage, the same material that human noses and ears are made of.

Scuba divers photograph a whale shark. Whale sharks usually swim slowly near the surface and have even been hit by ships.
© Jeffrey L. Rotman/Corbis

Answer: Hammerhead sharks got their name because their heads look like hammers.

Builders in the Sea

A coral is a soft little sea animal that looks like a bit of jelly. It is no bigger than the end of your little finger. At one end it has a mouth surrounded by little arms called 'tentacles'. The tentacles gather food. When they touch a tiny plant or animal floating nearby, they pull these inside the mouth.

(Top) Orange cup coral; (bottom) yellow and gray coral.

The baby coral swims through the water until it finds a place to build its house, and then it never swims again. Using special glue from inside its body, it sticks itself to a rock or to another piece of coral. Once it is stuck, it starts to build itself a house with a juice from its body that turns into a kind of stone. The hard little shell houses are called coral too.

In the ocean where the water is warm, the coral grows in lovely ocean gardens. It grows in just about every colour and shape you can think of.

SEARCH LIGHT

Two parts of the animal are called coral. What are they?

It may grow to look like lace, a fan, a leaf, a brain, the horns of a deer, or a ribbon.

One day a bud will grow on the coral. This bud grows into a new coral animal. After many years there are so many coral houses built on top of one another and next to each other that they become a great wall called a 'reef'.

Sometimes coral may grow together to form a reef hundreds of kilometres long. The largest coral reef in the world is the Great Barrier Reef near Australia. It is more than 2,000 kilometres long.

DID YOU KNOW?
The Great Barrier Reef is the largest structure ever built by living things. It is longer than the Great Wall of China and much wider.

There is an amazing variety of sea life on and around the Great Barrier Reef. There are about 400 types of hard coral, about 215 types of birds, and more than 1,500 types of fish, many with bright colours and unusual shapes.

Answer: Coral refers to the soft jelly-like animal living inside the hard shell, as well as to the shell itself. People also call many of these shells stuck together 'coral'.

Flashing Lights!

It is very dark deep below the surface of the oceans of the world. This dark area is called the '**abyssal** zone'. It is a black, soundless place where the water is very still. This zone lies thousands of metres below the water's surface.

You wouldn't think it, but there are many kinds of living things to be found in the abyss. For a very long time, people believed that nothing could live down there because there isn't any light. But scientists who investigated the deep sea found plenty of life!

Many forms of life were discovered near cracks on the ocean floor. These are called 'rift communities'. The huge cracks, or fissures, are between two of the **plates** that make up the Earth's crust. These fissures are hot-water vents that raise the temperature of the water around them. The fissures are rich in **minerals**.

Deep-sea anglerfish.
© Bruce Robinson/Corbis

Deep-sea animals include certain kinds of squid, octopuses, worms, and fish. Because it is difficult to study animals at such levels, not much is known about their behaviour or surroundings. But it is known that deep-sea animals have special features that allow them to live in conditions in which other animals could not. These features are called **adaptations**.

SEARCH LIGHT

Fill in the gap:
The deepest part of the ocean is called the _____ zone.

Many deep-sea fish and other creatures flash with their own lights. This ability to give off light is called 'bioluminescence'. It is an adaptation for living in the darkness of the deep sea. Some deep-sea animals have coloured lights on different parts of the body. Their bodies keep flashing on and off. It is possible that the animals are speaking to each other with their lights.

DID YOU KNOW?
Icefish, which live in the coldest and darkest waters, make a substance that keeps their blood from freezing.

Tube worms are just one example of the many types of life found deep in the ocean. Tube worms are large red worms that live inside white tubes that are attached to the ocean floor.
© F. Grassle, Woods Hole Oceanographic Institution

Boneless Blobs
of the Sea

A jellyfish is not a fish at all. Unlike fish it has no bones, and most of its body is like jelly. It does not have a brain or a heart. What it does have is a set of **tentacles** that can sting its prey - or a person!

Jellyfish are related to corals and sea anemones. They can be found in all oceans. There are about 200 kinds of jellyfish, in different forms, sizes, and colours. Some jellyfish are barely large enough to be seen. Others can be more than two metres around. Jellyfish may be transparent or brown, pink, white, or blue. Some kinds glow in the dark sea.

A jellyfish usually has the shape of an umbrella. It can have a few or many tentacles. Sometimes it has simple eyes around the edge of the 'umbrella'. The mouth and the stomach are in the middle of the 'umbrella'. The jellyfish has simple muscles on the underside that **contract** the body, much like the closing of an umbrella. This helps it swim.

Inside the tentacles of a jellyfish are poisonous stinging cells. These cells can stun small animals, which the jellyfish then pulls into its mouth. Some jellyfish feed on tiny animals and plants that their bodies catch as they drift through the water.

Some jellyfish can be very dangerous to humans. Even a small sting from the jellyfish called sea wasps can cause death within a few minutes. It's best just to look at jellyfish from a distance and not get too close.

Jellyfish in dark waters.
© Jeffrey L. Rotman/Corbis

SEARCH LIGHT

Can you think of one way that jellyfish and fish are similar? What's one way that they're different?

DID YOU KNOW?
Sometimes a jelly-like blob breaks away from a jellyfish and grows into another adult jellyfish.

Jellyfish sometimes sting swimmers who accidentally brush up against them in the water. Even dead jellyfish that have washed up on the beach can be dangerous and should not be touched.
© Danny Lehman/Corbis

Answer: The most obvious thing that jellyfish and fish share is their ocean home. One big difference between them is that jellyfish have no bones but fish do.

Shell-Dwelling Animals

There are many different shelled animals. The smallest live in shells as tiny as the letter 'O'. The largest, such as the giant squids, weigh more than two tonnes! Some of these animals belong to a group called 'molluscs'. And you might be surprised to know that there are about 100,000 kinds of them!

Most molluscs - such as snails, clams, oysters, and mussels - have shells. But some, such as octopuses and squid, have little or none at all. And not all kinds of animals with shells are molluscs. Crabs and lobsters have shells, but they are not molluscs.

Although most molluscs live in the water, some are found on land. Snails live in forests and gardens.

Newborn molluscs are squishy and helpless. They need protection from enemies that would eat them. They get this protection from the shell they build around themselves. Shells are really one-room houses that molluscs build out of their own bodies. It's as easy for them to do this as it is for you to grow fingernails. Each shell has room for just one animal.

Snail on a child's hand.
© Lance Nelson/Corbis

DID YOU KNOW?
Molluscs have been a popular food for thousands of years. Scientists have found old piles of shells, some over three metres tall, where ancient people threw the rubbish from their meals of clams and oysters.

Molluscs eat tiny bits of food that float with the moving water. They also eat the **algae** that cover rocks. Part of this food is used to build their bodies. The rest helps them build their shells. A mollusc and its shell keep growing as long as the mollusc lives.

When a mollusc dies, it leaves behind its shell. That is why most of the shells you find on the beach are empty. Mollusc shells can last for thousands of years - a reminder of how long molluscs have been living on the Earth.

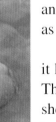
SEARCH LIGHT

Which of the following are molluscs?
- crabs
- snails
- prawns
- oysters
- squids

Mussels, pictured here in a tide pool, are a kind of mollusc. Mussels are found all over the world, mostly in cool seas.
© Kennan Ward/Corbis

Answer: Snails, oysters, and squids are all molluscs.

Eight-Armed Wonders

People used to tell scary stories about a deep-sea monster that wrapped its many long arms around a ship and dragged it down to the bottom of the ocean. They called the monster a 'devilfish'.

Today we know that this wasn't a monster at all. It was an octopus - an animal with eight arms that lives in the ocean. Octopuses are members of an animal group called molluscs, which includes squid, clams, and oysters.

There are nearly 50 kinds of octopus. Some are only a few centimetres long. The largest is longer than 9 metres and may weigh more than 68 kilos. But no octopus grows large enough to attack a ship!

An octopus usually lives alone amongst the rocks on the bottom of the ocean. Sometimes it moves rocks with its long arms, or **tentacles**, to make a little cave for itself. On the underside of each of its tentacles are many little round suckers, or **suction** cups. These help the octopus climb over rocks and hold on to things.

Octopuses like to eat shellfish such as crabs,

Suckers on the underside of the tentacle of a giant Pacific octopus.
© Stuart Westmorland/Corbis

SEARCH LIGHT

What are two ways that an octopus can escape from an enemy?

lobsters, and mussels. An octopus will crawl about on its rubbery tentacles as it looks for food. But it can also swim very fast. An octopus sometimes hunts fish, chasing them until they are too tired to swim anymore. Then the octopus tightly wraps its arms around the fish and eats them.

But the octopus has enemies too. It usually tries to hide from them. Many octopuses can hide by changing colour to match the area around them. If that doesn't work, the octopus shoots black ink into the water around it. The cloudy water confuses the enemy and helps the octopus get away.

DID YOU KNOW?
Octopuses are very smart. In fact, next to dolphins and whales, the common octopus is perhaps the smartest animal living in the ocean!

An octopus has eight arms, or tentacles. Its name comes from a Greek word that means 'eight-footed'.
© Stephen Frink/Corbis

Answer: It can change colour and squirt ink into the water.

Plants or Animals?

Sponges are strange animals. They don't have the body parts - inside or outside - that we expect an animal to have. They don't even move around. Instead, they stay attached to an underwater rock or coral reef, just like plants. For a long time, people thought sponges were plants. Scientists decided that sponges are animals only after watching them eating food by drawing it into their bodies.

There are nearly 5,000 different kinds of sponges. Most live in the sea, but a few like freshwater. Sponges may be flat like spreading moss. Or they may look like trees with branching arms. Some are as tiny as a bean, while others are as tall as a person. Some are smooth and mushy, while others are rough, hard, and prickly. Some are dull and drab, while others are brightly coloured.

A sponge gets oxygen to breathe and food particles to eat by straining water through its body. Sometimes fish, shrimp, and other creatures live inside a sponge. A few sponges attach themselves to crab shells and go wherever the crab goes.

People dive to collect sponges or pull them up with hooks. Later, the sponges are dried, cleaned, and trimmed. The fleshy parts are thrown away, and only the 'spongy' skeleton is used. The ancient Greeks and Romans used sponges to pad their armour and helmets. People still use sponges for scrubbing themselves clean, for painting, and for making medicines. However, factory-made sponges have taken the place of natural sponges in most homes.

SEARCH LIGHT

Which of the following statements are true about sponges?
a) Sponges can be found mainly in the sea.
b) Sponges eat by straining the water around them.
c) The sponges in your house probably came from the sea.

DID YOU KNOW?
Not all sponges are spongy. Some have glass-like skeletons.

© Stephen Frink/Corbis
© Royalty-Free/Corbis

(Top) Vase sponge; (bottom) marine sponges.

A school of fish swims near some sponges. A few animals eat sponges, but most leave them alone because of their unpleasant taste and smell.
© Royalty-Free/Corbis

Answer: a) Sponges can be found mainly in the sea.
b) Sponges eat by straining the water around them.

Water-Loving Beasts

The American animal that most people call a buffalo is actually a bison. True buffalo live in warm places in Asia or Africa. The best known among them is the Indian buffalo. It's also called the water

Mud-caked buffalo in Kenya.
© Yann Arthus-Bertrand/Corbis

buffalo. That's because these animals love to lie in the water or in mud. This helps them to stay cool and keep the flies away. Buffalo eat mostly grass.

Asian water buffalo have been reared and used by people for many years. They carry loads and pull carts. Some help farmers to plough fields, especially in India and East Asia. But that's not all. Some people in Asia eat buffalo meat. They use its skin for making leather goods. Buttons, bangles and many other things are made from the buffalo's horns. And buffalo milk is rich and full of cream.

The water buffalo of Asia are heavily built and look like oxen. Some may be taller than 1.5 metres at the shoulder. The smallest buffalo are the *anoa* from Indonesia and the *tamarau* from the Philippines. They are just about 1 metre high.

All buffalo have horns, but not all buffalo horns are the same. Some curve backwards. Some curve inwards. The Asian water buffalo and the African Cape buffalo have the biggest horns. The horns of the *anoa* are short and nearly straight.

Sadly, there are very few Cape buffalo left. They were thought to be dangerous to humans and have been over-hunted.

SEARCH LIGHT

The African or Cape buffalo are large animals with large horns. They were once hunted to the point of being endangered. Why do you think people were hunting them?

DID YOU KNOW?
Mozzarella cheese used to be made from water buffalo milk. True mozzarella still is.

In China, as in other parts of the world, water buffalo like this one help plough the field.
© Vince Streano/Corbis

Answer: Cape buffalo were over-hunted for two main reasons. First, hunters enjoyed having the Cape buffalo - like other large animals - as a trophy, mainly for its large horns. Second, people were afraid of the Cape buffalo and thought it was dangerous. So, like wolves and snakes in other countries, the buffalo were often killed on sight.

181

Kings of the River

Underneath the water in the rivers of Africa, a giant animal moves along the muddy bottom and eats water plants. It's named after a horse, looks something like a pig, and is larger than a crocodile. It's the king of the river, the hippopotamus. Its name is a combination of two Greek words that join together to mean 'river horse'.

An African folktale describes how God created the hippopotamus and told it to cut grass for the other animals. When the hippo discovered how hot Africa was, it asked God if it could stay in the water during the day and cut grass at night when it was cool. God agreed. However, he was worried that the hippo might eat the river's fish. The hippo, however, ate only plants. At night, hippos still go ashore and wander in herds, eating grass.

SEARCH LIGHT

Find and correct the mistake in the following sentence: When a hippo goes underwater, it constantly blows water out of its nostrils.

(Top) A herd of hippos in Botswana; (bottom) Fully submerged hippopotamus.

DID YOU KNOW?
Baby hippos are born in the water and can swim before they can walk.

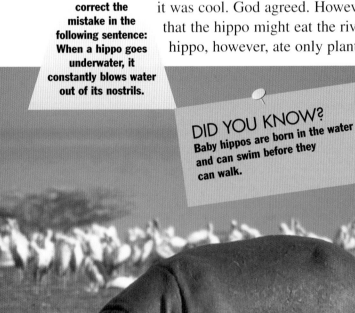

Hippos have barrel-shaped bodies, short legs, and four toes on each foot. Adult hippos can weigh more than 2,700 kilos. The biggest hippos may reach 4.6 metres in length and stand 1.5 metres tall at the shoulder. Although the hippo looks clumsy on land, it is well equipped for life in the water. It swims easily, and when it stays underwater, little flaps of skin close its **nostrils**.

When a hippo is mostly **submerged**, the only things you can see are its rounded eyes, tiny ears, and raised nostrils. Sometimes a hippo lifts its head out of the water and roars. When that happens, you can see its enormous red mouth and very long teeth.

Because of the hippo's great size, its only enemies are lions and people.

A hippopotamus stands along the shore of Lake Manyara in Tanzania.
© Wolfgang Kaehler/Corbis

Answer: When a hippo goes underwater, little flaps of skin close its nostrils.

Mermaids of Yore?

Stories about mermaids tell of creatures that have the head and body of a human and the tail of a fish. These stories may have come from people who saw manatees swimming and didn't know what they were.

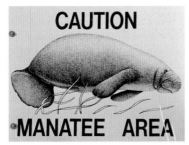

Boater's warning sign.
© Catherine Karnow/Corbis

A manatee is a large stoutly built animal with a **tapered** body that ends in a flat rounded tail. Adults grow to about 3 metres long and 360-545 kilos. The manatee has a thick tough skin and is nearly hairless. It uses its flippers for turning, holding food, moving along the bottom of rivers, and holding its young.

Manatees, especially the mothers and their calves, talk to each other using chirps, grunts, and squeaks. The other members of a group communicate by touching **muzzle** to muzzle. Manatees may live alone or in groups of 15 to 20.

They live in shallow waters along the coasts of oceans or in rivers that are rich in the plants they eat. The Caribbean manatee lives from the coasts of the southeastern United States to those of northern South America. The Amazonian manatee, as you might guess, lives in the Amazon River and other nearby freshwater. And the African manatee is found in the coastal waters and slow-moving rivers of tropical West Africa.

Manatees have small eyes and can't see very well. They don't move very fast either. Since manatees can't **tolerate** cool temperatures, they live in warm waters - places where lots of people like to live as well. Many manatees have been killed or injured when people drive their motorboats into the manatees' feeding areas. The manatees can't see the boats and don't move fast enough to get out of their way.

SEARCH LIGHT

Mother manatees and their calves communicate through
a) chirps, grunts, and squeaks.
b) snaps, crackles, and pops.
c) dings, rattles, and creaks.

DID YOU KNOW?
The manatee has an unlikely close relative on land: the elephant. It's thought that the manatee's early ancestor was a plant-eating wading animal.

The slow-moving manatee lives in warm shallow coastal waters. Because manatees can't see very well, they are often injured by motorboats in their feeding areas.
© Douglas Faulkner/Corbis

Answer: a) chirps, grunts, and squeaks.

The Town Builders

Muskrats are ratlike rodents that look a little like small beavers and live in water. The animal gets its name from the two musk **glands** under its tail. The glands give off a heavy, musky smell. Muskrats were originally found only in North America. People took them to Europe and Asia about 100 years ago, and they soon made themselves at home in those regions as well.

Muskrats build their houses in water, as a part of a 'town'. Mounds of mud, bulrushes, and other plants are heaped up into a dome-shaped structure. This rises above the surface of the water. The animals dig tunnels from under the water up into the mound. They then hollow out a room at the top, a few inches above the waterline.

Muskrats also dig narrow **channels** through the surrounding plant growth. The channels connect to each other and to other mounds. Muskrats can sometimes be seen swimming along these channels. They feed on different kinds of **sedges**, reeds, and roots of water plants, as well as **mussels**, crayfish, salamanders, and fish.

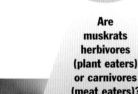

SEARCH LIGHT

Are muskrats herbivores (plant eaters) or carnivores (meat eaters)?

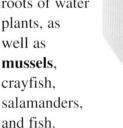

DID YOU KNOW?

Muskrats have been known to hold their breath underwater for 20 minutes or more.

Muskrats have small eyes and ears and a long scaly flat tail. They use the tail as a **rudder** for steering or changing direction while swimming. The hind feet are partially webbed and are used as paddles.

Muskrat fur is waterproof and keeps the animals warm. Muskrats continue to be trapped because of the quality of that fur. Because of that, there are far fewer muskrats today than there were in the past.

Muskrats look like a cross between a rat and a beaver. They live in water where they build a home of mud and plants that rises above the water's surface.
© Scott Nielsen/Bruce Coleman

Answer: Actually, muskrats eat both plants and meat, which makes them omnivores (animals that eat all foods).

The Whale Horses

In the cold Arctic seas of Europe, Asia, and North America, there lives a large creature called the 'walrus'. Its name is an English version of the **Scandinavian** word *hvalros*, meaning 'whale horse'.

Group of walruses gathered on rocks.
© Wolfgang Kaehler/Corbis

The walrus has a stocky body topped by a rounded head. It has small eyes like those of a pig and a short broad mouth. Its mouth is covered with stiff whiskers. Every year, the walrus grows a new set of whiskers. An adult walrus can grow to twice the length of a Ping-Pong table.

All walruses have long **tusks** growing on each side of the mouth. The tusks are very handy. The walrus uses them to fight, cut holes in ice, and pull itself out of water. Walruses spend nearly their whole life at sea. However, they often climb onto ice or rocky islands to rest and to have babies.

The walrus has flippers. In the water the flippers help the animal swim. On land the walrus uses them to walk. The walrus also uses its flippers to hold prey such as fish, but clams are its favourite food. Sometimes the animal feeds on young seals, though this happens only when it fails to find other food.

Walruses are social animals and live in groups of more than 100 members. There are two types of walrus, named for the two major oceans where they live: the Pacific walrus and the Atlantic walrus. The Pacific walrus is heavier and has longer tusks than the Atlantic walrus.

In the late 20th century, efforts were made to protect walruses. This helped increase the population of the Pacific walrus.

SEARCH LIGHT

Fill in the gap:
All walruses have _____ growing from the sides of their mouths that help them fight, cut holes in the ice, and drag themselves out of the water.

DID YOU KNOW?
The scientific name for the walrus, *Odobenus rosmarus*, translates into English as 'tooth-walking sea horse'.

Walruses are known for their long tusks. They use their flippers to help them walk on land.
© W. Perry Conway/Corbis

Answer: All walruses have tusks growing from the sides of their mouths that help them fight, cut holes in the ice, and drag themselves out of the water.

WHALES

The Biggest Animals of All

Whales live in the water. They look like fish. They swim like fish. But they aren't fish at all. Whales are 'aquatic mammals'. 'Aquatic' means they live in water. Mammals are warm-blooded creatures that give birth to live young ones and feed them with milk.

Whales can't stay under the water all the time as fish do. They have to come up for air from time to time. They breathe through blowholes at the top of their heads. When their warm breath hits the colder air outside, it makes a cloud of mist called the whale's 'spout'. You can spot a whale by its spout.

Fish can't make sounds. But whales can make two kinds of sounds. The first sounds like a bark, or a whistle, or sometimes a scream. Whales make these sounds to speak to each other. Some whales also make very loud, low sounds that other whales can hear from many miles away. This sound can be heard only under water.

(Top) Killer whale; (bottom) Beluga whales.

The biggest whale of all is the blue whale. It can be 34 metres long and weigh around 152 tonnes. That's more than ten buses put together! Even a baby blue whale is huge.

Finding food is a simple matter for blue whales. They just swim along with their huge mouths open, and thousands of tiny sea creatures flow in. But blue whales have no teeth. Instead, they have strings of hardened skin, like our fingernails, that hang from the roof of the mouth. This hardened skin is called '**baleen**' and is used as a strainer to let out the water while holding back the sea creatures captured in the whale's mouth.

SEARCH LIGHT

This humpback whale sails above the water as it grabs a breath of air. This act is called 'breaching'.
© Brandon D. Cole/Corbis

Why do you suppose that some whales' sounds can be heard only under water? (Hint: Who's listening?)

DID YOU KNOW?
Some whales leave the water and park themselves on a beach. They may stay there so long that they die. Strangely, other whales often join the 'beached' whale - possibly to keep the first one company, according to some researchers.

Answer: Whales 'talk' to other whales, so it makes sense that their sounds would be heard where the whales spend most of their time - under the water.

Uncover the mystery of everyday marvels, from rocks to rainbows

Science and Nature

Science and Nature

TABLE OF CONTENTS

Building Blocks
of Matter

Everything in the world is made up of molecules. Our bodies, our clothes, our houses, animals, plants, air, water, sky - everything. Molecules are so small, though, that we can't see them with our naked eyes.

But molecules aren't the smallest things. Molecules are made up of atoms, which are even smaller. Atoms are so small that it would take more than a billion atoms to fill the space taken up by one pea!

The word 'atom' comes from the Greek word *atomos,* meaning '**indivisible**'. But despite what their name suggests, atoms can indeed be divided into smaller pieces. Each atom has a **core**, called a 'nucleus'. Around the nucleus swarm tiny **particles** called 'electrons'. The nucleus itself is made up of other small particles called 'protons' and 'neutrons'. And these protons and neutrons are made up of even smaller things called 'quarks'. So, for now at least, quarks are among the smallest known things in the universe.

DID YOU KNOW?
Quarks are so small that scientists have to make up new ways to describe them. They talk about the different 'flavours' of quarks - not chocolate or pistachio but 'up', 'down', 'charm', 'strange', 'top' and 'bottom'.

SEARCH LIGHT

True or false? Atoms are the smallest things of all.

Answer: FALSE. Atoms can be split into electrons, neutrons, and protons, all of which are smaller than an atom itself. And quarks are even smaller still.

189

Same Stuff, Different Forms

Did you know that many of the things you may see or use every day - such as the water in a glass, the air in a football, and even the hard metal in a toy car - are **potential** transformers?

The substances that these things are made of can take the form of a solid, a liquid, or a gas. The form they take depends mostly on their temperature. When water gets cold enough, it becomes a hard solid we call 'ice'. When it gets hot enough, it becomes a wispy gas we call 'steam'. Many other substances behave the same way when they are heated or cooled enough.

A solid holds its own size and shape without needing a container. If you pour water into an ice tray and freeze it, the water will keep the shape of the cube-shaped moulds in the tray. You can think of the solid metal in a toy car as frozen too, but its melting temperature is much higher than the temperatures we live in. The person who made the car poured very hot liquid metal into a car-shaped mould and let it cool down and freeze.

A liquid does not hold its own shape. If you pour a half litre of water into a tall vase or a shallow bowl, it will take the shape of its container. But that water does keep its own size. It measures a half litre. Everyday liquids such as milk, paint, and petrol act this same way.

Gases do not keep their own shape or their own size. When air is pumped into a football, it takes the shape and size of the ball. As more air is pumped in, the ball gets harder but not much bigger. The air changes its size to fit the space inside the ball.

SEARCH LIGHT

Write down whether each item in the list describes a solid (S), a liquid (L), or a gas (G). Some may match more than one state.

- melts
- freezes
- has its own shape
- floats in air
- pours
- spreads out
- has an odour

Answer: melts = S; freezes = L; has its own shape = S; floats in air = G; pours = L; spreads out = L, G; has an odour = G

Sounds That See
in the Dark

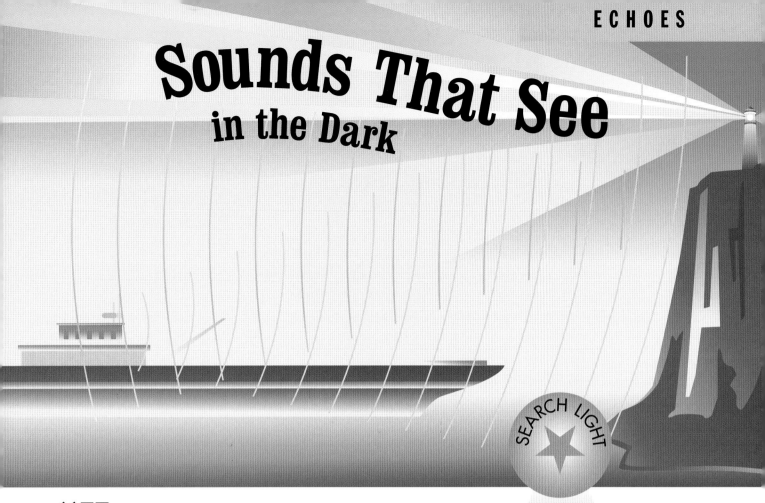

SEARCH LIGHT

Which animal uses sound to 'see'?

"Hel-l-o-o-o-o-o!'

A boy hears an echo coming from the hills.

'Echo, talk to me,' he calls.

'...to me,' repeats the echo. '...to me...to me...to me.'

What is an echo? It's a sound you make that bounces back to you from hills or other surfaces. But how can a sound bounce? It's not a ball.

Actually, sound is a wave in the air. If you could see air in the same way as water, you'd see the waves that sounds make. Sound waves bounce only if they hit something big and solid like the side of a hill or the walls of a cave.

What if nothing stops the sound waves? Then they just get smaller and smaller. Or they are absorbed by soft things such as carpets, curtains, or large pieces of furniture. That's why we don't usually hear echoes in the house.

Did you know that echoes can help some animals 'see' in the dark?

In pitch-black caves bats fly easily, never bumping into anything, and even catching tiny insects in the air. As they fly they make tiny whistle-like sounds. These sounds bounce back to them. The direction of the echo and the time it takes for it to return tell the bats exactly where things are as they fly.

Human beings have learned to harness echoes for navigation, too. Submarines travelling underwater use sonar to bounce sounds off of solid objects so that they can tell where those objects are located - like undersea bats!

DID YOU KNOW?
It is said that a duck's quack is the only sound that doesn't echo. If you happen to have a duck and a long hallway, you could test this theory yourself.

Answer: Bats use echoes to tell what is around them in the dark.
Dolphins do the same thing underwater.

The Power of Life

Without energy in our bodies, we wouldn't be able to do anything. We couldn't walk, talk, or even play. Energy is usable power. And all energy is related to some kind of motion.

All living things need energy, no matter what they do. Plants get their energy from sunlight. The energy is stored in **chemicals** inside the plant. This happens in a process called 'photosynthesis'.

Animals that eat plants take in the energy stored in plants. The energy is then stored in chemicals inside the animals as 'food energy'. The same happens when animals eat other animals.

Plants and animals use food energy every day as they grow and do the work of being a plant or an animal. So plants have to keep **absorbing** sunlight, and animals have to keep eating plants or other animals.

It isn't only living things that have energy. A dead tree has hidden energy. When we burn its wood it gives off warmth, or 'heat energy'. The Sun also makes heat energy as it constantly burns.

The Sun gives off not just heat but also light, as 'light energy'. The battery in a torch makes it shine, **generating** light energy. But if we put the same battery in a radio, we get music. A battery's energy is known as 'electrical energy'. And in a toy car that electrical energy produces movement, or 'kinetic energy'.

If we couldn't use heat, light, or electrical energy, we wouldn't be able to drive cars or cook food. We wouldn't have light at night. Basically, we'd have to use the energy of our own bodies. And that would mean eating a lot more and doing a lot less.

SEARCH LIGHT

These sentences are mixed up. See if you can sort them out.

Heat energy comes from things people or animals eat.

Food energy comes from things that burn.

**Answer: Heat energy comes from things that burn.
Food energy comes from things people or animals eat.**

The Science of Their Changing Colours

Trees that shed their leaves every year are called 'deciduous' trees. New leaves grow again in spring.

Scientists think that plants get rid of things they can't use any more. After a flower has helped to make seeds for a plant, its petals fall off. And soon after leaves have lost their green material, called 'chlorophyll', they also fall off.

The chlorophyll in leaves uses sunlight to make sugar out of water and carbon dioxide, a gas in the air. Plants need carbon dioxide to live and grow. When leaves use carbon dioxide, another gas called 'oxygen' is produced. Plants don't need all the oxygen they produce, so they let most of it go.

Animals and humans need oxygen to live. Their bodies use oxygen, and what do you think they produce? Yes, carbon dioxide. When animals and humans breathe out, they let the carbon dioxide go.

It's easy to see that plants, animals, and humans help each other in this way.

In countries where the weather cools down in autumn, plants lose their chlorophyll, and their leaves may turn yellow or red. The yellow colour was in the leaves all summer, but there was so much green in the leaves that the yellow was hidden.

Yellow leaves turn red only if they have lots of sugar in their sap and the sun shines on them. The more sugar a leaf has, the redder it becomes. If a leaf is kept in the shade, it will stay yellow, even if it has a lot of sugar.

SEARCH LIGHT

Find and correct the mistake:
Leaves turn red if they contain a lot of carbon dioxide when the sun shines on them.

Answer: Leaves turn red if they contain a lot of sugar when the sun shines on them.

Hot and Cold

SEARCH LIGHT

Temperature
measures how
much
a) heat something has.
b) chill something has.
c) pressure something has.

We can use our fingers, our tongue, or almost any part of our skin to feel just how hot or how cold something is. This is important because our bodies need just the right amount of heat so that we can live comfortably.

When it's cold and we want to make a room warmer, we turn on the heater. In the summer when it's hot and we want to make the room cooler, do we add cold to the room?

No. We take away some of the heat. We say something is cold when it doesn't have much heat. The less heat it has, the colder it is.

Air conditioners suck hot air from a room. Pipes inside the air conditioners take a lot of heat out of the air, making it cold. Then a blower fans the cooled air into the room again.

When we want to know exactly how hot or how cold something is, we use a thermometer. A thermometer tells us about temperature - that is, how hot something is. Some countries measure temperature in 'degrees Celsius (°C)'. Others use a different measuring system of 'degrees Fahrenheit (°F)'.

We can use thermometers to measure air temperature, oven temperature, even body temperature. And your body temperature tells not only whether you feel hot or cold but whether you're healthy.

DID YOU KNOW?
If you test too-hot bath water with your foot, you're likely to burn that foot. That's because it takes longer for your foot to recognize temperature than it does your hand.

Answer: a) heat something has.

Diamond Drops of Water

Susan and her mother had come to the park for an early morning walk. The weather had been nice and warm recently. The nights were still and there was hardly a cloud in the sky.

© W. Perry Conway/Corbis

The park's grass glittered and winked. 'Are those diamonds?' Susan asked. It looked as if someone had sprinkled tiny diamonds all across the grass during the night.

Susan bent down to touch one of the glittering points. 'It's water!' she cried out in surprise. 'How did it get here? Did it rain last night?'

'No, this isn't rainwater. It's dew.'

'What's dew?' Susan was eager to know.

'It came from the air. All air has got some water in it, you know,' said Mum.

'But I don't see any water in the air,' said Susan, looking around.

'No, of course you don't. It's in the form of **vapour**, like fog, only very light,' said Mum.

'So how does the water get onto the grass?'

'You know that steam turns into water again if it touches something cold, right?' Susan nodded. 'Well, on certain nights the air is warm and full of moisture,' Mum continued, 'but the grass and the ground are cool. So when the vapour in the warm air touches these cooler surfaces...'

'...it changes to water drops on the grass,' finished Susan. 'That must be why sometimes in the morning our car is covered with tiny drops of water.'

'That's right,' Mum smiled. 'Now let's get going on that walk!'

DID YOU KNOW?
People used to think that tiny spider webs in the grass were actually the beds of fairies. This is because the webs, covered with dew, looked like magic nets.

© Julie Habel/Corbis

Answer: When warm air touches the cool ground, the water in the air turns into drops of dew.

Floating Water

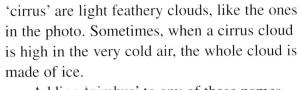

Which of the following describes a cumulonimbus cloud?
a) cloud on the ground
b) sleet cloud
c) fog
d) thundercloud

Have you ever looked up at the clouds and wondered what they're made of?

Well, they're made of water - thousands of litres of water, floating high in the sky.

It's easier to believe this when you know that cloud water takes the form of tiny droplets. The droplets are so tiny that you couldn't see one if it was separated from all the others.

Sometimes the water droplets join together around tiny pieces of dust in the air. These droplets become bigger and bigger as more of them collect. When they become too heavy to float, they fall - 'plop!' That's rain!

There are three main kinds of cloud. 'Cumulus' are the small puffballs or great woolly-looking clouds that are flat on the bottom. 'Stratus' are low clouds, usually streaky or without much shape. And

© W. Perry Conway/Corbis

'cirrus' are light feathery clouds, like the ones in the photo. Sometimes, when a cirrus cloud is high in the very cold air, the whole cloud is made of ice.

Adding 'nimbus' to any of these names changes it to mean a rain cloud. Tall white cottony rain clouds are called 'cumulonimbus', or thunderclouds. They often bring thunderstorms. Flat grey rain clouds are called 'nimbostratus'. They usually bring only rain.

Snow, **sleet**, and **hail** also fall from clouds. Snow and sleet usually fall on cold winter days. Hailstones can fall even on a warm summer day.

And you may not realize it, but you've probably been right inside a cloud yourself. A cloud so close to the ground that we can walk through it is 'fog'.

DID YOU KNOW?
Being on 'cloud nine' means you are feeling especially good, flying high. One explanation for the term comes from the military, where cloud types were numbered. Type nine was a tall thundercloud, and jets would have to fly very high to get over one.

Answer: d) thundercloud

Arcs of Colour

If you've ever looked at a rainbow and wondered how all those bright colours got into the sky, you're not alone.

The ancient Greeks thought these **arcs** of colour were signs from the gods to warn people that terrible wars or storms were going to happen. The Norse people believed a rainbow was a bridge the gods used to walk down from the sky to the Earth. Other legends said there was a pot of gold waiting at the end of a rainbow.

But as beautiful as rainbows are, they aren't magic. And they aren't solid enough to walk on. In fact, a rainbow is just coloured light. The seven colours are always the same and appear in the same order: red, orange, yellow, green, blue, indigo (a very deep blue), and violet. The name 'Roy G. Biv' helps you remember the first letters and the order of the colours.

Rainbows often appear after or at the end of a storm - when the Sun is shining again but there is still some rain in the air. The sunlight looks white, but all seven rainbow colours are mixed together in it. So when a beam of sunlight passes through the raindrops, it's broken into the seven different colours.

But you don't have to wait for rain to see rainbows. They can show up in the spray of a fountain or a waterfall, or you can make your own with a hosepipe. Set the nozzle to create a spray, aim it away from the Sun, and then stand between the Sun and the spray. You've got an instant rainbow!

SEARCH LIGHT

How can the name 'Roy G. Biv' help you remember the colours of the rainbow?

DID YOU KNOW?

Contrary to some legends, there really is no 'end' of a rainbow. Rainbows are actually full circles. But because we can see only a limited distance, to the horizon of Earth and sky, we see only part of the circle.

© Jeff Vanuga/Corbis

Answer: The name gives you the first letter of each of the colours of the rainbow, in the order that they occur in the rainbow. Like this: Red Orange Yellow Green Blue Indigo Violet.

Nature's Fireworks

It can be fun playing in gentle rain, splashing in puddles and chasing raindrops. But this would be a dangerous thing to do if there were thunderclouds above.

Thunderclouds are the large, dark, often fast-moving clouds that come out during storms. Thunderclouds rumble mightily during storms, and that rumbling indicates the presence of lightning. The rumbling is the sound lightning makes as it arcs across the sky.

During a thunderstorm, electricity collects in the clouds. And often this electricity is released as lightning. It's dangerous to be outside when there is a risk of lightning because it can quite easily kill someone from miles away. People have died from lightning strikes even though the storm the lightning has come from was barely visible on the **horizon**.

Lightning bolts frequently race to the ground, drawn by objects such as trees and lampposts, which are especially good conductors of electricity. Lightning is most attracted to tall objects, which is why trees, buildings, and radio towers are often struck.

Actually there are two parts to a lightning strike. The bolt from the sky is the part we don't see, because it is so fast and faint. The part we do see is the return strike. This is a bright flash of lightning that jumps up out of the ground to meet the lightning coming down and then races up to the base of the clouds.

Lightning can hurt or kill people who are struck by it. If you ever are caught in a thunderstorm, go indoors quickly or get into a car. Lightning that hits a car travels harmlessly into the ground.

True or false?
In a thunderstorm, it's a good idea to take shelter under a tree.

© A & J Verkaik/Corbis

DID YOU KNOW?
Florida is known as the 'lightning capital of the world'. Every year, lightning strikes in Florida more often than in any other state in the United States. Also lightning kills more people in Florida than in any other state.

Answer: FALSE. A tree is likely to be struck by lightning in a storm. It's better to get inside a car or a house, which will protect you even if the lightning strikes.

Nature's Fury

A cyclone is a **rotating** storm that can be hundreds of kilometres wide. These storms can be very destructive. The winds in a cyclone usually blow at more than 120 kilometres per hour.

When a cyclone starts in the warmer waters of the Atlantic Ocean, it is called a 'hurricane'. In the western Pacific Ocean, it is known as a 'typhoon'.

From above, a cyclone looks like a huge spinning doughnut of clouds. The centre of the storm, the doughnut hole, is called the 'eye'. The eye is quiet and cloudless. When the eye passes overhead, it might seem like the storm has ended. But within an hour or two, the eye passes and the other side of the storm hits.

With its strong winds a cyclone also brings flooding rains and sometimes very high ocean waves. When a cyclone hits land, it causes severe damage. The combination of wind, rain, and waves can knock down trees, flatten houses, and wash away roads.

Most cyclones start over **tropical** oceans because areas of warm water are their source of energy. Strong rotating winds that start on land are called a 'tornado'. A tornado, such as the one pictured here, starts for different reasons and is smaller than a cyclone. But a tornado also has very strong winds, so it too can be very destructive. It can knock a train off its track or lift a house straight into the air. Fortunately, tornadoes usually die soon after they start.

SEARCH LIGHT

Fill in the gap: The quietest part of a cyclone is the _____, where there are no winds or clouds.

DID YOU KNOW?
The best way for scientists to learn a cyclone's size and strength is to fly a plane through it. That's the surest way - but certainly not the safest!

Paul and LindaMarie Ambrose/Taxi/Getty Images

Answer: The quietest part of a cyclone is the eye, where there are no winds or clouds.

Killer Downpour

Rain seems to make things cleaner, doesn't it? Rain helps flowers grow and helps keep plants green. It washes the dust off cars and houses. It makes roads look shiny and it leaves a fresh smell in the air.

But rain can be dirty. That's because, as the rain falls, it gathers up any **pollution** that's in the air. It can leave cars looking streaky and windows looking spotty.

Some rain will even ruin the paint on cars. It will damage or kill the plants it falls on and the fish living in lakes that are fed by rain. Such rain is called 'acid rain'.

Scientist testing polluted lake water containing melted acid snow.
© Ted Spiegel/Corbis

This is what happens. We burn fuels such as coal, gas, and oil in our factories. This releases gases containing **elements** such as sulphur, carbon, and nitrogen into the air. These combine with moisture in the air to form such damaging substances as sulphuric acid, carbonic acid, and nitric acid. When it rains, these acids fall to earth with the water.

Acid doesn't fall to earth only in the form of rain. It can also fall as snow, sleet, and hail. It can even be in fog.

Acid rain harms many forms of life, including human life. It also damages buildings. The acid eats through stone, metal, and concrete. Acid rain has damaged some of the world's great monuments, including the **cathedrals** of Europe, the Colosseum in Rome, and the Taj Mahal in India.

The unhealthy branch on the left shows the damage that acid rain can do to plants.
© Ted Spiegel/Corbis

DID YOU KNOW?
Acid rain destroys trees. We need trees to make oxygen and to get rid of carbon dioxide, which can be poisonous to us. Just a quarter of a hectare of trees gets rid of 2.2 tonnes of carbon dioxide a year.

SEARCH LIGHT

Acid rain can cause
a) water to become polluted.
b) fish to die.
c) damage to buildings.
d) plants to die.
e) all of the above.

Answer: e) all of the above.

Movement
on the Seas

The sea never seems to sit still. Its waves rise and fall. On beaches they push forward and fall back. But what makes ocean water into waves?

Most waves are created by the wind. The wind blows along the surface of the water and forces waves in the same direction. The top of a wave is called the 'crest' and the lowest part in between the crests is known as the 'trough'. When waves roll through the open ocean, they're called 'swell'. As they reach the shore, their crests get higher and closer together and finally topple over. Then they're called 'breakers' or 'surf'.

A gentle wind makes long waves that don't rise very high. But stronger winds push harder on the water and create taller waves. Big storms mean strong winds, and that means huge, powerful waves.

Major storms at sea, called 'hurricanes' or 'typhoons', can cause enormous waves. Some are so big that they can smash seaside houses into pieces, or tip over ships that get in their way. During violent storms, waves have been known to reach to the tops of lighthouses and to toss boats completely out of the water.

The most destructive waves are tsunamis, but they're quite different from other waves. Tsunamis - also wrongly called 'tidal waves' - are not caused by tides or by the wind. These huge waves are created by underwater earthquakes or volcanic eruptions.

SEARCH LIGHT

'Breakers' is another word for
a) surf.
b) trough.
c) crest.

Without waves, the very popular sport of surfing wouldn't be possible. Riding a surfboard in waves like these requires great balance, skill, and a lot of nerve!
© Rick Doyle/Corbis

DID YOU KNOW?
According to researchers in Canada, the tallest ocean wave ever recorded was 34 metres high.

Answer: a) surf.

Waves of Destruction

A powerful earthquake struck the coast of Chile in 1960. Frightened, people got into their boats and went to the harbour to escape the disaster. Soon enormous waves caused by the earthquake rose up from the sea. These violent waves were each more than three stories high. They destroyed all the boats and killed the people in them. The waves then travelled for 15 hours across the Pacific Ocean to Hilo in Hawaii, where they destroyed more property.

These waves are known as 'tsunamis', from the Japanese for 'harbour wave'.

A tsunami is a large destructive wave created by the shock from an earthquake or volcanic eruption. The impact of a **meteorite** could also create a tsunami. Tsunamis travel fast and have the force to destroy entire coastal communities within moments.

A tsunami can travel at speeds of 725 kilometres per hour or more (as fast as a jet plane) and packs tremendous force. As a tsunami approaches land, it grows larger. It continues to travel until its energy is completely used up. All low-lying coastal areas are **vulnerable** to a tsunami disaster.

In July 1998 a tsunami **devastated** the northwest coast of Papua New Guinea. It was caused by an earthquake 19 kilometres offshore that measured 7.0 on the Richter scale. (The biggest earthquakes have not reached higher than 9.0.) The tsunami swept away three coastal villages. Afterwards, nothing remained but sand.

SEARCH LIGHT

Which of these does *not* cause a tsunami?
a) earthquake
b) volcanic eruption
c) high winds

DID YOU KNOW?
When tsunamis strike land, they generally first suck all the water out of any harbours.

Answer: c) high winds

Studying the Earth

How did the Earth get its shape?

What was the world like millions of years ago?

What is the Earth made of?

Why do earthquakes happen?

These are some of the many questions that geologists try to answer. Geologists are people who study the Earth's structure and its history. The word 'geology' comes from Greek words meaning 'earth science'.

Geology is an important science. Geologists help people find useful fossil fuels, such as oil and coal, which lie hidden in the Earth's crust. Geologists also help find out where earthquakes are likely to happen. This helps people choose the safest place to put up buildings.

Because there are so many things about the Earth that geologists study, geology is divided into many separate areas. For instance, the study of physical geology looks at the changes that take place inside the Earth and the reasons for those changes. Geochemistry is concerned with the chemical **elements** that make up rocks, soil, and **minerals**. Petrology deals with rocks themselves.

Did you know that palaeontology is a form of geology? Palaeontologists study life forms that existed on Earth millions of years ago, from the tiniest **bacteria** to enormous dinosaurs. But because these creatures died so many millions of years ago, their bodies have turned into fossils - living things preserved as rock.

SEARCH LIGHT

Match the scientist with what she studies:

geologist	Earth
petrologist	fossils
geochemist	rocks
palaeontologist	chemicals in rocks

To most of us, this landscape is beautiful. But to a geologist, it also tells the story of millions of years of the Earth's history.

© Layne Kennedy/Corbis

DID YOU KNOW?
About 39 tonnes of minerals go into building the average six-room house.

Answer: geologist—Earth, petrologist—rocks, geochemist—chemicals in rocks, palaeontologist—fossils

The Earth's Building Blocks

You might think that rocks are fairly dull. But rocks tell the history of the Earth, including stories of giant explosions, mountains rising from the sea, and buried forests turning to stone.

Most rocks are combinations of one or more **minerals**. Minerals are inorganic, which means they are not made by living things. Yet they are extremely important to all living things. Some minerals are metals, such as iron and gold. Others are non-metallic, like quartz and calcite.

Some rocks contain the hardened **remains** of animals and plants. Limestone rock is usually made up mostly of bits and pieces of fossil shells and skeletons of sea creatures.

All rocks fall into one of three groups, depending on how they are formed. Igneous rocks are formed from cooling magma, which is the lava released in a volcanic eruption. The earliest rocks on Earth were igneous.

But rocks don't stay the same forever. They break down into small pieces because of the effects of wind, water, and ice. And when small pieces of rock settle together, they're known as 'sediment'. As layers of sediment settle on top of each other over many years, their weight squeezes the pieces together into solid sedimentary rock. Both photos show the very common sedimentary rock called 'sandstone', which is cemented sand.

The third group of rocks gets its name from the word 'metamorphosis', which means 'change'. Metamorphic rocks are created when extreme temperatures or pressures cause changes in igneous or sedimentary rocks. Marble is a metamorphic rock formed from intensely squeezed and heated limestone. And limestone, you'll remember, began as seashells and skeletons. This is another amazing Earth story told by a rock!

Sandstone canyon.
© Scott T. Smith/Corbis

SEARCH LIGHT

Minerals are inorganic, which means they are not _____.

DID YOU KNOW?

Gold is the most easily shaped of all metals. It can be hammered until it is just 1 ten thousandth of a millimetre thick. And 30 grams of gold can be drawn into a wire more than 64 kilometres long.

Sandstone is fairly easily worn away by rushing water. Here you see a deep, narrow sandstone formation called a 'slot canyon'.
© David Muench/Corbis

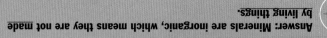

Answer: Minerals are inorganic, which means they are not made by living things.

The Remains
of Tiny Shells

The material we call 'chalk' was formed during the time when dinosaurs lived on Earth. At that time the oceans were rising higher and higher until finally they covered most of the land.

Drawing chalk, an entirely different material from natural chalk.
© Michael T. Sedam/Corbis

Billions of tiny animals lived in those oceans. They were so small you could not have seen them - they were even smaller than the full stop at the end of this sentence. These tiny creatures had shells made from the **element** calcium. When they died, their shells fell to the bottom of the sea. After thousands of years, there were many layers of shells on the ocean floor.

As more and more of the tiny shells pressed down from the top, those on the bottom became harder and began to stick together. Eventually the shells changed into a **mineral** called 'calcite', the main ingredient of the rock known as 'limestone'.

Many millions of years passed after the first chalk was made. The Earth's surface changed its shape, and the land and sea developed new coastlines. This left many chalk layers on dry land, both in the middle of **continents** and by the sea. In the south of England there are chalk cliffs 244 metres high. These are the famous White Cliffs of Dover, and they are almost solid chalk!

If you had a piece of chalk from those cliffs, you could use it to write on a chalkboard. But the chalk that is used in classrooms is not dug from the cliffs or the ground. It is made in factories by mixing several different materials together.

DID YOU KNOW?
Much of the chalk on Earth dates from 66 million to 144 million years ago. So much chalk comes from this time, in fact, that the whole period was named the Cretaceous Period, from the Latin word for 'chalk'.

SEARCH LIGHT

Why does it take millions of years to make chalk?

The fabulous White Cliffs of Dover in England are made up of chalk millions of years old.
© Bob Krist/Corbis

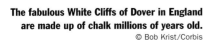
Answer: Many shells have to pile up to be heavy enough to press the bottom ones together and change them into stone.

The Nitty-Gritty

SEARCH LIGHT

True or false? Sand can be used to clean buildings.

You can find sand at the edge of lakes, the bottoms of rivers, and the seaside. You can find it in mountain valleys, deserts, and of course a sandpit. Where does all this sand come from?

Sand is created when rocks break into tiny, tiny pieces. For example, wind, ice, and rain knock against high mountain cliffs. Slowly, over millions of years, these forces break off pieces of rock. The pieces bounce down the mountainside and break off other pieces of rock - while they're also breaking into smaller and smaller pieces themselves. This isn't sand yet, but it's getting there.

Rivers and glaciers are also good at making sand. A river's water rushes along, carrying rocks with it and breaking them into little pieces. The ice of a glacier grinds away at the rocks it slowly moves across.

Another great sand maker is the ocean. Every day, all over the world, tides rise and fall, pushing against rocks over and over. Waves tear at the rocks along the shore, wearing them down.

Thanks to the weather, water, and ice, some of these broken rocks finally get so small that they become what we call 'sand'.

Now that you have all this sand, what can you do with it? Sand is used for paving roads. Bricks made with sand are harder and stronger than other bricks. Sand is also used to filter (or clean) water. When it's sprayed with great force against stone or brick, it can grind away thick layers of dirt or paint through a process called 'sandblasting'.

And, of course, sand is great for building sandcastles!

DID YOU KNOW?
Once a year the Harrison Hot Springs resort in British Columbia, Canada, holds the world sand sculpting championship. The rules say sculptures can be made only of water and sand, and they be finished in under 100 work hours.

Mounds or ridges of sand like these are called 'sand dunes'. They're caused by the combined action of wind and gravity.
© Dave G. Houser/Corbis

Answer: TRUE. Sandblasting is a powerful process for cleaning stone or brick.

The Hardest-Working Gemstones in the World

Diamonds were made millions and millions of years ago when fuming volcanoes melted the **element** called 'carbon' inside some rocks. Gigantic masses of earth pressed the carbon tightly. The hot melted carbon was squeezed so tightly that by the time it cooled, it had changed into the hard **gemstones** called 'diamonds'.

Some diamonds are found in the gravel and sand near rivers. Others are left in mountains by **glaciers**. Most diamonds are mined from rocks deep underground, mostly in Africa. The country of South Africa is the major source of diamonds used in jewellery.

Fill in the gap: Diamonds are so hard that only _____ can cut them.

Diamond jewellery.
© Lynn Goldsmith/Corbis

Diamonds usually look like pieces of glass or dull stones when they're first taken out of the ground. They must be cut and shaped to be used in jewellery. And diamonds are so hard that nothing can cut them except another diamond.

Using diamond-edged tools, the diamond cutter carefully shapes and polishes the diamond so that it has straight edges and smooth surfaces. These edges and surfaces help the diamond reflect light so that it sparkles and flashes with tiny bursts of colour.

Diamonds often seem to flash like white fire. But there are diamonds that have other colours. Red, blue, and green diamonds are difficult to find. Yellow, orange, and violet diamonds are more common. Sometimes people even find black diamonds.

Only the clearest diamonds become glittering gems. But because of their hardness, even dull-looking diamonds are still valuable as cutting tools. These are called '**industrial** diamonds'. Only about 25 per cent of all diamonds are fine enough to become jewels, so most of the world's diamonds are the hard-working industrial ones.

DID YOU KNOW?
The Hope diamond is one of the biggest blue diamonds known in the world. Unfortunately it is supposed to be cursed. Several of its owners have died tragically or have had very bad luck.

Raw diamonds look like chunks of glass when they're first found.
© Dave G. Houser/Corbis

Mountains of Smoke and Fire

Deep under the Earth's surface, it's so hot that even rock melts. Sometimes this molten rock, called 'magma', is pushed up to the surface. At this point it is referred to as 'lava'. And the opening or vent that lets the lava out is a volcano.

A volcano may explode violently, throwing out rocks for miles around. Or it may push lava out so that it flows away, cools, and hardens. Some volcanoes release clouds of poisonous gas or huge clouds of ash. Volcanoes can even do all these things underwater.

Most volcanoes have been around for a very long time. Many haven't erupted for years and have cooled off. Volcanoes that are not going to erupt again are called 'dead volcanoes'.

Some volcanoes still give off smoke. These 'sleeping volcanoes' may 'wake up' one day and erupt again. Mount Vesuvius in Italy slept for a thousand years. But one day in AD 79 it suddenly woke up. Its eruption hurled out hot ash and rocky fragments that buried the city of Pompeii. A hot mudflow buried nearby Herculaneum. Because the remains are so well preserved, the area has been named a World Heritage site.

But not all volcanoes are destructive. When a volcano throws out vast amounts of lava and **debris**, it piles up into a mountain. The Hawaiian Islands and the island of Iceland were created in this way.

Other volcanoes help provide heat and energy. Many Icelandic homes get their hot water from springs heated by volcanic steam. This steam can also be used to produce electricity. Plants grow very well in the rich soil left by volcanoes. And valuable gems, such as diamonds, can sometimes be found in the rocks that are thrown out by volcanoes.

SEARCH LIGHT

Which of the following is *not* produced by volcanoes?

a) lava d) ash
b) oil   e) steam
c) gas

DID YOU KNOW?
The remains of ancient Pompeii and the other cities buried by the eruption of Mount Vesuvius were amazingly well preserved. Loaves of bread that were baking at the time have been found. These discoveries marked the beginning of the modern science of archaeology.

© Douglas Peebles/Corbis

Answer: b) oil

Ancient Life in Stone

Would you like to see something that lived millions of years ago? You can if you find a fossil.

The **remains** or traces of plants, animals, and even **bacteria** that are preserved in stone are called 'fossils'. If you've ever pressed a coin into some clay and then removed it, you've seen the sort of image that's found in many fossils. The original thing isn't there anymore, but there's an **impression** of it left in the stone.

Many fossils are easy to recognize as the living things they once were. The plant fossil in the smaller photo here, for example, looks like a tracing of a fern leaf.

Usually the harder portions of an **organism** are the parts that last long enough to turn into fossils. Sometimes the hard structures are preserved almost whole. For instance, entire fossilized dinosaur bones have been petrified, or changed into a stony substance.

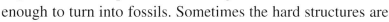

Fossilized fern.
© Wolfgang Kaehler/Corbis

SEARCH LIGHT

It's unusual to see an animal fossil that shows more than just the bones. Why do you think bones are usually the best-preserved parts?

Fossils are not always easy to find. Only a small fraction of all ancient life ever turned into fossils. And the fossils that did form are often buried deep underground.

You can tell that the fossils in the big photo used to be fish. However, they died millions of years ago. They sank to the riverbed and were covered with soft mud. Their flesh wasted away but their bones were held together by the mud.

Eventually the river dried up. It was filled with dust and dirt blown by the wind. The bones of the fish stayed where they were. Slowly, the mud from the riverbed turned to stone.

Finally, someone found this fossil while digging where the river used to be.

DID YOU KNOW?

Over millions of years, many plant and animal remains have turned into the coal, oil, and natural gas we use for fuel. These underground energy sources are known as 'fossil fuels'.

This fossil shows a rare picture of life in action millions of years ago. Look carefully and you can see that a big fish was eating a smaller one when they both died.
© Layne Kennedy/Corbis

Answer: It takes a long time for a fossil to form. Bones last much longer than flesh and organs do. So only the bones are left by the time the animal turns into a fossil.

Giants of the Past

The word 'dinosaur' means 'terrible lizard'. This name is given to lizardlike creatures that lived long, long ago. Many of the dinosaurs were the largest and scariest creatures that ever walked on land. All of them, large and small, were part of the animal group known as 'reptiles'. The dinosaurs were the ancient cousins of today's crocodiles, snakes, and lizards.

You may be familiar with the brontosaur, or 'thunder lizard'. What you may not know is that this dinosaur is now called apatosaur, meaning 'dishonest lizard'. A mix-up in **fossil** bones gave scientists the wrong idea of what it looked like. The apatosaur was still fairly impressive: it was as much as 21 metres long. No matter what you call it, this creature certainly must have sounded like thunder when it walked.

There were many different kinds of dinosaurs:

The tyrannosaur (*Tyrannosaurus rex*) was the 'king of the lizards' and was as long as a fire engine. For many years the tyrannosaur was thought to be the largest carnivore, or meat-eating animal, ever to have walked on Earth. But the giganotosaur was an even larger carnivore!

The anatosaur is called the 'duck lizard' because it had a bill like a duck - though there were 2,000 un-duck-like teeth in its cheeks!

The triceratops was the 'three-horned lizard.' Many of these dinosaurs once lived in the western United States.

There were many other kinds of dinosaurs - more than 1,000 different **species**. And they once lived almost everywhere in the world.

A Mystery Disappearance

SEARCH LIGHT

Many of the dinosaurs that once roamed the Earth were so big and strong that they didn't need to be afraid of any living thing. So why are there no dinosaurs today?

Some scientists think that when new kinds of plants began to grow on Earth, dinosaurs couldn't eat them. New kinds of animals smaller than dinosaurs also appeared during this time. They may have been able to survive better than the dinosaurs. It's also possible that disease killed them by the millions.

Not all scientists think that all dinosaurs died at once. Another explanation is that a changing **climate** killed them. We know that when they were living, the weather began to change. Summers grew shorter and winters grew colder. In some places, heat waves dried up rivers and swamps. Elsewhere, new lakes and rivers appeared, and many places were flooded. Some dinosaurs may have died because it gradually became too cold or too hot for them.

Many scientists believe that dinosaurs died because an **asteroid** struck the Earth about 65 million years ago. The dust raised by the impact would have blocked out sunlight for months, so that plants stopped growing and the temperature dropped. As a result, plant-eating dinosaurs would have died from lack of food, as would the meat eaters that hunted them.

Some scientists think that many dinosaurs **evolved** into birds. So the next time you see a robin, consider that you may be looking at a dinosaur's relative.

Which of the following is *not* thought to be a reason for the disappearance of dinosaurs?
a) an asteroid striking Earth
b) climate change
c) disease
d) poisoned plants
e) flood

DID YOU KNOW?
Scientists think that some dinosaurs swallowed rocks, just as some birds do, to help break up food in their stomachs.

Dinosaur tracks remain, but scientists still don't know what happened to the giant creatures that made them.
© Tom Bean/Corbis

Answer: e) flood

The Tyrant King

SEARCH LIGHT

Find and correct the error in the following sentence: *Tyrannosaurus rex* means 'tyrant wizard king'.

It was longer than a bus, weighed more than 3.6 tonnes, and had teeth up to 30 centimetres long. The tyrannosaur may have died out 65 million years ago, but it is still one of the largest meat-eating land animals that ever lived. It's no wonder that the first scientist who discovered this frightening creature's bones called it *Tyrannosaurus rex*: '**tyrant** lizard king'.

Dinosaurs were not true lizards. However, when scientists first discovered tyrannosaur **fossils**, they did believe that such a dangerous-looking animal would have been a powerful and cruel bully amongst the dinosaurs. The tyrannosaur's jagged teeth and huge jaws make it clear that the tyrannosaur was a powerful carnivore, or meat eater.

Tyrannosaurs lived mainly in what is now North America and Asia. The creature was about 12 metres long from its head to its thick and heavy tail. The tyrannosaur probably stooped forward, with the big tail balancing its weight when it walked.

The tyrannosaur had large, powerful rear legs but small front arms. These forearms wouldn't even have been able to reach its mouth. So the tyrannosaur probably planted its clawed rear feet on a dead animal, bit hard, and ripped the flesh away from the **carcass**.

The tyrannosaur is one of the most popular of all dinosaurs, thanks to films and books. But scientists still don't know a lot about the beast. Did it hunt by sight or by smell? Was tyrannosaur a hunter at all, or did it just eat the dead animals it found? Was it a fast runner?

With so many questions, we're still getting to know the tyrannosaur - but from a safe distance!

DID YOU KNOW?

Tyrannosaur fossils show features that support the theory that dinosaurs may be the distant ancestors of birds. For instance, its bones were very lightweight for their size, just as birds' are. And its walking posture resembles that of modern birds.

Sue, the famous *T. rex* in Chicago's Field Museum, was sick when she was alive. Researchers say that she suffered from gout, a painful disease that causes swelling in bones and joints.
Courtesy, Field Museum

Ancient Elephants

Believe it or not, thousands of years ago some elephants wore heavy fur coats.

Actually, the mammoth was an ancestor of the modern elephant. And mastodons were distant relatives of the mammoth. Neither of these animals is around today. But at one time they roamed the Earth in great numbers.

We know a lot about these ancient creatures because scientists have found many frozen mammoth bodies, especially in the icy area of Russia known as Siberia. Both beasts largely died out at the end of the last Ice Age, about 10,000 years ago. The mammoth didn't show up until about 1 1/2 million years ago.

Mastodons and mammoths were a lot alike, but mastodons were on the planet first. They appeared about 20 million years ago. They were smaller than mammoths and had thick legs like pillars. Mastodons were covered with long reddish brown hair.

SEARCH LIGHT

Mammoths and mastodons are related to
a) horses.
b) elephants.
c) dinosaurs.

DID YOU KNOW?
In 1816, when coal-gas lights were introduced, one of the first museum exhibits to be lit with the new invention was a mastodon skeleton.

Mammoths were the size of modern elephants. The woolly mammoth had a thick furry yellowish brown undercoat with longer bristly hair over it. Like the mastodon, the mammoth had small ears and very long tusks. Despite these dangerous tusks, both animals ate only grass and other plants. The tusks may have been for shovelling snow and ice to uncover food.

Mastodons and mammoths were around at the same time as early humans. The people of the day hunted the animals, but hunting didn't make them die out. Scientists think that the mastodon and the mammoth vanished because the **glaciers** of the Ice Age destroyed much of the vegetation they relied on as food.

This woolly mammoth was painted as part of a museum exhibit. But primitive artists first painted these creatures on the walls of caves.
© Jonathan Blair/Corbis

Answer: b) elephants.

Inventing New Plants

Luther Burbank grew up on a farm in the United States. Although he went only to secondary school, he read Charles Darwin's ideas about how living things change over time. Burbank wanted to understand why different plants have different kinds of fruit and flowers and how they might be changed to grow better ones.

In the 1870s most people thought it wasn't possible to make new kinds of plants. But Burbank surprised them by creating hundreds of new varieties, including a white blackberry that was so clear, its seeds could be seen through its skin. Burbank grew a tomato on a potato vine and called it a 'pomato'. He combined a plum tree and an apricot tree to make a new fruit called a 'plumcot'.

Burbank produced many plants by 'grafting'. He took a small twig from one plant and put it into a cut he made on a different plant. The plant with roots controlled the size of the new plant, while the twig grew into branches with flowers and fruit. Sometimes he produced completely new kinds of plants by cross-pollination. He did this by putting **pollen** from the flowers of one type of plant onto the sticky part of the flowers of another type of plant.

Getting the new plants he wanted was not easy. The white blackberry took Burbank 65,000 attempts to get it right. And he spent eight years cross-pollinating different types of daisy to turn a small yellowish daisy into a tall snow-white flower with a yellow centre. The result was the famous Shasta daisy.

Burbank's work produced many useful plants. And his experiments added greatly to the understanding of how features pass from parents to offspring.

Benefitting today from Burbank's work with plants.
© Lynda Richardson/Corbis

DID YOU KNOW?

Luther Burbank developed more than 220 new varieties of trees, vegetables, fruits, flowers, and grasses.

SEARCH LIGHT

Find and correct the mistake in the following sentence: Rafting is a way of making a new plant by sticking a twig from one plant into a cut on another plant.

© Corbis

Answer: Grafting is a way of making a new plant by sticking a twig from one plant into a cut on another plant.

Discovering a New Kind of Science

The French scientist Marie Curie became the first woman to win the Nobel Prize - one of the greatest honours in the world. What's more, she was the first person ever to win the prize twice.

Marie Curie was born in Poland. She moved to France and studied at the great university known as the Sorbonne. She was one of the best students there. She worked very hard - often late into the night, sometimes eating little more than bread, butter, and tea.

She married Pierre Curie after completing her science and maths degree. Pierre was also a scientist, and the two worked together. Another scientist, named Henri Becquerel, had already discovered that certain types of material send out tiny 'bullets' of energy all the time. Marie Curie called this action 'radioactivity'.

These strange radioactive **particles** were far too small to be seen, but it was possible to take a kind of photograph of them. Marie Curie studied radioactivity and discovered two new **elements** that were radioactive: polonium and radium.

Over the years, Marie Curie's discoveries about radioactivity have proved extremely important in many ways. Radioactivity helps doctors identify and treat diseases. A major form of power generation based on nuclear energy has been developed, a process involving radioactivity. And in geology, radioactivity is used to determine the age of ancient rocks.

Marie Curie's entire life was spent working for science. She fell ill and eventually died because of working so closely with radioactive materials. She knew about the risk, but she felt her work was too important to stop. Marie Curie was awarded the Nobel Prize in 1903 for her work on radioactivity and in 1911 for discovering radium.

SEARCH LIGHT

True or false? Marie Curie's research led to her death.

DID YOU KNOW?
Not only did Marie Curie win the Nobel Prize twice, but her daughter and son-in-law, Irène and Frédéric Joliot-Curie, shared the Nobel Prize in 1935.

© Bettmann/Corbis

Answer: TRUE. Marie Curie's work with radioactive materials damaged her blood and caused her death.

The Theory of Evolution

All cultures tell a story about how life on Earth began. Most traditions and religions say that creation happened in a particular event. But what does science tell us? A scientist named Charles Darwin came up with a very different idea about the origin of humans and other creatures.

In 1831, at the age of 22, Darwin set out from England on a scientific expedition aboard a ship called the *Beagle*. He sailed to the coast of South America and the Pacific islands, including the Galapagos.

On the trip, Darwin studied many **species**, or groups, of plants and animals. He also studied fossils - rocks that carry imprints of ancient plants and animals. The fossils showed that plants and animals living on Earth long ago were different from the same types of plants and animals that lived in his own time. Darwin wondered why the old species had disappeared and the new species had developed.

After much thought, this is what Darwin decided. Living things must work hard for food and shelter, so only the ones that do this best will survive. Small individual strengths, such as being bigger or faster, can be the key to survival. And these strengths are passed on to the individuals' offspring. Helpful individual differences add up over time to make the whole species change, or evolve.

Darwin and his ideas being made fun of in a magazine.
© Archivo Iconographic/Corbis

© Bettmann/Corbis

This was Darwin's famous **theory** of **evolution**. He also believed that, over time, the same species living in different surroundings could evolve into two separate species.

Darwin published his theory in his books *On the Origin of Species* and *The Descent of Man*. He proposed that all living things, including humans, have slowly evolved from earlier species. Many people do not accept Darwin's theory. But it is still the most widely accepted scientific theory.

DID YOU KNOW?
A skull that may be from one of our earliest human ancestors was recently found in the Sahel region of Africa. The skull is between 6 million and 7 million years old, more than a million years older than any skulls found before.

SEARCH LIGHT

Fill in the gap: Darwin's theory of evolution says that species of living things _____ over time.

Answer: Darwin's theory of evolution says that species of living things change (or evolve) over time.

Get the inside story on gadgets and systems past and present

Technology
and Inventions

Technology and Inventions

TABLE OF CONTENTS

Before There Were Automobiles

Long ago, most people had to walk wherever they wanted to go on land. Later, when large animals began to be **domesticated,** some people rode on camels, horses, donkeys, oxen, and even elephants.

Then came the discovery of wheels. The people of Mesopotamia (now in Iraq) built wheeled carts nearly 5,000 years ago. But so far the earliest cart that has actually been found is one made later than those in Mesopotamia, by people in ancient Rome. It was simply a flat board. At first, people pulled carts themselves. Later, they trained animals to do this.

As people used more and more carts, they had to make roads on which the carts could travel easily. In Europe and North America, carts developed into great covered wagons and then into stagecoaches. Pulled by four or six fast horses, stagecoaches first bounced and rolled along the roads in the mid-1600s. They became an important method of public transport during the 19th century.

It wasn't until the steam engine was invented that a better means of transportation was developed. This was the railway train. Steam **locomotives** used steam pressure from boiling water to turn their wheels.

The first passenger train service began in England in 1825. Soon trains were carrying hundreds of thousands of people wherever iron tracks were laid.

The first motorcars were not built until the late 1890s. Some of the earliest were made in the United States and England, though they were slow and broke down a lot. They looked much like carts with fancy wheels. What most of us would recognize as a motorcar wouldn't come along for several more years.

SEARCH LIGHT

What were the first things used by people to get around?
a) their own feet
b) carts
c) donkeys

DID YOU KNOW?
In the days of stagecoaches, a 560-kilometre journey could take 36 hours and 24 changes of horses. Today it would take less than six hours and one tank of petrol.

Answer: a) their own feet

How Henry Ford Made the American Car

Henry Ford was born near Dearborn, Michigan, U.S., in July 1863. As a boy, he loved to play with watches, clocks, and machines - good experience for the person who would build the first affordable car.

Cars had already been built in Europe when Ford experimented with his first **vehicle** in 1899. It had wheels like a bicycle's and a petrol-powered engine that made it move. It was called a Quadricycle and had only two speeds and no reverse.

Within four years Ford had started the Ford Motor Company. His ideas about making cars would change history.

Car makers at the time used parts others had made and put them all together. Ford's company made each and every part that went into their cars. What's more, they made sure that each kind of part was exactly the same.

In 1908 Ford introduced the Model T car. This car worked well and was not costly. It was a big success, but the company couldn't make them quickly enough to satisfy Henry Ford.

In 1913 he started a large factory that made use of his most important idea: the assembly line. Instead of having workers go from car to car, the cars moved slowly down a line while workers stood in place adding parts to them. Each worker added a different part until a whole car was put together.

This meant more cars could be built more quickly at a lower cost. By 1918 half of all cars in the United States were Model Ts. Ford's company had become the largest automobile manufacturer in the world. And Ford had revolutionized the process of **manufacturing**.

SEARCH LIGHT

True or false? Henry Ford built the very first automobile.

DID YOU KNOW? Henry Ford is reported to have once said that his customers could get a Model T in 'any colour they like, as long as it's black'.

Henry Ford's first car was the Quadricycle, seen here with Ford driving. It had only two forward speeds and could not back up.
© Underwood & Underwood/Corbis

Answer: FALSE. Henry Ford built the first inexpensive automobile. Gottlieb Daimler, a German, gets credit for building the very first automobile.

The First Flights

From the earliest times people wanted to fly, but no one knew how. Some people thought it would help if their arms were more like bird wings. So they strapped large feathery wings to their arms. Not one left the ground. A few even tried machines with flapping wings, called 'ornithopters'. These didn't work either.

Then in 1799 a British scientist named Sir George Cayley wrote a book and drew pictures explaining how birds use their wings and the speed of the wind to fly. About a hundred years later, two American brothers named Orville and Wilbur Wright read Cayley's book. Although they were bicycle makers, they decided to build a flying machine.

The Wright brothers' machine, *Flyer I*, had the strong light wings of a **glider**, a petrol-powered engine, and two **propellers**. Then, from a list of places where strong winds blow, they selected the Kill Devil Hills near Kitty Hawk, North Carolina, U.S., as the site of their experiment.

In 1903 Orville, lying flat on the lower wing of *Flyer I*, flew a distance of 37 metres. That first flight lasted only 12 seconds. The next year the Wrights managed to fly their second 'aeroplane', *Flyer II*, nearly 5 kilometres over a period of 5 minutes and 4 seconds.

Soon Glenn Curtiss, another American bicycle maker, made a faster airplane called the '1909 type'. Not long after that Louis Blériot from France did something no one had tried before. He flew his plane across the English Channel. He was the first man to fly across the sea.

The age of flight had begun.

SEARCH LIGHT

What modern machine's name sounds a lot like 'ornithopter', the flapping-wing machine that people tried to fly?

DID YOU KNOW?
In 1986 Dick Rutan and Jeana Yeager made the first non-stop round-the-world flight in an airplane. They did the whole trip without refuelling.

The Wright brothers had read that wind was very important for flying. That's why they chose the windy hill in North Carolina to test their machines.
© Bettmann/Corbis

Answer: How about the 'helicopter'? The '-opter' part of both words means 'wing'. A helicopter's name means 'whirling wing'. An ornithopter's name means 'bird wing'.

221

From Rafts to Ocean Liners

Today's ocean liners are a popular way for people to get from one place to another and have a holiday on the way.
© Corbis

DID YOU KNOW?
In 1947 the Norwegian scientist Thor Heyerdahl and a small crew sailed across more than 8,000 kilometres of ocean on a balsawood raft called the *Kon-Tiki*. It was an experiment to see whether ancient Americans could have settled some Pacific islands.

We don't know exactly how the first transport over water happened. But it's not hard to imagine how it might have come about.

Long ago, people used anything that would float to move things across water, including bundles of reeds, large jars, and covered baskets.

Perhaps one day someone tied three or four logs together and made a raft. Maybe someone else hollowed out a log as a type of **canoe**. These log boats could be moved by people paddling with their hands. Later they might have used a stick or a pole to make their boat move faster.

SEARCH LIGHT

From each pair, pick the boat that was developed first:
a) raft or sailing boat
b) submarine or canoe
c) paddle steamer or rowing boat

Whoever put the first sail on a boat made a wonderful discovery. Sailing was faster and easier than paddling because it caught the wind and used it to move the boat.

Eventually, someone built a ship that used a sail and long paddles, called 'oars'. When there was little or no wind, the sailors rowed with the oars. In time, sailors learned to turn, or 'set', a sail to make the boat go in almost any direction they wanted.

Later, paddles were used in giant wheels that moved large boats through the water. A steam engine powered these paddle wheels, which were too heavy to turn by hand. Steamboats cruised rivers, lakes, and oceans all over the world.

Today, ships and boats use many different types of engine. Most ships use oil to **generate** power. Some submarines run on nuclear power. But on warm days, many people still enjoy travelling on water by paddling, sailing, and even rafting.

Answer: a) raft b) canoe c) rowing boat

Silent Stalkers of the Sea

SEARCH LIGHT

Fill in the gaps: Submarines need _____ that don't use up _____.

Because they are meant to spend most of their time underwater, submarines are designed and built quite differently from other ships.

Submarines must be airtight so that water can't get inside them when they **submerge**. They also need to have strong **hulls** because the pressure of seawater at great depths is strong enough to crush ships. And submarines need special engines that don't use air when they are underwater. Otherwise, they would quickly run out of air and shut down! So most modern subs are powered by electric batteries when they're submerged. Some are powered by nuclear energy.

Because a submarine is completely closed up, it must have special instruments to act as its eyes and ears underwater. A periscope is a viewing **device** that can be raised up out of the water to allow the submarine officers to see what is around them. Another special system, sonar, 'hears' what is under the water by sending out sound waves that bounce off everything in their path. These echoes send a sound-picture back to the sub.

But why build submarines in the first place? Well, submarines have been very useful in times of war. They can hide underwater and take enemy ships by surprise.

Submarines have peaceful uses too. Scientists use smaller submarines, called 'submersibles', to explore the huge ocean floors and the creatures that live there. People also use submersibles to search for sunken ships and lost treasure. The luxury liner *Titanic* was discovered and explored with a submersible 73 years after it sank in the Atlantic Ocean.

DID YOU KNOW?
The *Nautilus*, the first nuclear sub, was once caught by a fishing net. The fishing boat and its unhappy crew were towed for several kilometres before the situation was sorted out.

When a submarine travels above the water, officers can stand on top of the conning tower. This is the raised deck of the ship.
© George Hall/Corbis

Answer: Submarines need engines that don't use up air.

Turning Trees to Paper

The pages in your exercise book are made of paper that came from a factory. So are the pages of this book.

The factory got the paper from a paper mill. The mill probably made the paper from logs. And the logs were cut from trees that grew in a forest. Pine trees are often used to make paper.

If you visit a **traditional** paper mill, you will see people working at large noisy machines that peel bark off the logs and then cut the wood into smaller pieces. Other machines press and grind this wood into very tiny pieces that can be mashed together like potatoes. This gooey stuff is called 'wood **pulp**'.

After it is mixed with water, the pulp flows onto a screen where the water drains off, leaving a thin wet sheet of pulp.

Big hot rollers press and then dry this wet pulp as it moves along **conveyor belts**. At the end of the line, the dried pulp comes out as giant rolls of paper. These giant rolls are what the paper factories make into the products that you use every day, such as newspapers, paper towels, and the pages of books that you read.

Because we use so much paper, we must be careful how many trees we cut down to make it. Fortunately, nowadays, a lot of used paper can be remade into new paper by **recycling**. You can help save trees by recycling the magazines, newspapers, and other paper that you use in school and at home.

> **DID YOU KNOW?**
> According to Chinese historical records, the first paper was made from tree bark, hemp (a plant used to make rope), rags, and fishing nets.

SEARCH LIGHT

Starting with a tree in a forest, arrange these mixed-up steps in the order they should happen in papermaking: (*Start*) tree → chop down tree, dry, peel bark, roll out sheets, cut up wood, press flat, grind into pulp

In a paper mill like this, the rolls of paper are sometimes as big as the trees they are made from.
© Philip Gould/Corbis

Answer: tree → chop down tree → peel bark → cut up wood → grind into pulp → press flat → dry → roll out sheets

Gutenberg's Gift

Before about 550 years ago, very few people owned books. In fact, there weren't many books to own. In those days, most books had to be written out by hand. Some books were printed by using wooden blocks with the letters of an entire page hand-carved into each block. The carved side of the block was dipped in ink and pressed onto paper. Both handwritten and woodblock-printed books took a lot of time, energy, and money. Only rich people could afford to buy them.

Then, in the 1450s, a man in Germany named Johannes Gutenberg had an idea for printing books faster.

First, he produced small blocks of metal with one raised backwards-facing letter on each block. These blocks with their raised letters were called 'type'. He then spelled out words and sentences by lining up the individual pieces of type in holders.

The second part of his invention was the printing press. This was basically a 'bed' in which the lines of type could be laid out to create a page. When he inked the lines of type and then used a large plate to press them against a sheet of paper, lines of words were printed on the paper.

Gutenberg's movable type and printing press, unlike carved woodblocks, meant that he could take his lines apart and reuse the letters. Once he had carved enough sets of individual letters, he didn't have to carve new ones to make new pages.

The Bible was one of the earliest books printed by using Gutenberg's movable type. By 1500 the printing presses of Europe had produced about 6 million books!

> **DID YOU KNOW?**
> The Chinese actually invented a kind of movable type 400 years before Gutenberg. But Chinese writing uses thousands of characters and they didn't invent a press, so the invention wasn't a success.

SEARCH LIGHT

Why did Gutenberg make the letters on individual pieces of type face backwards? (Hint: Think about looking at writing in a mirror.)

The artist had to imagine Gutenberg and his first page of print. But the printing press in the background is a fairly accurate image of what the inventor worked with.

© Bettmann/Corbis

Answer: When the letters face backwards on the blocks, they come out facing forwards on the paper. Try it yourself!

Books to Touch

More than 175 years ago in France, a young Louis Braille thought of a way to help blind people read and write. He himself could not see. He had hurt his eyes when he was just 3 years old. He was playing with his father's tools, and one of them blinded him forever.

Fortunately, Louis was a clever child. When he was 10 years old, he won a **scholarship** to the National Institute for Blind Children in Paris.

At the school Louis heard about how Captain Barbier, an army officer, had invented a system of writing that used dots. It was called 'night writing', and it helped soldiers read messages in the dark. These messages were of small bump-like dots pressed on a sheet of paper. The dots were easy to make and could be felt quickly.

Louis decided to use similar dots to make an alphabet for the blind. It was slow to be accepted but eventually was a great success. His alphabet used 63 different dot patterns to represent letters, numbers, punctuation, and several other useful signs. People could even learn to read music by feeling dots.

Today blind people all over the world can learn the Braille alphabet. Look at these dots:

Louis Braille invented his Braille alphabet when he was 15. At that age, how many years had he been blind?

In an actual Braille book, the tips of your fingers would be able to cover each small group of dots.

Can you guess what this pattern of dot letters spells?

It spells the words 'I can read'.

DID YOU KNOW?
On their Web site, the American Foundation for the Blind has a great area where you can learn Braille yourself. Go to http://afb.org and click on 'Braille Bug'.

Louis Braille completed his raised-dot alphabet for the blind when he was only 15 years old. People can even learn to read music through the Braille system.
Will and Deni McIntyre/Photo Researchers, Inc.

Answer: Louis Braille had been blind for 12 years when he invented his alphabet.

Eyes That Hear, Speech That's Seen

Mary: 'Can you come to the shop with me?'

Sara: 'I'll ask my mother'.

If Mary and Sara were like most girls you know, their conversation would not be unusual. But Mary and Sara are deaf, which means that they can't hear. However, they can understand each other.

How?

Well, one way that people who are deaf communicate is by using sign language. Sign language replaces spoken words with finger and

Deaf child learning to speak using touch, sight, and imitation.
© Nathan Benn/Corbis

hand movements, **gestures**, and facial expressions. People using sign language can actually talk faster than if they were speaking out loud.

Another way people who are deaf may communicate is through lip-reading. People who lip-read have learned to recognize spoken words by reading the shapes and movements speakers make with their lips, mouths, and tongues. Lip-readers usually speak out loud themselves even though they can't hear what others say.

Some people who are deaf use hearing aids or cochlear **implants** to help them hear the sounds and words that others hear. (The cochlea is part of the ear.) Hearing aids usually fit outside the ear and make sounds louder. Cochlear implants are inside the ear and use electrical signals to imitate sounds for the brain. Often children and adults with hearing aids or implants have lessons to learn to speak as hearing people do.

There are many schools for children who are deaf or hearing-**impaired**. There they may learn all or some of the skills of lip-reading, sign language, **oral** speech, and the use of hearing aids and implants. Older students may attend Gallaudet University in Washington, D.C., U.S., a university especially for people who are deaf.

DID YOU KNOW?
Some famous people have been deaf: Juliette Gordon Low, who founded the Girl Scouts; 1995 Miss America Heather Whitestone; and LeRoy Colombo, who, as a lifeguard, saved 907 people.

SEARCH LIGHT

This article mentions several ways in which people who are deaf can know what another person is saying. One is lip-reading. What is one of the others?

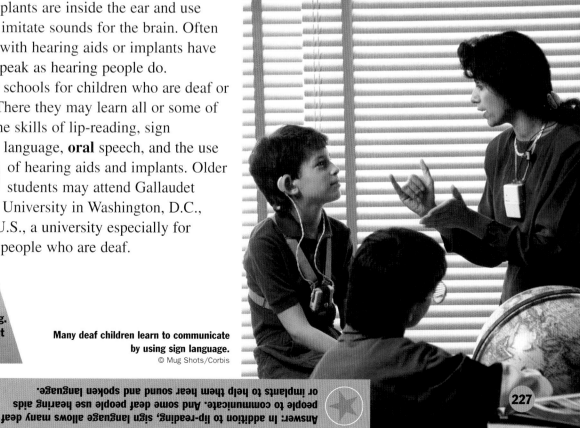

Many deaf children learn to communicate by using sign language.
© Mug Shots/Corbis

Answer: In addition to lip-reading, sign language allows many deaf people to communicate. And some deaf people use hearing aids or implants to help them hear sound and spoken language.

227

Staying in
Touch

The telephone is the most popular communication **device** of all time.

Alexander Graham Bell invented the telephone in 1876. In 11 years there were more than 150,000 telephones in the United States and 26,000 in the United Kingdom. In 2001 there were an estimated 1,400,000,000 telephones worldwide.

Traditional telephones have three main parts: a **transmitter**, a receiver, and a dialler. There is also a switch hook, which hangs up and disconnects the call.

When you speak into the phone, the transmitter changes the sound of your voice into an electrical signal. The transmitter is basically a tiny **microphone** in the mouthpiece. On the other end of the call, the receiver in the listener's earpiece changes that electrical signal back into sound. The receiver is a tiny vibrating disk, and the electrical signal vibrates the disk to make the sounds of the caller's voice.

When you make a call, the phone's dialler sends a series of clicks or tones to a switching office. On a rotating dial phone, dialling the number 3 causes three clicks to interrupt the normal sound on the line (the dial tone). On a touchtone phone, a pushed number interrupts the dial tone with a new sound. These interruptions are a form of code. The telephone exchange 'reads' the code and sends the call to the right telephone receiver.

Since the 1990s, mobile phones have become hugely popular worldwide. Mobile phones connect with small transmitter-receivers that each control an area, or 'cell'. As a person moves from one cell to the next, the mobile phone switches the signal it receives to the new cell.

SEARCH LIGHT

A telephone receiver is a
a) vibrating disk.
b) dial tone.
c) tiny microphone.

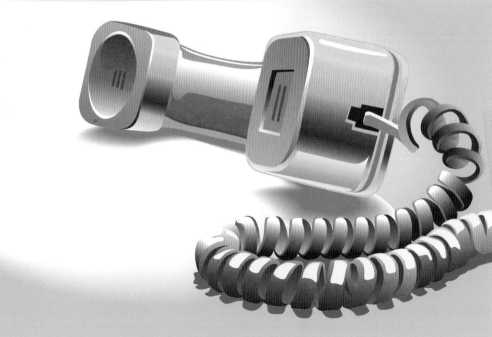

DID YOU KNOW?
Deaf and hard-of-hearing people can use telephone-like devices that turn their typed message into sound and the other person's voice into type. One such device is a TTY (for *TeleTYpes*), and another is a TDD (Telecommunications Device for the Deaf).

Answer: a) vibrating disk.

The Machines
That Solve Problems

The first computers were expensive room-sized machines that only business and government offices could afford. Today most computers are smaller, and many people have one in their own home or school. These 'personal computers' (PCs) first appeared in the mid-1970s.

A Palm Pilot, one of the tiny but powerful modern computers.
© RNT Productions/Corbis

Find and correct the mistake in the following sentence: A set of instructions that a computer uses to solve problems and do work is called 'memory'.

Computers can find the answers to many maths problems and can simplify work that has many steps and would otherwise take lots of time. They can do this because they can remember, in order, the individual steps of even long and complicated instructions.

The sets of instructions for computers are called 'programs' or 'software'. A computer's brain is its microprocessor - a tiny electronic **device** that reads and carries out the program's instructions.

Because they are programmed in advance, you can use computers to solve maths problems, remember facts, and play games. Computers can also help you draw, write essays, and make your own greeting cards.

DID YOU KNOW?
It was a weaving machine, a loom, that led to the first computers. At one time, looms used punched cards to set weaving patterns. Early computers used this system of coding in their 'programming languages'.

Computers need two kinds of memory. 'Main memory' is what handles the information that the computer is using as it is doing its work. Main memory operates amazingly fast and powerfully to speed up a computer's work. The second kind of computer memory is **storage** for its programs and for the results of its operations. The most important storage space is on the computer's hard drive, or hard disk. CD-ROMs and floppy disks are removable storage devices.

Since 1990 very small computers have been developed. Today there are laptop or notebook computers, as well as handheld computers. Handheld computers weigh only a few grams, but they can handle more **data** more quickly than most of the first giant computers.

© Ariel Skelley/Corbis

Answer: A set of instructions that a computer uses to solve problems and do work is called a 'program' [or 'software'].

229

Network of People

You can do things with your friends and family even when they are thousands of kilometres away simply by sitting at your computer. The Internet makes this possible.

As the name suggests, the Internet is like a large net whose every strand connects to a different computer. It is an international web linking millions of computer users around the world. Together with the World Wide Web (WWW, or Web), it is used for sending and receiving e-mail and for sharing information on almost any topic.

The Web is an enormous electronic library from which anyone connected to the Internet can receive information. It is organised into tens of millions of sites, each identified by an electronic address called the 'uniform resource locator' (URL). The Web allows you to view photographs and films, listen to songs and hear people speak, and find out about **countless** different things you never knew before.

The Internet has come a long way since 1969, when it all began. At that time the U.S. Defense Department was testing **methods** of making their computers survive a military attack. Soon their networks were extended to various research computers around the United States and then to countries around the world.

By early 1990 the Internet and the World Wide Web had entered homes. Today many people wonder how they ever managed without the Internet.

SEARCH LIGHT

The Internet
is more than
a) 10 years old.
b) 20 years old.
c) 30 years old.

DID YOU KNOW?
Radio took about 38 years to gain 50 million listeners. TV took about 13 years to have 50 million viewers. The Internet took only 4 years to get 50 million users.

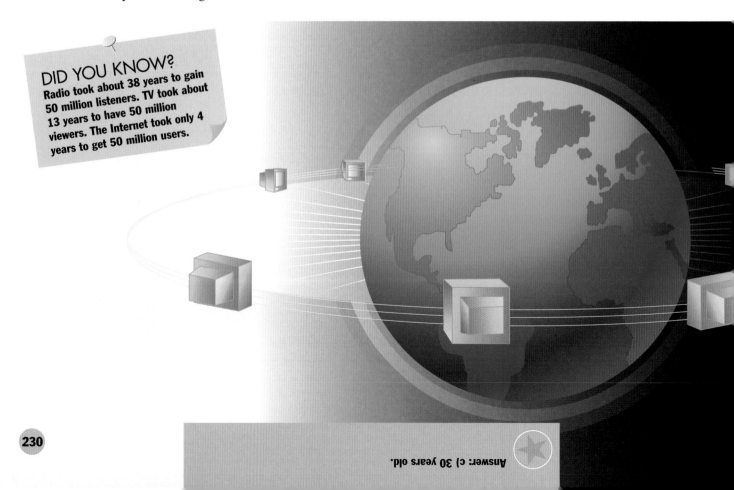

Answer: c) 30 years old.

Cables, Fuses, Wires, and Energy

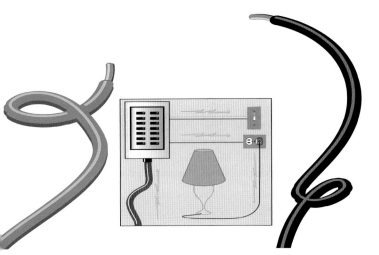

SEARCH LIGHT

Fill in
the gaps:
To prevent
shocks, electric
wires should be
wrapped with
_____ or _____.

You can't see electricity, but you know it's there when you watch an electric light go on, hear the telephone ring, or watch the television.

Electricity comes into your house through thick wires called 'cables'. These join a **fuse** box. From the fuse box run all the electric wires for your house. Each wire connects to a plug socket or a switch. From there, electricity passes along the plugs and leads that go into an appliance, lamp, or television.

Electricity moves easily along things made of metal, such as silver, copper, or iron. That's why copper wires are used to carry the electricity. Electricity doesn't pass through rubber or plastic. That's why wires carrying electricity are usually coated with rubber or plastic.

This coating is important, because electricity will flow wherever it can. When it is loose, it can be very dangerous. It can cause shocks, start fires, or even kill.

Did you know that electricity can be used to make a magnet?

If a wire is wound into a coil and wrapped around a piece of iron, the iron will become a magnet when electricity is sent through the coil. The iron will then attract other things made of iron and steel. Such a magnet is called an 'electromagnet'.

As soon as the electricity is turned off, the electromagnet isn't a magnet anymore. If the magnet is holding something when the electricity is turned off, that thing will drop.

DID YOU KNOW?
Although Thomas Edison is better known for his light bulb, films, and phonograph, his first invention was an electric voting machine.

Energy in the Air

Wind power has been used for many hundreds of years. Its energy has filled the sails of ships and powered machines that grind grain, pump water, drain marshes, saw wood, and make paper. Wind provides a clean and endless source of energy.

In the 1890s windmills in Denmark became the first to use wind power to generate electricity. But it took the major energy crisis of the 1970s to focus people's thoughts seriously again on using wind energy to produce electricity.

Windmills provide power to make electricity when their sails are turned by wind blowing against them. Originally, the sails were long narrow sheets of canvas stretched over a wooden frame. Later windmills used different materials and designs. Usually there are four sails shaped like large blades.

When the sails turn, the axle they are attached to turns as well, much as car wheels turn on their axles. The axle causes various **gears** to turn, which then causes a large crankshaft to turn. The crankshaft is a long pole running along the length of the windmill tower. At its other end the crankshaft is attached to a generator, a motor that can make and store electricity. So when the wind blows, the generator runs - making electricity.

Today, modern efficient wind machines called 'wind turbines' are used to generate electricity. These machines have from one to four blades and operate at high speeds. The first of these wind turbines appeared in the mid-1990s.

Traditional windmills in the Netherlands.
© ML Sinibaldi/Corbis

SEARCH LIGHT

Which of the following are advantages of wind power?
It's inexpensive.
It works everywhere.
It's clean.
It's endless.

DID YOU KNOW?
The total wind power of our atmosphere, at any one time, is estimated to be 3.6 billion kilowatts. That's enough energy to light 36 billion light bulbs all at once.

Hundreds of wind turbines like these in Denmark are set up on 'wind farms' in constantly windy areas to produce large amounts of electricity.
© Adam Woolfitt/Corbis

Answer: Wind power is inexpensive, clean, and endless. Unfortunately, it's not a usable way to generate power in areas with little or no wind.

Energy from Heat

SEARCH LIGHT

Energy means power - the power to do work. And thermal, or heat, energy can do a lot of work. When heat is applied to water, for instance, it makes the water boil. Boiling water then changes to vapour, or steam, which can apply great force as it escapes a container. Large quantities of steam powered the earliest train engines.

Fill in the gap: When steam escapes, it gives a mighty push. This push is so strong that it was used to move the early _____ engines.

The most important source of thermal energy for our Earth is the Sun's rays. This '**solar** energy' is used to heat houses, water, and, in some countries, ovens used for cooking. Solar power can even be **converted** to electricity and stored for later use.

To people, the second most important source of thermal energy is the store of natural fuels on and in the Earth. When these fuels (mainly coal, oil, gas, and wood) are burned, they produce heat. This heat can be used for warmth, made to power a machine directly, or converted into electricity. For example, a car engine burns petroleum (an oil product) for direct thermal power. In some areas, coal is burned to produce the electricity that powers people's homes.

(Top) Sun's heat focussed and used for cooking on solar oven by Tibetan monk. (Bottom) Locomotive fireman shovels coal to burn, boiling water to produce steam power.

DID YOU KNOW?
Hot-air ballooning, a popular sport in the 1960s, relies on thermal power. A gas burner heats air that is then fed into a large airtight balloon. And because hot air rises, the balloon rises up and away - carrying people or cargo along in its basket or container.

In a very few parts of the world, an interesting third form of heat energy comes from 'living' heat inside the Earth itself. This 'geothermal energy' comes from such sources as natural hot springs and the heat of active volcanoes ('geo' means 'earth'). Naturally escaping steam and hot water are used to heat and power homes and businesses in Reykjavik, Iceland. And though volcanoes are mostly too hot to tap directly, worldwide experiments continue as other major fuel supplies **dwindle**.

The intense power of the Earth's heat energy sometimes bursts into geysers - hot springs that send roaring columns of steam and boiling water high above the surface. This geyser is the famous Old Faithful in Yellowstone National Park in Wyoming, U.S.

Answer: When steam escapes, it gives a mighty push. This push is so strong that it was used to move the early train engines.

Streams of Energy

We have only to hear the roar of a waterfall to guess at the power of water. Its force is also clear anytime we see the damage caused by floods. But the water power can be extremely useful as well as destructive.

One excellent aspect of water power is that the water can be reused. Unlike such fuels as coal and oil, water does not get used up when **harnessed** for power. And it doesn't pollute the air either.

The power of water lies not in the water itself but in the flow of water. The power produced by water depends upon the water's weight and its height of fall, called 'head'. Generally, the faster that water moves, the more power it can generate. That's why water flowing from a higher place to a lower place, as a waterfall does, can produce so much energy.

© Hubert Stadler/Corbis

Since ancient times people have used the energy of water to grind wheat and other grains. They first **devised** the waterwheel, a wheel with paddles around its rim. As the photograph shows, the wheel was mounted on a frame over a river. The flowing water striking the blades turned the wheel.

Later, larger waterwheels were used to run machines in factories. They were not very reliable, however. Floodwaters could create too much power, whereas long rainless periods left the factories without any power at all.

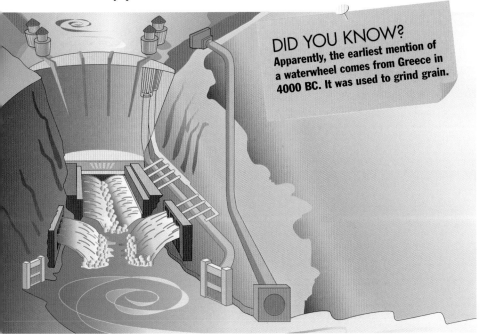

DID YOU KNOW?
Apparently, the earliest mention of a waterwheel comes from Greece in 4000 BC. It was used to grind grain.

Today, streamlined metal waterwheels called 'turbines' help produce electricity. The electricity produced by water is called 'hydroelectric power' ('hydro' means 'water'). Enormous dams, like the one pictured here, provide this **superior** source of electricity.

SEARCH LIGHT

Fill in the gap:
Unlike petrol or coal, water power doesn't cause air _____.

Answer: Unlike petrol or coal, water power doesn't cause air pollution.

Big Energy from a Small Source

All **matter** is made up of tiny particles called 'molecules'. In turn, all molecules are made up of even tinier particles called 'atoms'.

The central part of an atom is called a 'nucleus'. When the nucleus splits in two, it produces enormous energy. This breaking apart is called 'nuclear fission'. If two nuclei join and form a bigger nucleus - in a process called 'nuclear fusion' - even more energy is produced.

The nuclear energy released from fission and fusion is called 'radiation'. Radiation - the process of giving off **rays** - is a powerful spreading of heat, light, sound, or even invisible beams.

One of the first uses of nuclear energy was to build deadly weapons. Atomic bombs built during World War II and dropped on Hiroshima and Nagasaki in Japan largely destroyed those cities and killed many thousands of people. People worldwide now try to make sure that this will never happen again.

Today, however, nuclear energy has many helpful uses. Nuclear power plants produce low-cost electricity. Nuclear energy also fuels submarines. And it has also allowed doctors to see more details inside the body than ever before.

But nuclear energy has its **drawbacks**. Nuclear energy produces nuclear waste. Living beings exposed to the waste can suffer from radiation poisoning. They may experience damaged blood and organs, effects that can be deadly. And the radiation can remain active for thousands of years wherever nuclear waste is thrown away.

Unfortunately, no country has yet discovered the perfect way to store nuclear waste. But the benefits make it worthwhile to keep trying.

SEARCH LIGHT

What is the main problem with nuclear energy?

DID YOU KNOW?
We all actually enjoy the benefits of nuclear energy every day. The Sun, like all stars, is simply a giant nuclear power plant. Its heat and light are the products of nuclear energy.

Nuclear power plant on the coast of California, U.S.
© Galen Rowell/Corbis

Answer: Nuclear energy produces poisonous waste that remains deadly for generations. No one has yet come up with a safe and highly reliable way to get rid of the waste.

235

From the Ground
to the Petrol Station

SEARCH LIGHT

Up comes the thick black oil from the oil well and...out pours the petrol into your family's car. But how does the oil become fuel for vehicles?

Petroleum, or crude oil, is oil as it is found deep within the Earth. This raw form has many unwanted substances in it that must eventually be removed in a process called 'refining'.

From wells drilled deep into the ground, the oil often goes through long underground pipelines. There are pipelines in some very surprising places - under streets, mountains, deserts, frozen lands, and even lakes and rivers.

Pumping stations keep the thick oil moving through the pipes. Each station gives the oil enough of a push for it to reach the next station. There are pumping stations built all along the pipelines. Here and there along the pipelines, oil is directed into smaller pipes that take it to huge storage tanks.

Put the different stages in the correct order, beginning with the oil well. (Start) oil well → pipelines, petrol station, pipelines, refinery, storage tank, pumping station

From the storage tanks, the oil goes to a **refinery**, where it is heated until it is very hot. The hot oil is separated into many different substances. The heavy part that settles down at the bottom is used for road building. Other parts become machine oils and waxes. **Paraffin** and petrol also separate as the oil is heated. Finally, the lightest parts of the oil - cooking gas and other types of gas - are collected.

From the refineries, more pipelines carry oil to round storage tanks in tank farms. Petrol tankers fill up at the storage tanks and take the fuel to petrol stations, where people can fill the tanks in their cars.

DID YOU KNOW?
The trans-Alaska pipeline carries 88,000 barrels of oil every hour. The oil makes a 1,290-kilometre journey to the port town of Valdez in Alaska.

Answer: oil well → pipelines → pumping station → storage tank → refinery → pipelines → petrol station

Harming Our Environment

Have you ever seen black smoke pouring out of factory chimneys, turning the sky a dirty grey colour? This is air pollution. Cars, lorries, buses, and even lawnmowers release gases and particles that pollute the air too. Smoke from fires and barbeques also pollutes the air.

Land pollution, water pollution, and even noise pollution are also big problems. Factories and ordinary people may thoughtlessly dump rubbish and **waste** on land or in water. And when farm chemicals that kill insect pests or help crops grow sink into the ground and water, they pollute too. And noise pollution is created by loud machines and honking horns.

Ocean life isn't safe from pollution. The picture you see here shows a crew cleaning up a polluted seashore after an oil spill. Ships carrying petroleum sometimes have accidents, and their oil spills into the ocean.

Dirty air, land, and water are dangerous. Dirty air, or **smog**, is hard to breathe and makes people and animals sick. Dirty water makes people and animals sick when they drink it or wash or live in it. It also kills plants. If land takes in too much waste, nothing will grow on it and it becomes unfit to live on.

Stopping pollution isn't easy. Most people find it hard to change the way they live, even if they want to. And governments and big companies find it even harder to change, since the changes are often unpopular or expensive.

Even small changes help, however. Reusing things instead of throwing them away helps. Using less water every day helps. So does **recycling**. And perhaps in the future people will use cleaner forms of energy, such as wind power and solar energy.

SEARCH LIGHT

Match each item to the kind of pollution it creates.

litter	air
smog	land
oil spill	noise
car honking	water

© Chinch Gryniewicz—Ecoscene/Corbis

DID YOU KNOW?
It's estimated that the energy saved by recycling just one glass bottle would light up a light bulb for four hours.

Answer: litter = land   smog = air
oil spill = water   car honking = noise

Making Cloth

'**S**hu-dul-ig! Shu-dul-og!'

The shuttle in this weaver's left hand flies back and forth, carrying its thread.

A shuttle is part of a loom, a machine that makes cloth. Cloth is composed of threads crisscrossing each other.

'Warp' threads run up and down lengthwise on the loom. The shuttle carries the 'weft' thread back and forth, passing it over and under the sets of warp thread. This is how simple cloth like muslin is woven. Making patterned and other complicated cloth is a more complex weaving process.

The threads for weaving cloth are made of fibres - thin, wispy strands often tangled together. Some fibres come from animals, some from plants, and some from synthetic (artificial) sources. Fine silk fibres come from the cocoon of a silkworm - actually the caterpillar stage of a moth. People learned to spin fibres into threads a very long time ago.

The most commonly used animal fibre is wool. Most wool is the hair of sheep, but some comes from goats, camels, llamas, and several other animals. Woollen cloth keeps you nice and warm when it's cold outside.

Cotton is a plant fibre. Some cotton fibres are so thin that just about half a kilo of them can be spun into a thread about 160 kilometres long! Work clothing and summer clothes are often made of cotton.

Fine silk cloth is shiny and smooth. It is more expensive than cotton because silkworms need a lot of care. And each silkworm makes only a small amount of silk.

Today, weaving by hand has become mostly a specialized **craft**. As with much other manufacturing, modern cloth is usually produced by machines.

SEARCH LIGHT

Which of the following descriptions matches the term 'weft'?
a) cross threads
b) up-and-down threads
c) weaving machine
d) source of silk

DID YOU KNOW?
The strongest piece of weaving anywhere is a spider web. One strand of spider silk is thought to be stronger than an equal-sized piece of steel.

© Dave Bartruff/Corbis

Answer: a) cross threads

Charting the Year

A calendar, like a clock, provides a way to count time - though calendars count days and months rather than minutes and hours. The modern calendar has 12 months of 30 or 31 days each (February has 28, sometimes 29). The calendar year has 365 days, which is about how long it takes the Earth to circle the Sun once. That makes it a **solar** calendar.

Today's calendar, with a few changes, has been in use since 1582. Pope Gregory XIII had it designed to correct errors in the previous calendar. For this reason it is called the 'Gregorian calendar'.

The oldest calendars were used to work out when to plant, harvest, and store crops. These were often '**lunar** calendars', based on the number of days it took the Moon to appear full and then **dwindle** away again.

The traditional Chinese calendar is a lunar calendar. It has 354 days, with months of either 29 or 30 days.

Many calendars have religious origins. In Central and South America, the ancient Aztec and Mayan calendars marked **ritual** days and celebrations. Jews, Muslims, and Hindus have religious calendars - each with a different number of days and months.

All these calendars have one thing in common: they're wrong. None of them measures the Earth's yearlong journey around the Sun precisely. Extra days must be added to keep the count in step with the actual seasons. We add an extra day to February every four years. (Actually, even our corrections are wrong. Once every 400 years we *don't* add that day.) But if we didn't make some kind of correction, we'd eventually have New Year's Eve in the middle of the year!

Jewish calendar (in Hebrew) from the 1800s.
© Archivo Iconografico, S.A./Corbis

DID YOU KNOW?
The Chinese calendar names each year for one of 12 animals. In order, these are: rat, ox, tiger, hare, dragon, snake, horse, sheep, monkey, fowl, dog, and pig. The year 2003 is the Year of the Sheep (or Ram), 2004 the Year of the Monkey, and so on.

SEARCH LIGHT

What was probably the earliest use for calendars?

This ancient Aztec calendar stone weighs about 25 tons. Its central image of the Aztec sun god, Tonatiuh, indicates the important role religion plays in how major civilizations measure time.
© Randy Faris/Corbis

Answer: The earliest calendars were likely used to tell the right time to plant and harvest crops.

Understanding Size and Distance

SEARCH LIGHT

Guess which unit of measure was originally defined as equal to 'an average throwing stone'.
a) a pound
b) a cup
c) an inch

How far away from you is the nearest chair? You can make your own measurement to find out how many shoes away the chair is.

Stand up where you are and face the chair. Count 'one' for your right shoe. Now place the heel of your left shoe against the toe of your right shoe and count 'two'. Continue stepping, heel-to-toe, right then left, counting each shoe length, until you get to the chair.

Centuries ago, people did just what you are doing now. They used parts of the body to measure things. An inch was about the width of a man's thumb. A foot was the length of his foot. A yard was the distance from the tip of his nose to the end of his thumb when his arm was stretched out. But since everyone's thumbs, feet, and arms were different sizes, so were everyone's inches, feet, and yards!

Finally, in the 1800s, all these terms were standardised - that is, everyone in England agreed on a specific definition for each one. They became part of the English system of measurement, called the British **Imperial** System.

We also use another system, called the 'metric system'. This measures in centimetres and metres, grams and kilograms, and litres. All these measurements can be multiplied or divided by 10. Fortunately, most of the world accepts the metric system or the Imperial system as the **standard** of measurement. So, we know today that one measurement will mean the same thing, no matter where it is used or who's doing the measuring.

DID YOU KNOW?
A NASA probe to Mars ended up crashing because the two teams of scientists working on it used different measurement systems. One team used metric and the other used the Imperial system, so directions given to the probe sent it too close to the planet.

Answer: a) a pound. Though people agreed on a pound as the weight of 'an average throwing stone,' there were actually as many different 'pounds' as there were people!

Drawing with Light

DID YOU KNOW?
The first photograph - a farmhouse with some fruit trees - was taken in about 1826 by a French inventor, Joseph Nicéphore Niépce.

The word 'photography' comes from two ancient Greek words: *photo*, for 'light', and *graph*, for 'writing' or 'drawing'.

Photography, the process of taking pictures, requires a camera. But a camera may be any dark lightproof box with a small opening at one end that lets in light. Most cameras have glass **lenses** to help focus the light into the back of the box on the section that holds the film.

Cameras work basically as our eyes do. Light enters the front and shines a picture on the back.

In your eye, light enters through an opening called the 'pupil'. The camera's opening is its aperture. Your iris controls how much light enters your eye. The camera's shutter does the same. In eyes and in most cameras, the light then passes through a lens. In your eye, the picture is produced on the retina, the back lining of the eye. In a camera, the film receives and captures the image.

Photographic film is special material that has been treated with chemicals to make it **sensitive** to light. Light shining on film changes the film's chemical makeup. Depending on how much light shines on each part of the film, different shades or colours result.

Finally, in photography, developing the film creates the photograph. Film that has been exposed to light is processed with chemicals that **fix** the image on special paper.

Today, digital cameras don't use film. Instead, they translate the image into numbers recorded on a disk inside the camera. A personal computer decodes these numbers and displays a picture.

SEARCH LIGHT

Match the parts of the camera to the similar parts of an eye:

1. pupil   a) lens
2. iris   b) film
3. lens   c) shutter
4. retina   d) aperture

Answer: 1d; 2c; 3a; 4b

Photos That Move

SEARCH LIGHT

True or false? Films are really just a long string of photographs.

Sitting in a darkened cinema, caught up in the adventures of Harry Potter and Hermione Granger, you might find it difficult to believe that you're watching a series of still photographs. These still photos are projected onto the screen so fast, one after another, that you're tricked into seeing movement. This is why early on they were called 'motion pictures' or 'movies'.

DID YOU KNOW?
When a system that added sound to silent films was invented, the major film companies thought it would be a big failure. One small company, Warner Brothers, thought it might be interesting and soon produced the first 'talking pictures'.

Film for shooting cinema comes in long wound **spools** or **cartridges**. The film takes pictures at either 18 or 24 shots per second. Sometimes there are three or four cameras that shoot a scene from different angles. Sound is recorded at the same time but with separate equipment.

Later, the film is **edited** by cutting out parts that the director doesn't want. The parts being kept are then put together to tell the story. The finished film, with the sound and the pictures joined together, is shown as a continuous piece.

Film-making is a long and complicated process, involving many people. The actors are the most visible, but there are many others as well. The director has total control over how the story is filmed. A whole crew of people help with costumes, choreography, lighting, sound, camera operations, special effects, and the actors' makeup and hairstyles.

After the film has been shot, there are different people to edit it and other people who advertise the movie. Finally, the film reaches the cinemas. There you buy your popcorn or other refreshments and settle into your seat to enjoy the magic world of the finished film.

Answer: **TRUE. When the string of photos is flashed by quickly, the pictures appear to move.**

Thank You, Mr Marconi

Before there was television, people got much of their news and entertainment from the radio. And many still do!

Invention of the radio began in 1896 when the Italian scientist Guglielmo Marconi **patented** a wireless **telegraph** process. Marconi knew that energy can travel in invisible waves through the air and that these waves can be captured electronically to send and receive signals. His invention allowed people to send messages to each other over great distances without having to be connected by wires.

> **DID YOU KNOW?**
> On 30 October 1938, the eve of Halloween, actor-director Orson Welles's radio drama *The War of the Worlds* accidentally convinced many American listeners that Earth was being invaded by Martians!

A Marconi wireless telegraph set (1912), the 'parent' of the voice-transmitting radio.
© Underwood & Underwood/Corbis

Marconi and others added to his invention, working out how to add sound to these messages to make the first radios. These were used simply for sending and receiving messages. During World War I the armed forces used radios for this purpose. It was after the war that radio became popular as a means of entertainment.

During the 1920s radio stations were set up all over the world. In the early days, most of the radio programmes gave news or **broadcast** lectures and some music. As more and more people started to listen to the radio, more popular entertainment programmes were added. These included comedies, dramas, game shows, mysteries, soap operas, and shows for children.

Radio shows remained very popular until the 1950s. That's when television began to catch on. As it happens, television actually works in the same basic ways that radio does! It uses special equipment to send and receive pictures and sound in the form of electronic signals.

Today, radio **technology** is used in many ways. Cordless telephones, mobile phones, and garage-door openers all use radio technology. And radio entertainment programmes are still going strong.

SEARCH LIGHT

Fill in the gap: After World War I, radio developed from a two-way communication tool into a popular instrument for _____.

Guglielmo Marconi, seen here in 1922, received the 1909 Nobel Prize for Physics for his development of a way to send electronic signals without using wires.
© Bettmann/Corbis

Answer: After World War I, radio developed from a two-way communication tool into a popular instrument for entertainment.

243

The World in a Box

The British Broadcasting Corporation (BBC) offered the first public television (TV) programming in 1936. But World War II stalled the development and popularity of the new invention.

At first, people preferred radio to the small, fuzzy black and white pictures and poor sound of early TV. Very few people could even receive the programmes. In the United States, when the 1947 World Series of baseball was shown on TV, many Americans watched and afterward decided to buy TV sets. The turning point in Great Britain came with the televised coronation of Queen Elizabeth II in 1953.

The first TV programmes - mostly news reports, comedies, variety shows, soap operas, and dramas - were based on popular radio shows. Gradually, detective programmes, game shows, sports, films, and children's programmes joined the line-up.

In some countries, independent businesses called 'networks' - groups of stations linked together - choose TV programming and make money by selling advertising time. In other countries, people buy a TV and radio licence, which helps pay for government-sponsored programming. Another system, called 'cable TV', often sells subscriptions that allow viewers to watch their shows.

Broadcast TV works much as radio does. Special equipment changes images and sound into electrical signals. These signals are sent through the air and are received by individual **aerials**, which pass the signals on to the TV sets. There they are read and changed back into images and sound.

The TV technology keeps changing. Colour TV became popular in the mid-1960s, and cable TV and videocassette recorders (VCRs) spread during the '80s. Today, advances such as digital videodiscs (DVDs), high-definition TV, and satellite dishes provide even better picture and sound.

Earth-orbiting satellites have improved TV broadcasting. In fact, the only things that haven't changed much are the kinds of shows people watch and enjoy!

Big-screen TV and video recording have made the viewing experience very different from TV's early days. Now we can watch ourselves on TV!
© Jose Luis Pelaez, Inc./Corbis

DID YOU KNOW?

All the first television shows were live. You saw everything as it was happening, and if people made mistakes, you saw those, too.

Answer: TRUE. Early TV had poor picture and sound quality, and people preferred to listen to radio and use their imaginations.

Looking to Nature for Remedies

SEARCH LIGHT

Find and correct the mistake in the following sentence: Many medicines today still come from the bark of animals.

Two visitors watched a jaguar fall off its tree limb and lie quietly on the ground. Their guide in this South American forest had brought the cat down with a blowgun dart tipped with curare. Made from certain trees in the jungle, curare **paralyses** the muscles in the body.

When scientists heard about this remarkable poison, they experimented with it. Although large doses of curare are deadly, they found that tiny doses can help people relax during **surgery**.

Many years ago, a doctor might have treated stomach-ache with a medicine containing a pinch of gold dust, a spoonful of ash from a dried lizard, 20 powdered beetles, some burned cat's hair, and two mashed onions!

Not all the old recipes for medicine were as bad as this one. Usually medicines were made from tree bark and leaves, berries and seeds, roots, and flowers. The value of some 'folk remedies' has not been proved scientifically, but many modern drugs have been developed from plants, animals, and **minerals**.

The photograph, for example, shows a common flower called 'foxglove'. Its leaves are used to make 'digitalis', which helps people with heart disease. Pods of the opium poppy are used to make painkillers.

Not so long ago, a very important medicine was discovered in mouldy bread. This medicine, penicillin, and others like it are called 'antibiotics'. They help fight many diseases by killing **bacteria**.

Today, most medicines are synthesized. This means that they are made from combinations of chemicals rather than from plants or animals. This method is much more **economical** and allows scientists to create much larger supplies of important medicines.

DID YOU KNOW?
Deadly nightshade is a highly poisonous plant that was often used in small amounts as a medicine. It is closely related to the tomato.

© Eric Crichton/Corbis

Answer: Many medicines today still come from the bark of trees.

Exploring the Sky

The stars we see in the night sky look like little points of light. But they are vastly larger than they look. Almost all of them are much bigger than our Earth. The stars look tiny because they're very far away. If you rode in the fastest rocket for your entire life, you wouldn't make it even halfway to the closest star.

Fortunately, telescopes let us explore the stars without leaving the Earth.

A simple telescope is tube-shaped and has a special kind of **magnifying** glass, called a '**lens**', at each end. Other telescopes use mirrors or both lenses and mirrors to enlarge the faraway view. Lenses and mirrors gather the light from an object, making it seem brighter and easier to see.

Telescopes make stars and planets seem closer. And telescopes let us see much farther than we normally can. Through a simple telescope you can see the rings of the planet Saturn, as well as galaxies outside our own Milky Way. Giant telescopes on mountaintops can view objects much farther away and see with much greater detail. Their lenses and mirrors are often enormous and therefore enormously powerful.

Some modern telescopes don't even look like the ones most of us might look through. These devices, which must travel into space beyond Earth's atmosphere, can sense light and other **radiation** that's invisible to unaided human eyes. These sensitive instruments, such as the Infrared Space Observatory and the Hubble Space Telescope (pictured here), have shown scientists such wonders as the dust in space between galaxies and the births and deaths of stars.

> **DID YOU KNOW?**
> Special radio telescopes 'listen' to the radio signals produced by stars, galaxies, and other objects. One group in New Mexico, U.S., includes 27 'dish' antennas spread over 40 kilometres.

SEARCH LIGHT

Find and correct the mistake in the following sentence: Telescopes make faraway objects seem faster than they look with the unaided eye.

Behind the Hubble Space Telescope, you can see the Earth's atmosphere outlined.
NASA

Answer: Telescopes make faraway objects seem closer than they look with the unaided eye.

Tour the world of imagination and creativity

The Arts

The Arts
TABLE OF CONTENTS

Art of the Mind's Eye

(Left) Navajo man making a sand painting. (Right) Classroom artist-in-training.

A painting is a two-dimensional, or flat, work of visual art. It is created by applying some form of colour or paint to a surface.

Some artists paint what they see around them. Others paint pictures that they see in their imagination. The idea on which a painting is based is called its 'theme'.

Some paintings have a religious theme. For example, one of the most famous paintings in the world, Leonardo da Vinci's 'Last Supper', shows Jesus Christ sharing his final meal with his disciples.

Other paintings show famous legends and events in history. Or they show **landscapes**, animals, or even scenes from daily life. Many Chinese scroll paintings take landscapes and nature as their themes.

Artists also paint portraits, or pictures of people. Sometimes they paint pictures of themselves. Such paintings are called 'self-portraits'.

Some painters express ideas and feelings through lines, shapes, colours, and textures that don't look like anything you could recognize. Such paintings are called 'abstract paintings'.

Painters use many materials in their work. These include oil paints, **acrylics,** watercolours, **pastels**, inks, dyes, and enamel paints. Painters use different tools to apply these colours, like brushes of various sizes and flexible tools called 'palette knives'.

You probably know that many paintings are made on canvas or paper. But paintings can also be applied to different surfaces. Murals are paintings on walls, both indoors and outdoors. Frescoes are wall paintings made on wet plaster. And some American Indians paint without paint in an art known as 'sand painting'.

In Islamic countries and in East Asia, especially Japan, Korea, and China, the art of beautiful writing, which is called 'calligraphy', is considered a skill equal to painting. Calligraphy is usually done in ink, using a brush.

Young artist works on a painting in a public exhibit at the Palace of Fine Arts in Santiago, Chile.
© Pablo Corral V/Corbis

SEARCH LIGHT

Find and correct the mistake in the following sentence: Calligraphy is a self-portrait done in ink.

Answer: Calligraphy is beautiful writing done in ink.

Artist of the Floating World

Ando Hiroshige was a Japanese painter and printmaker who was especially famous for his pictures of landscapes. Hiroshige was one of the *ukiyo-e* painters. '*Ukiyo-e*' is a Japanese term that means 'pictures of the floating world'.

DID YOU KNOW?
The Tokaido Road had been in use for over 700 years when Hiroshige began to make pictures of it.

This painting, called 'Festival Day', is from Hiroshige's Tokaido Road series. In it, holiday travellers climb to a restaurant perched on a scenic lookout.
© Asian Art & Archaeology, Inc./Corbis

Hiroshige was born in 1797. When he was 14, Hiroshige joined the school of the *ukiyo-e* master Utagawa Toyohiro. He graduated as an artist from the school at only 15. His first work was published six years later, in 1818.

Hiroshige probably created more than 5,000 **prints** during his lifetime. His life as an artist was divided into three stages. The first stage was when he was a student. He followed the style of his teachers in making prints of people. He drew girls, actors, and **samurai**, or warriors.

During the second stage Hiroshige made **landscape** designs and prints of birds and flowers. His best works during this time were 55 landscape prints called the 'Fifty-three Stations of the Tokaido'. Tokaido was a road that connected the Japanese cities of Osaka, Kyoto, and Edo (now called Tokyo). Along the road were 53 towns. Inns in each town provided lodging, food, and gifts for travellers. Hiroshige made one print for each town, as well as one each for the beginning of the road and the arrival in Kyoto. Many people bought copies of the prints. Hiroshige was soon one of the most popular *ukiyo-e* artists of all time.

In the last stage of his work, Hiroshige illustrated more landscapes, some empty and some with people in them. But he did far too much work, and his later work wasn't his best.

It has been estimated that Hiroshige created more than 5,000 prints. He knew how to create very simply and beautifully what he saw.

Answer: Hiroshige was famous for his pictures of stops along the Tokaido Road.

Murals of Mexico

When he was only 10 years old, Diego Rivera received a government scholarship to study art at the Academy of San Carlos in Mexico City. This would be the beginning of a brilliant career as an artist.

Later, Rivera studied in Spain, and in 1909 he moved to Paris. There he became friends with important painters such as Pablo Picasso and Georges Braque. While in France, Rivera began using simple forms and bold colours in his paintings.

Rivera returned to Mexico in 1921 after meeting fellow Mexican painter David Alfaro Siqueiros. The two shared a goal. They decided to create a new, uniquely Mexican kind of art based on **revolutionary** themes. They wanted this art to decorate public buildings, so they decided to paint murals. Murals are paintings done on walls, on either the inside or the outside of buildings. Rivera painted his first important mural, 'Creation', for the National Preparatory School in Mexico City.

Rivera's many murals in his home country celebrated Mexican history and life. His paintings featured native Indians, Spanish **conquistadores**, Mexican peasants, factory workers, and famous philosophers, politicians, and other public figures. He liked to show how farming, industry, and culture were all connected in people's lives. His human figures had a flattened appearance and were outlined to emphasize their shape. His works were brightly coloured and crowded with figures, which made his huge murals seem even larger.

Rivera was in the United States from 1930 to 1934. There he painted murals for the California School of Fine Arts in San Francisco, the Detroit Institute of Arts, and Rockefeller Center in New York City.

Rivera's wife, Frida Kahlo, was also an important painter.

DID YOU KNOW?
The owners of Rockefeller Center in New York City destroyed Rivera's mural there because it featured communist leader Vladimir I. Lenin. That mural would now be worth millions. Rivera later painted a copy in Mexico City.

Like many of Rivera's murals, this one focuses on the life and labours of the working class. This mural, called 'Pan American Unity', is painted on a wall at City College of San Francisco.

Answer: a) bold colours

The 3-D Art

Classical bronze sculpture by Donatello of Italian military figure Gattamelata.
© Elio Ciol/Corbis

Sculpture is a **three-dimensional** visual art. Paintings, drawings, and photographs are all two-dimensional, or flat. Sculptures are most often shaped by carving, moulding, or **welding** materials. Some are formed by making a cast - that is, by pouring a liquid into a mould and letting it harden.

Sculpture, like other arts, is often made to express thoughts or feelings. People who look at it might respond with thoughts or feelings of their own. Because it can have shape and **texture**, sculpture may appeal to our sense of touch.

Some sculptures are realistic. Until the middle of the 20th century, most sculpture was meant to look like some person or thing. The giant stone faces on Easter Island, like much traditional sculpture, may have been meant to honour gods or heroes. Other famous realistic sculptures include Michelangelo's 'David' and Auguste Rodin's 'The Thinker'.

Some modern sculptures may be **abstract**. This means they only hint at an object or an idea. They may not look like people or things you would recognize. These sculptures try to communicate a pure feeling or idea.

Sculptures come in all sizes, shapes, textures, and materials. Sculptors may use soft materials such as clay, wax, or wood or harder materials such as stone or metal. Sometimes the materials aren't even meant to last. One artist makes sculptures out of milk!

The modern sculptor Alexander Calder made sculptures that hang in the air. He called these 'mobiles' which means 'moving things'.

Another modern sculptor, named Christo, makes sculptures by wrapping such things as bridges, buildings, and even small islands in fabric and plastic.

SEARCH LIGHT

Fill in the gaps: Sculpture is different from painting. A painting is _____, but a sculpture is _____ - _____.

DID YOU KNOW?

Mount Rushmore National Memorial, in South Dakota, is a huge hillside carving by Gutzon Borglum of the faces of four U.S. presidents. If those presidents' whole bodies were carved too, they'd stand over 137 metres tall. Abraham Lincoln's nose by itself is over 6 metres long.

Modern sculpture, such as Claes Oldenberg's 'Clothespin' (in Philadelphia, Pennsylvania, U.S.), often places common objects in unusual situations to make us see and think about them differently.
© Robert Holmes/Corbis.

Answer: Sculpture is different from painting. A painting is flat, but a sculpture is three-dimensional.

The Modern Michelangelo

SEARCH LIGHT

Fill in the gaps:
The officials who studied and judged art felt that Rodin's first major work was _____ and _____.

The French sculptor Auguste Rodin was interested in art even as a boy. At age 10 he started drawing. By the time he was 15, Rodin had discovered the art of **sculpture**.

Rodin started out working for building decorators. He did decorative stonework on the outside of buildings. Later, Rodin became a sculptor's assistant. He worked with the sculptor A.-E. Carrier-Belleuse.

In 1864, at age 24, Rodin publically showed his first major sculpture, 'The Man with the Broken Nose'. The official art **critics** of the time did not like it. They believed art should be about beauty. To them, Rodin's sculpture was about something 'ugly' and ordinary.

At age 35, Rodin went to Italy to study the work of the famous painter Michelangelo. He learned a great deal about the human form. His work began to look even more realistic. It seemed to be full of movement and drama.

When he was 37 years old, Rodin sculpted 'The Age of Bronze'. It was so unusual and realistic that people said he must have moulded it on a real person! After years of struggle Rodin finally had become known as a great sculptor.

Rodin's sculptures were usually **cast** in bronze or carved from marble. The bronze pieces could be duplicated many times, using an original piece that was moulded in clay.

The sculpture that Rodin is probably best known for is his statue 'The Thinker', shown in the photo here. Like almost all of his sculptures, it shows a person in a natural, everyday pose. But Rodin's work seems to show a reality and truth that people may not have noticed before. Many people still find that his work **symbolizes** the things that we all experience and feel.

DID YOU KNOW?
One of Rodin's most important sculptures, 'The Gates of Hell', was actually used as the doors of an art museum. Within it are many smaller sculptures. Many of them were early versions of what became some of Rodin's finest works.

© Owen Franken/Corbis

Answer: The officials who studied and judged art felt that Rodin's first major work was ugly and ordinary.

Traditions of Creativity

Most of us have been to museums that display art by famous painters and sculptors. But another sort of artwork is common to almost every culture - the arts and crafts of non-famous but skilled people who carry on the traditions of their ancestors.

Folk art has its name because it's made by the 'folk', or common people, rather than by professional artists. Farmers, shepherds, fisher folk, and tradespeople who live away from cities are often the creators of folk art. Some are very skilled. European sailors used to carve beautiful scrimshaw - delicately engraved pieces of whalebone or **ivory**. Today, people in India, Ghana, Indonesia, and other places make beautiful fabrics in patterns unique to their regions.

Hand-painted eggs from Ukraine, in eastern Europe.
© Craig Aurness/Corbis

Native American Hopi artists carve kachina dolls, representing spirits of ancestors. Children learn about the kachina spirits while they play with the dolls.
© Tom Bean/Corbis

In less **industrialized** countries in Asia, Africa, and Latin America, many folk arts and crafts are exported, and craftspeople can often make a living from them. Many of these countries support their craftspeople, usually by helping them to sell their work.

Folk artists typically produce useful things such as furniture, toys, jewellery, clothing, musical instruments, weapons, religious symbols, and household tools. They craft these objects from easy-to-find or **recycled** materials such as wire, wood, and natural **fibres**. Some people even make food into art.

Every region of the world has produced folk art in unique styles. Folk art frequently reflects the traditional wisdom, religious beliefs, and **superstitions** of a society. The art often focuses on important yet common events - births, marriages, funerals, and holidays.

SEARCH LIGHT

What material is used to make scrimshaw?

DID YOU KNOW?
As part of the Mexican festival called the Day of the Dead - el Día de los Muertos - sugar is formed into skeletons, coffins, and angels. These tasty pieces of folk art often serve as toys before they are eaten!

Answer: Scrimshaw uses whalebone or ivory as a surface for carvings.

The Art of Building

The Cathedral of Notre-Dame de Paris (begun in 1163), an example of Gothic architecture.
© Bill Ross/Corbis

Thousands of years ago, early human beings lived in caves or other natural shelters. As time passed, people learned new skills, developed new tools, and were able to build simple structures.

As societies developed, they needed more kinds of building. Soon forts, barns, schools, bridges, tombs, and temples were being built, using a variety of materials. Gradually, creating buildings became an activity for experts - an art and occupation that came to be known as 'architecture'.

Today architecture is a **refined** art requiring a lot of training, years of practice, and plenty of talent. An architect's work is to imagine and plan a building and then to supervise its construction.

The architect must keep many things in mind. For example, how is the building going to be used and by whom? Where will it be located? What would be the best materials to use? How much money will construction cost?

Architects try to create buildings that people like to look at as well as to live, work, and play in. And changing styles affect architecture just as happens in other arts. The next time you see or walk around a city, notice the various styles of building. You'll find many differences between those designed recently and those of even 50 or 100 years ago. Different countries and cultures also produce different styles of architecture.

People today are still amazed at the buildings created by long-ago architects. The **majestic** pyramids in Egypt, the Great Wall of China, the temple at Angkor Wat in Cambodia, and the Taj Mahal in India are some of the architectural wonders you can study and visit.

© Dallas and John Heaton/Corbis

SEARCH LIGHT

Fill in the gap: Architecture is the art of _____.

The architect of the Baha'i House of Worship in India designed it to look like India's national flower. It has thus come to be called the Lotus Temple. Fine architecture is in tune with its cultural environment.

Answer: Architecture is the art of building.

Grand Architect

Ieoh Ming Pei is one of the most important modern **architects**. He has created many major buildings throughout the world. And his style and ideas have strongly influenced the work of many other architects. He has specialized in building multi-storey structures in cities.

I.M. Pei was born in Canton, China, in 1917. He went to America to study but couldn't return to China when World War II started. So most of his work has been in North America and Europe.

I.M. Pei on site during construction at the Louvre, Paris.
© Owen Franken/Corbis

© Richard List/Corbis

In the 1940s Pei began working as a professional architect. He worked on such important projects as the Mile High Center in Denver, Colorado.

In 1955 Pei formed his own architectural practice, I.M. Pei & Associates. The practice's early work included a museum in Syracuse, New York, that was actually four buildings joined by bridges. He also created a design for a new type of airport control tower that was widely used.

SEARCH LIGHT

According to the article, which building is not one that Pei designed?
a) East Building of the National Gallery of Art
b) John Hancock Tower
c) Sears Tower

Pei's buildings are often tall, with lots of glass and steel. The designs combine simple **geometric** shapes, especially rectangles and triangles.

But his buildings are not dull or simple. In many of them, you can see the building supports or building materials, and these are their only decoration. The way that concrete, glass, and steel look together creates interesting designs on the sides of Pei's buildings. Special reflective glass also adds to the designs. He often combines different shapes and emphasizes the picture these shapes make in the **skyline**.

DID YOU KNOW?
We think of the pyramids as being old stone structures in Egypt or Mexico. But Pei built a new glass pyramid as the entrance to the famous Louvre Museum in Paris just a few years ago.

Some of Pei's most famous work includes the John Hancock Tower in Boston, the East Building of the National Gallery of Art in Washington, D.C., and the glass **pyramid** at the Louvre Museum in Paris, shown in the photograph here.

Answer: c) Sears Tower

Music-Making Methods

DID YOU KNOW?
One of the oldest musical instruments ever found was an animal bone flute more than 40,000 years old.

SEARCH LIGHT

Which instrument group is missing?
percussion
electronic
wind
stringed

Any **device** that is made to produce a musical sound is a musical instrument. This includes everything from a simple rubber band strung between two nails to the most complex electronic **synthesizer**.

There are thousands of different kinds of musical instruments. For convenience, they are sometimes divided into percussion, stringed, keyboard, wind, and electronic instruments.

Percussion instruments make music when somebody strikes, shakes, or scrapes them. Drums, rattles, and bells are percussion instruments.

Guitars, violins, harps, and sitars are all stringed instruments. They are plucked, played with a **bow**, or strummed to produce music.

On keyboard instruments, notes are played by pressing keys, pushing buttons, or flipping levers. Pianos, organs, and accordions are keyboard instruments.

You can probably guess how wind instruments work. They're played by blowing air to produce notes. Some examples are flutes, saxophones, bagpipes, trumpets, and clarinets.

Until recently, all music had to be sung or played in person. In the 18th century, people began to find ways to play music automatically. They created musical clocks, player pianos, and music boxes. With the help of water power, clockwork, and steam, these instruments made music without needing people to play them.

In the late 1800s, the earliest recording devices were invented. These allowed people to make copies of musical performances.

After the mid-20th century, inventors began to create electronic versions of some older instruments, such as guitars and pianos. They also built electronic instruments that made music in whole new ways. These instruments were called 'synthesizers' because they artificially made, or synthesized, music. Most recently, the computer has become another electronic device to be used as an instrument.

Answer: The keyboard group is the missing category.

A Company of Players

SEARCH LIGHT

The title calls an orchestra 'a company of players'. Another kind of company you've probably heard of is a business. What do you think a business and an orchestra have in common?

DID YOU KNOW?
The gamelan is the traditional orchestra of Java and Bali in Indonesia. Its instruments and music are mostly gongs and other tuned instruments that are struck. The human voice is sometimes an important 'instrument' too.

The orchestra at my school was busy practising. I brought my younger brother, Jeff, to watch. Jeff had never seen an orchestra before.

'Which person is the orchestra?' he asked me.

I smiled and said, 'Why don't you ask them?'

Jeff went up to a boy with a big fat brass tuba in his arms.

'Are you the orchestra?' Jeff asked.

'No,' the boy answered. He put his mouth to the mouthpiece, blew into it, and played a few loud notes.

'That sounds like a lorry's horn!' Jeff said.

He went to a girl who held a cello between her knees. It looked like a large violin.

'Are you the orchestra?' he asked.

She shook her head and drew a **bow** across the strings.

'That sounds like grandpa humming,' said Jeff.

Next he came to a boy standing behind two giant pots.

'Are those pots the orchestra?' he asked.

'No. They're kettledrums,' the boy said. He thumped two booming notes with a pair of mallets.

Behind him Jeff heard a 'tap-tap-tap'.

He turned around to see a woman tapping a long thin stick on a music stand. Everyone became very quiet.

'That's the conductor,' the drummer whispered. 'And that stick is her baton. She tells us how to play.'

The players all watched as the conductor's arms began to move slowly up and down. The musicians began to play, and music filled the room.

Jeff smiled.

I could tell what he was thinking. Now he knew who the orchestra was. They all were. The conductor and all the musicians with all their instruments together made the orchestra.

Answer: For one thing, both a business and an orchestra need members who cooperate in order to do their best work.

Music of Everyday Life

Pete Seeger, musician of the folk movement of the 1950s and '60s.
© Neal Preston/Corbis

Have you played or sung 'London Bridge Is Falling Down', 'Ring a Ring O'Roses', or 'Frère Jacques'? If you have, then you're part of the folk music tradition. In the case of nursery rhymes and musical games, that tradition can date back for hundreds of years!

Folk music is the shared music of a group or community of people. It's everyday music that was often created as part of children's games or as a way to make work easier. Some songs were sung at parties or weddings. Some were used to celebrate births or **mourn** deaths. And some were used as part of religious services.

Folk music is learned and passed on by everyone, not just musicians. Many folk performers don't study music in school, but they learn songs by listening to others play and sing.

Because it usually isn't written down, folk music changes as it travels between people and countries. Songs are created or lost, and some change because of people's poor memories. Other songs are rewritten to match new times, situations, and ideas. In the United States, some jazz, blues, and **gospel** tunes have their roots in folk songs brought over hundreds of years ago by African slaves.

In the 1960s in North America, musicians such as Pete Seeger, Bob Dylan, and Joan Baez performed folk music accompanied by guitars. Today this type of 'folk' and 'folk rock' music remains very popular. And through it the Western folk tradition continues to excite and inspire new generations.

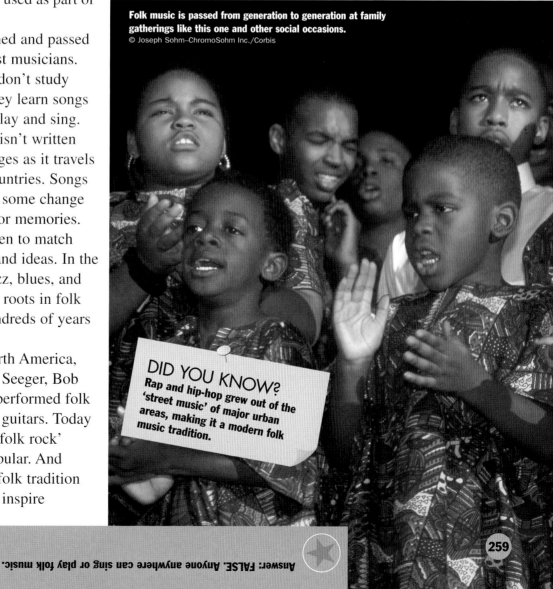

Folk music is passed from generation to generation at family gatherings like this one and other social occasions.
© Joseph Sohm–ChromoSohm Inc./Corbis

DID YOU KNOW?
Rap and hip-hop grew out of the 'street music' of major urban areas, making it a modern folk music tradition.

Answer: FALSE. Anyone anywhere can sing or play folk music.

The South African Sound

In the past 20 years, the music of South Africa has spread all over the world. In part that's thanks to Ladysmith Black Mambazo, the country's most popular singing group. But to find out what Ladysmith is and what 'mambazo' means, we have to go back to South African mining towns in the 1960s.

Working in the mines kept black workers far from their homes and their families. So on Saturday nights they entertained themselves by holding singing contests featuring traditional Zulu harmonies.

That was how a young man named Joseph Shabalala discovered his singing talent. In 1964, Shabalala kept having a dream in which he heard a special harmony. To create that sound, he formed a music group with his brothers, Headman and Jockey, and some cousins and friends.

They called themselves Ladysmith Black Mambazo because Ladysmith is Shabalala's hometown, and the black ox is the strongest animal on a farm. The group 'chopped down' their competition in every singing contest, so they added the name Mambazo, which is a kind of ax.

SEARCH LIGHT

What does 'Mambazo' mean in the name Ladysmith Black Mambazo?

Years later American musician Paul Simon heard the group's singing and later met the members in South Africa. They performed on Simon's 1986 album *Graceland* and toured with him, sharing their music with people everywhere. A year later Ladysmith Black Mambazo won a Grammy - an American music award - and today they're Africa's top-selling music group.

Shabalala also keeps the folk music of South Africa alive by teaching the traditional songs to young children.

DID YOU KNOW?
Ladysmith Black Mambazo has recorded songs for many films, including *The Lion King II*, and has performed for both the pope and the queen of England.

AP/Wide World Photos

Answer: Mambazo is a type of ax, used in the name because the group 'cut down' their singing competitors.

Music of an Era

Popular music is basically what its name says it is - music that is enjoyed by a very large number of people. But the modern term 'popular music' refers more particularly to music that's made by a musical entertainment business specifically in order to be sold.

Popular music (or 'pop' music) has roots in the music halls and **vaudeville** theatres of England and the United States. However, the modern popular music **industry** was truly launched with radio programming in the 20th century. Jazz music began to be heard widely in the 1920s. Country and western music's audience grew in the '20s as well. In the 1930s and '40s, big-band music was popular, and singers such as Frank Sinatra and Ella Fitzgerald found international fame.

In the mid-1950s, American rock and roll performers such as Elvis Presley and Chuck Berry commanded worldwide attention. By the 1960s, English bands such as the Beatles and the Rolling Stones were taking popular music in new directions. Rock strongly influenced disco, reggae, punk, rap, hip-hop, and other styles in the late 20th century.

Radio and the recording industry introduced non-Western cultures to these new forms of popular music. Traditional songs were performed in new styles, and at the same time, traditional instruments gave the new music an entirely different sound. This mixing of styles and sounds became 'world music' and 'worldbeat'.

Today worldbeat blends a wide range of sounds and rhythms. Shubha Mudgal combines India's folk and classical traditions with rock music. The Gipsy Kings mingle pop music with Spain's traditional flamenco. And popular music continues to evolve.

Popular music includes many different styles from many different places. The multiracial South African group Johnny Clegg and Savuka gave a strong European pop flavour to traditional Zulu music and added Zulu Inhlangwini dancing.
© Henry Diltz/Corbis

(From left) Famed reggae musician Bob Marley of Jamaica; Celtic-New Age singer Enya of Ireland; and pop singer-songwriter Phil Collins of England.
(Left) © Jeff Albertson/Corbis; (centre and right) © Reuters NewMedia Inc./Corbis

DID YOU KNOW?
The most-recorded song is 'Yesterday' by John Lennon and Paul McCartney of the Beatles. But before the tune had any words put to it, the writers referred to it as 'Scrambled Eggs'.

Answer: FALSE. Rock music is one of a number of kinds of popular music.

The Music of Change

Jazz music is very hard to define because it changes all the time. It has its roots in America's folk traditions, especially in the music of slaves taken from Africa. But today musicians from many countries play jazz and make their own contributions to it.

Early jazz borrowed from slaves' field hollers (a kind of musical calling-out) and work songs and from African American **hymns** and spirituals. Soon it adopted music from funeral processions and popular dance music.

Jazz funeral in New Orleans, Louisiana.
© Philip Gould/Corbis

DID YOU KNOW?

'Cool', 'bad', 'fly', 'the bomb' (later 'da bomb'), and 'dj' are all slang words that came from jazz.

Dixieland is a jazz style that grew up in New Orleans, Louisiana. Groups such as the Preservation Jazz Band continue to play in this musical tradition.
© Robert Holmes/Corbis

The first jazz recording was made in 1917 by the Original Dixieland Jazz Band. Dixieland grew up in New Orleans, Louisiana, and has a big brassy sound. It features trumpets, saxophones, trombones, and other wind instruments.

Chicago and New York City emerged as major jazz centres. Talented musicians such as Bix Beiderbecke and Louis Armstrong formed bands. And jazz spread to Europe. France especially welcomed jazz music and musicians - many not valued in the United States simply because they were black.

Jazz has also been richly influenced by women, especially as singers. Billie Holiday, Sarah Vaughan, and Ella Fitzgerald are just a few of the classics.

In the 1930s and '40s, jazz focused on rhythm, melody, and a smoother sound. Glenn Miller, Benny Goodman, Duke Ellington, and Count Basie earned fame for their 'big band' jazz orchestra styles.

In the mid-20th century, jazz changed again as mood, feeling, and complex musical imaginings dominated. Miles Davis, Charlie Parker, and John Coltrane led this 'cool' style of jazz. Davis later helped introduce 'jazz **fusion**', blending rock and other popular music with his jazz.

Jazz today is more varied than ever before. And jazz keeps growing in many directions.

SEARCH LIGHT

Who were the people most responsible for creating jazz?

Answer: Jazz began with the songs, chants, and music of African slaves in America.

An Aristocrat of Jazz

Count Basie in 1982.
© Roger Ressmeyer/Corbis

Young William Basie began studying music with his mother. He was later taught the organ by pianist Fats Waller. Waller himself was a well-known jazz musician.

Basie started his career playing piano on the vaudeville stage. Vaudeville was performed in a chain of theatres in the United States during the late 19th and early 20th centuries. Vaudeville shows provided an entertaining mixture of dancing, singing, comedy, and magic acts.

When Basie was about 23 years old, he went to Kansas City, Missouri. It was there that he formed his first jazz band. Basie's nine-piece band was distinct because it highlighted the **rhythm** instruments. The bass fiddle, drums, guitar, and Basie's piano became the core sound of his music. Basie had once played bass himself, and he developed a four-beat 'walking' style of rhythm. This even beat provided a light, simple, and relaxed musical **foundation**. It also helped the harmonies and melodies in his songs stand out. Basie's rhythm section set the pattern that modern jazz accompanying styles would follow.

Basie and his band played at many nightclubs and often did radio broadcasts. One night a radio announcer called him 'Count' Basie, to liken him to another fine bandleader with an **aristocratic** nickname, Duke Ellington. From that point on the band gained in popularity.

The Basie band's popular early numbers included 'Lady Be Good', 'Shoe Shine Boy', 'One O'Clock Jump', and 'Jumpin' at the Woodside'. He formed another orchestra in the 1950s that was more **sophisticated**. Those musicians could read music and perform very difficult pieces. This group's hits included 'Alright, Okay, You Win' and 'April in Paris'.

© Bettmann/Corbis

DID YOU KNOW?
Before he was a count, Basie was a baron. His first band was called the Barons of Rhythm.

Answer: FALSE. 'Count' was Basie's nickname.

Rock Guitarist

Carlos Santana was born in Mexico in 1947. He came by his interest in music naturally, since his father played violin in a traditional Mexican mariachi band. At about 7 years old, Carlos began to study guitar. He tried to copy the music of famous guitarists he heard on the radio.

As time passed, Carlos grew more interested in rock music and the blues. He began playing in bands as a teenager, and even after his family moved to California, he returned to Mexico to play in clubs and bars. In San Francisco in 1966, Carlos founded a group with five other musicians. The group's name, the Santana Blues Band, was later shortened to Santana.

In three years the group shot to fame when it performed at the historic 1969 Woodstock rock festival in the United States. The band became known for mixing jazz and Latin music into a rock sound. Carlos' own playing featured a unique, exciting electric guitar sound. His long and complex guitar solos varied and developed a single musical **theme**.

SEARCH LIGHT

Which three styles of music has Carlos Santana combined in his own work?

The group's first three albums were all major hits. The music was **vivid** and sparked the audience's imagination. On later albums the band continued to experiment with mixing jazz and rock.

© Reuters NewMedia Inc./Corbis

In 1998 the group was named to the Rock and Roll Hall of Fame. The following year Carlos Santana released *Supernatural*. On this CD he performed songs with such top performers as Eric Clapton, Lauryn Hill, Dave Matthews, and Rob Thomas of Matchbox 20. The CD sold more than 20 million copies, Santana's greatest success ever. And it introduced a new generation of listeners to him.

DID YOU KNOW?

Carlos Santana's hit album *Supernatural* reflected the continuing influence of Latin music in his own. Many songs on that CD, as on his earlier recordings, were sung in Spanish.

Answer: Santana's music combines jazz, Latin music, and rock.

A Very Formal Music

String quartet playing chamber music.
© Charles O'Rear/Corbis

In the West (Europe and the Americas) the term 'classical music' usually refers to sonatas, chamber music, operas, and symphonies from the late 1700s through the 1800s.

Classical music is a very **formal** kind of music. This makes classical different from forms such as jazz or folk music. Classical music has set fairly complex patterns that all classical composers (writers of music) and musicians understand and follow.

A sonata is made up of three parts that focus, in different ways, on a main musical theme, or special tune. The first part presents the theme. In the second part the theme is developed and played in different ways. The third part repeats the theme.

A symphony is a longer **composition** created to be played by an **orchestra**. A symphony has several sections called 'movements'. One movement is usually in the form of a sonata.

Chamber music was originally created for a smaller private audience. This kind of music uses fewer musicians and features delicate musical patterns.

© Kevin Fleming/Corbis

An opera is basically a play acted to music. The **dialogue** is sung, not spoken, and is accompanied by an orchestra.

The music of the great classical composers is still popular today. You may know the names or music of such composers as Beethoven, Mozart, and Bach.

Non-Western cultures have different forms of classical music. In China, classical music refers to ancient music that existed before the influence of Western art forms. India's two forms of classical music, Hindustani music and Carnatic music, are hundreds of years old. In Central Asia classical music comes from the medieval court music of such centres as Bukhara and Samarkand, two cities in Uzbekistan.

DID YOU KNOW?
Before the classical period in Western music, most formal music was either religious chanting or the music of the courts of kings and queens. Court music frequently accompanied complex dances.

Answer: A symphony is a long piece of music played by an orchestra.

A Life Filled with Music

When he was only 3 years old in Salzburg, Austria, Wolfgang Amadeus Mozart used to join his elder sister, Maria Anna, for her music lessons. But by the time he was 5, Mozart was making up his own music.

In the 18th century, when Mozart lived, most people didn't believe that a little boy could write such beautiful music. They thought Mozart's father had secretly written it.

So to test him, they asked young Mozart to stay in a room alone for a week. At the end of the week, Mozart had written a new piece of choir music. People agreed that this child was a musical genius.

Music from Mozart's opera *Don Giovanni*.
© Bettmann/Corbis

Mozart studied, taught, played, and wrote music all his life. His music was often joyous, sometimes grim. But it was always beautiful. Mozart used the orchestra's players and instruments in ways no one else had done before.

© Archivo Iconografico. S.A./Corbis

Mozart often blended popular and classical music to create new styles of music, especially in the opera. He could compose in many musical styles and could play equally well on the organ, the harpsichord, the piano, and the violin. Mozart could hear a piece once and then play it from memory, sometimes rewriting and improving it as he played.

Although he died when he was still a young man, Mozart wrote 16 operas, 41 symphonies, and more than 500 other pieces of music. Some of his most famous works include the operas *The Marriage of Figaro*, *Don Giovanni*, and *The Magic Flute* and the 'Jupiter' Symphony.

SEARCH LIGHT

How old was Mozart when he began writing his own music?
a) 15
b) 5
c) 8

DID YOU KNOW?
In the late 1990s, some parents played Mozart for their babies, even while they were still in the womb. They thought Mozart's music would make children more intelligent, but there's no evidence to prove this notion.

Answer: b) 5

Moving to Rhythms

(Top) Balinese dancers from Indonesia. (Bottom) Gitaga drummers and dancers of Burundi.

Thousands of years ago, early groups of people came together to dance. Hundreds of years ago, people danced at great functions in the courts of kings. Today, when people gather at social events, they still dance.

Originally there were two kinds of dance, social dance and what else?

Dancing is one of the oldest and most popular of forms of human **expression**. Originally, there were two kinds of dance. Social dances were performed on special occasions, such as births or marriages. Religious dances were performed to ask the gods for help, such as to provide rain or cure the sick.

Over the years, many early forms developed into folk dances. These continue to be enjoyed to traditional music. Some dances, however, became the specialty of professional artists. This kind of dance tends to be more theatrical and creative.

Ballet dancing developed in Europe, where it became an especially graceful art form. Ballet dancers must train constantly for years to master difficult steps, turns, and leaps. With great strength and beauty, ballet dancers can tell a story through their movements. *Swan Lake* is one such famous story ballet about a princess who turned into a swan.

Twentieth-century modern dance in the West took a different approach. Often it didn't try to tell a story. Instead, the dancers worked to express pure emotions or ideas. And where ballet conveys a sense of lightness, modern dance seems much more 'earthbound'.

In Asia, different traditions arose, producing classical dance-dramas that are highly **stylized** or formal. Some Asian dances involve not only **intricate** steps but detailed hand and arm movements as well. India's classical dance has more than 4,000 *mudra*s, or gestures portraying complex actions, emotions, and relationships. In Thailand, one traditional dance is performed with lit candles.

DID YOU KNOW?
Tap dance, a major feature of musical theatre, apparently developed from very mixed sources. These include the traditional clog dance of northern England, the jigs and flings of Ireland and Scotland, and the rhythmic foot stamping of African dances.

Native American girl doing a traditional dance.
© Lindsay Hebberd/Corbis

Answer: Religious dance was the other kind of dance besides social dance.

America's
Prima Ballerina

Delicate, **effortlessly** graceful, radiant, and enchanting - that is how Maria Tallchief has been described. Many people consider her America's finest ballerina ever.

Maria Tallchief was born in 1925, in the small town of Fairfax, Oklahoma. She spent the first eight years of her life in northeastern Oklahoma. Her father was a member of the Osage tribe of American Indians. Her mother was of Irish and Scottish **descent**.

Tallchief enjoyed the Osage ceremonial dances. She loved music and dancing. She trained as a pianist but her heart was in dancing.

When her family moved to Los Angeles, she studied dance. One of Tallchief's teachers, dancer Bronislava Nijinska, was strict. She always said, 'When you sleep, sleep like a ballerina. Even on the street waiting for a bus, stand like a ballerina'.

Tallchief receiving National Medal of Arts from President Bill Clinton in 1999.
AP/Wide World Photos

Maria Tallchief's dancing in *Firebird* became her most famous work.
© Hulton-Deutsch Collection/Corbis

SEARCH LIGHT

Which of these is not the name of a ballet?
a) Serenade
b) Woman of the Year
c) Gaîté Parisienne
d) Scheherazade

DID YOU KNOW?
Maria's sister, Marjorie Tallchief, was a successful ballerina as well. She was the first American to become a lead dancer with the Paris Opéra Ballet. And she and Maria worked together many times over the years.

Tallchief worked hard for five years and then joined the Ballet Russe de Monte Carlo. She danced in many ballets and even gave solo performances. Some of these solos were in *Scheherazade* and **choreographer** George Balanchine's *Serenade* and *Firebird*.

Tallchief married Balanchine in 1946, and soon they were both working with the company that became the New York City Ballet. Tallchief was so popular that she had to give as many as eight performances in a week! She was the prima ballerina (main female dancer) with NYCB for most of the next 20 years.

In 1953 she was honoured as America's 'Woman of the Year'. That same year her home state of Oklahoma honoured her achievements and her Native American identity by naming her Wa-Xthe-Thomba, meaning 'Woman of Two Worlds'.

Tallchief retired from dancing in 1965. She felt it was time to pass on to young dancers what she had learned about the art that she loved.

Answer: b) Woman of the Year

Writing for the Ages

© Royalty-Free/Corbis

Literature is writing that is good enough or important enough to last for tens, hundreds, or even thousands of years. It's valuable work that people make sure is heard, read, and passed down from generation to generation.

People usually think of literature as novels such as *Kidnapped*, the poetry of Emily Dickinson, or the plays of William Shakespeare. But even books for young readers, such as *The Cat in the Hat* or *Alice's Adventures in Wonderland*, can be literature. Literature also includes philosophy and history, letters and essays, even journals like *The Diary of Anne Frank*. Some literature tells a story; some literature makes a point; and some literature just uses words and language in an exciting or memorable way. Some literature does all these things at once.

Not all literature started on the page. Ancient stories of heroes like Beowulf and Odysseus were spoken first and written down later. Speeches such as Martin Luther King, Jr.'s *I Have a Dream* can also be literature.

But just writing something down doesn't make it literature. We don't usually think of such useful but disposable things as phone books, menus, or game instructions as literature. Even books come and go - many that you see in shops today won't be around decades from now. Most newspaper articles are read once and tossed aside, but if their topics are important or their writing is very good, those articles might be collected into a book to be preserved and reread. They're on their way to becoming literature!

© Kelly-Mooney Photography/Corbis

SEARCH LIGHT

Which of the following would have the best chance of someday being considered literature?
a) phone book
b) restaurant menu
c) your diary
d) CD-ROM instructions

Answer: c) your diary

The Man Who Created Wonderland

Not many people curl up in their favourite chair to read a maths book. But in the 1800s, a maths lecturer named Charles Dodgson wrote two children's books that are still popular today. Using the pen name 'Lewis Carroll', Dodgson dreamed up *Alice's Adventures in Wonderland* and its sequel, *Through the Looking-Glass*.

As a boy growing up in the English countryside, Lewis Carroll (as we'll refer to Dodgson) loved mathematical puzzles. As an adult, that love led him to teach maths at the University of Oxford.

Carroll never married, but he loved entertaining children. He was especially fond of the daughters of the **dean** of his college - Alice, Lorina, and Edith Liddell. Carroll often took the girls on boating and picnic trips and amused them by making up stories and drawing pictures. One story told of a young girl named Alice who fell down a rabbit hole into Wonderland, a magical place where nothing was as it seemed.

Lewis Carroll (Charles Dodgson).
© Bettmann/Corbis

Lewis Carroll's characters from *Alice's Adventures in Wonderland* are still some of the most popular in the world.
© Craig Lovell/Corbis

Young Alice Liddell asked Carroll to write the story down. He did, filling it with his imagination and humour and also with his knack for puzzles and word games. It became *Alice's Adventures in Wonderland*, a wild tale that includes an anxious White Rabbit, a vanishing Cheshire Cat, and a tea party thrown by a Mad Hatter.

Carroll had not intended to publish the story as a book, but his friends talked him into it. Readers loved the strange and silly adventures, and so Carroll continued Alice's tale in *Through the Looking-Glass*. By the time he died, Carroll's two Alice books were the most popular children's books in England.

SEARCH LIGHT

Fill in the gaps: In addition to being an author, Lewis Carroll was a _____ _____.

DID YOU KNOW?
Dodgson invented the name Lewis Carroll by taking his first and middle names, Charles Lutwidge, and translating them into Latin as *Carolus Ludovicus*. Then he reversed them and translated the Latin back into English.

Life Re-created on a Stage

Actors in traditional Japanese Kabuki drama.
© Charles & Josette Lenars/Corbis

Plays and drama in some form have been a part of all cultures throughout the world for all of human history. The making and overall experience of a dramatic performance is called 'theatre'.

At first, theatre was part of religious celebrations. Until several hundred years ago, most people couldn't read. Seeing the religious stories acted out helped them better understand their religions.

Theatre gradually developed into an art form. Plays were written and performed for entertainment and to communicate ideas. As theatre developed, so did a whole group of professional artists around it. Today the theatre employs a great many creative people doing different jobs to make and run a play.

The playwright is the person who writes the words and basic actions of a play - this is called a 'script'. The play's director reads the script and thinks of a way to turn the words and actions into a live performance. The actors learn the lines of the script and pretend to be the characters in the story.

Another important group of theatre artists are the designers. These behind-the-scenes people invent and build the environment of the play: the actors' costumes and makeup, the special lighting, any sound or music that's needed, props or properties (objects) used in the play, and the set or scenery the play is performed on. The stage set consists of the background, the furniture, and the artificial rooms that are built onstage.

All these people and elements build a fascinating dramatic world. Whether the audience is watching a Japanese Kabuki drama or a professional Shakespeare production or a school play, they partake, for a time, in the very special world of the imagination.

SEARCH LIGHT

Fill in the gap:
The _____ decides how best to perform the story of the play.

DID YOU KNOW?

The Mousetrap, a mystery play by Agatha Christie, has been running in London for more than 50 years - longer than any other play.

Theatrical performances most often take place indoors. But people often enjoy outdoor stagings, especially when the weather is pleasant. This one in Toronto, Ontario, Canada, is a play by William Shakespeare.
© Bob Krust/Corbis

A Commanding Actress

Dame Judi Dench is one of England's most famous and admired actresses.

Judith Olivia Dench was born in 1934. In 1957 she had her professional stage **debut** as Hamlet's love, Ophelia, in William Shakespeare's play *Hamlet.* Her performance and delivery were delicate but intelligent, and the character came alive for audiences.

Although a fairly small woman, Dench has always been known for her **commanding** presence onstage. She has acted with the Royal Shakespeare Company and other major theatres. Dench has also played modern roles during her stage career. She created the role of the odd but lovable Sally Bowles in the first London production of the musical *Cabaret* (1968). But Shakespeare has been her specialty.

Outside Great Britain, people probably know Dench best for her role as the stern spy chief 'M' in the James Bond movies. In 1997 the film *Mrs. Brown* brought her wide international attention. She played Queen Victoria in that film. In 1998 she played another queen, Queen Elizabeth I, in the film *Shakespeare in Love.* For this she won an Academy Award for best supporting actress. She won the same award from the British Academy of Film and Television Arts (BAFTA) - one of many she was awarded.

The great strength that Dench communicates has marked her acting style. In addition, however, she gives touchingly personal life to the characters she plays, whether they are grand historical figures or everyday people. Her two popular television series, 'A Fine Romance' and 'As Time Goes By', show off her skill at playing ordinary women.

Judi Dench has always considered the stage her first love. For her remarkable contribution to theatre and films, Dench was honoured with a knighthood as Dame Commander of the British Empire in 1988.

In 1994 Judi Dench played the actress Irina Arkadina in the classic Russian play *The Seagull,* written by Anton Chekhov.
© Robbie Jack/Corbis

SEARCH LIGHT

Dame Judi Dench has made a number of films and some TV programs, but her greatest love is the _____.

DID YOU KNOW?

Dame Judi Dench's first appearance onstage was as a snail in a production at the Mount School.

Dreams on the Big Screen

When Thomas A. Edison introduced a moving picture machine in 1894, only one person at a time could watch his Kinetoscope. But soon films were being projected onto a large screen for large audiences.

The earliest films were silent. Words were put up on the screen between scenes to show the **dialogues** or to help explain the action. Cinemas often used a pipe organ to provide live music.

The first feature film was *The Great Train Robbery*, a 10-minute action film made in 1903. Audiences were thrilled with this silent story of the hold-up of a moving train. Some people even fainted during the final scene when an actor turned and fired his gun at the camera.

In 1927 *The Jazz Singer* marked the beginning of sound in cinema. The first 'talkies' were hard to understand. But the **technology** improved, and by 1931 very few silent pictures were still being made.

American gangster films, westerns, horror films, and musicals became very popular. Cartoons were also popular, especially those made by Walt Disney's company. Film classics from Europe include Jean Renoir's dramas and Sergei Eisenstein's war epics. In the 1950s many people began to think of some directors as the 'authors' of their films. Directors of this sort include Alfred Hitchcock, Satyajit Ray, Ingmar Bergman, and Federico Fellini.

Today India and Hong Kong have large film industries. And countries such as Iran, Mexico, Taiwan, France, Spain, and Japan produce especially beautiful, interesting films. In the late 20th century both Australia and Ireland became known for their sensitive and witty films. And, of course, America is the home of the grand and expensive **blockbuster**.

The Kobal Collection–Kennedy Miller

© Bettmann/Corbis

The Kobal Collection–Biograf Jan Sverak/Portobello Pictures

The Kobal Collection–Melampo Cinematografica/Sergio Strizzi

(Clockwise from top) *The Great Train Robbery* (1903); Italian actor-writer-director Roberto Benigni's *La Vita è Bella* (1997; *Life Is Beautiful*); Czech director Jan Sverak's *Kolya* (1996); and Australian director John Duigan's *Flirting* (1989).

SEARCH LIGHT

Which musical instrument often provided music in cinemas during silent films?

DID YOU KNOW? The amazing effect of parting the Red Sea in Cecil B. DeMille's 1923 film *The Ten Commandments* was created by using an 18-metre tub of jelly.

Director Alfred Hitchcock's *Spellbound* (1945).
© John Springer Collection/Corbis

Answer: The pipe organ often accompanied silent films.

Indian Cinema
for the World

Satyajit Ray is probably India's best-known film director and screenwriter. His sensitive and visually interesting works let the world see Indian cinema as more than simple entertainment.

Ray was born in Calcutta, India, in 1921. He started out working as an illustrator for books and advertising. At one point he illustrated the Bengali novel *Pather Panchali* - in English, *The Song of the Road*. It tells the story of Apu, the poor son of a priest. Apu wants to be a novelist and travels from his small village to the city of Calcutta. The story shows the conflict between traditional and modern life.

Ray was interested in making a film of *Pather Panchali*. And a famous French director, Jean Renoir, encouraged him. Ray started work on the film in 1952, using friends as actors and film crew.

Satyajit Ray.
Camera Press

SEARCH LIGHT

How did Ray start out?
a) as an illustrator
b) as a writer
c) as a director

He at first used his own money, but the West Bengal government eventually supplied the rest.

Ray completed the film in 1955. It was a tremendous success. *Pather Panchali* won a major award at the 1956 Cannes International Film Festival. After this, Ray became a very popular and respected filmmaker.

Most of his films are about the struggles of poor people. They also focus on the challenges of the modern world. Ray made all kinds of films: comedies, tragedies, romances, musicals, and detective stories. All of his films, however, show his insight into how people behave and what they go through.

Ray also wrote many short stories and books. But he is best remembered as the person who woke up the world to the possibilities of fine filmmaking in India.

Satyajit Ray's 1977 film *Shatranj ke Khilari* (in English, *The Chess Players*) was his first one made in the Hindi language. It deals with the effect of the West on India.
Nimai Ghosh

DID YOU KNOW?
Because Ray had so little money for his first movie, his film crew worked for free. This seemed all right, since none of the crew had ever worked on a film before.

Answer: a) as an illustrator

A Grand Musical Play

Outdoor performance of the opera *Aida* by Giuseppe Verdi.
© Gail Mooney/Corbis

Like a play, an opera is a story acted out onstage. But in an opera the performers sing their lines instead of speaking them. An opera is also different from a musical because opera performers usually don't speak at all. Their songs don't happen between conversations, but rather their songs are the conversations. The music an orchestra plays for an opera is as important to the overall effect as the singing.

SEARCH LIGHT

Find and correct the error in the following sentence: In an opera, performers usually speak their lines.

Traditional opera tells a big story in a grand way. The story is usually serious, though there are comic operas too. Many operas tell tragic tales of lovers who are kept apart. Richard Wagner's *Tristan und Isolde* is one of these. Some operas, like Wolfgang Amadeus Mozart's *The Magic Flute*, tell stories of mystery and enchantment. Comic operas, such as Giaocchino Rossetti's *The Barber of Seville*, often feature silly situations and people.

In the late 1800s, W.S. Gilbert and Arthur Sullivan wrote comic operas that made fun of people from various walks of life. One of the most popular of their light operas, or operettas, was *The Pirates of Penzance*. But today's opera composers continue the dramatic spirit of classic opera, even though their subjects have changed.

A special form of opera developed in China during the late 18th century. It is called *jingxi*, and English speakers know it as Peking opera. Its performers use larger-than-life movements to **portray** their characters. The rhythmic beating of clappers marks time for movements, and the performance may feature acrobatic fighting scenes.

***Jingxi*, known in English as Peking opera, is a spectacular musical and dramatic show.**
© Marc Garanger/Corbis

DID YOU KNOW?
Classic operas are usually performed in the language they were written in. Today, if the audience doesn't speak the language of the opera, the opera company may show the singers' words in the audience's language on a screen above the stage.

Answer: In an opera, performers usually sing their lines.

Australia's Golden Voice

Opera singer Joan Sutherland was born in Sydney, Australia, on 7 November 1926. She was a musical child and studied piano and music with her mother. At about age 20 Sutherland won a singing competition and began studying professionally.

© Bettmann/Corbis

DID YOU KNOW?
Sutherland's nickname to her fans was 'La Stupenda' because of her stupendous (fantastic) talent.

SEARCH LIGHT

True or false? Joan Sutherland never needed any training to become a great singer.

A year later Sutherland made her first appearance as a singer in a performance of Henry Purcell's opera *Dido and Aeneas*. She played the lead female role of Dido.

Sutherland won many prizes in singing competitions, and she used the money to move to London. There she studied at the Royal College of Music. In 1952 she became a member of the company of the Royal Opera, Covent Garden. She made her first appearance there in Wolfgang Amadeus Mozart's *The Magic Flute*.

In 1961 Sutherland performed in Gaetano Donizetti's *Lucia di Lammermoor* at the **Metropolitan** Opera, New York City. Lucia was a difficult role. On one hand it required the singer to do some extremely tricky vocal **gymnastics**. In addition to that, it was a major acting challenge. Sutherland performed it so well that her fame spread around the world. She was soon performing in major opera houses all over Europe.

Sutherland was admired as a coloratura soprano. Sopranos are female singers with very high voices. Coloratura singers have to have a very light and flexible voice. They must be able to sing complex series of notes very rapidly.

Sutherland was one of the most successful opera stars of her day. In 1978 she was knighted as a Dame Commander of the British Empire. She retired from the stage in 1990, at the age of 64.

Answer: FALSE. Sutherland continued to train throughout her career.

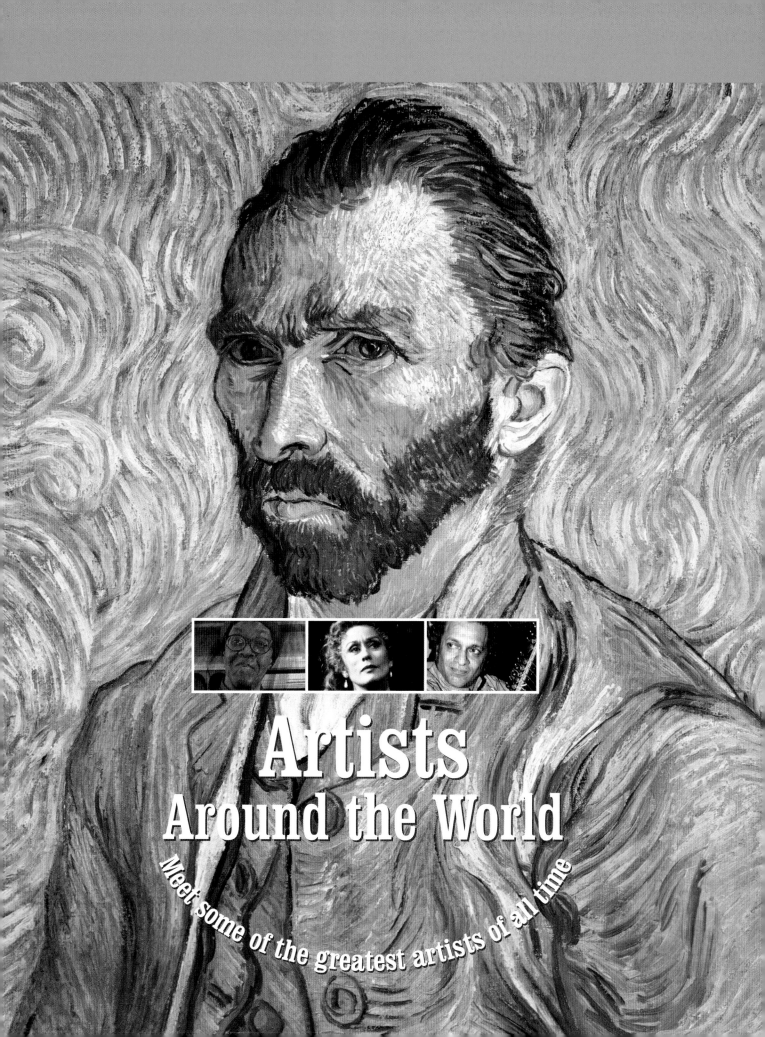

Artists
Around the World

Meet some of the greatest artists of all time

Artists Around the World

TABLE OF CONTENTS

Lonely Landscapes

Xia Gui is known today as one of China's greatest masters of **landscape** painting. He painted rapidly, using short, sharp strokes of the brush. Most of his landscapes were done in shades of black, but a few had light washes of colour added to them.

Xia was probably the official court painter to either the emperor Ningzong or the emperor Lizong (or maybe both). That means he would have lived about the end of the 12th century to the beginning of the 13th century.

Together with his friend and fellow artist Ma Yuan, Xia founded the Ma-Xia school of painting. This group followed a tradition of very simple landscape painting, with little happening in the landscape and few details. By showing only selected features, such as mountain peaks and twisted trees, they aimed to create a feeling of unlimited space and quiet drama. The Ma-Xia school had a great influence on later artists.

Most of Xia's surviving works are album leaves. These were single sheets of usually square paper, occasionally glued onto fans. The paintings were done on silk, mainly in shades of black ink. In each landscape there are distant hills in the upper left corner and a closer view of land in the lower right corner. In the centre, groups of trees reach into the empty space all around. The empty space was always an important feature of Xia's work.

Xia was also a master at **composing** works on the hand scroll. These are viewed by unrolling the scroll from one end to the other, then rerolling the scroll as you view it. The effect is like a continuous imaginary journey through the scenery of nature.

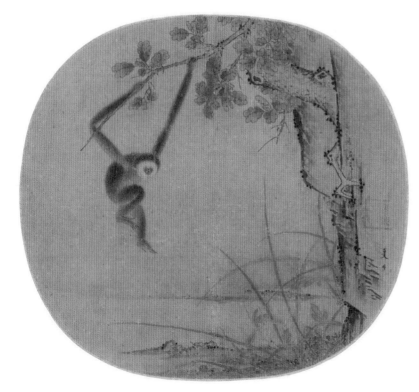

The painting here, known as 'Swinging Gibbon', is said to be by Xia Gui. The next generation of painters did not value Xia's work. But about 50 years after that, one critic wrote: 'His works have an exciting [stimulating] quality,...a remarkable achievement.'

© The Cleveland Museum of Art 2001

DID YOU KNOW?

Xia Gui and his fellow artists used a dramatic kind of brushwork called 'axe stroke'. It was named this because it looked like the chop mark of an axe on wood.

SEARCH LIGHT

Fill in the gaps: Xia Gui made his paintings on album leaves and _____ _____.

Answer: Xia Gui made his paintings on album leaves and hand scrolls.

Home-style Architect

Hassan Fathy is famous as a **humanitarian** architect. He built homes and buildings that put people's needs first. Fathy was born in 1900 in Alexandria, Egypt. He studied there and began his career in Egypt.

Fathy's goal was to build **affordable** housing for local Egyptian people. He felt that many European building methods and designs that had come into his country were not well suited to it. He thought houses should be built from local materials, according to local designs, and with traditional methods. By building in this way he lowered the cost of his houses and respected the culture of the area as well. In addition, traditional methods and materials tended to suit the local climate best.

Because Egypt is a very hot country, it is important to plan houses that are as cool as possible. Fathy's buildings often had thick walls (to keep out the heat) surrounding an interior courtyard. Air scoops on the roof caught winds from the desert and funnelled them down through the buildings. By these methods, Fathy managed to cool his buildings naturally.

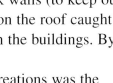

SEARCH LIGHT

The New Gourna Village was built from
a) sticks.
b) straw.
c) mud.

Hassan Fathy.
Courtesy of the Aga Khan Trust for Culture

One of Fathy's most famous creations was the New Gourna Village near Luxor, Egypt. The original village was near the **archaeological** digs of ancient Luxor and had to be relocated. Fathy trained the local people in the ancient tradition of mud brick construction. The people then built homes for themselves that were made almost entirely from mud bricks and that kept all the good features of their former homes.

Fathy died in 1989, but his work has inspired many young architects in the Middle East. He promoted ideas that adapted traditional styles and methods to the needs of the present day.

The Sadat Resthouse (built in Garf Huseyn, Egypt, in 1981) shows some of Hassan Fathy's trademark features. Here you can see the thick walls and air scoops that help cool the building naturally.

DID YOU KNOW?
Hassan Fathy is quoted as having said: 'Architecture is music frozen in place and music is architecture frozen in time.' What do you think he meant by this?

Courtesy of the Aga Khan Trust for Cult<None>ure

Answer: c) mud.

Genius of European Art

Once there was a small boy in Florence who loved to watch painters and sculptors at work. He wanted to be an artist, but his father did not like the idea. Little did the man know that his son Michelangelo would become one of the world's most famous artists.

Michelangelo began training as an artist at age 13. He was so interested in his art that he often forgot to eat and slept on the floor beside his unfinished artwork. He refused help, even on big projects, so some works took years to complete. Many were never finished.

Michelangelo worked in Rome and Florence. In Rome he was **commissioned** to carve a Pietà. This is a marble statue showing the Virgin Mary supporting the dead Christ on her knees. The finished work, known as the 'Madonna della Pietà', made him famous. And in Florence, Michelangelo spent two years working on a huge block of marble. From it he carved 'David', one of the world's finest and best-known sculptures.

Between 1508 and 1512 Michelangelo created his most famous work, the paintings on the ceiling of the Sistine Chapel in the Vatican in Rome. He painted much of the ceiling lying on his back in a tight cramped position. The **fresco** paintings of figures and events from the Bible are huge and splendid. The wall behind the altar **depicts** the Last Judgment of humanity by God.

Michelangelo was so admired that he became the first European artist whose life story was written during his own lifetime.

(Top) Portrait of Michelangelo. (Bottom) Michelangelo's frescoes on the Sistine Chapel ceiling and west wall (behind the altar).

David was the name of Michelangelo's
a) teacher.
b) student.
c) statue.

DID YOU KNOW?
Despite all the time that went into his artwork, Michelangelo found time to design buildings, write poems, and even create defensive structures for Florence.

Michelangelo's 'David' is being cleaned and repaired. It is often considered the finest example of the Renaissance ideal. During the Renaissance ('Rebirth'), art and literature blossomed richly.

Answer: c) statue.

The Brilliant Colours of Mexico

Mexican painter Frida Kahlo's life was filled with struggles. But her dazzlingly colourful **self-portraits** reflect Kahlo's power and confidence in the face of her hardships.

When Kahlo was a child she had polio, and the disease kept her right leg from growing properly. Then, when she was 18, Kahlo was in a terrible bus accident. For the rest of her life she had many operations to try to correct both of these problems.

Kahlo began to paint while she was recovering from the bus accident. Her paintings were often dramatic self-portraits that showed Kahlo's powerful feelings about herself and the world she lived in. Their brilliant colours reflect Kahlo's bold attitude toward life.

Before the bus accident, Kahlo had met the famous Mexican painter Diego Rivera while he was painting a **mural** at her school. Later she showed Rivera some of her paintings and he encouraged her to keep working at her art.

> **Frida Kahlo's most famous paintings were**
> a) murals.
> b) self-portraits.
> c) buses.

> **DID YOU KNOW?**
> Kahlo was very proudly Mexican. She often wore very decorative Mexican jewellery and native clothing. Her hairstyle, piled high on her head, was also in the style of the people of the Mexican state of Oaxaca.

Kahlo and Rivera were married in 1929. They travelled to the United States where Rivera had received **commissions** for murals. Kahlo kept painting and met many important people of the time. The artist Pablo Picasso admired her work. And many of her well-known friends helped her show her paintings in Europe and America.

Kahlo's work was called 'surrealistic' by some. Surrealism is a style of art that has a strange dreamlike quality. Kahlo, however, said that her paintings were the reality that she felt and that they spanned both reality and dreams.

In the spring of 1953 Kahlo had the only exhibition of her work in Mexico. She died one year later. Today her house in Coyoacán is the Frida Kahlo Museum.

Frida Kahlo was the first Hispanic woman to be featured on a U.S. postage stamp. The stamp, seen here being unveiled, featured one of her famous self-portraits.
© AFP/Corbis

Answer: b) self-portraits.

Sunflowers
and Starry Nights

Vincent van Gogh was a Dutch artist of the 19th century and is now considered to be one of the greatest painters in the world. Van Gogh painted what he saw around him - trees, flowers, people, and buildings. He visited museums and met with other painters. But van Gogh had his own way of painting. He said he 'wanted to look at nature under a brighter sky.'

Self-portrait of van Gogh, painted in 1889.
© Archivo Iconografico, S.A./Corbis

SEARCH LIGHT

How many paintings did van Gogh sell in his lifetime?
a) 80
b) 700
c) 1

In van Gogh's paintings, the southern French town of Arles is like no other place in the world. The skies are bluer and the sun is brighter. The orchards in bloom are pinker and greener. The cobblestone streets are more cobbled and stony. His pictures seem to be flooded with a golden light.

Van Gogh wanted wonderful colour in his pictures. His paintings called 'Sunflowers', 'Irises', and 'Starry Night' are among the most famous pictures he painted and are filled with brilliant colours. He tried to keep to the outward appearance of his subjects, yet his feelings about them exploded in strong colour and bold lines.

Van Gogh's style was direct, forceful, and natural. He worked with great speed and excitement. He was set on capturing an effect or a mood while it possessed him. He told his brother that if anyone said a painting was done too quickly, 'you can reply that they have looked at it too fast.'

Van Gogh painted for just ten years. But during this time he did more than 800 paintings in oil colours and 700 drawings. Surprisingly, he sold only one painting while he lived. People did not understand the way he painted. His work was too unusual and alive with energy.

Now the whole world knows he was a great artist.

DID YOU KNOW?
In 1990 van Gogh's 'Portrait of Dr. Gachet' sold for approximately £51.5 million - the most ever paid for a single painting.

Van Gogh's paintings of sunflowers are probably some of the most famous paintings in the world. You may even have seen them on T-shirts and coffee mugs. This is a photo of an original, painted in 1889.
© Christie's Images/Corbis

Answer: c) 1

Painter to the King
and to the People

Goya's self-portrait at the age of 69.
© Francis G. Mayer/Corbis

As a young man in Spain, Francisco de Goya worked as a bull-fighter. But his great love was painting. After studying art in Rome, Goya returned to Spain and worked as a **tapestry** designer. Soon his talents attracted attention and he began painting portraits of wealthy Spaniards. By 1786 Goya had become a 'painter to the king of Spain'.

But Goya became tired of painting pictures of dukes and duchesses and the royal family. Most of the people of Spain were poor and often hungry. Constant wars made their lives worse. Wanting to portray this 'everyday' world, Goya began to draw and paint images of the poor and hardworking people of Spain.

Goya didn't make the men and women in his art look prettier or more important than they were. His paintings show people as they looked after a life of hard work. Goya included the lines in their faces and the sadness in their lives. He showed their bent backs and their worn clothes. This style of painting people and scenes from daily life is called 'realism'.

Goya's pictures of everyday life include some pleasant moments such as this one, titled 'Two Boys with Two Mastiffs'. (As you've probably guessed, a mastiff is a large breed of dog.)
© Archivo Iconografico, S.A./Corbis

The subjects of Goya's paintings did not always please the king and the people of the royal court. They thought he should paint only famous people and beautiful things. In fact, his 'Disasters of War' series of etchings was so realistic and **gory** that it was not shown until over 35 years after Goya's death. But today, hundreds of years later, the power and honesty of Goya's 'everyday' paintings still impress and move viewers.

SEARCH LIGHT

Why is Goya's art called 'realism'?

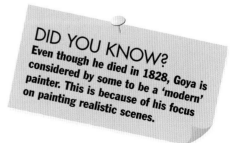

DID YOU KNOW?
Even though he died in 1828, Goya is considered by some to be a 'modern' painter. This is because of his focus on painting realistic scenes.

Answer: Goya's painting style was called 'realism' because he showed ordinary people as they really were.

Exploring
with an Artist

There's a story which says that the artist Pablo Picasso started to draw before he learned to speak. While this is probably only a story, it does suggest how important art was to Picasso.

Picasso was born in Spain in 1881 but lived much of his life in France. He was an inventor and an explorer. But he didn't invent machines or explore strange places. He explored and invented with art. He painted with his fingers, made drawings with a rusty nail, and even made a bull's head from the handlebars and seat of a bicycle. He was able to work anywhere at any time of the day or night.

Picasso's big studio was a sort of jungle - a jungle of paint cans, brushes, chalk, pottery, coloured pencils, and crayons, among many other things. Rolls of heavy paper and canvas, picture frames and easels, and tools for cutting designs on heavy board lay scattered about like rubbish. But to Picasso it was all **inspiration**.

He painted Spanish bullfighting,

Visitors viewing Picasso's painting 'Mandolin, Fruit Bowl, and Plaster Arm'.
© AFP/Corbis

SEARCH LIGHT

What does it mean to say that Picasso's studio was a jungle? (Hint: Jungles are hard to walk through.)

horse races, and clowns. He painted happy pictures in warm colours (such as pink) and sad, lonely ones in cool colours (such as dark blue). He sometimes painted people and animals the way they were. But more often he painted them from his imagination.

The art style that Picasso and fellow artist Georges Braque invented is called Cubism. They painted people and things so that all parts and sides could be seen at the same time. Cubists often created pictures from simple shapes such as squares or cubes.

DID YOU KNOW?
Picasso was probably the single most influential figure in 20th-century Western art. And he worked for 80 of his 91 years. He experimented with a large variety of styles in a number of artistic mediums.

In 2001 the works of Picasso were shown for the first time in China. These children are practising drawing by imitating some Picasso prints. A large photo of the artist looks on from the wall.
© Reuters NewMedia Inc./Corbis

Answer: Picasso's studio was so cluttered with art supplies that it was difficult to move around in it. Just as jungles are rich and dense with plant and animal life, so his studio was crowded with materials that helped him create.

Creator
of Fantastical Fictions

Can you imagine a garden where a beautiful poppy flower has the power to unravel time? Or a pool where if you gaze too long into it, you could merge with your reflection? Jorge Luis Borges imagined these things and more as he created **fantastical** worlds with his words.

Borges on his 82nd birthday, in 1981.
© Bettmann/Corbis

Borges was born in 1899, in Buenos Aires, Argentina. His father was a lawyer and his mother was a teacher. His English-born grandmother told him many stories. Borges was educated at home by an English governess and learned English before Spanish.

At age 20 Borges started writing poems, essays, and a biography. But when his father died in 1938, Borges had to take up a job as a librarian to support the family. The same year, Borges suffered a severe head wound that left him near death, unable to speak, and afraid he was insane. This experience seems to have freed in him a great creativity. When he finished his library work, he would spend the rest of the day reading and writing.

Borges' dreamlike short stories would later make him famous when they were collected in the books *Ficciones* (*Fictions*) and *The Aleph and Other Stories, 1933-69*. He also wrote political articles that angered the Argentine government and cost him his library job.

In 1956 Borges received Argentina's national prize for literature. But he had been losing his eyesight for decades because of a rare disease and by this time he was completely blind. Still, he created stories by having his mother and friends write as he **dictated**. Some of his best work was produced this way, including *El libro de los seres imaginarios* (*The Book of Imaginary Beings*).

SEARCH LIGHT

Although Borges is famous as a Spanish-language writer, what language did he learn first?

Uruguayan President Jorge Batlle (left) and Argentine Chancellor Adalberto Rodríguez Giavariani admire a portrait of Jorge Luis Borges painted by Jorge Demirjian.
AP/Wide World Photos

Answer: Because his governess was English, Borges learned English before Spanish.

Aboriginal Poet

She was born Kathleen Jean Mary Ruska, but she's known in the Aboriginal language as Oodgeroo Noonuccal. Her Aboriginal last name, Noonuccal, is the name of her clan. Kath Walker, the name she wrote under for most of her career, became a famous Australian Aboriginal writer and political protester. In fact, when her book of poetry, *We Are Going,* came out in 1964, she became the first Aboriginal woman to be published.

Kath Walker (Aboriginal name Oodgeroo Noonuccal) as an older woman.
National Archives of Australia/Canberra, Act, Australia

DID YOU KNOW?
Walker was left-handed, but her teachers in school forced her to write with her right hand. Not long ago, this practice was common in many places. Right-handedness was thought to be somehow 'better' and 'normal'.

Walker grew up in Queensland, Australia, where many of the ancient Aboriginal customs were still practiced. At the time Walker was growing up, Aboriginal people had few rights in Australia. She was allowed to go to school only through the primary grades.

When she was 13, Walker began work as a maid. At 16 she wanted to become a nurse but wasn't allowed to because she was Aboriginal. What Walker did instead was work hard for Aboriginal rights. In 1967 she was successful in getting the anti-Aboriginal sections removed from the Australian constitution. In recognition of her efforts, she was awarded the MBE (Member of the Order of the British Empire) in 1970. Walker would later give back this award to protest further discrimination against Aboriginal people. After 1981 most of her work was published under her Aboriginal name.

SEARCH LIGHT

Find and correct the mistake in the following sentence: Walker was the first Aboriginal woman to be noticed.

Walker described her poetry as easy to understand, with simple rhymes and images. Her work focuses on the troubles of the Aboriginal people. Below is a sample of her poetry.

> But I'll tell instead of brave and fine
> when lives of black and white entwine.
> And men in brotherhood combine,
> this would I tell you, son of mine.

As a young woman, Kath Walker was angry about how Aboriginal people were treated. She then began working to have the laws made more fair - and she succeeded in many ways.

National Archives of Australia/Canberra, Act, Australia

Answer: Walker was the first Aboriginal woman to be published.

The Letter
Writer's Stories

SEARCH LIGHT

Latin American writer Isabel Allende was born in 1942, in Lima, Peru. Her many books, written in Spanish, have been translated into several languages. Her works feature a **technique** called 'magic realism' - the use of fantasy and myth in realistic fiction. Her stories reflect her own experiences and also look at the role of women in Latin America.

Isabel Allende's uncle was Salvador Allende, president of Chile. She was a journalist there, as well as a short-story writer. In 1973, Salvador Allende was murdered during a time of political problems. Under the new government, Isabel Allende was threatened, and she and her husband and children were forced to flee to Venezuela. They ended up spending 13 years there.

In 1981, while still in **exile**, she started writing a letter to her dying grandfather. She wrote about childhood memories and the people who had touched their lives. This letter turned into her first novel, *La casa de los espíritus* (1982; *The House of the Spirits*). It was followed by the novels *De amor y de sombra* (1984; *Of Love and Shadows*), *Eva Luna* (1987), and *El plan infinito* (1991; *The Infinite Plan*).

Most of Allende's stories have a political **aspect** and include a number of exiles. Allende calls these people the '**marginals**'. She says that they are exiled from the big umbrella of society. They have the courage to stand on the edge of life and not be sheltered or protected.

In 1990, Allende was able to return to Chile. But she was heartbroken when her young daughter became sick and died of a terrible blood disease. Out of her sorrow came a book, *Paula* (1994). It was Allende's first **non-fiction** book and it went on to become a bestseller.

> **Why do you suppose that Isabel Allende often writes about people who are exiles?**

> **DID YOU KNOW?**
> After *Paula* was published, Allende suffered from severe writer's block. 'Writer's block' is the term used when a writer is unable to think what to write or how to write it. Allende eventually broke through by writing another non-fiction work.

© Ed Kashi/Corbis

Answer: Isabel Allende and her family became exiles themselves. It's not unusual for writers to draw on their own experiences for their work - even if it's fiction.

Writer of Life-Changing Stories

The famous English author Charles Dickens lived more than 100 years ago. Many of the stories he wrote were about how hard life could be for children. And many changes were made because of his books.

Some of Dickens' stories tell about how some children were treated badly in schools, at home, and at work. At his own school, his teacher beat him with a cane for laughing too loudly. Dickens was barely a teenager when he had to quit school and take a job away from home. His father had spent too much money and could not pay it back. He used many of his own experiences when he wrote his book *David Copperfield*.

When Dickens' stories were first read, some people were angry. Others were ashamed. Such stories as *Oliver Twist* made them think seriously. They realized that children should be treated kindly and should have fun as well as study hard. They should not be made to leave home and go to work when they are very young.

One of Dickens' best-known stories is called *A Christmas Carol*. It tells about a rich man called Scrooge who doesn't like Christmas. In fact, he doesn't like very much at all, except for making money. In the story, Scrooge learns that his life is better when he helps others and spends time enjoying their company.

People still like to read Dickens' books, not just to find out what life was like a long time ago but for the wonderful stories that they tell. Some are funny, like his *Pickwick Papers*. Some are family stories, such as *David Copperfield* and *Great Expectations*. And some of his books are historical stories, like *A Tale of Two Cities*.

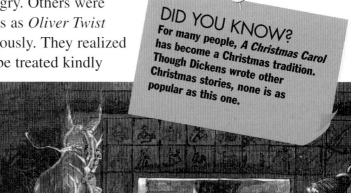

Charles Dickens.
© Bettmann/Corbis

SEARCH LIGHT

True or false? Dickens' stories were entirely imaginary creations.

DID YOU KNOW?
For many people, *A Christmas Carol* has become a Christmas tradition. Though Dickens wrote other Christmas stories, none is as popular as this one.

In this illustration from Dickens' *A Christmas Carol*, the miserly Ebenezer Scrooge is visited by the miserable ghost of his former partner, Jacob Marley.
© Bettmann/Corbis

Answer: FALSE. Dickens used experiences from his own life and the lives of unfortunate children for some of his stories.

Journey to Everywhere

Imagine exploring a distant land in a giant balloon. You could drift over mountains and waterfalls, deep blue lakes, and flaming volcanoes.

A French writer named Jules Verne imagined such a journey many years ago. He wrote about it in a book called *Five Weeks in a Balloon* (1863). It was his first adventure story about strange journeys. People liked the story so much that Verne decided to write more. The next one was called *A Journey to the Centre of the Earth* (1864). It was about all the wonderful and scary things people might find inside the Earth.

As a young boy Verne often went sailing with his brother on the River Loire in France. Verne would imagine that he was sailing a huge **yacht** on a voyage of discovery. Verne wrote about his imaginary adventures in the sea in *Twenty Thousand Leagues Under the Sea* (1870). He named his imaginary submarine the *Nautilus*, after an actual submarine built in 1800. In *From the Earth to the Moon* (1865) he wrote about travelling to the Moon in a rocketship long before powered flight was even possible.

People have said that Verne invented the future. It would be more accurate to say that he invented **science fiction**. Verne himself said that he was fortunate to live and write in a time when new discoveries and inventions were being made. He kept up with advances in geography and science to get ideas for his stories. Verne believed the discoveries he studied would someday make his imaginary journeys a reality.

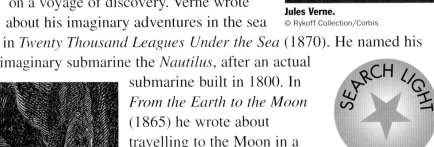

Jules Verne.
© Rykoff Collection/Corbis

DID YOU KNOW?
Not long after the success of Verne's book *Around the World in 80 Days* (1873), journalist Nellie Bly attempted the around-the-world journey. She finished in 72 days.

SEARCH LIGHT

How did studying geography and science help Verne's writing? (Hint: He liked to write about things that might happen.)

Like many of Jules Verne's novels, *Twenty Thousand Leagues Under the Sea* is filled with fantastical creatures and exciting places.
© Bettmann/Corbis

Answer: Studying geography helped Verne set his fantasy stories in realistic places to make them seem more real. His knowledge of science helped his invented machines seem more possible.

Poet Laureate
of India

Rabindranath Tagore, born in 1861 in Calcutta, India, started writing poems when he was only 8 years old. He grew up to be the first Indian writer to receive the Nobel Prize for Literature.

Tagore studied in India and London, England. In 1890 he published *Manasi*, his first collection of truly fine poems. In 1891 he went to East Bengal (now Bangladesh) to help manage his family's lands. He found the village people kind but very poor. Tagore wrote many poems and stories about their condition. He also wrote about the beautiful Bengali countryside, especially the Padma River.

Tagore wrote in new forms of verse and in the common language of the Bengali people, rather than in **classical** styles. His writings became very popular amongst all Bengalis. His poems of 1901-07 reflect his great sadness at the death of his wife and two of his children. In 1910 he wrote a little book of devotional songs called *Gitanjali*. It was translated into many languages and became a huge success. In 1913 he won the Nobel Prize for Literature.

Tagore produced 22 collections of writings during his life. He wrote songs, plays, short stories, and books, and he composed music. He also founded a school in rural West Bengal that combined European and Indian traditions. It later became Vishva-Bharati University.

In 1915 the British government knighted Tagore. Four years later he gave up his knighthood after a terrible shooting of Indians by British soldiers. All his life he spoke out against British rule of India.

Tagore lectured and read his works to people in many countries from about 1912. And at about age 70 he took up painting and became one of India's finest artists.

DID YOU KNOW?

Rabindranath Tagore's father was a major Hindu thinker. He founded a quiet getaway in rural West Bengal (a state of India), where his son set up his experimental school.

SEARCH LIGHT

Rabindranath Tagore is famous as the first Indian to do what?

© E.O. Hoppé/Corbis

Rabindranath Tagore, seen here with his granddaughter in 1929, is generally considered the most outstanding artist of modern India.

Answer: Tagore is famous for being the first Indian to win the Nobel Prize for Literature.

Haiku Master

SEARCH LIGHT

Basho's name came from his
a) cottage.
b) village.
c) lord.

The poet Basho was born Matsuo Munefusa in 1644. He is considered to be the greatest of the Japanese *haiku* poets. Basho took his name from the Japanese term *basho-an*, meaning 'cottage of the plantain tree' (a plantain is like a banana). This was a simple place where the poet liked to go to be by himself.

Haiku is a traditional form of Japanese poetry that puts great emotion in just a few words. *Haiku* poems have only three lines and a total of only 17 syllables. And they are often about nature.

Although he was interested in poetry from a young age, Matsuo wasn't always a poet. He started out as a **samurai** warrior in the service of a local lord. But after his lord's death in 1666, Matsuo gave up being a warrior and focused on creating poetry. He moved to Japan's capital, Tokyo (at that time called Edo), and soon became well known as a poet and **critic**.

Basho brought a new style of *haiku* to Japanese poetry. In the past, it had basically been a hobby and not very serious, but Basho brought his Buddhist beliefs to his writing. He looked with interest at small things and showed the connections between all things. His new-style *haiku* compared two separate physical events. In the following *haiku*, for example, he links nightfall with the landing of a black crow.

On a withered branch A crow has alighted: Nightfall in autumn.

(Note: Unlike the original, this **translation** has only 16 syllables.)

Basho wrote poems as he traveled around the islands of Japan. He wrote about the sights and landscapes he saw, and these poems are considered some of his best.

DID YOU KNOW?
A term often used to describe Basho's poetry is *sabi*. The word refers to a love of the old, the faded, and the little-noticed.

Answer: a) cottage.

The Nobel Laureate

When Wole Soyinka was a child, his grandfather told him how to deal with a bully. 'Even if you are beaten, challenge him again. I promise you, either you will defeat him or he will run away.'

These words turned out to be true for Wole Soyinka, the first black African writer to win the Nobel Prize for Literature. The bully he fought - with his words, not his fists - was the Nigerian military government. Even when the government put him into prison, he continued to write his stories, novels, essays, poetry, and plays.

Soyinka was born in 1934 in Nigeria. His full name is Akinwande Oluwole Soyinka. His large family is of Yoruba heritage. And having a big family, he got to listen to lots of stories - about battles, religion, legends, and family.

Soyinka attended university in England but returned to Nigeria to study African drama. He also taught drama and literature at Nigerian universities. In 1960 he founded a theatre group, where he put on his own plays and even acted in some. His first important play, *A Dance of the Forests*, was about Nigerian independence. In *The Lion and the Jewel*, Soyinka made fun of Westernized African school teachers.

During the Nigerian **civil war**, Soyinka worked for a cease-fire and was arrested because of his work and writings. The government placed him in a cell all by himself for over a year. Only his own ideas kept him entertained. These ideas became some of his later books.

Soyinka's plays draw on Nigerian culture, dance, poetry, music, and myths. These elements combine with his wide knowledge and his strong political beliefs to create powerful dramatic images and ideas.

Wole Soyinka in 1986.
© Jacques Langevin/Corbis

SEARCH LIGHT

Fill in the gap: Soyinka was imprisoned for disagreeing with the Nigerian _____.

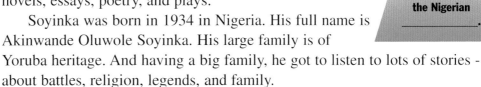

Soyinka's plays have been staged worldwide. *Death and the King's Horseman* (shown here at the Goodman Theatre in Chicago, Illinois, U.S.) dramatizes the conflict between Western morals and African culture and traditions.
The Goodman Theatre; photo by James C. Clark

DID YOU KNOW?
Soyinka often refers to the Yoruba god Ogun as an important figure for him, his writing, and his people. He describes Ogun as 'the god of creativity and destruction'. Ogun is traditionally the god of war, the hunt, and ironworking.

Answer: Soyinka was imprisoned for disagreeing with the Nigerian government.

A Life of Letters and Literature

SEARCH LIGHT

Fill in the gap: Dickinson often sent her poems in _____ to her friends.

Emily Dickinson, one of America's greatest poets, was born in 1830 in Massachusetts, U.S. She had many friends, though she did not often leave her home to meet them. After 1865 she seldom left her room, appearing only occasionally and briefly in a white dress when guests visited downstairs.

Dickinson spent a great deal of time writing to her friends. The greatest excitement in Dickinson's life was in her **vivid** imagination. She included many of her best poems in the letters she wrote. She also wrote or copied poems into little booklets that she made by sewing pages together.

For the time in which she lived, Dickinson's poems were unusual. Most of them are about familiar things such as love and friendship, nature and death. But her rhymes are often not quite exact, and some of her poems are like a puzzle. But many people find great beauty and truth in her words.

Her poems are especially remarkable because of the strong effect they have, even though they're usually very brief. She stripped away unnecessary words and made sure that those that remained were **energetic** and exact. She also liked to place a familiar word in an unusual position to 'surprise' us and to make us pay attention.

Many people think that the poems of Emily Dickinson are among the best ever written by an American poet. It seems strange, then, that only seven of her poems were published while she was alive. It was Dickinson's sister, Lavinia, who first published her poems in a book. She called it *Poems by Emily Dickinson*. It was published in 1890, four years after Emily died.

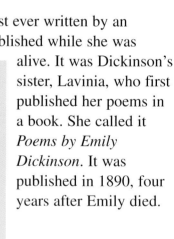

DID YOU KNOW?

Here is a sample of Dickinson's poetry:
The bee is not afraid of me,
I know the butterfly;
The pretty people in the woods
Receive me cordially.
The brooks laugh louder when I come,
The breezes madder play.
Wherefore, mine eyes, thy silver mists?
Wherefore, O summer's day?

Answer: Dickinson often sent her poems in letters to her friends.

Prized Poet
of Illinois

Gwendolyn Brooks was born in 1917 and grew up in Chicago, Illinois, U.S. That city would play a major part in the life and work of this important American poet. She began writing poetry when she was just 7 years old. By the time she was in her early teens, her writing was being published in magazines.

Brooks, an African American, attended what was then the leading secondary school for white children in Chicago. This was very unusual at the time. She was later transferred to an all-black school and then to an **integrated** school. These experiences gave her an insight into the relationships between black people and white people that strongly influenced her work.

Brooks's first published book, *A Street in Bronzeville* (1945), won rave reviews. Its poems made the ordinary life of her neighbours seem special to the reader. In 1950, Brooks won the Pulitzer Prize for Poetry with *Annie Allen*. She was the first African American poet to win this award. The book's poems focus on an African American girl growing up in Chicago.

In the late 1960s, Brooks's poetry became more **political**. She began to think that 'black

Gwendolyn Brooks with her first published book, *A Street in Bronzeville* (1945).
AP/Wide World Photos

poets should write as blacks, about blacks, and address themselves to blacks.' In 1968 she published *In the Mecca*. The book's long title poem reflects the pain and struggle of African American people living in the Mecca, a vast block of flats that had become part of a **slum**.

Brooks wrote many more books. She was honoured as **poet laureate** of Illinois (1968) and held a similar position for the whole United States (1985-86). Throughout her life Brooks remained strongly committed to teaching about the power of poetry and to encouraging young writers.

SEARCH LIGHT

Gwendolyn Brooks was the first African American poet to
a) win the Nobel Prize.
b) be published in the United States.
c) win the Pulitzer Prize.

© Bettmann/Corbis

Answer: c) win the Pulitzer Prize.

The Writer and the Mississippi River

A one time Mississippi River boat pilot, Mark Twain became one of America's greatest authors. His *Tom Sawyer*, *Huckleberry Finn*, and *Life on the Mississippi* rank high on any list of great American books.

Mark Twain was born Samuel Langhorne Clemens in 1835. He grew up in Hannibal, Missouri, on the Mississippi River. From this river town he gathered the material for his most famous stories. Young Tom Sawyer, for instance, was a combination of several boys - including himself.

During his life, he held jobs that he would turn into material for his writing. His work as a riverboat pilot gave him experience he used to write *Life on the Mississippi*. When he began working as a newspaper reporter, he began using the pen-name Mark Twain. It is an old river term meaning two fathoms, or 12 feet, of water - a depth that was not very safe for riverboats.

One of his stories, 'The Celebrated Jumping Frog of Calaveras County', was printed in many newspapers. It was a popular story, and Twain travelled as a roving reporter and then on a lecture tour. After these travels he wrote *The Innocents Abroad*, which made him famous.

Twain was known as a humourist. But behind his mask of humour lay a serious view of life. He had known the sadness of poverty, the early death of his father and later his brother Henry, and the loss of a daughter. One of his most famous novels, *Huckleberry Finn*, is sometimes thought of as a child's book. But its heartbreak and wisdom are appreciated best by adults. Another of his famous novels, *Tom Sawyer*, is mostly a young person's book that adults can also read with pleasure.

SEARCH LIGHT

'Half twain' means 'mark twain plus half a mark' and equals 15 feet. So how much is a mark?

Mark Twain.
© Bettmann/Corbis

DID YOU KNOW?
Mark Twain's words are quoted frequently for both their wisdom and their humour. In one of his books, he wrote: 'Man is the Animal that Blushes. He is the only one that does it - or has occasion to.' What do you suppose he meant?

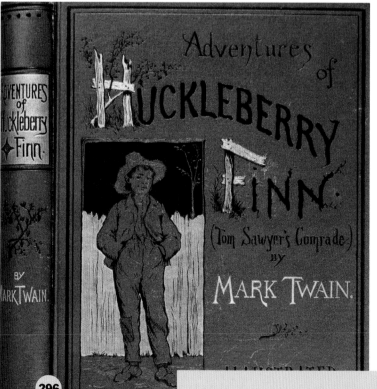

Huckleberry Finn is considered by many to be Twain's finest work. But from time to time it is banned in schools or libraries because of racial issues in the book.
© Stapleton Collection/Corbis

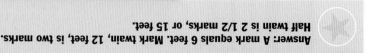

Answer: A mark equals 6 feet. Mark twain, 12 feet, is two marks. Half twain is 2 1/2 marks, or 15 feet.

Theatrical Ballerina

SEARCH LIGHT

Find and correct the mistake in the following sentence: Elssler's style of ballet borrowed from break dance traditions.

Fanny Elssler was a famous Austrian dancer who brought energy and drama to her performances. She was born in 1810, in Vienna, Austria, and studied ballet from a young age. As a child, Elssler appeared with her sister in several ballets at Vienna's Kärntnerthor Theatre.

When she was a young adult, Elssler became famous worldwide thanks to her energetic spirit onstage and her remarkable pointe work (dancing on the points of the toes). She made her Paris Opéra debut in 1834 in Jean Coralli's ballet *La Tempête,* a dance version of William Shakespeare's play *The Tempest.*

Before Elssler came along, most ballet was 'classical ballet', which featured light graceful dance, like that performed by Elssler's greatest rival dancer, Marie Taglioni. But Elssler introduced theatrical, or 'character', ballet, which borrowed from folk dance traditions and even mime. She performed a Polish folk dance called the 'cracovienne' in the ballet *La Gypsy.* And because some Gypsies were associated with Spain, she got the nickname 'the Spaniard from the north'.

Elssler spent the later part of her career touring the United States, England, Germany, Italy, and Russia. Because of her long world tours, Elssler had to break her agreement with the Paris Opéra, and so she could not return to dance in France. Her worldwide tour ended up lasting more than ten years.

Elssler retired from the ballet in 1851. Her last years were spent in her native Vienna. During her career she was unequalled as a 'character' dancer with amazing dramatic powers.

DID YOU KNOW?
Elssler and her sister danced at Marie Taglioni's debut, in Taglioni's father's ballet troupe.

Fanny Elssler was known for her great dramatic skill. She was one of the first ballerinas to tour the United States. She was noted for her Spanish dances and often performed with her sister Therese.
© Archivo Iconografico, S.A./Corbis

Answer: Elssler's style of ballet borrowed from folk dance traditions.

'The Divine Sarah'

Sarah Bernhardt, called 'the Divine Sarah' by playwright Oscar Wilde, was one of the greatest French actresses of the 19th century - and one of the most famous actresses of all time.

In 1861, at age 17, Bernhardt was enrolled in the acting course at the Paris Conservatoire. She admired some of her teachers. But she considered the school's methods too old-fashioned. Through a family friend, Bernhardt was accepted into the national theatre company, the Comédie-Française. But she soon had to leave because she slapped a senior actress who had been rude to her younger sister. After a period when she questioned her talent for acting, Bernhardt joined the Odéon theatre and, in six years, established her reputation as an actress.

Sarah Bernhardt in the title role of Victorien Sardou's play *Theodora*.
© Hulton-Deutsch Collection/Corbis

Building on her success, Bernhardt returned to the Comédie-Française. When she played the title role in Jean Racine's *Phédre*, she surprised the critics with the passion of her performance and was given excellent reviews. From that point on, she was a star. She performed in France and internationally. And she was in demand for new plays by major writers of the day, as well as for classics such as William Shakespeare's works. She even played a number of male roles, including Hamlet.

Bernhardt possessed a wide emotional range and could show sensitive detail in her acting. Her grace, striking looks, and charm gave her a **commanding** stage **presence**. And her unique voice was sometimes described as sounding like a 'golden bell'. Her popularity also increased because of her dramatic personality offstage.

In 1915 an earlier injury worsened and her right leg had to be removed. She continued to act, however, playing parts she could perform while seated.

Poster of Sarah Bernhardt from the early 1900s.
© Historical Picture Archive/Corbis

DID YOU KNOW?
Bernhardt liked to keep her fans entertained and shocked, so she let it be known that she slept in a coffin every night. Though she slept mostly in an ordinary bed, she did pose for photographs 'asleep' in her coffin.

SEARCH LIGHT

Why do you think Sarah Bernhardt was nicknamed 'the Divine Sarah'?

Answer: Her wonderful acting, striking looks, and beautiful voice made Sarah Bernhardt seem to some like a goddess.

Living for Music

Can you imagine composing music without being able to hear it? Beethoven, one of the greatest music composers ever born, created much of his best music late in life, after he had become totally deaf.

Ludwig van Beethoven was born in 1770 in Bonn, Germany. Music was very important in his family. His grandfather and his father were professional singers in the choir of the **archbishop** in Bonn. Young Beethoven was given the opportunity to play the organ at court as soon as he was old enough to work. The archbishop liked his music so much that he sent him to Vienna to learn from Wolfgang Amadeus Mozart. After hearing Beethoven play, Mozart told his friends: 'This young man will make a great name for himself in the world.'

At that time people usually thought of the piano as an instrument for playing music for singers. But Beethoven composed such beautiful piano music that it stood on its own as a work of art. Beethoven's music was a bridge between a strict musical tradition and a freer, more deeply emotional style of music. He also brought new ideas and life to such classical music forms as the sonata, symphony, concerto, and quartet. Some of his best-known works include the *Moonlight Sonata*, the *Pastoral* and *Eroica* symphonies, and the *Emperor Concerto*.

After some years Beethoven realized that he couldn't hear things clearly any more - not even what he was playing. Doctors told him he would never be cured. Beethoven stopped playing in public and kept away from people. But he still heard music in his mind and he wrote down his musical ideas in his notebooks. These books contained some of his finest music.

Beethoven's own handwritten music for his *Eroica* symphony.

Mansell/Timepix

SEARCH LIGHT

Beethoven was Mozart's
a) teacher.
b) student.
c) father.

DID YOU KNOW?
Beethoven's musical works marked the beginnings of Romantic music. That sounds like music about love. But 'romantic' more broadly describes art that is concerned with expressing emotions, dramatic things in life, and the individual person's experience.

© Archivo Iconografico, S.A./Corbis

Answer: b) student.

Music at His Fingertips

Which instrument did Ravi Shankar play and make famous?
a) sitar
b) drums
c) cymbals

In 1930, at age 10, Ravi Shankar and other family members joined his eldest brother's Indian dance **troupe** in Paris, France. The boy lived in France for over five years and studied dance and music.

Shankar gave up dance at age 18. He returned to India and studied the sitar

Ravi Shankar and daughter Anoushka performing at a charity concert in Kuala Lumpur, Malaysia, in 2001.
© AFP/Corbis

for seven years under master musician Ustad Allauddin Khan. The sitar is a large long-necked stringed instrument, played from a seated position.

In 1944 Shankar began composing film music. A bit later he became music director of All India Radio. His audience grew within India. And when his musical **score** for Satyajit Ray's 1955 film *Pather Panchali* won major awards, Shankar gained worldwide notice.

Shankar first toured the United States and England in 1956. Over the next ten years his audiences grew from small groups of Indian immigrants to sold-out concerts at New York City's Philharmonic Hall. As Shankar's fame increased, so did the popularity of Indian music. Sitar music is very different from music of the West. So it was exciting for Shankar and others to combine the two traditions to make altogether new sounds.

DID YOU KNOW?
The most frequently played South Asian musical form for sitar is called a *raga*. The sitarist, accompanied by *tabla* (drum) and *tamboura* (droning lute), plays a particular set of notes in a very specific way to create a unique mood.

Shankar met and worked with many famous Western musicians who played a variety of styles. He played with jazz musicians, classical violinist Yehudi Menuhin, pianist and **conductor** André Previn, and experimental composer Philip Glass. His most famous musical association was with rock musician George Harrison of the Beatles. Harrison studied sitar under Shankar in India. Harrison's fame and influence allowed him to introduce Shankar and Indian music to a vast audience in the West.

Shankar continues to compose and perform. And he remains one of the most highly regarded musicians in the world.

In 1971 George Harrison organized the Concert for Bangladesh. Ravi Shankar and many other musicians performed to raise money for the starving people of that country.
© Henry Diltz/Corbis

A Vision in Motion

Film-maker Akira Kurosawa got his start working as an assistant director for a Japanese film studio. In 1943 he wrote and directed his first feature film, *Sanshiro Sugata*. The story of 19th-century **judo** masters became very popular with Japanese audiences.

Kurosawa's fame grew in 1948 with his film *Yoidore tenshi* (*Drunken Angel*).

Kurosawa with American directors Francis Ford Coppola and George Lucas.
© The Kobal Collection—Toho/Kurosawa

The film is about an alcoholic doctor who helps the poor fight against disease and **gangsters**. It stars Toshiro Mifune, who appeared in most of Kurosawa's films. In 1951 *Rashomon* made Kurosawa the first world-famous Japanese film-maker. The film won the Grand Prix at the Venice Film Festival and the Academy Award for best foreign film.

Many consider Kurosawa's best film to be *Ikiru* (*To Live*), from 1952. It follows a man who has only a few months to live and spends his last days helping the poor. Two years later Kurosawa released his most popular film: *Shichinin no samurai* (*Seven Samurai*). The film is a **tribute** to American westerns - but with **samurai** warriors instead of cowboys. In fact, it was later remade in the United States as the western *The Magnificent Seven*.

Many of Kurosawa's films were set in historical Japan. But his work was popular in Japan and throughout the world. It combined artistic ideas, emotions, and images with plenty of action and drama to keep viewers entertained.

Kurosawa died in 1998. The Kurosawa Akira **Memorial** Satellite Studio has been opened on the Japanese island of Kyushu. It was there that he filmed several of his masterpieces, including *Ran* and *Kagemusha*.

SEARCH LIGHT

Which of the following films is called *Seven Samurai* in English?
a) *Shichinin no samurai*
b) *Yoidore tenshi*
c) *Ikiru*

DID YOU KNOW?
Kurosawa was well known for making classic European literature into films with Japanese settings. For example, *Kumonosu-jo* (*The Throne of Blood*) was adapted from William Shakespeare's *Macbeth* and told from a Japanese viewpoint.

Kurosawa's film *Ran* ('Chaos') is felt by many to be his finest work. It is a version of Shakespeare's play *King Lear* set in 16th-century Japan.
© The Kobal Collection/Herald Ace-Nippon—Herald-Greenwich

Answer: a) *Shichinin no samurai*

New Zealand's Opera Star

Kiri Te Kanawa was born in 1944 in New Zealand. At the age of 5 weeks, she was adopted. Her adoptive and biological mothers were both of British descent. Her adoptive and biological fathers were Maori (native New Zealanders).

Te Kanawa's mother discovered very early that her daughter was musical. So her parents sent her to a school where a well-known singer taught music. After leaving school Te Kanawa won various singing competitions in New Zealand and Australia.

By the 1970s Te Kanawa was world famous as a **soprano** diva (leading female vocalist) of opera. Her first big success was in Wolfgang Amadeus Mozart's opera *The Marriage of Figaro*. She performed in many Mozart operas after that.

Te Kanawa made her first appearance at the Metropolitan Opera in New York City quite by accident. The lead star playing Desdemona in Giuseppe Verdi's *Otello* suddenly fell ill. Te Kanawa was asked to perform instead, with only three hours to rehearse! She did such a splendid job that everyone raved about her performance.

Te Kanawa filming a video.
© Le Poer Trench Michael—Sygma/Corbis

SEARCH LIGHT

True or false? Te Kanawa's voice is described as tenor.

In 1981 Te Kanawa sang at the wedding of Britain's Prince Charles and Princess Diana. She sang George Frideric Handel's 'Let the Bright **Seraphim**'. This performance was seen on television by millions of viewers all over the world.

Te Kanawa is particularly known for the warmth of her soprano voice and her engaging personality on the stage. She has made a number of recordings. Most of these are of classical pieces, but she has also recorded traditional Maori songs from her New Zealand childhood.

In 1982 Te Kanawa was given a British noble title. She was made Dame Kiri Te Kanawa for the joy her singing had brought to so many.

Dame Kiri Te Kanawa appears here in Richard Strauss's comedic opera *Arabella*.
© Robbie Jack/Corbis

DID YOU KNOW?
In 1990, during a tour of Australia and New Zealand, Kiri Te Kanawa performed at an outdoor concert in the city of Auckland. An audience of 140,000 people attended.

Answer: FALSE. She is a soprano.

Centre Stage of Qawwali

Nusrat Fateh Ali Khan was considered one of the greatest singers of the music known as *qawwali*. Begun in Persia (present-day Iran) hundreds of years ago, *qawwali* music is based on Sufi Muslim poems about deep religious faith expressed through love. It has simple melodies and forceful rhythms.

Nusrat Fateh Ali Khan in concert.
Michael Harder Photography

*Qawwal*s (singers of *qawwali*) traditionally perform their songs at **shrines**. A *qawwal* must learn all the Sufi poems. He often makes up more *qawwali*s by using phrases and passages from different poems to create a new expression or idea. The singing includes much shouting and dancing.

Nusrat Fateh Ali Khan was born in 1948 in Pakistan. His father and two of his uncles were also famous *qawwal*s who sang in the classical style. Khan received music lessons from his father. When his father died in 1964, Khan sang in the *qawwali* style for the first time at his father's funeral. Two years later Khan gave his first public performance, singing with his uncles.

Khan sang in a very high range (a family trademark) and had a powerfully expressive voice. He was noted for his melodic creativity and had been known to perform for 10 hours. By the early 1970s Khan was recognized throughout Pakistan as the outstanding *qawwal* of his time. He sang at a world music concert in the United Kingdom in 1985. Soon he was performing regularly throughout Europe.

In 1996 Khan recorded songs for several American films. He also appeared on music television shows and performed songs that appealed specifically to Western audiences. Some people felt that he had betrayed the music's Islamic heritage. But Khan said he had given up nothing to share his musical heritage with a wider audience.

SEARCH LIGHT

Fill in the gaps:
Qawwali music is based on _____ _____.

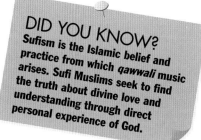

DID YOU KNOW?
Sufism is the Islamic belief and practice from which *qawwali* music arises. Sufi Muslims seek to find the truth about divine love and understanding through direct personal experience of God.

Here, Nusrat Fateh Ali Khan and Party perform in a 1993 concert. The term 'party' is a general term for the group of musicians who play for the *qawwal*.
© BALDEV/Corbis Sygma

Answer: *Qawwali* music is based on Sufi poetry.

Enriching American Dance

Alvin Ailey in 1983.
© Bettmann/Corbis

Alvin Ailey was born in 1931, in Texas, U.S. As a child, he helped his mother pick cotton to earn money. They moved to Los Angeles when Ailey was about 11 years old.

In Los Angeles, Ailey discovered dance during a school field trip to a ballet performance. He began to study with the dance teacher Lester Horton and joined the Lester Horton Dance Theater in 1949. When Horton died four years later Ailey became the director of the company. However, the next year the company broke up and Ailey moved to New York City.

SEARCH LIGHT

Ailey began his professional dancing in
a) the 1950s.
b) the 1940s.
c) the 1980s.

In New York Ailey danced in many performances and worked with some famous dance **choreographers**. They included Martha Graham and Hanya Holm. Ailey's own modern dancing combined what he learned from Lester Horton with African and Afro-Caribbean styles.

In 1958 Ailey formed the Alvin Ailey American Dance Theater. Most of its members were African Americans, like Ailey. One of the company's early performances was a work by Ailey called *Revelations*. The dance is set to American **Negro spirituals**, and it has become the company's most popular work.

Since the 1960s Ailey's company has performed around the United States and the world. Its popularity made Ailey one of the most famous American choreographers in the world and encouraged people everywhere to appreciate and enjoy modern dance.

Alvin Ailey died in 1989, but the Alvin Ailey American Dance Theater continues to **flourish**. And just as Ailey hoped, the company he founded has expanded from a troupe of mostly black performers to a rich multi-ethnic mix.

Alvin Ailey's dance *Revelations* is the company's signature piece. Since it is set to the religious music of his childhood, the name is quite appropriate. Revelation is the name of the last book of the Christian New Testament.
© Hulton-Deutsch Collection/Corbis

DID YOU KNOW?
Ailey choreographed 79 ballets during his lifetime. Altogether, however, the Alvin Ailey American Dance Theater has performed over 170 works created by more than 65 choreographers.

Answer: b) the 1940s.

Satchmo - Jazz Superstar

SEARCH LIGHT

What is unusual about scat? (Hint: Bee dee wa scabba doo.)

In the early 20th century, a young African American boy sang and danced on a street in New Orleans, Louisiana. He wanted to earn some money because his family was very poor. That boy, Louis Daniel Armstrong, would become one of the world's most famous jazz trumpet players.

Armstrong warming up on his trumpet in 1956.
© Ted Streshinsky/Corbis

Armstrong loved music and tried various instruments before finally choosing the cornet. The cornet looks like a trumpet but is shaped like a cone. Armstrong became the leader of his school band. Jazz was just becoming popular, and as a teenager he learned music by listening to pieces played by famous jazz musicians. Later he learned to read music.

Armstrong played with jazz bands in Chicago and New York City. He recorded his first solo pieces, 'Chimes Blues' and 'Tears', in Chicago. In New York he changed from the cornet to the trumpet. He thought the trumpet had a brighter sound and a more flamboyant look. By the time Armstrong was 28 years old he had become very famous. He toured the world as a trumpet soloist with big bands.

Louis Armstrong was nicknamed 'Satchmo' by his fellow musicians. Short for 'Satchel Mouth', the name suggested that his mouth was as wide as a satchel (a large school bag). But the friendly teasing was a sign of the great respect jazz musicians had for Armstrong's talent. His creativity, ability to express emotion, and superior **technical** skill were universally admired.

Armstrong is also remembered as one of the inventors of what is called 'scat'. Sometimes, while singing a **lyric**, he would sing without using words. He would sing a string of sounds instead. His scat singing and gravelly voice became as well known as his face and trumpet.

DID YOU KNOW?
Louis Armstrong was known for his musical quotations. That is, he was known for honouring other musicians by slipping pieces of their music into his performances.

Louis Armstrong (centre) also performed in a number of films. This picture is from *High Society*, a 1956 film starring the singer Bing Crosby (seated, far left), Frank Sinatra, and Grace Kelly.
The Kobal Collection/MGM

Answer: Scat is singing that uses sounds rather than real words.

Muppet Master

As a puppeteer and creator of the Muppets, Jim Henson delighted, entertained, and educated several generations of children and adults.

Henson was born in Mississippi, U.S., in 1936. He grew up in Washington, D.C., and began his career as a puppeteer while in secondary school there. Later he and his wife had a short puppet show on local television called 'Sam and Friends'. While he was still in university, Henson put together a team of puppeteers who performed in commercials and on TV.

In 1969 the Children's Television Workshop created a TV show with Henson called 'Sesame Street'. The program featured his 'Muppets' and included such now well-known characters as Kermit the Frog, Grover, Big Bird, and Cookie Monster. Young viewers loved the Muppets. But 'Sesame Street' also proved Henson's belief that learning could be fun.

The Muppets are a unique form of puppetry that was new to television. Often it takes two people to operate a Muppet since the head and each arm may require a human hand to move them. The larger Muppets, like Snuffleupagus and Big Bird, are actually costumed actors. The puppeteer who controls each Muppet also provides the character's voice. Henson operated and voiced Kermit himself for 35 years.

'Sesame Street' was so successful that in 1976 Henson created 'The Muppet Show' - a TV programme for both adults and children. The Muppets have appeared in several films as well, including *The Muppet Movie* and *Muppets from Space*.

Sadly, Henson died suddenly of pneumonia in 1990. But his Muppets continue to perform today, with Henson's son Brian leading the company.

Jim Henson's granddaughters Katrina (left) and Virginia Henson with Kermit the Frog when he was given his own star on the Hollywood Walk of Fame in 2002.
© Reuters Newmedia Inc./Corbis

SEARCH LIGHT

Henson's first TV show was called
a) 'Cheers'.
b) 'Sam and Friends'.
c) 'The Banana Bunch'.

DID YOU KNOW?
Kermit the Frog's original eyes were made from a Ping-Pong ball cut in half.

Jim Henson, seen here among some of his Muppets, was a favourite with both children and adults. Some adults enjoyed Henson's work from the time they were children themselves.

Answer: b) 'Sam and Friends'.

Celebrate the stories that have moved the world for centuries

Legends,
Myths, and Folktales

Legends, Myths, and Folktales

TABLE OF CONTENTS

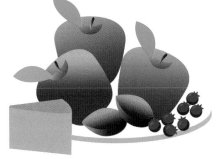

Stories of Wonders and Everyday Life

DID YOU KNOW?
Your school probably has its own legend. Most likely it's about a former student or teacher known for his or her unusual or amazing behaviour. Check with your teacher to see if he or she knows about a school legend.

In very ancient times, people needed help to explain the mysteries of life. They didn't have scientists or other experts to tell them why different things happened. So the way they grew to understand these mysteries was through stories called 'myths'.

Today when we call something a myth, we usually mean that it isn't true. But that's often because we don't believe the very old stories. People used to believe in myths very strongly.

Some of the most familiar European myths come from ancient Greece. The gods and goddesses of Greek religion all had stories about them that explained just why things were the way they were.

World religions today have their own mythologies. Hinduism, for example, is filled with wondrous tales of gods and heroes, such as the elephant-headed god Ganesha, who represents good luck. One Bible story tells how Moses led the original Jews out of slavery in Egypt. And the famous stories of Jesus stand as examples to Christians of a perfect life.

Myths are closely related to several other kinds of stories that teach us lessons. These include folktales, legends, fables, and fairy tales.

Folktales are very much like myths, though they are usually about ordinary characters in unusual situations.

Legends resemble folktales and myths, but they're usually linked to a particular place or person that is real or imaginary.

Fables teach lessons by telling stories with animal characters.

Fairy tales sometimes carry a message about right and wrong. But often they're simply exciting, magical stories.

SEARCH LIGHT

Which of the following is a story about ordinary people doing unusual things?
a) myth
b) fable
c) folktale

Answer: c) folktale

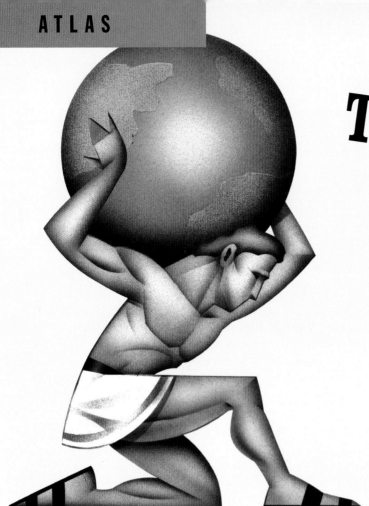

The Bearer of the World

SEARCH LIGHT

Find and correct the mistakes in the following sentence: Hercules agreed to get three golden apples for Atlas if Atlas would hold the heavens and Earth on his shoulders for a while.

Long, long ago, Zeus, the king of the ancient Greek gods, was very angry with Atlas, one of the Titans (the children of Heaven and Earth). He was angry because Atlas had tried to fight with him. So Zeus ordered Atlas to stand forever holding the heavens and the Earth on his shoulders!

Atlas wanted to get rid of his tiresome job. He almost managed this when the Greek hero Hercules came to ask for his help. Hercules was supposed to get three golden apples that were guarded by a dragon in a garden. Atlas agreed to get the apples if Hercules would hold the heavens and the Earth on his shoulders while he was gone.

When Atlas returned, he told Hercules to keep the job. Hercules agreed. But he asked Atlas to hold the world for just a minute while he found a shoulder-pad for himself. As soon as Atlas lifted the world onto his shoulders, Hercules picked up the golden apples and ran away. Some stories say that thunder is Atlas shouting after Hercules to come back. Most pictures of Atlas show him carrying the world.

This is an ancient Greek story. But today, when we want to learn about the world, we look in a book called an 'atlas'. Here we can see the shapes of countries, the rivers that flow in each country, and where the continents are.

DID YOU KNOW?
Atlas is also the name of a range of mountains in north-western Africa. In one story, Atlas was the king of that area. But he was a bad host to the Greek hero Perseus, who showed him the Gorgon's head. Looking at the Gorgon turned men to stone.

Answer: Atlas agreed to get three golden apples for Hercules if Hercules would hold the heavens and Earth on his shoulders for a while.

Beasts of Fire and Mist

SEARCH LIGHT

Which of the following is not breathed out by dragons?
a) ice
b) fire
c) mist

According to a popular story, there was once a terrible dragon in a city where many people lived. It had huge wings like a bat. The flapping of its wings could be heard for miles. It could kill an ox with a single blow. Its eyes flashed and it breathed fire.

Every year, the people of the city had to offer the dragon a girl to eat, or it would kill everyone. One year it was the turn of Princess Sabra to face the dragon. George, the youngest and bravest of the champions who protected the Christian church, came forward to save her. He wounded the dragon with his magic sword, Ascalon. The princess threw her sash around the dragon's neck and pulled the beast to the marketplace, where George killed it with a single blow. George later became the **patron saint** of England.

People used to believe in all kinds of dragons. The beasts roamed the land, swishing their great scaly tails. They flashed fiery glances from their enormous eyes. They blew rings of poisonous smoke and breathed out flames of fire without ever burning their tongues!

In China and other Asian countries, on the other hand, the dragon, or *long*, is considered good, lucky, and a powerful protector of people. The Chinese emperors adopted the dragon as their symbol. Dragons are linked with water and they breathe out mist and clouds instead of smoke and fire. You can see huge, colourful paper dragons being carried during the Chinese New Year and other celebrations. Maybe stories of dragons started because people found dinosaur bones and didn't know what they were. The bones would have looked like they came from monsters.

DID YOU KNOW?
There are some real dragons alive today. They are the giant Komodo dragons, 3-metre-long lizards that live in Indonesia.

Answer: a) ice

Who Will Marry Mousie?

Who did the father mouse want his daughter to marry?
a) the Sun
b) a mouse
c) the wind

There was once a charming girl mouse who knew everything a young mouse should know. She could gnaw holes, climb high shelves, and squeeze into small spaces.

Her father thought that a smart young mouse would make a fine husband for his daughter. But her mother had other ideas. 'My daughter is finer than anyone in the world. She will not marry a mouse!'

So the three of them went on a journey to the Sun's palace.

'Great Sun,' the mother said. 'Our daughter is so special we want her to marry someone who is greater than all others.'

'I am honoured,' answered the Sun. 'But there is someone greater than I.' As he spoke, a cloud spread itself over the Sun's face.

'I am not really good enough for your daughter,' replied the cloud. 'There is someone more powerful than I.'

As he spoke, the wind swept the cloud across the sky. Now the mother asked the wind to marry her daughter.

But the wind said, 'The wall is greater than I am. He has the power to stop me.'

But the wall said, 'I should not be the husband of such a delightful young girl. It's true that I can stop the wind, which can toss the clouds, which can cover the Sun. But there is someone even greater.'

'Who?' asked the mother.

'A mouse,' said the wall. 'A mouse can pass through me or under me. If you want a son-in-law who is the greatest in all the world, find a mouse.'

So the three mice went home happily, and the daughter married a mouse.

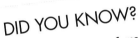

DID YOU KNOW?

There have been many famous mice in children's stories, including Mickey and Minnie Mouse, Mighty Mouse, Speedy Gonzales, Mrs Tittlemouse, Motor Mouse, Danger Mouse, the Tailor of Gloucester, and the Two Bad Mice.

Answer: b) a mouse

Animal Stories That Teach

True or false? The dog lost his meat because he was hungry.

Aesop's fables are animal stories that were told in Greece almost 2,500 years ago. They are stories about animals or birds that speak and act like people. Each of these stories tells us a useful truth about everyday life. These truths are called 'morals'.

One of Aesop's fables is about a greedy dog.

A dog had a piece of meat in his mouth and was carrying it home. On the way, the dog looked into a pond and saw his own reflection. It looked like another dog with a second piece of meat. 'Why should *he* eat such good meat?' thought the dog. 'I want that piece too.'

The dog opened his mouth to grab the other piece of meat, and his piece dropped into the water and disappeared. When the greedy dog saw the meat disappear, he put his tail between his legs and crept away.

The moral of this fable is: 'Be careful, or you may lose what you have by grabbing something that isn't there.'

Here is another fable, about a fox.

Strolling through the woods one day, a fox saw a juicy bunch of grapes hanging from a high vine.

'Just the thing for a thirsty fox,' he said to himself.

The fox jumped as high as he could, but he could not reach the grapes. He tried again and again. Each time he just missed the tasty-looking fruit. 'Oh well,' he thought. 'Those grapes are probably sour anyway.' And he went away without the grapes.

The term 'sour grapes' comes from this Aesop's fable about the fox. It refers to the attitude some people show when they sneer at something they can't have.

DID YOU KNOW?
The next time someone says something is 'fabulous', you can tell them that the word 'fabulous' comes from the word 'fable'. It means 'amazing' or 'larger-than-life', or even 'imaginary', like a fable.

Answer: FALSE. The dog lost his meat because he was greedy.

The Country Mouse and the Town Mouse

Once, a small grey mouse lived in the country. He had to find food to store for the winter, but when he had stored enough, he thought: 'I'll ask my cousin from town to visit. He might enjoy a holiday.'

At dinner the town mouse asked: 'Is this all you have to eat, a few acorns?'

The country mouse nodded **humbly**.

The next morning the town mouse woke up shivering. 'I was so cold I nearly froze. Come and visit me in town. We'll wine and dine, and I have a nice cosy mouse hole where we can sleep.'

The two set off. It was late when they arrived at the great house. There had been a banquet that day, and the table was still covered with good things to eat.

'Sit down,' invited the town mouse. 'I will bring you some delicious food.'

Then someone opened the door, and in dashed three big dogs, growling and sniffing, and the owners of the house entered.

Two voices shouted: 'Who has been at this table?'

The mice ran all around the room until they found a small hole in a wall where they could hide. Hours later, when the dogs and people finally left the room, the country mouse came out cautiously.

'Thank you for your hospitality, but I like my acorns and my cold winter winds far better than your grand food and warm house. At home, I can sleep in peace and comfort. Here there's always fear to take your appetite away!'

SEARCH LIGHT

Did the country mouse get more to eat at his house or at the house of the town mouse?

DID YOU KNOW?

Real field mice sometimes do move into people's houses to spend the winter and then move back outdoors when the warm weather returns.

Answer: The town mouse had more food to choose from, but the country mouse didn't get a chance to eat much of it.

The Golem of Prague

SEARCH LIGHT

The golem
was a
a) clay beast.
b) clay man.
c) clay toy.

Many hundreds of years ago there lived many Jewish families in the city of Prague. Although they worked hard, many people in Prague didn't like them. Sometimes Jewish businesses were raided. Sometimes their homes were burned. And sometimes they were killed.

In that time there was a wise rabbi, a great teacher, living in Prague. His name was Rabbi Loew. He knew a way to help his people. He would build a man of clay. He would make the Golem.

Rabbi Loew shaped clay into the form of a man's body. And when he was done, he walked around the clay man seven times, chanting, 'Shanti, Shanti, Dahat, Dahat.' The Golem then opened his eyes and sat up.

'Golem,' said Rabbi Loew. 'I've made you so you can help and protect my people.' The Golem nodded.

'Every day I'll tell you what to do,' continued Rabbi Loew.

At first the Golem was a great gift to the Jewish families of Prague. He helped them in their work and protected them. But the Golem wanted more. So Rabbi Loew taught him to read. But reading about people made him want even more. He wanted to be human.

Rabbi Loew couldn't make the Golem human. The Golem became angry and began to attack the people he had earlier helped. He became a monster.

Rabbi Loew had no choice but to chase the Golem from Prague. No one knows what happened to the Golem. And no one knows where he is today.

Answer: b) clay man.

King Arthur's
Knights of the Round Table

It is said that, long ago, the British people needed a king. One day, the legend goes, a rock appeared with a sword caught in it.

A sign said: 'Whoever Can Pull This Sword from This Rock Will Be Rightful King of the Britons.'

The strongest men in the kingdom tried to pull the sword out of the rock. It would not move. Then along came a young boy called Arthur. He had not heard about the sword in the rock. Thinking he would borrow the sword for his stepbrother, who had gone off to war, Arthur stepped up to the rock. He pulled. The sword slid out easily.

Merlin the magician had placed the sword in the rock. He had kept it there by magic. Only Arthur could remove it. The sword was called Excalibur. Merlin had been Arthur's teacher. He knew that Arthur would be the best king for Britain.

SEARCH LIGHT

Find and correct the mistake in the following sentence: The name of Arthur's famous sword was Lancelot.

DID YOU KNOW?
Although the Arthur story is a legend, there might really have been a 6th-century military leader who led the British against invaders.

As king, Arthur needed people to help him rule wisely. He decided he would ask the strongest and bravest men to help him. He sent messengers to look for these strong and brave men.

Many men came to help Arthur. He asked them to promise to be fair, to keep their word and to protect the weak. They became Arthur's Knights of the Round Table. Lancelot would become the greatest of all the Knights of the Round Table. But Arthur made the table round for a reason. It meant that everyone seated was equal there, and no one could sit at the 'head' of the table.

King Arthur's legend also says that if Britain is ever in danger, he will come back and save the people once again.

Odysseus and the Cyclops

Long ago, the Greek king Odysseus was sailing home from war with his men. Along the way, they stopped at an island where one-eyed man-eating giants called Cyclops lived.

Odysseus and his men wandered into a cave belonging to the Cyclops Polyphemus. At **twilight** Polyphemus returned with his flocks of sheep. When Polyphemus and all the sheep were inside, he picked up a huge stone and closed the mouth of the cave. Odysseus and his men were trapped!

Polyphemus ate up two of Odysseus' men and fell fast asleep. In the morning he ate two more men and, after blocking the mouth of the cave, went off with his sheep. The stone was too heavy for the men to move. Odysseus, however, thought of a plan. He sharpened the branch of an olive tree.

When Polyphemus came home that night, Odysseus offered him wine. The Cyclops drank it and asked Odysseus' name.

Odysseus answered, 'People call me Nobody.'

'Your gift, Nobody, is that I shall eat you last,' said Polyphemus. And, drunk with wine, he fell fast asleep.

Odysseus then took the great sharp branch and drove it into the sleeping giant's eye, blinding him. When Polyphemus cried out for help, the other Cyclops shouted, 'Who is hurting you?'

'Nobody,' screamed Polyphemus.

'Well, then you don't need any help from us,' said the other giants.

Meanwhile, Odysseus and each of his men **lashed** together three sheep. Under the middle sheep, each man clung to the **fleece**. Finally everybody was hidden.

Polyphemus did not think of feeling under the bellies of the sheep. And so the men escaped to their ship and continued their long journey home.

SEARCH LIGHT

How many eyes does the Cyclops have?
a) a million
b) ten
c) one

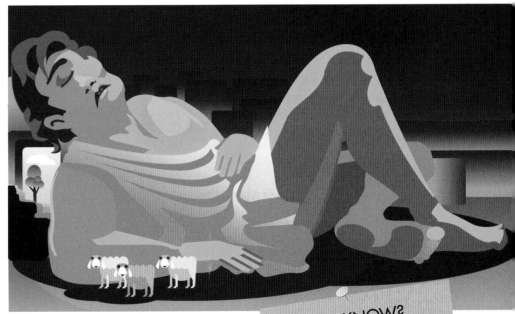

DID YOU KNOW?
Some scientists think the legend of Cyclops might have developed when people found elephant bones and didn't know what they were. The elephant skull has a large hole that looks like a single eye socket.

Answer: c) one

The Trojan Horse

More than 3,000 years ago the Greeks and the Trojans fought a long and terrible war. For about ten years the Greek army camped outside the city of Troy. The strong wall around the city stopped them from getting in.

There were many battles during those years. The Greek soldiers tried to knock down the wall. They couldn't. They tried to climb over it, but the Trojans always pushed them away. Then the Greeks thought of a trick. They started building a very big horse made of wood.

Watching this, the Trojans were puzzled. They were even more puzzled one morning when they saw that the Greek army had gone away. Only the strange wooden horse was standing outside their gates.

The Trojans went out to look at it. They liked the beautiful wooden horse so they pulled it inside the walls. They thought the war was over because the Greeks had left. They put away their swords and spears. They sang and danced around the horse.

Finally, the Trojans went to sleep. Then the Greeks played their trick. The Greek soldiers had hidden inside the hollow wooden horse. That night, they climbed out of the horse and opened the gates of Troy to all the other Greek soldiers.

The Greeks caught the Trojans completely by surprise and captured the city of Troy. Even today, we often call a tricky inside attack a 'Trojan horse'.

DID YOU KNOW?
From this story we get the expression 'Beware of Greeks bearing gifts'. Can you guess why?

SEARCH LIGHT

Correct the mistake in the following sentence: The Greeks built a large woollen horse to trick the Trojans.

Answer: The Greeks built a large wooden horse to trick the Trojans.

The Thunder God

SEARCH LIGHT

Which day of the week is named for Thor?

Long ago, in Europe's northern lands of ice and snow, most people believed that Thor was king of all the gods. Thor was the mighty god of thunder and the sky. He was the eldest son of Odin. Thursday, the fifth day of the week, is named after him (Thor's day).

Thor had a red beard and was very tall and strong. He had a magic belt that made him doubly strong whenever he wore it. He used his strength to protect people from giants and evil fairies.

His hammer, called Mjollnir, was his main weapon and produced lightning bolts. Thor had to wear special iron gloves to hold it. It would always return to him after killing the person it was thrown at. It could split a mountain in half or kill all the frost giants in one blow.

Thor travelled in a **chariot** that was drawn by two goats. One of them was called Tooth-Gnasher and the other was Tooth-Grinder. Whenever it moved across the sky, the chariot produced thunder, and glowing sparks flew from its wheels.

Soldiers worshiped Thor because of his strength. Peasants and farmers worshiped him because he made rain for their crops.

DID YOU KNOW?

Thor's qualities may sound like some fictional superheroes you've heard of before. In fact, Thor himself has appeared as a comic book superhero.

Answer: Thursday (Thor's day) is named for the Norse god.

The Bear and the Old Man

DID YOU KNOW?
Many people enjoy eating cooked turnip tops, also called 'turnip greens'. They become less bitter, but still taste interesting.

SEARCH LIGHT

Find and correct the mistake in the following sentence: The bear didn't like turnip tops because they tasted sour.

There was a time when bears and people got along well together. One day an old man was out planting turnips in a field near his house. As he was working, a bear came out of the woods.

'What are you doing in my field, Old Man?' asked the bear.

'I'm planting turnips,' he replied. 'Do you mind if I use your field, Bear?'

'No,' said the bear. 'Just share the turnips with me when you are done.'

When the time came to harvest the turnips, the bear asked, 'Where's my share, Old Man?'

'I've decided to split them with you, half and half,' said the old man. 'You can have the tops, Bear, and I'll keep the roots.'

This sounded fair, but when the bear ate the green turnip tops, he found them **bitter**. He realized he'd been tricked - for turnip roots were sweet.

The next year, the old man was again in the field.

'Old Man,' he said. 'You tricked me last year. I want my fair share this year, and this time I want the roots.'

'Okay, Bear,' said the old man. 'This year I'm planting rye. When it's grown you shall have the roots and I'll take the tops.'

The bear was pleased with himself, thinking he had made a good deal. But rye is a grain, and the food is at the top of its stems. When he tried eating the rye roots, he discovered that they had no taste. He realized that he been tricked once again. And ever since, bears and people have not got along.

Answer: The bear didn't like turnip tops because they tasted bitter.

Yeh-Shen

SEARCH LIGHT

Fill in
the gaps:
Instead of a
fairy godmother,
such as Cinderella
had, Yeh-Shen had a

_____

to help her.

DID YOU KNOW?
A 9th-century-AD Chinese version of this classic story is one of the earliest known. There are about 300 different variations of the Cinderella story.

Once there was a man with a beautiful daughter called Yeh-Shen. **Alas**, before the girl grew up, her father died. So Yeh-Shen was brought up by her stepmother.

Now the stepmother already had a daughter of her own. So the stepmother gave Yeh-Shen all the hardest jobs. Yeh-Shen had no friends other than a golden fish, a carp. Yeh-Shen always shared what she had with her friend the carp.

One day the stepmother discovered Yeh-Shen's secret friend. She caught the fish and cooked it for breakfast. As Yeh-Shen gathered up the bones of the fish, the skeleton told her that it could grant wishes.

Yeh-Shen was eager to go to the Spring Festival. But Yeh-Shen's stepmother refused to let her go. She was afraid that pretty Yeh-Shen would get all the attention and her own daughter would get none. So Yeh-Shen asked the bones for help. As soon as she said the words, she was dressed in a gown of peacock feathers. On her feet were beautiful golden slippers.

At the festival Yeh-Shen danced and danced and had a wonderful time. But when she saw her stepmother approaching, she was frightened and ran away, leaving behind one golden slipper.

The next morning everyone was talking about the beautiful stranger. The **magistrate** announced that his son wanted to marry the woman whose foot fitted the slipper. But though many tried, no one's foot would fit.

When the magistrate saw Yeh-Shen, he asked her to try on the slipper. The slipper fitted perfectly. Yeh-Shen and the magistrate's son were married and lived happily together all their lives.

Answer: Instead of a fairy godmother, such as Cinderella had,
Yeh-Shen had a magic skeleton (or fish skeleton) to help her.

The Stonecutter

DID YOU KNOW?
Stonecutters may have lived simple lives, but they have contributed to some very grand structures. For example, stonecutters played a major role in building the Great Pyramids of Egypt.

There was once a poor stonecutter who went daily to the mountain near his house and cut stone to use in building houses. One morning he saw a palace being built and immediately realized how **humble** his life was.

'Oh, if only I could have that palace, then I would truly be happy.'

And suddenly it was true. Unknown to the stonecutter, the spirit of the mountain had granted his wish. The stonecutter was happy, but soon he realized that even princes get hot in the Sun.

'Oh, if only I could be like the Sun, then I would truly be happy.' And suddenly it was true.

The stonecutter was again very happy. But one day a cloud drifted in front of him and blocked all his glorious rays.

'Oh, if only I could be like this cloud, then I would truly be happy.' And suddenly it was true.

But he grew tired of being a cloud, for every day the wind blew him around.

'Oh, if only I could be like the wind, then I would truly be happy.' And suddenly it was true.

One day he ran into the mountain, which wouldn't move no matter how hard he blew.

'Oh, if only I could be like the mountain, then I would truly be happy.' And suddenly it was true.

But a tiny itch bothered him. When he looked down, he saw a stonecutter chipping away pieces of stone.

Then he knew where happiness lay. 'Oh, if only I could be a stonecutter, then I would be content for the rest of my life.' And suddenly it was true.

And he was finally truly happy.

SEARCH LIGHT

Put these in the order they occur in the story: mountain, Sun, prince, cloud, stonecutter, wind

Answer: stonecutter, prince, Sun, cloud, wind, mountain, stonecutter

The Tiger in the Trap

Once there was a traveller. He was just getting ready to stop for the night when he heard a low moaning. He found a tiger trapped in a deep pit.

The tiger saw the man and begged, 'Please free me from this trap, and I will be grateful to you for the rest of my life.'

The traveller agreed and lowered a large branch into the pit for the tiger to climb out. As soon as the tiger was free, he fell upon the man.

'Wait!' said the traveller. 'I thought you were going to be grateful to me.'

'It was men who trapped me,' answered the tiger. 'So a man should suffer for it.'

Just then a **hare** hopped by and asked what was happening. The tiger explained and then asked if the hare agreed with him.

'First I have to see the pit. Where were you?' the hare asked the tiger.

'Down here,' the tiger replied and jumped into the pit.

'Was the branch there too?' asked the hare.

'No,' said the tiger. And so the hare took the branch away.

Then the hare turned to the traveller and told him to be on his way.

The tiger cried out in **dismay** as the man walked off down the trail. 'How could you betray me?'

'I judge each according to his own and not by his fellows,' answered the hare. 'You have the fate you deserve and so does the man.'

DID YOU KNOW?

Despite the many stories, tigers seldom eat people. Usually a tiger attacks a person only if the tiger is sick or is unable to hunt its natural prey.

SEARCH LIGHT

Why did the tiger want to eat the man?

Answer: Other men had trapped the tiger so the tiger thought this man should pay for it.

The Monkey
and the
String of Pearls

DID YOU KNOW?
Some animals really do like jewellery. Birds such as magpies often steal and collect shiny things like aluminium foil or silver chain.

SEARCH LIGHT

Fill in the gap: The first monkey stole the pearls so she could look _____.

One of the most popular kinds of stories in South Asia are called Jataka tales. They tell about the past lives of the Buddha, in both human and animal form. Similar South Asian tales occur in Hindu and other non-Buddhist literature. All these stories aim to teach a lesson, as does this one.

The king and queen decided to have a swim one beautiful day. The queen did not want to lose her jewellery so she took off her pearls and gave them to a handmaid. The handmaid soon grew tired in the warm sun and fell asleep.

A monkey had been watching and quickly ran down the tree, snatched the necklace, and raced back up into the branches. The monkey thought she looked **regal** in the pearls. 'Aren't I beautiful?' she said to herself.

When the maid awoke she noticed that the pearls were missing. 'The queen's necklace has been stolen!' she cried.

But no matter how hard the king's guards looked, they couldn't find the thief. The captain of the guards was puzzled. He decided to put out glass necklaces in the hope of catching his thief.

When the other monkeys saw the many glass necklaces lying on the ground, they quickly snatched them up and chattered happily to themselves, 'Oh, don't we look stunning?'

All except the first monkey. She reached into her hiding place for the string of pearls and put it on. 'Your necklaces are just glass,' she teased, 'but mine is made of pearls.'

This was what the captain of the guards had been waiting for, and he and his men sprang from their hiding places and caught the monkey. They returned the string of pearls to their queen and let the rest of the monkeys keep the glass necklaces.

Answer: The first monkey stole the pearls so she could look regal.

The Poor Man and the Flask of Oil

SEARCH LIGHT

Why, in the olden days, would a man who sold oil be wealthy?

About the 8th century, the writer Ibn al-Muqaffa made a famous Arabic translation of the South Asian stories known as tales of Bidpai. The translation was called the *Kalilah wa Dimnah* (after the two jackals in the book's first story, Kalilah and Dimnah). It provided a treasure of tales and parables that would appear throughout Islamic literature. This is one of those well-known tales.

A poor man lived next to a rich man who sold oil for a living. The poor man envied his neighbour's wealth and riches and often talked about them. So the rich man gave the poor man a **flask** of oil as a gift.

The poor man was delighted. 'I could sell the oil,' thought the poor man. 'Then I would have enough money to buy five goats.'

Later he thought some more. 'With five goats,' he said to himself, 'a man would be rich enough to have a wife.' He liked this thought so much he added to it.

'Of course, my wife would be beautiful and give me a fine son.'

But then the poor man had a thought that worried him. 'What if my son is lazy because his father is a wealthy man? What if he refuses to obey me and disgraces me?'

This thought made the poor man so angry that he began stomping around his hut, swinging his staff. 'Why, if my son refuses to obey me, then I'll teach him a lesson. I'll beat him with my **staff**.'

As the staff swung about, it nudged the flask of oil off its shelf. The flask crashed to the ground and broke, spilling its contents on the dirt. The man looked at the shards of the flask, realizing that his dreams were now just as broken. And once more he was just a poor man living next to a wealthy neighbour.

DID YOU KNOW?
Oil merchants are still quite wealthy even today. Of course, now they sell the kind of oil used to make petrol.

Answer: Oil has long been used as a fuel for lamps and was very valuable when there wasn't yet any electricity.

Moni Mekhala
and Ream Eyso

DID YOU KNOW?
In North American Indian mythology, a spirit called the Thunderbird watered the Earth. Lightning was believed to flash from its beak, and rolling thunder came from the beating of its wings.

At one time, both the goddess Moni Mekhala and the giant Ream Eyso were studying with the same teacher. This teacher was very wise.

After a few years of teaching them both, the wise teacher decided to hold a contest for her students. She asked them to bring her a full glass of dew the next morning. Whoever brought her a glass full of dew first would win a prize, a magic ball.

Both got up very early and went to gather their glasses of dew.

Ream Eyso was quite pleased with himself. 'Surely my idea of pouring the dew off the leaves is brilliant,' he said.

Moni Mekhala had actually started the night before by laying a scarf on the grass. 'This worked beautifully,' she said as she wrung the scarf out into a cup.

The goddess won the magic ball, and the giant was given a magic axe as a second prize. Ream Eyso was jealous of Moni Mekhala. So he took his axe and threw it at the goddess. It made a terrible rumble as it flew through the air.

Moni Mekhala heard the noise and held up her magic ball. She caused the ball to strike the giant with great, jagged sparks of fire. The fire made him so hot that he dripped large drops of sweat all over the ground.

Even today you can hear the rumble and see the sparks as Ream Eyso's sweat falls to the ground.

SEARCH LIGHT

What natural occurrence does this story explain?

Answer: This story explains the source of thunder, lightning, and rain.

How Kangaroo Got His Tail

SEARCH LIGHT

Match up the animals with their descriptions.
Kangaroo Wombat
sleeps outside
sleeps in a hole
flat head
long tail

Long ago, before kangaroos had long tails and before wombats had flat heads, the animals played and lived together.

Kangaroo and Wombat were great friends and spent every day together. But at night, each one liked to sleep in a different way. Wombat liked to sleep indoors, warm and snug. Kangaroo liked to sleep outdoors, beneath the stars. Each thought his way of sleeping was the best.

Then, one night, a terrible storm cracked open the sky, and harsh winds and rain **scoured** the land. Kangaroo was outside and was miserable in the cold, wet night. He knocked on Wombat's house and called to Wombat to let him come in to warm up. But Wombat thought about the amount of space Kangaroo would take up, so he refused to let him in.

Kangaroo was very angry about being locked out in the storm. He picked up a big rock and dropped it through the roof of Wombat's house.

'There,' Kangaroo shouted. 'Now your house will be damp all the time.'

The rock landed on Wombat's head and flattened his brow. Wombat grabbed a spear and threw it as hard as he could at Kangaroo. The spear pierced the end of Kangaroo's tail.

No matter how hard Kangaroo pulled, the spear wouldn't come out, and his tail just stretched longer and longer.

Since that day, Kangaroo and Wombat have not been friends. Kangaroo still has a big tail and sleeps outside. And Wombat still has a flat head and sleeps in a hole.

DID YOU KNOW?
Not all kangaroos sleep on the ground. Tree kangaroos sleep and spend much time in trees rather than on the ground. And when they are on the ground, they walk rather than hop.

Answer: Kangaroo: *sleeps outside, long tail* **Wombat: *sleeps in a hole, flat head***

Ananse and the Wisdom Pot

Ananse the spider was far and wide considered to be the wisest of all animals, and many animals came to him with their problems and questions.

After a while, Ananse grew tired of answering so many questions and decided he would have to do something to regain his peace and quiet. So he put all of his wisdom into a giant pot. He strapped the pot to his belly. He planned to carry the pot to a branch of a tall tree where all the animals could go to get their own answers to their questions.

But as he was climbing the tree, the pot kept getting in the way of his legs and slowed him down. Ntikume, one of Ananse's many sons, saw this. He suggested that Ananse strap the pot to his back instead, where it wouldn't be in his way.

When Ananse heard this he was furious. He couldn't **tolerate** the thought that his son should have a better idea than his own. So Ananse grabbed the pot and flung it to the ground, where it shattered into a thousand pieces.

Ever since then, wisdom has been scattered all over the world for many people to find.

SEARCH LIGHT

Who is Ntikume?

DID YOU KNOW?
The West African character Ananse (or Anansi) also appears in Jamaican tales. This shows how folktales travelled from Africa with the slave trade to the West Indies.

Answer: Ntikume is one of Ananse's many sons.

The Monkey Court

Once two young friends were walking along together when they saw a large piece of meat. Each boy thought he had seen the meat first, so each thought he deserved to have it. The two argued over the meat. And though they both thought it right to share, they thought that the other should take the smaller portion. They agreed to take their **dispute** to the Monkey Court.

Now Monkey saw them coming and he realized that here was a real chance for him. So he put on his wisest face and listened patiently to their story.

When the two boys had finished talking, Monkey said, 'I shall divide the meat equally between you.' With that, Monkey tore the meat in two and was about to hand it over when he noticed that the two pieces were uneven.

'I will fix this so that each of you gets the same amount of meat,' said Monkey. And with that he took a bite from the larger piece of meat. But once more he noticed that the two pieces were uneven. And no matter how carefully Monkey bit the pieces of meat, one piece always ended up being bigger. Finally there were only two small pieces of meat.

At that point Monkey said, 'It is time for me to take my fee for being your judge. These two tiny pieces of meat will do just fine.' And with that he sent the two hungry, and wiser, boys on their way.

DID YOU KNOW? In many African tales, the monkey and several other animals are clever and the human beings are usually shown to be foolish.

SEARCH LIGHT

Why do you think the two boys expected Monkey to solve problems for them?

Answer: Monkey had a reputation for being clever, as you see from the story. So the boys expected that he could solve their problems. But instead, he outsmarted them whilst teaching them a lesson about being greedy.

Jackal Gets Away

SEARCH LIGHT

Why do you think Jackal was afraid of Lion?

DID YOU KNOW?

Like many African trickster characters, Jackal is a clever underdog figure, smaller and weaker than his rival. Jackal's target - Lion in this story - is usually sincere, hardworking, and slow-witted.

Jackal was known for his cleverness and often used his wits to trick other animals. He especially enjoyed playing tricks on mighty Lion. But one day Lion almost put an end to all of Jackal's pranks.

Jackal was walking along, feeling **smug** while thinking about how he had just tricked Hyena out of a meal. He was not paying attention to where he was going, and instead he was laughing about how clever he was.

Only when it was too late did Jackal realize that he had walked right into Lion's **territory**. He was about to turn and run when he saw Lion just a few steps away. Lion was staring at him, and not looking at all friendly. Jackal knew he was in serious trouble for he could never hope to outrun Lion when he was this close.

But Jackal didn't panic. Instead he started wailing out loud and digging at the ground. 'Oh, Lion. What will we do? Those rocks over there are falling and they'll surely crush us both.'

Lion quickly looked at the rocks, and indeed they did seem to be tilting in a frightening way. He had never paid much attention to them before. He didn't realize that this was how they always looked.

'Quick, Lion,' cried Jackal, 'use your mighty strength to stop the rocks while I go find a log to prop them up.'

Lion threw his huge shoulder against the rocks and pushed with all his might.

We'll never know how long he stayed there before he realized that Jackal had tricked him once again. Perhaps he's still there.

Answer: Not only might lions eat jackals, but lions don't like other predators to be in their territory.

Rabbit Throws Away His Sandal

SEARCH LIGHT

Which animal is not in the story?
a) dog
b) skunk
c) snake

Rabbit was the wisest of all the animals, and so he was their mayor. Although he was a good leader, he wasn't well liked because he used his wits to play tricks on the other animals.

One morning all the animals decided they would get rid of Rabbit and his tricks. They gathered outside of Rabbit's burrow, planning to grab him and tear him to pieces as soon as he came out.

But Rabbit heard them grumbling. He called back, 'I'll be out as soon as I find my sandals.'

It was still dark as the Sun had yet to rise. The animals all began to shout, 'Rabbit, hurry up. We need your help.'

Rabbit called back, 'I've found one sandal, but it's broken and it'll take time to fix it.'

Jaguar, who was quite impatient, said, 'Throw it out here and I'll fix it while you look for the other sandal.'

Jaguar grabbed the object that flew out of the burrow and tossed it into bushes.

After a while, Skunk said, 'What's keeping you, Rabbit?' But no one answered.

Then Vulture said, 'Snake, slither into that hole and see what's keeping Rabbit.'

Snake did just that. But he could see very quickly that he was alone in the burrow. 'There's no one here. Rabbit's disappeared.'

Then from the bushes everyone heard Rabbit laugh. They realized he had tricked them once again. They had been so eager waiting for Rabbit that no one noticed he had thrown himself out instead of his sandal.

DID YOU KNOW?
Rabbits appear in the folktales of several different cultures. For instance the Brer ('Brother') Rabbit of African American tales grew out of an African character, Hare. Both are clever, like Rabbit in this Mayan story from Central America.

Answer: a) dog

The Tale of a Lumberjack

If somebody told you that a giant woodsman had created a 160 kilometre-long inlet to float logs to a mill, would you believe it? Probably not, but it makes a good story.

Stories like that are called 'tall tales', and an imaginary giant lumberjack named Paul Bunyan figures in many American tall tales. A lumberjack is a man who earns his living by cutting down trees. Paul was so big and powerful that he could make hills, lakes, and rivers whenever he wanted to. In fact, he's supposed to have created the Grand Canyon and the Great Lakes.

Paul Bunyan was so big that when he sneezed, a whole hillside of pine trees would fall over. Being such a large man, Paul would get very hungry. He was especially fond of pancakes. The frying pan for making them was so big that people would skate around it with slabs of bacon tied to their feet to grease it.

Paul had a famous helper that he found during the 'blue winter'. People called it the 'blue winter' because the snow that fell was all blue! One night Paul heard an animal crying. When he looked outside, he saw a pair of silky blue ears sticking out of the snow. Paul pulled and pulled. Out of the blue snow came a baby blue ox!

Paul took the ox home with him and named it Babe. When Babe grew up, he was nearly as big as a small mountain.

One story tells of a road with so many curves in it that people didn't know whether they were coming or going. Paul laughed and picked up one end of the road and tied it to Babe. Babe tugged and pulled all the curves out of the road.

DID YOU KNOW?
The legend of Paul Bunyan may have come from stories that real lumberjacks told around the fire on cold evenings.

Answer: FALSE. As far as anyone knows there never was an actual lumberjack named Paul Bunyan.

How Crow Brought Daylight to the World

There was a time when the world of the north was always in darkness. The people wished for light and Crow told them he had seen daylight on one of his many travels.

'Please bring us some daylight,' the people begged Crow.

Crow flew for many miles. Just when he thought he couldn't fly any more, he saw daylight ahead of him.

When he reached daylight, he landed in a tree to rest. While Crow was resting, the chief's daughter came along. Crow turned himself into a speck of dust and landed on the girl's **parka**. Then Crow heard a baby crying.

'What's wrong?' the girl asked her young brother.

Crow drifted into the baby's ear and whispered: 'Tell her you want a ball of daylight to play with.'

The chief's daughter tied a piece of string to a ball of daylight and gave it to her brother to play with. When the girl carried her brother and the ball of daylight outside, Crow turned back into a bird, grabbed the ball by its string and flew away.

When he arrived home, the people were overjoyed. 'We have daylight!' they cheered. 'We can see the whole world.'

But Crow warned them: 'It is just a small ball of daylight. It will need to rest every now and then, so you won't have daylight for the whole year.'

And that is why the people of the frozen north have half a year of daylight and half a year of darkness.

SEARCH LIGHT

Fill in the gap: This story explains why there is daylight for only _____ the year in the far north.

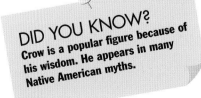

DID YOU KNOW?
Crow is a popular figure because of his wisdom. He appears in many Native American myths.

Answer: This story explains why there is daylight for only half the year in the far north.

333

Coyote Brings Fire

DID YOU KNOW?
Coyote, like several other animals in folktales of different cultures, is a 'trickster' character. Tricksters are often heroes, are usually smart, are sometimes magical, and often get tripped up by their own pride.

Many long years ago fire belonged only to the Fire People. This was a problem for the Animal People during the winter when the winds blew cold. So one year the animals got together to talk about their problem.

'If we don't have fire this winter, then many of our aged grandparents will die,' said Squirrel. 'Let's ask Coyote what we should do. He's clever and always has a plan.'

Coyote listened to the other animals and then told them he had an idea. He told the other animals to be ready to make a great noise when he swished his tail. Coyote led them up into the hills where the Fire People lived. Alone, Coyote dragged himself into the firelight of the Fire People's camp.

'Who's there?' growled one of the Fire People. And then, 'No fear, it's just sorry Coyote.'

As soon as everything was quiet, Coyote swished his tail. At once a great wailing arose all around the camp.

The Fire People jumped up thinking they were being attacked. Coyote then grabbed a piece of fire with his mouth and bounded off down the hill. One of the Fire People reached out and grabbed Coyote's tail, **scorching** it white.

Coyote tossed the fire to Squirrel, who was waiting. The Fire People almost caught Squirrel. The heat from their bodies was so strong that it curled Squirrel's tail. But Squirrel quickly passed the fire to Wood, who swallowed it. Try as they might, the Fire People couldn't make Wood spit out the fire.

Later, Coyote showed the other animals how, whenever they wanted fire, all they had to do was rub two sticks together and Wood would release the fire for them.

SEARCH LIGHT

The animals wanted fire because
a) they wanted to cook.
b) they wanted to stay warm.
c) they were jealous.

Answer: b) they wanted to stay warm.

Why Possum's Tail Is Bare

Possum once had a bushy tail covered with thick, glossy fur. In conversation, he always managed to mention his tail: 'When I was brushing my beautiful tail yesterday, you'll never guess what I saw...'

The other animals were tired of hearing about Possum's tail. But Rabbit said: 'Don't worry, I have a plan.'

The next day Rabbit announced that there was going to be a grand dance. 'We'll want to do something special with your tail,' he said to Possum.

'First,' said Rabbit, 'we need to wash and comb your tail.'

So they dipped Possum's tail in the river, and then Rabbit pulled a pine cone through Possum's tail fur.

'Ouch!' cried Possum. 'You're hurting me.'

'I can stop if you want me to,' replied Rabbit.

'No, no,' said Possum. 'Keep working on my tail.'

So Rabbit kept pulling the pine cone sharply over Possum's tail.

'Now we'll just wrap your tail in this red ribbon,' Rabbit told him.

Possum was so excited. As soon as he reached the dance, he untied the ribbon. And as he did so, all the other animals started to laugh.

'What's so funny?' shouted Possum. Then he looked at his tail. It was as bare and smooth as Snake's back. Rabbit had pulled all the fur off Possum's tail!

'Oh, oh!' wailed Possum and fainted on his back.

And that's why, when you see Possum today, his tail is bare, and if you scare him he rolls over onto his back.

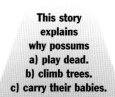

SEARCH LIGHT

This story explains why possums
a) play dead.
b) climb trees.
c) carry their babies.

Answer: a) play dead.

Raven and Crow's Potlatch

SEARCH LIGHT

Fill in the gaps: Before tricking Crow, Raven asks _____ and _____ for help.

Raven was a crafty fellow, always playing tricks. All during the autumn he teased the other animals as they gathered food. When winter came Raven realized what a fool he'd been. He was cold and hungry.

So Raven went to see Squirrel. 'Friend,' he called. 'Won't you share some of your food?'

'No!' said Squirrel. 'You made fun of me, and now you can starve.'

Disappointed, Raven went to see Bear. 'Friend Bear,' called Raven. 'Won't you share some food with your poor friend Raven?'

But Bear was asleep, and he'd eaten all his food before settling in for his winter sleep.

Raven was hungrier than ever. He thought hard and decided to visit his cousin Crow. 'Why Crow, aren't you ready?' he asked.

'Ready for what?' Crow asked.

'Your **potlatch** feast. All the animals will be here soon. They can't wait to hear you sing.'

Now Crow was vain about his voice, so he was very excited.

Raven went out and invited all the animals to the potlatch. 'Come to my potlatch. There'll be mountains of food.'

Soon all the animals had gathered, and they began to stuff themselves with Crow's food. Crow sang until all he could do was croak. By the time he had finished, Crow was hungry. He wasn't worried, though, because every guest at a potlatch has to invite the host to a thank-you feast.

But while he waited all winter long, Crow was never invited to any feasts. All the animals thought that the potlatch had been Raven's, so Raven was treated to feasts. And Crow has never stopped being hungry. You can still see him today wherever people are, begging for food in his harsh, croaking voice.

DID YOU KNOW?
This story may have developed or at least changed after Pacific American Indians came into contact with white traders. In earlier Indian traditions, guests at potlatch feasts were not expected to invite the host to a feast in return.

Answer: Before tricking Crow, Raven asks Squirrel and Bear for help.

Investigate the beliefs and faiths of people everywhere

Religions Around the World

Religions Around the World

TABLE OF CONTENTS

Belief in a Higher Power

There are many people in the world who believe in a god or gods. Others do not use the word 'god' but still believe that there are other, greater forces at work in their lives. The way groups of people worship these forces or their gods forms what we call a 'religion'.

Worshippers in Nepal celebrate Buddha Jayanti, honouring the Buddha's birth, death, and Enlightenment.
© Macduff Everton/Corbis

Many different religions are practised around the world. Major religions today include Christianity, Islam, Judaism, Hinduism, Daoism, Sikhism, and Buddhism. Most religions try to answer the same basic questions: How was the world created? What is the meaning of human life? Why do people die and what happens afterward? Why is there evil? How should people behave?

Many religions have buildings set aside for worship. In these temples, cathedrals, mosques, and churches, activities such as prayer, **sacrifice**, and other forms of worship take place.

At different times in history, followers of one religion have tried to make others believe in that religion. Sometimes this was done by peaceful means. Often, however, it was done by force - sometimes by 'holy wars'.

For instance, between 1095 and 1292, European Christians led a number of **crusades** against Muslims. In these crusades Christians tried to take control of the holy city of Jerusalem and other places they associated with the life of Jesus Christ. Muslims also carried out holy wars, or jihads. At various times Muslims spread into much of the Middle East and parts of Europe and Asia.

Most religions, however, encourage their followers to live peacefully with people of other religions. And, in fact, they share many **aspects** in common. These include **rituals** to perform, prayers to recite, places to visit or avoid, days that are holy, holy books to read and study, and leaders to follow.

DID YOU KNOW?

India is the birthplace of several world religions. Buddhism, Hinduism, Jainism, and Sikhism all began there.

Roman Catholics worship together in a service called 'mass'. Here the mass is being led by Pope John Paul II, world leader of the church, in Saint Peter's Basilica in Rome, Italy.
© Vittorino Rastelli/Corbis

One World, Many Beliefs

Stained-glass image showing a Christian artist's idea of God the Father, with angels.
© Royalty-Free/Corbis

How did the universe start? How did life on Earth begin?

For thousands of years people have searched for the answers to such questions. Some people believe that science will solve the mysteries. But in the earliest times, science could not explain natural events such as earthquakes and storms, day and night, and life and death. People believed that these things were the work of beings greater and more powerful than humans: the gods.

Today many people still seek an understanding of life through the worship of a god or gods. They often feel that their faith helps them live better lives.

Some religions, such as Judaism, Christianity, and Islam, teach that there is only one God, a **supreme** being who made the universe and controls the world. This is called 'monotheism', from the Greek words for 'one' and 'God'. The worship of several powerful gods is called 'polytheism', because 'poly' means 'many'. Ancient Greeks and Romans believed in many gods, whom we know today from ancient **myths** and art.

People from different places and cultures have their own names for their gods. The God of the ancient Jews was called Yahweh. Muslims use the Arabic word for God, Allah. Hindus believe in a large number of gods and goddesses (female gods). Each of them has a different personality and controls a different **aspect** of life. They believe these gods are forms of one supreme god. One popular Hindu god is the elephant-headed Ganesha.

Many Hindus appeal to Ganesha when they begin an important new project.

The behaviour of a god can vary from religion to religion. Some religions may see their god or gods as unforgiving and cruel. Others consider their god to be merciful and kind. But all gods play a part in helping people understand their world.

SEARCH LIGHT

Fill in the gap: The Hindu god of successful beginnings is _____.

In many world religions, worshippers like this woman in Hong Kong burn incense to honour their gods.
© Royalty-Free/Corbis

DID YOU KNOW?
Not only did the ancient Egyptians believe in a large family of gods, but they also believed that their pharaoh, or king, was a god.

Answer: The Hindu god of successful beginnings is Ganesha.

A Life Apart

Most major religions have a tradition of monasticism. Monasticism comes from the Greek word for 'living alone'. So monks - men who practice monasticism - are people who choose to live apart from society. This allows them to devote themselves to a religious life. Women who choose this way of life are called 'nuns'.

Not all monks and nuns live entirely by themselves. Many live in communities with other monks or nuns. These community homes are usually called 'monasteries' or, for nuns, 'convents'. Life in a religious community generally focuses on prayer, **meditation**, and religious works. Monks and nuns may concentrate on building a personal relationship with God. They may work to purify their thought and reach spiritual perfection.

Some monks do live all by themselves as **hermits**. And some wander from place to place their entire lives. But whether they live in a community or by themselves, all monks and nuns give up certain of life's pleasures. Many don't own property or have any money. Others force themselves to face certain challenges, such as **fasting** or other physical discomforts.

Monks and nuns choose to live apart so that they won't be distracted by life. Usually, they are unmarried, since having a family requires great dedication and time. The monastic life allows people to focus as much of themselves as possible on God and on the **salvation** their religion promises.

Many monks and nuns do still take part in the world around them. For example, they may serve as teachers, social workers, missionaries, or nurses. In earlier times monks were often among the few people who could read and write. So they're responsible for having preserved much of written world history and culture.

DID YOU KNOW?
One Christian monastery in the United States specializes in training dogs. The monks there feel that the connection between dogs and humans, as well as the focus on discipline and responsibility, helps them spiritually.

SEARCH LIGHT

True or false? Only Christians can be monks.

Answer: FALSE. Almost all the world's major religions have some tradition of monasticism.

Eternal Battle of Good and Evil

Over 2,700 years ago, a man named Zoroaster lived in Persia (modern Iran). At that time people worshipped many gods. Zoroaster's beliefs opposed this way of thinking.

Zoroaster denied the power of lesser gods and honoured one god as supreme - Ahura Mazda, also called Ormazd. The power of evil he named Ahriman. Zoroaster preached that a struggle between the two resulted in the creation of the world. Since its creation, the whole world has been involved in the battle between good and evil, light and darkness. Each human being struggles between good and evil. After a person dies, the soul crosses a bridge and passes into either heaven or hell.

Zoroastrians also believe that the history of the world is a vast drama divided into four periods of 3,000 years each. At the end of the first 3,000 years, the creation of the world takes place. At the end of the second, Ahriman arrives to corrupt the creation. In the third period, he triumphs but finds himself trapped in creation and doomed to cause his own destruction. In the fourth period, religion comes to Earth through the birth of Zoroaster.

SEARCH LIGHT

Who represents good in Zoroastrianism, Ahura Mazda or Ahriman?

Each 1,000 years thereafter, a new **prophet** will appear. The last of these will bring the final judgment and a new world.

Islamic armies invaded Iran about 1,400 years ago. Eventually, most Zoroastrians left Iran and settled in India around Bombay (now called Mumbai). These people came to be known as Parsis. The Parsis grew into a rich and highly educated community.

The holy book of the Zoroastrians is the *Avesta*. The central feature of their temples is a sacred fire that burns night and day and is never allowed to die out.

DID YOU KNOW?
Zoroaster is sometimes credited with having created the practice of astrology. Astrologers 'read' the heavens in order to predict events and determine people's characters.

Between the ages of 7 and 11, children are initiated into the Zoroastrian religion in a ceremony called *navjote*. Here, priests oversee this young Parsi (Indian Zoroastrian) boy's *navjote*.
© Tim Page/Corbis

Answer: Ahura Mazda represents good in Zoroastrianism.

Religion of Israel

The Jews call themselves 'Israel', which in Hebrew means 'the people chosen by God'. According to Jewish holy writings, the one God promised Abraham, the father of all Jews: 'I will make of thee a great nation.' In return, that nation, Israel, was to obey God forever.

Lighting the menorah in celebration of the Jewish festival of Hanukkah.
© Richard T. Nowitz/Corbis

Later, when the people of Israel were enslaved in Egypt, a leader named Moses freed them and led the Jews to a new home. While going there, they made an agreement with God in the form of the **commandments**, God's laws. The commandments remind the Jewish people of their responsibilities to God and to each other.

All of this is written in the Hebrew Bible (known as the Old Testament to Christians). The most important section of the Hebrew Bible is the Torah - also called the Five Books of Moses, or Pentateuch. The Torah contains the religious ideas, history, ceremonies, and **rituals** of Judaism.

When a Jewish boy turns 13, he must read from the Torah in public. This makes him a Bar Mitzvah, or 'son of the commandment'. Girls celebrate their Bas Mitzvah, or Bat Mitzvah, which takes place after their 12th birthday.

Jews worship in synagogues, where services include the reading of the Scriptures, praying, and offering blessings and thanks to God. Important Jewish holidays are Purim, Rosh Hoshanah, and Hanukkah. The festival of Passover begins with a religious meal.

Today there are different groups within Judaism. **Orthodox** Jews dress, eat, live, and worship very much like their ancestors did hundreds of years ago. **Conservative** Jews worship much like Orthodox Jews but live by more relaxed rules. Reform Jews worship in more modern ways, with even fewer rules about how they live their daily lives.

SEARCH LIGHT

Correct the mistake in the following sentence: The most important part of the Jewish Bible is called the Bat Mitzvah.

DID YOU KNOW?
Many Jews keep 'kosher', which means they observe special laws about the food they eat. There are strict rules for how food is prepared and whether certain foods can be eaten in combination or at all.

Young Jewish boys all over the world celebrate their Bar Mitzvah. This young man carries the Torah at the Western Wall in Jerusalem as part of his celebration.
© Richard T. Nowitz/Corbis

Answer: The most important part of the Jewish Bible is called the Torah.

343

Father of Many Nations

The first book of the Bible tells the story of Abraham. This honoured leader is important in the major religious **traditions** of the Jews, Christians, and Muslims.

According to the account in the Bible, God came to Abraham one day and told him: 'I will make of thee a great nation.' God commanded him to leave his home in Mesopotamia (modern Iraq) for an unknown land, which would belong to Abraham and his descendants.

At the age of 75, Abraham started on this journey, bringing his wife, Sarah, and some other companions. They reached the '**Promised Land**', then known as Canaan, in what is now Israel.

Because Abraham and Sarah were so old when they settled there, they thought they couldn't have children. So Sarah gave Abraham her slave Hagar to have a child with, and Hagar gave birth to a son, Ishmael. But God had promised Abraham and Sarah their own child. When Abraham was 100 years old and Sarah was 90, their son, Isaac, was born. Sarah later sent Hagar and Ishmael away to live in the desert. Many consider Ishmael the first of the Arab people.

God tested Abraham by ordering him to kill Isaac as a sacrifice. Abraham was upset, but he was ready to obey. God stopped Abraham, however, and, because of his obedience, blessed him and his descendants. Isaac inherited the Promised Land after his father died and is considered to be the father of the Jewish people.

Abraham died when he was 175 years old and was buried next to Sarah. Abraham is still respected and honoured by Christians, Jews, and Muslims. They honour him as the father of their religion and as a great **prophet**.

SEARCH LIGHT

How old was Abraham when he went on his journey to Canaan?
a) 175
b) 100
c) 75

DID YOU KNOW?
Islamic tradition says that Abraham, assisted by his son Ishmael, built the Kaaba, the holiest of Muslim shrines, in the centre of the Great Mosque in Mecca, Saudi Arabia.

Answer: c) 75

Yahweh's Messenger

According to the Jewish Bible, the Hebrew people first went to Egypt in search of food during a great **famine**. Eventually, the Egyptians came to fear the Hebrews and enslaved them. At one point the pharaoh, the ruler of Egypt, ordered that all newborn male Hebrews be killed. Moses was born about this time, more than 3,000 years ago.

According to the Bible, Moses' parents set him afloat on the Nile River in a reed basket. The pharaoh's daughter found the child while she was bathing. Moses thus grew up in the Egyptian court. One day he learned that he was a Hebrew. He went out to visit his people and saw the hard life they led. Moses saw an Egyptian **overseer** beating a Hebrew slave, and he killed the overseer. He realized that he would have to flee.

Moses found shelter with a priest, married the priest's daughter, and became a shepherd. While looking after the flock, Moses heard God for the first time. God spoke to him from a burning bush on Mount Sinai, identifying himself as Yahweh. He told Moses to go back to Egypt and demand that the pharaoh set the Hebrews free.

Moses tried. But when the pharaoh refused, Yahweh punished the Egyptians with ten plagues. The tenth took the life of the pharaoh's eldest son, so the pharaoh ordered the Hebrews to leave.

Through much hardship, Moses led his people toward the Promised Land of Canaan. At Mount Sinai, Yahweh told Moses to go up the mountain. There Moses received the Ten **Commandments**. These laws and others told the Hebrews how to live. They became part of the Torah, the first five books of the Bible, and bound Jews to God.

SEARCH LIGHT

True or false? Moses grew up in the Egyptian court of the pharaoh.

DID YOU KNOW?
The Bible says that as Moses and the Hebrews fled the Egyptian soldiers chasing them, they came to a body of water believed to be the Red Sea. Yahweh created a dry path for the Hebrews to cross, but he drowned the Egyptian soldiers who followed.

The famous artist Michelangelo created this sculpture of Moses, the founder of the religious community of Israel.
© John Heseltine/Corbis

Answer: TRUE.

Following Jesus Christ

More than two billion people around the world follow the teachings of Jesus Christ. They call themselves Christians. And their religion, Christianity, is the world's most widespread religion.

Christianity developed from Judaism about 2,000 years ago. Over the years it has split into many groups. This is because, at various times, Christians disagreed among themselves about some of their beliefs. The major branches of Christianity include the Roman Catholic church, Protestant churches, and the Eastern Orthodox church.

Despite the divisions, there are many things these groups agree on. They all have the same holy book, the Bible. The Christian Bible is divided into the Old Testament and the New Testament, which is about the life and teachings of Jesus Christ. Nearly all Christian churches have leaders, or clergy. In different churches they may be called priests, ministers, or pastors, among other titles. Clergy give their church members guidance and perform official duties at services of **worship**.

SEARCH LIGHT

Christians celebrate Christmas to honour Jesus Christ's
a) birth.
b) death.
c) resurrection.

Most Christians believe in the Trinity as well. The word comes from Latin and means 'three'. It describes the three individual **aspects** of the one God. The three are: God the Father, who created everything; God the Son (Jesus Christ), who died to save humankind; and God the Holy Spirit, who inspires people's thoughts and actions.

And all Christians celebrate certain holy days. Christmas marks the birth of Jesus, and Easter honours Jesus' resurrection, when he rose from the dead. The Friday before Easter is called Good Friday. It is the anniversary of Jesus' death.

DID YOU KNOW?
Although Christianity is widespread today, its followers were pursued and tormented in the religion's early days. Sometimes they were killed if they were discovered to be Christians.

Answer: a) birth.

The Son of God

Almost everything we know about Jesus Christ comes from the Christian Bible. Jesus was a Jew, born to Mary more than 2,000 years ago in Bethlehem. Christians believe that Jesus was the son of God. The New Testament **Gospels** of the Christian Bible tell the story of Jesus' life and teachings.

Mosaic picture of Jesus Christ in the cathedral in Cefalù, Sicily, Italy.
© Mimmo Jodice/Corbis

Jesus grew up in Nazareth, in what is now Israel. When he was 12 his parents took him to Jerusalem for the feast of Passover. Suddenly they discovered that he was missing. They finally found Jesus talking in the Temple with the learned men, who were amazed at how wise he was.

Like his earthly father, Joseph, he became a carpenter. When Jesus was about 30 years old, he began **preaching** about God. He is also said to have begun performing miracles. In one miracle Jesus fed 5,000 people with just five loaves of bread and two fish.

Jesus was kind to the poor and the sick. He was also kind to people who were disliked by others. He taught that all people should love each other just as they love their families and themselves. Jesus taught about the kingdom of God. Some people thought this meant that Jesus would try to rule a kingdom here on earth. The rulers of the land thought Jesus might try to seize power from them. So at age 33 Jesus was arrested, killed on a cross, and buried. But visitors to his tomb found it empty.

According to the Gospels, Jesus rose from the dead and was taken back up to heaven.

First, however, he appeared many times to his followers. His followers became known as Christians, and their religion is called Christianity. They see Jesus' death as a **sacrifice** for all people.

SEARCH LIGHT

Fill in the gap:
Jesus taught that people should love each other as much as they love their families and _____.

DID YOU KNOW?
'Christ' was originally a title that came from the Greek word *christos*. *Christos* is a translation from the Hebrew term *meshiah* (or Messiah), meaning 'the anointed one', and refers to the king whom the Jews expected to come.

This stained-glass window in a church in Palo Alto, California, U.S., shows one of Jesus' miracles. This and other major events from Jesus' life are often subjects of Christian art.
© Steve Skjold/Photo Edit

Answer: Jesus taught that people should love each other as much as they love their families and themselves.

Mother of Jesus

Christians worldwide honour Mary, the mother of Jesus. She is known as Saint Mary and the Virgin Mary. But not much is known about Mary's life. What we do know comes from the New Testament of the Christian Bible.

The Bible first mentions Mary as a young girl living in Nazareth, a town north of Jerusalem in Palestine (now in Israel). She was engaged to marry Joseph, a local carpenter. One day an angel came to her and told her that she had been chosen to give birth to God's son. Later Mary gave birth to Jesus.

King Herod heard that a newborn baby would one day become king of the Jews in Herod's own kingdom. Herod ordered all babies under the age of 2 to be killed. Joseph was warned by an angel in a dream, and he fled with Mary and Jesus to Egypt.

Mary appears again at the wedding at Cana, where Jesus performed his first miracle. She was also one of the few followers who did not run away in fear when Jesus Christ died on the cross. The New Testament Book of John describes how Jesus spoke to John and to Mary from the cross, telling them to look after each other. After that, Mary is mentioned as one of the people who devoted themselves to prayer after Jesus rose to heaven. She also took part in the early growth of the church.

But over the centuries, the mother of Jesus has become recognized as a holy person second only to Jesus in the Roman Catholic, Eastern Orthodox, and other churches. Her position has also influenced the lives of women in Christian cultures.

A Pietà (image of the Virgin Mary and the dead Christ), by Luis de Morales.
© Archivo Iconografico, S.A./Corbis

SEARCH LIGHT

True or false? Saint Mary is Jesus' mother.

DID YOU KNOW?
Throughout the history of Christianity, many people have claimed to have seen Mary. One of the most famous visions was reported in 1917 by three children at Fatima, Portugal.

Mary, often called the Madonna ('Lady'), has been a favourite subject of artists for centuries. Images of Mary and the baby Jesus are a frequent theme, as in Fra Angelico's 'Madonna of Humility', seen here.
© Francis G. Mayer/Corbis

Answer: TRUE.

A Branch of Christianity

Christianity has been divided into many **denominations**, or different church organizations within one religion. Roman Catholicism is one of the oldest of these and has the largest following. It dates back to the 1st century AD, when it was founded by followers of Jesus Christ.

The headquarters of the church is Vatican City, located in Rome, Italy. The head of the church is the Pope, who is the **bishop** of Rome. He is the highest authority for all Catholics. The name Roman Catholicism comes from the religion's base in Rome and from a Greek term meaning 'universal'.

The chief worship service of the Roman Catholic church is called the 'mass'. The first part of the service involves readings from the Bible and a sermon, or religious lecture. The second half involves communion, when the priest stands at the altar and repeats what Christ did and said at his Last Supper on the night before he died. For Catholics the bread and wine taken during this part of the mass are the body and blood of Christ.

Roman Catholics believe in holy people called 'saints' and seek their help in times of need. The most honoured of Catholic saints is Mary, the mother of Jesus. Like all Christians, Catholics consider the Bible the holiest of their religious books.

Catholics are expected to attend mass every Sunday and on major feast days, called 'holy days of **obligation**'. These holy days include Christmas, when Christians celebrate the birth of Jesus.

(Top) Nun of the order of Sisters of Mother Teresa, who help the poor worldwide.
(Bottom) Catholic procession through the streets of Lagos, Nigeria.

SEARCH LIGHT

The word Catholic comes from a Greek term meaning what?
a) 'national'
b) 'universal'
c) 'local'

DID YOU KNOW?
At one time, because of disagreements in the Roman Catholic church, there were two popes at the same time - one in Rome and the other in France.

Roman Catholics everywhere celebrate mass. These people worship in the historic Spanish mission church of San José de Gracia in Las Trampas, New Mexico, U.S. It was built in 1760.
© Craig Aurness/Corbis

Answer: b) 'universal'

Jewish and Christian Scriptures

© Richard T. Nowitz/Corbis

© CLEO Photography/Photo Edit

Jews and Christians call their scriptures, or holy books, the Bible. But their Bibles are not the same. What Jews call the Bible forms what Christians call the Old Testament. The Christian Bible also contains the New Testament. Both the Old Testament and the New are collections of shorter sections called 'books'.

The Jewish Bible tells the history of Israel. It is grouped into three sections: the Law, the Prophets, and the Writings.

SEARCH LIGHT

Correct the mistake in the following sentence: The founding of Israel is described in the New Testament.

(Left) Family shares the bible. (Right) Torah scrolls in the main synagogue in Jerusalem.

The first five books, the Law, are also known to Jews as the Torah. The Law describes how the world and people came to be and how Israel was founded. It contains the story of Moses, the Ten Commandments (instructions for life and worship), and other teachings. The section called the Prophets contains the later history of Israel as well as messages passed from God to the Jewish people. The Writings include history, songs and hymns, **psalms**, poetry, stories, and wise sayings.

The New Testament of Christianity tells the story of Jesus Christ and his followers. It is shorter than the Old Testament. There are four sections in the New Testament: the Gospels, the Acts, the Epistles, and Revelation.

The Gospels describe Christ's life, death, and resurrection (raising from the dead). In the Acts of the Apostles, the story and teachings of Jesus' disciples, or followers, are told. The Epistles are letters that various leaders of the early Christian church wrote. The Book of Revelation talks about the end of the world and the events that will take place before the end comes.

None of the original Bible documents still exist. The Bible **texts** are copies of copies that were handed down over many generations.

DID YOU KNOW?
In 1947 a young shepherd found the first of the documents called the Dead Sea Scrolls in a cave in Judaea (now in Israel). These documents come from about Jesus' time. They hold versions of some biblical writings, as well as many texts never seen before.

The Bible was one of the first books printed by Johannes Gutenberg on the first printing press. This is one of the few remaining copies.
© David Young-Wolff/Photo Edit

Answer: The founding of Israel is described in the Old Testament.

The Religion of Muhammad

Islam is a major world religion. It was founded in Arabia about 1,400 years ago by a man called Muhammad. Followers of Islam are called Muslims. There are more than a billion Muslims in the world.

Palestinian Muslim women pray during Ramadan outside the Dome of the Rock, in Jerusalem.
© AFP/Corbis

Muslims believe that the archangel Gabriel brought Muhammad many messages from God (Allah in Arabic). Most people in Arabia at that time believed in many gods. But the messages told Muhammad that there was only one God. Muslims believe Muhammad was the last of God's prophets, in a line that began with Adam and continued through Abraham, Moses, and Jesus.

The messages to Muhammad were collected in a book called the Koran, or Qur'an. The Koran says that God is stern but forgiving and asks everyone to worship only him. Muslims believe that when they die, they are judged according to their actions.

Islam has five duties that every Muslim should perform. These five Pillars of Islam instruct Muslims to make known their faith in God, pray daily, give to the poor, **fast,** and make a **pilgrimage** to the holy city of Mecca once during their lifetime if possible.

A Muslim must pray five times a day, either alone or with others in a mosque, the Muslim place of worship. Special group prayers are said in mosques every Friday. Fasting takes place during Ramadan, the holy month during which God is said to have revealed the Koran. During fasting, Muslims may not eat or drink between sunrise and sunset.

Mecca is the holy city of Islam where Muhammad was born and where Abraham built a shrine called the Kaaba. Only Muslims may enter Mecca. The yearly pilgrimage to Mecca is called the *hajj* and is celebrated in the festival of Id al-Adha.

SEARCH LIGHT

Which of the following is not one of the five Pillars of Islam?
a) fasting
b) prayer
c) faith
d) pilgrimage
e) singing
f) giving to the poor

DID YOU KNOW?
Medina, in Saudi Arabia, is celebrated as the first Muslim community. From there, Islam spread throughout Arabia. Only Muslims are allowed to enter the city.

Islam has spread throughout the world, as Muhammad had intended. These Muslims are praying together in a mosque in Sarajevo, in Bosnia and Herzegovina.
© Dean Conger/Corbis

Answer: e) singing

Islam's Prophet

Muhammad was born in Mecca about 1,400 years ago. During his life he established Islam, one of the world's major religions.

Mecca was a **prosperous** and important centre of trade. Muhammad was a merchant and married a wealthy widow. When he was older, he spent many nights praying in a cave in a hill near Mecca. Muslims believe that on one such night he was visited by the archangel Gabriel, who brought him God's message.

Muhammad believed that God wanted him to deliver God's teachings to the Arab people. These teachings are recorded in Islam's holy book, the Koran. His family and friends accepted Muhammad as the last of a series of **prophets** of God that began with Adam and continued through Abraham, Moses, and Jesus. He then began to preach publicly in Mecca. His religion came to be called Islam, which means 'submission to God'. The believers were called Muslims, which means 'those who have submitted'.

Muhammad said that there was only one God, called Allah in the Arabic language. At that time most Arabs worshipped many different gods. Some people disliked Muhammad's idea and planned to kill him, so he moved to the city of Medina. In his new home he began **converting** people to Islam. After fighting a war with his enemies, Muhammad returned to Mecca and convinced everyone there to become Muslims. Many Arabs then became Muslims, and gradually Muhammad became the leader of Arabia.

Eventually, Islam split into different branches. All Muslims, however, look upon Muhammad as an example of an ideal of human life. They honour three cities connected with him: Mecca (his birthplace), Medina (the first Muslim community), and Jerusalem (which he supposedly visited on a journey to heaven).

DID YOU KNOW?
All Muslims try to make a journey to Mecca at least once in their lifetime.

The shrine known as the Kaaba, in the holy city of Mecca, is considered by Muslims to be the holiest place on Earth. The yearly *hajj* (or pilgrimage to Mecca) is undertaken by over a million worshippers. Daily prayers are said in the direction of Mecca and the Kaaba.
© AFP/Corbis

Holy Book of Islam

True or false? Muhammad wrote down the entire Koran.

Followers of the religion called Islam (Muslims) believe that God spoke to the Prophet Muhammad through the angel Gabriel. Muhammad received these messages for about 20 years. God, called Allah in Arabic, sent the messages so that Arabs would have a holy book in their own language. Muhammad and his followers memorized the messages and sometimes wrote them down. Altogether they're called the Koran, or Qur'an, which means '**recitation**' or 'reading' in Arabic.

After Muhammad's death, Muslims were afraid that the knowledge in the Koran would be lost. So Uthman, the third caliph (Islamic ruler), ordered a single, official version of the Koran to be created.

The Koran's 114 chapters are not presented in the order they were revealed to Muhammad. The chapters are called *surah*s. The *surah*s have different lengths, but each begins with a prayer and is written in a poetic tone.

(Top) Young Nigerian girl reads the Koran with other students. (Bottom) Students in Islamabad, Pakistan, at a *madrasah* (Muslim school of higher learning).

According to the Koran, there is only one God and all Muslims should obey God and his word. The Koran also reflects a belief in the **resurrection** from the dead, in angels and devils, and in heaven and hell. All people will be judged by God. The book also says that God's message to Muhammad is both a warning and a promise. It's a warning to those who refuse to believe in the one God. But it also promises spiritual rewards to those who believe in God and do his will.

For Muslims, the Koran is the true word of God and the final word in all matters of law and religion. It is also considered to be without any error in what it teaches.

DID YOU KNOW?

Many inside and outside portions of the Taj Mahal in India are inlaid with verses of the Koran. Calligraphy (artistic lettering) is a major Islamic art form. Some forms of Islam do not allow artistic images of living things, though the Koran does not mention this.

This beautifully illuminated (decorated) copy of the Koran was made in the 18th century for the sultan of Morocco.
© Corbis

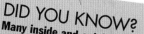

A Simple Faith

The Baha'i faith is a fairly new religion with followers throughout the world. It grew out of Islam, the religion founded by Muhammad. After Muhammad's death, the Islamic religion split into two groups, Sunnites and Shiites. Some Muslims (as followers of Islam are called) used the title of 'bab' (Arabic for 'gateway') for their religious leaders. The most famous use of the term was by a Persian (Iranian) Shiite named Mirza Ali Mohammad, who declared himself 'the Bab' in 1844.

One of the Bab's earliest followers was Mirza Hoseyn Ali Nuri, who took the name Baha Ullah. In 1863 he declared himself to be the messenger of God whom the Bab had predicted would come. Most of the Bab's followers believed him. Baha Ullah later founded the Baha'i faith. He made his eldest son, Abd ol-Baha (Abdul Baha), the leader of the Baha'i community.

SEARCH LIGHT

Fill in the gaps:

_____ was the founder of the Baha'i faith.

Abd ol-Baha (Abdul Baha), first leader of the Baha'i faith, who is called the 'Center of the Covenant' and 'Architect of the Administrative Order'.
© Baha'i World Centre

The Baha'i faith teaches that a person's purpose in life is to worship God through prayer and meditation and seeks to unite all people in one religion. Those who follow this faith believe that people must also work to end racial, class, and religious unfairness. They believe that the founders of the world's great religions are all messengers of God. These messengers include Moses, the Buddha, Jesus, Muhammad, and Baha Ullah. They also believe there will be more messengers of God in the future. Followers of this religion do not drink alcohol, and they must seek permission from parents to marry.

Baha'i followers attend local spiritual assemblies to worship. There are also several impressive Baha'i temples located around the world. Baha'i services are extremely simple. There is no preaching. Instead, there are readings from the scriptures.

DID YOU KNOW?
Most Baha'i temples are nine-sided domes. These features suggest both the differences between and the unity of all people.

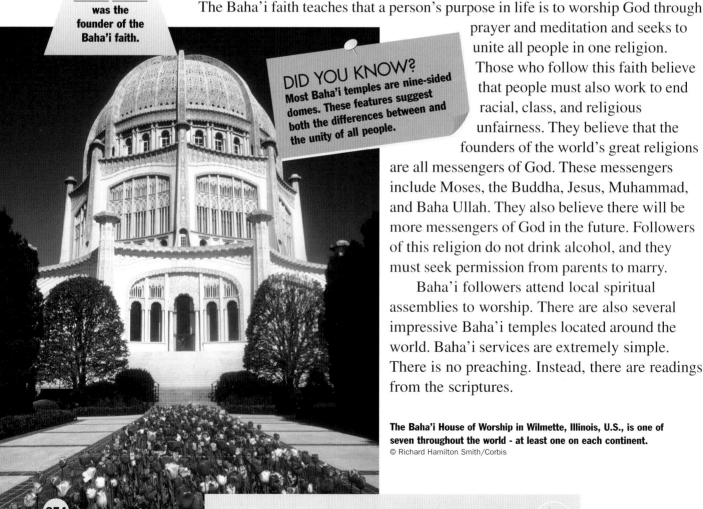

The Baha'i House of Worship in Wilmette, Illinois, U.S., is one of seven throughout the world - at least one on each continent.
© Richard Hamilton Smith/Corbis

Ancient Religion
of South Asia

Hinduism is a religion, but it is also a culture and a way of life. Over 800 million people, mostly in India and Nepal, practise Hinduism.

Hindu devotees pray as they bathe in the holy Ganges River.
© AFP/Corbis

The roots of Hinduism go back more than 3,000 years. Since that time it has grown into many different **sects**. The beliefs of one Hindu might not be the same as those of another. But Hinduism is generally very accepting of differences between these subgroups.

Brahman is the one supreme power in Hinduism, but most Hindus believe there are many gods. Most important among these gods are Vishnu, Shiva, Brahma, and Shakti. Each of the different gods has influence over a different part of life. For example, the elephant-headed god Ganesha helps remove difficulties. Lakshmi is the goddess of wealth. Shiva is one of the main and most complex Hindu gods. He both destroys things and rebuilds them.

Meditation is a very important part of Hinduism. It encourages relaxation and concentration to free the mind. Other forms of worship include chanting hymns and performing small **sacrifices** to the gods. There are also many holy books in Hinduism. The most famous and important one is the Bhagavadgita.

Most Hindus believe that human souls are reborn after death. The Hindu law of *karma* says that what a person does in one life affects his or her future life. In Hinduism the purpose of life is to do good things in order to free yourself from the cycle of rebirth.

Another important Hindu view is *ahimsa*, which means 'non-injury' to all living things. This has led to the well-known Hindu respect for the cow.

SEARCH LIGHT

Fill in the gap. The Hindu concept of *karma* has to do with the cycle of _____.

DID YOU KNOW?
Hindus consider the Ganges River, or Ganga, to be a holy place. Every year, hundreds of thousands of people bathe in the Ganges during a festival called a *mela*.

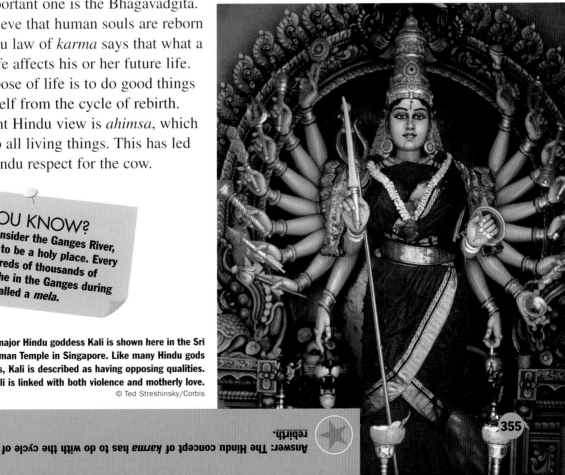

The major Hindu goddess Kali is shown here in the Sri Veeramakaliamman Temple in Singapore. Like many Hindu gods and goddesses, Kali is described as having opposing qualities. For instance, Kali is linked with both violence and motherly love.
© Ted Streshinsky/Corbis

Answer: The Hindu concept of *karma* has to do with the cycle of rebirth.

355

The Teacher of Hinduism

'**A**rise! Awake! And stop not 'til your goal is reached!' This was Vivekananda's call to the people of the world. His highest goal was to strive for self-perfection. And he felt that working to benefit **humanity** was the most honourable activity.

Vivekananda was born in India as Narendranath Datta in 1863. He was an active and curious child who questioned everything. He was fascinated by Hindu monks. He wondered how they could leave home and wander about the world.

Vivekananda in 1900.
Courtesy of the Vedanta Society of Southern California

'Have you seen God?' young Narendranath asked every holy man he met. He had heard people talk about God and pray to him, but no one said they had seen God.

One day, a holy Hindu man called Ramakrishna told Narendranath, 'Yes, I see God as I see you.' Sri Ramakrishna's honesty removed Narendranath's doubts.

Narendranath took the name Vivekananda, gave up everything, and travelled throughout India as a wandering monk. He felt very sad at the condition of the poor people of his country. He tried to find help to better their lives.

In 1893 Vivekananda attended the **Parliament** of Religions in Chicago, Illinois, in the United States. When he addressed the audience as 'sisters and brothers of America', everyone clapped. They listened as he talked about Hindu philosophy, about God, and about how all religions lead to the same goal of knowing God.

After travelling in the United States and in England for three years, Vivekananda returned to India with some of his Western followers. There he founded the Ramakrishna Mission. Still in service today, the mission works both to improve the lives of poor and uneducated Indians and to spread the vision of a Hinduism active in society.

SEARCH LIGHT

What was Vivekananda's original name?

DID YOU KNOW?
Vivekananda's travels through the United States and England led to great interest in Hinduism there. The Ramakrishna Mission has also helped make its version of Hinduism widely known and now has branches in many parts of the world.

Vivekananda founded the Ramakrishna Mission in 1897, the same year this photograph was taken. The next year, the Vedanta Society of the City of New York was founded. This organization is the oldest branch of the mission in the United States.
Courtesy of the Vedanta Society of Southern California

The Teachings of the Buddha

The religion that developed in ancient India around the teachings of Siddhartha Gautama, the Buddha, is called Buddhism. His teachings offered a way to achieve **Enlightenment**, and he attracted many followers. After his death, temples were built in his honour and his religion spread through much of Asia, especially China, Korea, and Japan. It has spread to Western countries too.

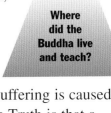

SEARCH LIGHT

Where did the Buddha live and teach?

The Buddha taught about the Four Noble Truths, which became the basis of Buddhism. The First Noble Truth is that life is made up of pain and suffering. The Second Noble Truth is that all suffering is caused by a person's desires, by wanting. The Third Noble Truth is that a person can be free from these self-centred desires. The freedom from desire is called Nirvana, or Enlightenment. The Fourth Noble Truth is called the Eightfold Path.

To follow the Eightfold Path means that a person follows a Middle Way between a life of luxury and a life of unnecessary poverty. Following this path eventually leads to a life free from suffering. The eight parts of the Path are: right understanding (of the Four Noble Truths), right thought, right speech, right action (including non-violence), right way of living (occupations in line with Buddhist beliefs), right effort, right mindfulness (attention), and right concentration (**meditation**).

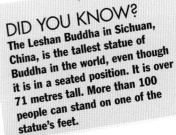

(Top) Buddhist nuns in Dharmshala, India, where Tibet's Dalai Lama and others fled from their homeland in 1959. (Bottom) Student monks holding bowls to receive alms (offerings) in Bagan, Myanmar.

DID YOU KNOW?
The Leshan Buddha in Sichuan, China, is the tallest statue of Buddha in the world, even though it is in a seated position. It is over 71 metres tall. More than 100 people can stand on one of the statue's feet.

The Buddha's teachings weren't written down until 300 years after his death. By then the religion had split into a number of groups, each with a different understanding of the Buddha's teachings. And today Buddhist monks, nuns, and priests carry the teachings forward as they understand them.

In southwestern China, Buddhists may worship at temples such as this one in Kunming, in Yunnan province.
© Royalty-Free/Corbis

Answer: The Buddha lived and taught in ancient India.

The Enlightened One

The term 'buddha' means '**enlightened** one' - one who understands truths beyond the everyday world. It is not a name but rather a title of respect. 'The Buddha' or the name Gautama refers to the founder of the religion called Buddhism. If you see an image of him, he looks peaceful, wise, and full of love.

Gautama was the son of a king. He was born long ago near what's now the border of Nepal and India. His personal name was Siddhartha. Before his birth, his mother had a strange dream about a beautiful white elephant. The holy men predicted that the queen would have a son who would grow up to be either a king or a buddha.

When he was 29 years old, Siddhartha saw four sights that left him thinking about the purpose of life. He saw a weak old man with a walking stick. Another day he saw a sick man, and another day a dead body. Then Siddhartha saw a holy man looking very calm.

Siddhartha decided to give up the life of a prince. He left his home in search of truth. At one point he decided to sit under a tree until he became enlightened. He wanted to understand the truth about the spirit and about life. Finally, at the age of 35, Siddhartha reached enlightenment. He became the Buddha. The tree he sat under is called the bodhi ('enlightenment') tree.

Buddha spent the rest of his life teaching people a way of thought and living that involved **meditation** and a freedom from suffering. While he did not claim to be a god, some people do pray to him. Many people live their lives according to Buddhist teachings

DID YOU KNOW?
The teachings of the world's great religious leaders often overlap. The Buddha taught that people should 'consider others as yourself'. Similarly, Jesus Christ taught that people should 'do unto others as you would have others do unto you'.

SEARCH LIGHT

Fill in the gaps. The word 'buddha' means '_____'.

Answer: The word 'buddha' means 'enlightened one'.

Tibet's Great Teacher

The word '*lama*' means 'teacher' in the Tibetan language. Lamas are religious leaders who are usually great teachers or heads of **monasteries**. In the Mongolian language, '*dalai*' means 'ocean', and stands for a vast 'sea of wisdom'. The Dalai Lama is head of the leading Tibetan Buddhist group called the Yellow Hat order. He's also the religious leader of Tibet. Until 1959, the Dalai Lama was the head of the Tibetan government as well.

Which of the following is a good translation of the title Dalai Lama?
a) religious leader
b) yellow teacher
c) wisest teacher

Tibetans believe that some lamas are reborn as other lamas. The Dalai Lama is considered to be the human form of Avalokiteshvara. Avalokiteshvara is a *bodhisattva* (a Buddha-to-be) known especially for his kindness and mercy towards humans. The first Dalai Lama was Dge-'dun-grub-pa. All the Dalai Lamas that followed him are believed to be his reincarnations (rebirths).

How do the Tibetans know that the Dalai Lama has been reborn? The rebirth may happen days or even years after a Dalai Lama has died. Special attention is paid to a dying Dalai Lama's words and to any unusual signs during his death. Also, one special priest is believed to have visions and other **mystical** knowledge about a newly reborn Dalai Lama. A careful search based on these clues takes place. Often two or more boys may be examined before the new Dalai Lama is finally announced. The new Dalai Lama is trained at a monastery from an early age. A chosen adult rules the state until the young Dalai Lama has been educated.

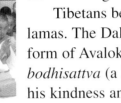

Children observing the 14th Dalai Lama as he visits Sarnath, Uttar Pradesh, India, in January 2003.
© AP/Wide World

Since 1959, the present (14th) Dalai Lama has lived in **exile** in Dharmsala, India. He and some followers left after a failed Tibetan rebellion against the Chinese government, which had invaded Tibet in 1950. Since then the Dalai Lama has worked hard but peacefully for Tibet's independence.

DID YOU KNOW?
In 1989 the present Dalai Lama was awarded the Nobel Prize for Peace. This honoured his non-violent efforts to end Chinese domination of Tibet.

The present Dalai Lama teaches, lectures, and speaks to thousands of people worldwide. If he had not been exiled from Tibet, he would have led a quiet and protected life. But today he is a popular and well-spoken representative of the Buddhist religion and Tibetan independence.
© AP/Wide World

Answer: c) wisest teacher

Teaching Non-violence

Jainism is one of three major ancient religions of India, along with Buddhism and Hinduism. Jainism was founded more than 2,500 years ago by Mahavira. He probably lived at the same time as Siddhartha Gautama, who founded Buddhism.

The term Jainism comes from the word Jina, which means 'conqueror'. Jains believe that it is possible to fight earthly desires and physical needs to reach a stage of perfect understanding and purity. They work towards this **perfection** by taking vows that help them live properly. Jains try to reach a point where they no longer depend on the world or their bodies for anything. A person who reaches this stage is called a Jina.

In Jainism all living things have value. Jains believe in *ahimsa*, or non-violence, which means they cannot harm any living creature. As a result of this belief, most Jains are **vegetarians**.

Jainism has both **lay** followers (regular believers) and monks and nuns. All Jains are forbidden to lie, steal, and eat meals at night. But Jain monks and nuns also follow other very strict rules as they try to achieve a perfect inner state. They do not marry, and they keep few or no possessions. Most Jains are lay followers. They may marry, but they are expected to avoid certain foods and to keep few possessions. They are also expected to avoid unnecessary travel and pleasure, to **fast**, and to serve their fellow Jains, especially the monks and nuns and the poor.

Many lay followers also worship or make offerings to past Jinas and to various gods and goddesses. There are about 4 million followers of Jainism today in India and 100,000 in other countries.

SEARCH LIGHT

True or false? Jains are vegetarians.

Jain worshipper pouring a milk offering on a huge Indian statue of Bahubali, the first human of this world-age to gain perfection and release from worldly needs.
© Chris Lisle/Corbis

This Jain priest stands before a statuette of Mahavira, founder of Jainism. His name means 'great hero', and he is honoured as the last of the 24 Jinas.
© Charles & Josette Lenars/Corbis

DID YOU KNOW?
Jain non-violence includes insects. Many monks own nothing but a small broom to sweep insects from their paths and a mouth-and-nose covering to prevent them from swallowing or inhaling small insects.

Answer: TRUE. Most Jains do not eat meat.

A South Asian Religion

Sikhism is a religion founded by Guru Nanak in the late 15th century in India. The word 'guru' means 'teacher'. The word 'Sikh' means 'disciple' or 'learner'.

Teacher helping two Sikh boys with lessons.
© Annie Griffiths Belt/Corbis

Guru Nanak was the first Sikh guru. There were nine gurus after him. The fifth Sikh guru, Arjun, wrote down his own **hymns** and those of the earlier gurus. The last guru, Gobind Singh (also called Gobind Rai), added his own hymns. He said that after his death the book in which the hymns were written would take the place of the Sikh guru. This book became the holy book of the Sikhs, called the *Adi Granth*, or *Granth Sahib*.

Sikhs call their places of worship *gurdwara*s ('gateways to the guru'). The chief *gurdwara* is the Golden Temple, built in 1604 in Amritsar, India. Sikhs eat together in the *gurdwara* as a sign of the equality of all kinds of people.

Sikhism includes **aspects** of two other religions, Hinduism and Islam. From Hinduism comes belief in a cycle of birth, death, and rebirth. Another Hindu feature is the concept of *karma*, which says that a person's previous life affects the present one. Islam's influence can be seen in Sikhism's description of God as the One, the Truth, the Creator, the immortal, the formless, and the ever present.

Most Sikh boys and girls will become part of the Khalsa, the Sikh **order** of soldier-scholar-saints. After that, men must not cut their hair, must wear short trousers (even under their longer outer trousers) and a steel bracelet, and must carry a comb and a sword. Sikhs are not permitted to use liquor, tobacco, or drugs.

DID YOU KNOW?
Sikhs treat their holy book, the *Adi Granth*, as a living guru. The book is awakened in the morning and draped in fine things. Followers place offerings before it. It is put to rest in the evening.

SEARCH LIGHT

Which of the following is the holy book of the Sikhs?
a) Guru Nanek
b) *Adi Granth*
c) Amritsar

Much of Sikh worship is an individual activity. This woman - part of a Sikh settlement in New Mexico, U.S. - is meditating in her home.
© Buddy Mays/Corbis

The Spirit World

A shaman is a person believed to have extraordinary powers. 'Shaman' means 'he who knows'. It is thought that a shaman can predict what's going to happen in the future. A shaman goes into a trance to enter the spirit world and performs special rituals to cure sick people. Because of this, the shaman acts as the people's doctor and priest.

Religious beliefs in which the shaman plays a major role are called 'shamanism'. However, the believers don't refer to their belief in this way. Shamanism is simply a term that groups together certain religious beliefs.

Shamans from Goshal village in northern India being greeted by Manali village elder (left) during festival.
© Lindsay Hebberd/Corbis

In general, followers of shamanism believe that everyone has a soul. A person falls ill when the soul leaves the body for some reason. It then becomes the job of the shaman to enter the world of spirits, get hold of the runaway soul, and bring it back to the body of the sick person.

It is believed that the spirits choose the man or woman who is to act as a shaman. The spirits first tell the person in a dream that he or she has been chosen. If the person refuses to become a shaman, he or she is made sick by the spirit until he or she gives in. People chosen as shamans typically have some unusual feature. For example, they might have an extra tooth or an extra finger.

People in very different parts of the world practise shamanism or have religions with very similar features. These include groups in North and South America, India, Australia, the Pacific Islands, and China. The greatest number of people who practise a pure shamanism live in northern Asia, mostly in the Russian region of Siberia.

DID YOU KNOW?

Dance and drama play an important part in the activities of a shaman. The north Asian shaman becomes a fascinating sight, with his cloak floating in the light of a fire. He becomes actor, dancer, singer, and storyteller.

SEARCH LIGHT

True or false? Shamans often have an unusual physical feature.

On the Southeast Asian island of Borneo, some people practise shamanistic traditional religions. Here a ceremonial dance is performed by a shaman of the Dayak people.
© Charles & Josette Lenars/Corbis

Answer: TRUE.

Religion of Magic and Spirits

Many people in Haiti believe in the religion known as Vodun or, among most outsiders, Voodoo. Vodun came to Haiti more than 300 years ago when large numbers of people from Africa were taken there to work as slaves. As time passed, the beliefs of the African slaves mingled with those of Haiti's French plantation owners, who were mostly Roman Catholics.

Those who practice Vodun believe that there is one god and many kinds of spirits, called *loa*. The purpose of Vodun is to serve these spirits and keep their goodwill. The spirits serve as a link between people and the god whom the Haitians call Bondye.

During ceremonies the *loa* may take control of (possess) a believer. That person then may do **ritual** dances, accept animal **sacrifices** for the spirit, and offer important advice to others. Otherwise the *loa* is a combination guardian angel and **patron saint**.

A Vodun priest is called a *houngan*, and a priestess (female priest) is called a *mambo*. They lead ceremonies in which people play drums, sing, dance, pray, prepare food, and sacrifice animals. The leaders also act as counsellors, healers, and expert protectors against sorcery or witchcraft. Important Vodun spirits are honoured on feast days of different Roman Catholic saints, and the spirits of ancestors are honoured on All Saint's Day and All Souls' Day.

Many Haitians believe in zombis. A zombi is either a dead person's bodiless soul that is used for magical purposes or a dead body raised magically from the grave to be a slave.

SEARCH LIGHT

Vodun is a mixture of African beliefs and what other religion?
a) Judaism
b) Hinduism
c) Roman Catholicism

DID YOU KNOW?
Hollywood horror movies did much to create misunderstandings about 'Voodoo' and fear of its followers. It has often been shown as an evil and terrifying religion.

These women in Togo, in West Africa, are being received into the Vodun tradition in a secret ritual ceremony. Many people were taken as slaves from Togo to the West Indies, where Vodun is also a major religious tradition.
© Caroline Penn/Corbis

Teacher of Great Wisdom

Confucius was a Chinese teacher and thinker. He believed in understanding and learning, and in people's ability to improve themselves. In China, Confucius' ideas have been important for thousands of years. There, he is known as Kongzi, which means 'Master Kong'.

Confucianism is often called a religion, but it is really a system of **values** for living a good life. Confucius spoke more about goodness than about God. His teaching focused on how people could make themselves better in their lifetimes. He also taught about the importance of honouring one's parents and ruler.

Confucius was born to a poor family in 551 BC, more than 2,500 years ago. His father died when he was 3 years old. After that his mother educated him in music, shooting with a bow and arrow, arithmetic, chariot riding, and calligraphy (the art of handwriting). Confucius also studied Chinese poetry and history. All these things helped him become a good teacher.

In China during Confucius' time, parents sometimes hired special **tutors** to educate their children. Only the wealthy could afford tutors, and poor children had fewer chances for education. Confucius wanted to make education available to all because he believed everyone needed to acquire knowledge and build character. He believed that education was the best way to understand yourself and improve the world.

Confucius spent his whole life learning and teaching so that he could change society for the better. Many of his wise sayings were collected in a work called the *Analects*. Today, many East Asian countries celebrate Confucius' birthday as a holiday.

DID YOU KNOW?
You may have heard of one of Confucius' famous sayings: 'A journey of a thousand miles begins with a single step.' What do you think he meant by that?

Answer: b) learning and self-improvement.

The Religion of Laozi

Over 2,500 years ago, there lived a wise **philosopher** in China. His name was Laozi. Laozi (also spelled Lao-tzu) lived in a time of battles and great social troubles. His teachings, therefore, offered a way to bring nature and human life into harmony.

The *Yin* and *Yang* symbol, suggesting the way opposites join to make up the wholeness of life.

SEARCH LIGHT

Daoism began in
a) China.
b) Vietnam.
c) Korea.

The teachings of Laozi and others became the religion known as Daoism (or Taoism). According to Daoist tradition, Laozi wrote a book on Daoism known as *Daodejing*, or 'Classic of the Way of Power'. The main purpose of this book was to advise the king on how to rule his kingdom.

Today Laozi is honoured as a saint by his followers in mainland China, Taiwan, Vietnam, Japan, and Korea. The followers of Daoism believe in the Dao (meaning the 'way'), which is understood as a natural force and the source of all things in the universe. In Daoism death is a natural process and results in a person's returning to his or her source, the Dao.

Daoism states that a human being is part of a universe based on the spiritual principles of *Yin* and *Yang*. *Yin* and *Yang* mean the 'dark side' and 'sunny side' of a hill. Together they create the wholeness of nature. A human being carries both *Yin* and *Yang* in his or her body and must balance them in daily activities through personal discipline.

While Daoism teaches the freedom of the individual, it also stresses the duties of the community toward its people and the duties of government toward its citizens. This is just one more example of the balance of Yin and Yang.

Daoism and Confucianism are very different systems. But together, for thousands of years, they have been major influences on Chinese culture.

DID YOU KNOW?
In Daoist belief, *Yin* is thought of as earth, female, and dark. It is represented by the tiger, the colour orange, and a broken line. *Yang* is thought of as heaven, male, and light. It is represented by the dragon, the colour azure, and an unbroken line.

During the Chinese New Year celebration, Daoists in Kowloon pray and make offerings at the Wong Tai Sin temple.
© Dave G. Houser/Corbis

Answer: a) China.

A Very Japanese Religion

Nearly all the followers of the Shinto religion are natives of a single country: Japan. There is no clear indication when Shinto began. It is basically as ancient as the Japanese people themselves.

Shinto is a loose set of beliefs and attitudes held by most Japanese about themselves, their families, and their ancestors. Shinto has no central holy book. No single group or individual created the religion. But its beliefs were strongly influenced by several Eastern religions. These include Confucianism, Daoism, and Buddhism. In fact, most Shinto followers are also active Buddhists.

Shinto monk visits shrine on Mount Haguro in Japan.
© Chris Rainier/Corbis

Shintoists honour and worship powers called *kami*. These may be gods, forces of mercy, certain ancestors, or other powers considered to be **divine**. *Kami* can't be known or explained. But they are believed to be the source of human life. And they guide people to live in harmony with the truth.

Each family or community has a specific *kami* that acts as the group's guardian. Many *kami* are connected to objects and creatures of nature, as well as to particular areas and family groups. Believers' own ancestors are also deeply honoured and worshipped.

Unlike many religions, Shinto has no regularly scheduled services or meetings for worship. Worshippers may visit their *kami's* **shrines** (or others) anytime they want to - some go every day. Several festivals and ceremonies during the year bring believers together. Shintoists celebrate births and weddings in special ceremonies.

The major Shinto celebrations are the Spring Festival, the Autumn Festival (a kind of harvest festival), and the Annual Festival (New Year celebration) with a Divine Procession, or parade. Each grand festival has a specific order of **rituals** to be carried out.

SEARCH LIGHT

True or false? In Shintoism, forces of nature may be worshipped.

DID YOU KNOW?
In Shinto mythology, the sun goddess Amaterasu has long held a special place. She is the guardian *kami* of the Japanese royal house.

In Shinto tradition, Inari is the god of rice cultivation and merchants. The Fushimi Inari shrine near Kyoto, Japan, is one of the most famous of many Inari shrines.
© David Samuel Robbins/Corbis

Answer: **TRUE.**

Visit the continent at the crossroads of many cultures

Views of Europe

Views of Europe

TABLE OF CONTENTS

Britannica®

LEARNING LIBRARY

Have a great trip!

Unity in Diversity

Which of these rivers can be found in Europe?
a) Rhône
b) Mississippi
c) Nile

COUNTRIES OF EUROPE
1. Albania
2. Andorra
3. Austria
4. Belarus
5. Belgium
6. Bosnia and Herzegovina
7. Bulgaria
8. Croatia
9. Cyprus
10. Czech Republic
11. Denmark
12. England
13. Estonia
14. Finland
15. France
16. Germany
17. Greece
18. Hungary
19. Iceland
20. Ireland
21. Italy
22. Latvia
23. Liechtenstein
24. Lithuania
25. Luxembourg
26. Macedonia
27. Malta
28. Moldova
29. Monaco
30. Netherlands
31. Northern Ireland
32. Norway
33. Poland
34. Portugal
35. Romania
36. Russia (part)
37. San Marino
38. Scotland
39. Serbia and Montenegro
40. Slovakia
41. Slovenia
42. Spain
43. Sweden
44. Switzerland
45. Ukraine
46. Vatican City
47. Wales

Stonehenge, a mysterious ancient monument in southern England.
© Royalty-Free/Corbis

Europe is a continent of many countries and many different peoples. Much of it is made up of islands and peninsulas. A peninsula is a piece of land surrounded by water on three sides. Europe's islands include Iceland and the British Isles in the Atlantic Ocean and Corsica, Crete, Malta, and Cyprus in the Mediterranean Sea. Europe's main peninsulas are the Scandinavian, Iberian, Italian, Balkan, and Jutland peninsulas.

Europe also has many mountain ranges. Important ones are the Pyrenees, the Alps, the Apennines, the Carpathians, and the Balkans. Its long rivers include the Volga, the Danube, the Don, the Rhine, the Rhône, and the Oder. These rivers and the **canals** that connect many of them have carried people and products for many, many years.

The rivers also provide water for Europe's farms. Wheat and barley are two of Europe's major crops. Southern Europe specializes in fruits, vegetables, olives, and wines. Other crops include oats, maize, sugar-beets, and potatoes.

Europe is one of the world's major industrial regions. In fact, the **Industrial Revolution** began in Europe. Today the factories of Europe make many products, including electrical goods, motor vehicles, aircraft, and computers.

In the first half of the 20th century, Europe was the centre of two world wars. After World War II, many Eastern European countries had **communist** governments while many in Western Europe had **democratic** governments. By the early 21st century, most Western European countries had joined together to form the European Union (EU). Many EU countries share the same money - called the 'euro'. Most Eastern European countries want to join the EU too.

Leaning Tower of Pisa, a famous tilting building in Pisa, Italy.
© Royalty-Free/Corbis

DID YOU KNOW?
Did you know that the automobile was invented in Europe? A German man named Benz came up with the first true petrol-powered car. He named it after his daughter, Mercedes.

Answer: a) Rhône

Life on the Iberian Peninsula

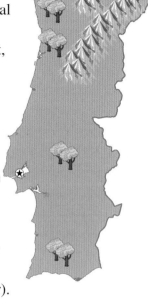

Lisbon

Portugal is a small country in south-western Europe. Its capital is Lisbon, and its only neighbour is Spain. Together, Spain and Portugal make up the Iberian **Peninsula**.

Northern Portugal is quite hilly, with many oak, beech, chestnut, and pine forests. Southern Portugal has mostly **plateaus** and plains. Brush and grasslands cover the plains of the south. Portuguese farmers grow wheat, maize, potatoes, and grapes. And although olives grow wild in Portugal, many farmers also plant their own olive trees. Portugal's many cork oak trees provide much of the world's supply of cork. Portugal is also famous for its many varieties of wine, including port and Madeira.

Summers in Portugal are dry and mild. Many tourists go to Portugal in the summer to see the beautiful museums, castles, and old churches. Others go to tour historic cities, such as Lisbon, Coimbra, and Porto. And many go to enjoy Portugal's many beaches.

The national sport of Portugal is *futebol* (football, or soccer). Portuguese bullfighting is also very popular. It is different from bullfighting in other countries, however. Portuguese bullfighters don't kill the bull in the ring. Folk music and folk dancing are popular traditions, and most villages have their own *terreiro*, or dance floor. One of the most popular regional dances is the *fandango*. The Portuguese are especially fond of *fado*, a traditional folk song that reflects a sad mood.

Portugal is also famous for its explorers. Ferdinand Magellan led the first expedition to sail around the world, and Vasco da Gama opened up a trade route around Africa to Asia.

SEARCH LIGHT

Portugal shares much of its culture with the people of Spain. Why do you think this is true?

DID YOU KNOW?

The capital of Portugal was once moved to another country on another continent. From 1807 to 1821, Rio de Janeiro in Brazil was Portugal's capital. Brazil was a Portuguese colony at the time.

Many people travel to Portugal to enjoy the country's beautiful sunny beaches.
© Nik Wheeler/Corbis

Answer: The only country to share a border with Portugal is Spain. So the Portuguese people have had much more contact with the Spanish than any other people.

A Distinctive European Country

Spain is a country in the south-western corner of Europe. The capital city is Madrid. Spain borders Portugal and France, but most of the country lies along the Mediterranean Sea and the Atlantic Ocean. The country's beautiful beaches are favourite European holiday spots.

Spain's history is rich and complex. It differs in many ways from other Western European countries. For instance, several Islamic states were formed on its territory, some lasting for centuries. Most other Islamic states lie farther to the east, in the Middle East, or to the south, in North Africa. Modern Spain's cultural variety shows in the different languages spoken there, including Catalan, Basque, Gallego, and, of course, Spanish.

In the 1500s and 1600s, Spain was a world power. It had a powerful navy called the Spanish Armada, and it was the first country to **colonize** much of the Americas. That's why so many people in South America, Central America, Mexico, and the United States speak Spanish and are of Hispanic **heritage**.

Spain features seafood in much of its cooking, with dishes such as paella, a fish-and-rice dish. Spanish farmers are major producers of pork, poultry, beef, and lamb. They also grow wheat, barley, maize, sugar-beets, beans, and olives. Spain also grows grapes for its large wine industry.

Bullfighting has long been a favourite pastime of Spaniards. And football (soccer) is also very popular. Another activity found in Spain is the music and dancing known as *flamenco*. *Flamenco* came to Spain with the Caló (Gitano) people, more commonly known as Gypsies. It is played on guitar as the dancers click wooden castanets and stamp their feet rhythmically.

SEARCH LIGHT

Why is the Spanish language spoken in so many countries?

DID YOU KNOW?
With all the rock stars that have come from the United States and England, you might think that the guitar was invented there. The modern electric guitar was invented in the States, but the guitar itself probably originated in Spain in the early 1500s.

This village in Spain overlooks one of the country's many vineyards.
© Patrick Ward/Corbis

Answer: Spain conquered many other areas of the world during its Golden Age in the 1500s and 1600s. Those areas eventually adopted many Spanish customs, as well as the language.

Heart of a Language and Culture

English is one of the world's most widely spoken languages. This is partly because it was the language of the British Empire. The empire once controlled so much of the world that it was said that the Sun never set on the British Empire.

England, the birthplace of English, takes up most of the island of Great Britain. It is one of the four lands that form the United Kingdom. The English that people speak there today is quite different from the English that was spoken long ago. If you were to read a book by Geoffrey Chaucer, one of the early writers of English, someone would have to explain to you what many of the words mean.

England has produced many famous writers since Chaucer. They include such poets as John Milton and Percy Bysshe Shelley, and such novelists as Jane Austen and Charles Dickens. England is also known for its theatre. That art has remained important since the time of the playwright William Shakespeare more than 400 years ago.

England's Oxford and Cambridge are two of the oldest universities in the world. The country's contributions to classical and folk music, as well as to rock-and-roll, are also important. It's hard to imagine what rock would be like without English performers such as the Beatles, the Rolling Stones, and David Bowie.

The English people also invented two of the world's most popular sports: football (known as 'soccer' in the United States) and cricket.

London

DID YOU KNOW?
The English language has changed a lot over the years. The following are two versions of the same sentence from the story *Beowulf*.
Old English:
Wæs se grimma gæst Grendel haten.
Modern English:
Grendel was the name of this grim demon.

The English countryside contains many small villages such as this one in the south-central Cotswold district.
© Nik Wheeler/Corbis

SEARCH LIGHT

Find and correct the mistake in the following sentence: William Shakespeare was a famous English novelist.

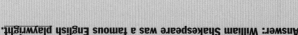

Answer: William Shakespeare was a famous English playwright.

City on the Thames

London is the capital of the United Kingdom. It lies in south-eastern England on the banks of the River Thames. Long ago, the Romans built a city near the mouth of the river. They called it Londinium. That's how London got its name.

Guards parade in front of Buckingham Palace.
© Graham Tim—Corbis/Sygma

Tourists and Londoners alike use London's public transportation system. The red double-decker buses are recognized worldwide. And the city's underground railway - called the 'tube' - has been reliably shuttling passengers throughout London since 1884. The city is full of **monuments,** historic buildings, and other interesting sights. The Tower of London is one of the city's oldest structures. It was built by William the Conqueror as a fortress. It also served as a prison, and its famous prisoners included Sir Walter Raleigh and Elizabeth I, before she became queen. The tower is now a museum that contains England's crown jewels.

SEARCH LIGHT

Find and correct the mistake in the following sentence: Britain's kings and queens are crowned in Buckingham Palace.

Other famous buildings include the Houses of **Parliament** (also called Westminster Palace). This building has 1,100 rooms and over three kilometres of **corridors**. It also has a tower clock called Big Ben, whose huge bell weighs more than 13 tonnes. Nearby is Westminster Abbey, an ancient church where British kings and queens are crowned. Buckingham Palace is the home of the queen of England.

London's British Museum is the oldest museum in the United Kingdom. It has a vast collection of objects from all round the world. It also has one of the world's largest libraries. Another well-known museum is Madame Tussaud's, which has wax statues of famous people.

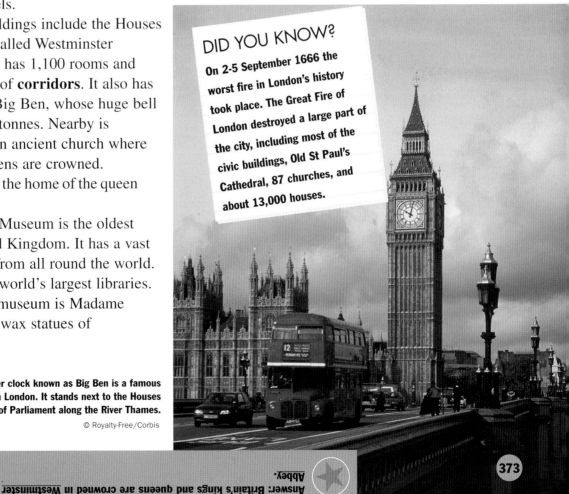

DID YOU KNOW?
On 2-5 September 1666 the worst fire in London's history took place. The Great Fire of London destroyed a large part of the city, including most of the civic buildings, Old St Paul's Cathedral, 87 churches, and about 13,000 houses.

The tower clock known as Big Ben is a famous sight in London. It stands next to the Houses of Parliament along the River Thames.
© Royalty-Free/Corbis

Answer: Britain's kings and queens are crowned in Westminster Abbey.

Land of Mountains and Heath

Scotland is a nation famous for its natural beauty. It lies on the northernmost part of the larger of the two main British Isles. Pinewood forests dot the area known as the Highlands. Dwarf willows grow on the highest slopes of the Grampian Mountains just below the snow-covered peaks. But perhaps the most famous of Scotland's plant life is the heather, a kind of **heath**. The word heath is also used to describe the wild wide-open stretches of rough land of Scotland's countryside.

Scotland has been part of the United Kingdom since the 18th century. Its capital is Edinburgh. Scotland's largest city is Glasgow, an industrial centre.

The country has made many cultural contributions to the world. Writer Robert Louis Stevenson wrote the well-loved *Treasure Island* as well as the horror story *Dr. Jekyll and Mr. Hyde*. And poet Robert Burns is claimed by Scots as their national poet.

Many visitors to Scotland go there to see its castles and **abbeys**. Tourists to Scotland enjoy the country's wildlife. Deer, foxes, badgers, and wildcats can be seen in the countryside. Golden eagles, peregrine falcons, and kestrels fly overhead. Almost half the world's gray seals breed off the coast in Scottish waters. And sometimes whales can be seen too.

Many tourists also visit the country's largest lake, Loch Ness. Though its famous Loch Ness monster is probably just a legend, many sightings of the monster have been reported. And the possibility that it may exist continues to fascinate many people.

SEARCH LIGHT

Fill in the gaps: Although many people visit Scotland to see its castles and _____, the country is best known for its natural _____.

DID YOU KNOW?
Haggis, a national dish of Scotland, isn't for everyone. It's a large round sausage made of the liver, heart, and lungs of a sheep, all chopped and mixed with fat and oatmeal and packed into a sheep's stomach and boiled.

A Scottish farmer stands in a pasture with one of his Highland cattle. His knee-length pleated skirt, called a 'kilt', is part of the traditional clothing of men from Scotland.
© Dewitt Jones/Corbis

Answer: Although many people visit Scotland to see its castles and abbeys, the country is best known for its natural beauty.

The Emerald Isle

Belfast

Dublin

Ireland is a land with no snakes. Legend has it that St Patrick **banished** them all. But the real reason is that Ireland is an island and snakes have not lived there at least since the last Ice Age, thousands of years ago.

Ireland is the smaller of the two British Isles of north-western Europe. The smaller northern part of Ireland is called Northern Ireland and is part of the United Kingdom of Great Britain and Northern Ireland. Northern Ireland's capital is Belfast. The larger part of Ireland is called the Republic of Ireland, but it is usually simply called Ireland or Eire. Its capital is the city of Dublin.

Because of its location in the Atlantic Ocean, Ireland has a mild **climate** most of the year. It rains quite often, with the hilly parts of the island getting nearly 254 centimetres of rain each year. Much of the land is covered with grass and green moss. Some people describe Ireland as the Emerald Isle because it is so beautifully green. The green lowlands and mild climate make Ireland a good place to rear cattle and sheep. Barley, wheat, and potatoes also grow well. In fact, potatoes were once almost the only food people ate. But in the 1840s, disease ruined the potato crop and many people starved or left Ireland for other countries, especially the United States.

Ireland was once a colony of Great Britain. It gained its independence in the 20th century, although Northern Ireland remains part of the United Kingdom. Ireland is very popular with tourists, and Irish music and culture are famous throughout the world.

DID YOU KNOW?
The best-known characters in Irish folklore are fairies called 'leprechauns'. According to legend, they are little old men who live alone and make shoes. They also are supposed to have a hidden pot of gold, which they guard carefully.

SEARCH LIGHT

How did Ireland get its nickname of the Emerald Isle?

Cattle graze in a field in County Kerry, Ireland.
© Galen Rowell/Corbis

Answer: Ireland is such a green and beautiful island that people have for a long time called it the Emerald Isle.

Land of the Song

SEARCH LIGHT

In the Welsh language, the name for the country of Wales is
a) 'Eisteddfod'.
b) 'Caerdydd'.
c) 'Cymru'.

Wales's capital city, Cardiff, had its beginnings in Cardiff Castle. This stone keep, the strongest part of the castle, was built in the 12th century.
© Neil Beer/Corbis

Wales is a beautiful land of hills, valleys, and ancient castles. Located on the western edge of the island of Great Britain, it's one of the four countries that today make up the United Kingdom. Wales is called 'Cymru' (pronounced 'Coomrie') in the Welsh language, and its capital, Cardiff, is called 'Caerdydd'. Many people still speak Welsh, but Wales's main language is English.

The rough Welsh countryside was created long ago by rivers of ice called 'glaciers'. Wales's many mountains - including the highest one, Snowdon - were formed mostly from volcanic rock. Along the coast are fabulous cliffs overlooking pebbled and sandy beaches. Seabirds and shorebirds are commonly seen, and bottlenose dolphins live in Cardigan Bay off the west coast.

Coal mining was once the most important part of the Welsh economy. Today, very little coal is still mined in Wales. Many more people now work in manufacturing, especially in the car, chemical, and electronics industries.

Many tourists visit Wales to see its parks and castles and to attend its many music festivals. The largest is the annual Eisteddfod, a celebration of poetry and music that began in 1176. Music is so important in Wales that it is called the 'land of the song'. Choral (group) singing is especially popular amongst the Welsh people.

Nearly 2,000 years ago the ancient Romans built a small fort where the Welsh capital, Cardiff, now stands. Hundreds of years later, invaders from England built a castle on that same site. Cardiff eventually grew there and became an important shipping centre. Cardiff Castle remains one of the city's most impressive buildings.

Cardiff

Answer: c) 'Cymru'.

Country of
Castles, Wine, and History

For hundreds of years France was one of the most prized countries of Western Europe. One reason is that France has wonderful farmland. Many types of crops and plants are grown in France because of the plentiful water from France's rivers. And the French have made good use of their generous harvests - fine French cooking has long been internationally appreciated.

But France may be even better known for its wines. There are miles of lovely green vineyards - areas for growing grapes. The **champagnes** and wines made from these grapes are famous throughout the world.

The French river valleys are full of historic and beautiful old castles, called *chateaux*. These were built of stone, with thick walls that protected the people inside from attacks. At first the *chateaux* were used as forts, but later they were used as homes for the **nobility**. The king and the nobility ruled France until they were overthrown in the French Revolution of 1789. Ten years later the famous leader Napoleon began his rule of France.

Many tourists visit France to see its famous monuments and cathedrals and its beautiful countryside. Some popular spots, such as the palace of Versailles, are located outside the capital city of Paris. Others, such as the Eiffel Tower and the Cathedral of Notre Dame, are inside Paris. Other big French cities include Marseille, Lyon, and Nice.

France is separated from England by a narrow body of water called the English Channel. Today high-speed trains travel between the two countries through the Channel Tunnel, which was built underneath the Channel.

SEARCH LIGHT

Find and correct the mistake in the following sentence: Today high-speed trains travel through the tunnel underneath the English Channel that connects France with Belgium.

Vineyards, where grapes are grown for wine, surround a village in eastern France. French wine is prized all over the world. This village is part of the region that produces wine called Burgundy.
© Michael Busselle/Corbis

DID YOU KNOW?
French writers have won more Nobel Prizes for Literature than writers from any other country.

Answer: Today high-speed trains travel through the tunnel underneath the English Channel that connects France with England.

Belgium's Beautiful Capital

On the banks of Senne River lies Brussels, the capital of Belgium. There is much to see in this historic city known for its lace and chocolate. A more recent feature also sets Belgium apart: together with Strasbourg, France, it's the centre of the European **Parliament**.

★ **Brussels**

One of Brussels' most beautiful old buildings is the Town Hall. It has a tower with the statue of St Michael, the **patron saint** of Brussels. Opposite the Town Hall across the square known as the Grand Place is the King's House. It's now a history museum. On a hill, rising above the modern buildings, is the Church of St Michael and St Gudule. It was built more than 500 years ago.

One of the most popular sights in Brussels is a small bronze fountain in the shape of a naked little boy. He is often called the city's 'oldest citizen' because he has been around since 1619. Other places to visit include the Royal Palace, the Palace of Justice, and the Opera House. There's also the Palace of the Nation, which is the Belgian parliament house.

An unusual and interesting structure in Brussels is the Atomium. It shows how the atoms of a molecule of iron fit together. It is almost 100 metres high and is made of shining metal. It was built for the International Exhibition of Brussels, a fair held in 1958.

Chocolate is not the only kind of food that comes from Brussels. According to some experts, the vegetable called Brussels sprout was first there 800 years ago.

SEARCH LIGHT

The river that flows past Brussels is called the
a) Seine.
b) Senne.
c) Severn.

DID YOU KNOW?
Like many people worldwide, Belgians enjoy fried potatoes (French fries, or chips). But they prefer to eat them with mayonnaise rather than ketchup or some other sauce.

Flowers are sold in Grand Place, a beautiful public square in the city of Brussels. The square began as a marketplace during the Middle Ages.
© Bettmann/Corbis

Answer: b) Senne.

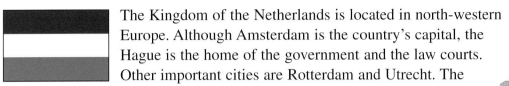

Country of Windmills and Dykes

The Kingdom of the Netherlands is located in north-western Europe. Although Amsterdam is the country's capital, the Hague is the home of the government and the law courts. Other important cities are Rotterdam and Utrecht. The Netherlands is also known as Holland, and its people are called the Dutch.

Much of the Netherlands is made up of 'reclaimed land'. This means that lakes, marshes, and low-lying land located at or below **sea level** have been drained and made into usable dry land. Such areas are called 'polders'. The polders are surrounded by dams called 'dykes'. Without the dykes, much of the Netherlands would be flooded. People once used windmills to help drain water from flooded lands. Many windmills still dot the landscape. But today electric or **diesel** pumps are used to pump the water out.

Several rivers flow through the centre of the Netherlands. They used to be filled with lobsters and fish, but water pollution has killed many of these animals. Many seabirds and other sea creatures such as **molluscs** can be found in coastal areas.

For a long time, the Netherlands has been known for producing flowers, especially tulips. The butter, cheese, and condensed milk from the country's dairy farms are also famous the world over. Hundreds of years ago, Dutch seamen were the leading merchants of Europe. Today, **commercial** ships still keep the harbours and ports of the Netherlands very busy.

Art has a long tradition in the Netherlands. The most famous Dutch painters are Rembrandt and Vincent van Gogh.

DID YOU KNOW?
Tulips are grown all over the Netherlands, and the country is famous for them.

SEARCH LIGHT

A polder is a
a) windmill.
b) land area that was once under water.
c) machine used to pump water out.

The many windmills in the Netherlands were once used to drain water from the land.

© Larry Lee Photography/Corbis

Answer: b) land area that was once under water.

A Country Reunited

Although Germany, in the heart of central Europe, has a long history, it is actually a young country. For many years various princes, dukes, and bishops ruled small states in the region. It was not until 1871 that these became united as a single nation.

Germany has produced many renowned musicians, writers, artists, scientists, and athletes. Such figures include writer Johann Wolfgang von Goethe and composer Ludwig van Beethoven.

In the early 20th century, Germany became involved in two world wars. The country was on the losing side of World War I and as a result suffered through difficult times. Many of the people were unhappy, and some supported Adolf Hitler, who wanted to make Germany strong again. As the leader of the Nazi Party he soon took control of the country. Germany then tried to conquer several neighbouring countries. The conflict over these actions developed into World War II.

After Germany was defeated in 1945, the country was divided into East and West Germany. East Germany became a **communist** country and West Germany became a **democracy**. Berlin, the former capital of Germany, was itself divided in 1961 by the Berlin Wall, built by the East German government. Many families were split up and could no longer visit each other.

In 1989 the Berlin Wall fell and the communist government of East Germany came to an end. On 3 October 1990, Germany became one country again. Berlin became its new, undivided capital.

SEARCH LIGHT

When did Germany become a unified country? (Hint: there is more than one answer!)
a) 1871
b) 1550
c) 1776
d) 1990

Houses line a river at Schiltach, a village in the Black Forest region of Germany. The region is named for its thick groves of trees.
© Richard Klune/Corbis

DID YOU KNOW?
For German children, the highlight of the Christmas season is St Nicholas Day (6 December). The night before, they leave a shoe outside their bedroom door or by the fireplace. St Nicholas comes during the night to fill the shoes with sweets and gifts.

Answer: Germany first became unified in 1871 and again in 1990.

Snow and Chocolates

Switzerland's great beauty draws visitors from all over the world to see its snow-capped mountain ranges, blue lakes, green pastures, and the tall trees covering the mountainsides. Switzerland is a country in central Europe. Bern is its capital city, and its people are the Swiss. Its neighbouring countries are Germany, Austria, Liechtenstein, Italy, and France. Because of its close contact with these countries, Switzerland's official languages include German, Italian, and French.

The mountains known as the Alps cover more than half of Switzerland. The Jura Mountains occupy more than a tenth of the country. The Mittelland **plateau** is a flatland that lies between the two mountain ranges. Because it has so many mountains, Switzerland has bridges and tunnels that help people travel within the country. The tunnels that run through the Alps are amongst the world's longest.

High up in the Alps you'll find snow and ice all year long. With so much snow, Switzerland has become known for its winter sports. People travel from all over the world to ski, skate, and sledge in the **resort** towns of St Moritz, Gstaad, and Interlaken. The mountain resorts are also popular in summer for activities such as boating, swimming, hiking, and mountain climbing.

The highest grape-growing area of central Europe is located in the Swiss Alps, at an **altitude** of 1,190 metres. Some people know Switzerland better for its watches and cheese, both of which are world famous. But what is most important to many other people are the delicious chocolates the Swiss make!

Bern

SEARCH LIGHT

Why would a country like Switzerland be popular for winter sports? (Hint: Think of the land.)

DID YOU KNOW?
When the new 56-kilometre-long Gotthard Tunnel opens in 2011, it will be the longest railway tunnel in existence. One of the longest road tunnels also happens to be in Switzerland and is also called Gotthard - the 16-kilometre-long St Gotthard Tunnel.

The Matterhorn, a mountain peak in the Alps, rises above a valley in Switzerland.
© Royalty-Free/Corbis

Answer: Some mountains in Switzerland have snow on them year-round, and many lakes freeze. This makes it ideal for sports such as skiing, skating, and sledging.

City of Music

Vienna, the capital of Austria, is famous for its music and its splendid buildings, especially the museums and palaces. What you might find surprising is that Vienna today looks very much like it did hundreds of years ago.

Visitors can take a trip through the city streets in a horse-drawn carriage called a 'fiacre'. No well-dressed fiacre driver would be seen without a colourful shirt and an old-fashioned black hat, according to tradition.

One of Vienna's most impressive sights is the spire of St Stephen's **Cathedral**, which looms over the city. The cathedral bell weighs 20 tonnes. The metal used to make it was melted down from cannons that were captured from the Turkish army in 1711.

Another important building is the State Opera, where many great composers have heard their works performed. That is where the opera composers Richard Wagner and Giuseppe Verdi conducted and where Gustav Mahler was a director. The State Opera opened in 1869 with a performance of Wolfgang Amadeus Mozart's *Don Giovanni*.

Museums have been made from the houses in which the famous **composers** Joseph Haydn, Mozart, Ludwig van Beethoven, Franz Schubert, and Johann Strauss lived and worked. Before they became famous, Haydn and Schubert were members of the Vienna Boys' Choir. The choir was started in 1498 and still performs in the Hofburg Chapel on Sunday mornings. So now you know why Vienna is called one of the music capitals of the world.

DID YOU KNOW?
The Viennese coffeehouse has been a tradition for three centuries. At one time, artists and celebrities gathered at famous literary and theatrical cafés. The word 'café', in fact, comes from a Turkish word meaning 'coffee'.

SEARCH LIGHT

Fill in the gap: Because of the many famous composers who have lived there, Vienna is known as one of the _____ capitals of the world.

One of the many historic buildings in Vienna is the Schonbrunn Palace. The palace was once the home of many Austrian rulers but is now a museum.
© Adam Woolfitt/Corbis

Answer: Because of the many famous composers who have lived there, Vienna is known as one of the music capitals of the world.

★ Prague

New Beginnings
in a Historic Land

On 1 January 1993, the nation of Czechoslovakia did a remarkable thing - the former **communist** country split peacefully into two free and independent countries. The eastern section became Slovakia. The western provinces, Bohemia and Moravia, became the Czech Republic. The Czech Republic is the larger of the two new countries. Its capital is Prague.

The Czech Republic has many hills and mountains. These include the Sumava, Ore, Sudeten, and Krkonose mountains. The country is noted for its karst region - a limestone area with many sinkholes, caverns, and underground passages and lakes. Many people visit the Czech Republic especially to participate in winter sports. Others go there for fishing and hunting and to enjoy the beauty of the mountains. Among the country's wildlife, the mouflon, an endangered mountain sheep, is reared in game reserves.

Farming is very important in the Czech Republic. The most important crops are sugar beets, wheat, barley, potatoes, and maize. Northern Bohemia is known for a plant called the 'hop', used in flavouring drinks. The Czech Republic also has many factories that manufacture iron, steel, aluminium, fertilizers, and cement. Cotton, wool, and **synthetic** fibres are also produced and made into clothing.

The Czechs are known for traditional crafts. They make beautiful glass and **porcelain** objects and are especially known for their fine **crystal.** Some people make pretty lace, and others make delightful wood carvings. And among the many Czechs who have contributed to the arts are the novelist Franz Kafka, **composer** Antonin Dvorak, and poster artist Alphonse Mucha. Playwright Vaclav Havel became the first president of the independent Czech Republic.

The village of Telc is in southern Moravia, one of the two provinces that make up the Czech Republic.
© Dave Ball/Corbis

SEARCH LIGHT

Is the Czech Republic larger or smaller than Czechoslovakia?

DID YOU KNOW?
The Czech Republic has been greatly affected by acid rain. Because of this pollution, many trees have been cut down. By the end of the 20th century, nearly three-fifths of the republic's forests had been destroyed or seriously damaged.

Answer: The Czech Republic is smaller than Czechoslovakia.

Country in the Heart of Europe

If people had asked 'Where is Poland?' at different times during the past 1,000 years, they would have been given many different answers.

In the mid-1500s, for example, Poland was the largest country in Europe. But at other times, there was no Polish state at all! In the late 1700s, Poland was no longer a separate country after it had been divided up by the countries of Russia, Prussia, and Austria. The boundaries of modern Poland were marked out in 1945. Its constitution (laws of government) of 1791 is the oldest in Europe.

About two-thirds of Poland's more than 38 million people live in cities. Warsaw, the capital, is the largest city. Other important cities include Lodz, Gdansk, and Krakow. About 90 per cent of Poles are Roman Catholics. They are especially proud because in 1978 Karol Jozef Wojtyla became Pope John Paul II, the first Polish leader of the Catholic church.

Polish ham is one of the country's most famous exports. In addition to rearing pigs, farmers also rear cattle and sheep throughout the country. Nearly half of Poland's land is used for farming.

Poland has had a changeable history, with shifting boundaries, but it's always enjoyed a rich cultural heritage. In literature Polish poet Czeslaw Milosz won the 1980 Nobel Prize for Literature, and poet Wislawa Szymborska won it in 1996. Frédéric Chopin, a famous composer, was from Poland. And one of the most famous scientists in history, Mikolaj Kopernik, was born in Poland. You may know this great astronomer as Nicolaus Copernicus.

DID YOU KNOW?
During World War II, the Nazis avoided Rozwadow, Poland, because they believed many people there had typhus, a deadly disease. But doctors there had simply injected people with harmless bacteria that looked like typhus in blood tests. This saved many lives.

The port of Gdansk is one of the largest cities in Poland.
© Bernard and Catherine Desjeux/Corbis

Answer: Poland has been divided and ruled by different countries at various times in its history. The two countries that most recently controlled Poland were Russia and Germany.

Bay of Smokes

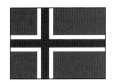

Reykjavik is the capital and largest town of Iceland, a small island country in the North Atlantic Ocean. The word Reykjavik means 'bay of smokes'. The city's name comes from the steaming hot springs nearby. The town is heated by the hot water carried by pipes from these springs. The water is heated by the many volcanoes underneath Iceland.

Reykjavik

Even though the city is very far north, it has a fairly mild climate. However, winters are long and very dark. Much of Iceland's area outside the city is covered by **glaciers**.

According to legend, a Viking named Ingolfur Arnarson founded the city about 1,200 years ago. For many years, Reykjavik remained a small fishing village. It was occupied and ruled by the Danes, the people of Denmark. Today Reykjavik is a major fishing port. It is also Iceland's main centre for business. Not surprising for a fishing city, Reykjavik's chief industries are processing fish and building ships.

Iceland has one of the highest **literacy** rates in the world. Almost all the people can read. Iceland has a rich literary tradition, and Icelandic **sagas** date from the 13th century. Folklore is also popular, especially stories about trolls.

The city has many museums and art galleries. The country's traditional cuisine includes many seafood dishes and *skyr*, a dessert made from skimmed milk and served with fresh bilberries.

SEARCH LIGHT

Who were the first people in Iceland?

This power plant produces heat for the city of Reykjavik by using steam from hot springs.
© Roger Ressmeyer/Corbis

DID YOU KNOW?
Apparently it's not uncommon for workers in Iceland to hire a medium to help them if something goes wrong during a construction project. A medium is someone who claims to be able to talk to supernatural creatures.

Answer: The Vikings were the first people in Iceland.

City of the Little Mermaid

Copenhagen is Denmark's capital and largest city. It is located on two islands: Zealand and Amager. Denmark is an unusual country because it's made up of a peninsula (Jutland) and over 400 islands. What used to be Copenhagen's city centre is located on a little island called Slotsholmen (meaning 'castle **islet**').

In 1167, Bishop Absalon of Roskilde had a fortress built on Slotsholmen. This was the beginning of the city. The Christiansborg Palace replaced the fortress, and now it houses the Danish **parliament** and the Supreme Court. Today the Danish royal family live in the Amalienborg Palace.

To the west of Slotsholmen is the Town Hall. It has a very interesting feature. Apart from the usual offices, it also has Jens Olsen's **astronomical** clock. This huge clock shows the time in different parts of the world. It also shows the **orbits** of the planets and two different calendars.

Nearby is Charlottenborg Palace, the home of the Royal Academy of Fine Arts. The palace was built in the 17th century. Close to it is Tivoli, a world-famous amusement park that opened in 1843.

Copenhagen

SEARCH LIGHT

Fill in the gap: The city of Copenhagen lies on two _____.

If you go farther north, you'll see the Citadel, a military **fortress** still used by the Danish army even though it was built nearly 400 years ago. In the harbour outside the fortress is the statue of the Little Mermaid. It is said to be the symbol of the city. The story of the Little Mermaid is a fairy tale written by Hans Christian Andersen, who spent many years of his life in Copenhagen.

DID YOU KNOW?
In World War II, when the Germans occupied Copenhagen, the Danish king rode daily through the city on his horse to give his people courage. When asked why the king had no bodyguard, a boy supposedly said: 'All of Denmark is his bodyguard.'

City natives and visitors alike enjoy the Tivoli Gardens in Copenhagen. Besides its pretty flowers and fountains, Tivoli has restaurants, open-air theatres, and an amusement park with rides and games.
© Steve Raymer/Corbis

Answer: The city of Copenhagen lies on two islands.

Land of Fjords and Mountains

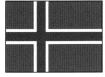

Norway is a country in northern Europe. It lies on the western half of a **peninsula** it shares with Sweden. Together with Denmark, these countries are known as Scandinavia. The many arms of the sea that stretch into Norway are called 'fjords'. The longest and deepest of these is Sogne Fjord. Almost every part of the country is close to the sea or a fjord.

Norway is also covered with mountains. The two highest peaks are Galdhopiggen and Glittertind. Each of them is more than 2,460 metres tall. **Glaciers** can be found in some of the mountain ranges. The Jostedals Glacier is the largest in Europe.

Norway is a leading producer of **oil**, which comes from the North Sea. Many people work in **forestry**, harvesting trees for **timber**. Most of Norway's forests contain evergreen trees, such as pine and spruce. In the south, however, the forests contain ash, birch, and aspen trees. Elk, wild reindeer, lemmings, and wolverines live in the mountains and forests.

Fishing is a major **industry** in coastal areas. Other countries buy fish from Norway, especially frozen cod, canned sardines, and herrings. And whales can be seen too, off the Norwegian coast. Norway's long seafaring tradition includes many famous explorers, such as the Viking explorer Leif Eriksson and the adventurer-scientist Thor Heyerdahl.

Some of Norway's native Sami people (also called Lapps) still practise traditional reindeer herding. Most of the people of Norway speak either Bokmal or Nynorsk, though many also speak English. Painter Edvard Munch, playwright Henrik Ibsen, and composer Edvard Grieg are famous Norwegians who have made important contributions to the arts.

Oslo

SEARCH LIGHT

Fill in the gaps: Two major Norwegian languages are _____ and _____ .

DID YOU KNOW?
A vast ocean current carries warm water to Norway's coast. This usually keeps the fjords from freezing, even in areas that are north of the Arctic Circle.

Many long narrow arms of the sea called 'fjords' stretch into the western part of Norway. Here a woman looks down on Geiranger Fjord.
© Bo Zaunders/Corbis

Answer: Two major Norwegian languages are Bokmal and Nynorsk.

Scandinavia's Largest Country

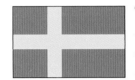

The Kingdom of Sweden in northern Europe is the largest of the Scandinavian countries. **Scandinavia** is the area occupied by Sweden, Norway, and Denmark. Norway and Finland are on Sweden's borders. The rest of the country is bounded by water.

The capital of Sweden is Stockholm, nicknamed the 'Venice of the north'. Like that Italian city, Stockholm has many waterways and bridges. Sweden has many rivers and lakes. And rivers provide half of the country's electric power. The rivers and lakes also contain many varieties of fish.

Sweden is a cold country. But the temperature in each part of the country depends on the **elevation** of the land and how close it is to the sea. The weather is warmer near the sea and colder on the mountains. Evergreen forests of spruce and pine cover more than half of Sweden. In the south there are also deciduous trees (trees that lose their leaves). Because of its rich forests, Sweden is known for its timber, wood **pulp**, paper, and furniture industries.

Stockholm

SEARCH LIGHT

As well as fish, what do Swedes get from their rivers that helps them in their everyday lives?

Within its forests Sweden has many different kinds of animals and birds. There are hares, weasels, shrews, foxes, ermine, and elk. Snipes, plovers, wagtails, partridges, ptarmigans, grouse, and woodcocks are just some of Sweden's many birds.

The Swedes celebrate many special festivals. On December 13 they celebrate St Lucia's Day. On that day young girls wear green wreaths with lighted candles on their heads and serve coffee and buns to older family members. Midsummer's Eve is celebrated with singing and dancing on about June 24, around the time of the longest day of the year.

DID YOU KNOW?
Although Sweden can be cold, you may still want to consider moving there when you get older. By law, all Swedish citizens get at least five weeks of paid holiday a year.

Much of Stockholm, the capital of Sweden, is built on islands. The islands are connected to each other and to city districts on the mainland by old bridges and modern overpasses.
© Macduff Everton/Corbis

Answer: Half of Sweden's electricity comes from its rivers. As the rivers flow through large dams, the water turns motors known as 'turbines'. The turbines make electricity.

The Largest Country in the World

Russia is the largest country in the world - nearly twice the size of China or the United States. In fact, Russia is so large it stretches across two **continents** - Europe and Asia.

Until 1917, Russian **tsars**, such as Peter the Great and Catherine the Great, had long ruled the country. The communist nation known as the Soviet Union was founded in 1922, and Russia was its largest and most important republic. The Soviet Union dissolved in 1991, however, and Russia became an independent country again.

Most of Russia is covered by large rolling plains. Across the plains flow Russia's rivers, including the Volga, the longest river in Europe. 'Mother Volga' flows into the Caspian Sea, the world's largest **inland** body of water. Many of the other rivers drain into the Arctic Ocean or into Lake Baikal, the world's deepest lake. More than one-fifth of all the world's fresh water is in Lake Baikal. That's more water than there is in all five of the Great Lakes in North America put together.

Roughly 145 million people live in Russia. About three-fourths of them live in cities. Moscow, the capital, is the largest city. It has more than 8 million citizens. St Petersburg is the second largest city, with more than 4 million people. Both cities have many world-famous museums and buildings.

Russians have contributed greatly to the arts. The works of writers Aleksandr Pushkin, Leo Tolstoy, and Anton Chekhov are still popular today. So is the music of composer Pyotr Ilich Tchaikovsky. And Russian ballet companies have trained some of the world's most gifted dancers, including Anna Pavlova and Mikhail Baryshnikov.

SEARCH LIGHT

Which country has a greater land area than Russia?
a) United States
b) China
c) Romania

DID YOU KNOW?
It would take the water from all the rivers in the world a whole year to fill Russia's Lake Baikal just once.

St Basil's Cathedral is a colourful landmark in Moscow, the capital of Russia.
© Jose Fuste Raga/Corbis

Answer: No other country is larger than Russia.

'Little Paris'

Bucharest, the capital of Romania, has many public squares. A square is an open area that's formed where two or more streets meet. Many of the city's streets and **boulevards** lead into squares. The famous Revolution Square contains the former royal palace and Cretulescu Church, which was built in 1725. It is one of the most beautiful squares in the city. With its tree-lined boulevards and varied **architecture**, Bucharest was once known as 'Little Paris'.

★ Bucharest

You can experience some of the city's long history in many of its old buildings. The Antim Monastery and the churches of Stavropoleos and Saint Spiridon are treasured for their age and for their fine architecture. The University of Bucharest was founded in 1694.

Bucharest also has preserved much of its history in its many museums. Two of the most popular are the Museum of the History of the City of Bucharest and the National Art Museum, which is now in the royal palace. Some tourists prefer the Village Museum. It is an open-air building near the Arch of Triumph that displays many kinds of peasant houses.

There is much to do in the city, even after the museums close.

Bucharest has a national **philharmonic** orchestra, as well as the 'I.L. Caragiale', the National Theatre, which is named after a famous Romanian playwright. There are also a Theatre of Opera and a Ballet of Romania. A typical Romanian meal enjoyed before or after going to the theatre might include a type of cornmeal bread called *mamaliga* with cheese and sour cream.

DID YOU KNOW?

In his novel *Dracula*, Bram Stoker based the character of the famous vampire on a Romanian prince, Vlad Tepes. The Romanian word *tepes* means 'stake'. In English the prince is known as Vlad the Impaler.

Bucharest is the capital and largest city of Romania. It is the centre of business, government, and the arts for the country.
© Sandro Vannini/Corbis

Bulgarian Capital
of Today and Yesterday

Sofia is the capital of the Eastern European country of Bulgaria. It is also the largest city in the country. It lies in a valley in the western part of Bulgaria.

Sofia has had many different names. When the Romans conquered it long, long ago, they called it Serdica. This name came from the Serdi, a tribe of people who had settled there. When it became part of Bulgaria, it was called Sredets. That name means 'in the middle', and it refers to the position of the city in the centre of the Balkan Peninsula. The Turks conquered Bulgaria in the late 1300s. And about that time the city was given the name Sofia, after its St Sofia church. In the Greek language, *sofia* means 'wisdom'.

Like many old cities, Sofia has an old section and a new one. The old section has narrow streets and small houses that are built close to each other. There are many **mosques** in this part of the city. They were built when Bulgaria was ruled by the Turks.

The modern part of the city has large apartment buildings and wide avenues. Most people in Sofia live in these buildings. There are similar apartments and broad roads in the suburbs too.

If you like history, you'd like to visit the churches of St George, Boyana, and St Sofia. You can also see the Alexander Nevsky Cathedral in Sofia. It was built to honour the Russians who helped Bulgaria to become an independent country in the 1870s.

SEARCH LIGHT

Choose the answer that puts the city's different names in order from earliest to most recent.
a) Sredets, Sofia, and Serdica
b) Serdica, Sofia, and Sredets
c) Serdica, Sredets, and Sofia

DID YOU KNOW?
In Bulgaria, Christmas is celebrated on two days, December 25 and 26. Under communism, religious holidays weren't allowed. So people invented a supposedly 'non-religious' holiday, and they celebrated it the day after Christmas.

Sofia is a busy but beautiful city. Its buildings display a mixture of many different styles of architecture.
© Sandro Vannini/Corbis

Answer: c) Serdica, Sredets, and Sofia

A Country of Many Cultures

Belgrade

The country of Serbia and Montenegro was called Yugoslavia until 2003. It lies on the Balkan **Peninsula** in south-eastern Europe. The country is made up of two republics. One is Serbia, of which the capital is Belgrade. The other is Montenegro, of which the capital is Podgorica. Until the 1990s Yugoslavia included several other regions that are now independent countries. These were Croatia, Slovenia, Macedonia, and Bosnia and Herzegovina.

Before the 20th century, the country was ruled by many different powers. This made it a country with many **diverse** cultures. The Slavs, the Turks, the Italians, and the Austrians have all influenced the food, folk costumes, and buildings of the country. This large mix of people has sometimes caused problems. In the 1990s there was a war between the Serbs, the Croats, and the Bosnians, and there were many wars earlier in the 20th century. By the beginning of the 21st century, much of the fighting had ended, and the country was beginning to rebuild itself.

The many mountains of Serbia and Montenegro include the Balkan Mountains and the Dinaric Alps. Daravica, at more than 2,400 metres, is the country's highest peak. People raise sheep and goats in the mountain pastures. The main flatland area in the country is the Mid-Danube Plain. It is the most fertile region for growing crops. The main crops are maize, sugar beets, and wheat. Fruits and vegetables are also grown.

Many people go to Serbia to see its very old churches and visit its mineral springs. Montenegro's seacoast, with its beautiful landscape and old stone houses, is also popular.

SEARCH LIGHT

Serbia and Montenegro was called Yugoslavia before it took its current name. When did it change its name?

DID YOU KNOW?
The country was a founding member of the World Chess Federation in 1924. Today, 161 countries belong to the federation, and it is one of the most widespread sports organisations in the world.

Mountains rise up sharply from the coast of Serbia and Montenegro.
© Otto Lang/Corbis

Answer: 2003

Borderland Country

Ukraine has one of the largest populations of any European country. It is located at the eastern edge of Europe, near Asia (the word Ukraine means 'borderland' or 'bordering country'). Ukraine's capital is Kiev, an ancient city that was founded more than 1,000 years ago.

Ukraine is a rather flat country, with only a few mountains. Its major mountains are the Carpathians in the west and the Crimean Mountains in the south. It also contains a portion of the Polissya (also known as the Pripet Marshes), the largest swamp in Europe. The **marshes** have a great variety of wildlife, including elk, wolves, lynx, mouflon (wild sheep), and wild boars.

Ukraine has a rich tradition of oral literature, complete with heroic stories and songs that remain popular today. Ukraine's folk traditions can be seen in the country's many festivals. At the festivals people in brightly coloured folk costumes perform traditional dances and music. The country's written language is similar to Russian and uses the **Cyrillic** alphabet.

The region that is now Ukraine has a long history. Many years ago Kiev was the centre of a country called Kievan Rus. In the 1700s Ukraine came under the control of the Russian **tsars**. In the 19th century it was the main site for battles in the Crimean War between Russia and the Ottoman Turks. Ukraine became part of the Soviet Union in the early 20th century. It was known as the country's breadbasket because it produced large amounts of grain (particularly wheat). In 1991, with the fall of the Soviet Union, Ukraine became an independent country.

SEARCH LIGHT

Ukraine was the centre of what war in the 19th century between Russia and the Ottoman Empire?

DID YOU KNOW?
The Ukrainian city of Chernobyl was the site of the world's worst nuclear power station accident. The accident occurred in April 1986.

Ukrainian folk dancers perform in traditional costumes.
© David Cumming; Eye Ubiquitous/Corbis

Land of Islands

The country of Greece is surrounded on three sides by seas. To the south is the Mediterranean Sea, to the west is the Ionian Sea, and to the east is the Aegean Sea. More than 2,000 islands in the Ionian and Aegean seas belong to Greece, but people live on only about 170 of them. The islands are divided into two groups - the Ionian Islands and the Aegean Islands - depending on which sea they're in.

As well as its many islands, Greece also has many mountains. The tallest is Mount Olympus. It is 2,917 metres high. Zeus, Ares, Athena, and all the other Greek gods and goddesses were said to live on Mount Olympus.

SEARCH LIGHT

Fill in the gap: Greece includes about _____ islands, though not all have people living on them.
a) 3,000
b) 9,750
c) 2,000

Greece was the ancient birthplace of Western civilization. The Greeks learned to read and write more than 3,000 years ago. And it was in Greece that the Olympic Games began about 3,500 years ago. The first modern Olympic Games were held in Athens in 1896.

Many great thinkers and philosophers, such as Socrates, Plato, and Aristotle, came from ancient Greece. The country also produced such poets and playwrights as Homer and Sophocles, as well as famous historians such as Herodotus and Thucydides. Pythagoras was one of the earliest mathematicians, and Hippocrates is considered the father of modern Western medicine. Greece was also known for its famous speakers, called 'orators'. One of the most famous was Demosthenes.

Many rare plants grow in Greece, and medicines are made from some of them. But probably the most important plants are the olive trees of Greece. Much of the olive oil bought by people all round the world comes from Greece.

DID YOU KNOW? Even today doctors take the oath of Hippocrates, a famous early Greek doctor. They promise to do no harm and to follow the highest standards in their work.

Whitewashed houses line the hillside of the island of Santorini in Greece.
© ML Sinibaldi/Corbis

City of the Acropolis

How did the first public buildings of modern Athens show the Greeks' respect for the past?

One of the first things you notice in Athens, the capital of Greece, is a flat-topped mass of rock at the city's centre. It's called the Acropolis and is more than 162 metres high. At the top are buildings that were built very long ago. One of them, the famous Parthenon, was built in honour of the goddess Athena. The city was named after her.

Not too far away is the Theatre of Dionysus. This was the city's drama centre. It had 13,000 seats arranged in 67 rows. Nearby is the Odeum theatre, which seated 5,000 people. It is now used for the Athens summer festival of music and drama.

Theatre was very important to the ancient Greeks. When these theatres were built thousands of years ago, the actors wore masks when they performed. The types of plays they performed are called classical Greek tragedies and comedies. These are still performed today.

The modern city grew from the small town at the base of the Acropolis. Many newer parts of the city have been built in the last hundred years or so. Some public buildings were made of white marble to match the buildings on the Acropolis. Today Constitution Square is the centre of the city. And the Old Royal Palace that stands on one side of it is the home of the Greek **parliament**.

When the Olympic Games were revived in 1896, the first Games were held in Athens in the newly remodelled 70,000-seat Panathenaic Stadium. It was originally built in 329 BC for the Panathenea athletic contests, part of ancient Athens' most important festival.

DID YOU KNOW?

So many tourists visit the Acropolis every year that buses are no longer allowed to drive to the top. The exhaust from the buses was polluting the buildings and causing them to fall apart.

The Theatre of Dionysus in Athens is more than 2,300 years old. If you had lived in ancient Athens, you'd probably have gone to see plays in this huge stone theatre. The whole community was expected to attend performances there.
© Michael Nicholson/Corbis

Answer: They were made of white marble to match the ancient buildings of the Acropolis.

A Tourist's Delight

The country of Italy in south-central Europe has a rich history and many interesting places to visit. Rome, Italy's capital, is one of the world's oldest cities. Other historic Italian cities are Milan, Naples, Florence, and Venice, which has many canals.

Rome

In Rome the Colosseum is an **arena** where many years ago thousands of people went to watch **gladiators** fight. Vatican City lies within Rome too. It's the world headquarters (seat) of the Roman Catholic church and is where the pope lives. The Sistine **Chapel** in the Vatican is one of the most beautiful buildings in Europe. The ceiling and walls have famous paintings by the famous artist Michelangelo.

Pisa in central Italy is best known for its leaning tower. Soon after its construction started, the ground underneath sank. The Leaning Tower of Pisa leans over so much that to climb its stairs you have to lean in the opposite direction. Engineers have stopped it from sinking. They could have straightened out the whole tower, but then it wouldn't be such fun to visit.

DID YOU KNOW?
For many people, it's impossible to imagine a world without Italian food – especially pizza and spaghetti.

On the island of Sicily in southern Italy is Mount Etna, an active volcano. A thin column of smoke always rises from it, and sometimes red-hot lava spills out. Perhaps even more famous are the breathtaking snow-covered Italian Alps in northern Italy. These mountains aren't volcanoes, though. People travel from all over the world to enjoy winter sports in the Alps.

Italy's wine, food, arts, and culture are prized around the world. Famous Italians include artist Leonardo da Vinci, writers Dante and Petrarch, scientist Galileo, and filmmaker Federico Fellini.

Visitors come from all over the world to see the famous works of art in Florence and other Italian cities.
© William Manning/Corbis

SEARCH LIGHT

Which of the following can all be found in Italy?
a) Milan, Sicily, Rome, and Mount Everest
b) Mount Vesuvius, Paris, and the Statue of Liberty
c) Mount Etna, Pisa, and the Alps

Answer: c) Mount Etna, Pisa, and the Alps

Explore some of the world's oldest and most intriguing countries and cities

Views of Asia, Australia, and New Zealand

Views of Asia, Australia, and New Zealand

TABLE OF CONTENTS

Britannica LEARNING LIBRARY

Have a great trip!

The Largest Continent

SEARCH LIGHT

True or false?
The highest point on Earth is in Asia.

COUNTRIES OF ASIA
1. Afghanistan
2. Armenia
3. Azerbaijan
4. Bahrain
5. Bangladesh
6. Bhutan
7. Brunei
8. Cambodia
9. China
10. East Timor
11. Georgia
12. India
13. Indonesia
14. Iran
15. Iraq
16. Israel
17. Japan
18. Jordan
19. Kazakhstan
20. Kuwait
21. Kyrgyzstan
22. Laos
23. Lebanon
24. Malaysia
25. Maldives
26. Mongolia
27. Myanmar
28. Nepal
29. North Korea
30. Oman
31. Pakistan
32. Philippines
33. Qatar
34. Russia (part)
35. Saudi Arabia
36. Singapore
37. South Korea
38. Sri Lanka
39. Syria
40. Taiwan
41. Tajikistan
42. Thailand
43. Turkey
44. Turkmenistan
45. United Arab Emirates
46. Uzbekistan
47. Vietnam
48. Yemen

Asia is the world's largest continent. It covers about one-third of the Earth's land and has about three-fifths of the world's population. Japan, China, India, and Taiwan are some of the most familiar of Asia's nearly 50 countries. In fact, Asia is so big that it's often easier to talk about the **regions** rather than the countries of Asia. The region names commonly used are North Asia, Central Asia, East Asia, Southeast Asia, South Asia, and South-west Asia (the last is one usually called the Middle East).

Most of the continent is made up of mountains and **tablelands**. The Himalayan mountain chain in South Asia includes the highest point on Earth, Mount Everest. The Earth's lowest point, the Dead Sea, is in Asia too.

Asia is home to many kinds of animals. Reindeer, Arctic foxes and hares, seals, walruses, and lemmings can be found in the far north. Elk, brown bears, and sables live in the cool forests. Antelope, wild sheep, and goats are found in the **steppes** and deserts. Black bears, pandas, tigers, and monkeys can be found in southern and eastern Asia. Southern Asia is also noted for elephants, leopards, crocodiles, cobras, and peacocks.

Northern Asia has very cold winters and cool summers. It is covered by tundra - vast treeless plains common in cold regions. Central Asia has cold winters and hot summers with little rainfall. Southern Asia has a warm climate all year, with a lot of rain. There are rainforests all across southern Asia. And nearly all Asian countries share one very important food plant: rice.

Statue of Buddha in Si Satchanalai, Thailand.
© Royalty-Free/Corbis

DID YOU KNOW?
Asia is the birthplace of all the major religions of the world.

Answer: TRUE. The world's tallest mountain, Mount Everest, is in Asia.

Asia's Largest Country

The People's Republic of China is Asia's largest country and has more people than any other country in the world - more than a billion and a quarter! The capital city is Beijing. Han (or Mandarin) is the most widely spoken language of China's several dozen languages. The Chinese civilization is one of the world's oldest and has produced such famous thinkers as Confucius.

Parts of China are very mountainous, as is the **Plateau** of Tibet in south-western China. One part of the plateau is called 'the Roof of the World'. China is so big that some parts are scorching hot deserts while it rains almost every day in some south-eastern regions. Many boats and ships carry people and goods on China's major rivers - the Huang He, Yangtze, and Xi. China also has many railroads as well as three of the world's longest highways.

China's enormous and varied land area supports many plants and animals. Some Chinese animals have become **extinct** in the rest of the world, including the giant salamander, the giant panda, and the great paddlefish. Many of China's trees provide useful substances. The tung tree and the camphor tree produce valuable oils. The lacquer (or varnish) tree produces substances used in making wooden objects. And from the star anise tree comes a food flavouring. In addition, Chinese farmers produce more rice than does any other country.

SEARCH LIGHT

Find and correct the mistake in the following sentence: The People's Republic of China is the largest country in Asia and has the most people: more than a million and a quarter.

People around the world enjoy eating Chinese food. But China has many more traditional and **regional** dishes than most non-Chinese know about. In addition to rice and noodles, Chinese dishes include delicacies such as steamed chicken feet and hundred-year-old eggs.

DID YOU KNOW?

You may think of pasta as an Italian dish, but actually it was created in China. So were fireworks, compasses, silk, chopsticks, crossbows, paper, and paper money.

Rice is one of the most important crops grown in China. Farmers use terraced fields such as these to grow rice on hillsides.
© Keren Su/Corbis

Answer: The People's Republic of China is the largest country in Asia and has the most people in the world: more than a billion and a quarter.

Ancient China's
Giant Guardian

SEARCH LIGHT

Why did the Chinese emperors have the Great Wall built?

The Great Wall of China is the largest structure humans have ever built. Chinese **emperors** had the wall built to guard the country from raids or invasions. It runs from east to west for more than 6,400 kilometres as it stretches across the mountains and valleys of northern China. It is about 6 metres thick at its base and as tall as a house. The entire wall is made of earth and stones. The wall also had watchtowers placed along its length.

Different parts of the wall were built at different times, but all of it was finished long before there were machines to help with the building. Thousands of men worked to build the wall. Many of them died while working on it.

Tourists visiting the Great Wall of China.
© Dean Conger/Corbis

After the Great Wall was built, the people of China felt safer. If an enemy approached the wall, smoke signals would be passed from watchtower to watchtower. A signal fire would be lighted if an attack came at night. An alarm would be sounded, and the emperor's army would rush to defend the wall.

But the Great Wall didn't always provide protection. Because the wall was so long, some parts of it were guarded better than others. Sometimes enemies broke through. Finally, the Chinese stopped depending on their wall.

Today the Great Wall is a great attraction for visitors to China. In 1987, UNESCO (the United Nations Educational, Scientific, and Cultural Organization) named the Great Wall a World Heritage site.

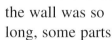

DID YOU KNOW?
The Great Wall of China can be seen from outer space.

The Great Wall of China is one of the most remarkable structures on Earth. It is more than 6,400 kilometres long and is one of the largest construction projects ever carried out. Work on parts of the wall began more than 2,500 years ago.
© Keren Su/Corbis

Answer: The emperors had the wall built to keep out the people who were raiding northern China.

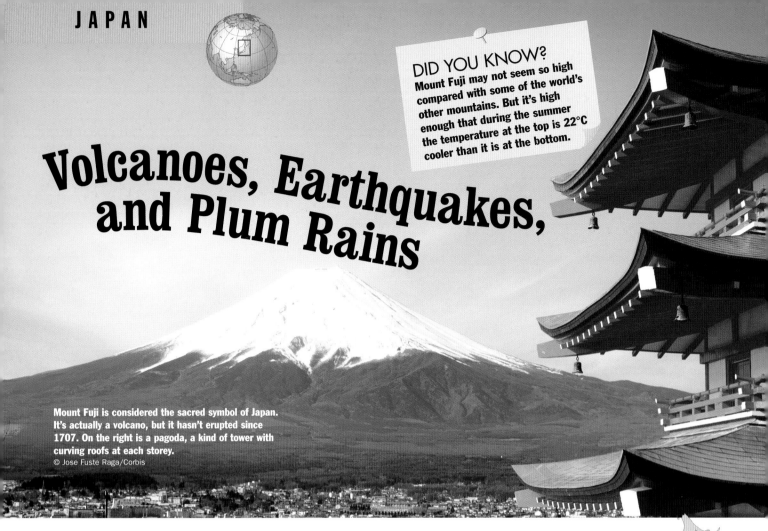

JAPAN

Volcanoes, Earthquakes, and Plum Rains

DID YOU KNOW?
Mount Fuji may not seem so high compared with some of the world's other mountains. But it's high enough that during the summer the temperature at the top is 22°C cooler than it is at the bottom.

Mount Fuji is considered the sacred symbol of Japan. It's actually a volcano, but it hasn't erupted since 1707. On the right is a pagoda, a kind of tower with curving roofs at each storey.
© Jose Fuste Raga/Corbis

Japan is made up of a string of islands that stretches for about 2,400 kilometres along the coast of north-eastern Asia in the Pacific Ocean. The four main islands are Honshu, Hokkaido, Kyushu, and Shikoku. The largest of them is Honshu.

Most of the islands are covered with hills and mountains. Many of the mountains are volcanoes. Some of them are active, and some are 'asleep'. Mount Fuji is a sleeping, or dormant, volcano. It is Japan's highest mountain, reaching a height of 3,776 metres. Rivers flowing past the volcanoes get so much **acid** in them that they can't be used to water crops.

There are many lush forests in Japan. Japanese cherry trees, famous for their spring blossoms, are planted throughout the country. The forests stay beautifully green because it rains and snows so much in Japan. Most parts of the country get more than 100 centimetres of rain each year. The summer rains are called *baiu*, which means 'plum rain'. They are called that because they begin at the time when the plums ripen. Some parts of Japan get many centimetres of snow each winter.

Many kinds of wild animal can be found in Japan's forested areas. These animals include bears, badgers, otters, mink, deer, and foxes. Japan has many **wildlife sanctuaries** to protect all these wonderful creatures.

Did you know that there are about 1,000 earth tremors in Japan every year? Fortunately, most are not very strong, though violent earthquakes do occur sometimes. When that happens, there is a danger of tsunamis, giant tidal waves along the coasts.

Tokyo

SEARCH LIGHT

The largest island in Japan is
a) Honshu.
b) Kyushu.
c) Hokkaido.

402

Answer: a) Honshu.

An Asian
Land Divided

North Korea

South Korea

Pyongyang ⭐

Seoul ⭐

The Korean **peninsula** is a land of beautiful mountains. For a long time it was a single country. Today it is divided into two countries - North Korea and South Korea. But though they are separate, they share a border and a common history that stretches back thousands of years.

Korea has a rich culture that was influenced by China, especially in early times. The Buddhist and Confucian religions came to Korea from China. Over the years, however, Korea developed a culture that is very much its own. For example, even though it once used the Chinese system of writing, the Korean language isn't closely related to any other language. And Korean music sounds quite different from other East Asian music. In the folk music called *p'ansori*, a singer-storyteller performs with a drummer. In dance and other music, the *kayagum*, a stringed instrument, is an original Korean favourite. Many people around the world love to eat Korean food - especially tasty barbecued meat and a spicy cabbage dish called *kimchee*.

In 1948, after World War II, the Korean peninsula was officially divided into North Korea and South Korea. North Korea became a **communist** country, but South Korea did not. In 1950 a war broke out between the two. This was the Korean War, which ended in 1953 with the two Koreas remaining separate.

Both North and South Korea have been rebuilt since the war. In 2000 the two countries held talks about joining together again.

People were finally allowed to cross between them and meet family members they had not seen since the war, almost 50 years before.

SEARCH LIGHT

True or false?
The Korean peninsula became a communist country in 1948.

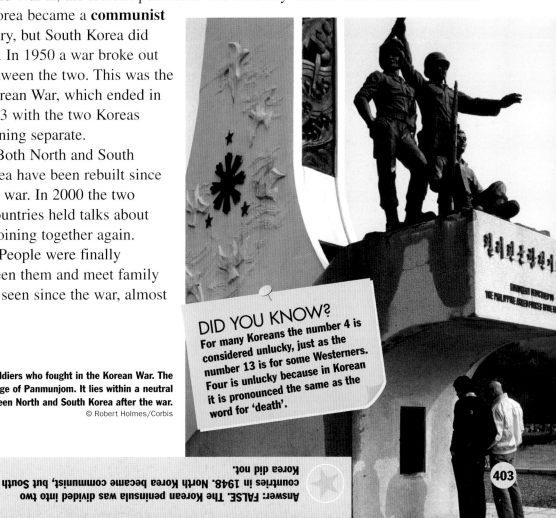

This monument honours soldiers who fought in the Korean War. The memorial stands near the village of Panmunjom. It lies within a neutral zone established between North and South Korea after the war.
© Robert Holmes/Corbis

DID YOU KNOW?
For many Koreans the number 4 is considered unlucky, just as the number 13 is for some Westerners. Four is unlucky because in Korean it is pronounced the same as the word for 'death'.

Answer: FALSE. The Korean peninsula was divided into two countries in 1948. North Korea became communist, but South Korea did not.

403

The City of Lady Penh

Phnom Penh is the capital of the Kingdom of Cambodia in Southeast Asia. It is located at the meeting point of three rivers: the Basak, the Sab, and the Mekong.

Phnom Penh is more than 500 years old. According to legend, a woman named Lady Penh was walking on a hill and found a bronze statue of the Buddha, the founder of the Buddhist religion. There she started the town of Phnom Penh, which means 'Penh Hill'. Her ashes, it is said, were kept in a **pagoda** at the top of the hill.

Phnom Penh was built around the Preah Morokot pagoda. Its floor is paved with tiles of solid silver. The pagoda is built like a tower, with several stories. At the edge of every story, the roof curves upward. It and other stately buildings are near the Royal Palace, where the king and his family live.

There are many museums in Phnom Penh. The National Museum has a fine collection of art by the Khmer people, who make up more than 85 percent of the population of Cambodia. The Tuol Sleng Museum is devoted to the memory of the many Cambodians who were killed in the 1970s by Cambodia's communist government. This was a terrible time in the history of the city and country.

The Royal Ballet of Phnom Penh is known the world over. Its ballets are inspired by ancient Buddhist and Hindu legends. There was a time when the dancers performed only for the Cambodian royal family. Now everyone can enjoy them.

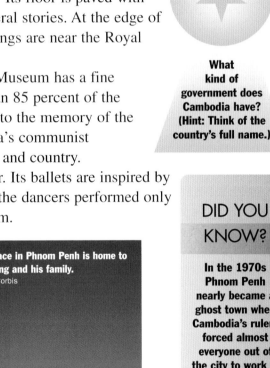

Phnom Penh

SEARCH LIGHT

What kind of government does Cambodia have? (Hint: Think of the country's full name.)

DID YOU KNOW?

In the 1970s Phnom Penh nearly became a ghost town when Cambodia's rulers forced almost everyone out of the city to work in farm fields.

The Royal Palace in Phnom Penh is home to Cambodia's king and his family.
© Nevada Wier/Corbis

Answer: Cambodia is a kingdom, so in theory it is ruled by a king or a queen. However, in modern times most monarchs have government officials and lawmakers to help run the country.

Cambodia's Treasured Temple

Angkor Wat is a **temple** in the Southeast Asian country of Cambodia. The word *angkor* means 'capital', and *wat* means '**monastery**'. Angkor Wat is more than 800 years old. It is the world's largest religious structure.

The Khmer people are native to Cambodia, and the city of Angkor was once the capital of the Khmer Empire. King Suryavarman II built Angkor Wat. He dedicated the temple to the three Hindu gods Brahma, Vishnu, and Shiva. It was not just a temple but also the government centre of Suryavarman II's empire.

The temple walls are covered with sculptures of Hindu gods. They also show scenes from ancient Khmer history. In addition, there are hundreds of carved statues of *apsara*s, or 'heavenly dancers'. They are seen wearing beautiful costumes, jewellery, and crowns.

About 20 years after the complex was built, a foreign army attacked the Khmers and **looted** the city. King Jayavarman VII, who was ruling the Khmer, felt that the gods had failed him. He became a Buddhist and built a new capital nearby called Angkor Thom. Angkor Wat then became a Buddhist **shrine**. Many of the statues and carvings were replaced by Buddhist art.

After many years, however, the forest grew and covered Angkor Wat. Most people forgot all about it. A French explorer named Henri Mouhot rediscovered the city while travelling on the Mekong River in 1858. In 1992 UNESCO (the United Nations Educational, Scientific and Cultural Organization) named the entire Angkor area a World Heritage site. Today Angkor Wat is one of the main attractions for visitors to Cambodia.

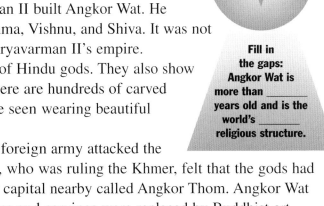

SEARCH LIGHT

Fill in the gaps: Angkor Wat is more than _____ years old and is the world's _____ religious structure.

DID YOU KNOW?
When UNESCO named Angkor Wat a World Heritage site, it meant that the place has major importance for the entire world. Being a World Heritage site makes it easier for countries to cooperate to protect a cultural or natural treasure.

Tree roots growing on the Ta Prohm temple, part of the temple centre at Angkor, Cambodia.
© Royalty-Free/Corbis

Answer: Angkor Wat is more than 800 years old and is the world's largest religious structure.

Island Nation of Southeast Asia

Jakarta

The Republic of Indonesia is a country of islands lying between the Indian and Pacific oceans. Its capital is Jakarta on the island of Java.

Indonesia is made up of about 13,670 islands, though some are shared with other countries. The largest island is New Guinea, which Indonesia shares with Papua New Guinea. Parts of Borneo, the second largest island in the group, belong to Malaysia and Brunei. Sumatra, Java, and Celebes are the other major islands of Indonesia. Most of Indonesia's people live on these five islands.

Most of the islands are mountainous. Only about one-tenth of the land is used for growing crops, but many of the people make their living from farming. Rice is the main crop grown there. Other crops include coffee, tea, tobacco, and spices. There are also many palm and rubber trees in Indonesia. The country produces many things made of palm oil and is a major supplier of natural rubber.

The **climate** in Indonesia is hot and **humid.** Rain falls heavily throughout the year. Because of that, much of Indonesia is full of rainforests. Mangrove tree swamps are common along the coasts.

Indonesia is known for more than its **natural resources**, though. The people of Indonesia practice special decorative arts throughout the islands. Perhaps the most popular art with tourists is batik, a special way of dyeing fabric. Indonesians are also known for their traditional dance and puppet performances. Puppetry is one of the favourite arts of the islanders themselves.

DID YOU KNOW?
Indonesia has more than 200 active volcanoes. Among them is the famous Krakatoa. When it erupted more than a hundred years ago the explosions were heard thousands of miles away.

SEARCH LIGHT

Fill in the gap: Indonesia is a country made up of about 13,670 _____.

Indonesians use a process called 'batik' to dye fabrics. The results can be quite colourful.

The Lion City

The Republic of Singapore is a small island nation in Southeast Asia. Singapore is also the name of the country's main island and of its capital city. Legend says that a prince named the island Singapura, meaning 'lion city', because he thought he saw a lion there.

DID YOU KNOW?
If you want to give a gift to someone from Singapore, you shouldn't give a clock or a handkerchief. These objects are linked with death or funerals. Umbrellas are not good gifts either - they are associated with accidents.

Singapore Island and about 60 little nearby islands make up the country. All these islands lie off the southern tip of the Malay **Peninsula**. Singapore Island is shaped like a diamond. It is linked to the country of Malaysia on the Malay Peninsula by a road and railway that cross the water of the Johor **Strait**.

As of 1995, almost 3 million people lived in this small island nation. That makes Singapore one of the most crowded countries in the world. But Singapore is also one of the most well-to-do Asian nations because it has been a busy world shipping port for a long time. People have moved there from all parts of Asia, giving Singapore a rich and varied cultural **heritage**. Most people speak the Malay language, but Mandarin Chinese, Tamil (an Indian language), and English are also official languages.

Singapore's weather is hot and very rainy - a typical **monsoon** climate. The lowlands often flood when it rains hard, but the rainy weather is good for plants. While only a few of Singapore's native plants remain, patches of original rainforests still survive. There are some original **mangrove** forests on the main island's north-western side. And people often call Singapore city the 'Garden City' because of its many parks, gardens, and tree-lined streets.

SEARCH LIGHT

Singapore has four official languages - Malay, Mandarin Chinese, Tamil (an Indian language), and English. Most countries have one or two. Why do you think Singapore has so many?

Singapore is sometimes known as the 'Lion City'. Its symbol is a merlion, a creature that is half lion and half fish.
© Earl & Nazima Kowall/Corbis

Answer: Singapore's four official languages reflect the fact that people from many different cultures have moved there. Also, being a busy and successful world port means that people from all over the world live, work, and pass through Singapore.

City of Angels

Bangkok is the capital of Thailand and the country's largest and most important port. The Thai people call the city Krung Thep, which means 'city of angels'. Bangkok spreads across both sides of the Chao Phraya River. From the river a network of **canals** spreads through the city.

The Grand Palace, where the kings of Thailand once lived, stands on the river's east bank. The palace is surrounded by walls. Also within these walls is Wat Phra Kaeo, a temple full of Thai art treasures. It holds the Emerald Buddha, the holiest statue of the Buddha in all of Thailand.

There are many other Buddhist temples, or *wat*s, along the banks of the Chao Phraya River. A *wat* usually has living quarters for monks, **shrines** for **meditation**, towers, and a meeting place. Some of the *wat*s are decorated with beautiful carvings. The Temple of Dawn, or Wat Arun, is one of these.

Wat Pho is the oldest and largest *wat* in Bangkok. It has the largest reclining Buddha and the largest collection of Buddha images in Thailand. People call Wat Pho the first university in Thailand. An early king had **texts** carved in stone and set around the temple so that people could read and learn from them.

In Bangkok's famous floating markets, merchants sell fruits, vegetables, flowers, and other items from boats in the canals. Shoppers step from boat to boat as they look at all the things to buy.

SEARCH LIGHT

The name Krung Thep means
a) 'grand palace'.
b) 'city of angels'.
c) 'emerald Buddha'.

DID YOU KNOW?
The full official Thai name for Bangkok has more than 160 letters. According to some sources, it is the longest name of any place in the world.

These Buddhist monks walk on the grounds of one of Bangkok's famous temples, the Wat Phra Kaeo. Inside the temple is a sacred image called the Emerald Buddha. Buddhism is the city's main religion.
© Paul Almasy/Corbis

Answer: b) 'city of angels'.

North and South

The Socialist Republic of Vietnam is located in Southeast Asia, near China, Laos, and Cambodia. It is made up of what for many years were two countries: North Vietnam (the Democratic Republic of Vietnam) and South Vietnam (the Republic of Vietnam). After a long war, the two countries were reunited in 1976. The capital of Vietnam is Hanoi.

Most people know of Vietnam because of its wars. The one that led to the reunification of North and South Vietnam began in the 1950s. The **communists** who ruled North Vietnam wanted to bring the two countries together under their leadership. South Vietnam, with support from the United States, tried to stop them. During the late 1960s and the early 1970s, both the Vietnamese and the Americans suffered great losses. Many people were killed, and Vietnamese cities and much of the countryside were badly damaged. South Vietnam surrendered to North Vietnam in 1975.

In spite of the troubles Vietnam has faced, it still has a number of interesting places to visit. Hanoi has centuries-old temples as well as modern art and history museums. Bustling Ho Chi Minh City (formerly Saigon, capital of South Vietnam) has Buddhist **pagodas** and a **cathedral** among its attractions.

Most of Vietnam's people are farmers. Much of the farmland is used for growing rice. There are also farms that grow coffee, tea, rubber, sugarcane, soybeans, and coconuts. The people often eat meals of rice with fish.

DID YOU KNOW?
French is one of the languages spoken in Vietnam, and French cooking is part of Vietnam's cuisine. Sound odd? France once ruled the country as a colony, until the Vietnamese gained their independence in the 1950s.

SEARCH LIGHT

Fill in the gaps: Present-day Vietnam is the result of joining _____ and _____ Vietnam in the 1970s.

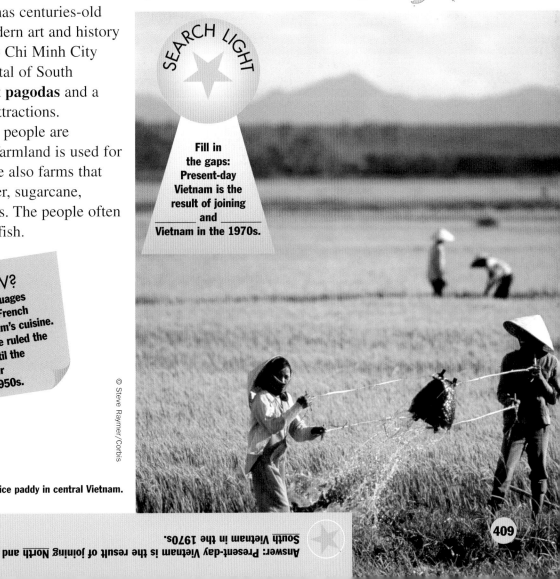

© Steve Raymer/Corbis

Farmers work in a rice paddy in central Vietnam.

Mountain Country

Afghanistan is a dry country in southern Central Asia. Kabul is Afghanistan's capital city. Mountains cover a large part of the country. The Pamir Mountains rise in the north-east, and the giant Hindu Kush range spreads across the country from north-east to south-west. Many of Afghanistan's rivers get their water from the melting snow and **glaciers** in the mountains. The Kabul River provides water for the fertile valleys and **basins** around the cities of Kabul and Jalalabad.

Kabul

Not much of Afghanistan's land can be used for farming, though. It is either too rocky or too dry. Only farmers who live in the river valleys where water is available are able to grow crops. They mostly grow wheat, maize, grapes, and rice. Instead of farming, many people raise herds of sheep, goats, cattle, or camels.

SEARCH LIGHT

For centuries Afghanistan was ruled by a king. It suffered a long civil war in the 1980s when the Soviet Union supported Afghanistan's **communist** government. In the 1990s a Muslim group overthrew the government and then fought amongst themselves. Finally one group, called the Taliban, took control. They made many strict laws and took away a lot of the Afghan people's rights. Many people around the world were upset by this.

Unscramble these words connected with Afghanistan:
- blaKu
- niHud shuK
- tinamouns

In 2001 the United States was attacked by terrorists. The U.S. government blamed the terrorism on al-Qaeda, a Muslim group supported by the Taliban. A few weeks later the United States, Britain, and other allies attacked Afghanistan and forced the Taliban from power. The new government restored many of the rights of the Afghan people that the Taliban had taken away.

DID YOU KNOW?

Conflict is not new to Afghanistan. During the 1800s, Russia and England supported different tribal groups in Afghanistan. This led to many battles and wars in the region. The Europeans called this contest the 'Great Game'.

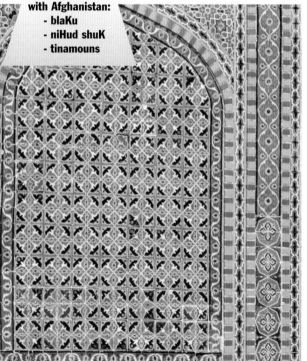

Complex designs cover a wall of a mosque in the city of Mazar-e Sharif, Afghanistan. Many Muslims believe that inside the mosque is the tomb of Ali, the son-in-law of Muhammad, the founder of the Islamic religion.
© Charles & Josette Lenars/Corbis

Answer: - blaKu = Kabul
- niHud shuK = Hindu Kush
- tinamouns = mountains

Land of the Bengals

Bangladesh is a small densely populated country in South Asia. It's also a young country, born only in 1971. Before that it was called East Pakistan. But the area it lies in is traditionally known as Bengal.

East Pakistan was part of the country of Pakistan. The people of East Pakistan wanted their freedom, and they won it after fighting a war with the help of the neighbouring country of India. Today Bangladesh shares a language (Bengali) and culture with the Indian state of West Bengal. Most of the people are of the Islamic faith, though a number are Hindu.

Bangladesh is generally hot and **humid**. Two major rivers - the Ganges (Ganga) and the Brahmaputra - come together there as the Padma River. Summer brings heavy rains. Every two or three years the Brahmaputra River floods the countryside, killing many people and damaging crops and houses.

Bangladesh's capital, Dhaka, is divided into Old and New Dhaka. In Old Dhaka you can see many styles of buildings, most notably Mughal (Islamic) monuments, gardens, and mosques. In the maze of crowded narrow lanes, bazaars sell everything from bracelets to silk to books.

In the **fertile** central region of Bangladesh, many crops are grown. These include rice and jute, a fibre often used to make sacks and mats. Jute is sold to other countries. Parts of Bangladesh are covered with forests - bamboo trees in the east and mangrove swamps along the coast. Elephants, bears, deer, and monkeys live in the forests and grasslands. But the country's best-known animal is the Bengal tiger - larger than all the big cats except the Siberian tiger.

SEARCH LIGHT

People are trying to save the Bengal tiger by saving its habitat. Why would that help? (Hint: What does the forest do for the tiger?)

DID YOU KNOW? One of the most popular sports in this land of tigers and jute is kite flying.

This young woman is picking tea leaves in a field in Bangladesh. Tea is one of the country's major crops.
© Roger Wood/Corbis

Answer: Without forests in which to hide and hunt for food, tigers would die. So by saving the place where the Bengal tiger lives and gets its prey, we have a better chance of saving the animal as well.

City in the Heart of the Himalayas

Thimphu is the capital of Bhutan, a small country in South Asia. It is a small city located in a valley in the heart of the Himalaya Mountains.

The people of Thimphu are not allowed to build houses in just any way they choose. There are strict rules for how all buildings must look. Buildings must be a certain height, and they have to follow the traditional building style of Bhutan. The similar-looking buildings give Thimphu a special look.

The Tashi Chho *dzong* is a good example of the Bhutanese style of building. It is styled like a fortress, but it was originally a **monastery**. It's been remodelled and now also houses the offices of the royal government.

Farming is very important to the people of Thimphu. All **fertile** soil is used for growing crops - even the land around the royal palace. The main crops are rice, maize, and wheat.

Tourists usually like to visit the vegetable market in Thimphu. At one end of the market, you'll find people selling **handicrafts** and other locally made items. These include Buddhist prayer wheels and flags, baskets, hand-woven and hand-knitted clothes, and many different kinds of hats. Another interesting place is the memorial *chorten*, or small **shrine**, at the temple called Changangkha Lhakhang. And you should make time to go up the hill known as Sangay Gang. From there you'll get a spectacular view of Thimphu.

SEARCH LIGHT

Fill in the gap: Thimphu sits high above sea level in a valley of the _____ Mountains.

DID YOU KNOW?

The government of Bhutan limits the number of tourists who can enter the country. One result is that Thimphu is a quiet city with little of the crowding common in other capitals.

Schoolchildren sit on a hill above Thimphu. Before the 1960s the city had no formal schools except ones that taught religion. But since then great progress has been made in non-religious education.
© Karan Kapoor/Corbis

Answer: Thimphu sits high above sea level in a valley of the Himalaya Mountains.

Land of Temples and Shrines

India is a country of more than a billion people. The people speak dozens of languages, including Hindi, Bengali, Telugu, and Tamil. Many also speak English. The country is the birthplace of two major religions: Hinduism and Buddhism. Both were founded in ancient times, but many people in India still practice them, especially Hinduism. Other religions in India include Islam, Christianity, and Sikhism. The country's capital is New Delhi.

New Delhi

People from all over the world travel to India to see its many beautiful and historic buildings. Long ago, for instance, Buddhists built dome-shaped **shrines** called *stupa*s. These were built in places where the founder of the religion, the Buddha, lived, visited, or preached. Some of the most famous *stupa*s are at Sanchi and Sarnath. A *chaitya* is a Buddhist temple, or place where people pray together. There are some beautiful *chaitya*s among a group of caves carved out of cliffs at Ajanta. The Ajanta caves are also known for their paintings. Though the paintings are about 2,000 years old, they still look bright and beautiful.

India also has several Hindu rock temples. The Kailash Temple at Ellora is carved out of solid rock. So are the sculptured temples of Khajuraho. The stone *ratha*s, or shrines, in Mahabalipuram are also remarkable.

Many tourists like to see India's grand **mausoleums**, where important people are buried. The Taj Mahal, one of the most beautiful sites in the world, is the mausoleum complex Emperor Shah Jahan built for his queen in the 1600s.

DID YOU KNOW?
In India's capital, New Delhi, is a slender five-storey-tall tower built by early Muslim kings. It's in a group of buildings called the Qutub Minar. The Muslim conquerors made the buildings and tower from pieces of Hindu and Jain temples.

SEARCH LIGHT

True or false? A *chaitya* is a place where Hindus pray.

The Buddhist religion began in India many years ago. These caves in western India were used as temples and monasteries by early followers of the religion. The walls of the caves are covered with religious paintings.
© David Gurr—Eye Ubiquitous/Corbis

Answer: FALSE. A *chaitya* is a place where Buddhists pray.

Wonder of the World

Several hundred years ago most of India was conquered and ruled by the Mughals, who followed the religion of Islam. When the emperor Jahangir ruled over northern India, his son, Prince Khurram, married Arjumand Banu Baygam. Prince Khurram called his wife Mumtaz Mahal, meaning 'chosen one of the palace'. The two were almost always together, and together they had 14 children.

Prince Khurram became emperor in 1628 and was called Emperor Shah Jahan. But three years later, Mumtaz Mahal died while having a baby. Shah Jahan was heartbroken. He decided to build the most beautiful monument to his wife. He had the best **architects** design it in a perfect blend of Indian, Persian, and Islamic styles. Beginning in about 1632, over 20,000 workers laboured for 22 years to create what was to become one of the wonders of the world.

The great monument was called the Taj Mahal (a form of Mumtaz Mahal's name). It was built in the city of Agra, India, the capital of Shah Jahan's empire. Its several buildings sit in a large garden on the south bank of the Yamuna River. From the garden's south gateway you can see the front of the white marble **mausoleum**. It contains the tombs of Mumtaz Mahal and Shah Jahan. The mausoleum stands on a high marble platform surrounded by four minarets, or towers. Many of its walls and pillars shimmer with **inlaid** gemstones, including lapis lazuli, jade, crystal, turquoise, and amethyst. And verses from the Koran (the Muslim holy book) appear on many parts of the Taj.

Many visitors still come to the Taj Mahal. To help protect and care for it for many years to come, the Taj was made a World Heritage site in 1983.

DID YOU KNOW?
According to tradition, Shah Jahan planned to have a tomb built for himself across the river from the Taj Mahal, with a bridge connecting the two. But he was removed from power and imprisoned by his son before his plan could be carried out.

Visitors flock to see the breathtaking Taj Mahal in Agra, India. Many people in the city claim to be descendants of the 20,000 workers who built the structure.
© Vince Streano/Corbis

A Young Country with an Ancient History

Pakistan is a country in South Asia. India is its largest neighbour. For many years Pakistan and India were a single country known as British India. Pakistan was created to provide a separate homeland for India's Muslims. It became an independent country in 1947. Its capital is Islamabad.

Islamabad

Pakistan was established in two sections, East Pakistan and West Pakistan. Later, in 1971, East Pakistan became a separate country called Bangladesh.

Although Pakistan is a young country, it has a rich history. It was the site of the ancient Indus civilization. This was one of the largest of the early city-based civilizations. Pakistan is also home to many historic **mosques**, tombs, and **shrines**. Some of these are hundreds of years old.

Pakistan is a rugged place. In the north are the mountains of the Karakoram Range and the Himalayas. Some of the world's tallest mountains are part of these ranges. Huge **glaciers** and roaring rivers cross this landscape. Other parts of the country are very dry. Pakistan's natural plant life is mainly grass and bushes. But on the slopes of the Himalayas, oak, cherry, cedar, and pine trees grow. Brown bears, black Himalayan bears, leopards, and wild sheep are found in the northern mountains. The rare snow leopard is found there also.

Most of Pakistan's people speak Urdu. But Punjabi, Sindhi, Pashto, and Balochi are also spoken. Many people can also speak English.

Many Pakistanis are farmers. They grow rice and cotton. Some people make a living from forestry and fishing. Others make beautiful carpets and do fine **embroidery**.

DID YOU KNOW?

The official emblem, or symbol, of Pakistan features the crescent-and-star symbol of the national religion, Islam. The emblem also displays what were originally Pakistan's four main crops: cotton, tea, wheat, and jute.

SEARCH LIGHT

True or false? Pakistan used to be part of India.

A group sets up camp in the Karakoram Range in Pakistan.
© Galen Rowell/Corbis

Answer: TRUE.

Island Nation of
Natural Riches

The cloth of your shirt or the lead in your pencil may be from Sri Lanka! Tea is another famous **export** of this island nation.

Sri Lanka lies just south of India in the Indian Ocean. For hundreds of years, it was called Ceylon. In 1972 its name was changed to Sri Lanka. Colombo is Sri Lanka's capital, but the country's **legislature** and law courts are based in the city of Sri Jayewardenepura Kotte.

Most Sri Lankans are farmers. Because the country has a tropical **climate**, with high **humidity** and plenty of rainfall, it is easy to grow rice, tea, sugarcane, rubber trees, and coconut palms. Sri Lankans mine precious gems such as sapphires and rubies. They also produce graphite, the material used to make pencil leads and other products.

Sri Lanka was ruled by different countries for hundreds of years. The Portuguese were the first Europeans to conquer the island. They arrived in 1505. Then the Dutch gained control by promising to help drive the Portuguese away. Finally, in 1802 the British took over the island. They ruled for almost 150 years. Each of these countries wanted to **colonize** the island so they could make money trading its natural goods.

Despite long years of foreign rule, the Sri Lankan people have preserved their traditional sculpture, painting, and **architecture**. The ancient religions of Buddhism and Hinduism have strongly influenced the arts in Sri Lanka. The country's many Buddhist and Hindu temples, with their dramatic ceremonies, are a focus of the island's cultural life.

DID YOU KNOW?
In Sri Lanka some people believe it's bad luck to have a chameleon (a kind of lizard) cross your path.

SEARCH LIGHT

Which of these products does Sri Lanka sell to other countries?
a) tea, tobacco, and coconuts
b) tea, coconuts, and gold
c) tea, rubber, and gems

People in Sri Lanka practice a traditional form of fishing using stilts.
© Torleif Svensson/Corbis

416

Answer: c) tea, rubber, and gems

City of Cafés

Yerevan is one of the world's oldest cities. A fortress was built there in 783 BC. Yerevan is the capital of Armenia, a country at the north-western edge of Asia. The Hrazdan River divides the city. In early times the city became an important stop for traders. In modern times dams have been built on the river to supply electric power for the city's many **industries**.

Republic Square lies at the centre of the city. Yerevan spreads out from the riverbank to the slopes of the surrounding hills. The peaks of Mount Aragats, Mount Azhdaak, and Mount Ararat can be seen from the city. All three are 'dead' volcanoes. Mount Ararat is traditionally considered the place where Noah's ark came to a rest at the end of the flood described in the Jewish and Christian Bible. Most of the houses in the city are pink because they are made with pink 'tuff' stones from the volcanoes.

Yerevan's many museums include the National Art Gallery and the Children's Art Gallery. There is also a painters' **bazaar** during weekends where paintings are sold at reasonable prices. The Matenadaran archives houses books that were written long ago. It has a wonderful collection of old illustrated **manuscripts**. The Erebuni Museum contains many historical objects, including coins and ancient tools.

One of the most unforgettable things about Yerevan is its many cafés. In summer there are so many outdoor cafés that it's often hard to tell where one ends and the next one begins!

SEARCH LIGHT

Find and correct the mistake in the following sentence: Yerevan is famous for being one of the world's largest cities.

DID YOU KNOW?
Many Armenians hold Mount Ararat sacred. They believe their ancestors were the first people to appear in the world - and therefore on the mountain - after the great flood described in the Bible.

Yerevan is an attractive city in a fine natural setting framed by 'dead' volcanoes, including the snow-capped peaks of Mount Ararat. Many of the city's buildings were made using local stone of various colours, especially pink.

© Dean Conger/Corbis

417

Answer: Yerevan is famous for being one of the world's oldest cities.

Modern Persia

The country of Iran, in south-western Asia, was the centre of a mighty empire in ancient times. Today it is a strict Islamic **republic**, meaning that its laws are based on the religion of Islam. Many people in the countries around Iran also follow Islam. However, most Iranians follow Shi'ah Islam, a form that is less common elsewhere. The country's capital is the ancient city of Tehran.

The people of the region have always called the land Iran, but outsiders gave it the name Persia. The name came from the province of Pars, or Persis, where some of the early kings of the region had their capital. In about 550 BC one of those kings, Cyrus the Great, expanded his kingdom and created the Persian Empire. The empire lasted for more than 200 years until the great Macedonian empire-builder Alexander the Great defeated the last Persian ruler. After that, the region changed hands many times.

All the different groups that ruled Iran through the centuries contributed to its rich culture. One of Iran's best-known poets was Omar Khayyam. He wrote beautiful poems that are still read today. Iran is also famous for its miniature paintings, silver work, and Persian rugs. Iran continues to produce these traditional crafts, but it has worked to develop modern **industries** as well.

Iran relies on selling its petroleum and natural gas for much of its income. The country also produces chemicals from those two substances. Iran borders the Persian Gulf and the Caspian Sea, and fisheries there provide jobs for some Iranians.

SEARCH LIGHT

Find and correct the mistake in the following sentence: Iran was once the centre of the mighty Ottoman Empire.

DID YOU KNOW?

The religion of Zoroastrianism was founded in Iran by a man named Zoroaster, or Zarathushtra, more than 2,500 years ago.

Shop windows in Tehran, Iran, display jewellery and other goods.
© Shepard Sherbell/Corbis

Answer: Iran was once the centre of the mighty Persian Empire.

City of Arabian Nights

Have you heard the stories of *The Arabian Nights*? Did you know that most of the stories are set in Baghdad? Baghdad is the capital of Iraq. It lies on the banks of the Tigris River.

People have lived in the area where Baghdad now stands for about 4,000 years. The city itself, however, did not develop until many years later. About 1,200 years ago a Muslim caliph (leader) named al-Mansur chose a village called Baghdad for his capital. The new city was built within rounded walls. At the centre stood the caliph's palace and a grand **mosque**. People called Baghdad the City of Peace or the Round City. During the reign of a later caliph named Harun al-Rashid, Baghdad was said to be the richest and most beautiful city in the world. The stories in *The Arabian Nights* tell about the glory of Baghdad during this period.

Today Baghdad is one of the largest cities in the Middle East. It is also a centre of the art and culture of the religion of Islam. It has many mosques, museums, and libraries. People go to the Awqaf Library to study Arabic history and literature. The Iraqi National Museum has a famous collection of items from the country's early history.

DID YOU KNOW?
The caliphs of Baghdad in the 800s and 900s AD were great supporters of the game of chess. The city was home to some of the world's best players.

Despite its many advantages, Baghdad has faced many problems in recent times. After Iraq invaded Kuwait in 1990, the United States and other countries bombed Baghdad and other parts of Iraq. Parts of the city were destroyed. Baghdad was damaged again in 2003, during another war with the United States. Once again the people of Baghdad had to work to rebuild their city.

SEARCH LIGHT

Unscramble these words that have to do with Baghdad:
- phical
- qlra
- squome
- diMled tEas

Most of the people of Baghdad follow the religion of Islam. The city has many mosques, or houses of worship for Muslims.
© Charles & Josette Lenars/Corbis

Answer: - phical = caliph   - qlra = Iraq   - squome = mosque   - diMled tEas = Middle East

The Jewish State

Although Israel did not become a country until 1948, the region where it is located, formerly called Palestine, has a rich history. It was the ancient home of the Jewish people, and for many hundreds of years it has been home to Arabs. The region, especially the city of Jerusalem, is important to people of the Christian, Jewish, and Islamic faiths.

Jerusalem

Much of Israel is a desert. But there are also well-watered areas where crops can grow. Israel's major crops are citrus fruits, flowers, and vegetables. An important feature of Israel is the Jordan River. It rises in the north and flows south into Lake Tiberias (the Sea of Galilee) and then into the Dead Sea, a large salt lake.

Israel was created as a country where Jews could rule themselves and live without fear of **persecution**. But this caused problems for the Arabs already living on the land. These people, called Palestinians, felt that the land was being taken away from them. The neighbouring Arab countries also objected to a Jewish state in Palestine and tried to overrun the country just after it was founded.

Israel won that war as well as several others. During one war Israel took control of areas called the Gaza Strip and the West Bank. Palestinians there want to form their own state. They also want control of part of Jerusalem, which Israel claims as its capital. The Israelis and the Palestinians have tried to settle their differences peacefully, but conflicts between the two groups continued into the 21st century.

DID YOU KNOW?
Salt water is buoyant - that is, it makes things float. The Dead Sea is so salty that when you swim in it, you float even if you don't want to.

SEARCH LIGHT

Fill in the gap: Israel's founding as a Jewish state caused problems for the _____, the Arab people already living in the same area.

Several cities were located on the shores of Lake Tiberias in northern Israel in ancient times. The lake is called the Sea of Galilee in the Bible.
© David G. Houser/Corbis

Answer: Israel's founding as a Jewish state caused problems for the Palestinians, the Arab people already living in the same area.

Holy City

Jerusalem is a very holy city for Jews, Christians, and Muslims. The section of Jerusalem called the Old City is full of churches, **mosques**, and **synagogues**. People have lived in the Old City for nearly 5,000 years.

There are many sounds in the Old City. You can hear the ringing of church

The Church of the Holy Sepulchre.
© Michael Nicholson/Corbis

bells and the Muslim call to prayer from the **minarets**. You can also hear the sound of chanting at the Western Wall. The wall is the only remaining part of an ancient Jewish temple. Because of the sound of the prayers offered there, the wall is often called the Wailing Wall. Above it is the Temple Mount, which is sacred to Muslims. It is the site of the beautiful gold-capped **shrine** called the Dome of the Rock. It is said that Muhammad, the founder of Islam, made his journey to heaven from this site.

To the north of the Temple Mount lies Via Dolorosa, or Street of Sorrows. This is believed to be the path Jesus walked while carrying the cross. It ends at the Church of the Holy **Sepulchre**. This church is the most important shrine for Christians. It is said to have been built over the place where Jesus died, was buried, and rose from the dead.

Because of Jerusalem's religious importance, control of the city has long been disputed. Israel claims Jerusalem as its capital, but some people disagree with this claim. Among them is a group called the Palestinians, who live in East Jerusalem and nearby territories. Some of them want a separate state created for Palestinians, and they want part of Jerusalem to be its capital.

Jerusalem is holy to which three religions?
a) Islam, Buddhism, and Hinduism
b) Islam, Hinduism, and Judaism
c) Islam, Christianity, and Judaism

DID YOU KNOW?
People called Canaanites built the original town of Jerusalem. Their name comes from either a word meaning 'merchant' or another word meaning 'red wool'. The Canaanites were merchants famous for their red and purple dyes.

Jews pray at the Western Wall. The Dome of the Rock is in the background.
© Richard T. Nowitz/Corbis

Answer: c) Islam, Christianity, and Judaism

City on Seven Hills

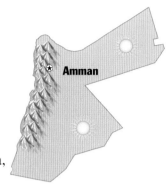

Amman is the capital of the Hashemite Kingdom of Jordan. 'Hashemite' means that the ruling family is **descended** from the Prophet Muhammad. The city is spread over seven hills, called *jabal*s in the Arabic language. Most of Amman's historical sites are clustered in the downtown area, at the bottom of the *jabal*s.

An ancient **citadel** towers over the city of Amman. It is at the top of Al-Qala Hill. Al-Qasr is the most imposing building of the citadel. Al-Qasr means 'the palace'. Nearby is the Jordan Archaeological Museum. It has many exhibits from the **prehistoric** age up to recent times. Probably its most famous possessions are the Dead Sea Scrolls. These ancient **manuscripts** are about 2,000 years old, and they include parts of the Torah (the first five books of the Hebrew Bible) and other writings.

At the bottom of Al-Qala Hill is a Roman **amphitheatre**. The theatre was cut into the northern side of a hill and can seat 6,000 people. It is still used to stage shows, and it has two museums. The Jordan Folklore Museum has many things that tell us how the people of Jordan used to live. The Museum of Popular Traditions has traditional costumes and antique jewellery. Many of the costumes feature beautiful **embroidery**. The odeum is another theatre, nearly as old as the Roman one. It seats just 500 people. Romans used it as a concert hall, and it's still used for concerts.

Visitors to Amman enjoy the city's many bazaars (markets) called *souk*s. Each *souk* sells different things. The gold *souk* is greatly admired.

In the Arabic language, *jabal* means
a) hill.
b) bazaar.
c) theatre.

DID YOU KNOW?
Nearly 2,400 years ago the Egyptian king Ptolemy II Philadelphus took over the city of Amman. He decided to rename it. The name he chose? Philadelphia, for himself.

Houses in Amman, Jordan, cover a hill above an ancient Roman amphitheatre. This huge outdoor theatre was built more than 1,800 years ago and is remarkably well preserved.
© Adam Woolfitt/Corbis

Answer: a) hill.

The City of Wells

Beirut, the capital of Lebanon, lies on the coast of the Mediterranean Sea. It is the country's chief port and largest city. Until the late 20th century, Beirut was a social and cultural centre of the Middle East. In many ways, the city was a complicated mix of peoples and ideas. People from all over the world have attended its schools, colleges, and universities, including the American University of Beirut.

Beirut

Long ago the city was part of a region called Phoenicia. The Phoenicians called the city Be'erot, which means 'wells', because of its underground supply of water. It was one of the most attractive cities in the Middle East. For a long time Beirut was the most important port in the eastern Mediterranean. Its location made it a natural **crossroads** between Asia and Europe.

But Lebanon has been torn apart by many wars and conflicts. Much of Beirut was destroyed in a **civil war** that lasted from 1975 to 1991. Some parts of the city have been rebuilt now. Traditional two-story houses with red-tiled roofs sit side by side with fashionable new houses. Many houses and buildings, though, are still in bad shape and need to be repaired.

Despite the destruction, there are many things to see in Beirut. The American University of Beirut Museum, the Nicolas Sursock Museum, and the National Museum are some of them. At the National Museum you can see objects that are thousands of years old. The city also has many shopping centres and a large number of cafés where you can relax and enjoy Lebanese food, such as *baba ganouj* (aubergine dip) or *tabbouleh* (cracked-wheat salad).

DID YOU KNOW?
The city of Beirut has been damaged and rebuilt several times in its long history. Once, about 1,500 years ago, it was destroyed by an earthquake and a tidal wave.

SEARCH LIGHT

What event led to the destruction of large parts of the city of Beirut in the late 20th century?

A street vendor carries his goods on a bicycle through the streets of Beirut.
D. Mace/Robert Harding Picture Library

Answer: The civil war in Lebanon, which lasted from 1975 until 1991, destroyed much of Beirut.

Holiest City of Islam

Mecca is the holiest city for followers of the religion of Islam. The city, located in Saudi Arabia, is the birthplace of the Prophet Muhammad, the founder of Islam. Muslims all over the world face in the direction of Mecca five times each day to pray.

Mecca ← **Riyadh** ★

The Haram, or Great Mosque, and the Kaaba are the most important places in Mecca. The **mosque** is said to be a copy of God's house in heaven. It can hold a million worshippers. The Kaaba lies in the central courtyard of the mosque. It is a cube-shaped **shrine** made of black stone and wood. This is the holiest shrine of Islam. It is the object toward which Muslims pray when facing Mecca, and it is the most important site for Muslim **pilgrims** to visit when they go to the city. Muslims call the pilgrimage, or journey, to Mecca the *hajj*. All adult Muslims are supposed to try to make the trip at least once.

There are numerous sites from Islamic history in Mecca. Mount Hira, in the north-eastern part of the city, has a cave where Muhammad went to **meditate** in private before he became a **prophet**. Muslims believe he received the first verse of the Koran, the holy book of Islam, in this cave.

Mecca changed greatly in the 20th century. The areas surrounding the Great Mosque were cleared. New houses were built. The streets were made wider, and new tunnels were built to handle more traffic. Like Riyadh (the nation's capital), Mecca is now one of the largest and most modern cities in Saudi Arabia.

SEARCH LIGHT

Fill in the gaps: Muslims go to Mecca to see the birthplace of the
_____.

DID YOU KNOW?
There are more than 1 billion Muslims in the world today. Every year, about 2 million Muslims, from nearly every country of the world, make the pilgrimage to Mecca.

Hundreds of thousands of people gather at the Great Mosque in Mecca on the 27th night of the Muslim holy month of Ramadan. Muslims believe that the Prophet Muhammad first received the Koran on that night many years ago.
© AFP/Corbis

Answer: Muslims go to Mecca to see the birthplace of the Prophet Muhammad.

Pearl of the East

Damascus is the capital of Syria and one of the oldest cities in the world. Travellers who visited Damascus in the past wrote about its many trees, its olive groves, and its streams and fountains. Some of these parks and gardens still exist. And for this reason people still call Damascus the 'Pearl of the East'.

In the old part of Damascus, many people live very much as people did hundreds of years ago. Most of them still live in small single-storey houses built close together. Rising above them are the graceful minarets (towers) and domes of the city's many **mosques**, where believers in the religion of Islam worship. The Great Mosque of Damascus is the oldest surviving stone mosque in the world.

One of the most colourful areas of Damascus is the region of the khans and **bazaars**. Long ago khans were trade, storage, and resting places for camel **caravans**. The Khan Asa'ad Pasha is a beautiful building. It has a striking gate and a black-and-white marble top supported by marble pillars. It is still a centre of trade. The bazaars are lined with shops, stalls, and cafés. They're filled with the noise of people bargaining for the best deal.

SEARCH LIGHT

Why would the streets in the Damascus bazaars have names like the Street of the Spice Men?

Many streets in the bazaar were once devoted to particular trades. You could find the Street of the Saddlers, Street of the Slipper Merchants, and Street of the Water-Pipe Makers. You could also find the Street of the Spice Men, Street of the Dyers, and many others. The longest and busiest of them all was the famous Street Called Straight. It is mentioned in the Bible.

DID YOU KNOW?
Damascus is believed to be the world's oldest continuously inhabited city. People have apparently lived there since about 2500 BC.

The minarets, or towers, of the Ommayed Mosque rise above the surrounding buildings in Damascus, Syria.
© Charles & Josette Lenars/Corbis

Answer: Having the streets named after what was sold there made it easier for shoppers to find what they were looking for.

City on Two Continents

Istanbul is the only city in the world that sits on two continents. It is divided by the Bosporus Strait - a narrow stretch of water that separates Europe from Asia. So part of Istanbul lies in Asia and part in Europe. The city has been a gateway between Asia and Europe for centuries. Today it is the largest city in Turkey and its most important port.

Istanbul has a long history. In the 7th century BC the Greeks built a **colony** on the site and called it Byzantium. For more than 1,000 years, beginning in the 4th century AD, the city was the capital of the Byzantine Empire. It became known as Constantinople during this period. In 1453 the Turks of the Ottoman Empire conquered Constantinople and made it their capital. After the fall of the Ottoman Empire, Turkey became a **republic** in 1923. The capital was then moved to Ankara. Istanbul took its current name in 1930.

Fires, earthquakes, and invasions have greatly damaged Istanbul over the years, but the old part of the city still has many historic sights. One of these is Topkapi Palace, where the Ottoman **sultans** lived. Another landmark is the Hagia Sophia, which was built as a church almost 1,500 years ago. It later became a **mosque** and is now a museum.

Of the many mosques built by the Ottomans, the Blue Mosque is the most famous. Another interesting place to visit is the Grand **Bazaar**. It has shops selling gold, carpets, **ceramics**, copper, brass, and hundreds of other items.

DID YOU KNOW?
Two bridges spanning the Bosporus Strait connect Istanbul's European and Asian sides. So you can actually walk from one continent to another!

SEARCH LIGHT

Istanbul was formerly known as
a) Constantinople and Ottoman.
b) Byzantium and Constantinople.
c) Bosporus and Byzantium.

The Hagia Sophia, in the background, and the Blue Mosque are two of the best-known sights in Istanbul.
© Danny Lehman/Corbis

Answer: b) Byzantium and Constantinople.

Island Continent

The island continent of Australia lies between the Indian and Pacific oceans. Australia is the smallest, flattest, and driest continent. And it has fewer people than other **inhabited** continents. Australia is both a continent and a country, and the map shows you the country's states.

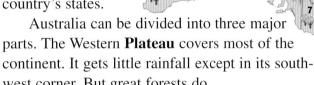

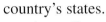

Australia can be divided into three major parts. The Western **Plateau** covers most of the continent. It gets little rainfall except in its southwest corner. But great forests do grow there. Elsewhere on the plateau, wells are the only way to get water. The Eastern Uplands run along the east coast. And the Interior Lowlands lie in between.

One of the most famous symbols of Australia is the natural formation known as Ayers Rock, also called Uluru. The site is sacred to the Aboriginal people. It lies in a national park at the centre of the country.
© Catherine Karnow/Corbis

There you'll find the colourful 335-metre-tall Ayers Rock, also called by its Aboriginal name, Uluru.

STATES OF AUSTRALIA

1. Australian Capital Territory
2. New South Wales
3. Northern Territory
4. Queensland
5. South Australia
6. Tasmania
7. Victoria
8. Western Australia

More than half of the country has been turned into pastures for animals, mostly sheep. Australia has the largest number of sheep in the world and produces more wool than any other country. Australia also has many animals that are not found anywhere else in the world. Two well-known examples are the koala and the kangaroo. The duck-billed platypus and the echidna are two unusual egg-laying mammals.

Many visitors go diving along Australia's Great Barrier Reef, the largest coral **reef** in the world. It stretches for miles and has an amazing display of fish. However, scientists are worried that the reef may be damaged if world climate changes cause the temperature of the sea to rise.

Australians are often called 'Aussies', and most are of European **heritage**. But there is also a large native Aboriginal population. Most Aboriginals live outside the cities in the inner part of the country called the Outback. Today the Aboriginals make boomerangs to sell to tourists, although they originally used them for hunting.

DID YOU KNOW?
Australia is probably the only modern country where so many people can trace their families back to murderers and thieves. Great Britain used to send some of its prisoners to Australia, thousands of miles away, so they wouldn't be able to get back home.

Male Red Kangaroo at Alice Springs.
© Eric and David Hosking/Corbis

SEARCH LIGHT

Find and correct the mistake in the following sentence: Australia has many animals that are not found anywhere else in the world. Two well-known ones are the buffalo and the spider.

Answer: Australia has many animals that are not found anywhere else in the world. Two well-known ones are the koala and the kangaroo.

427

A Magnificent
Harbour City

Sydney is Australia's largest city and one of the most important ports in the South Pacific Ocean. It's also the capital of the state of New South Wales. Sydney is built on low hills surrounding a wonderful harbour on Australia's south-eastern coast. Its beaches are very popular, especially for surfing. And in 2000 the city hosted the Summer Olympic Games.

Sydney Cove is the small sheltered inlet where Australia's first permanent European settlement began. It used to be Sydney's shipping centre, and its old landing place (or quay) is now a tourist centre called Circular Quay. The quay has many walkways, cafés, parks, and docks for the ferries that crisscross the harbour. The nearby Sydney Opera House has a glittering white roof that looks like seashells. Besides opera, the Opera House presents plays, classical music concerts, ballets, and films. Darling Harbour just west of downtown has an aquarium, museums, and gardens.

Sydney Harbour Bridge and The Rocks, a historic district in Sydney.
© Royalty-Free/Corbis

DID YOU KNOW?

Central Sydney is known as 'Eora Country'. The area's Aboriginal people used the word *eora*, meaning 'from this place', to tell the first British settlers where they came from. Today, many Aboriginal people in Sydney call themselves Eora.

The oldest part of Sydney is called The Rocks. This historic district has **cobbled** streets lined with houses that were built by the first British settlers. The Rocks draws crowds of shoppers during the weekend market and has many galleries selling arts and crafts. Here you'll also find the Museum of Contemporary Art.

Macquarie Street is known for its early public buildings. The street is named after the governor who had them built. Landmarks include the **Parliament** House, Sydney Hospital, the Mint Building (which used to produce money), and the beautiful Hyde Park Barracks (which used to house soldiers). Nearby, the large grassy field called the Domain, which was once set aside for public ceremonies, today provides a place for lunchtime sports and candlelight Christmas caroling.

Boats zoom past the Sydney Opera House, a major centre for performing arts of all kinds in Sydney. Its white curved roof looks like seashells or the sails of yachts.
© Paul A. Souders/Corbis

Land of the Long White Cloud

New Zealand is an island country in the South Pacific Ocean. Though it looks close to Australia on maps, the two countries are actually more than 1,600 kilometres apart. New Zealand has two main islands, called North and South Island. Cook **Strait**, a narrow stretch of sea, separates the two. Wellington, the capital city, is on North Island. It lies farther south than any other national capital in the world. New Zealand's largest city, Auckland, is also on North Island.

Both islands have mountains and hills. The Southern Alps is a long chain of mountains on South Island. The mountains trap the moist ocean air, and they are often wrapped in clouds. The first people to live in New Zealand, the Maori, called the country Aotearoa, meaning 'land of the long white cloud'.

New Zealand is known for Merino sheep, which are famous for their wool. Huge sheep ranches are scattered among the hills on South Island. New Zealand also produces excellent butter, cheese, and meat.

New Zealand has unique wildlife. The long-beaked kiwi, a bird that cannot fly, is found only in New Zealand. The bird is one of the country's national symbols - and New Zealanders themselves are sometimes even called Kiwis.

Traditional Maori culture has survived, but now it's blended with the European culture of modern New Zealand. You can still hear traditional Maori music played on the flute and see traditional Maori dances. Wood carving, painting, and making things of woven **flax** are Maori crafts.

SEARCH LIGHT

Who were the first people to live in New Zealand?

DID YOU KNOW?
New Zealand is home to a place with one of the longest names in the world, a hill called Taumatawhakatangihangakoauauotamateaturipuka kapikimaungahoronukupokaiwhenua-kitanatahu.

A gondola car rides high above the harbour at Queenstown, New Zealand.
© Royalty-Free/Corbis

Answer: Long before Europeans arrived in New Zealand, the islands were inhabited by the Maori. The Maori came to New Zealand from the group of islands called Polynesia.

A Visit to New Zealand's Capital

Wellington is the capital of New Zealand, an island country near Australia. It lies on the shores and green hills surrounding a beautiful bay. The city's centre is called Civic Square. It is made up of a group of buildings with an open square in the middle. The buildings include the National Library, the City Gallery, and Capital Discovery Place - a science and **technology** museum for children.

From Civic Square, you can reach Lambton Harbour by going across the

City-to-Sea Bridge. The bridge is decorated with carvings and lovely artwork - all of it created by Maori artists. The Maori are the original people of New Zealand. From the street named Lambton **Quay**, visitors often take a cable car to reach the **botanical** gardens located in the hills above Wellington. The cable car ride provides some of the best views of the city.

Botanical gardens in Wellington, New Zealand.
© Paul A. Souders/Corbis

The botanical gardens have many trees and plants not seen elsewhere. They also have many varieties of roses on display. The Bolton Memorial Park, a burial site for some of Wellington's first settlers, is located within the gardens. Along a section of the city's shoreline is the Oriental Parade. It is a beautiful place that is often crowded with joggers, cyclists, sunbathers, and swimmers. Many people swim out to the large fountain anchored offshore.

Wellington is home to the National Museum of New Zealand (Te Papa Tongarewa). Also popular is the Colonial Cottage Museum, the family home of Katherine Mansfield, one of New Zealand's most famous authors.

DID YOU KNOW?
Wellington is a centre of New Zealand's growing cinema industry. Many films are shot in and near the city.

Green hills surround the city of Wellington. Its harbour serves as a major port for New Zealand.
© Dallas and John Heaton/Corbis

Answer: c) the Louvre. (The Louvre is a museum in Paris, France.)

Discover the continent that is as diverse as it is magnificent

Views of Africa

Views of Africa

TABLE OF CONTENTS

Have a great trip!

Land of Splendour

Alabaster sphinx at Memphis, Egypt.
© Roger Wood/Corbis

Africa's **splendour** is seen in its dramatic landscapes, its amazing animal life, and its **diverse** human culture. The African continent is the home of more than 800 million people living in more than 50 countries. Africa is the second largest continent on Earth, after Asia.

Africa's long coastline is shaped by the Atlantic and Indian oceans and the Mediterranean and Red seas. In the north of the continent lies the Sahara. It is the world's largest desert and covers almost all of northern Africa. Located in south-western Africa are two other major deserts, the Kalahari and the Namib.

The African continent has two major rivers, the Nile and the Congo. The Nile is the longest river in the world. At the southern end of the Nile is Lake Victoria, Africa's largest lake. Not far to the south-east of Lake Victoria is Mount Kilimanjaro, the highest point in Africa. One of the world's major waterfalls, Victoria Falls, is also in Africa.

Africa is known for its wildlife. There are elephants, rhinoceroses, hippopotamuses, lions, and leopards. Other animals include antelope, gazelles, giraffes, baboons, gorillas, hyenas, and chimpanzees. Most of these animals live in Africa's open grasslands or in tropical rainforests.

The people of Africa belong to hundreds of **ethnic** groups. Each group has its own language, traditions, religion, arts, and history. During its political history, Africa has been the site of Egyptian dynasties, African kingdoms, European colonies, and independent countries.

Giraffe, Kenya.
© Royalty-Free/Corbis

SEARCH LIGHT

Find and correct the mistake in the following sentence: Africa is one of the smallest continents.

COUNTRIES OF AFRICA

1. Algeria
2. Angola
3. Benin
4. Botswana
5. Burkina Faso
6. Burundi
7. Cameroon
8. Central African Republic
9. Chad
10. Comoros
11. Congo, Dem. Rep. of the*
12. Congo, Republic of the
13. Côte d'Ivoire
14. Djibouti
15. Egypt
16. Equatorial Guinea
17. Eritrea
18. Ethiopia
19. Gabon
20. Gambia
21. Ghana
22. Guinea
23. Guinea-Bissau
24. Kenya
25. Lesotho
26. Liberia
27. Libya
28. Madagascar
29. Malawi
30. Mali
31. Mauritania
32. Mayotte (France)
33. Morocco
34. Mozambique
35. Namibia
36. Niger
37. Nigeria
38. Rwanda
39. São Tomé and Príncipe
40. Senegal
41. Seychelles
42. Sierra Leone
43. Somalia
44. South Africa
45. Sudan
46. Swaziland
47. Tanzania
48. Togo
49. Tunisia
50. Uganda
51. Western Sahara †
52. Zambia
53. Zimbabwe

* Full name is the Democratic Republic of the Congo (formerly Zaire)
† Annexed by Morocco
Islands of Cape Verde, Mauritius, Réunion off map

Two Countries, One Name

Congo (Brazzaville).

Congo (Kinshasa).

As long as 25,000 years ago, people began to live in the forests of the Congo River **basin** in west-central Africa. They gathered food from the forests and dug up roots to eat.

Today the Congo basin contains two countries separated by the Congo River. Both of the countries are called Congo. To tell them apart, they are sometimes referred to by the names of their capital cities. One of the countries is called Congo (Brazzaville), and the other is Congo (Kinshasa). Congo (Brazzaville) is officially known as the Republic of the Congo. Congo (Kinshasa) is officially called the Democratic Republic of the Congo.

Women gather firewood in the Democratic Republic of the Congo, which is also called Congo (Kinshasa). More than two-thirds of the people live in small towns and villages.
© Gallo Images/Corbis

DID YOU KNOW?
The Congo River is one of the great rivers of the world. Only the Amazon River (in South America) drains a larger area than the Congo River does.

The Congo region got its name from the Kongo, or Bakongo, one of the main groups of people who live there. These people have been in the area for centuries, from the time when the Congo was ruled by various kingdoms.

The Portuguese arrived in the kingdom called Kongo in 1483. At first the newcomers were friendly to the people of the kingdom. By the 1530s, however, the Portuguese were sending the Kongolese away as slaves.

SEARCH LIGHT

How did the Congo get its name?

By the late 1800s other European countries had become interested in the Congo region. They valued the Congo River as a route for trade between the west coast of Africa and the interior part of the continent. The French and the Belgians took over different parts of the Congo. The local people didn't win their independence until 1960. Though free, each of the two Congos faced many problems. Both countries experienced periods of fierce internal fighting and struggles for power.

Answer: It was named for the Kongo, or Bakongo, people, who have lived there for centuries.

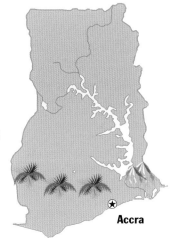

Accra

Gold Coast of Africa

The country of Ghana has so much gold that it was once called the Gold Coast of Africa. It still has the largest gold **reserves** in the world. Ghana is in western Africa. Accra is its capital and largest city.

Ghana has coastal plains in the south, **savannah** in the north, and hills and rainforests in between. The oddly shaped baobab tree grows in the savannah and coastal plains. There you will also find giant anthills, some of which are over 4 metres high. In the rainforests are tall trees such as the mahogany. And there are many kinds of animals - lions, leopards, elephants, buffalo, monkeys, and snakes, to name a few.

Many of Ghana's people work in fishing, logging, or gold mining. Farming is very important as well. Much of the farmland is used for growing cacao. These trees produce cocoa beans, which are used to make chocolate. Cacao, timber, and gold are sold to other countries.

Long ago the Almoravids from northern Africa conquered Ghana and forced its people to become slaves. Since then, many other groups have gone to Ghana. The Portuguese arrived in the 1400s. They traded in gold, ivory, and slaves. Later came the British, the French, the Dutch, the Swedes, and the Danes. In 1901 the British made the Gold Coast a **colony**. In 1957 the colony won its independence and became the new country of Ghana. Today Ghana is one of Africa's leading **democracies**.

SEARCH LIGHT

Why do you think people from so many other countries wanted to take over Ghana? (Hint: Think of Ghana's former name.)

DID YOU KNOW?

Ghana's weavers are famous for their colourful kente cloth, which is made in narrow strips in beautiful patterns. The patterns have such names as 'thousand shields', 'the lion catcher', and 'gold dust'. The strips are sewn together to make clothing.

These miners work at the Ashanti gold mine in Obuasi, Ghana. Ghana has long been one of the world's leading producers of gold. Mining provides work for many of Ghana's people.
© Penny Tweedie/Corbis

Answer: Ghana was called the Gold Coast for its vast reserves of gold. Throughout its history, many different people have wanted to control Ghana so that they could take its gold.

From Trading Post to Modern City

Accra is the capital of the West African country of Ghana. It lies on the coast of the Gulf of Guinea, which is part of the Atlantic Ocean. The city is built partly on a low cliff. The rest of it spreads northward across the Accra plains.

Accra reflects the cultures of the many people who have settled in the area where it now stands. The Ga people had villages there when the Portuguese arrived in 1482. The British, the Danes, and the Dutch came later. The Europeans built **fortified** trading posts along the coast. They traded in gold, ivory, and slaves. Because of the area's gold, it became known as the Gold Coast. In 1877 Accra became the capital of the British Gold Coast colony.

Children in Ghana enjoying a game called *mancala*, **played with stones and cups.**
© Margaret Courtney-Clarke/Corbis

DID YOU KNOW?
Accra's name comes from *nkran*, a word in the language of the Akan people of Ghana. *Nkran* are black ants that are found all over the city and the surrounding area.

SEARCH LIGHT

Which of the following can be said of Accra?
a) The British once ruled there.
b) It is located on the Pacific Ocean.
c) Part of the city is built on a cliff.

Accra lies along the Gold Coast, an area in southern Ghana that has rich deposits of gold. The Portuguese built this strong fort, now called Elmina Castle, in the Gold Coast in 1482. They wanted to keep all of the area's gold trade for themselves.
© Liba Taylor/Panos Pictures

The Gold Coast gained its independence from British rule in 1957 and took the name Ghana. Accra became the capital of the new country. Today it is a modern city of more than 1.5 million people.

Accra is Ghana's business and educational centre. The national museum and national **archives** and the Accra Central Library are located in the city. The University of Ghana is in nearby Legon. Black Star Square is the site of the Independence Arch. This large square is used for parades. For those who like sport, Accra has a football stadium and a racecourse. Not far from Accra are the Aburi **Botanical** Gardens, which were created by the British more than 100 years ago. And the city's large open markets receive most of the food supply each day.

Answer: The British once ruled there.
Part of the city is built on a cliff.

Forests and Minerals

Guinea is a country in western Africa on the Atlantic Ocean. Its capital city, Conakry, is a major port. Ships stop there to load up on Guinea's minerals and other products and transport them to markets around the world.

Conakry

The land is divided into four main areas. A flat plain lies along the coast. Northern Guinea has open grasslands called savannahs. The grass there grows as high as three metres during the rainy season. To the east the Fouta Djallon **highlands** rise sharply from the plain. In the south-east is a hilly area with large forests. There are valuable teak, mahogany, and ebony trees in this area. But much of the forest is becoming open grassland because people have cut down many of the trees so that they can use the land for farming.

Most people in Guinea work as farmers, growing their own food. They grow rice, cassava, sweet potatoes, bananas, coffee, pineapples, peanuts, yams, and maize. Some crops are grown to sell to other countries. Guinea also has large amounts of such minerals as bauxite, iron ore, gold, and diamonds. These are mined and sold to other countries.

The people of Guinea belong to several different groups. In the Fouta Djallon region many people are Fulani. In northern Guinea are the Malinke. Other major groups in the country are the Susu, the Kissi, and the Kpelle. Until 1958 Guinea was a **colony** of France. Because of this the official language in Guinea is French. But many African languages are spoken there as well.

DID YOU KNOW?

All three of western Africa's major rivers begin in Guinea. The country's Fouta Djallon region is the source of the Niger, the Gambia, and the Senegal rivers.

SEARCH LIGHT

True or false? Most of the people in Guinea work as miners.

The savannahs of northern Guinea have some trees scattered among the grasses.
© David Reed/Panos Pictures

437

Answer: FALSE. Most of the country's people are farmers.

LIBERIA

Africa's
Oldest Republic

In the 1820s some Americans who opposed slavery bought land in West Africa. They used it to create a new country for freed slaves, whose ancestors had been taken from Africa. This country was called Liberia. Its government was set up as a **republic** modelled on the United States government. Liberia is now the oldest republic in Africa. Despite the origins of the country, most of its citizens are not the descendants of former slaves.

Today you can find out about Liberia's past by visiting the Malima Gorblah Village and Besao Village. These villages preserve the country's old culture. They are like living museums of Liberia's past.

Liberia's climate is warm and humid all year and rainy from May to October. The country's forests and rolling hills are home to such wild animals as monkeys, chimpanzees, antelopes, elephants, crocodiles, and poisonous snakes. There are two rare animals found in Liberia. One is the pygmy hippopotamus, which looks like a baby hippo even when it is fully grown. The other is the manatee, a big seal-shaped **mammal** that lives in the water.

The rubber trees, coffee, and cocoa that grow in Liberia provide products that can be sold to other countries. Liberian farmers also grow rice, sugarcane, bananas, and yams. Liberia is rich in mineral resources. It is one of the world's leading producers of iron ore.

Liberia suffered through a **civil war** in the early 1990s. It made life dangerous and difficult for many people. The war officially ended in 1996, but some fighting has continued.

Monrovia

SEARCH LIGHT

Fill in the gap: Liberia is the oldest _____ in Africa.

Women try to catch fish in a small pond north of Monrovia, Liberia. Fish are a major source of protein for many Liberians.
© Jan Dago/Magnum Photos

DID YOU KNOW?
Liberia means 'land of the free', a fitting name for a country created for freed slaves.

438

Answer: Liberia is the oldest republic in Africa.

Land of
500 Languages

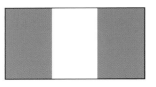

Abuja

Nigeria is a country on the west coast of Africa. It's a place of great variety, in both land and people. More people call Nigeria home than any other country on the continent. There are about 250 different groups of people living there. And they all have unique traditions, ways of life, and languages. More than 500 different languages are spoken in Nigeria. But English is the official language.

The weather is not the same in all parts of the country. Some areas get a lot of rain. Other areas are very dry. Because there are different kinds of weather in different parts of the country, there are many kinds of animals and plants. There are thick **rainforests** as well as **mangrove** and freshwater swamps. There is also open grassland called the 'savannah'. There are small trees all over the **vast** savannah.

Once, camels, antelope, hyenas, lions, baboons, and giraffes lived in the savannah. Red river hogs, forest elephants, and chimpanzees lived in the rainforest. Animals found in both forest and savannah included leopards, monkeys, gorillas, and wild pigs. Today these animals generally are found only in special parks.

Nigeria has many cities. The capital of Nigeria used to be Lagos. But in 1991 the capital changed to Abuja. Lagos is a very large coastal city with many businesses. But Abuja is in the middle of the country, which makes it easier for people to travel there. Lagos was overcrowded, too, and Abuja had more open land for building.

SEARCH LIGHT

True or false? Nigeria is a very rainy country.

Wase Rock rises sharply above the surrounding countryside near Wase, Nigeria. This part of the country consists of savannah, or open grassland, with scattered short trees.
© Bruce Paton/Panos Pictures

DID YOU KNOW?
It is said that more twins are born in Nigeria than anywhere else in the world. Twins are so common that they usually get the same set of names. For example, the Yoruba people usually name their twins Taiwo and Kehinde.

Answer: FALSE. Parts of the country do get a lot of rain, but parts of it are very dry.

Land of Teranga

Dakar

Long ago there was a house packed with men and women. They were inspected and priced like animals. The weaker ones died, and the stronger ones were shipped to the Americas to work as slaves. This slave house was on Gorée Island, which lies off the coast of Senegal, in westernmost Africa. Exactly what went on there is not known for sure. But Senegal was at one time involved in selling Africans as slaves.

But that was long ago. Today Senegal's culture is known for its *teranga,* a spirit of warm welcome toward outsiders. *Teranga* means 'hospitality', or 'welcoming heart', in the language of the Wolof. Many different groups of people make up the Senegalese nation. The Wolof are one of the largest of Senegal's seven main **ethnic** groups.

Despite their different backgrounds, the people of Senegal tend to live in similar ways. Most of the people practice the religion of Islam. And most live in small villages in the countryside. Each village has a water source, a mosque (Islamic house of worship), and a public gathering place. France ruled Senegal until 1960. The different groups of Senegal speak several different African languages, but French is still widely used as a common language. This helps people from different groups talk to each other.

Senegal is one of the world's main producers of peanuts. The country has wide rivers and good soil. The light-coloured sandy soil in the north-western part of the country is especially good for growing peanuts. Dakar, the country's capital, is a major centre for the peanut trade.

A Soninke mother and child stand in the doorway of a traditional-style mud house on a bank of the Senegal River. Like most of the other peoples in Senegal, the Soninke are Muslim.
© Margaret Courtney-Clarke/Corbis

DID YOU KNOW?
Léopold Senghor, the first president of independent Senegal, was also an important writer. He was a leading poet of a movement that celebrated African culture.

Ancient Country in Africa's Horn

Not very long ago, a lot of people in Ethiopia, a country in eastern Africa, went hungry. In 1992-93 the Ethiopian government had to ask countries to donate food for its people. Some 10 million people faced starvation. Although many countries helped, hundreds of thousands of Ethiopians still suffered. Many later died because they had no food.

Most Ethiopians are farmers. But sometimes the government makes bad decisions on how to use the country's farmland. That's one reason why there's not always enough food to meet the needs of the people. Another reason is lack of rain. Ethiopia has two rainy seasons. But once in a while it suffers from droughts, times when it does not rain enough. Often Ethiopia must buy food from other countries. But Ethiopia sells things such as sugarcane, beeswax, leather goods, and coffee. Ethiopia is the place where coffee first came from.

Ethiopia is one of the oldest countries in Africa. It lies within a region that's called the Horn of Africa because on a map it looks like an animal's horn. The capital is Addis Ababa. Most of the people in Ethiopia are Christian. Some follow Islam. Others follow traditional animism, the belief that there is life in the forces of nature or even in **inanimate** objects.

One of the exciting things in Ethiopia is the rich variety of wildlife. But many of the animals have become rare, including lions, leopards, elephants, giraffes, rhinoceroses, and wild buffalo. In order to protect the remaining animals, the government has set aside 20 special parks and **sanctuaries**.

SEARCH LIGHT

Find and correct the mistake in the following sentence. Ethiopia is a young country located in the Horn of Africa region of eastern Africa.

DID YOU KNOW?
In the early 1970s the remains of some of the bones of 'Lucy' were found in Ethiopia. Lucy is believed to be an early ancestor of humans who lived between 3 million and 4 million years ago.

A village lies in a typically rugged part of Ethiopia's landscape.
© Jacques Langevin–Corbis/Sygma

The City Called 'New Flower'

If you visit Ethiopia by plane, you will probably land in Addis Ababa. The city is the capital of Ethiopia and its largest city. Addis Ababa sits high in the mountains at an **elevation** of about 2,450 metres above sea level. It is the highest city in Africa.

At one time in Ethiopia's history, a town called Entoto was the capital. This town had a cold **climate** but lacked enough firewood to provide heat for the people. The wife of Emperor Menilek II wanted him to build a house at a nearby hot springs. The emperor did so, and a new city was founded around it in 1887. The emperor's wife named the new city Addis Ababa, which means 'New Flower'.

Wedding party, Addis Ababa.
© Michael S. Lewis/Corbis

As the population of Addis Ababa grew, that city experienced a shortage of firewood too. To help solve this problem, a large number of eucalyptus trees were imported from Australia. The eucalyptus trees eventually grew in number and now provide a forest for the city's needs.

Today Addis Ababa is the **headquarters** of several international organizations. One of them is the United Nations Economic Commission for Africa. Another one is the African Union. This league includes many African nations that work together to improve their economies and governments.

As a national capital, Addis Ababa has many of Ethiopia's government buildings. The city is also an important educational and commercial centre too. Addis Ababa University was started in 1950. And goods such as textiles, plastics, and wood products are **manufactured** in the city. Addis Ababa is also the site of one of Africa's largest open-air markets.

SEARCH LIGHT

How did Addis Ababa get so many eucalyptus trees?

DID YOU KNOW?
Many of the places in Addis Ababa don't have regular addresses. Many of the city's streets don't even have names. So if you go to Addis Ababa, be sure to get a guide.

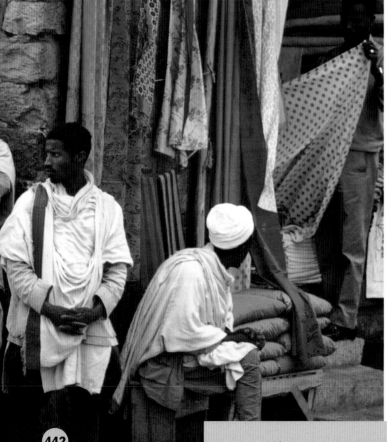

Merchants sell traditional textiles at an outdoor market in Addis Ababa.
© Carl & Ann Purcell/Corbis

Answer: The city had many of the trees brought over from Australia to provide a source of firewood. Over time, the trees grew in number.

Cradle of Humanity

Some of the very earliest humans are believed to have lived in Kenya. That is why some people call the country the 'cradle of humanity'.

Kenya is a country in East Africa. Its capital is Nairobi. The country has a beautiful natural landscape with great variety. There are sandy beaches, huge mountains, rolling grassland, and deserts. A long deep valley cuts through western Kenya. It is part of the Great Rift Valley, a very long series of cracks in the Earth's surface. It runs from south-western Asia through East Africa. Part of Kenya's south-eastern border lies along the Indian Ocean. Lake Victoria makes up part of Kenya's western borders. It's the largest lake in Africa.

The Kenyans are mostly farmers. In the Mount Elgon region, coffee and tea are grown and then sold to other countries. Mount Elgon is a volcano that no longer erupts. The soil in this volcanic region is especially good for growing crops. In the evergreen forests in the west are valuable trees such as cedar and podo. In the south of the country, most of the forests have been cut down.

Kenya's wildlife safaris are world famous. Many tourists visit the country to see the wide range of wild animals, including lions, leopards, elephants, giraffes, gazelles, baboons, and many others. In the rivers there are hippopotamuses, crocodiles, and many fish and spiny lobsters. Many of the animals that live in Kenya are very rare. The country has set up more than 50 national parks and preserves to protect its wildlife.

A group of Masai men perform a traditional dance in Kenya. All young Masai men are brought up to learn the group's customs. They are also encouraged to develop strength, courage, and endurance - traits for which the Masai warriors are noted throughout the world.
© Wendy Stone/Corbis

SEARCH LIGHT

Find and correct the error in the following sentence: Kenyan farmers are mainly known for their rice and cabbage crops.

DID YOU KNOW?
Every year more than a million wildebeest, a kind of African antelope, pass through Kenya.

Answer: Kenyan farmers are mainly known for their coffee and tea crops.

From Swamp to Capital City

Nairobi used to be a swampy place. But this swamp would one day become the capital city of Kenya in East Africa. The name Nairobi comes from a water hole that the Masai people of Kenya called Enkare Nairobi. Enkare Nairobi means 'cold water'.

In the late 1890s, the British established a settlement there while building a railway across southern Kenya. This railway still runs through Nairobi. It connects Lake Victoria, on the border with Uganda, to Mombasa, Kenya's major **port** on the Indian Ocean. When the British took control of Kenya in 1905, Nairobi was made its capital city. Under British rule, Nairobi grew into a trading centre and a large city. It remained the capital when Kenya became free from the British in 1963.

A mosque in Nairobi.
© Stephen Frink/Corbis

DID YOU KNOW?
Nairobi is the largest city between Johannesburg, South Africa, in the far south of the continent, and Cairo, Egypt, in northern Africa.

Today Nairobi is an important centre for education. The University of Nairobi and its Kenyatta University College are among the major schools in the city. Visitors go to see the National Museum of Kenya, McMillan Memorial Library, and Kenya National Theatre. The **tourism** industry is important to the city's economy.

Just a few miles south of the city is Nairobi National Park. It's a large beautiful park set aside to protect the area's wild animals. It was the first such park established in Kenya. Tourists go to see the park's lions, black rhinoceroses, gazelles, giraffes, antelope, and zebras, as well as hundreds of kinds of birds. Near the main gate is a small zoo. Keepers there take care of baby elephants and black rhinoceroses.

SEARCH LIGHT

Enkare Nairobi means
a) swampy place.
b) cold water.
c) hot city.

Once just a swamp, Nairobi is now a large city with modern buildings.
© Adrian Arbib/Corbis

Answer: b) cold water.

An Island Paradise

The Republic of Seychelles is a country made up of about 115 islands in the Indian Ocean off the east coast of Africa. Victoria is its capital city and the only shipping port. It lies on Mahé, the country's largest island.

Victoria

The Seychelles is made up of two main island groups. The Mahé group has 40 islands. These islands are rocky and hilly, with narrow strips of coastline. The other group consists of low islands built up from the rock-hard skeletons of countless coral animals. These coral islands have almost no water, and very few people live on them.

Mahé is home to the great majority of the country's people. Most of the people are Creole, with a mixture of Asian, African, and European heritage. The French and then the British used to rule the islands. The Seychelles was given its independence by Britain in 1976. Creole, English, and French are all national languages.

The islands have very little good farmland. Tree products such as coconuts and cinnamon bark are the main crops. Fishing is a very important industry. The people catch the fish, pack them into cans, and ship them around the world.

The islands are especially rich in beautiful **tropical** scenery. Coconut palm trees grow along the coast on most of the islands. Giant tortoises and green sea turtles live along the coasts. Sharks are found in the ocean. The seafaring frigate bird spends time on the islands. Tourism is the Seychelles' biggest industry, with visitors attracted by the country's beaches, wildlife, and greenery.

SEARCH LIGHT

About how many islands make up the Republic of Seychelles?

The rocky islands of the Seychelles are rugged and beautiful.
© Nik Wheeler/Corbis

DID YOU KNOW?
The coco de mer, or double coconut tree, is found only in the Seychelles. Its nut can weigh almost 25 kilos and is the largest seed in the world.

Answer: The country consists of about 115 islands.

Seaside Somalian Capital

Mogadishu is the capital of Somalia, a country in eastern Africa. The city lies along the Indian Ocean. Mogadishu is a major port. It is also the largest city in the country.

A big part of the city is in ruins today. It is hard to think that at one time Mogadishu was a lively city with bright whitewashed walls. There were beautiful **mosques** topped by tall towers called 'minarets'. But years of internal fighting in Somalia have left the city a ghost of its former self.

Schoolchildren listen to a lesson in a classroom in Mogadishu.
© David Turnley/Corbis

Arab settlers from the Persian Gulf set up the city in about the 10th century. The city traded goods with the Arab states, the Portuguese, and the leaders of Muscat (Oman) in the Middle East. The city's trade grew to include Persia, India, and China. During that time the city grew wealthy and powerful. In the 16th century, the Portuguese saw the success of the city and wanted to own it. But they were never able to take it over. In the late 19th century, Italy was in charge of the city.

In 1960 Mogadishu became the capital of Somalia. By that time Somalia was independent. Building began in the new city. The style of the old buildings and mosques mixed well with the style of the new ones.

But a **civil war** broke out in Somalia starting in the 1980s. Many people died during the fighting, and there was damage everywhere.

DID YOU KNOW?
Mogadishu's prominent location has made it a port of call for many travellers. In the early 15th century, the famous Chinese admiral Zheng He stopped there on three of his voyages throughout the Indian Ocean.

SEARCH LIGHT

Find and correct the mistake in the following sentence: Mogadishu, the capital of Somalia, is a young city.

Answer: Mogadishu, the capital of Somalia, is an old city.

Kampala

City on the Hill of Antelopes

Kampala is the capital and largest city of Uganda, a country of East Africa. It lies in the southern part of the country, north of Lake Victoria. Kampala spreads over a number of hills. The rulers of the powerful Buganda kingdom of the 1800s kept antelope on the slopes. In the local language, Kampala means 'the hill of antelopes'.

Buganda came under the control of the British in the 1890s. The British chose Kampala as the site of their headquarters. For a while they controlled all of what is now Uganda from a fort on Old Kampala Hill. When Uganda gained independence from Great Britain in 1962, Kampala became the capital.

Kampala is Uganda's centre for business. It lies on **fertile** farmland and is the main market for the Lake Victoria region. Coffee, cotton, tea, tobacco, and sugar are sold there. And most of Uganda's large companies have their offices in the city.

Kampala serves as the religious centre for Uganda as well. Some well-known Christian churches in the city include the Namirembe Anglican **Cathedral** and Rubaga and St Peter's Roman Catholic cathedrals. Kampala's many **mosques** include the white Kibuli Mosque. It also has Hindu temples.

If you ever visit Kampala, make sure to go to the Uganda Museum. It has a collection of historical musical instruments that you can play. You'll also find a number of art galleries in the city. Northeast of Kampala, a place called Nyero is famous for a different kind of art. There you can see rock paintings that date back hundreds of years. No one knows for sure who made them.

SEARCH LIGHT

Fill in the gap: Kampala is built on a series of _____.

DID YOU KNOW?

The Kasubi Tombs, on a hill overlooking Kampala, are the burial place of the kings of the Buganda kingdom.

Ugandans shop for bananas at a market in Kampala. The city lies within Uganda's most important farming region.
© David and Peter Turnley/Corbis

Answer: Kampala is built on a series of hills.

Desert Land on the Sea

Algiers

Algeria is a country on the north coast of Africa. It is the 2nd largest country in Africa and the 11th largest country in the world. The country's capital is Algiers.

The northern part of Algeria is on the Mediterranean Sea. This area is known as the Tell. Two mountain ranges separate the coastal area in the north from the Sahara in the south. About four-fifths of Algeria's land lies within the Sahara, the largest desert in the world. Two huge sandy areas known as 'ergs' cover most of Algeria's desert. Not much grows on the desert's surface. But there are valuable minerals, **oil**, and gas underground.

Rainfall is very rare in the desert. At times, areas in the Sahara get no rain for years. There are also dry streambeds known as *wadi*s in the desert. If it rains, the *wadi*s quickly fill with water.

Most of Algeria's people live in the northern part of the country, where the climate is mild. That area receives enough water from rivers and rainfall to water the crops and provide people with water for drinking and industry. The people in Algeria are mostly Arabs, but many are Berbers. The ancestors of the Berbers lived in the area before the Arabs arrived.

Algeria was a French colony for more than 100 years. Hundreds of thousands of French people settled there. After a war against the French, the Algerians gained their independence in 1962. Most of the French then left the country.

SEARCH LIGHT

A *wadi* is a
a) northern part of the country.
b) dry streambed.
c) wide field of sand.

DID YOU KNOW?

The name Sahara comes from the Arabic word *sahra*, which means 'desert'.

This trans-Saharan highway winds through the desert in Algeria. Historically, travelling through the Sahara was very slow and dangerous. But year by year modern roadways have been extended farther along the ancient trade routes into the desert.

© Robert Holmes/Corbis

Answer: b) dry streambed.

The Pharaohs and the Pyramids

Nearly 5,000 years ago there was a kingdom by the Nile River in a place called Egypt. The king was known as the pharaoh. People thought of him as a god.

The people of Egypt developed a great **civilization**. They built ships and sailed to other countries. They made great buildings. They carved and painted lovely pictures. And they developed a system of writing.

Three Egyptian kings - Khufu, his son Khafre, and his grandson Menkure - each ordered the people to build him a pyramid. The pyramids were to be the kings' **tombs**. A pyramid is a large structure with a square base and four sides shaped like triangles. The sides slope upward and meet in a point at the top.

After a king died, his body was carefully prepared and wrapped in many layers of cloth. (A body prepared in this way is called a 'mummy'.) Then it was placed in a splendid coffin that was placed in a room in the middle of the pyramid. The Egyptians believed in an afterlife. So they put all the pharaoh's treasures in the room too, for him to use in the afterlife. After that, the doors were sealed with stones.

The pyramids of the pharaohs can still be seen today. They stand by the Nile River near a town called Giza. The first pyramid to be built is perhaps the largest structure ever made by people. It is called the Great Pyramid. The other two pyramids stand beside it. It took thousands of workers many years to build the pyramids. But since the Egyptians had no heavy machinery, no one knows exactly how they were built.

DID YOU KNOW?
More than 2 million blocks of stone had to be cut, transported, and assembled to create the Great Pyramid.

In ancient times the pyramids built near Giza, Egypt, were counted among the Seven Wonders of the World.

© Larry Lee Photography/Corbis

SEARCH LIGHT

Fill in the gap: Three kings of Egypt ordered that giant _____ be built to use as their tombs.

Answer: Three kings of Egypt ordered that giant pyramids be built to use as their tombs.

Joining Two Seas for a Shortcut

The Suez Canal is one of the most important waterways that people have ever made. The **canal** is located in Egypt. It joins the Mediterranean Sea and the Red Sea and separates the continents of Africa and Asia. It offers the shortest route for ships sailing between Europe and the lands on the Indian and western Pacific oceans, such as Australia and large parts of Asia. Before the canal was built, ships travelling between these parts of the world had to sail all the way around Africa.

Watching a ship pass through the Suez Canal.
© David & Peter Turnley/Corbis

Beginning about 3,900 years ago, people dug several canals roughly in the area of the Suez Canal. But none of them joined the Mediterranean and Red seas directly. The Suez Canal was created by joining a series of lakes across the **Isthmus** of Suez to form one long water passage between the two seas.

The Suez Canal has eight major bends. In some places it has been widened to form double channels called 'bypasses'. These allow ships travelling in opposite directions to pass each other. In the canal ships travel in groups and follow rules to prevent accidents. Each ship moves at a set speed, leaving a fixed gap between it and the next ship in the group. This keeps the ships from knocking against each other. A tugboat follows each large ship. The entire trip takes between 12 and 18 hours.

SEARCH LIGHT

Fill in the gaps:
The Suez Canal joins the _____ Sea with the _____ Sea.

On average, 50 ships cross through the Suez Canal each day. Nearly 20,000 trips are made in a year. Most of the vessels using the canal are small tankers and cargo ships, though some passenger liners and warships also use the waterway.

Cargo ships like this one make up a large part of the traffic in the Suez Canal.
Hubertus Kauns/Superstock

DID YOU KNOW?

By taking the Suez Canal shortcut, a ship travelling from London, England, to Bombay, India, cuts more than 8,000 kilometres off its trip.

Answer: The Suez Canal joins the Mediterranean Sea with the Red Sea.

Oil Country of Africa

Libya was once a poor country. Then in 1959 petroleum, or crude **oil**, was discovered in the desert. This made Libya one of the richest countries in North Africa. Some of the largest oil deposits in the world are in Libya. The capital city of Libya is Tripoli. It is located on the coast of the Mediterranean Sea and is one of Libya's major ports.

Libya has three main regions: the Sahara, Tripolitania, and Cyrenaica. The largest is the desert land of the Sahara, which is one of the driest places on Earth. There are very few plants in the Sahara. However, date palms grow in the oases, such as those found around the town of Sabha. An oasis is a **fertile** place in the desert where water can be found. Most Libyans live in Tripolitania, in the north-west. Many of the people keep sheep and goats. They also grow barley, wheat, tobacco, dates, figs, grapes, and olives. In Cyrenaica, in the north-east, the Akhdar Mountains and some oases are the main features.

Many people in Libya identify themselves with traditional tribes, or *qabilah*s. The Berbers, the original people of Libya, were mostly coastal farmers. Today, however, most Libyans have a mixed Berber and Arabic **heritage**.

Libya became an independent country in 1951. It was ruled by a king until 1969. In that year a group of army officers led by Muammar al-Qaddafi took control of the country. Many people outside Libya have criticized Qaddafi for supporting terrorists and using his army to attack other countries.

SEARCH LIGHT

Libya has been a much wealthier country since
a) oil was discovered.
b) gold was discovered.
c) water was discovered.

A lake lined with palm trees forms an oasis in the Libyan desert.
Doug McKinlay/Lonely Planet Images

DID YOU KNOW?
The highest temperature ever recorded on Earth was measured at Al-Aziziyah, Libya. One day in September 1922, the temperature soared to 58°C.

Answer: a) oil was discovered.

Built for Victory

★ Rabat

Rabat is the capital city of Morocco, a country in North Africa. It is located on the coast of the Atlantic Ocean. Modern Rabat has a rich mixture of cultures reflecting African, Arab, Islamic, and French influences.

Rabat has ancient roots. The city started out almost 900 years ago as a camp for Muslims who wanted to sail across the sea to fight in Spain. Later, the camp was named Ribat al-Fath, which means 'camp of victory'. A wall was built to protect the camp. Within the wall the city of Rabat began to grow.

Large parts of the old wall are still standing. Within them are the old town and the Jewish quarter. The Oudia Gate and the Tower of Hassan also stand as impressive monuments of the past.

France and Spain each controlled sections of Morocco for part of the 20th century. The country gained its independence in 1956. Rabat now houses government offices, universities, and art schools. The king of Morocco lives in Rabat for part of the year.

It's a short ride by road or rail to Casablanca, which is Morocco's largest city and its chief port. Like Rabat, it was once a base for pirates who attacked European ships. The Portuguese put a stop to the piracy in 1468. They later built a new town in the area called Casa Branca. The French called it Maison Blanche, and the Spanish called it Casablanca. All these names mean the same thing: 'white house'.

SEARCH LIGHT

What ruler lives in the city of Rabat today?

A wall built hundreds of years ago still surrounds part of the city of Rabat.
© Nik Wheeler/Corbis

DID YOU KNOW?
The name Rabat comes from the Arabic word *ribat*. That word is often translated as 'camp' but can also mean 'monastery'. In North Africa it refers to a place were Muslim soldiers would gather either to study or to prepare for holy war.

452

Giant of Africa

The largest country in Africa is the Sudan. It is the tenth largest country in the world. The Sudan is located in north-eastern Africa. Khartoum is the capital city. It sits at the point where the Blue Nile and White Nile rivers join together to form the mighty Nile River. The Sudan is one of the hottest places in the world. In Khartoum temperatures higher than 38°C may be recorded during any month of the year.

There are 19 major **ethnic** groups in the Sudan. More than 100 languages and **dialects** are spoken in the country. Many of the people either farm or rear camels and cattle. Roughly 10 per cent of the people live as **nomads**. Amongst all groups poetry and song are respected art forms. Both often reflect the country's mixed Arab and African **heritage**.

In 1956 the Sudan gained its independence from the United Kingdom. But fighting broke out almost immediately. The people living in southern Sudan opposed the new government, which was controlled by northerners. The southerners are typically black Africans who practise traditional African religions or Christianity. The northerners are typically of mixed ethnic origins. They speak a version of Arabic and practise Islam. The fighting continued until 1972, when the southerners were given control of their local government. But war broke out again in 1983. In 2002, the two sides agreed to stop the war, but fighting continued in some parts of the country.

SEARCH LIGHT

Fill in the gaps: Fighting in the Sudan has been mainly between people living in the _____ and people living in the _____.

DID YOU KNOW?
The name 'Sudan' comes from the Arabic term *bilad al-sudan*, which means 'land of the blacks'. This term was once used to describe all settled African lands south of the Sahara (a large desert in northern Africa).

Sudanese men rest on a wall near their camels, which are considered a symbol of wealth. Many people in the Sudan raise camels for their milk and meat as well as for transportation.
© Jonathan Blair/Corbis

Land of Oil and Diamonds

Angola is a large country on the south-western coast of Africa. The Atlantic Ocean is its western boundary. Four countries shape its borders on land. Its capital is Luanda, a large city on the coast.

Luanda

Most of Angola is a high **plateau** covered by savannahs, which are open grasslands with scattered trees. Roaming this land are leopards, lions, hyenas, elephants, and hippopotamuses. You may also see giraffes, zebras, and monkeys. With such rich wildlife, Angola has many national parks and nature **reserves**. However, some of the animals are in danger of disappearing because of hunting and other reasons. These animals include elephants, gorillas, chimpanzees, and black rhinoceroses.

The two largest groups of people in Angola are the Ovimbundu and the Mbundu. These two groups, and others, speak different languages that together are called Bantu languages. Almost all of the people also speak Portuguese, the country's official language.

Angola has many natural resources. Two of them - oil and diamonds - are major parts of the country's **economy**. Angola sells these products to other countries. But more people work in farming than in any other job. They grow **cassava**, maize, sugarcane, bananas, and coffee. In the south-west they rear cattle.

SEARCH LIGHT

Portuguese explorers reached Angola in 1483. Over time, the Portuguese developed a **colony**. They ruled for almost 500 years. During much of this time, the Portuguese sent millions of Africans away from the colony to work as slaves. After years of fighting the Portuguese, Angola finally won its independence in 1975. But afterward the country struggled off and on with fighting inside its borders.

How were the Portuguese able to take control of Angola and stay in power there? (Hint: What would the Portuguese have brought with them to fight with?)

DID YOU KNOW?
Angola is rich in tropical woods such as mahogany, rosewood, and black ebony. These woods are used to make fine furniture.

An Angolan woman wears traditional dress.
Giacomo Pirozzi/Panos Pictures

Answer: In the 15th century, when Portugal conquered Angola, the Bantu-speaking peoples didn't have guns or cannons. The Portuguese had both.

The Jewel of the Kalahari

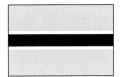

Botswana was once one of the poorest countries in Africa. It used to be called Bechuanaland. After gaining independence from Great Britain in 1966, it was renamed Botswana. The new name came from that of the main group of people living there, the Tswana, or Batswana. In 1967 large **deposits** of diamonds were discovered in the region. Suddenly Botswana was one of Africa's richest countries.

Botswana is located in southern Africa. Its capital city is Gabarone. Most of the country's area is a dry region called the Kalahari. This is known as the sandveld, or 'thirstland'. The thirstland is different from a true desert because it has some grass and trees. In eastern Botswana there are rocky ranges of hills.

In the north-west is the Okavango River, which flows in from Namibia. It has been called 'the river that never finds the sea' because it ends in Botswana instead of flowing into the ocean. The place where it ends is called the Okavango **delta**. This huge swampy area has thick clumps of **papyrus** and much wildlife, including lions, hippopotamuses, and zebras. Many of the animals are protected in the Moremi Wildlife Reserve.

Botswana has forests in the north and east. Some of the trees produce fruits such as the marula or nuts such as the mongongo, which are important to the diet of the local people. Their diet also includes beans, meat, and **porridge** made with sorghum or maize. Some people eat dried caterpillars as a snack!

SEARCH LIGHT

Why did Botswana become one of Africa's wealthiest countries?

DID YOU KNOW?
The San people of the Kalahari speak an unusual language. It's called a 'click language' because it has many clicking sounds as parts of words. It is nearly impossible to speak that language if you don't learn it while you are growing up.

Many people in Botswana live in small towns and villages such as this one in the Okavango delta region of the country.
© Yann Arthus-Bertrand/Corbis

Answer: Diamonds were discovered in Botswana.

Island Sanctuary

The Republic of Madagascar lies more than 400 kilometres off the south-eastern coast of Africa in the Indian Ocean. It occupies the fourth largest island in the world; only Greenland, New Guinea, and Borneo are larger. The capital of Madagascar is Antananarivo. It is located in the centre of the country.

Antananarivo

Even though Madagascar is so close to Africa, its people are not mainly African. The first people to live on the island were Malagasy people from Indonesia, almost 5,000 kilometres to the east. They arrived in about AD 700. People from Africa, Europe, and other parts of Southeast Asia came later. The people of Madagascar are still called Malagasy, but today their culture is a unique mix of Asian and African influences.

About half of the Malagasy follow Christianity. Most of the rest practise a traditional religion that has been passed down through the years. These people believe that the dead can reward or punish the living. They bury the dead in richly decorated tombs. They spend more time, money, and care on building tombs than they do on their houses.

For thousands of years Madagascar was covered with forests. But over time most of the trees have been cut down to make room for rice fields. The loss of the forests has been difficult for many of the animals of Madagascar - especially the lemurs. Lemurs look something like monkeys with long bushy tails. They are found in the wild only in Madagascar and on nearby islands. Madagascar also has many unique kinds of birds, chameleons, and butterflies. There are about 800 types of butterflies alone!

Rice fields line a hillside in Madagascar.
© Chris Hellier/Corbis

SEARCH LIGHT

Where did the first people to live in Madagascar come from?

DID YOU KNOW?
The coelacanth, a fish thought to have been extinct for 60 million years, was found in the waters near Madagascar in the 1900s. Such animals are sometimes called 'living fossils' because their appearance and other physical traits have not changed for millions of years.

Answer: The first people to live in Madagascar came from Indonesia.

On Malawi's
Fertile Plains

The capital of Malawi, a country in southern Africa, is Lilongwe. It is largely a planned city. It was not founded until 1947, when it was established as a trading centre. The city is in the central part of the country. In the late 1960s the leaders of Malawi decided to try to develop this central area of the country further. As part of their plan, they moved the capital from Zomba to Lilongwe in 1975.

In addition to being a government centre, Lilongwe provides a market for local farmers to sell their crops. Some of the country's best farmland surrounds Lilongwe. This region produces tobacco, the main crop that Malawi sells to other countries. In Lilongwe you can visit the tobacco auction floors, where large amounts of tobacco are sold.

The city has two main sections, the old city and Capital Hill. The old city has the central market, cafés, and restaurants. People go there regularly to shop. The newer part of the city, on Capital Hill, has government buildings, hotels, and **embassies**. Between the two sections of the city is a nature sanctuary, which provides protection for the native animals and plants. The sanctuary covers about 148 hectares and is home to many different kinds of birds.

Because of its central location, many people travel through Lilongwe on their way to other parts of the country. The city has an international airport. It also has rail connections to Salima in the east and the Zambian border on the west.

DID YOU KNOW?
Although it is Malawi's capital, Lilongwe is only the second largest city in the country. Blantyre, in the south, is the largest city in Malawi and also the main centre of industry and commerce.

Tobacco is sold at an auction in Lilongwe. The city is the centre of Malawi's tobacco processing and trading industries. Malawi is one of Africa's top tobacco producers.

David Else/Lonely Planet Images

SEARCH LIGHT

Find and correct the mistake in the following sentence: Lilongwe is where coffee, the country's main crop, is sold.

Answer: Lilongwe is where tobacco, the country's main crop, is sold.

Namibia's Windy Corner

Windhoek is the capital city of Namibia, a country in southern Africa. The city lies at a height of more than 1,654 metres. It is surrounded by a ring of hills. These hills protect it from the most violent of the dry winds blowing in from the Kalahari Desert to the east and the Namib Desert to the west. The city's name comes from a German word that means 'windy corner'. Windhoek is free of fiercely blowing winds for less than four months of the year.

The Herero and Khoekhoe peoples were among the first settlers in the region. Before the Europeans arrived, the city was called Aigams. This name means 'hot water' and referred to the **hot springs** in the area. Germany claimed the town for itself in 1890. South Africa took over the region, then known as South West Africa, 25 years later. When Namibia became independent in 1990, Windhoek was made the nation's capital.

Windhoek is also the country's chief economic centre. It sits in the middle of the grazing lands of the Karakul sheep. The skins of very young Karakul lambs are processed and transported by a number of furriers in Windhoek. This business employs many people in the city.

Windhoek has several interesting places and buildings to visit. The Alte Feste (Old Fort), built by the Germans, is one of the oldest buildings in the city. It is now a history museum. Christuskirche is an attractive church that was also built during German colonial times. And the city's St George's Cathedral is the smallest functional **cathedral** in southern Africa.

SEARCH LIGHT

Among the area's first residents were
a) Germans and South Africans.
b) Aigams and Namib.
c) Herero and Khoekhoe.

DID YOU KNOW?
The country's first university, the University of Namibia, was founded in Windhoek in 1992.

These buildings on a street in Windhoek display a mixture of styles, some modern and some from the time when Germany controlled the town.
© Royalty-Free/Corbis

Answer: c) Herero and Khoekhoe.

A People Apart

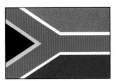

For several hundred years, most of South Africa's people had few freedoms. There are four main groups of South Africans today: black Africans, white Africans, people whose families came from India, and people of mixed origins. The whites make up a fairly small number of the country's people. But for a long time they held all the power. Non - whites had many of their basic rights taken away.

In the 1650s, the Dutch set up the first permanent European settlement in South Africa. The British and Dutch fought for control over the area during the 1800s. In 1910 the British established the Union of South Africa. Black Africans, the **majority** of the population, were not allowed to vote or hold political office.

In 1948 the government introduced a policy called apartheid. The word apartheid means 'apartness' in the Dutch language of Afrikaans. This policy gave most of the country's land to white people. Black Africans and other nonwhites were forced to live in separate areas and could enter areas where whites lived only if they had a pass. They had separate and worse schools and could hold only certain jobs. They could not vote or take part in government.

One of the leaders in the fight against apartheid was Nelson Mandela. Because of this, the government jailed him from 1962 to 1990. But black Africans continued to support Mandela. The country began to do away with apartheid in 1990. Mandela became South Africa's president in 1991, and he became a symbol of freedom throughout the world. The country's laws now support equal rights for everyone. But South Africa is still recovering from the effects of the many years of apartheid.

SEARCH LIGHT

Find and correct the mistake in the following sentence: Under apartheid, most of South Africa's land was reserved for nonwhites.

President Nelson Mandela celebrates with a choir after signing South Africa's new constitution in December 1996. The constitution promised equal rights for all of the country's people.
© Charles O'Rear/Corbis

DID YOU KNOW?
Mahatma Gandhi led his first political protest in South Africa. Before Gandhi began fighting for India's independence from Britain, he lived for a time in South Africa. He helped the Indians who lived there fight for their rights.

Answer: Under apartheid, most of South Africa's land was reserved for whites.

City in a Garden

Harare is the capital of the African country of Zimbabwe. It lies on a broad high ridge called the Highveld in the country's north-eastern garden region. Harare is green with trees and bright with flowers.

The city was founded in 1890. It was named Salisbury after Lord Salisbury, the British prime minister. As with much of southern Africa, Zimbabwe came under British rule in the late 1890s. The city developed only after 1899, when a railway line was established from the port of Beira in Mozambique to the east.

There were many industries that were started in Salisbury after World War II. People started moving into this city, and gradually the population grew. The city itself is modern and well planned, with high-rise buildings and tree-lined avenues.

In 1980 the new government of independent Zimbabwe renamed the city Harare. This honoured Chief Neharawe, who originally occupied this area with his people. The word Harare means 'one that does not sleep' in the Shona language.

Harare is still the centre of Zimbabwe's industry and **commerce**. It is the main place where crops from the surrounding farmlands are received and then distributed. There are also important gold mines nearby.

The University of Zimbabwe is located in Harare. The city is also home to the National Archives, which displays historical documents. At the National Gallery of Zimbabwe you can see an impressive collection of African painting and sculpture. And every year the city holds the Harare International Festival of the Arts. At this festival you can see all kinds of artistic performances, from traditional dancing and drumming to the plays of William Shakespeare.

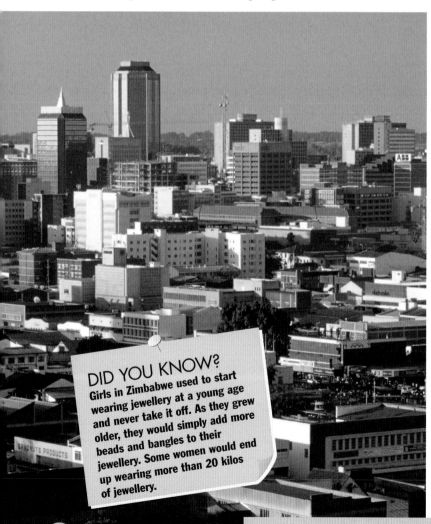

DID YOU KNOW?
Girls in Zimbabwe used to start wearing jewellery at a young age and never take it off. As they grew older, they would simply add more beads and bangles to their jewellery. Some women would end up wearing more than 20 kilos of jewellery.

SEARCH LIGHT

Harare is located on the
a) high seas.
b) Highveld.
c) highway.

Modern high-rise buildings loom over the city of Harare, Zimbabwe.
Richard I'Anson/Lonely Planet Images

Answer: b) Highveld.

From North to South America, explore the great variety of the Western Hemisphere

Views of the Americas

Views of the Americas
TABLE OF CONTENTS

Britannica®
LEARNING LIBRARY

Have a great trip!

Land of Plenty

Morning light on Mount Rushmore, South Dakota, U.S.
© Paul A. Souders/Corbis

North America is the third largest continent. Three countries - Canada, the United States, and Mexico - make up most of it. The countries of Central America are also usually considered part of North America. They occupy a narrow strip of land that connects North America to South America. Several islands, including Greenland in the north and the West Indies in the south, are part of North America too.

Because it's so large, the continent has many different types of climate. Most of Greenland is covered with ice all the time - even in summer. But the southern islands and countries are usually hot and humid. In between there are both deserts and rainy areas, but most places have warm summers and cold winters.

North America is rich in **natural resources**. Forests cover a large part of the land. The **fertile** soils of Canada, the United States, and Mexico produce large amounts of maize, cotton, soybeans, tobacco, wheat, and other crops. The continent is also rich in minerals such as coal, iron ore, copper, natural gas, **oil**, and silver.

The history of the continent goes back thousands of years. Scientists believe that people from Asia crossed over to Alaska more than 20,000 years ago and then moved southward. Their **descendants** eventually established great civilizations, such as that of the Maya in Central America and the Aztec in Mexico. The first Europeans in the region were the Vikings, who settled in Greenland in about the 900s. It wasn't until 1492 that explorers from other parts of Europe began to arrive.

COUNTRIES OF NORTH AMERICA
1. Canada
2. Greenland
3. Mexico
4. United States
5. West Indies
6. Central America*

*Countries of Central America are Belize, Costa Rica, El Salvador, Guatemala, Honduras, Nicaragua, and Panama (see page 473) U.S. state of Hawaii off map

DID YOU KNOW?
More dinosaur fossils have been found in North America than on any other continent.

Dzoonokwa Totem Pole in Thunderbird Park, Victoria, British Columbia, Canada.
© Gunter Marx Photography/Corbis

Answer: c) Asians

Frozen Island

Greenland is the world's largest island. It sits in the North Atlantic Ocean between Iceland (to the east) and the islands of the Canadian north (to the west). Most of Greenland lies within the Arctic Circle. Its northern tip is only 800 kilometres from the North Pole. The capital city is Nuuk.

Greenland is almost entirely covered in ice. In some places the ice is 3,000 metres thick. Some of the ice is so deep that it is actually below the level of the sea around the island. The people live on the seacoast highlands that are free of ice. Greenland's open land is called 'tundra'. It has very few trees, and grasses, grass-like plants called 'sedges', and moss-like lichens are the main plants.

The weather in Greenland is cold and may change quickly from sunshine to blizzards. Normal winter temperatures are –6°C in the south and –33°C in the north. Even in the warmest parts of the island, summer temperatures hover around 7°C.

Aside from people, only seven kinds of **mammals** brave Greenland's cold weather on land. They are polar bears, musk oxen, reindeer, arctic foxes, snow hares, ermines, and lemmings. Seals and whales gather in the ocean waters, and Greenlanders once depended on them for food. Nowadays they are more likely to fish for cod, salmon, flounder, and halibut.

Nuuk

SEARCH LIGHT

Most of Greenland's surface is covered by
a) rice.
b) ice.
c) trees.

Most Greenlanders are of Inuit (Eskimo) **heritage**. They moved there from North America between 4000 BC and AD 1000. In the early 1700s Denmark **colonized** Greenland, and the Danes still control it today.

DID YOU KNOW?

The first European settlement in Greenland was founded in 986 by the Viking explorer Erik the Red. About 15 years later, his son Leif Eriksson sailed west from Greenland and became one of the first Europeans to reach North America.

Fishing boats are moored in a harbour in Sisimiut, Greenland.
© Deanna Swaney/Lonely Planet Images

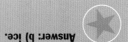

Answer: b) ice.

The Land of Long Winters

Canada is the second largest country in the world in terms of land size, after Russia. But it has fewer people than many other countries that are much smaller. This is because much of Canada is a very cold place with long winters. In the northern islands it is often freezing cold even in summer.

Canada has a low **population** for its size. It is one of the world's wealthier countries. Much of the country's wealth lies in its many mines and forests. Minerals such as coal, copper, nickel, and iron ore are found in the mines. Farming is also very important. Canada grows a large amount of grain. It sells a lot of wheat and other products to other countries.

Most Canadians live in towns and cities. Toronto is the largest city in Canada. If you went there, you could see one of the world's tallest structures, the CN Tower, soaring above the skyline. Montreal is one of Canada's oldest cities and has many historical buildings. It also has an important seaport, even though it is nearly 1,500 kilometres from the Atlantic Ocean!

Canada's official languages are English and French. But many other languages are spoken there, including Inukitut (the language of the Inuit, or Eskimos) and other Canadian Indian languages. Canadian Indians are also known as First Nations people.

If you visit Canada, you should try to see Niagara Falls. These beautiful waterfalls, on the border between Canada and the United States, were once one of the most famous honeymoon spots in North America.

SEARCH LIGHT

What is the only country larger than Canada?

DID YOU KNOW?
Churchill, Manitoba, on Hudson Bay, is sometimes called 'the polar bear capital of the world'. Every fall thousands of bears gather along the shore, waiting for the bay to freeze so that they can walk out onto the ice to hunt seals.

Banff National Park in Alberta is one of Canada's major tourist destinations.
© David Muench/Corbis

Answer: Russia.

A Welcoming Northern Capital

Ottawa, the capital of Canada, is one of the country's most attractive cities. It is located on the south side of the Ottawa River in the province of Ontario. Across the river is the province of Quebec.

Since Ottawa is the centre of the country's government, it is the public face of Canada for many people. The city has been kept lovely and welcoming. It has many parks and rivers, bicycle paths, museums, art galleries, and universities. Some of Ottawa's historic buildings go back to the early 1800s. The Château Laurier is one of these. It is a house built in the style of a grand French **château**. Behind it rises Major's Hill Park, Ottawa's oldest park. This is the best place to view the city and to see up and down the Ottawa River.

Dozens of different languages are spoken in Ottawa. But most people speak either French or English, the official languages of Canada.

Château Laurier, Ottawa, Ontario.
© Richard T. Nowitz/Corbis

Many years ago French explorers and hunters travelled through the area that is now Ottawa. Only a few people lived there until the early 1800s. By that time the British ruled the territory. They decided they wanted a route for their ships to be able to travel from the Ottawa River to Lake Ontario, so they built the Rideau Canal. The city of Ottawa began as a base for the workers who built the **canal**. It was called Bytown then but later became Ottawa. It became the capital of Canada in the mid-1800s.

DID YOU KNOW?
The city of Ottawa was named after an Indian group that once lived in the region. The Ottawa were known as great traders. The name Ottawa means 'to trade' or 'the at-home-anywhere people'.

SEARCH LIGHT

Find and correct the mistake in the following sentence: French and Canadian are the official languages of Canada.

The Rideau Canal in Ottawa is the world's longest outdoor ice-skating rink.
© Cheryl Conlon/Lonely Planet Images

Answer: French and English are the official languages of Canada.

La Belle Province

Quebec is both the oldest and the largest in land area of Canada's ten provinces. It's the home of two attractive port cities and a countryside that is covered with forests, rivers, and lakes. No wonder it's known in French as La Belle Province, 'the beautiful province'.

Quebec City is the capital of Quebec province and the oldest city in Canada. It lies at the point where the St Lawrence and Saint-Charles rivers meet.

Ice cream sign written in French and English, in Quebec City.
© Richard T. Nowitz/Corbis

The name Quebec comes from the Algonquian Indian word for 'where the river narrows'. About 240 kilometres southwest of Quebec City is Montreal, the largest city in the province. It's also Canada's second largest city.

The first European to visit the area was Jacques Cartier of France. In 1534 he landed at the site of a Huron Indian village. But it was another 70 years before the French settled in the area. In 1608 Samuel de Champlain founded the city of Quebec, establishing the first permanent **colony** in the region. It served as a fur-trading post for beaver, mink, and other pelts.

During the next 150 years, the French and British fought over Quebec and Montreal. Eventually, a treaty in 1763 granted the area to the British. During the American Revolution, the American colonists tried to seize control of the area. But the British held onto it.

Eight out of every ten people in Quebec are of French **ancestry**. Because of this, both French and English are spoken in Quebec. The people of the province also practice different religions. Generally, the people of French origins are Roman Catholic and those of English origins are Protestant.

DID YOU KNOW?
The Magdalen Islands in the Gulf of St Lawrence are one of Quebec's most popular vacation spots. People come to see the islands' many birds and mammals, especially the seals, who arrive every spring to have their young.

There are many beautiful buildings in the Old Quebec historic area of Quebec City. The historic hotel Château Frontenac towers over the area.
© Ron Watts/Corbis

Answer: It's an Algonquian Indian word for 'where the river narrows'.

Melting Pot of Many Cultures

Dear Class,

We are in Boston, on the north-eastern coast of the United States, visiting my brother Rex after a few busy days of sightseeing. We've already been to New York City and Niagara Falls. Later we're going to take a look at the Grand Canyon, Hollywood, and Disneyland. Rex teaches history in one of the universities here. He's invited some of his friends to meet us. One of them is from Austria, and another is from Poland. The rest are from Japan, India, and Italy. I tell him that I'm confused. 'Don't you have any American friends?' I ask Rex.

He laughs. 'They're all Americans.'

Helmut, his friend from Austria, says, 'Didn't you know that America has people from all over the world?'

'That's why people often describe America as a "melting pot" of many cultures,' says Tajima, from Japan.

'People come here for many reasons. Some become citizens. But students from all over the world also come here to study. I have students from Indonesia, Australia, Iran, and even Iceland in my college,' says Rex.

'But who were the first to come here?'

Rex's Indian friend, Samir, says the first people who came here were from Asia, more than 20,000 years ago. The American Indians (Native Americans) are their **descendants**. About 500 years ago, Spanish settlers arrived from Europe. Other Europeans followed - from England, Ireland, and Germany and then from Italy, Poland, Russia, Sweden, Greece, and elsewhere. People from Africa were first brought over as slaves. People from every corner of the world have made America what it is today.

Tonight we're going out for a Lebanese meal. I can't wait!

Your classmate,

Lydia

Italian immigrants arriving at New York's Ellis Island.
© Bettmann/Corbis

SEARCH LIGHT

Fill in the gap with the correct phrase: When people call America a 'melting pot', they mean people from _____ live there.

DID YOU KNOW?
Christopher Columbus often gets credit as having been the first European in the Americas. But many researchers believe he was about 500 years too late. They think Leif Ericson, the Viking explorer, landed in North America first.

New U.S. citizens recite the Pledge of Allegiance during a ceremony held in Orange Bowl Stadium in Miami, Florida.
© Bettmann/Corbis

Answer: When people call America a 'melting pot', they mean people from all over the world live there.

Crossroads
of the Pacific

It is said that no place on Earth has better weather than Honolulu. In the course of an entire year, the temperature rarely gets below 14°C or above 31°C. And the sun is usually shining. Honolulu is the capital of Hawaii, a state made up of islands in the middle of the Pacific Ocean. Hawaii became the 50th American state in 1959.

Iolani Palace, Honolulu, Hawaii.
© Michael T. Sedam/Corbis

Honolulu is on Oahu Island. Like Hawaii's other large islands, Oahu formed from material that spewed up from volcanoes on the ocean floor. Diamond Head, the crater, or centre, of an old volcano, is one of the best-known landmarks in the Pacific. It got the name Diamond Head when some British sailors found crystals on its slopes and mistakenly thought they were diamonds!

Polynesian people from other Pacific islands were probably the first settlers in Honolulu, but Europeans did not arrive until 1794. That is when Captain William Brown of the British ship *Butterworth* entered the harbour.

Today the modern city of Honolulu is a major port. In the Hawaiian language, its name means 'protected bay'. It is also called 'the crossroads of the Pacific' because of the many ships and airplanes that stop there.

Sun, sand, and sea attract many tourists to Waikiki Beach. Most visitors also go to see the USS *Arizona*, a sunken battleship. It was left in place as a memorial to all the people who died in Japan's attack on Pearl Harbor on 7 December 1941. This attack is what brought the United States into World War II.

SEARCH LIGHT

Diamond Head
is a
a) sunken battleship.
b) rare gem.
c) crater of a volcano.

DID YOU KNOW?
There are only 12 letters in the Hawaiian alphabet. A, E, I, O, and U are the vowels, and H, K, L, M, N, P, and W are the consonants.

Waikiki Beach, with Diamond Head in the background, is the centre for tourism in Honolulu. There are many big resorts along the beach, and people come from all over the world to enjoy swimming and surfing in the waters of the Pacific Ocean.

© Craig Aurness/Corbis

Answer: c) crater of a volcano.

The Great Culture Mart

Many people describe New York City as the centre of culture in the United States. That's because no matter what you're interested in, you'll find it in New York. Whether it's theatre, music, ballet, or museums, the city has some of the very best to offer.

The street called Broadway in New York became the centre of American theatre in the mid-19th century. The number, size, and fame of the Broadway theatres grew as New York City grew. In the 1890s the brilliantly lighted street became known as 'the Great White Way'. Beyond these theatres the city offers free performances of the plays of William Shakespeare in Central Park. Operas and concerts are also held in the park.

New York City has a number of famous entertainment venues for performances of all kinds. The city's concert halls include those at the Lincoln Center for the Performing Arts as well as Carnegie Hall and Radio City Music Hall. The groups that perform in these halls include the Metropolitan Opera, the New York City Opera, and the New York **Philharmonic**. The New York City Ballet also performs at Lincoln Center, in the New York State Theater.

Dinosaur skeletons on exhibit at the American Museum of Natural History.
© Michael S. Yamashita/Corbis

Museums are another important part of New York City's cultural life. The Metropolitan Museum of Art, the Museum of Modern Art, and the Guggenheim Museum are among the city's art museums. You can also spend many hours in the American Museum of Natural History and its Rose Center for Earth and Space Science. With all of these resources, there is always plenty to do in New York City.

SEARCH LIGHT

Fill in the gaps: Carnegie Hall is a famous ____ ____ in New York City.

DID YOU KNOW?
The Brooklyn Children's Museum was one of the world's first museums designed specifically for children. It was also one of the first to offer interactive activities for children.

The Metropolitan Museum of Art is a favourite spot for visitors and New Yorkers alike. More than 5 million people visit the museum each year.
© Bob Krist/Corbis

Early Greek Art

Winslow Homer

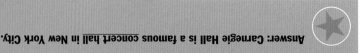

Answer: Carnegie Hall is a famous concert hall in New York City.

Ring of Fire

Mexico is a large North American country with ancient cities, beautiful beaches, and snow-capped mountains. Many of the mountains are volcanoes. They are part of the 'Ring of Fire', a chain of volcanoes that form a circle around the Pacific Ocean.

Mexico City

The mountains are just one part of Mexico's diverse **geography**, which also includes deserts, grasslands, and tropical forests. The tropical forests, in southern Mexico, are home to such animals as monkeys, parrots, and jaguars. Deer, coyotes, snakes, and armadillos are found in the dry north.

Mexico's history goes back thousands of years. The native Indian Olmec were the first to establish a **civilization** in what is now Mexico. They lived in central Mexico from about 1200 to 400 BC. The Maya, Toltec, and Aztec later built their own cities. The Aztec city of Tenochtitlán was built on the site of what is now Mexico City, the country's capital.

In the 1500s Spanish conquistadores (soldiers) took over from the Aztec, and Spain ruled Mexico for several hundred years. The country gained its independence in the early 1900s. Because of this history, Mexican culture is part Indian and part Spanish. Although Spanish is the official language, there are about 50 other local languages spoken.

On 2 November, the *Dia de los Muertos* (Day of the Dead) is observed. Also called All Souls' Day, it is a time when families visit the graves of their dead ancestors. Another popular holiday is *Cinco de Mayo* (5 May), which celebrates a Mexican victory against an invading French army.

SEARCH LIGHT

Find and correct the error in the following sentence: Mexico is part of the 'Ring of Gold', the circle of volcanoes that rings the Pacific Ocean.

DID YOU KNOW?

The Aztec introduced the Spanish conquistadores to chocolate and other foods that soon became favourites around the world after the conquistadores took them back to Europe.

The tower of the Great Palace and surrounding ruins are part of an ancient city in Mexico built by the Mayan people.
© ML Sinibaldi/Corbis

Answer: Mexico is part of the 'Ring of Fire', the circle of volcanoes that rings the Pacific Ocean.

Sinking City
of Palaces

Mexico City is the capital of Mexico and one of the world's largest cities, with more than 8 million people. It was founded in 1325 as the capital of the Aztec people. The Aztec city was called Tenochtitlán, which means 'Place of the High Priest Tenoch'.

Tenochtitlán was built on small islands in Lake Texcoco. After Spanish conquerors arrived in the 16th century, they began draining the lake in order to use the land. Today most of the water is gone, but the soil is soft and some of the city's streets and buildings are sinking. Since 1900 the city has sunk about 9 metres!

Mexico City is high above sea level - about 2,240 metres. However, it is surrounded by mountain ranges that are much higher. Dust and smoke from cars, fires, and factories are trapped by the mountains and pollute the city's air. The city also lies within an earthquake zone. An earthquake in 1985 destroyed many buildings and killed thousands of people. But most of the city's ancient monuments and palaces remained unharmed.

The floating gardens of Xochimilco.
© Peter M. Wilson/Corbis

Many of these monuments are located around a square called the Zócalo. They include the National Palace and the Metropolitan **Cathedral**. In another part of the city, Chapultepec Park includes a castle, a zoo, and a fun fair. The Pink Zone ('Zona Rosa') is one of Mexico City's main tourist and entertainment areas. It is the home of orchestras, art galleries, museums, theatre groups, and dance companies.

Another interesting area to visit is Xochimilco, with its floating gardens. These are rafts made out of reeds on which plants and flowers are grown. The famous Aztec pyramids of Teotihuacán are located north-east of the city.

DID YOU KNOW?
Mexico City has more than 350 distinct *colonias*, or neighbourhoods. The city is so large that when you take a taxi, you have to tell the driver the *colonia* of your destination as well as the street address!

SEARCH LIGHT

Mexico City was founded by
a) the Aztec.
b) the Inca.
c) the Maya.

The centre of Mexico City is a square popularly known as the Zócalo. The square is surrounded by many splendid public buildings.
© Randy Faris/Corbis

Answer: a) the Aztec.

The Isthmus Nations

Fill in the gap: Because of Central America's colonial past, most of its people speak _____.

Central America is an **isthmus** that lies between the Pacific Ocean and the Caribbean Sea. Seven countries lie within its boundaries - Belize, Guatemala, El Salvador, Honduras, Nicaragua, Costa Rica, and Panama. Together this cluster of nations stretches from North to South America. The countries share a long and proud history that reaches back thousands of years to the civilizations of the Maya and other native Indian peoples.

The Maya built great cities in northern Central America from about AD 200 to 900, but then they began to decline. When Spanish explorers arrived in the 16th century there were few Maya left. The Spanish soon established **colonies** in the area and ruled them for about 300 years before granting them independence. Because of this, most Central Americans speak Spanish, though many Indians speak their native languages. English is the official language of Belize, which was ruled by England for many years.

Today the people of the region are very diverse. Some are descended from Europeans, while others are of Asian or black African **ancestry** or Maya. Most are mestizos - people of mixed Indian and European ancestry.

Central America is mainly hilly and has many mountains. Swamps, rainforests, and lowlands extend along both coasts. There are many volcanoes, and the region has frequent earthquakes. Most people live along the western side.

Central America has many fascinating plants and animals, particularly in its rainforests. Jaguars and ocelots prowl the forest floors. Spider and howler monkeys scramble through the trees and climb vines called 'lianas'. Manatees swim in the rivers. Parrots chatter and insects buzz. Beautiful orchids bloom in clearings, and unusual fruits and nuts are found everywhere.

COUNTRIES OF CENTRAL AMERICA
1. Belize
2. Costa Rica
3. El Salvador
4. Guatemala
5. Honduras
6. Nicaragua
7. Panama

Mayan painted tripod plate.
© Bowers Museum of Cultural Art/Corbis

DID YOU KNOW?
No place in Central America is more than 200 kilometres from the sea. At its narrowest point, in Panama, the isthmus is only 48 kilometres across.

Blue poison dart frog.
© Kevin Schafer/Corbis

The ruins of the stone-stepped Temple of the Jaguar stand at the archaeological site at Tikal, Guatemala.
© John Noble/Corbis

Land of the Quetzal

Guatemala is a country in Central America. It was once home to the great Mayan civilization, which ruled from about AD 250 to 900. Today Mayan Indians make up about half of Guatemala's population, and they still have a great influence on its culture. Their crafts, dances, music, and religious ceremonies are similar to those from hundreds of years ago.

Guatemala City

Along with the Mayan Indians, the population of Guatemala includes the Ladinos, who have mixed Spanish and Mayan Indian heritage. While the Mayan Indians tend to live in the rural highlands, most Ladinos live in cities. The Ladinos tend to be wealthier than the Indians.

Spanish is the country's most widely spoken language, but one in three Guatemalans speaks an Indian language. Most of the people are Roman Catholic, but many Indians mix Catholic beliefs with traditional religious practices. The town of Esquipulas, in eastern Guatemala, is home to the Black Christ, the most important Catholic shrine in Central America. It was named for the dark wood from which it was carved. Guatemala's many religious festivals include the popular Easter celebrations in the town of Antigua Guatemala.

The land of Guatemala includes mountains, volcanoes, grasslands, and rainforests. The wildlife of the rainforests includes the quetzal, the colourful national bird. There are also many snakes, crocodiles, and iguanas.

Farming is important in Guatemala. Many farmers grow maize, beans, and squash to feed themselves and their families. Other farmers raise coffee, bananas, sugar-cane, cotton, and cattle to sell to other countries.

SEARCH LIGHT

Fill in the gap: Most people in Guatemala have at least some _____ ancestry.
a) French
b) Quetzal
c) Mayan Indian

DID YOU KNOW?
Guatemala has three continuously active volcanoes: Santa María, Fuego, and Pacaya. In 1902, Santa María erupted for 19 days in a row.

For gorgeous feathers, few birds surpass the quetzal. Found in rainforests from southern Mexico to Bolivia, the quetzal was the sacred bird of the ancient Maya and Aztec. Today it is the national symbol of Guatemala (whose monetary unit is the quetzal).
© Michael & Patricia Fogden/Corbis

Answer: c) Mayan Indian

Volcanoes and Earthquakes in Central America

Nicaragua is the largest country in Central America, the strip of land that connects North and South America. The capital and largest city of Nicaragua is Managua.

Nicaragua has two large lakes, Managua and Nicaragua. The area around the lakes is dotted with about 40 volcanoes. Some of the volcanoes are still active. Nicaragua also experiences many earthquakes, which can be very destructive.

Managua

The most **fertile** farmland in the country lies near the volcanoes. The soil is rich with **minerals** from volcanic ash. Because of that, people have lived in the area for thousands of years. The early people who lived there found this soil perfect for growing beans and maize. They were also skilled craftsmen and left behind stone carvings, pottery, and gold jewellery.

But they also discovered the power of the volcanoes. Scientists have found footprints that were left many years ago by people who were fleeing from the lava and ash of an erupting volcano.

Spanish explorers arrived in Nicaragua in the 1500s. The native Indians who lived there resisted, but eventually the Spanish conquered the land. Nicaragua was named for Nicarao, an Indian chief who led the fight against the Spanish. The country finally gained independence from the Spanish in the 1800s.

Many Nicaraguans are farmers, still growing the traditional maize and beans. They also produce coffee, cotton, beef, and bananas, which are sold to other countries. Only a small portion of the land is actually used for farming, however. More than one-fourth of the country is covered with rainforest.

DID YOU KNOW?
Association football, or soccer, is the most popular sport in all Central American countries except for Nicaragua, where baseball is the national pastime.

SEARCH LIGHT

Why do you suppose Spanish is the official language of Nicaragua?

© Corbis

Ash clouds rise into the air during an eruption of Cerro Negro, Nicaragua's most active volcano.

Answer: The Spanish conquered much of South and Central America in the 1500s and ruled the region for many centuries. For that reason Spanish is still the official language of Nicaragua, even though Spain no longer controls the country.

Land of
Many Fish

Panama City is the capital of the small Central American country of Panama. It lies on the Gulf of Panama near the Panama **Canal**. Panama City used to be a small Indian fishing village. The Spanish name for the city, *Panamá*, means 'many fish'.

A Spanish soldier named Pedro Arias Dávila founded Panama City in 1519. It was the first European settlement on the Pacific coast of the Americas. After the Panama Canal opened in 1914, the city became an important centre for world trade.

To understand what the city looked like centuries ago, you can visit the area known as San Felipe. Some people call it Casco Viejo, which means 'old city'. Here you'll see many buildings from the **colonial** days. In the building called the Salón Bolívar, the soldier Simón Bolívar worked on ways to unify the South American countries newly freed from Spanish rule. In 1997 the United Nations Educational, Scientific and Cultural Organization named the old section of Panama City a World Heritage site. This means that

SEARCH LIGHT

What turned Panama City from a small fishing village into a centre for world trade?

it is an important cultural site that should be protected and preserved.

But it's the canal that connects the Atlantic Ocean with the Pacific Ocean that most visitors want to see. Every day ships from all over the world take the trip through the narrow canal. The ships carry **cargo** and passengers between countries. The canal saves them a journey of thousands of kilometres around the southern tip of South America

Colonial architecture is a prominent feature of the San Felipe neighbourhood of Panama City.
© Alfredo Maiquez/Lonely Planet Images

DID YOU KNOW?
Because of the way Panama curves, a very strange thing happens when you pass through the Panama Canal. Travelling through the canal from the Atlantic to the Pacific actually takes you from west to east instead of the other way around. So when you exit, even though you're on the west side of the country, you're farther east than when you started.

Answer: The building of the Panama Canal turned Panama City into a world trading centre.

A Major World Waterway

(Top) Construction of the Panama Canal; (bottom) Two men stand in front of canal locks under construction in 1913 as part of the Panama Canal project.

The Panama Canal is one of the most important artificial waterways in the world. It's located in the Central American country of Panama. The canal cuts through a narrow strip of land to connect the Atlantic and Pacific oceans. It is about 80 kilometres long.

The Panama Canal can cut thousands of kilometres from a ship's voyage. Ships travelling between the east and west coasts of the United States, for example, can shorten their trip by more than 14,500 kilometres. Without the canal, they would have to go around the southern tip of South America.

Many different kinds of goods are shipped through the canal. Thousands of ships carry more than 180 million tonnes of **cargo** through it each year. The most important goods include crude **oil** and grains.

The Panama Canal uses what is called a lock system. Locks are huge tanks with gates at each end. They are used to raise or lower boats from one water level to another. This is necessary because the lake through which the canal passes is at a higher level than the oceans.

First a boat enters the lock, and the gate is closed behind it. If the boat needs to rise to a higher level, water is added to the lock. As the water rises, the boat floats higher. When the lock is full of water, the gate in front of the boat is opened. The boat can then travel out onto the higher part of the canal. The process is reversed for boats going in the other direction. It takes about nine hours for a ship to go through the canal.

DID YOU KNOW?
Boats pay to use the canal, just as cars do on some roads. A large cruise ship might pay more than £60,000. A man named Richard Halliburton paid the lowest toll ever recorded. He paid just about 22 pence when he swam the length of the canal in 1928.

SEARCH LIGHT

How long does it take a ship to pass through the Panama Canal?

A small tugboat leads a large ship out of one of the Panama Canal's locks.

© Danny Lehman/Corbis

477

Jewel of the Caribbean

The island of Puerto Rico is a self-governing commonwealth of the United States. This means it has the right to make its own laws, but it has some ties with the United States. Puerto Ricans are American citizens, but they do not elect representatives to the U.S. Congress or pay U.S. taxes.

San Juan

Located in the West Indies, Puerto Rico lies in the northern Caribbean Sea. The island is mostly hilly, though it is flatter along the coast. Most of the people live in the coastal area. Rainforests cover parts of the north. Many of the island's trees were cut down for lumber or farming. Special plans now encourage **conservation**. New forests have been planted with such fast-growing trees as eucalyptus, teak, and Honduran pine.

Puerto Rico was known as Borinquén to the native Arawak Indians who settled on the island hundreds of years ago. Their **descendants** were living there when in 1493 Christopher Columbus became the first European to reach the island. Columbus claimed the island for Spain, and soon Spaniards had established a settlement there.

DID YOU KNOW?

Puerto Rico is home to a kind of frog called the *coquí*. It was named after its loud croak, which sounds like 'Ko-kee! Ko-kee!' This much-loved frog has become a symbol of the island.

Puerto Rico was a Spanish colony for almost four centuries. At the end of the 1800s, the United States defeated Spain in the Spanish-American War. Afterward the island was turned over to the United States. In 1951 the island became a commonwealth. Some people on the island want it to become a U.S. state, but in elections most of the people have voted against this.

SEARCH LIGHT

True or false? Puerto Rico is one of the 50 states of the United States.

San Juan is the capital and largest city of Puerto Rico. In the 17th and 18th centuries, walls were added to protect it. The San Juan Gate was once the main entrance to the city.
© Wolfgang Kaehler/Corbis

Answer: FALSE. Puerto Rico is an American commonwealth.

Sugarcane and Politics

The country of Cuba is part of the West Indies, a group of islands in the Caribbean Sea. The country is made up of one main island and about 1,600 smaller islands. The capital is Havana, on the north-western coast of the main island.

Many Cubans are farmers. For a long time the most valuable crop has been sugarcane. Sugarcane grows as a tall, thick grass, and it is from this plant that we get sugar. Cuba also produces tobacco, and Cuban cigars are famous worldwide. Other major crops are coffee, rice, and tropical fruits. Although making sugar from cane is still important, many factories have been closed. Tourism is now the largest source of income for Cuba.

Cubans speak Spanish, and the country's culture reflects its Spanish background. The island was claimed for Spain by Christopher Columbus in 1492 and was ruled by Spain until the 1890s. African culture has also influenced Cuba. Many Africans were taken to the island long ago to work as slaves on the sugar plantations.

Cuba saw major changes when Fidel Castro took over the government in 1959. Castro was strongly **communist**, and he developed a close relationship with the government of the Soviet Union. This caused problems between Cuba and its neighbour the United States, since the United States strongly disagreed with the political ideas of the Soviet Union. In fact, Cuba was nearly the centre of a nuclear war between the United States and the Soviet Union in 1962. The problems remained even after the Soviet Union collapsed in 1991.

DID YOU KNOW?

Large stalks of sugarcane are often sold in fruit markets in Cuba. For children it's a treat to have a small section of sugarcane to suck on, like an ice lolly.

More than 2 million people live in Havana, Cuba's capital city.

© Bob Krist/Corbis

SEARCH LIGHT

True or false? Cuba is ruled by Spain.

Answer: FALSE. Cuba was ruled by Spain for many years but gained independence in the 1890s.

The Unknown Continent

Scientists believe that millions of years ago South America and Africa were part of the same ancient **landmass** now known as Gondwanaland. In fact, if you view South America and Africa as puzzle pieces, you'd see that the two continents fit roughly together. Slowly, South America broke away and began to drift westward. Today the **Isthmus** of Panama links South America to North America. The South American mainland is divided into 12 independent countries and one dependent state.

The Andes Mountains, one of the longest and highest mountain ranges in the world, lie in South America. The continent also features the Guiana Highlands and the Brazilian Highlands, which contain some of the oldest rocks on Earth. The River Amazon in South America is one of the greatest rivers of the world. A huge quantity of the world's freshwater flows through the Amazon **basin**. The river makes the **lush** Amazon rainforest possible.

For thousands of years South America was **isolated** from the rest of the world. Outsiders didn't know about ancient peoples such as the Inca who lived on that continent. Then in 1498 Christopher Columbus landed in South America. Spanish and Portuguese **colonizers** and adventurers followed. They **converted** many of the native Indians to Christianity. Nowadays most South Americans speak Spanish or Portuguese.

South America's many unusual animals - such as llamas, alpacas, jaguars, sloths, and armadillos - were new to the first visiting Europeans. Today many people visit South America to see its rainforests and to enjoy its rich animal life.

The bright green emerald tree boa is native to the Amazon Basin of South America.
© David A. Northcott/Corbis

COUNTRIES OF SOUTH AMERICA
1. Argentina
2. Bolivia
3. Brazil
4. Chile
5. Colombia
6. Ecuador
7. French Guiana
8. Guyana
9. Paraguay
10. Peru
11. Suriname
12. Uruguay
13. Venezuela

Rio de Janeiro, Brazil.
© Richard T. Nowitz/Corbis

SEARCH LIGHT

True or false?
a) Christopher Columbus landed in South America.
b) South America was once connected to Africa.
c) South America is attached to North America.

Answer: These are all true statements.

A Close Look
at River Life

At the heart of South America lies the Amazon River **basin**. It is nearly as large as the United States, but few people live there. Nonetheless, the area is full of living things. They are all part of a giant **tropical** forest called the rainforest. There are so many plants, animals, birds, and insects there that no one has been able to list them all! Some of them exist nowhere else in the world.

The rainforest is a very important place. It helps control the world's **climate** by absorbing gases in the air that can cause a problem called **global warming**. It also provides a home for the many animals in the area.

Emerald tree boa in the Amazon basin.
© David A. Northcott/Corbis

SEARCH LIGHT

Find and correct the error in the following sentence: The Amazon rainforest has many trees, plants, animals, people, and insects.

There are brightly coloured birds, including green and yellow parrots with red heads, pink flamingos, and beautiful hummingbirds. There are also millions of butterflies, some as big as small birds.

The treetops are alive with playful monkeys. On the ground are funny-looking animals called tapirs that resemble hairy pigs. There are also animals that you wouldn't enjoy meeting. The spotted jaguar, a large member of the cat family, is one. The anaconda is another. It is one of the world's largest snakes and can swallow a whole deer in one gulp! There are also huge hairy spiders, many-legged centipedes, and army ants that eat almost everything that they find.

It's not a good idea to swim in the Amazon River. What looks like a floating log might actually be a dangerous crocodile. There are electric eels that can hurt a person with an electric shock. And there are harmless-looking fish called piranhas that are actually quite ferocious, though they don't usually bother people.

DID YOU KNOW?
Many of the plants found in the Amazon rainforest contain substances that can be used as medicine to fight diseases such as cancer. These plants are not found anywhere else in the world.

The Amazon is home to many different types of wildlife, including the green-cheeked Amazon parrot.
© Eric and David Hosking/Corbis

Answer: The Amazon rainforest has many trees, plants, animals, birds, and insects.

World-Class Mountains

Andean condors.
© Galen Rowell/Corbis

The Andes are the tallest mountains in the Western **Hemisphere**. The highest peak, Mount Aconcagua in Argentina, is about 6,960 metres high. The mountains run north to south for the entire length of South America - 8,900 kilometres in all. They separate a narrow strip of land along the west coast from the rest of the continent.

The Andes region is made up of many high **plateaus** surrounded by even higher peaks. In some sections, the chain separates into two ranges. The Cordillera Oriental is the eastern mountain range, and the Cordillera Occidental is the western range.

Because of the extreme **altitudes**, the mountains can be a very difficult place to live. There are few plants above 4,900 metres, but between 2,400 and 3,500 metres there is plenty of good farming. This is the zone where most of the people of the Andes live and where most of the cities are. Just above this zone is where llamas and alpacas are raised. These relatives of the camel are valuable for their wool and for other purposes. At higher elevations there is less oxygen to breathe. Few people live at heights greater than 3,700 metres. Sheepherders, though, sometimes live as high as 5,000 metres.

SEARCH LIGHT

Mount Everest, the world's highest mountain, is over 8,800 metres tall. How much taller than Mount Aconcagua is it?
a) about 180 metres
b) about 4,880 metres
c) about 1,830 metres

The best-known people ever to live in the Andes were the Inca. When Europeans arrived in the mountains in the 1500s, the Inca ruled much of the area. Remains of the magnificent Inca city called Machu Picchu can still be seen in the mountains of Peru.

DID YOU KNOW?

Andean condors are among the largest flying birds on Earth. Their wings measure 3 metres across from tip to tip and are strong enough to allow these giants to fly as many as 320 kilometres a day looking for food.

Mount Fitzroy and Mount Torre belong to the part of the Andes Mountains in south-western Argentina. Altogether, the Andes Mountains pass through seven different countries in South America.
© Francesc Muntada/Corbis

Answer: c) about 1,830 metres

Columbus' South American Namesake

Colombia, in South America, is the only American nation named for Christopher Columbus. Its capital city, Bogotá, sits on a high **plateau** in the Andes Mountains.

Colombia is a land of beaches, deserts, jungles, grasslands, and mountains. The Andes range runs the length of the country. Southeast of the mountains, rivers crisscross the lush green Amazon rainforest. In the east are grasslands called the Llanos.

Since Colombia lies close to the **equator**, its climate is generally hot. But it's cooler in the highlands. The rainforest gets more than 250 centimetres of rain annually. The Llanos region has dry and wet seasons.

Bogotá

Colombia is home to many different kinds of plant and animal. There are more than 130,000 different plants in the country, including a kind of water lily called *Victoria amazonica*. Its leaves are large and strong enough to support a child. Just some of the animals found in Colombia include jaguars, ocelots, peccaries, tapirs, deer, anteaters, monkeys, and the rare spectacled bear. There are more than 1,550 kinds of birds in Colombia. That's more than Europe and North America have combined. These birds include the huge Andean condor and the tiny hummingbird.

Before the Spaniards landed in the area in the 1500s, there were many Indian tribes living there. They crafted gold and made stone sculptures. The Spaniards took the people's lands and made them slaves. Many other Indians died of disease. Finally, the people **revolted**, and Colombia became free in 1813. Spanish is still the official language of Colombia.

SEARCH LIGHT

True or false? There are more kinds of birds found in Colombia than in all of North America.

DID YOU KNOW?
Colombia is among the world's leading producers of emeralds. The mysterious beauty of these fiery green gemstones has inspired many legends. They were long believed to cure certain illnesses.

Trays of coffee beans are dried in the sunshine on the roof of a farm building in north-western Colombia. Colombia grows much of the world's supply of coffee beans.
© Jeremy Horner/Corbis

Answer: TRUE. Colombia has more kinds of birds than Europe and North America have combined.

Land of the Inca

Peru is a large South American country that lies just south of the **equator**. In the west it has a long coastline on the Pacific Ocean. Many of Peru's major cities are located on a narrow strip of flat land along the coast. Among them is Lima, the capital. Eastern Peru is part of the huge **basin** of the Amazon River. It is nearly covered with rainforests. Between the coast and the Amazon region are the Andes. Some peaks in this mountain range reach higher than 3,000 metres. High in the Andes is Lake Titicaca, one of the largest lakes in South America.

Lima

Around AD 1200 a group of Indians called the Inca formed the city of Cuzco in what is now Peru. From there they set out to conquer other Indian peoples along South America's west coast. Eventually the Inca ruled over as many as 12 million people. But their great **empire** was destroyed when Spanish soldiers seized the land in the 1530s. Spain ruled until Peru won its independence almost 300 years later.

Today Peru still has many reminders of the Inca. The country's name comes from a word meaning 'land of abundance' in Quechua, the Inca language. The name refers to the riches that the Inca got from the land, including great amounts of gold. Indians who still speak the Quechua language make up about half of Peru's population. And in the Andes there is Machu Picchu. The remarkable stone remains of this Inca settlement attract visitors from all over the world.

SEARCH LIGHT

Unscramble these words having to do with Peru.
- deAns
- caIn
- mazonA

DID YOU KNOW?
Peru is known for two domesticated animals that are native to the Andes, llamas and alpacas. These animals are surefooted climbers well suited for life in the mountains.

A Peruvian girl displays a style of traditional dress that is still worn among some of the country's inhabitants.
© James Sparshatt/Corbis

Answer: deAns = Andes
caIn = Inca
mazonA = Amazon

Secret of the Andes

SEARCH LIGHT

Why did the Inca abandon Machu Picchu?

A long time ago, a group of people who worshipped the Sun lived in South America. They constructed incredible stone buildings high in the Andes, a chain of mountains in the western part of the continent. These people were the Inca. Their most famous creation was Machu Picchu, in the mountains of Peru.

Religious centre, Machu Picchu.
© Craig Lovell/Corbis

The Inca ruled a large **empire** and had a lot of gold. Their fame reached far and wide. Even the rulers of Spain heard about their 'land of gold'. In the 1500s the Spanish invaded the Inca empire. The invaders killed many people, took their gold, and destroyed their religious buildings. The Spanish invasion brought an end to the Inca empire.

Although the Inca had no written records, they left behind **archaeological** clues about their lifestyle. One big clue is Machu Picchu. At some point the Inca **abandoned** the site. No one is sure why. Some people think it's because the site didn't have enough water. After Machu Picchu was abandoned, trees and plants grew over it. This kept it hidden from the Spanish during their invasion. The site remained unknown to people outside of the Andes until an archaeologist found it in 1911.

If you visit Machu Picchu, you'll find great temples and palaces. You'll also see dozens of stepped **terraces** for farming all around the site. There are also a plaza (square), houses, and a cemetery. Walkways and thousands of stone steps connect the different parts of the site. These structures were probably built in the 1400s and 1500s. But amazingly, almost all of them are still in very good shape. The Inca must have been some builders!

DID YOU KNOW?

The name Machu Picchu means 'old peak' in Quechua, the language of the Inca.

© Jim Zuckerman/Corbis

For hundreds of years Machu Picchu was known only to a few people who lived nearby. The rest of the world learned about the site only when an archaeologist named Hiram Bingham discovered it in 1911.

Answer: It's still not certain, but it could have been because of a lack of water.

Half of South America

Brazil, the largest country in South America, took its name from brazilwood. The first European settlers in Brazil shipped a lot of brazilwood back to Europe, where it was used to produce valuable red dyes.

Brazil covers nearly half of the continent. It has a long coastline along the Atlantic Ocean. It shares borders with every South American country except Chile and Ecuador. The capital of Brazil is Brasília. Two other Brazilian cities - São Paulo and Rio de Janeiro - rank among the world's largest. Both of these cities lie on the coast. The River Amazon is a key natural feature of Brazil. It is the largest river in the world in terms of the amount of water it carries. More than 1,000 tributaries, or smaller rivers, empty into the Amazon. During the river's annual flood, it pours more than 174 million litres of water per second into the Atlantic Ocean.

The lush Amazon rainforest covers much of the river's huge **basin**. This rainforest contains the most varied plant life on Earth. Nearly 50,000 kinds of animal are also found there. So many different kinds of plant and animal live in the forest that many of them haven't been named yet!

Brazil's national sport is football. The Brazilian team has won the World Cup soccer championship five times. Pelé, a Brazilian national hero, is considered to be one of the greatest soccer players ever.

Rio de Janeiro is the second largest city in Brazil. It is located on the Atlantic Ocean in the south-eastern part of the country.
© Richard T. Nowitz/Corbis

SEARCH LIGHT

Which of the following can be said of Brazil?
- It makes up half of South America.
- It's named for a tree.
- The national sport is basketball.
- The Nile River is in Brazil.

DID YOU KNOW?
The large and gentle monkey called the 'muriqui' is found only in the eastern forests of Brazil. It is one of the world's most endangered animals.

Answer: It makes up half of South America, and it's named for a tree.

The Once-Forgotten Land

Not long ago nobody knew much about Paraguay, a country in South America. For much of the 1800s and 1900s Paraguay was ruled by **dictators** who kept the country isolated from the rest of the world. But in the 1990s the country began to open up and encourage visitors.

Paraguay is located in the south-central part of South America. Its capital is Asunción. The country is surrounded by land, and rivers provide the only way to get to the Atlantic Ocean. This makes the rivers very important to Paraguay. In fact, the country's name may come from an Indian word meaning 'river that gives birth to the sea'.

Asunción

The Paraguay River divides the country into two natural parts. To the east the land is mostly wooded hills and grassy plains. To the west is a dry, flat region called the Chaco Boreal. It is part of the larger Gran Chaco region, which extends into Bolivia and Argentina.

The wild animals of Paraguay include bats, monkeys, armadillos, anteaters, otters, jaguars, and nutrias, which are rats that can live in water. In the Chaco there are a small number of Chacoan peccaries, which look something like wild pigs. Scientists thought these animals were **extinct** until some living ones were found in the early 1970s.

The people of Paraguay live mostly in the east. More of them work in farming than in any other kind of job. They grow sugarcane, **cassava**, maize, rice, and tobacco. They also produce a tea called 'yerba maté', which is popular in Paraguay and neighbouring countries.

SEARCH LIGHT

For a long time most people knew little about Paraguay. Why?

DID YOU KNOW?
The first people to live in what is now Paraguay were the Guaraní Indians. Today many of Paraguay's people speak two languages - Guaraní and Spanish.

Traditional Latino dancing is showcased at an outdoor plaza (square) in Asunción, Paraguay.
© Sarah JH Hubbard/Lonely Planet Images

Answer: Paraguay was run by dictators for much of the 1800s and 1900s. These leaders didn't let the country's people have much contact with people in other countries.

487

A Long and Narrow Land

No other country has a shape like Chile's. The country stretches along South America's Pacific coast for a long 4,300 kilometres but is only a skinny 180 kilometres wide. Chile controls Easter Island in the Pacific and claims part of Antarctica as well. Its capital is Santiago.

Most of Chile is dominated by the Andes Mountains. Many people there raise llamas and alpacas for wool. But the country is so long that it has many habitats other than the **alpine**. The north is mainly desert. Some **cacti** and shrubs grow there. Central Chile is **temperate** and has land that's good for farming. Most of Chile's people live there. The area is known for its unique *matorral* habitat, with mixed trees, shrubs, cacti, and grass. But people have cleared away much of this growth for firewood. Very few people live in the far south. There are grasslands suitable for raising **livestock** in the area called Chilean Patagonia. But most of the region is rugged and quite cold.

Chile faces many kinds of natural disasters, including volcanic eruptions, earthquakes, and **tsunamis**. In the winter there are fierce storms and floods. Summer often brings **drought**.

Like much of South America, Chile was **colonized** by Spain in the 1500s. The country won independence in the early 1800s. But the long period of Spanish rule had a lasting effect. Most Chileans are mestizos, a mix of Spanish and American Indian ancestry. And most people speak Spanish.

* Santiago

SEARCH LIGHT

Fill in the gap: Chile is about _____ longer than it is wide.
a) 2.5 times
b) 250 times
c) 25 times

Llamas graze near a snow-capped volcano in northern Chile. People use llamas to carry things. Llamas are also used as a source of food, wool, and hides.
© Graham Neden–Ecoscene/Corbis

DID YOU KNOW?
The Atacama Desert in northern Chile is perhaps the driest place on Earth. Some parts of the desert have not had a drop of rain for hundreds of years.

Answer: c) 25 times

Land of Giants

Easter Island is located in the eastern part of the Pacific Ocean. The people who live on the island call it Rapa Nui. But the first European visitors to land there, the Dutch, named it Paaseiland, meaning 'Easter Island', because they arrived on Easter Sunday. Today Easter Island is a part of the South American country of Chile.

SEARCH LIGHT

How did Easter Island get its name?

Easter Island is only 23 kilometres long and 11 kilometres wide. It lies 3,500 kilometres west of Chile. Although the island is small and isolated, it is famous throughout the world for its huge stone statues of people. They are called *moai*. There are more than 600 *moai* on the island. They stand on giant stone platforms called *ahu*s. Some of the *ahu*s have as many as a dozen statues.

All of the *moai* were carved after about AD 700. Some of them have rounded heads and stubby bodies. One famous *moai* is a lifelike figure of a kneeling man. The statues

A line of *moai* statues.
G. Renner/Robert Harding Picture Library

made at a later date are very tall and slim. These *moai* have a huge **topknot** called a *pukao* on the top of their heads. Most of them are between 3 and 6 metres tall. One statue from this period is almost 10 metres high. It is made from a single block of stone that weighs nearly 74 tonnes. The *pukao* on its head alone weighs about 10 tonnes. One unfinished statue is about 21 metres tall. Its back is still attached to the rock from which it was carved.

Stone statues called *moai* stand on a slope of Rano Raraku, a volcano on Easter Island.

© James L. Amos/Corbis

DID YOU KNOW?

No one is sure why the Easter Island statues were carved or what they mean. Many people believe that the statues honoured important people who were revered as gods after their death.

Home of the Gaucho

At the southern end of South America lies Argentina, the second largest country on the continent - only Brazil is larger. The capital is Buenos Aires.

The landscape of Argentina is **diverse**, with four main regions. The mountains of the Andes rise in the north-west. The dry Gran Chaco lowlands lie in the north. In the south is the cold dry region of Patagonia. The Pampas grasslands cover the heart of the country.

The Pampas has rich soil and lots of rainfall. It is there that you'll find most of Argentina's farms and ranches. It's also where you'll find gauchos - the famous Argentine cowboys. In the 1700s and 1800s these wandering horsemen hunted large herds of escaped horses and cattle that roamed over the Pampas. Argentine writers celebrated the gauchos in poems and stories. Today the gauchos have a more settled lifestyle, working on the farms and ranches.

The Argentine people are as diverse as the land. The first people who arrived in what is now Argentina were American Indians (Native Americans). They travelled there from North America thousands of years ago. Today most of the population is European. The largest groups are from Spain, Italy, France, Britain, Germany, Poland, and Russia.

Spanish is the national language of Argentina. But because Argentina has so many **immigrants** from different parts of Europe, many other European languages are also spoken. Some Indian languages can be heard as well.

Buenos Aires ★

DID YOU KNOW?
Dance and music are important parts of Argentine culture. The tango, a very dramatic dance, was created in Argentina in the 1800s. Today it is performed all over the world.

SEARCH LIGHT

Find and correct the mistakes in the following sentence: The first people who lived in Argentina were Spanish immigrants from Europe.

Ranchers on horseback drive cattle in Patagonia, the largest region of Argentina.
© Corbis

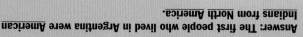
Answer: The first people who lived in Argentina were American Indians from North America.

Remarkable
People in History

Learn about famous lives from different times and places

Remarkable People in History
TABLE OF CONTENTS

The Emperor
and the Right Way of Living

Some 2,200 years ago, the emperor Ashoka ruled India. Like many ancient rulers, he expanded his empire by conquering new lands. But unlike most rulers, Ashoka suddenly turned his back on warfare and began to govern according to the non-violent beliefs of Buddhism.

It is said that Ashoka became a Buddhist when he saw the horrors caused by the wars he'd led. After that, he decided to serve his subjects and all humanity instead of conquering others. He called this 'conquest by *dharma*'. In India *dharma* means the 'right way of living' and 'universal truth.' This included being honest, truthful, and kind. It also meant being merciful, generous, and thoughtful.

The emperor himself would often tour the countryside, preaching his belief in *dharma* to the people. Ashoka also appointed '*dharma* ministers' to help relieve people's sufferings. These ministers were assigned to look after the special needs of women and people living in religious communities.

Ashoka passed laws to prevent cruelty to animals and had hospitals built for both people and animals. He also started construction projects to make all people's lives easier. Trees were planted on roadsides, wells were dug, and watering sheds and rest houses were built.

The only recognition Ashoka wanted was for people to remember that he had ruled according to *dharma*. To preserve his ideas, Ashoka had his teachings carved on rocks and pillars (columns) in public areas. These inscriptions are called the Rock **Edicts** and Pillar Edicts. The most famous is the lion pillar found at Sarnath, which has become India's national emblem.

SEARCH LIGHT

Ashoka was an Indian
a) mathematician.
b) emperor.
c) priest.

DID YOU KNOW?
Despite his reputation as a kind and generous ruler, some stories describe Ashoka as cruel and ruthless. According to one story, he had all his brothers killed in order to seize the throne.

Sarnath, an archaeological site in northern India, is said to be the place where the Buddha first preached to his followers. Ashoka built this stupa (shrine) and others, as well as pillars, to honor the event.
© Brian A. Vikander/Corbis

Rome's Remarkable General and Statesman

Julius Caesar was a brilliant general and a gifted writer. But most important, he helped create the ancient Roman Empire.

Early in his career Caesar formed a **bond** with the two most powerful men in Rome, the wealthy Crassus and the General Pompey. In 59 BC they helped elect Caesar as one of Rome's two consuls, the government's highest rank. After a year as consul, Caesar left Rome to govern Gaul (now France). There he earned a reputation as a military leader. He stopped uprisings and invasions, and he even landed in Britain. Caesar also wrote detailed accounts of his battles.

While Caesar was in Gaul, Crassus was killed. Pompey now controlled Rome, and he turned against Caesar. He declared Caesar a criminal and ordered him to break up his army. Instead, Caesar declared war and marched to Rome. Pompey fled to Greece.

SEARCH LIGHT

Fill in the blank: Caesar took power in Rome after defeating _____, his former political supporter.

Sculpture of Julius Caesar, in the National Museum in Naples.
© Bettmann/Corbis

At that time Rome was governed by a senate (a supreme council). But Caesar felt the government was corrupt and needed a strong leader. In 49 BC he declared himself **dictator,** and he spent five years fighting a civil war against Pompey to make his rule secure. Some of the Roman senators worried that Caesar had too much power. On March 15, 44 BC, they murdered Caesar on the floor of the Senate.

In the short time he led Rome, Caesar proved to be a great statesman. The changes he made helped begin the 500-year Roman Empire. And for almost 2,000 years after his death, some world leaders used a form of the title 'caesar' (such as 'Kaiser' in Germany and 'czar' in Russia).

DID YOU KNOW?
In William Shakespeare's play *Julius Caesar*, Caesar is told to "beware the ides of March". The ides refers to the time around the 15th of the month. Today those famous words are sometimes used as a warning.

By crossing over the stream known as the Rubicon in 49 BC, Caesar basically declared war against the Roman Senate. 'Crossing the Rubicon', the subject of this engraving, became a phrase that means taking a step from which there's no turning back.
© Bettmann/Corbis

Answer: Caesar took power in Rome after defeating Pompey, his former political supporter.

The Man Who Changed Cuba

In the 1950s General Fulgencio Batista ruled the Caribbean island of Cuba. His rule was harsh and often violent, and some large American companies grew rich while many Cubans remained poor. Fidel Castro was a young lawyer who believed Batista's rule was unfair. There were no free elections in Cuba, so Castro organized a military force to overthrow Batista.

Fidel Castro in 1960.
© Bettmann/Corbis

Castro bought guns with his own money and attacked Batista's forces in 1953. The attack failed badly, and after two years in prison Castro went to Mexico to make a new plan. Soon he and about 80 other **rebels** arrived in Cuba. They hid in the mountains and fought a **guerrilla** war using small-scale battles and making hit-and-run attacks. Batista finally fled Cuba in 1959.

Castro became Cuba's leader and created a **communist** government to control all parts of Cuba's life. After a while, the people lost many of the same rights that Batista had taken away, and Cuban businesses did not create new wealth. Many Cubans left their homeland or tried to do so. But Castro also greatly increased many benefits to the Cuban people. Education and health services were free, and every citizen was guaranteed work.

SEARCH LIGHT

True or false? The United States has also supported Castro's rule in Cuba.

The United States, Cuba's near neighbor, strongly opposed Castro's government. They even tried to overthrow it in 1961. And in 1962 Cuba was at the center of a dangerous clash between the United States and the **Soviet Union**. Castro had let Soviet **nuclear weapons** be set up in Cuba.

Today Cuba is one of the last communist countries in the world. In the late 20th century there was unrest among Cubans, and Castro relaxed some of his strictest controls. Still, after more than 40 years, he remains Cuba's powerful leader.

DID YOU KNOW?
Castro was a very good baseball player. It is said he once even tried out for the Senators, a professional baseball team in Washington, D.C.

Fidel Castro still speaks out strongly against people who disagree with his communist government in Cuba. Here he speaks at a rally in 2003.
© AFP/Corbis

Answer: FALSE. Since the early 1960s, the United States has opposed Castro and has supported attempts to overthrow him.

The Father of Europe

During the Middle Ages (about AD 500-1500) one of the most powerful European kings was Charlemagne. Charlemagne was a Frank. The Franks were a people who lived in parts of modern France and Germany. When he became the one and only ruler of the Frankish lands in AD 771, Charlemagne wanted to make his kingdom bigger and stronger. He also wanted to spread Christianity and protect the Roman Catholic church.

Illuminated (richly decorated) manuscript showing Charlemagne meeting Pope Adrian I.
© Archivo Iconografico, S.A./Corbis

With this plan in mind, Charlemagne spent 30 years battling the Saxons, another Germanic people. In these and many other wars, Charlemagne gained control over much of western Europe, including what is now France, Switzerland, Belgium, the Netherlands, and half of Italy and Germany.

In the year 800, the **Pope** crowned Charlemagne the emperor of the Romans. This made him the first of many emperors who would rule until 1806. Charlemagne reorganized the government in his empire. He worked with leaders of the church to improve the church and government. And he sent out special agents to make sure that his laws were being obeyed.

Charlemagne brought about many improvements in the kingdom. He set up a new money system and reformed the law courts. He built a large court library and set up a school at his palace court. He was concerned with educating the ordinary people and improving the learning of priests. He hoped education would make his people better Christians.

Charlemagne died in 814. Today he is remembered as one of the most important rulers in European history. In fact, he's sometimes called the father of Europe.

SEARCH LIGHT

Which of these did Charlemagne **not** build?
a) pyramids
b) schools
c) libraries

DID YOU KNOW?
Charlemagne enjoyed swimming. He even built a palace on a hot spring that he used for bathing with friends.

Charlemagne's empire survived for only a brief time after he died. But no other ruler in the European Middle Ages had such a deep and long-lasting effect.
© Ali Meyer/Corbis

Answer: a) pyramids

Queen of Egypt

SEARCH LIGHT

How many times did Cleopatra rule Egypt?

She spoke nine languages, was a good mathematician, and had a great head for business. And she would use both her intelligence and her beauty to hold on to power. Today, Cleopatra VII Thea Philopator of Egypt is still an amazing historical figure.

Cleopatra was the second daughter of King Ptolemy XII. When her father died in 51 BC, 18-year-old Cleopatra was supposed to rule Egypt with her 15-year-old brother, Ptolemy XIII. In a few years, her brother's supporters drove Cleopatra from power. But later the Roman leader Julius Caesar helped her get her throne back. War soon broke out. In 47 BC Cleopatra's brother and co-ruler drowned. By law she couldn't rule alone, so she married her 11-year-old brother.

Cleopatra returned to Rome to live with Caesar and had a son by him named Caesarion. But Caesar was murdered in 44 BC, and Cleopatra lost her strongest supporter. She soon went back to Egypt. With Caesar dead, the two most powerful men in Rome were Octavian and Mark Antony. When Antony wanted to invade Persia, he invited Cleopatra to meet him.

Antony quickly fell in love with Cleopatra and married her. But he was also married to Octavian's sister. An angry Octavian declared war against Antony and eventually defeated him. Antony died in Cleopatra's arms.

Cleopatra did not want to live without Antony. The story is that she had an asp (a kind of snake) brought to her, and when it bit her, Cleopatra died at the age of 39. The Egyptians believed that death by snakebite made you **immortal**. Cleopatra didn't live forever, but her legend has lasted more than 2,000 years.

DID YOU KNOW?
William Shakespeare wrote a play about Egypt's most famous queen, called *Antony and Cleopatra.*

This image of the Egyptian queen Cleopatra appears on a temple of the goddess Hathor in Dandarah, Egypt. Hathor was the goddess of the sky, of women, and of love.
The Art Archive

Answer: Cleopatra ruled Egypt twice.

A Clever, Courageous Queen

When Elizabeth I became queen of England, few thought she would last very long. But Elizabeth I not only ruled for almost half a century. She became one of England's greatest rulers.

Elizabeth was the daughter of Anne Boleyn, King Henry VIII's second wife. Henry also had a daughter, Mary, from his first marriage, and he would have a son, Edward, from his third. After Henry's death, Edward ruled for a short time until he died. Mary ruled for three years before she too died. In 1558 Elizabeth became the queen of England at age 25.

At the time, England was poor, weak, and torn by **conflict** between different groups. The people hoped Elizabeth would marry a strong man who would guide her. But Elizabeth had no desire to share her power. She was determined to be a successful queen, so she gathered experienced and trustworthy advisers. Elizabeth herself had a good education and was very clever and brave.

The queen encouraged English sailors to travel to distant parts of the world. Captains such as Francis Drake brought back riches and found new trade routes to the Americas, Asia, and Africa. As trade developed with other lands, England grew wealthy. Under Elizabeth, England also experienced a Renaissance, or 'rebirth' of the arts. Some of the famous writers of the period were William Shakespeare, Christopher Marlowe, Francis Bacon, Edmund Spenser, and John Donne.

By the time Elizabeth died in 1603, England had become both rich and strong. The 45 years of her **reign** became known as the Elizabethan Age.

SEARCH LIGHT

Elizabeth ruled England only after her
a) two sisters ruled.
b) sister and brother ruled.
c) two brothers ruled.

Oil painting of Elizabeth I with members of her court.
© Stapleton Collection/Corbis

DID YOU KNOW?
During Elizabeth's rule, Spain attacked England with a great fleet of ships called the Spanish Armada. England's victory over the Spanish forces saved the country from becoming part of the Spanish empire.

Elizabeth I, popularly known as Good Queen Bess, became queen after the death of her half sister in 1558. She loved showy clothing and jewels.
© Archivo Iconografico, S.A./Corbis

Answer: b) sister and brother ruled.

The Dragon Lady

One of the most powerful women in Chinese history was Cixi. She controlled China for more than 40 years in the late 1800s. Cixi was so **ruthless** and dangerous that some people called her the Dragon Lady.

In Western countries such as Great Britain and the United States, Cixi was also known as the Empress Dowager. But she was never really an empress. She was just the mother of the emperor's only son. When the emperor died, she helped her 6-year-old son, who was heir to the throne, rule China. She still had power when her son was old enough to rule by himself. Then he died, and the Dragon Lady made sure her 4-year-old nephew became the new emperor. This was against the law, but she helped him rule too.

The Dragon Lady lived in a group of palace buildings called the Forbidden City, within the city of Beijing. Only the servants who lived there too ever saw Cixi.

She spoke to all her visitors from a large red throne shaped like a dragon that was hidden behind a silk screen. Every one of her orders ended with the warning "Hear and obey".

Under Cixi the Chinese government became very dishonest. Many believed that Cixi had many people murdered. In 1908, when the Dragon Lady was dying, she had her nephew, the emperor, poisoned. She wanted to make sure that he died first and thus would never rule without her.

SEARCH LIGHT

Did anybody ever see the Empress of China?

DID YOU KNOW?

The Dragon Lady wore solid gold shields on her very long fingernails to keep them from breaking.

Known in the West as the Empress Dowager, Cixi controlled the political life of China for many decades. The nation was fairly stable under her influence, but the government was dishonest and did not make changes that were needed to benefit the people.
© Hulton-Deutsch Collection/Corbis

Answer: Only the servants living within the Forbidden City ever saw the Empress of China.

Founder of Pakistan

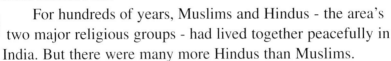

Mohammed Ali Jinnah was born in Karachi in 1876. At that time the city was part of India, and India was controlled by the British. When Jinnah was a young man, his parents sent him to London to gain business experience. Instead, he studied law and learned about the British system of government. After his studies, he returned to India and began to practice law in Bombay (now Mumbai). It was about this time that the people of India began to seek freedom from British rule.

For hundreds of years, Muslims and Hindus - the area's two major religious groups - had lived together peacefully in India. But there were many more Hindus than Muslims. Because of this, many Muslims feared that they might not be treated equally once India became an independent country.

Although Jinnah was Muslim, at first he didn't think there was anything to be afraid of. But as time passed, he began to feel that the Muslims in India should have their own country. So Jinnah began to work hard to make a Muslim nation out of part of India's land. The new country would be called Pakistan.

In 1947 the British government agreed to the formation of Pakistan. India became independent from Britain in August of that year, and a section of the country became Pakistan. Jinnah was chosen as Pakistan's first head of state, but he served for only a year before he died. Despite his short rule, Jinnah's people loved him. And because he helped create Pakistan, Jinnah is considered the Father of Pakistan.

SEARCH LIGHT

For which people did Jinnah want to build a country?

Mohammed Ali Jinnah.
© Bettmann/Corbis

DID YOU KNOW?
When Jinnah was a law student in London, he worked to help Dadabhai Naoroji become the first Indian member of the British Parliament.

Mohammed Ali Jinnah founded the state of Pakistan in 1947. Here, Pakistani soldiers in 1993 hang a portrait of Jinnah as part of preparations for Pakistan Day in March.
© Reuters NewMedia Inc./Corbis

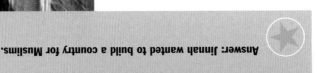
Answer: Jinnah wanted to build a country for Muslims.

A Fighter for Rights

South African leader Nelson Mandela was a fighter. He fought against apartheid. Apartheid was an official policy of the government of South Africa that separated people according to their race and colour.

During World War II, Mandela joined the African National Congress (ANC), and he later became one of its leaders. This organization had one aim - to fight for the freedom of the black people in South Africa.

Mandela didn't want to use violence in the ANC's fight against the government. However, after the police killed unarmed Africans, Mandela changed his mind. He argued for using **sabotage** against the government - that is, secretly working to undermine and destroy it. At the same time, the South African government outlawed the ANC. In 1962 the government decided that Mandela was guilty of acts against the government. He was sentenced to five years in prison. The following year, he was found guilty of more charges and sentenced to life imprisonment.

By the 1980s, more and more people had heard about Mandela's hopes for South Africa. They began to **campaign** for his release from prison. Countries and organizations all over the world gave him their support. Early in 1990, South Africa's president, F.W. de Klerk, ordered Mandela's release. President de Klerk, together with Mandela, worked to change South Africa into a country where all races would have equal rights.

South Africa held its first elections open to people of all races in 1994. Mandela and the ANC won the elections, and Mandela became the country's first black president.

Nelson Mandela in 1990.
© David Turnley/Corbis

SEARCH LIGHT

True or false? Mandela spent his life in prison.

DID YOU KNOW?
In 1993 Nelson Mandela and F.W. de Klerk were jointly awarded the Nobel Prize for Peace for ending the apartheid system.

Nelson Mandela spent nearly 30 years of his life as a political prisoner. Four years after his release he ran for president of South Africa. He was elected in April 1994.
© Peter Turnley/Corbis

Answer: FALSE. He served a large part of his life - almost 30 years - in prison.

Architect of Modern China

Mao Zedong was born in 1893 in China's Hunan province. Mao's father had been born a poor peasant, but he became wealthy as a farmer and grain dealer. Only limited education was available where Mao grew up. So, at the age of 13, he left school to work on his family's farm. He later ran away to attend school in the provincial capital, where he discovered new ideas from Chinese and Western thinkers.

Mao Zedong in 1967.
© Bettmann/Corbis

Mao briefly served in the army during the Chinese Revolution (1911-12). This uprising overthrew the ruling Manchu **dynasty** and turned China into a **republic**. After that there were many years of fighting between different groups who wanted to rule China. This time was known as the 'warlord period'.

After the war, Mao returned to school, ending up at Beijing University, where he worked in the library. There he became involved in the May Fourth Movement of 1919. This was the beginning of China's move towards communism. In communism, property is owned by the state or community, and all citizens are supposed to have a share in the nation's wealth.

SEARCH LIGHT

Was Mao's family rich or poor?

In the 1920s, Mao helped create the Chinese Communist Party (CCP). He started a communist revolution among peasants in the countryside. The CCP broke away from the Nationalist Party. The Nationalists thought that the Chinese should decide their own future, but they opposed communism. The Red Army, Mao's military force, began fighting them and gathering strength in the late 1920s.

DID YOU KNOW?
During World War II, Mao's communists and the Nationalists joined together to fight against Japan's invasion of China.

Mao finally took control of the whole country in 1949 and became the chairman of the People's Republic of China. Although the lives of many poor people were improved under Mao, many others suffered and died during his efforts at reform and improvement. He died on September 9, 1976.

Mao Zedong, the leader of the Chinese communists, spent a great deal of time in the countryside trying to gain support for his ideas. Here, as a young man, he speaks to a group of his followers.
© Bettmann/Corbis

Answer: Actually, they were both. His father was born poor but later became a wealthy farmer and merchant.

Israel's First Woman
Prime Minister

In 1906, when Goldie Mabovitch was a child, poverty forced her family to move from Russia to the United States to find work. At school, she joined a group that wanted Jews to have their own country. This was known as Zionism. A few years later she and her husband, Morris Myerson, moved to Palestine, a Middle Eastern region then under British control.

Goldie Myerson became involved in political activities in Palestine. She **negotiated** protection for Jews who fled from Nazi Europe during World War II. After the war, she worked to help Jewish war refugees.

In 1948 part of Palestine became the State of Israel, and Goldie Myerson was one of the signers of Israel's declaration of independence. The surrounding Arab countries attacked Israel, but the new country defended itself and remained independent.

The following year she was elected to the Knesset, the Israeli **parliament**. Later she changed her last name from Myerson to 'Meir', a Hebrew word meaning 'to burn brightly'. She also became known as 'Golda' instead of Goldie.

Israeli Prime Minister Golda Meir in 1972.
© Hulton-Deutsch Collection/Corbis

Meir became the prime minister of Israel in February 1969. As prime minister, she worked hard for peace in the Middle East and travelled widely to meet with the leaders of many other countries.

But in 1973 Egypt and Syria's invasion of Israel led to another Arab-Israeli war. Though Israel eventually won the war, the whole country was stunned by the attack. Many Israelis felt Meir's government was to blame, and so she resigned as prime minister the following year.

DID YOU KNOW?
Golda Meir was 71 years old when she became the world's third female prime minister. The first two were Sirimavo R.D. Bandaranaike of Ceylon (now Sri Lanka) and Indira Gandhi of India.

Before she became Israel's prime minister, Golda Meir served as Israel's representative to the United Nations. In this photo, Meir helps a little girl light five candles to celebrate Israel's fifth anniversary.
© Bettmann/Corbis

Egypt's Man of Peace

When Muhammad Anwar el-Sadat was born in 1918, Egypt was still a British colony and was ruled by a sultan. But one day Sadat would rise to become Egypt's president.

Sadat was in the army during World War II. After that he joined an organization that wanted to overthrow the Egyptian **monarchy** and drive out the British. The organization was led by Gamal Abdel Nasser. In 1952 Nasser's group was successful, and Egypt gained its independence. Nasser became the country's first president, and Sadat twice served as his vice-president. When Nasser died in 1970, Sadat became president.

Egypt had lost control of the land lying between Egypt and Israel during a war with Israel in 1967. The two countries remained enemies after that. In six years Sadat ordered Egyptian forces to retake this land. Israel won the war that followed. But Sadat's actions made him very popular in Egypt and in other Arab countries.

Four years after the war, Sadat sought peace with Israel. He visited the country to share his peace plan. Later he held peace talks in the United States with the Israeli prime minister, Menachem Begin. Because of their efforts, Sadat and Begin shared the 1978 Nobel Prize for Peace.

The following year, Egypt and Israel signed a peace treaty - Israel's first with an Arab country. Sadat's actions were praised around the world. But many Egyptians and other Arabs opposed the treaty. In 1981 Sadat was killed by religious **extremists** during a military parade.

Anwar el-Sadat, reviewing a military parade, shortly before he was killed.
© Kevin Fleming/Corbis

SEARCH LIGHT

True or false? Sadat did not want Egypt to be run by a king.

DID YOU KNOW?
While Sadat was working to overthrow the Egyptian monarchy, he went to prison twice. The second time he was imprisoned, he taught himself French and English.

When Egypt and Israel were working to make peace, U.S. President Jimmy Carter was a great help. Here (from left to right) you see Sadat's wife, Jehan, and Sadat himself, with the U.S. first lady, Rosalynn Carter, and President Carter.
© Wally McNamee/Corbis

Answer: **TRUE.**

World Peacemaker

A peacemaker has to be impartial - that is, be fair and not take sides. U Thant was a true peacemaker. As the secretary-general of the United Nations between 1961 and 1971, he had the job of peacemaker among many warring countries.

U Thant was born in 1909 in Burma (now called Myanmar). 'U' is not a name but a term of respect similar to the English word 'Mister'. Thant means 'pure'. Thant was educated at the University of Rangoon. It was here that he met Thakin Nu, later called U Nu. U Nu went on to become the prime minister of Burma after World War II.

Nu recognized Thant's abilities and appointed him as a spokesman for the government. Later Thant became a **diplomat** when he was appointed a member of the Burmese representatives to the United Nations (UN). In 1957 he became his country's permanent representative to the UN, and he later served as vice president of the UN General Assembly.

When the UN's leader, the secretary-general, died in 1961, the United States and the Soviet Union could not agree on a new leader for the body. Though neither country got their first choice, they were able to settle on Thant as acceptable.

As secretary-general, Thant worked for peace around the world. In 1962 he aided in the removal of Soviet missiles from Cuba. He also helped to end the civil war in the Congo, and he established a peacekeeping force on Cyprus in the Mediterranean Sea. When India and Pakistan went to war in 1965, Thant flew to India to help negotiate the ceasefire.

SEARCH LIGHT

True or false? U is U Thant's first name.

DID YOU KNOW?

In 1976 an island in New York's East River, near the UN headquarters, was decorated with trees and flowers and called U Thant.

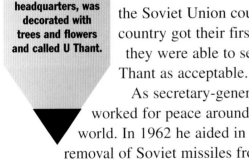

U Thant was a faithful Buddhist, and he applied a Buddhist attitude of focus and open-mindedness to his work at the United Nations.
© Bettmann/Corbis

Answer: FALSE. U has a meaning similar to the word 'Mister'.

A Young Girl and Her Diary

During World War II in Europe, the Nazis of Germany tried to destroy the Jewish people and their culture. The Nazis had taken control of many countries, including the Netherlands (Holland). In the city of Amsterdam, the Nazi threat forced a young Jewish girl and her family to spend two years in hiding. Anne Frank's moving diary of those years in hiding has since become a classic book.

Halfway through the war, the Nazis began sending Jews to prison camps. So in July 1942, Anne's family went into hiding in the back-room office and warehouse of Anne's father's business. Four other Jews hid with them in the small space, and non-Jewish friends smuggled food and other supplies to them.

Anne was 13 when she went into hiding. In her diary, she describes daily life in the secret rooms. She also writes about her own dreams and feelings while growing up in hiding.

SEARCH LIGHT

True or false? Anne Frank went on to write many other famous books.

Anne Frank.
Anne Frank House, Amsterdam and Anne Frank-Fonds, Basel—Hulton/Archive by Getty Images

The family never once left their hideout until the Nazi police discovered them in August 1944. Then the Frank family was moved to the concentration camp at Auschwitz in Poland, where Anne's mother died in 1945. Anne and her sister were sent to another camp, Bergen-Belsen, where they both died of typhus. Anne's father, Otto Frank, was the only family member who survived.

Friends had found Anne's diary in the hiding space. After the war, they gave it to her father, and he published it in 1947. Since then, Anne's story of courage and hope has inspired millions of readers. Today, the Frank family's hiding place in Amsterdam is a museum.

DID YOU KNOW?

A new English translation of Anne Frank's diary was published in 1995. The new edition has material that was not in the original version and is nearly one-third longer.

Anne Frank sits at her desk at school in 1940. She left school at the age of 13 to go into hiding.
Anne Frank House, Amsterdam and Anne Frank-Fonds, Basel—Hulton/Archive by Getty Images

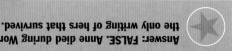

Answer: FALSE. Anne died during World War II, and her diary is the only writing of hers that survived.

Hero of Many Nations

In the early 1800s, in the country that would become Venezuela, there lived a man with a big dream. He wanted the countries of Spanish South America to become independent from Spain and join together as one strong country.

Portrait of Simón Bolívar by M.N. Bate.
© Bettmann/Corbis

This man was Simón Bolívar. For years he fought the Spanish in support of this dream, and many people came to help him from all over the world. Many of them sailed from Europe and searched all over South America to find him.

Bolívar was born in 1783. His **liberation** of New Granada - now Colombia, Ecuador, and parts of several other countries - is one of the most daring acts in the history of war. In the spring of 1819 he led a small army of 2,500 men through floodwaters and across icy mountain passes, through places where there were no paths at all. Tired and hungry, they finally arrived in Boyacá, near Bogotá, the capital of New Granada. There they surprised a big Spanish army. Fighting fiercely, they beat the Spanish and freed New Granada.

Bolívar fought many battles to free other countries in South America, including his native Venezuela. His dream of freeing the South American countries from Spain came true. But even if he was never able to join all the different countries together as one nation, he is one of the most important heroes in South America. The South American country of Bolivia was named in his honour.

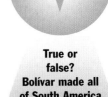

SEARCH LIGHT

True or false? Bolívar made all of South America come together as one nation.

DID YOU KNOW?
The money in Venezuela is named for the South American liberator Simón Bolívar. It's called the *bolívar*.

In addition to the countries that are now Colombia and Ecuador, Simón Bolívar and his troops won the independence of Venezuela and Peru.
© Bettmann/Corbis

Answer: FALSE. He did, however, help free many nations from Spanish rule.

Salt and Empires

In March of 1930, a 61-year-old Indian man started out on a long walk to the ocean. When people asked where he was going, Mohandas ('Mahatma') Gandhi replied, 'I am going to the ocean to get some salt.' Soon thousands joined him in a trip that lasted a month and became known as the 'Salt March'.

Mahatma Gandhi.
© Bettmann/Corbis

Mohandas K. Gandhi was a Hindu Indian who had studied law in London. India was controlled by Britain, and when Gandhi returned home he was angered by the poverty and inequality he saw in his country. Rather than fight the British with guns or bombs, Gandhi believed in simply refusing to obey unjust laws. For example, he urged Indians to make their own clothing so they wouldn't have to buy British goods. Hindus began to call Gandhi 'Mahatma', which means 'great soul'.

Most Indians could not afford to buy expensive British salt, but it was against the law for them to make their own. So Gandhi walked 300 kilometres to the sea to make salt from seawater. After the Salt March, the British put Gandhi in jail. It wasn't the first or the last time he was jailed for leading non-violent protests. Gandhi went to jail cheerfully. When he came out, he went back to teaching Indians how to regain control of their country by peaceful means. India finally won independence from Britain in 1947.

After India became independent, there was violence between the country's Hindu and Muslim populations. During the last year of his life, Gandhi worked to build peace between all the peoples of India.

SEARCH LIGHT

True or false? Gandhi's real name was Mahatma.

DID YOU KNOW?
In the Hindi language, Gandhi's principle of non-violence is known as *satyagraha*. The word means 'truth force'.

Mahatma Gandhi, leader of the Indian non-violent protest, marches with supporters to the shore at Dandi to collect salt in violation of the law. Following this action, he was jailed.
© Bettmann/Corbis

Answer: FALSE. Mohandas was his name. Mahatma was a title of respect.

Civil Rights Leader

Martin Luther King Jr riding a bus in Montgomery, Alabama, U.S., in 1956.
© Bettmann/Corbis

On 1 December 1955, in Montgomery, Alabama, U.S., a black woman called Rosa Parks was arrested. She had refused to give up her seat on a bus to a white man. At that time, the law said that black people had to sit only in certain sections of trains and buses and use different public toilets and even drinking fountains from the ones white people used. Rosa Parks' action sparked protests by black residents of the city. And Martin Luther King Jr was chosen to lead the protests.

SEARCH LIGHT

True or false? Martin Luther King Jr set off the Montgomery bus boycott.

King was a Baptist minister and a student of the Indian leader Mahatma Gandhi. He believed that non-violence was the most powerful way for people to make their point. This means demanding rights through peaceful methods, such as **strikes** and protests, not by fighting. The protests he led became known as the Montgomery bus **boycott**. The law was changed after a year of protests.

However, black people still didn't receive the same rights and privileges as white people. In 1963 King and his supporters were imprisoned because of their protests against **discrimination**. When he was freed, King and other **civil rights** leaders organized a march on Washington, D.C., the national capital. There, King delivered a powerful speech to hundreds of thousands of people, saying: 'I have a dream.' His dream was that one day all people would be equal, like brothers.

For his work on civil rights, King was awarded the Nobel Prize for Peace in 1964. Through all his struggles, King used only peaceful methods of protest. But in April 1968, King was shot dead in Memphis, Tennessee, by James Earl Ray.

Martin Luther King Jr led the march on Washington in 1963. His protests helped win important rights for African Americans.
© Bettmann/Corbis

DID YOU KNOW?
In 1977, King was posthumously (after his death) awarded the Presidential Medal of Freedom. This is the U.S. government's highest honour awarded to a person not in the military.

Around-the-World Voyager

Hundreds of years ago, only very brave men took the risk of travelling the open seas to reach unknown lands. Ferdinand Magellan was one such man.

Magellan was born into a **noble** family in Portugal in about 1480. When he was about 25, he joined the Portuguese navy, where he fought in numerous battles and saw many new places. But the king of Portugal refused to increase his **wages** after a decade of service, so Magellan went to work for the Spanish king.

At that time, Portugal controlled the sea route around Africa to the Indian Ocean to reach the rich Spice Islands (now called the East Indies). Magellan decided to sail west to find a new route to the islands. He set out in 1519, sailing across the Atlantic and down the coast of South America. He hoped to discover a passage to the ocean beyond South America. When he found it, he named it the Strait of Magellan. The ocean on the other side appeared calm and peaceful. Magellan called it the Pacific, from the Latin word for 'peaceful'.

An illustration of Ferdinand Magellan's ship *Victoria*.
Collection of the Bibliotheque Nationale; photo, © Erich Lessing/Art Resource, New York

SEARCH LIGHT

Unscramble the following words:
- utgroPal
- ciSpe sladIns
- fiPicac nOace

After 99 more days, Magellan's ship reached the island now known as Guam. Landing in the islands we call the Philippines, Magellan and his men fought with the islanders. Magellan was killed there on 27 April 1521.

A crewman, Juan Sebastián de Elcano, took command. The remaining crew sailed to the Spice Islands, loaded up with spices, and returned to Spain. In a voyage that took more than three years, they became the first men to circle the globe. But during that time, 200 men had died.

This painting from 1970 shows the Portuguese explorer Ferdinand Magellan. He led an expedition that was the first to travel all the way around the Earth.
The Art Archive/Marine Museum, Lisbon/Dagli Orti

DID YOU KNOW?
The Strait of Magellan isn't all that's been named for the famous explorer. Magellan's name remains a popular choice for other things. For instance, the space mission begun in 1989 to explore the planet Venus was called Magellan.

510

Answer: utgroPal = Portugal ciSpe sladIns = Spice Islands fiPicac nOace = Pacific Ocean

On Top of the World

On 29 May 1953, at 11.30 AM, Tenzing Norgay and Edmund Hillary became the first people to reach the **summit** of the highest mountain on Earth, Mount Everest.

Tenzing Norgay.
UPI—EB Inc.

Tenzing Norgay was born in 1914 in Tibet (now part of China). He later moved to Nepal and lived with the Sherpa people. Sherpas, who moved from Tibet to Nepal hundreds of years ago, have lived in high mountains for hundreds of years. Not far from Tenzing's adopted village rises the majestic Everest. It is part of the Himalaya Mountains and lies on the border between Nepal and Tibet. When Europeans went to Nepal to climb mountains, many Sherpas were hired to carry supplies for the mountain climbers. Because of their experience living in high mountains, they proved to be excellent guides and **mountaineers**.

At the age of 18, Tenzing moved to Darjeeling (Darjiling), in India. He hoped to earn his living carrying supplies for mountaineering expeditions. Three years later, he accompanied a survey team as a **porter** on an expedition to climb Mount Everest. During the next few years, he took part in more Everest expeditions than any other climber.

Working with so many different people, Tenzing learned to speak seven languages. Later he became a *sirdar*, or an organizer of porters. He continued to guide expeditions to Everest and inspired many mountaineers.

During their historic climb of Mount Everest in 1953, Edmund Hillary lost his footing and nearly died. Tenzing did not panic. He held the rope line tightly and planted his axe firmly in the ice. Later he simply said, 'Mountain climbers always help one another.'

For his courage and heroism and for having been one of the first people to scale Mount Everest, Tenzing was awarded the British George Cross and the Star of Nepal.

Fill in the gap: Someone who organizes porters for mountain climbing in the Himalayas is called a _____.

DID YOU KNOW?
Tenzing Norgay was the first man to be photographed on the summit of Everest. Since Tenzing could not operate a camera, Edmund Hillary took the photograph.

Here, Edmund Hillary (on the left) and Tenzing Norgay prepare for one part of their climb to the top of Mount Everest.
Royal Geographical Society; photo, Alfred Gregory

Answer: Someone who organizes porters for mountain climbing in the Himalayas is called a *sirdar.*

Mother
of the Poor and Dying

Was
Mother Teresa
Indian
by birth?

During her lifetime Mother Teresa became known worldwide for her kindness and her **charitable** work.

Mother Teresa was born Agnes Gonxha Bojaxhiu in Albania (now Macedonia) in 1910. When she was 18 years old, she decided to become a nun in the Roman Catholic church. She travelled to Ireland and there she joined the Institute of the Blessed Virgin Mary. She took **vows** promising to live a simple life and not to marry, and she became Sister Teresa.

The Institute had charity missions in India, and soon Sister Teresa sailed to the country to work as a teacher. Over the next 17 years, she taught in two schools in India, one of which was in Calcutta (now Kolkata). She saw firsthand the poverty and suffering of the people. She often said that she was inspired to make two important decisions in her life. One was to become a nun, and in 1946 the other was to devote her life to helping the sick and the poor.

As soon as her studies in nursing were finished, she began working with the people living in Calcutta's slums. She became an Indian citizen. And she became Mother Teresa when she founded the Missionaries of Charity. This was a new order of Roman Catholic nuns who wanted to help the sick, especially the dying and disabled.

Under Mother Teresa's guidance, the Missionaries of Charity opened centres all over the world. In these centres anyone could receive care, no matter what their religion. In 1979 Mother Teresa was awarded the Nobel Prize for Peace. Soon after her death, in 1997, the Roman Catholic church began the process to have Mother Teresa declared a saint.

DID YOU KNOW?
When Mother Teresa founded her religious order, the Missionaries of Charity, her Indian nuns adopted the *sari* as their habit, or official dress. The *sari* is a garment worn by most women of India, Pakistan, and Bangladesh.

Mother Teresa lived in poverty with some of India's poorest people. She made it her life's work to care for the country's poor and dying.
© Bettmann/Corbis

Answer: No. Mother Teresa was born in Albania (now Macedonia), near Greece. But she lived and worked in India and became an Indian citizen.

The First Modern Woman Doctor

SEARCH LIGHT

Fill in
the gaps:
In 1868 Blackwell
started the first
_____
for women.

Elizabeth Blackwell was born in England in 1821, but she moved to the United States with her family when she was 11. By the time she was 23, Blackwell had decided that she wanted to be a doctor. But at this time there were no female doctors in the United States.

It wasn't easy for Blackwell to study medicine. Most of the medical colleges she applied to turned her down. The men who taught medicine didn't think it was right for a woman to be a doctor. Finally, Blackwell was admitted to Geneva Medical College in New York. She was the only woman in a class of 150.

The other medical students made things difficult for Blackwell. They criticized her, refused to talk to her, and kept her from taking part in the classroom medical demonstrations. However, two years later, Blackwell was the best student in her class. In 1849 she became the first female doctor in the United States.

Photograph of Elizabeth Blackwell.
Courtesy, Hobart and William Smith Colleges

Despite this training, Blackwell could not get a job in any of the city hospitals. So she opened her own hospital, the New York Infirmary for Women and Children, in a district where many poor people lived. When the American Civil War broke out in 1861, Blackwell's hospital became a relief centre for wounded soldiers. She also helped select and train nurses for the war.

Blackwell worked to establish a medical school for women, so that other women could become doctors. In 1868 she opened the Woman's Medical College, the first of its kind in America.

DID YOU KNOW?
A year after Blackwell opened her hospital, her sister Emily came to work with her. She, too, had become a doctor.

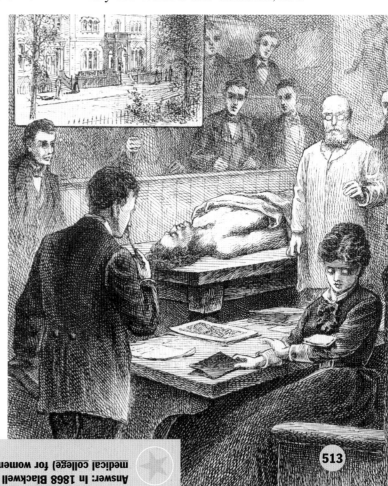

Elizabeth Blackwell was not only the first American woman doctor. She also became the first woman to have her name placed on the British medical register. This meant she was allowed to practise medicine in Great Britain.
© Bettmann/Corbis

Answer: In 1868 Blackwell started the first medical school (or medical college) for women.

Gold Medallist
in Athletics

When she won the 400-metre world championship in 1997, Cathy Freeman ran a victory lap carrying two flags. One was the flag of her country, Australia. The other was that of her people, the Aboriginals. The Aboriginals are the original people of Australia, who have suffered great mistreatment and injustice since the Europeans came to their country. Her choice to carry both flags was **controversial**. But it showed Freeman's strong sense of national and ethnic pride.

While Freeman was growing up in Queensland, her father encouraged her to start running. By the time she was 17, Freeman had won a gold medal at the 1990 Commonwealth Games and been named Young Australian of the Year. In 1992 she was the first Australian Aboriginal woman to compete in the Olympic Games.

At the 1994 Commonwealth Games, Freeman took home gold medals in the 400-metre and 200-metre races. Her win in the 200-metre race set a national record. Perhaps Freeman's greatest race was at the 1996 Olympic Games in Atlanta, Georgia, U.S. She ran against the world record holder, Marie-José Pérec of France. The two champions raced neck and neck. Finally, it was Pérec who shot ahead to the finish line.

SEARCH LIGHT

How many Olympic Games has Freeman competed in?
a) 1
b) 2
c) 3

Cathy Freeman holding the Olympic torch in 2000.
© Reuters NewMedia Inc./Corbis

In 1997 Freeman was named Australian of the Year. A year later, however, she injured her foot and had to withdraw from the Commonwealth Games. Freeman didn't let the injury stop her, and in 1999 she was running again. She came back and successfully defended her 400-metre world championship title. At the Sydney Olympics in 2000, Freeman had the great honour of lighting the Olympic torch. A week later her dream of Olympic gold came true when she won the 400-metre race in front of her fellow Australians. Again she took her victory lap proudly carrying both the Australian and Aboriginal flags.

DID YOU KNOW?
In a rush to get to her first track race, 8-year-old Cathy Freeman ran into a post and hurt her eye. She ran her first race with one eye closed and won it easily.

Cathy Freeman was the first Aboriginal to win an individual medal in an Olympic event. She won the 400-metre race at the 2000 Olympics in Sydney, Australia.
© Duomo/Corbis

Answer: c) 3

The Man Who Discovered Outer Space

Galileo Galilei was born in Pisa, Italy, in 1564. As a young man he became interested in mathematics and **astronomy**. He loved to experiment and try out new ideas.

Galileo.
© Bettmann/Corbis

A story claims that Galileo once dropped objects of different weights from the top of the famous Leaning Tower of Pisa. He wanted to prove that things fall at the same speed, no matter how much they weigh. But some of Galileo's ideas angered other scientists, so he left Pisa and went to Padua.

For years Galileo taught mathematics at the University of Padua. But in 1609 his career changed direction. Galileo heard about the telescope, a Dutch invention that could make distant objects appear closer. Galileo figured out how such a device would work and then used **lenses** from spectacle makers' shops to make his own telescopes. Galileo's telescopes were better than most and could make objects appear up to 20 times larger than what the naked eye could see.

Galileo began to look up into the night sky. In December 1609, with the help of his telescope, Galileo learned that the Moon's surface is rough and uneven. A month later he discovered four moons orbiting the planet Jupiter. Also, when Galileo studied Saturn, he noticed something mysterious about its appearance. Later scientists would learn that the planet's strange look was due to its large rings.

Using his telescopes, Galileo helped change how people looked up at space. Likewise, much of the modern science of **physics** is based on his ideas - especially his ideas about how objects of all sizes move and how helpful it is to test scientific ideas by experimenting.

> **Fill in the gap:** Galileo built his own _____, which was an improvement on others built earlier.

DID YOU KNOW?
Galileo agreed with Nicolaus Copernicus and Johannes Kepler that the Earth orbits the Sun. This upset the Roman Catholic church, and Galileo was forced to tell everyone he was wrong.

This fresco (a painting created on wet plaster) shows Galileo demonstrating his version of the telescope.
© Archivo Iconografico, S.A./Corbis

Answer: Galileo built his own telescope, which was an improvement on others built earlier.

515

The Woman Who Lived with Chimpanzees

In the 1940s a young English girl named Jane Goodall dreamed of living in the African forests among the animals she'd read about. As she grew older, Goodall began to make her dream come true.

In 1957, when she was about 23 years old, a school friend invited Goodall to Kenya, in Africa. While in Africa, Goodall met the famous scientist Dr Louis Leakey. At the time, Leakey was studying wild chimpanzees in order to find out more about the origins of human life. He was impressed by Goodall's interest in animals and encouraged her to study chimpanzees in Tanzania.

Some people thought that Goodall wouldn't last for more than a few months in the forest amongst the wild animals. But Goodall proved them wrong and ended up living in Tanzania for 15 years. During that time, the chimpanzees slowly became used to Goodall and finally allowed her to spend hours around them.

Jane Goodall presenting a stuffed toy monkey to United Nations Secretary-General Kofi Annan in 2002.
© AFP/Corbis

Being able to watch the chimpanzees up close allowed Goodall to discover many things about the animals that people did not know. Goodall saw chimpanzees use sticks as simple tools to draw termites and ants out of their nests. Goodall also found that all chimpanzees are different from each other in their behaviour and **natures**, just like people.

As a child, Jane Goodall grew up reading about wild animals. But as an adult, she ended up writing many books of her own. In them she shared what she learned from 15 years of living with the wild chimpanzees of Africa.

DID YOU KNOW?

Before Goodall's studies, scientists believed chimpanzees were vegetarians. But Goodall learned that they do sometimes hunt and eat meat.

Jane Goodall spent many years in Africa studying chimpanzees. She encountered this curious chimp at the Gombe Stream Research Center in Tanzania in 1972.
© Bettmann/Corbis

Answer: Tarzan, Mowgli, and Dr Dolittle all lived with animals.

Woman of Courage

Helen Keller became blind and deaf soon after she was born, but she still managed to learn to read, write, and speak.

Helen Keller in her later years.
EB Inc.

Helen was born in Alabama in the United States in 1880. At 19 months, she fell ill, probably with scarlet fever. She recovered but lost her eyesight and hearing. Since she couldn't hear other people, she didn't learn to speak.

When Helen was 6 years old, Alexander Graham Bell examined her. He was a doctor for speech correction as well as being the inventor of the telephone. Bell sent a special teacher, Anne Sullivan, to stay with Helen as her **governess**.

Sullivan was herself a remarkable woman. She was very patient and taught Helen that things had names. She taught Helen to finger spell the alphabet. By using finger spelling on Helen's palm, Sullivan helped Helen understand names for things that she could feel.

Helen was a hard worker and soon learned to read a form of the alphabet with her fingers. She started to read by feeling raised letters and words on cardboard. Later she learned **Braille**, a system of writing that many blind people use. Another teacher, Sarah Fuller, taught Helen to speak by having her feel people's lips and throats as they were talking.

Despite her blindness, Helen Keller wrote numerous articles and several books, including *The Story of My Life* and *Helen Keller's Journal*. Her early life with Anne Sullivan is the subject of a well-known play and film called *The Miracle Worker*.

Helen Keller died when she was 88 years old. She is remembered as a woman of great courage and intelligence.

SEARCH LIGHT

True or false? Helen Keller was born deaf and blind.

DID YOU KNOW?
As an adult, Helen Keller lectured all over the world. And her efforts to improve the treatment of deaf and blind people helped to stop the practice of putting people with physical disabilities into asylums for the mentally ill.

Helen Keller (on the left) is shown here reading the lips of her teacher, Anne Sullivan (on the right). Sullivan stayed with her pupil from 1887 until her own death in 1936.
© Corbis

Answer: FALSE. Helen Keller became deaf and blind after an illness when she was almost 2 years old.

The Man Who Conquered Disease

In the 1800s, the bite of a dog with rabies meant certain death for the person who had been bitten. In 1885, when a rabid dog bit a boy called Joseph Meister, his mother was desperate. She went to the only man she thought might be able to cure her son.

Pasteur had found that rabies was caused by a virus - a disease-causing **agent** so small it could not be seen, even under a microscope. He had already worked out a way to defeat the rabies virus in animals. But he had never tried his treatment on humans. Pasteur treated Joseph, and Joseph became the first person to be cured of rabies.

Scientist Louis Pasteur.
© Hulton-Deutsch Collection/Corbis

SEARCH LIGHT

Pasteurization refers to
a) a disease-causing organism.
b) a weak dose of a disease.
c) heating something to kill bacteria.

Pasteur devoted his life to solving the problems of industry, farming, and medicine. He discovered that if a liquid like milk is heated to a certain temperature for a few minutes, it takes longer to spoil. If milk is not treated in this way, tiny living organisms called 'bacteria' cause it to go bad. These organisms are killed by heat in a process that came to be called 'pasteurization'.

Pasteur also discovered that many diseases are caused by germs that enter the body from outside. In 1877 he tried to find a cure for anthrax, a disease that affects the lungs and kills cattle and sheep. Pasteur successfully developed the method known as 'immunization'. Immunization means giving a patient a weak dose of a virus that the patient can fight off. Then the patient's body knows how to stop an actual case of the disease.

DID YOU KNOW?
In 1868 Pasteur saved the French silk industry. Silk businesses were facing ruin because of a mysterious disease that attacked the silkworms. Pasteur worked out a way of detecting the disease and preventing it from spreading.

Louis Pasteur's discoveries are among the most important in the history of medical science. He is often known as the founder of microbiology - the study of simple life forms too small to be seen with the naked eye.
© Hulton-Deutsch Collection/Corbis

Answer: c) heating something to kill bacteria.

Football Star

One man, more than any other, has helped to make football (soccer) popular around the world. That man is Pelé. Pelé, whose real name is Edson Arantes do Nascimento, was born in 1940 in Brazil.

Pelé holding the international football award for 'Footballer of the Century'.
© AFP/Corbis

Pelé made his **debut** with the Santos Football Club in 1956. With Pelé playing forward, the team won several South American cups. In 1962 the team won its first world championship. Pelé also played for Brazil's national team and helped it to win the World Cup championship in 1958, 1962, and 1970.

Pelé played for which country?
a) Brazil
b) Peru
c) Colombia

Pelé was a brilliant player who possessed great speed and balance. He could guess the moves of other players and had good control of the ball. In addition to all this, he could kick a ball powerfully with either foot, or direct it with his head, straight into the goal.

Pelé scored a career total of 1,281 goals in 1,363 matches, with 139 in one year alone. He scored his 1,000th goal in 1969. Pelé's career made him a national hero in Brazil. His fans call him Pérola Negra, meaning 'Black Pearl'.

Although Pelé retired in 1974, he made a comeback the following year with a New York team, the Cosmos. He said he returned to 'make soccer truly popular in the United States'. He succeeded, becoming a star in the United States as well.

Pelé's skills did not stop on the football field. He has also written best-selling **autobiographies**, starred in several films, and composed music, including the whole soundtrack for the 1977 film *Pelé*.

DID YOU KNOW?
When Pelé first went for trials with the major league football teams, he was repeatedly turned down.

Pelé in action was so magical to watch that once two armies stopped fighting just to watch him play.
© AFP/Corbis

Answer: a) Brazil

Plays That Never Grow Old

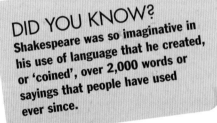

William Shakespeare is considered to be the greatest playwright in the English language and one of the most beloved playwrights in the world.

Not much is known about Shakespeare's life. He was born in Stratford-upon-Avon, England, in 1564. This was during the **reign** of Queen Elizabeth I. In his late 20s, Shakespeare went to the city of London to write and act. He joined a theatre **troupe** and began to write plays.

Over the next 20 years, Shakespeare wrote 38 plays and many poems. From his writing we can tell that he knew a lot about human feelings, as well as both city and country life. Most of the stories that Shakespeare told were known to his audience. But his characters and the way he told their stories in his plays attracted crowds of people to the Globe Theatre, where his troupe often performed.

A 2001 production of *A Midsummer Night's Dream* performed at the Albery Theatre in London.
© Archivo Iconografico, S.A./Corbis

DID YOU KNOW?
Shakespeare was so imaginative in his use of language that he created, or 'coined', over 2,000 words or sayings that people have used ever since.

Four hundred years later, people still enjoy reading Shakespeare's plays and seeing them onstage and in films. They quote his most famous lines (such as 'To be or not to be') and laugh and cry along with his characters. Shakespeare's plays have remained popular for several reasons. His characters show realistic human emotions. His **plots** are often complicated, but they always hold the audience's attention. And his language is powerful and poetic.

Some of Shakespeare's plays, such as *Hamlet*, have very sad endings. They are called 'tragedies'. Others, such as *A Midsummer Night's Dream*, are full of silly plots and have happy endings. They are the 'comedies'. Other Shakespeare plays, such as *Julius Caesar* or *Henry V*, are based on real-life figures and events. These are the 'histories'. And some plays, such as *Romeo and Juliet*, have a little bit of everything: romance, comedy, *and* tragedy.

SEARCH LIGHT

Which of the following describes a play with a happy ending?
a) tragedy
b) comedy
c) plot

William Shakespeare's plays have been popular for hundreds of years. Shown here is a portrait of the famous playwright.
© Robbie Jack/Corbis

Answer: b) comedy

abandon to leave without planning to return

abbey place where a community of monks or nuns live and work; also, the church serving that community

abdomen in insects, the end portion of the body that is behind the head and thorax (middle section)

absorb soak up

abstract (adjective) artistically communicating feelings or ideas about a subject, rather than creating a realistic image

abyssal unfathomable; of or relating to the bottom waters of the ocean depths

acid a chemical substance that produces a burning effect when interacting with some materials

acrobat performer who does tricks and physical routines that require strength, balance, and body control

acrylics type of paint

adaptation in biology, a change in an organism or its parts that allows the organism to survive better in its environment

aerial metallic rod or wire for sending or receiving radio waves or other energy signals

aerial acrobat performer who does tricks and feats above the ground or in the air, especially on a trapeze

affordable reasonable in price

agent something that produces an effect

aggressive openly hostile or tending to approach with great force or energy

agriculture farming

alas unfortunately or sadly

algae (singular: alga) group of organisms that are similar to plants and live mostly in the water

alpine relating to mountainous or hilly areas above the line where trees grow

altitude the distance of an object above a specific level (such as sea level) on a planet or other heavenly body

amphitheatre building with seats rising in curved rows around an open space where events such as games and plays take place

ancestry all the family members who lived before a particular individual

antenna (plural: antennae) in biology, a slender organ on the head of some insects and crustaceans (such as shrimps and lobsters) that allows them to sense their environment

anticlockwise in the direction opposite to the way a clock's hands move, as viewed from the front

antics playful or funny actions

arc a curved line

archaeology (adjective: archaeological) the science that deals with past human life as shown by fossils, tools, and other material left by ancient peoples

archbishop high-ranking priest in some Christian churches who oversees other bishops and church government in a very large area

architect person who designs and plans buildings and oversees their construction

architecture the art of designing and building structures, especially buildings that can be lived and worked in

archives place where public records or historical documents are kept

arena enclosed area used for public entertainment

aristocrat person of an upper class

artificial made by human beings rather than occurring in nature

aspect part, feature, or quality of something

asteroid small, often rocklike heavenly body orbiting the Sun

astronomy (adjective: astronomical) the science of the heavenly bodies and of their sizes, motions, and composition

atmosphere the envelope of gases that surrounds a planet

autobiography life story written by the person it is about

axis imaginary pole going through the centre of the Earth or other heavenly body

bacterium (plural: bacteria) tiny one-celled organism too small to see with the unaided eye

baleen a hardened substance from 0.6 to 3.6 metres long found in two rows along the upper jaws of certain whales

banish to force or drive away

barrier object that blocks access to another object or place; also, something that prevents something else from happening

basin in geography, the area of land drained by a river and its branches

bask to lie or relax in a warm place

bazaar marketplace where many kinds of goods are sold; *especially,* such a marketplace in Asia or Africa

bishop churchman ranking above a priest who oversees other clergy and carries out other official functions

bitter taste that is sharp and harsh, like a fruit that is not ripe

blockbuster huge, successful event

bond connection or friendship

botanical (noun: botany) having to do with plant life

boulevard wide avenue often having grass strips with trees along its centre or sides

bovine animal group that includes cattle, oxen, bison, and buffalo

bow a wooden rod with horsehairs stretched from end to end, used in playing a musical instrument such as a violin by stroking it

boycott the refusal to deal with a person, group, or country, usually in order to show disapproval or to force a change in behaviour

Braille a system of writing for the blind in which letters are represented by raised dots

bray to make a sound like the loud harsh call of a donkey

breadth width

brew to prepare by steeping (soaking) or boiling in hot water

broadcast send out a programme or message to a group, usually by radio, television, or the Internet

buff an off-white colour

burden weight or load to carry

burrow deep hole or tunnel made in the ground by an animal for shelter

bushman in Australia, a person who lives in the bush (wilderness)

cacti (singular: cactus) flowering plants of dry regions that have water-storing fleshy stems and, usually, sharp spines

calorie unit used to measure the amount of heat energy that food provides to the body

camouflage colours and patterns that allow a person, animal, or thing to blend in with its surroundings

campaign planned activities designed to lead to a particular result

canal artificial waterway for boats or for draining or supplying water to land

canoe a small light and narrow boat having sharp front and back ends and moved by paddling

canopy overhead covering

captive (noun: captivity) taken and held in a cage or as a prisoner

caravan group of pack animals or of vehicles travelling together one behind the other

carbohydrates plentiful, energy-producing natural substances that are formed by many food plants eaten by animals

carcass dead body or leftover parts of an animal

cargo goods transported in a ship, airplane, or other vehicle

cartridge sealed container

cassava tropical plant that has a thick underground root-like part and can be made into a number of foods

cast to form a shape by pouring a liquid into a mould and letting it harden

cathedral the main church of a district under the care of a bishop

ceramics objects made out of clay baked at high temperatures

cereal starchy seeds of certain grass plants grown for food

champagne a sparkling white wine

channel narrow waterway connecting two bodies of water

chapel small, sometimes private, place for prayer or special religious services

chariot ancient two-wheeled battle cart pulled by horses

charitable done to serve the needs of the poor or sick

château castle or large country house, especially in France

chemical one of the combined substances making up living and non-living things

choreographer creator of a dance

circulate flow

citadel castle or fortress that protects a city

citrus kind of tree or shrub grown in warm regions and having thick rind (skin) and fleshy fruits, including oranges, grapefruits, and lemons

civil rights the social and personal rights of a citizen

civil war war between opposing groups of citizens of the same country

civilization the way of life of a people at a particular time or place; also, a fairly advanced culture and technology

classical traditional in style

climate average weather in a particular area

clockwise in the direction that a clock's hands move, as viewed from the front

cloudburst sudden heavy rainfall

cobbled made of rounded stones larger than a pebble and smaller than a boulder

colony (plural: colonies; adjective: colonial; verb: colonize) 1) in general, a settlement established in a distant territory and controlled by a more powerful and expanding nation; 2) in biology, a group of similar organisms that live together in a particular place

comet chunk of frozen space debris that has a shiny tail and orbits the Sun

commanding grand and powerful

commandment law or rule for living

commerce (adjective: commercial) the buying and selling of goods, especially on a large scale and between different places

commission (verb) to order to be made; (noun) an order granting the power to perform various acts or duties

communism (adjective: communist) system of government in which all property is owned by the state or community and all 4 citizens are supposed to have a share in the total wealth

compose to create a literary, musical, or other artistic work

composer person who writes music

concentrated condensed, or made thicker, by removal of water

conductor the leader of an orchestra

conflict disagreement, struggle, or fighting

conquistador Spanish conqueror of Latin America

conservation the care and protection of something fragile, unique, and valuable, such as rare wildlife or ancient structures

conservative tending to safeguard existing views, conditions, or traditions

continent one of the largest of Earth's landmasses

contour the outline of a figure, body, or surface

contract to make smaller by tightening or squeezing together

controversial causing division or disagreement

convert to change; to win over to a new or different belief

conveyor belt a loop of material that can move objects from one worker or workstation to the next for the steps needed to make a product

core central part

corkscrew device with a handle and a spiral-twist metal piece, used for removing certain bottle stoppers

corridor passageway into which compartments or rooms open

countless too many to count

craft (noun) a skill or trade; (verb) to make skilfully, usually by hand

crater bowl-shaped dent in a surface

crest (adjective: crested) 1) in biology, an erect clump of fur or feathers, usually on an animal's head; 2) in geography, the upper edge or limit of something, such as the top of a mountain or a wave

critic person who studies and comments on the quality of or works of art

crossbreed to produce offspring from parents of two varieties or species

crossroads place where roads cross; also, a central meeting place or a decision-making point

crude oil oil taken from the ground and not yet cleaned or separated into different products; also called petroleum

cruise a pleasure trip on a large boat or ship

crusade campaign or cause taken up with passion and belief

crystal clear colourless glass of very good quality

cultivate in gardening and farming, to plant crops and to care for them as they grow

cutting in gardening and farming, a section of an adult plant capable of developing into a new individual

Cyrillic having to do with the alphabet for writing in Russian and other eastern European languages

dabble (adjective: dabbling) to reach with the bill to the bottom of shallow water in order to obtain food

data factual information or details

dean head of a division of a school or university

debris rubbish or fragments

debut first formal public appearance

decade ten-year period

delta large triangular area made of material deposited at the mouth of a river, where it empties into the sea

democracy (adjective: democratic) government in which the highest power is held by the citizens; they either use their power directly (usually by voting) or choose others to act for them

denomination religious organization based on beliefs; it joins church groups together to help govern them

depict to represent by a picture

deposit substance laid down by a natural process

descendant member of a recent age group of a family or similar division that began years earlier

descended related through a long line of ancestors

descent ancestry, heritage, or origin

devastate wreck or destroy

device tool or piece of equipment

devise work out, invent, or plan

dialect one of several varieties of a language used by the members of a particular group or class of people

dialogue conversation in a play, film, or written work

diameter the length of a straight line through the centre of an object

dictate to speak for another person to write down or for a machine to record

dictator person who rules with total power, often in a cruel or brutal way

diesel type of fuel-fed engine

digestive system parts of the body that work together to break down food into simpler forms that can be used by the body

diplomat person who works to keep up friendly relations between the governments of different countries

discrimination the treatment of some individuals or groups differently from others without any fair or proper reason

dismay sadness or disappointment

dispute to argue with

diverse varied; different

divine holy, godlike, or concerning God

dome large rounded structure shaped like half of a ball

domestic (adjective) tame, usually animal

domesticate (verb) tame; make an animal used to living with or working for humans

dominant main or leading

drastic huge or dramatic

drawback problem or bad side

drought long period of dry weather

dual having two aspects; double

dung animal waste

dwindle become smaller or less

dynasty series of rulers of the same family

echo to repeat or imitate a sound

eclipse darkening of the Sun, Moon, or other heavenly body by the shadow of another heavenly body

economical inexpensive and efficient

economy the system in a country or group by which goods are made, services are offered, and both are sold and used

ecosystem community of all the living things in a region, their physical environment, and all their interrelationships

edict law or order given by a ruler or leader

edit cut down to a different or shorter version

effortless easy and natural

element in science, one of the simplest substances that make up all matter

elevation the height of an object above sea level

embassy the living quarters or office of an ambassador (a person who officially represents his or her own government in a foreign country)

embroidery needlework done to decorate cloth

emperor (feminine: empress) the ruler of an empire

empire a major widespread area under a single government, or a number of territories or peoples under one supreme ruler

energetic lively or active

Enlightenment remarkably clear state of awareness, understanding, and inner peace

equator imaginary circle running east-to-west around the Earth that lies halfway between the North Pole and the South Pole

erode wear down

ethnic having to do with a large group of people who share a racial, national, tribal, religious, language, or cultural background

evaporate change into a vapour, or gaseous form, usually by means of heating

evolve (noun: evolution) change, especially over time

exile (noun) banishment or official separation

exotic unusual and unfamiliar

expanse large area

export to carry or send abroad, especially for sale in another country

expression communication, usually of emotions or ideas

extinct no longer existing

extremist person who holds unusually strong opinions or beliefs

famine drastic food shortage, often ending in starvation for many

fantastical highly imaginative and unrealistic

fast (noun) period of time when a person gives up or limits eating, often for religious reasons

ferocious fierce and wild

fertile rich and productive; able to yield quality crops in large quantities

fertilizer natural or artificial substance used to make soil better for growing crops

fibre strand or thread-like structure

fix in photography, to make an image lasting

flare (verb) to fan out or expand

flask container for liquid

flax the fibre from which linen cloth is made

fleece wool of an animal such as a sheep or a goat

flourish to grow successfully; to do well

fodder coarse food for farm animals

foliage the leaves of a plant

forefeet (singular: forefoot) the front feet of an animal with four or more feet

forestry the science and work of caring for forests

formal following a specific order or pattern

fortify to strengthen with weapons and by military defences

fortress well-defended place

fossil an imprint or other trace in rock of an animal, plant, or other living thing

foundation basis or groundwork

fragrance (adjective: fragrant) sweet, pleasant, and often flowery or fruity smell

fresco painting done on freshly spread moist plaster

frigid frozen or extremely cold

fuse an electrical safety device

fusion blending or combination

gangster member of a gang of criminals

gear a toothed wheel that works as part of a machine

gemstone natural material that can be cut and polished for use in jewellery

generate create, produce, or be the cause of

geography the natural physical features of an area; also, the study of the countries of the world and of the Earth's surface features

geometric based on straight lines, curves, and simple shapes such as circles and squares

gesture movement of the body, arms, hands, or legs to express feelings or thoughts

gills pair of breathing organs found in fish and some other water-dwelling animals

glacier a large river-like body of ice moving slowly down a slope or spreading over a land surface

gladiator in ancient Rome, a person who fought to the death as part of a public entertainment

gland structure in animals that produces special substances, such as sweat or oil or milk

glider a soaring aircraft similar to an airplane but without an engine

global warming increase in the average temperature on the planet Earth

gorge narrow steep-walled canyon

gory violent and bloody

Gospel one of the first four New Testament books, telling of the life, death, and resurrection (rising from the dead) of Jesus Christ

gospel genre of black American music that grew mostly from Christian church services, blues, and traditional spirituals

governess woman who teaches and trains a child in a private home

gravity force that attracts objects to each other, keeps people and objects anchored to the ground, and keeps planets circling the Sun

guerrilla person who is part of an independent fighting force that makes surprise raids behind enemy lines

gymnastics difficult physical exercises

habitat the physical environment in which a living thing dwells

hail small balls or lumps of ice that fall from the sky, as rain does

handicrafts articles, such as pottery, made by hand by an individual

handiwork creative product

hare rabbit-like animal

harness control, much as an animal may be hitched up and controlled by its harness

headquarters the governing and directing centre of an organization

heath low evergreen shrub with needle-like leaves and clusters of small flowers

hemisphere half of the planet Earth or of any other globe-shaped object

herb pleasant-smelling plant (such as mint, basil, thyme, coriander) often used in cooking, either in part or whole

heritage background or descent

hermit person who has withdrawn from society to live alone

highland high or mountainous land

horizon distant point where the land and the sky appear to meet

hot spring a source of hot water coming from underground

hull hard outer shell of a seed; also, the outer layer of a boat or ship

humanitarian devoted to the happiness and welfare of other people

humanity the human race

humble poor or meek

humidity (adjective: humid) moisture or dampness; *especially,* the amount of moisture in the air

husk usually thin, dry outer covering of a fruit or seed

hymn song of joy or praise, often to a god

immigrant person who goes to another country to live

immortal living or lasting forever

impaired damaged or limited

imperial having to do with an emperor or empire

impish playfully naughty

implant (noun) object inserted within living tissue; (verb) insert securely or deeply

import bring from a foreign place

impression mark or figure made by pressing one object onto the surface of another; also, the effect or feeling an object or person creates

inanimate not living

indivisible unable to be divided

industrial having to do with businesses that construct or produce something

Industrial Revolution period beginning in the 18th century in which the invention of machines changed forever the way people live and work

industrialized built-up and modernized through business and manufacturing

industry business and manufacturing

inhabited occupied; having residents

inlaid decorated with materials set into the surface

inland part of a country away from the coast

inspiration something that causes a particular thought, feeling, or idea

instinct natural tendency of a living thing to respond in a particular way to a situation

integrate (adjective: integrated) to combine two or more parts in order to create a more balanced whole; *especially,* to remove barriers that isolate one group of people from another

intricate complicated or detailed

investigate look into or study

islet small island

isolate to keep separate or alone

isthmus narrow strip of land connecting two larger land areas

ivory material that makes up elephant and walrus tusks

judo sport, developed from the Japanese fighting art of *jujitsu,* in which opponents use quick movements and careful positioning to try to throw each other to the ground

kernel whole grain or seed of a cereal plant

laboratory place where science tests and experiments are done

landmass large area of land

landscape picture showing views of nature and the countryside

larva (plural: larvae) wingless, often wormlike stage of many insects

lash to tie or attach

layperson (adjective: lay) person who belongs to a religious group but is not part of its official clergy (as a priest or minister is)

legislature an organized government group with the power to make laws

lens (plural: lenses) curved piece of glass that concentrates rays of light

liberation freedom

literacy the ability to read and write

litter group of newborn animals born to the same mother at the same time

livestock animals kept or reared, especially farm animals such as cattle, pigs, sheep, goats, and horses

locomotive railway vehicle that carries the engine that moves train cars along

loot to steal from a home or public place, especially during rioting or wartime

lunar having to do with the Moon

lung organ that helps some animals breathe air

lush rich with thick, plentiful growing plants

lyrics the words of a song

magistrate official who looks after the laws of a particular area

magnify make something appear larger

majestic grand or splendid

majority most; usually, more than half of a group of individual people or things

mammal class of warm-blooded animals that feed their young with milk from special mammary glands, have an internal backbone, and are more or less covered with hair

mangrove tropical tree or shrub that has partly exposed roots and grows thickly in areas of salty water

manufacture to make from raw materials, by hand or by machine

manuscript handwritten or typewritten document

marginal lying at or near the outer edge (margin) of some larger place, object, or group

marine having to do with the ocean

marmalade clear, usually sugary jelly containing pieces of fruit and fruit rind

marsh area of soft wet land usually overgrown by grasses and sedges

massive heavy or large

matter physical substance or material from which something is made

mausoleum large or fancy tomb

meal coarsely ground substance

medicinal used as a medicine

medieval period in European history from the 5th to about the 14th century AD

meditation (verb: meditate) quiet, focused concentration, meant to calm and clear the mind; sometimes used to reach a spiritual awareness

memorial something that keeps alive the memory of a person or event

meteorite a mass of material from space that reaches the Earth's surface

method way or system

microphone a device that changes sound to electrical signals, usually in order to record or send sound

migration movement from one country or place to another

minaret in Islamic architecture, the tall slender tower of a mosque, from which Muslims are called to prayer

mineral naturally occurring non-living substance; important nutrient for living things

mischievous playfully naughty

moccasin soft leather shoe first worn by Native American Indians

module independent unit made to be part of a larger structure

molecules the smallest possible pieces of a particular substance

mollusc any member of a group of animals that have no backbone and are usually enclosed in a shell (for example, snails, clams, or squids)

molten melted

monarchy form of government in which the ruler inherits the position and rules for life; monarchs include kings, queens, emperors, and tsars

monastery housing for people who have taken religious vows, especially for monks

monitor watch carefully and keep track of

monsoon regular period of heavy rainfall and wind, especially in southern Asia

monument stone or building set up in memory of a person or event

mosque Muslim place of worship

mountaineer mountain climber

mourn to feel great sorrow, usually because of a death or other loss

mural a painting on a wall

mussel kind of mollusc (shellfish)

muzzle (noun) animal's snout (projecting jaw and nose); also, fastening or covering for an animal's mouth to prevent it from biting or eating

mystical having to do with a person's direct spiritual connection with a god or other supernatural power

myth story that unfolds part of the world view of a people or is used to explain a belief or natural event

natural resources the materials or qualities supplied by nature (such as minerals or waterpower) that make a place valuable to people, usually for industrial and manufacturing purposes

nature inborn or instinctive way of behaving or thinking

nectar sweet liquid produced by plants and used by bees in making honey

negotiate to discuss and bargain with another in order to reach an agreement

Negro spiritual religious folk song developed among blacks in the southern United States

network complex system

nobility a nation's upper-class social group

noble of upper-class birth or rank

nocturnal active at night

nomad member of a people who have no permanent home but instead move from place to place, usually with the seasons and within a specific area

non-fiction literature that is based on fact rather than on imagination

nostril one of the outer openings of the nose

nuclear weapon explosive device that produces enormous power by splitting apart the centres of the tiny particles called 'atoms'

nuisance annoying or troublesome person, thing, or event

nursery place where plants are grown for farming, for scientific experiments, or for sale to the public

nutrient substance that a living thing needs in order to stay healthy and grow

obligation responsibility or duty

oddity unusual thing or quality

oil (or crude oil) liquid taken from the ground and not yet cleaned or separated into such products as petrol and paraffin; also called petroleum

oral having to do with the mouth

orbit (verb) to travel around an object; (noun) an object's path around another object

orchestra group of musicians playing together, usually with a leader called a 'conductor'

order religious community, usually requiring that its members take solemn vows promising duty and faithfulness

organism living thing

orthodox strictly obeying traditional rules, customs, or beliefs

overseer person in charge of others who are carrying out a task

overwhelm defeat, beat down, or swallow up

pagoda tower-like Asian temple or memorial building several storeys tall, with the edges of the roof at each level curving upwards

papyrus tall reed that grows in the Nile valley and that the ancient Egyptians used to make an early kind of paper

paraffin fuel for lanterns

paralyse make someone or something unable to move

parasite creature that lives on another, which it usually injures

parka hooded heavy jacket for very cold weather

parliament formal meeting for the discussion of a specific subject; also, a law-making body of some governments

particle tiny bit or piece

pastel type of drawing crayon

patent (verb) legally protect the rights to make, use, or sell an invention; (noun) document that legally protects the ownership and use of an invention

patron saint holy person whose spirit is believed to specially protect a group or place

peninsula a finger of land with water on three sides

perfection state of being without flaw or error

persecute (noun: persecution) to treat cruelly or harmfully for an extended period of time; *especially,* to make a person or group suffer because of their beliefs

pest plant or animal that is annoying or destructive

pesticide poison that kills insects dangerous to growing plants

phenomenon (plural phenomena) event or happening

philharmonic large orchestra that plays classical music

philosopher thinker or seeker after truth and understanding of basic concepts

photoelectric effect electrical effect produced when light strikes a metal surface

physics the science that deals with matter and energy and the way they interact

pied having blotches of two or more colours

pilgrim person who travels to a shrine or holy place to worship

pilgrimage journey made to a holy place to worship there

plantation large farming property, usually worked by resident labourers

plate in the Earth sciences, a large segment of the Earth's crust (outer layer) that is constantly in motion

plateau wide land area with a fairly level surface raised sharply above the land on at least one side

pleated folded and laid over another part of some material, especially a piece of cloth

plot the main story of a work of literature

poet laureate poet honoured by a country or other region as its most outstanding poet

political having to do with creating and controlling a government

pollen (verb: pollinate) very fine, dusty substance from flowers, important in reproduction of other plants

pollute (noun: pollution) to poison or make dirty, often with man-made waste

polo team sport played by hitting a wooden ball with mallets through goalposts while on horseback

pope the leader of the Roman Catholic church

population all the people living in a country or other specific area

porcelain hard white substance made of clay mixed with other materials; used especially for dishes

porridge soft food made by boiling grain meal or a vegetable in milk or water until it thickens

port protected harbour where ships dock to load or unload goods

porter person who carries baggage

portray to make a picture of, describe in words, or play the role of

potential possible

potlatch in the American Pacific Northwest, traditional American Indian feast where the host gives out many gifts to show wealth and generosity

poultry birds reared for their eggs or meat

preach to deliver a sermon; to urge to accept an idea or course of action

precious of great value or high price

predator (adjective: predatory) animal that lives by eating other animals

prehistoric having to do with times before written history

presence the strong and self-confident quality a person has that makes others focus on him or her

prey an animal eaten by another animal

print (noun) work of art made by a process that allows more than one copy of an image to be made

prism a piece of many-sided clear crystal

Promised Land in Judaism, the land of Canaan, which God promised to Abraham and Moses if the Hebrew people promised to worship only Him

propeller a device that uses blades that fan outwards from a central hub to propel (move) a vehicle, such as a boat or an airplane

prophet a holy person who acts as a messenger between God and people; also, a gifted person with the ability to accurately predict future events

prosperous wealthy

prowl creep about in a sneaky way, often while hunting

psalm a sacred song or poem used in worship; *especially*, one of the biblical poems collected in the Book of Psalms

pulp 1) in biology, the juicy fleshy part of a soft fruit; 2) in industry, a mashed-up paste, such as the raw plant material used in making paper

pygmy something very small for its kind

pyramid structure with a square base and four sloping triangle sides that meet in a point at the top

quay structure built along the bank of a waterway for use as a landing place

rabies serious disease of animals that is usually passed on through the bite of a sick (rabid) animal; its effects include extreme salivation, strange behaviour, and usually death

radiation energy sent out in the form of rays, waves, or particles

rainforest dense tropical woodland with a high yearly rainfall and very tall trees

ray beam

rebel person who fights against an existing power or way of doing things

recitation act of speaking or reading a piece of literature aloud

recycle to reuse, or to pass used or scrap material through various changes in order to create new useful products from it

reef raised length of rocks, coral, or sand at or near the surface of water

refined polished, complex, and advanced

refinery factory that treats crude petroleum and separates it into different parts

regal royal or noble

region (adjective: regional) general area; also, a specific district

reign the time during which a ruler is in power

remains (noun) parts that are left after time passes or some event occurs

republic form of government in which citizens are allowed to elect officials and representatives responsible for governing by law

reserve area of land set apart for some special purpose; also (usually plural: reserves), money or valuable items kept in hand or set apart until needed

resort (noun) holiday centre; fancy vacation spot

resurrection rising from the dead

revolt to rise up (often violently) against the power of a ruler or government

revolution activity or movement designed to make changes in a situation

rhythm regular pattern of sound

rind the usually hard or tough outer layer or 'skin' of a fruit or vegetable

ritual a formal custom or ceremony, often religious; the required form for such a ceremony

roam to travel or wander freely through a wide area

rodent major animal group that includes mice, squirrels, and other small gnawing animals

rotate (noun: rotation) spin or turn

rotation spinning or turning

rudder flat piece attached to the back of a boat or ship and used for steering

ruthless without pity

sabotage damage or destruction of property that interferes with an enemy's use of it

sacred holy

sacrifice an act of offering something of value to save or make up for something else

saga tale of historic or legendary figures and events of Norway and Iceland

salvation rescue from the power and effects of sin

samurai warrior class in Japan from about the 12th to the mid-19th century

sanctuary safe place

sap the liquid inside a plant

satellite natural or man-made object that circles another object, usually a planet

savage extremely violent

savannah hot, dry grassland with scattered trees

saw-toothed having an edge or outline like the teeth (cutting points) of a saw

scale in biology, one of the small, stiff, flat plates that form an outer covering on the body of some animals, especially fishes and reptiles

Scandinavia area in northern Europe that includes the countries of Denmark, Norway, and Sweden

scholarship an award of money to help pay for a person's education

science fiction stories that deal with the effects of real or imagined science on society or individuals

scorch to burn a surface, usually changing its colour

score in films, the background music that goes with the pictures on the screen

scorpion animal of the arachnid class (which includes spiders) that has a long body and a narrow sectioned tail with a poisonous stinger at the tip

scour to scrub hard

sculpture three-dimensional artwork, usually shaped by carving, moulding, or welding

sea level height of the surface of the sea

sect group following a person or a specific set of beliefs

sedge plant group found in marshes and related to grasses and rushes

self-portrait picture of the artist who painted or drew the picture; usually shows the face

semi-desert area that is much like a desert but has more rainfall

sensitive easily affected

sepulchre place of burial

seraphim in Christianity, Islam, and Judaism, special angels who guard God's throne

shears cutting device similar to scissors but usually larger

shrine place where honour or worship is offered to a saint or deity

skyline an outline of buildings or other large objects against the background of the sky

sleet frozen or partly frozen rain

slum crowded, dirty, run-down housing

smog dirty air, a word made by combining 'smoke' and 'fog' to describe how the air looks

smug conceited; full of oneself; self-satisfied

snout long projecting nose, like that of a pig; also, the long front part of the head of some animals, such as alligators

solar having to do with the Sun

solitary alone

sophisticated complicated or stylish

soprano the highest woman's singing voice; also, a person who sings in this voice

Soviet Union country of eastern Europe and northern Asia that existed from 1922 to 1991 and consisted of Russia and 14 other republics

space shuttle rocket-launched airplane-like vehicle that transports people to and from space

species group of living things that have certain characteristics in common and share a name

sphere ball or globe

splendour something very grand or beautiful

spool reel for winding lengths of materials such as tape, thread, or wire

spout tube, pipe, or hole through which liquid flows

squid sea mollusc that has a long thin body with eight short arms and two usually longer tentacles

staff wooden walking stick

stalk plant's main stem

standard commonly accepted amount or number

starchy containing starch, a natural substance that is made by green plants and is part of many foods

stationary unmoving

steppe land that is dry, usually rather level, and covered with grass

Stone Age the oldest period in which human beings are known to have existed, characterized by the making of stone tools

storage space to keep or hold on to things

strait narrow channel connecting two large bodies of water

strike temporary stopping of normal activities in protest against an act or condition

sturdy physically strong and healthy

stylized simplified or made to suggest natural forms but not imitate them

submerge put under water

suction holding onto something by sucking

sultan king or ruler, especially of a Muslim state

summit top or highest point

superior better than

supernova the explosion of a very large star during which it may become a billion times brighter than the Sun

superstition unproven belief usually based on a mistaken idea of how something is caused

supreme highest, best, and without limit

surgery a medical procedure or operation for treating a disease or condition

symbolize to stand for or mean

synagogue Jewish house of worship

synthesizer a tool or machine that creates things artificially; also, a machine for creating musical sounds artificially

synthetic produced artificially

tableland broad flat area of high land

tapered gradually becoming smaller or narrower towards one end

tapestry heavy cloth that has designs or pictures woven into it and that is often used as a wall hanging

technical having to do with the way a skilled individual handles the details of an art or craft

technique special way of doing something; *especially,* the way a skilled individual handles the details of an art or craft

technology scientific ideas and knowledge put to actual use in actions, machines, and processes

teeming crowded

telegraph a device for sending coded messages over long distances by using electrical signals

temperament personality or usual mood

temperate having mild weather

temple building used for worship

tentacle long arm-like structure on certain animals, usually found sticking out near the head or mouth and used especially for feeling or grasping

terrace area of hillside that has been levelled off to allow farming on the land

territorial protective of a territory or home area

territory area, especially an area claimed by an animal

text written work

texture the feel of a surface

theme main idea or musical element

theory in science, an idea or reasoned explanation for why things are as they are or why things happen as they do

thorax the middle of the three main divisions of the body of an insect

three-dimensional having depth (or thickness), in addition to width and height

timber wood that is cut down for use in building something

tolerate to put up with; also, to be able to survive

tomb special building or room in which a dead person is buried

topknot short mound of hair worn on the top of the head

tourism business of encouraging travel to a specific location and of managing services for visitors (including lodging, transport, food, and activities)

tradition custom; habit of belief or of living

traditional usual; well known because of custom or long-time use

translation version of a written work that has been changed from its original language into another

transmitter a device that sends messages or code

tribute gift, performance, or action meant to show appreciation, respect, or caring for someone or something

tropical having to do with the Earth's warmest and most humid (moist) climates

troupe company or group; *especially,* a working group of stage performers

tsar one of the emperors of Russia until 1917

tsunami huge ocean wave produced by an undersea earthquake or volcanic eruption

tuft 1) in plants, a small cluster of flexible leaves or fibres that are attached or close together at the base and free at the opposite end; 2) in animals, a short mound of fur

tundra treeless plain with few plants, most often in extremely cold regions

tusk long tooth that overhangs when the mouth is closed and serves for digging food or as a weapon

tutor a privately hired teacher

twilight the light between the end of day and the beginning of night; also, the name for that time of day

tyrant powerful and cruel ruler; also, someone who acts like a tyrant

unique very unusual or one of a kind

universal present or occurring everywhere

values morals or ideals

vapour a substance in the state of a gas (rather than a solid or liquid)

vast huge or spacious

vaudeville popular American form of entertainment from the 1890s to the 1930s, involving musical, dancing, comedy, magic, and other variety acts

vegetarian person or animal that does not eat flesh

vehicle a device or machine used to carry something

venom poison that comes from animals

veterinarian doctor who takes care of animals

vibrate to move rapidly back and forth or from side to side

vivid bright or dramatic

vow solemn promise or statement

vulnerable exposed or in danger

wages payment for work or services

warm-blooded having a body temperature that stays mostly unchanged and is not affected by the surrounding environment

waste materials that are unused or left over after some work or action is finished

waterproof not affected by water

weaned capable of and used to eating food rather than nursing

weld to join metal parts together with heat

wildlife sanctuary place of protection for animals and plants

worship (verb) to honour and show surrender and obedience to a god or supernatural power

yacht small ship or large boat used for pleasure cruising or racing

Harare (city in Zimbabwe) *page* **460**

hard drive, *also called* hard disk (computer science) computers *page* **229**

hares (mammals): *look under* rabbits and hares

Havana (city in Cuba)
Cuba *page* **479,**
photograph *page* **479**

Hawaiian geese (birds)
geese *page* **161**

hearing aids
deafness *page* **227**

hearing impairment: *look under* deafness

heat
thermal power *page* **233**
look under temperatures

heath (plant and landform)
Scotland *page* **374**

Hebrew Bible: *look under* Old Testament

helium (chemical element)
Jupiter *page* **22**

Henson, Jim (American puppeteer) *page* **306**

herbs: *look under* peppers; strawberries

Hercules (Greek myth)
Atlas *page* **310**

Herero (people)
Windhoek, Namibia *page* **458**

Herschel, Sir William (British-German astronomer)
Uranus *page* **24**

Hillary, Edmund (New Zealand explorer)
Tenzing Norgay *page* **511,**
photograph *page* **511**

Himalayas (mountains in Asia)
Pakistan *page* **415**
Tenzing Norgay *page* **511**
Thimphu *page* **412**

Hinduism (religion) *page* **355**
God *page* **340**
India *page* **413**

hip-hop (music and culture)
Did you know? *page* **259**

Hippocratic oath (ethical code)
Did you know? *page* **394**

hippopotamuses (mammals) *page* **182**
Liberia *page* **438**

Hiroshige, *also called* Ando Hiroshige (Japanese artist) *page* **250**

Hitler, Adolf (German ruler)
Germany *page* **380**

Holland (country): *look under* Netherlands, the

Holsteins (mammals)
cattle *page* **100,**
photograph *page* **100**

Holy Roman Empire (historic empire)
Charlemagne *page* **496**

holy wars
religion *page* **339**

Honduras (country)
Central America *page* **473**

honey
bees *page* **114**

honeycombs
bees photograph *page* **114**

Honolulu (city in the U.S.) *page* **469**

hooves (animal feet)
horses *page* **103**
look under ungulates

horseback riding
horses photograph *page* **103**

horses (mammals) *page* **103**

hot peppers
peppers *page* **153**

house cats (mammals): *look under* cats

'How Crow Brought Daylight to the World' (Inuit myth) *page* **333**

'How Kangaroo Got His Tail' (Australian folktale) *page* **327**

howler monkeys (mammals)
monkeys *page* **123**

Hubble Space Telescope
Pluto photograph *page* **26**
telescopes *page* **246,**
photograph *page* **246**
Venus *page* **19**

human beings
Did you know? *pages* **216, 441**
Kenya *page* **443**
temperatures *page* **194**

humpback whales (mammals)
whales photograph *page* **186**

hurricanes (wind storms): *look under* cyclones

hydroelectric power
water power *page* **234**